The
Working Parents' Handbook

How to Succeed at Work, Raise Your Kids, Maintain a Home, and Still Have Time for You

Katherine Murray

Manage life or it will manage you!

Katherine Murray

Park Avenue

An imprint of JIST Works, Inc.

The Working Parents' Handbook
How to Succeed at Work, Raise Your Kids, Maintain a Home, and Still Have Time for You
Copyright © 1996 by Katherine Murray

Published by **Park Avenue Productions**
An imprint of JIST Works, Inc.
720 N. Park Avenue
Indianapolis, IN 46202-3431
Phone: 317-264-3720   Fax: 317-264-3709
E-mail: JISTWorks@AOL.com
See back page of this book for other books of interest.

Interior Illustrations by Bruce Berrigan

Printed in the United States of America

99 98 97 96   5 4 3 2 1

Library of Congress Cataloging-in-Publication Data

Murray, Katherine, 1961-
    The working parents' handbook : how to succeed at work,
  raise your kids, maintain a home, and still have time for you   /
  Katherine Murray ;   interior illustrations by Bruce Berrigan.
      p. cm.
    Includes bibliographical references.
    ISBN 1-57112-075-0
    1. Working mothers—United States—Life skills guides.
  2. Parents—United States—Life skills guides.   3. Dual-career
  families—United States.   4. Work and family—United States.
  I. Title.
  HQ759.48.M85   1996
  646.7'0085—dc20   96-33851
                                                                CIP

ISBN: 1-57112-075-0

To all working parents,
everywhere

Acknowledgments

The process of writing a book is not unlike raising a child. (Except it's a lot quicker and a lot less expensive!) It requires the help, insight, and direction of a number of talented people. I'd like to thank all these special people who have made writing and publishing *The Working Parents' Handbook* a wonderful experience:

James Irizarry, publisher, for believing in the project from the start and seeing it through to a finished book.

Connie Horner, my dear friend, research assistant, and biggest source of encouragement. Without you, Connie, much of the research for this book would never have been done.

Dr. Ted Sharpe, who reviewed and made suggestions for the chapters dealing with emotional issues. Thank you for providing your expertise—it has greatly added to the book.

Sherri Emmons, editor extraordinaire, who made invaluable suggestions and improvements throughout the development and editing stages of this book. Thanks, Sherri.

Wendy Prescott, for the wonderful, inviting, and useable design. Her careful design and layout of all the many elements makes this a book readers will enjoy spending time with.

And most of all, to my children, Kelly, Christopher, and Cameron, who make my life more wonderful, more joyful, and more challenging than I ever dreamed possible. They have provided—unwittingly and, in some cases, unwillingly—many of the examples for this book. Whether I am in work mode (glasses on, at the computer) or in Mom mode (playing "Donkey Kong Country" or, yes, baking cookies), they are at the center of my heart. I am truly blessed to be their mother.

Thanks, Mom and Dad!

Many thanks to these mothers and fathers who contributed their real-life stories and experiences to make *The Working Parents' Handbook* a better book:

Louis Ater	Pat Jones
Bill Alfee	Toni Lee
Wendy Alfee	Lisa Levins
Victoria Baker	Karen Livisee
Donneal R. Cottrill	Carol Mauer
Pam Eakins	Peggy Norris
Patti Fleming	Staci Rich
Janet Gagneur	John Smith
Duane Hampton	Debra Spencer
Peggy Payne Hood	Kathy Strickland
Melinda Hornback	Dan Turner
Connie Horner	Reva Turner
April Hyden	Susan Wheatley

Table of Contents

Introduction

Picture this: Laura Petrie, tall, slim, and beautifully coifed, greets husband Rob just before his trip over the ottoman. Buddy and Sally rush over, laughing, as Rob completes his somersault, jumps to his feet, and, grinning broadly, shakes hands all around.

This is a man who's *worked* all day? There have been days when I would've just given up and stayed right there on the floor. "Day's over, I'm not moving," I'd say, and poor Laura would have to bring me dinner in the living room.

When Richie comes into the picture, he's greeted with warm smiles and attentive ears. No one's had a bad day. No one is so rushed that he hears, "Not now, Rich!" three times for every one, "What was it you wanted to tell me?" He's the pet of the Petrie household, and life, career, and family all seem to mix well.

Life in the '90s isn't much like a "Dick Van Dyke Show" episode. (It probably wasn't like that in the '60s, either.) Sometimes career and family mix about as well as oil and water. We have so many demands on our time that we struggle continually to prioritize our priorities. People get lost in the shuffle. Hurried and harried, we make choices that affect our lives—our earning potential, our futures, our families—before we really even understand that they *are* choices.

The Working Parents' Handbook is all about finding a balance—a workable balance—between home and office. No matter how harried you feel, there's hope. It *is* possible to have a career and kids at the same time; many of us are already doing it. How well we do it depends in large part on whether we've determined our family priorities, found a job that supports those priorities, and organized ourselves and our families to make sure we're headed toward the goals we want to reach.

Idealistic, perhaps, but not impossible.

Who Is This Book For?

The Working Parents' Handbook is a common-sense guide that bridges an important gap: the gap between home and work. If you're a parent who is considering a return to the workforce, a parent who has never worked and now has to, a parent who's in the market for a better job, a single parent shouldering both family and financial responsibilities, or a prospective parent considering the pros and cons of the life-career-baby triangle, you'll find insights, advice, practical information, and usable tips to help you sort out what's best for your family and for yourself.

In other words, if you are or will be a parent and you work, this book is for you.

What's in This Book?

Chapter 1, "**Priorities, Priorities**," gives you some basic information about what's happening today in American families and how other families are making it work. This chapter also presents tips for having a family discussion, weeding out the wants from the whining, determining your family's priorities, and designing a constructive family mission statement.

Chapter 2, "**Outside Looking In**," explores the point at which the needs of your family and the demands of the work world intersect. In this chapter you will rate various factors to identify the kind of job you want. How much do you need to make? How many hours can you be away? What benefits do you need? What about room for advancement? This chapter helps you weigh options and compare what you find with what your family needs. It also offers tips on conducting your job search and finding a "family-friendly" company.

Chapter 3, "**The Child-Care Issue**," addresses one of the biggest hurdles for most parents, especially those returning to the workforce for the first time as parents. Who can you trust to care for your children while you're at work? This chapter explores the options, from home-run day care to corporate-sponsored child care to grandma's house. There are other options, as well: the home office, the Mom-Dad-swing-shift circus act, and job sharing. This chapter helps you investigate all the choices and offers tips and checklists to help you make prepared decisions.

Chapter 4, "**Your Sitter Is on Line 1**," answers such questions as, How do you handle the first "Suzanne-just-threw up-on-the-family-room-carpet!" phone call? Should you run right home? How do you know when an emergency is an emergency? This chapter includes guidelines for responding to various situations from the office, and helps you prepare for emergencies *before* they happen.

Chapter 5, "**Inside Looking Out**," maps out that big first step: out the front door and into the office, and helps you navigate those trying first days with advice from other parents who've been there.

Chapter 6, "**Post-Parting Blues**," helps you gear up for the adjustment period ahead. Remember when you had that family meeting and designed your mission statement? Remember when everyone was happy to voice an opinion? Now, nobody's talking. Everyone's grumpy. The kids are getting sick. You're getting sick. You try to cover up the grayness you feel when you go to work, but you're afraid it shows. This chapter helps you understand what you're all going through and offers suggestions from experts on how to get back on course and stay there.

Chapter 7, "**On the Home Front**," deals with a common scenario: the house is going to pot! Your kids can write their names in the cat hair on the sofa. Three-meals' worth of dishes are piled in the sink. The trash is ripening in the garage because you forgot to put it out for the garbage pickup. Your home, once manageable, has become an unkempt reminder of how overly busy you are. This chapter helps you organize, prioritize, and delegate responsibilities so the necessary jobs get done. You'll find tips for chore sheets and allowance scales. Write-in calendars are provided so you can regiment important household tasks.

Chapter 8, "**Time for You**," helps you attempt the impossible: finding time for yourself. Maybe it's not logical, but it is fact: The more demands that are placed on your time, the more time you need to regroup. This chapter shows you how to grab some centering time and—even in the midst of a hectic schedule—take care of you. You can also reduce your stress and the demands on your time by taking charge of the dinnertime crazies and simplifying your responsibilities.

Chapter 9, "**Creating a Family-Friendly Workspace**," helps you become a family advocate even in the office. Many employers today recognize that, in order for their employees to be happy and excel at work, things must be okay at home; which means that many employers now offer a number of options to help support the work-family split. They are building on-site day-care centers, giving tuition assistance for preschools, and being more flexible about flex-time. This chapter tells you about what's being done to support families in the workplace and encourages you to explore what you can do in your office—from starting a parents-lunch-out once a month to putting up a parents' Q&A board where employees can find numbers for back-up baby-sitters, trade home-organizing tips, or arrange schedule swapping.

Appendixes

The final section of the book provides three quick references for additional information. Appendix A is a "Back-to-Work Checklist" that helps you hit all the major points before you start out that first day of work. Appendix B is a list of "Emergency Numbers for Home and Work." Appendix C closes the book with a listing of "Family-Friendly Resources," agencies and organizations dedicated to educating, empowering, and facilitating the growth of family-friendly workplaces.

Special Features

As we began researching this book, one fact became clear: Working parents are trying, and trying hard. Many of them have stories, tips, and suggestions to share. In this book, you'll find the voices of your peers—parents who are navigating uncharted waters, always with the best interest of their families at heart. Look for these special elements:

Best & Worst
Parents tell you what they think are the best—and worst—aspects of being a working parent.

Did I Tell You About the Time . . . ?
These include stories—funny and sometimes poignant—parents have shared.

From One Parent to Another

These are tips parents offer from tried-and-true experience.

TIP

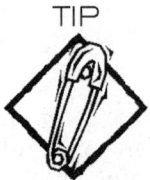

NOTE

NOTEPAD

PICK-UP

TIP

HOUSEHOLD

TIP

Additionally, you'll find tips, notes, sidebars, and checklists that provide information to support the chapter text and give you a chance to try out some of the recommended techniques. Household tips and pick-up tips in chapter 7 show how you can streamline your housekeeping efforts. Plus, we've thrown in some illustrations, just to keep things rolling.

Chapter 1

Priorities, Priorities

"When I was a kid, my parents moved a lot—but I always found them."
—Rodney Dangerfield

It's a staggering statistic: 77 million of us living in America today are parents. We represent a rainbow of ethnic backgrounds, educational levels, incomes, ages, and occupations. We have an incredible range of financial, emotional, practical, and physical needs. As you are ushering your 3-year-old out the door with her blanket and bunny, trying to get her into her car seat, thousands of parents just like you are doing the same thing all over the country. We all get those semi-hysterical phone calls from Grandma when Bradley swallows the cap to the glue. We all face sick days when we're not sick, and we all navigate the teacher-conference-or-managers'-meeting decisions.

The Balancing Act

Family consciousness is not a new thing, but it *is* speaking with a louder voice than it was a decade ago. Today more and more parents in the workforce are willing to exchange high-demand, high-stress careers for more holistically appealing lives. They want to go to PTA meetings once in a while. They want to make the cookies for the Boy Scout troop. They want to be the ones taking the baby's temperature and sponging her forehead when the flu hits and she really wants Mommy or Daddy.

In some cases, parents are willing to make a trade—less money, perhaps, or less responsibility in return for more freedom to be with their families. In other cases, the trade isn't necessary: Some do find jobs that enable them to set the priorities most important to them and balance work and home. The first step is setting the priorities.

Priority setting is a fairly simple task: You think about what's important to you as a family, discuss it, debate it if necessary, and decide. Voilà. Priorities. The challenge to setting your family priorities is finding the time to think about them. And anyone who's ever had a child to care for knows how unrealistic *that* can seem.

Early Mornings for Mom and Dad

As long as there have been jobs and kids, there have been parents trying to figure out how to balance the two. On a purely practical level, the chore is often close to impossible. Does this sound familiar?

6:00   Alarm rings. You hit the snooze button.

6:15   Alarm rings again. "Mom? Dad?" No, it's not the alarm. It's the kids.

6:20   One of you gets to shower; the other makes coffee. Hopefully you'll have time to switch places.

6:30   You break up a fight in the second bathroom. "Justin, you don't need to use Diana's curling iron."

7:00   Breakfast in concert. One makes lunches while the other serves cereal and Pop-Tarts.

7:10   Little Michael spills his juice. Again. Diana, trying to be helpful, grabs the closest thing she can get her hands on to mop it up. The closest thing happens to be the draft of the report you were working on last night.

7:20   Diana barely scoots out the door in time to catch the bus to junior high. Glancing down, you see she's forgotten her lunch. You'll have to drop it off on your way to the office.

7:30   Michael is still on his fourth spoonful of cereal. You bite your lip and try not to jump up and down screaming, "Hurry up! Hurry up!"

7:45   Your spouse is all packed and ready, with Justin and his bookbag waiting by the door. It's your turn to take Michael to preschool. A quick kiss, and they leave. Michael works on his seventh bite of cereal.

7:46   You can't stand it anymore. "Mike, I've got to get to the office on time today, and I've got to drop off Diana's lunch on my way. Are you just about finished eating?"

"Nunh-uh," Michael mumbles, chewing slowly.

You decide to be proactive. "Here," you say, "Let's take this Pop-Tart in the car. I know what I said about not eating in the new car, but we won't tell the other kids, okay? Come on—oh, we forgot to brush your teeth. Well, just remember to brush them twice as long tonight, all right?"

Picking up your briefcase (with the damp report inside) and scooping up Michael (with his tightly clutched Pop-Tart), you head for the door, destined to be at least 15 minutes late, even if traffic is smooth and you catch all the lights green.

Office Hours for Mom and Dad

By the time you get to the office, you're probably glad to be there. The meeting has started without you, so you pop open your briefcase, pull out the soggy report, and head down the hall toward the conference room. You pause at the door, take a deep breath, and walk in, smiling and as confident as possible. You've only missed a few minutes and are able to give your report and answer questions from the department managers. Much to your relief, things seem to go well, despite the morning's shaky start. After the meeting, your boss walks up. "A few of the managers asked for a copy of your report. Would you make a few copies and circulate them?"

"Uh, how about if I send them a copy by e-mail?" you ask, glancing down at the milk-stained report.

"That's fine," she says. She leans closer and points to your shoulder. "Um ... you have red streaks on your shirt...."

You glance down in horror. Cherry Pop-Tart. Thanks, Michael.

Of course, we bring with us to the office more than Pop-Tart fingerprints and milk-stained reports. We bring worries about sick children, day-care arrangements, upcoming doctor's appointments, and missed teacher conferences. Some of us bring guilt, too. And many of us never quite escape that torn feeling—that we should somehow be both at home and at work, care-taking and providing, doing it all.

Learn Those Lessons Well

Even the best parents are sometimes beset by doubts and guilts. Experts tell us that the quality—and, to some degree, the quantity—of the time we spend with our children is important. And we can rest assured that our presence in the workforce teaches our children some valuable lessons they might not otherwise learn:

- Our children learn about teamwork and cooperation.

- They learn how to set priorities.

- They discover how to make decisions.

- They develop an understanding of money.

- They find out about—and feel good about—what they have to offer the family.

- They see responsibility modeled in adults and learn to be responsible at home and at school.[1]

How Is America Parenting?

Parenting is hard work even when you aren't responsible for merging two different cultures, age groups, perspectives, and lifestyles. The switch back and forth from the work world to home life is akin to culture shock for many of us: We often go from Wall Street to "Sesame Street" in a matter of minutes.

In his study *Parents in Modern America: A Sociological Analysis*, done in the early 1970s, researcher E. E. LeMasters found that there are 13 characteristics all American parents share, no matter what ethnic, religious, educational, or financial group they belong to.[2] You'll probably recognize some of your challenges here:

1. We aren't sure what a "good parent" is. The role is ambiguous at best. It's up to each of us to decide for ourselves what successful parenting means.

2. We expect to be able to solve problems even professionals cannot.

3. Except for Lamaze classes (which don't help a whole lot when you're facing a 13-year-old who's cutting school) we get no formal parenting training.

4. Perhaps because we aren't realistically pre-pared, we have romantic ideas of parenting.

5. We have complete responsibility for our chil-dren but only partial authority.

6. We place extremely high standards on our-selves and on one another as parents.

7. We often must work with incomplete or con-flicting information in deciding how to resolve situations with our children.

8. We do not choose our children, which means we are responsible whether we want to be or not!

9. We have no models to follow for parenting in the '90s. We've been swayed this way and that by popular culture and the method of the moment, but each generation changes so much in its parenting styles that we are inventing the model as we go.

10. Although this may be the dawn of the family-friendly age, economics is still the bottom line. We must earn a living to be able to provide for our children, which sets the stage for some necessary trade-offs.

11. With the continued rise in the number of two-income families, we are adding more roles that compete with the demanding role of parenting.

12. Parenting is a no-quit endeavor. If you don't like your job, you can quit. If you don't like a movie, you can leave. If you don't like your spouse—well, I won't tell you what to do about your spouse. But once a parent, always a parent—for better *and* for worse.

13. The standards we set for our children are higher even than the bar we set for ourselves as parents. We want our children to do better, to have more, to be happier and more successful in life than we are. That's a pretty tall order—both for ourselves and for our kids.

BEST & WORST

Best: "Knowing I'm providing for my kids"

How Is America Working?

The responses families come up with to make their home lives work are as varied as their parenting styles and occupational circumstances. The following sections briefly review some of the different ways families balance work and home.

Two Parents, Two Careers

Many of us parenting today were raised very differently than our parents were. Before World War II, life was closer to "Ozzie and Harriet"; it's likely that our mothers were raised by mothers who stayed home and parented for a living. Such families are in the minority today. These days, all kinds of factors—the cost of living, the pursuit of self-fulfillment, societal pressures—contribute to our needs and desires to work outside the home.

The term *two-career family* covers many different arrangements. One parent might be the primary provider, while the other works part-time. Perhaps both parents are necessary breadwinners. Or one parent might work two jobs while the other works either full- or part-time.

Two-career families—especially those in which both parents work full-time—face unique challenges because of the conflicting demands placed on their limited time. There is much to be done, and there are only 24 hours in a day. Organization is mandatory. Teamwork is essential.

For practical how-to's and wherefore's on getting and keeping your house organized and your team members enlisted, see chapter 7.

One Parent, One Career

Statistics tell us that 31 percent of all households with children are currently headed by single parents—which means a single income—and single mothers outnumber single fathers 6 to 1.[3]

If you are the sole provider for your family, you face additional challenges. You are navigating work and family responsibilities without the support of another adult to share the load. For you, organization and teamwork—in this case, enlisting the help of your children—are supremely important. They can make the difference between you and yours being harried or happy.

According to a study published in Working Mother *magazine, a divorced mother's job has a positive effect on her children.[4] Research shows that families headed by working mothers tend to join in more recreational activities together, and that the children have a solid basis of self-esteem—perhaps because of the additional financial stability in the family or the mother's increased confidence and independence.*

Two Parents, One Career

The "traditional" family of the 1950s—June Cleaver, *et al.*—was represented by the male head-of-household, the female homemaker, and the young, carefree offspring. The '90s version of the traditional family is different. The working-outside-the-home parent may be Mom or Dad—or Mom *and* Dad. If one parent does stay home, he or she may do the carpool thing, the child-care thing, or the work-at-home thing.

Even in a two-parent, single-career family, there is balancing to be done. Both parents are still parents, after all. The parents are partners financially and emotionally, and the prioritizing and organization of the family are still important.

Alternatives

We've looked at some of the more obvious categories of working parents. But there are other options to be explored. Depending on what is most important to your family, you may want to think about one of these alternatives:

Working Different Shifts

According to the *Statistical Abstract of the United States 1995*, 17.8 percent of workers currently work shifts other than traditional daytime hours: 5.1 percent work the evening shift; 3.7 percent work nights; and 3.4 percent work a rotating shift—some days, some evenings, some nights.[5]

For families that place a priority on child care by Mom or Dad, this offsetting of shifts works well, especially while the kids are young. But the challenges are obvious, and parents have to make "couple time" a priority to keep this relationship happy and healthy.

Working at Home

Another growing segment of our parenting population is working at home. With computer technology and the ability to link home and office easily by modem, more employers are open to complete or partial work-at-home arrangements.

◆ ◆ ◆ ◆ ◆ ◆ ◆ ◆ ◆ ◆ ◆ ◆ ◆

"I'm home all day with my 3-year-old while my husband works. I start dinner about 4:00, and when Tom gets home at 5:15, I leave for work. When I get home at 1:30, he's asleep. I go to bed and when I wake up, Tom's already left for work. We aren't seeing each other much right now—I figure we've got another year or so of this—but at least we're able to raise Jonathan the way we want to."

◆ ◆ ◆ ◆ ◆ ◆ ◆ ◆ ◆ ◆ ◆ ◆ ◆

Some work-at-home parents are entrepreneurs; others have arrangements with their employers to work one or more days a week at home and still be eligible for benefits and other perks of employment.

Statistically, 3.2 percent of men and 3.5 percent of women in the workforce—parents or not—are working at home an average of 14.1 hours a week.[6]

From One Parent to Another
"If you miss your kids like I do, try to start a business in your home. Then you can earn some extra money, raise your kids the way you want, and not have the expense of baby-sitters and/or day care."
—Mother of two who works more than full-time

Setting Your Priorities

As you can see, there are many ways to balance the home-family equation. You may come up with something original, or you may try one or two different alternatives before you settle into a situation that really works for your family.

The first step is to go on a fact-finding mission: What are the priorities for your family? What are your goals? What's most important to you as a family, and to you as an individual?

Determining your family priorities is an important step in the process of balancing home and work. You must decide what you're working toward before you can begin moving toward it. Finding out what your family priorities are involves these steps:

1. Talk with your spouse to determine what your priorities are from a parental and financial-partnering standpoint.

2. Have a family meeting in which you invite— and record—input from all family members.

3. Review the list of priorities with your spouse and edit it into a family priority list.

4. Call a second family meeting and read the family priority list. From the list, write a family mission statement—a simple statement that explains what your family wants most to accomplish. Post the mission statement, along with household rules and chore lists (we'll get to those in chapter 7), on the family bulletin board.

Starting Out

The first step in determining your family priorities involves the parents in the house. If you are a single parent, you can sit down with a notebook and a pen and get right to work. If you have a partner, arrange a quiet time when the kids are busy or in bed, when you can have 30 minutes to an hour to talk uninterrupted.

Talking about family priorities cuts right to the heart of family life—why we married, what we wanted, who we've become, who we want to be, how we're raising our kids—and should be handled with gentleness and respect. Take as much time as you can—preferably a long, quiet evening or, even better, a weekend away—to focus on what's important to you as individuals, as a couple, and as a family. Don't try to squeeze in a quick discussion after a tough day at the office or at half-time during your daughter's basketball game.

Brainstorm a list of priorities—whatever comes to you—in no particular order. Don't force yourself to think of what is most important and then list other things in degrees of lesser importance. Just ask yourself (or your mate) "What's important for this family?" and write down whatever comes to mind. You can prioritize the items—and probably throw out a few and add others—when you go through the list later.

As you go through this brainstorming process, here are a few things to keep in mind:

 Different families will have different priorities, and those priorities will change as your children get older, as your financial needs increase or decrease, or as other opportunities present themselves.

 Don't expect your priorities and your partner's priorities to be identical. Go into the discussion expecting negotiation and compromise. If you think it's most important to get out of debt within two years and she thinks it's most important to have at least one parent home with the kids most of the time, that doesn't mean one of you is right and the other is wrong. What you're working on is not a list of your own priorities that everyone else in the family should fall in line with, but a collection of priorities that everyone agrees to (with the parents having the lion's share of the say).

 Everything counts. Write down whatever comes into your head at this stage, no matter how trivial. "Clean laundry" may not be high up on your priorities list, but if it occurs to you, write it down.

 Don't judge your partner's comments. If Sam says "Changing the oil in the riding mower" is one of the family priorities, write it down. There will be time for editing later. Just keep the ideas moving, and don't negate anything your partner finds important.

A Few Possible Family Priorities

- To be debt-free in five years

- To create a loving, happy home

- To spend time every week alone with each child

- To reserve one evening a week for ourselves as a couple

- To be able to purchase a house

- To save for our children's college education

- To be able to take a family vacation once a year

- To purchase a new van

- To be more active at church or in civic organizations

Having a Family Discussion

Once you have your parental list, the next step is to add the voices of the kids. What do they think is most important for your family? Their input is important, both for the perspective it will give you and for their need to be included in decisions that affect them and will ultimately require their support.

Including the kids in the discussion ensures that they feel part of the process: So when it's their turn to do the dishes and they'd rather watch TV, they understand the "whys" behind the chores and realize—somewhere deep down, underneath the compensatory grumbling—that everyone is doing his or her part to make sure the family's priorities are being honored.

Don't just spring a surprise family meeting on the kids. Make it an event. Publicize it. Order pizza, rent a movie (for afterward), do something special. Explain a few days before the meeting what you want to talk about—"We want to hear what you think is most important for our family"—so your kids have a chance to think about it on their own before the meeting. Remember, nobody thinks well on a pop quiz.

When you call the family meeting to order, don't expect absolute order. The first time I tried to have a family meeting with my three children, I made the mistake of doing it at dinner. My teenager made three or four cynical comments. My 7-year-old shouted out things like, "My bedtime is too early! I want to watch 'Beetlejuice' in the mornings, and you won't let me! Cameron drives me crazy!" And Cameron, the baby, threw his mashed potatoes on the carpet. I gave up and dejectedly went to get the carpet cleaner. Weeks passed before I drummed up the nerve to try again. With more thoughtful planning, and a more controlled environment, things went much more smoothly.

For best results, have an agenda. As the saying goes (and it is especially applicable with kids), "Act or be acted upon." Have a sense of humor about it, but get your point across: "Kids, you know I'm thinking about going back to work (or changing jobs, or whatever), and we're trying to decide what's most important for our family so we can make sure we're all happy and cared for while these changes are going on. We want to hear what's most important to you, and what you think is most important for our family."

You might be surprised at what you hear. Again, don't judge the answers, just write them down. If someone isn't talking, ask. "Bethany, what do you think is the most important thing in a family? What do you think is important for you to be happy?" Depending on the age of the child, she may or may not know the answer. (Some of us still haven't figured it out!) But whatever she says— even if she says nothing at all—you've let her know that her feelings are important and welcome as part of this family process. You're enlisting her understanding and participation—even if she's too young to really understand what's going on.

A Few Child-Offered Priorities

- No more peas at dinner.
- I want Mom to play Sega with me more often.
- New jeans.
- Cartoons.
- I want to go out with my friends more.
- My own room.

🧦 Drums.

🧦 A later bedtime.

🧦 Someone else to take out the trash.

After you write down the various priorities, wants, and needs that come raining down on you, take time to read back what you've written. Ask for clarification if you're not sure what was meant. "Bethany, you said 'dinner' was important. Did you mean just having it, or having it together as a family?" Make sure you understand what your kids think is important, even if you don't share their views. Remember, you're gathering facts here. You and your spouse (or just you, if you're a single parent) get to make the final cuts, taking everyone's wants and needs into consideration.

Separating Wants from Whining

Some of what you hear will be helpful. Some will be confusing. And some will be veiled—or perhaps not so veiled—attempts to make you feel guilty and give in to some privilege you have previously denied.

In our house, television is not a high priority. It especially is not a high priority for me, the Keeper of the TV Control. When Christopher tells me he needs to watch a particular cartoon in order to feel loved and happy, I file that comment in the "whining" category. He's pushing my buttons and that gets a parental veto. When he says it's important that I stay and watch during his Taekwondo class instead of dropping him off and running errands, I understand that he wants my involvement. He wants me to be proud of him, and he doesn't like to be dropped off. That comment I record as a want that is important and something I'll consider in the future.

We all know there's a fine line between direct communication and manipulation. Where that line

is in your family only you can know for sure. As you gather the information for your family priority list, however, don't leave anything out—even if you think it's manipulative. Just write it all down, and weed out the sneaky stuff later.

Editing the List

BEST &
WORST

Worst: "Finding time to attend school functions"

Now it's time for you and your partner in parenting to sit down and sift through the list you've compiled. Read through it individually once or twice; then go through it point by point. Some items you'll be able to consolidate; others you will want to omit. And you may think of others to add.

You may find your priorities falling into three general categories:

Financial

Emotional

Physical

Please note that Financial is listed first, not because it is more important than the emotional or physical needs of the family, but because it is more difficult to address the other needs when the family is in a state of financial crisis. Most of us return to the workforce at least in part for financial reasons. Additional financial benefits can make working with emotional and physical needs easier. And, on the flip side, emotional and physical needs can definitely be magnified in times of financial strain.

After you've thought about your family priorities and reached some kind of consensus, take a moment and fill out the Priority List provided at the end of this chapter.

Here's a sample priority list showing how the items are organized once the list is compiled and condensed:

Family Priority List

Financial Priorities

To add a new family room next spring.

To get Christine a car for her 16th birthday.

To save 10 percent of our annual salaries.

Emotional Priorities

To create an atmosphere of love, safety, and acceptance.

To cooperate with each other to help our household run smoothly.

To value the feelings of each family member.

To listen to each other.

To be willing to voice our opinions.

To respect others' opinions.

Physical Priorities

To be warm, safe, and cared for.

To be well fed.

To have comfortable, acceptable, and season-appropriate clothing.

To take good care of ourselves and stay as healthy as possible.

To follow household safety rules at all times.

One very important point: Now that you've created your priority list, you've got the basic information you need to make some important decisions about how to approach your work options. Remember, however, that every system needs to be reviewed and revised on a regular basis, and your family priority list is no exception. You will find that some things that are priorities now will drop off the list in the coming months and other priorities will arise. Be willing to review and revise whenever you see that a change is needed. Your family grows and changes continually, and so will their priorities and needs.

Did I Tell You About the Time . . . ?

"When our youngest daughter was 2, I asked the pharmacist if Stresstabs really worked. He said they did, and I was overjoyed. Curious at my reaction, he asked what kind of stress I was talking about. I replied, '2-year-old, toddler stress!' He said, 'Oh, no, ma'am. Stresstabs work for muscle stress, not mental stress! I think what you're looking for are tranquilizers!'"
—Mother of two who works part-time

Developing a Mission Statement

Now that you've determined what's most important to your family, you need to distill it down to a single mission statement that says clearly what you want to accomplish as a family. Do this in a group meeting. (Yes, I can hear your 10-year-old now: "Not *another* family meeting! I want to watch 'The Simpsons!'") Just one more time.

Take your priority list and read it aloud to the kids. Explain that you want to reduce the list to a simple statement about what's most important. Ask for input, and write the statement right there on the spot.

One family may focus more on emotional issues—feeling loved, safe, supported, accepted—while another may focus on practical issues—taking care of the house, getting out of debt, cooperating and getting along. There's no right or wrong, there's only what's most important for your family.

Here are a few examples:

 "Our mission as a family is to create an environment in which all family members feel loved, safe, and cared for."

 "Our mission as a family is to work together to create a loving, safe, and beautiful home."

 "Our mission as a family is to cooperate and help each other with the daily running of the household."

 "Our mission as a family is to encourage, strengthen, challenge, and support each other as we learn the lessons in our lives."

 "Our mission as a family is to work together to improve our financial situation so we can build the home we've always wanted."

Posting It

Well congratulate yourself, you've done it. You've made the change from reactive family living—that is, reacting to whatever situation comes along—to proactive family living—deciding what's important to you and making your decisions based on those priorities. You may or may not see the change right away, but it will be at the basis of every family decision you make, in terms of job hunting, chore assigning, or goal setting. Underneath it all, you'll know your family's mission statement— what's most important to you and why—and you'll be able to make your choices accordingly.

Family Priority List

Date: __/__/__

Financial Priorities

_____

_____

_____

_____

Emotional Priorities

_____

_____

_____

_____

Physical Priorities

_____

_____

_____

_____

Family Mission Statement

Date: __/__/__

Our mission as a family is to

_____

_____

_____

_____

Notes

1. Earl A. Grollman and Gerri L. Sweder, *The Working Parent Dilemma* (Boston: Beacon Press, 1983).

2. J. Ross Eshleman, *The Family: An Introduction* (Englewood Cliffs, NJ: Allyn & Bacon, 1974), pp. 511-512.

3. *The World Almanac 1995* (Mahwah, NJ: Funk & Wagnalls), p. 960.

4. *Working Mother* magazine (September 1995).

5. *Statistical Abstract of the United States 1995*, Tables 635 & 636.

6. Ibid.

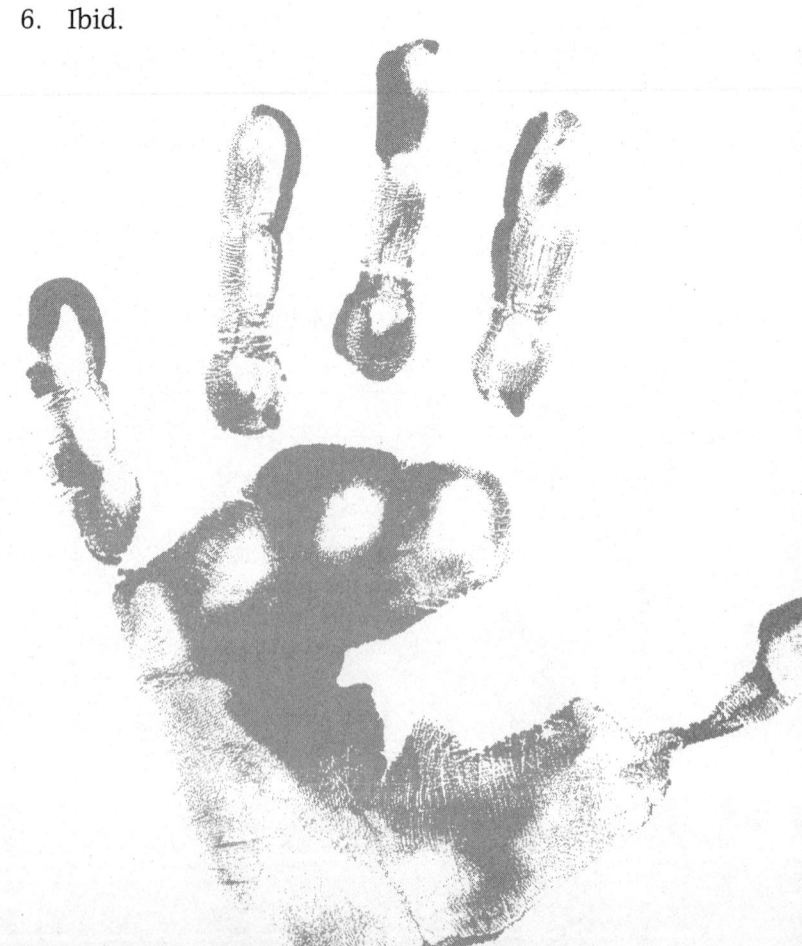

2

Outside Looking In

A man was late for work. *"What's the idea of being late?"* asked the boss.

"Well, the alarm clock woke up everybody but me this morning."

"What do you mean, the alarm clock woke up everybody in the family but you?"

"Well, there's eight in our family and the clock was set for seven."
—Ed Ford

This chapter is all about finding the right job, the one that uses your talents and meets both your needs and the needs of your family. First we'll take a look at what you decided is important for your family. Then we'll come up with a list of essentials for the "perfect" job. (I'm not promising that you'll find the perfect job right off the bat, but you have a lot better chance of finding it if you've figured out what it is.)

Maybe you already have a job and are reconsidering whether you've made the right choice or whether it's time for a different one: Statistics show that 44 percent of all working adults expect to be looking for a different job within the next three years.[1] Or you may be preparing to enter or reenter the workforce. In any case, coming at your job search from the "What's the right job for our family?" standpoint will help you find something that aligns with what is important in your life.

Stress-Busters

Looking for a job can be a full-time occupation. In fact, experts agree that the more focus and follow-up you're willing to invest in your job search, the more likely you are to get the job you want. When you add family responsibilities to the sometimes complex and often harrowing experience of looking for work, the result is often an extra helping of stress and a shortage of patience.

For that reason, let's start out with a few job search stress-busters.

 Remember that everything doesn't have to be done right now. When you feel the pressure to mail out 20 resumes, *and* write follow-up letters, *and* make those phone calls, *and* you're late for Todd's basketball practice, *and* Dana's bugging you to use the phone, stop before you see red and breathe. Five or six good, deep breaths will do it. Remind yourself that finding a job—like raising children—takes a steady investment of time, and the kinder you can be with yourself in the process, the better. Your family will thank you for it.

Keep things as organized as you can. Set up a job search work area in a corner of the family room, the den, or a home office where people won't make off with the paper, where your daughter won't color on the backs of your resumes, and your 3" by 5" note cards won't get shuffled or shredded into doilies.

Create a schedule for yourself that works with your family responsibilities. We all know how hard it is to grab time for ourselves, but when you're looking for work, it's imperative. Schedule time for reviewing want ads, making phone calls, writing follow-up letters, creating interview cards, and so on. Break these activities up to do at different times of the day, if you need to, but schedule them. You'll know you are accomplishing your goals, and the extra planning will help you look forward to the next step.

Review your progress at the end of the week. Keep a record each day (preferably in a day-planner or on a calendar) of who you contacted, when, what the result was, and what action you need to take. At the end of the week, go back and review all the contacts you made. Take time to honor the investment of brainpower, willpower, and energy it took to make all those connections and push yourself forward. That will give you the incentive (after a day or two off) to start fresh on Monday.

Learn to let it rest. Especially when it's a financial bind that is causing a sudden search for work, the temptation to get all caught up in the job search is very strong. As creatures of habit, we humans think only one thing at a time; and when that one thing has to do with money (especially a shortage of it), we can easily get obsessive. If you find yourself constantly thinking of your job search and your money situation, hold up a mental stop sign and look around you. Those kids over there, fighting over the TV, they'd rather play a game with you than hear about the frustrations of your job search. Your friend next door would surely like some help putting that wallpaper border up straight this time. There are many things in our lives besides our most current and most upsetting worry. We just need to remember to see them.

What Does Your Family Need?

In the last chapter, you came up with a family list of priorities that took into account what you and your partner (or you, yourself, if you're a single parent) feel is most important for your family's goals to be met. You solicited input from the kids, as well, making sure they knew they were included and welcomed as you developed both the priority list and your family's mission statement.

You should have a pretty good idea by now of what's important to your family and what isn't. That's going to be different for everyone, so there's no general guideline to follow on what works and what doesn't. Your list, whatever it says, and your mission statement will be your guiding factors when you're considering what your family needs as you find the job to match. But this brings up another question.

What About You?

Searching for a job is, after all, a singular undertaking. We don't look for jobs in groups (at least most people don't). The ideal job for you is going to be one that uses your talents, that gives you room to grow, that meets the needs of your family, and that gives you a sense of satisfaction.

Notice that *"meets the needs of your family"* is only one part of the equation.

Perhaps the best advice I ever heard on job searching is something a friend said to me a few years ago: "Spend a few minutes visualizing yourself in the place you're thinking about working. If you see yourself miserable and glum, forget it. If you see yourself contented and happy, consider it. If you see yourself frazzled and stressed out, run the other way!"

In other words, no matter what kind of situation you're up against, taking a job that makes you miserable is not going to help your family. Part of finding the right job for your family involves finding the right job for you: A happier you means a more supportive, funny, available parent, which translates into better times with the kids.

One mother whose two boys wanted her to "get them everything" for Christmas, answered this way:

"I asked them if they'd rather me work full-time so they could have more things, or would they rather me be home most of the time and just settle for fewer Christmas gifts. They quickly replied they'd much rather me be home with them."

Later in this chapter, you'll have a chance to identify some of the things that are most important to you in a job. The job you want is out there. You just need to know what you're looking for, so you know it when you find it.

These are the things I like to do:

1. _____
2. _____
3. _____
4. _____
5. _____
6. _____
7. _____
8. _____
9. _____
10. _____

What Do You Want to Keep?

When you begin looking for work, one thing is certain: Life is going to change. At first the kids may not believe it. Even though you did the family priority list thing and the mission statement, the idea that "Mom is going back to work" or "Dad is changing jobs" may not have sunk in. You might be asking for more help around the house so you can spend time on your job search. You might need the phone more (that will be *really* unpopular with your teenager), but the reality of "what's changing around here" won't seem real at first.

Before you start making sweeping changes, take a quiet look around—perhaps for a week or so—and see what works and what doesn't. I speak here from the experience of having used the wrong approach for years. I did everything around the house myself until a pressing deadline turned me into a stressed-out lunatic. I knew I was going about things the wrong way when my 14-year-old said, "Mom, the next time you go to the store, could you get me a new toothbrush?"

It was too much. "A new toothbrush?" I asked, incredulously. "A new toothbrush? Didn't I just get you one last month?"

She shrugged. The bicycle chain around her neck jangled. (Don't ask, it's the new look.) "I lost it," she mumbled.

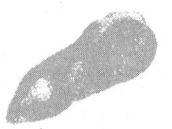

"Lost it? How do you lose a toothbrush? Well, in a room like yours, I can see how. Why don't you ever clean that room? And how come I'm the only one who ever cleans up anything around here? You'd think that as hard as I work, you kids ... "

And I was off. My daughter's eyes glazed and she glanced toward the nearest exit.

Luckily, I stopped myself before I started foaming at the mouth and they had to call in the Tranquilizer Squad. Thank goodness—for myself and my kids—those outbursts are rare events.

Here's the point: An ounce of prevention is worth a pound of cure. If I'd looked around my house in a moment of relative calm—or at least without the job search (or deadline) stress weighing on me—I would have seen that, yes, Christopher brings in the trash cans on Tuesdays and, okay, Kelly has been doing the dishes like I asked her to. They are helping. Where could they do more?

And when I calmly answered that question for myself, I could think about how to implement it without ranting, "Why don't you help more?" Instead, I could say, very politely, "This is what we all need to do to chip in and make this household work."

Ah ... much better.

What Will Have to Change?

If you're a parent, odds are you've said it: "There are only so many hours in the day!" If you're a parent who is working or who is contemplating returning to the workforce, you know that time is like money: we always need or want more and are never quite sure where it will come from.

If you are preparing for a return to work, you know things around the house will change. Already, as you gather your job search tools, think about contacts, read the papers, and talk to relatives, there are more demands on your time than ever before. When you find the job you're looking for, the demands on your time will be even greater. That's why now is a good time to think about what you'll want to change when you start working.

Some of the changes may be predicated on when and where you work. For example, if you work nights, you may need to have one of the older children help the younger children with bath time. Or if you have a long commute, you may need your spouse to start supper in the evening.

In this early stage, just looking around at what works now and what might need to change is the key. Make a list of who does what and file it away for the future family discussion on chore distribution (that's chapter 7).

Again, you may see things that you know will need to change—like the way Christopher throws his book bag and coat in the middle of the living room floor when he walks in from school. Tackle it now, if you want, but if you've got enough on your plate right now, write it in the "Needs to Change" column and institute it as a new rule at the next family meeting.

The Home Planner

Chore	Who Does It?
_____	_____
_____	_____
_____	_____
_____	_____
_____	_____
_____	_____
_____	_____
_____	_____
_____	_____
_____	_____
_____	_____
_____	_____

What Do We Need to Change?

_____

_____

_____

_____

_____

_____

_____

What's Out There?

The job force is expanding and changing every day. When our parents (or perhaps their parents) went to work, they were fairly certain that this would be the job they would hold for the rest of their lives. Jobs were almost exclusively performed on-site; there were few work-at-home occupations outside of home-service businesses and health-care professionals who made house calls.

BEST & WORST

Best:
"Double insurance coverage"

Today, as Walt Disney said, "If you can dream it, you can do it." All kinds of opportunities are opening up in cottage industries, home businesses, or businesses that truly exist somewhere in the phone lines of cyberspace. Computers have made all kinds of services lucrative and possible for people who want to stay home and work. They also make it feasible for employers to hire people who divide their time between work in the office and work at home: If they can take their files back and forth, what difference does it make whether they sit at this desk or that one?

The Home-Office Split

Not all employers are thrilled with the loss of control involved in setting employees free to work at home. Many do so grudgingly, and over time see the benefit of a happy employee who is more productive because he's able to balance the priorities in his life.

Studies have shown that of the 110 million employees in the United States, 19 million of them do at least some of their work at home. The number is not terribly high, but getting higher. The average number of hours they work at home ranges from 12 to just under 17 hours a week.

Work at Home for Someone Else or for Yourself?

If you're thinking about working at home, you might wonder why you'd rather be someone else's employee when you could work for yourself. Many of us have wondered the same thing. The following lists touch on a few of the basic differences:

When you are working for someone else:

- You are usually home only part of the time (one or two days a week).
- You can still "leave the office at the office."
- You draw a regular paycheck.
- You are covered on the company health plan.
- Any benefits that apply to a full-time employee apply to you (assuming you're working full-time).

When you are working for yourself:

- You may have start-up costs ranging from minimal to substantial.
- You are your own boss, which means Discipline, Discipline, Discipline!

> Everything that happens is yours to deal with.

> You need to meet with an accountant and an attorney to get started on the right foot.

> You've got to have a sound idea for a business that you know will go.

In both cases, you still need a plan for making sure the kids are cared for. You will still have demands on your time, and there will still be competing demands for your attention.

The decision of whether to work for yourself or for someone else is one that many people wrestle with throughout their careers. If you're not sure what you want to do, the safer road is to find a job that allows you to work at home part of the time. That way, you can see how you respond to the work style (some people find they have trouble keeping work and home separate when they occupy the same space) and ease into it with a smaller degree of risk.

Job Sharing

Working out an arrangement in which you are at home part of the time is not the only way a parent can find a job style that fits his or her family's needs. Other alternatives exist, including job sharing. In job sharing, more than one employee shares the same job, thus enabling the employer to get the same amount of work done, and two employees to have jobs (and, in some cases, benefits) and still be able to orchestrate the priorities in their lives.

From One Parent to Another
"The most important gift you can give your child is a good set of values. Let your children live with the consequences of their mistakes when they are young, and the consequences are not as life-impacting later."
—Mother of two who works full-time

Seasonal Jobs

If your talents or interests lead you into seasonal work, you have another option for the way you mix work and family. Teaching is a somewhat seasonal job that blends in well with family life— although any teacher will tell you that the number of hours spent working outside the classroom, grading papers, writing lesson plans, and designing projects, makes for a full-to-bursting day. The schedule a teacher follows, however, allows Mom or Dad to be home during the summer and on Christmas and spring vacations, to have relatively short work days (at least at-school work days), and to have weekends off.

Other kinds of seasonal jobs include retail sales, facility management, house painting, landscaping, and construction.

If You Need Time Off

As you begin your job search, you should be aware that the Family and Medical Leave Act was passed in 1993 to guarantee up to 12 weeks of time off for family members in certain situations. There are a few stipulations, though. Companies with fewer than 50 employees are not required to follow FMLA guidelines. All companies with more than 50 employees, and all government agencies, are required to give you up to 12 weeks of (usually unpaid) leave, although you may be able to work out vacation or sick time you haven't used in order to arrange for continuing salary. If you begin working for a company of 50 or more (or a government agency), you are protected by the Family and Medical Leave Act if you need to take time off for any of these circumstances:

- The birth of a child

- The crisis care of an immediate family member

- The adoption of a child

- Your own medical condition that keeps you from working

The FMLA applies to both women and men—moms and dads—and workers are guaranteed their same or equivalent positions when they return to work. If for some reason your position has been filled when you come back, you will be assigned a similar job with identical salary and benefits.

Setting Up Your Job Search

By now, you've spent some time thinking about the kind of job arrangement you'd like. Have you considered the type of job you'd like to have, the one that would use your talents and give you a chance to show what you can do? If not, a little brainstorming is in order.

In *The Very Quick Job Search* J. Michael Farr identifies six essential steps that will help you find the job you want quickly.[2]

1. **Know what you have to offer your employer.** What are your strengths? What can you bring to the job that someone else could not? Don't be afraid to give voice to your skills. That's not bragging, it's presenting yourself.

2. **Know what you want from a job.** Think of this in terms of both practicalities—type of work, location, people, pay—and personal accomplishments—challenge, creativity, advancement, opportunity.

If you aren't sure what kinds of jobs appeal to you, take a trip of the library and look through *America's Top 300 Jobs* or the *Occupational Outlook Handbook*.[3] These books will give you an overview of many of the jobs available in the United States today. Some may require additional education and/or training, but others won't.

3.   **Know where to look.** Fewer than 15
percent of all jobs are found through ads in
the newspaper. Where else is there? Contacts
are everywhere, you just need to know
where to find them. Friends, family,
acquaintances—even your son's parent's
friends or your daughter's troop leader—may
be the links that lead you to the job you
want.

See *The Very Quick Job Search* for
a wealth of practical ideas on how to
best find, organize, and act on your
job leads.[4]

4.   **Take your job search seriously.** Treat your
job search like a job. Research shows that the
harder you look for the job you want, the
more likely it is you will find it quickly.
Organize your job search information—
books, resumes, papers, note cards, business
cards, pens, calendars, day-planner—and put
it in a Hands-Off! area of your home. Maybe
it's in the kitchen; maybe it's a quiet spot in
the den. Set up your area and put armed
guards there if you have to, but protect it. No,
Sam *doesn't* need to color on the back of your
note cards. Treat your job search—and the
tools you need to complete it—as seriously as
you would any work assigned you by your
future employer.

5.   **Get out there.** Planning and researching
aren't easy, but they don't involve too much
risk. Most people dread the interview stage,
where they are setting appointments and
keeping them, and opening themselves up to
possible judgment and—gulp!—rejection. But
you won't get a job sitting in the house.
Eventually, you have to get out there and
interview.

The Very Quick Job Search has wonderful advice on how to make sure you don't get into a cat-and-mouse interview game: Make it a point to approach employers who aren't hiring.[5] They will be impressed with your foresight ("I know you're not hiring right now, but I'm really interested in your company and wanted to find out how I could submit my resume in case you have any openings...") and your initiative. The employer will not be looking for how you *don't* fit—as she might be if she's interviewing dozens of prospective employees—and will be more likely to see the strengths you could bring to the organization.

A Mental Health Minute

Sometimes—especially if you're returning to the workforce after several years of stirring Cream of Wheat—the hardest thing about the job search is opening the front door and walking out. You might feel that life has passed you by. Things you used to know are outdated. Things you hoped you'd know by now don't seem so important.

Okay, close the door. You're not quite ready yet. Get a pencil and a pad of paper, and make a list of all your strengths. I mean everything. If you're great with a can of cleanser, write it down. If you can sing like Pavarotti, write it down. If you've got computer skills or a good phone voice or don't get paper cuts easily, write it down. Fixing lawnmowers? It's a skill. Good at calming down your mother-in-law? It's a talent that will come in handy. Able to deliver three children to three different after-school activities and still have time to get the dog groomed? Believe me, that's a gift.

The point is that you've been doing things for years that you haven't necessarily seen as part of your skills set. Parenting is all about skills: people skills, management skills, coping skills, communication skills. There's literally nothing you've learned as a parent that won't translate in some useful way to your work.

When you've made your list, go get yourself a cup of coffee and look over the list long and hard. This is about you and what you have to offer. Be proud of it. All experience is useful experience, whether you've been paid for it monetarily or not. When you feel secure that what you have to offer an employer is *more* today than it was a few years ago *because of your experience*, go ahead and open the door and walk out. The world will be a better place for it.

6. **Keep in touch.** Once you've made the initial contact, whether it's a phone call, a dropped-off resume, or a full-blown interview, follow up. Send a thank-you card; wait a set period of time and follow up with a phone call. Get organized about your follow-ups, but make sure you don't let a contact drop until you're certain the position has been filled. And even if the decision was made for someone else, be pleasant about it and ask the employer to keep your resume on file. It's especially important not to burn bridges in the job world. You might be passing this way again someday.

Employer Possibilities

Here's a list of employers I'm interested in contacting:

1. _____
2. _____
3. _____
4. _____
5. _____
6. _____
7. _____
8. _____
9. _____
10. _____

What Can You Give Your Employer?

Somewhere in the back of your mind you should have a basic idea of what your family needs—financially, emotionally, and physically. Hopefully you've also spent some time thinking about the type of job that would make you happy: home or work, full-time or part-time, one that would enable you to use your hands or your brain—you get the idea.

One last step before you turn yourself loose on the world of prospective employers: Determine how far you're willing to go. What, in terms of hours and commitment, are you prepared to offer? Get a clear picture of this before you walk into that first interview, and you'll have not only a better chance of getting what you want but an increased probability that you'll recognize the "wrong" job right off the bat.

Defining "Can"

The word "can" can give us problems. In this context, the question "What can you give your employer?" does not mean "What is it humanly possible for you to give your employer?" but, rather, "In light of your family's priority list and mission statement, and taking into account the type of job you think would make you happy, what are you willing to give your employer?"

You "can" do all sorts of things. You can take a job because you feel you have to, right now (and sometimes those situations happen), and be miserable, underappreciated, and underpaid. You can work many more hours than you want to "for the money." You can show up when someone calls in sick, and you can frantically try to arrange for a baby-sitter on your days off when you're called in unexpectedly. You "can" do all those things.

What you're trying to do instead is be proactive about the type of job you select, so you get a job that fits what you and your family need, instead of taking a job "because you have to" and trying to make your family fit around it.

So consider what you're willing to invest in terms of time, commitment, and flexibility before you put that best foot forward. Being clear about what you want—and what you're offering—will help both you and your eventual employer make the right match.

Hours

Jobs come in all shapes and sizes, with all kinds of hourly commitments—from a few hours a week to nearly every waking moment. When you think about the hours you want to work, ask yourself these questions:

1. How many hours a week am I willing to work?

2. What time of day would be best?

3. Do I need to be home before or after school?

4. Do I need flexible time in the middle of the day?

5. Do I need to work a set schedule or is flex-time okay?

6. Do I want to work conventional workdays (Monday through Friday) or weekends?

Commitment

Some jobs want you to "sign on" for a specific period of time. You may have a contract or an agreement that a certain amount of time is a "probationary" period, after which you are instated as a full-time employee. In many organizations using a probationary period, your benefits won't be in full effect until the probationary period is over. The employer is trying to protect his or her investment in your training and wants to be sure you make it through the toughest part of the learning curve.

Commitment, from your side, means something a little different. How far up on your priority scale are you prepared to put your job, if it's the "right" job? A doctor must be willing to make a huge commitment: on-call every few nights, all night, answering pages in the middle of plays, school functions, and family dinners. Are you looking for a job you can "leave at the office," so when you're finished for the day you can simply turn off the lights and go home?

Different occupations, of course, require different degrees of commitment. Degree of commitment often means the difference between a "job" and a "career."

Generally, we are willing to make a commitment to something when we know it will pay us back long-term. In building a career, we invest time, effort, and even money. We take classes because we know the extra learning will make us more valuable to our employer. We agree to go to training seminars because we know we'll have a shot at management later.

If the job you're seeking is a short-term commitment—something to do while your kids are small, a second income to help you through a budget squeeze, or a specific answer to a need for something like additional insurance, outside companionship, or work experience—you might not be willing to make such a commitment. You don't want to be giving up 60 hours a week for a job you don't plan to be working at four months from now. You don't want to go in at 3:00 A.M. when the shift supervisor calls you.

Only you can decide what level of commitment you are willing to give your new job. There's no right or wrong, only what's comfortable for you and your family. The key is in thinking it through before you go to the interview. Know what you are offering before you get there.

Here are a few questions to ask when you're considering your commitment factor:

1. Where will this job fall in terms of our priority list?

2. Am I looking for a job that will become a career or am I looking for a part-time or temporary position?

3. Am I willing to continue my education to excel in this job?

Did I Tell You About the Time . . . ?

"I'm real proud of the five-car-carrier truck I drive. The kids think it's just the greatest thing. I was excited the day I got to bring it home and show it to them. My wife and kids were standing in the yard as I pulled the truck in the driveway. As they smiled and waved at me, I drove into the telephone wires and ripped them from the house. My wife stopped smiling."
—Father of two who works full-time

Flexibility

Flexibility is really an offshoot of commitment, because asking how flexible you're willing to be is really asking, "How much change are you willing to put up with?" Some families do well with changing or rotating schedules; others have trouble settling into a routine when Mom or Dad are always working different hours.

Some parents work on an as-needed basis. One mother, a substitute teacher in her local school system, says, "I only work when the kids are in school, and if I've got something else to do, I can do it."

Statistics show that 17 percent of the American workforce works hours other than traditional office hours.[6] Just under 4 percent of those workers have what they call "irregular" schedules that cannot be classified as either day, evening, night, or rotating shifts. If this type of arrangement is okay with you and your family—in some cases, it might nicely complement your spouse's work situation—know that before you go to the interview.

What about travel? Would you enjoy an occasional business trip, or would traveling put too much of a strain on your family?

Questions to ask about flexibility include these:

1. Can our family be flexible about my work schedule?

2. Do I need a job that is predictable, or can I be available on-call?

3. Am I willing to travel?

4. What does "flexibility" mean to me, and how flexible am I willing to be for the job I take?

I am willing to offer my employer:

Hours: _____

Overtime? _____

Flexible scheduling? _____

On-call? _____

Commitment:_____

_____

_____

Flexibility: _____

_____

_____

The "Ideal" Match

The whole idea behind thinking about what you want before you go looking for it is that the more you understand about what's important to you, the more likely you are to get it. And the more likely you are to know it when you see it. Hopefully, you'll also know when you've walked into the wrong place.

How many horror stories have you heard from people who have taken a job because they were afraid they couldn't find anything else? Maybe you've done it yourself. Many of us do it at least once in our working careers.

We've been weaving the picture of the ideal job. You know what your family needs. You've thought about your talents and aspirations. You've gotten an idea of what you're willing to give an employer in terms of time, commitment, and flexibility. Now, what is this ideal employer going to give you?

In Search of the Ideal Employer

Earlier, I mentioned that there are a number of ways to go about your job search. You might hear about job openings from friends or relatives. You might read about them in the paper. You might use an employment service, see something on-line, or catch an ad in an industry magazine. However you found it, you now have an interview.

Often we go into an interview—or the second, third, or fourth interview—thinking about what we have to offer, putting our best foot forward, appearing confident, capable, and sure. But you also need to think about what the company has to offer you. How will you know whether the company is one that will support your "family-is-important" lifestyle? There are a number of things you can look for (and ask about):

1. What is the average age of your employees?

2. Are there a number of young families here? How many?

3. What are your policies on sick days and personal days?

4. Do you have any alternative scheduling options, such as flex-time or job sharing?

5. Do you have any special child-care benefits, such as on-site day care, child-care subsidies (that's where the employer pays part of the child-care expense), summer programs, or back-up care?

These questions hit all the basics, and you'll probably know whether you're talking to a family-friendly employer as soon as you ask the first family-related question.

These are the things that are most important to me in an employer:

1. _____

2. _____

3. _____

4. _____

5. _____

6. _____

7. _____

8. _____

9. _____

10. _____

The Family-Friendly Workplace

How do you know whether the company you are interviewing with is one that is going to work for you and your family? In short, a family-friendly company will see that your family makes you a better candidate and not a lesser one. The person sitting opposite you in the interview will see the value in the many decisions you make in a day's time, the multitasking, organizing, and peacemaking qualities you bring to his or her team. He or she will look past the occasional trip to the orthodontist's office and the after-school phone calls in order to get the long-term benefit of an intelligent, capable, and dedicated employee. As one family-friendly employer put it,

"I knew when I interviewed Carol that I was in for a couple of years of babies being sick, deadlines getting stretched, and unexpected situations. But she was so creative and so talented, I knew that having her on board was worth all of that and more. Today, she's one of my best people. I've never regretted it for a minute."

Making a "Less-than-Ideal" Match Better

You may already have a job. Some things in that job might be great; others are less than you'd hoped for. Ask yourself the questions in this chapter as you think about your current job: Is it fitting the balance of home and work you'd hoped it would? Is there some rebalancing to be done? Don't feel as though you are stuck in the job with no hope of changing it. Things can always be changed.

A carefully thought-out conversation with your employer might help you understand his or her policies on family-related issues. It also might help clear the air if there are issues between you that need to be addressed. A great book for thinking about and then asking for what you want is *The Aladdin Factor*, by Jack Canfield and Mark Victor Hansen.[7] This book will help you identify what you're looking for, and show you how to ask for what you need in a clear, nonthreatening manner.

Summary

Your family is an asset, not a liability. The experience, dedication, and commitment you have invested in your family should be a benefit to your prospective employer, and not something you need to apologize for.

There still are employers out there who want to own the body, mind, and soul of an employee and who are threatened when an employee puts something else (like family) first. And those employers will find the employees they seek. But rest assured that there are many employers who look for the maturity, capability, commitment, and responsibility of an employee who seeks a challenging, progressive environment that fits in with his or her overall family and personal goals. Your job is to find them.

Notes

1. J. Michael Farr, *The Very Quick Job Search,* 2nd Edition (Indianapolis: JIST Works, 1996).

2. Ibid.

3. U.S. Department of Labor, *America's Top 300 Jobs* (Indianapolis: JIST Works, 1994); U.S. Department of Labor, *Occupational Outlook Handbook* (Indianapolis: JIST Works, 1994).

4. Farr, *The Very Quick Job Search.*

5. Ibid.

6. *Statistical Abstract of the United States 1995,* Table 635 (U.S. Government Printing Office, 1995).

7. Jack Canfield and Mark Victor Hansen, *The Aladdin Factor* (New York: Berkley Books, 1995).

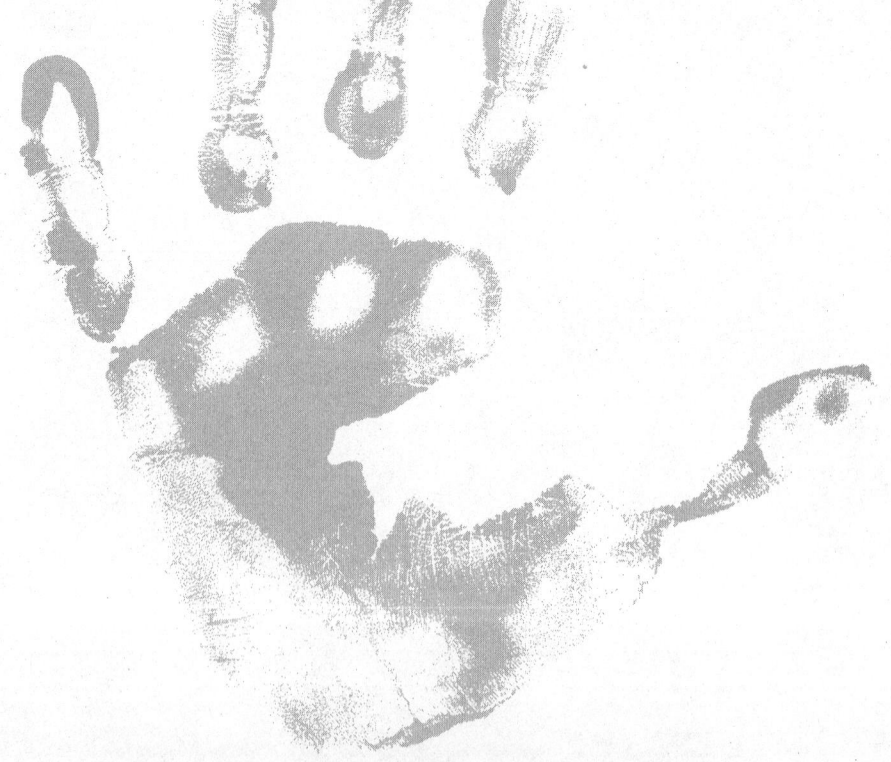

The Child-Care Issue

Translations from the Child

"I don't know why. He just hit me."
He hit his brother.
"I didn't hit him. I just sort of pushed him."
He hit his brother.
"I didn't do anything."
He hit his brother.
"Mo-m-m-my!"
His brother hit him.
—Robert Paul Smith

Finding child care you're happy with is one of the most important factors in balancing home and office life. If you're worried about your children while you're at work, you're not able to focus on the job at hand. If you have questions about the situation, about the caregiver, about your child's safety—any level of concern, no matter how small—that's going to affect the level of concentration you can bring first to your job search and then to your job.

If you've got child-care arrangements worked out so that you, your spouse, and your children are all cared for and supported, you are free to do and be your best in the workforce. That's good for you and will translate to a happier parent and happier kids.

BEST & WORST

Best: "My own paycheck!"

This chapter presents the different options available in finding child care. We will look at a number of practical situations and discuss the things to consider and ask about each. My best advice, however, is this: *Trust your instincts.* Only you know whether your child will thrive best in a preschool, in a home, with grandma, or in a day-care program. We will look at several situations here so that you can get a bird's-eye view of the different options and focus in on the one that seems a close match to what your family needs and wants.

What's Out There?

Just as children come in all shapes, sizes, and colors, there are all kinds of child-care arrangements. The trick is to investigate what's possible; look around in your area and find out what's available; look even closer and see what's feasible (in other words, what fits your budget); then answer the most important question: Which caregiver will give your child the love, support, and protection she needs when you are not there to give it to her?

This section explores several of the most popular child-care options. I've divided them into the following categories: baby-sitters, home day care, day-care centers, care by a friend or neighbor, care by a relative, and self-care.

What Are Parents Using?

In preparing this book, a colleague and I interviewed many working parents who were using each of the different child-care options.[1] There were definite favorites—such as home-style day care—and other, rarer occurrences—like the latch-key kid alternative. Child-care choices are predicated, of course, on the needs of the child, which vary from age to age and situation to situation.

Specifically, we found:

 6 percent of respondents had in-home baby-sitters;

 31 percent arranged their work hours so Mom and Dad took care of the kids and no day care was needed;

 25 percent took their children to home-run day care;

 14 percent used local day-care centers;

 6 percent relied on friends or neighbors;

 14 percent took their children to other family members (aunts, grandparents, etc.);

 6 percent of the parents interviewed allowed their children to stay home alone. (All of the parents in this category had children over the age of 10, usually with at least one teenager in the home.)[2]

Figure 3.1 shows the results of these informal interviews.

How Our Parents Responded

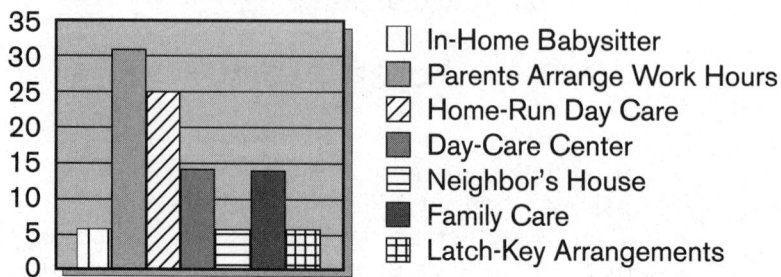

☐ In-Home Babysitter
▨ Parents Arrange Work Hours
▨ Home-Run Day Care
▨ Day-Care Center
☰ Neighbor's House
▨ Family Care
▦ Latch-Key Arrangements

Figure 3.1

Things to Consider

Many parents prefer to work out child-care arrangements themselves, so their children spend a minimum of time in someone else's care. A fairly high number of respondents—26 percent— said that they have arranged their work schedules so Mom has the kids when Dad is working and vice versa.

Home-run day care was the second most popular choice, showing up as the child-care solution for 25 percent of those interviewed.

Grandma or Grandpa is the logical next choice, with 14 percent relying on family members to fill in the gaps of child care. Another 6 percent had their children stay with neighbors until they were able to get home from work.

As you think about the type of child care that will work for you, several factors will weigh heavily:

 The ages of your children and the care they need

 The hours (both the number and the range of hours) you need child care

 the cost of different kinds of child care

Your Child's Age

It's no secret that children need care; and they need loving care no matter what age they are. Different ages bring different responsibilities, however. An infant needs one kind of care; a ninth-grader needs another.

Some parents arrange to work swing shifts so they can keep their child at home while he is an infant and then make day-care or preschool arrangements when he is old enough to want socialization. One mother puts it this way:

◆ ◆

"From the time Sara was born until she was 18 months old, my employer allowed me to work at home three days a week. Then, all of a sudden, when Sara turned one-and-a-half, Mom wasn't interesting anymore. She was ready to be social, and I began taking her to day care and went back to work at the office full-time. Things are great—we enjoy being together more than ever now that we're each doing our own thing."
—Mother of one who works full-time

◆ ◆

Your Hours

All working parents try set up the best possible child care for their child. For some, that means a little of this and a little of that. Your daughter might go to the baby-sitter's on Tuesday and Thursday and to preschool on Monday, Wednesday, and Friday mornings. Perhaps you are able to work at home those three afternoons, or she goes to a neighbor's house and you pick her up on your way home.

When you are thinking about the type of child care you need, think about the hours you'll be needing it. If you are just beginning to look for a job, you don't know the actual hours you will be working, but you will have an idea of what you're *willing* to work, which you can use as a guideline for the hours you'll need child care.

If your second-grader only needs someone to watch him from 3:00 P.M., when he gets off the bus, until 5:10, when you get home, you might be able to work it out with a neighbor for those couple of after-school hours a day. If you've got a toddler who needs full-time child care, you'll probably be looking for a home-run day care, a day-care center, a relative, or some kind of swing shift arrangement with your spouse. Remember that the key is to come up with the schedule and practical arrangements to support what is important to your family. So what if you do something different every day of the week, as long as everyone is okay with it? Or perhaps you will go the other way and keep a very regimented schedule. That's okay, too. The idea is to come up with a system that works for you and provides the best possible care for your children.

Your Budget

None of us would choose a particular kind of child care—especially if we thought it was substandard—simply because of the cost. More likely, if we are faced with child-care costs that are too high and the need to work, we will scramble like crazy to come up with as many options as we can find.

But different kinds of child care are going to cost differing amounts. Nannies—private, in-home caregivers acquired through a service—cost upwards of $200 a week. An in-home baby-sitter might charge half that, although other services, such as laundry or dishes, might be extra. In-home day care might range from $45 to $100 a week (maybe higher in some areas), and day-care centers offer a range of hours and choices that also put you in the $100 and up bracket. If you add another child, you're looking at $150 + a week in child-care expenses alone, which adds up quickly week after week after week.

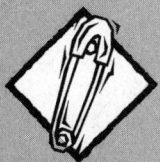

Many businesses today are willing to help parents by subsidizing the cost of day care. Talk to local day-care providers to see which businesses in your area participate in subsidized programs. And don't forget to ask about day-care subsidies as a benefit in your job interviews!

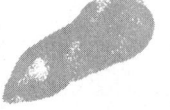

There is an option—or a combination of options—that will work for you. Keep looking until you find it. And once you make your child-care decisions, make it a point to reevaluate every so often. Nothing is set in stone, and the key to making things better is being able to look at them and ask yourself (and your kids) how everything is working out.

What Kind of Care Do We Need?

List each child's name and age and the type of care he or she needs; for example,

Brandon, 8, after-school care

Emily, 2, all day

How much can we afford to spend on child care?

Child-Care Options

Once you've established that you'll need to rely on someone other than yourself, your spouse, or your family for at least part of the time, you have a number of avenues to consider. You might want to allow your children to stay at home and have the caregiver come to them. You might take them to another person's home. Or you might enroll them in a day-care center. This section discusses those different options and gives you checklists for evaluating each.

In-Home Sitter

It may be every working parent's dream: your very own Mrs. Doubtfire, perhaps retired after many years of teaching school, searching for a special child she can love and care for and bake chocolate-chip cookies with. She comes to your home, she does the laundry and the dishes, she takes wonderful care of your kids, gets them to their appointments, lessons, and friend's houses on time, and starts dinner for you on the days you're running late.

The in-home sitter is a wonderful option provided (1) you can find just the right person and (2) you can afford her. Many in-home sitters do become members of the family, often taking on other household responsibilities in addition to caring for the children. One mother who has successfully worked with an in-home sitter for years has this tip to offer:

♦ ♦

"Make your sitter a part of your family. Treat her with respect, and never take advantage of her! There is mutual love between my children and our sitter, and I'm glad."
—Mother of two who works full-time

♦ ♦

Where can you find an in-home sitter? The answer depends on the type of sitter you're hoping for. Nannies, once a luxury, are now becoming more commonplace in the two-career family. You can contact an agency to interview a range of potential nannies and hire the one that best fits your household. How much will you pay for a nanny? That varies greatly, depending on the area you live in. But, generally, you should expect to pay a premium—$200 to $300 a week and higher—for premium, customized child care.

If you want to find an in-home sitter in a more informal undertaking, think about what type of sitter you're looking for. Your church is a good place to start. Other places to try include a local university (often they have a referral service for students looking for placements; someone majoring in education would be a logical choice as a sitter). Perhaps the most often-used source for good in-home care is the advice of friends and neighbors. Maybe your friend had a sitter who was wonderful last summer but won't be needing her services this summer. Keep your eyes and ears open and the right in-home sitter may come to you.

What are some things to look for in a good in-home sitter? Here is a list of considerations[3]:

 How interested is she in your child?

 How does she interact with the child? Is she listening attentively or focusing on other things?

 Does she seem to be creative?

 What does she think is the most important thing about caring for a child?

 Does your child seem to like her?

 Is she willing to drive to appointments or carpool if necessary?

 Will she do any other household chores?

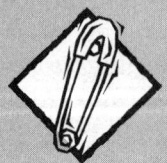

Before you hire an in-home sitter, invite her over to "play" at least twice in an informal setting. Let her interact with your children and give them a chance to get comfortable together, with you nearby.

Make sure, when you find the sitter who will work for your family, that you discuss how to resolve any issues that might arise. Talk about discipline, stresses, financial situations, and illness. Iron out the wrinkles up-front, as much as possible.

Remember, too, that an employee you have in your home is an employee nonetheless. Check with your accountant and make sure you've got the right paperwork filed with the IRS.

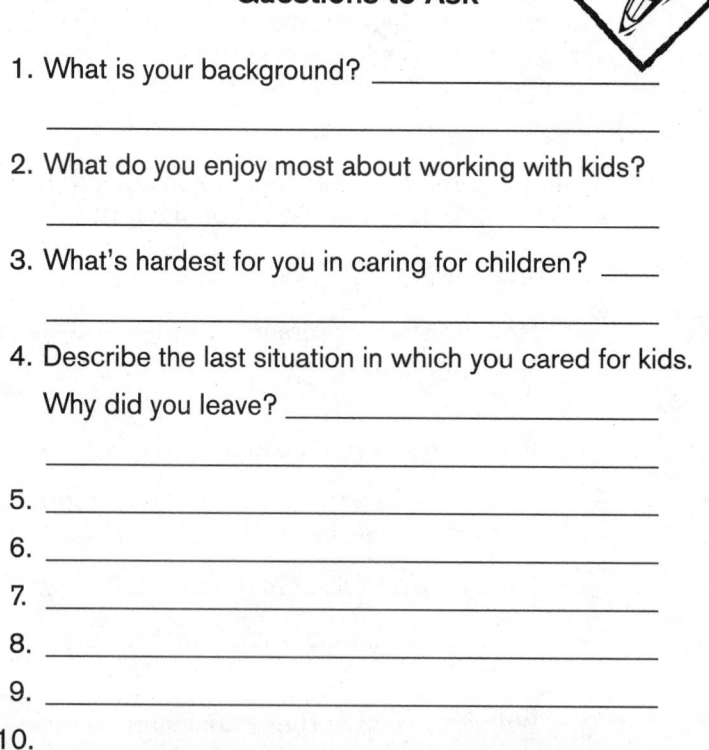

Questions to Ask

1. What is your background? _____

_____

2. What do you enjoy most about working with kids?

_____

3. What's hardest for you in caring for children? _____

_____

4. Describe the last situation in which you cared for kids.
   Why did you leave? _____

_____

5. _____

6. _____

7. _____

8. _____

9. _____

10. _____

The most important word of advice about hiring an in-home sitter is this: Get references and check them. It is possible to do this without affronting or insulting the prospective caregiver. Anyone who loves children will understand your need to be thorough in making sure you've hired the best possible person to care for your child.

Home Day Care

The second largest percentage of working parents we interviewed (25 percent) take their children to home-run day cares. This situation often is one in which the caregiver, usually a mother herself, takes four to ten children into her home on a full-time or part-time basis.

Home day care is done on a formal, accredited or an informal basis. Many cities have agencies that can give you the names, locations, and phone numbers of accredited home day cares in your area. An accredited home day-care center will follow guidelines determined by the agency, which usually keeps tabs on the number of children in the home, the ages of the children, the adult-to-children ratio, and meal plans. Additionally, the agency may provide information to caregivers on topics such as the importance of immunizations, planning healthy snacks, and how to reduce germs and colds with safe household products.

From One Parent to Another

"When you're looking at home day cares or day-care centers, don't take your child to every one you visit. Take him only to the two or three best. That will let him be part of the decision without overwhelming him with the ones you don't like."

—Mother of two who works full-time

How do you find a home-run day care? Start by looking for a child-care agency in your area. Look in the *Yellow Pages* under Child Care or even Preschools. You also may want to contact your local Child and Family Services division (a segment of your local government) to find out what agencies and services are available.

Friends and family are a good source of information on home-run day care, as are other parents at work or the parents of children in your child's class at school.

Once you've found a home-run day care you want to check out, go and visit by yourself first. Observe and ask about the following things:

 Is the overall atmosphere of the home happy or harried?

 Is there a separate "child area" with easels, tables and chairs, toys, and/or blocks where the children feel welcome to play with abandon?

 Does the day-care provider offer a set schedule during which she does different activities with the children?

 How does she handle nap time?

 What does she do when she has one or more sick children at home?

 How is discipline handled?

 Is there an outdoor, fenced play area with play equipment appropriate to the ages of the children?

Again, ask for references. The day-care provider can probably give you the names and numbers of the parents of some of her other charges. When you get the numbers, make the calls. The provider won't mind you checking, and the parents won't mind giving their input. Everyone understands the need to make sure one's children are protected and cared for.

Home Safe Home

One of the biggest differences between a day-care center and a home-run day care—besides the number of children—is the adherence to health and safety guidelines. In order to be licensed, day-care centers must meet with strict state requirements. If you are electing to use a home-run day care, you'll need to think about and ask about some safety issues yourself.

- Does the day-care provider have an adequate number of fire alarms and extinguishers?

- Does she have an exit plan that she explains to the children about where to go and what to do in case of fire?

- Does she teach the children how to call 911?

- Where do they go in case of inclement weather?

These are not issues that need to be resolved on your first visit, but they are important things to address before you begin dropping your child off in the morning.

The Day-Care Center

A smaller percentage (14 percent) of the parents we interviewed used day-care centers. But nationwide, day-care centers provide a massive amount of support to parents in a variety of occupations with a wide range of working hours. A day-care center typically cares for a large number of children, ranging in ages from 6 weeks to 12 years. (Not all day-care centers are licensed for infant care. Check the centers in your area to see which ones provide the services you need.)

A typical day in a day-care center is similar to that of a preschool, only longer. Your child will probably have circle time, story time, drawing and coloring, puzzle time, snack time, lunch time, nap time, music, and other activities. Some day-care centers focus strongly on academics and offer things like computer time (even for 2- and 3-year-olds), field trips, and Montessori-style lessons.

The Montessori method of teaching, designed by Sister Maria Montessori in the early 1900s, focuses on experiential learning. Children learn about measuring by spooning rice into a cup; they learn their letters by tracing the outline of the letter on a sandpaper block; they get the basics of mathematical operations by working with blocks and beads. This enables even pre-readers to grasp many of the basic concepts they'll learn later, all in fun, nonthreatening activities.

Many day-care centers offer activities or low-key learning experiences that are based on the Montessori method. Ask your day-care center how they handle academic issues. Experts agree that the primary focus for preschoolers should be on fun and socialization. They'll have plenty of time for academics later.

A good day-care center, like a happy home-run day-care situation, can be a terrific experience for your children. They might love the interaction; they might enjoy the stimulation; and many children of working parents like having their own "work" to go to.

The hours of day-care centers usually are limited, however, and parents who work nontraditional hours are often left to find other child care. There is a need today for 24-hour day-care centers, where children can spend the night if their parents work the graveyard shift; for weekend care, for parents in nontraditional occupations like retail or other service businesses; and for sick-child care, for the child "on the mend," not seriously ill but not recovered enough for school. These options are available, but not widely so. Their numbers are still small.

Parents' Wish Lists

The following items are on parents' wish lists for day care. The need is there, but the services are slow in coming:

 Extended hour care

Weekend care

24-hour care

 Drop-in care

Overnight care

 Sick-child care

Here are a few questions you will want to ask the director of the day-care center when you visit:

What is the overall mission statement of the day-care center?

Has a formal complaint of any kind ever been filed against the day-care center? If so, what was the situation and how was it resolved? If not, what should a parent do if he or she has a question or concern?

How accessible is the director of the center? What is the director's background, and what does she or he find most challenging about running the center successfully?

How does enrollment at the center compare to the enrollment a year ago? Is the enrollment growing? Have the necessary number of teachers and aides been added?

The following sections break down by age groups the things you might want to consider as you're looking for a day-care center for your child. Bear in mind that many of the issues will apply to any child-care arrangements you make, not only day-care centers. The key is to go in knowing what you're looking for; then you'll know it when you do (or don't) find it.

Infants and Toddlers

Babies need laps to sit on and hands to hold. One of the most important things for an infant or toddler in day care is that there be an adequate number of adults to care for the children present. Most states have strict requirements about the adult-to-child ratio, particularly where infants and toddlers are concerned. Check the requirement for your state, and make sure that any caregiver you investigate adheres strictly to state guidelines.

Here's a quick list of things to look for:

 Is the center a happy place? Is the atmosphere laughing and loving or tense and quiet?

 What kind of training does the staff participate in?

 Is there a nurse on-staff?

 How long have the infant and toddler teachers been with the staff? Children will bond with their caregivers, and a frequent turnover in teachers could be unsettling to your child. It also could be an indication that something is wrong with the management of the center.

 Are there plenty of cribs?

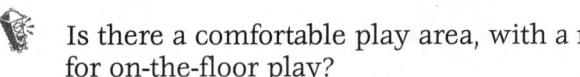 Is there a comfortable play area, with a rug for on-the-floor play?

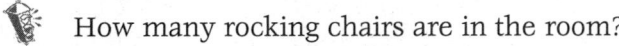 How many rocking chairs are in the room?

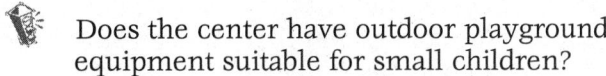 Does the center have outdoor playground equipment suitable for small children?

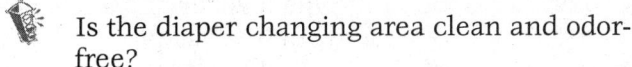 Is there a separate fenced play area apart from the older children's playground?

Is the diaper changing area clean and odor-free?

Ask to see any toys your child will be playing with. How do the teachers deter the spread of germs with the bunch of "chewers" they have in class every day?

Questions for Later

1. What items from home will you need to provide for your baby? _____

   _____

2. How many diapers does the center need on-hand?

   _____

3. What about bottles and pacifiers?

   _____

4. How does the center handle it when your child is on a prescription? _____

   _____

5. _____
6. _____
7. _____
8. _____
9. _____
10. _____

Preschoolers

If you're considering a day-care center for your preschooler, you'll have a different set of concerns on your checklist. The same safety and cleanliness issues apply, but there will be other things to watch for, as well.

 What is the class size? How many adults are available for your child's class? There may be one full-time teacher and a teacher's aide, depending on the age group and the number of children in the class.

 Are there child-sized tables and chairs? Most centers also have child-sized toilet facilities and are equipped for both small and middle-sized (school-aged) children.

 What does the staff do in the event of scrapes and bruises? At what point do they notify you? Is there an accident report form or some reporting policy they follow in case of an injury?

 What types of meals are offered? Licensed day-care centers must follow state guidelines for nutrition; these guidelines require that lunch menus be posted weekly, so parents can see what their children are eating during the day.

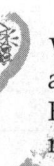 What happens during a typical day? Is there a balance between action and quiet times? How many times a day will your child be read to? Will he or she get to play on the playground? What happens on rainy or cold days?

What does the general learning atmosphere feel like? At preschool age, learning should be an exploration: you should see plenty of toys for "pretend"—dress-up clothes, toy kitchens, blocks. While preschoolers are apt to learn things like colors, shapes, numbers, and maybe letters, there shouldn't be any pressure on them to learn at this age. Preschool should be fun.

 How is discipline handled? If you don't see any signs of it going on around you, ask. Day-care centers usually use a "time-out" method to discipline. Get clear guidance on what's acceptable behavior and what is not.

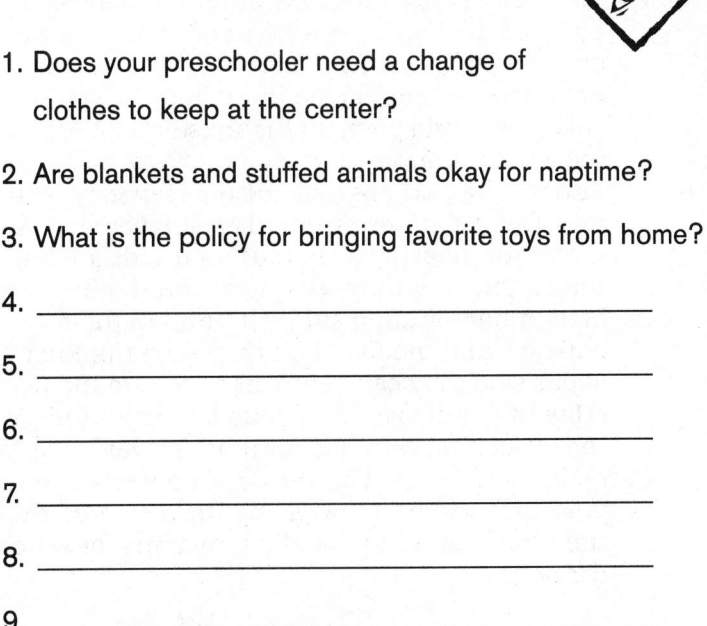

Questions for Later

1. Does your preschooler need a change of clothes to keep at the center?

2. Are blankets and stuffed animals okay for naptime?

3. What is the policy for bringing favorite toys from home?

4. _____

5. _____

6. _____

7. _____

8. _____

9. _____

10. _____

The School-Aged Child

Most day-care centers have some kind of after-school club or activity center for school-aged children. Some also offer transportation to and from area schools and provide field trips and other incentives— such as computer time—for older children.

When you're investigating a day-care center for your school-aged child, make sure you visit during the time the school-agers are in the building. See how the teacher (or teachers) handle the kids. Are the children kept busy? Are they working with age-appropriate materials, or are they using toys and building sets meant for younger children? Are there plenty of children in your child's age group, or is he one of the oldest or youngest? Sociability is an important factor in both what your child learns and how well he adjusts to his environment.

Many day-care centers have more school-agers enrolled during the summer and school vacations over the holidays. And many of these centers use field trips to keep the children busy. If you're okay with your child going to the museum on Monday, the zoo on Tuesday, the pool on Wednesday and Friday, and perhaps a picnic on Thursday, you may find a day-care center is just what you want for your school-aged child. If your kids are like mine, however, they want to spend the first month of summer vacation sitting around in their pajamas until noon, when they start thinking about who they can get to take them to the pool. (Hey, if I could get away with sitting around in my robe watching cartoons until noon every day, I'd do it, too!) Check with the day-care center to see if your kids will be allowed any unstructured time, time they can spend reading, relaxing, or watching cartoons.

Another important issue to explore if you're thinking about a day-care center for your school-aged child is what they do about discipline. Dealing with 10 or 12 jeering fourth graders is no small feat. How do the teachers handle it? Again, get very clear directions on what's acceptable and what's not, and—before you enroll her—go over the list with your child. Make sure you both know what you're walking into.

Questions for Later

1. Do you pick up after school?

2. If my child participates in sports, can you provide transportation to the center after practice?

3. Do you have any club activities, such as scouting or 4-H, available for school-agers at the center?

4. _____

5. _____

6. _____

7. _____

8. _____

9. _____

10. _____

Workplace Child Care

A decade ago, finding a day-care center in or around an office was nearly unheard of. Today, some large corporations have a day care on premises; others make arrangements with nearby centers to help offset child-care costs for employees or in other ways subsidize child care.

BEST & WORST

Worst: "Making arrangements when kids are off school"

In return for their family-friendly investment, these employers enjoy many benefits, including happier employees, less turnover, and higher productivity. Parents can easily have lunch with their children, be close by in case of bumps and bruises, and work with peace of mind knowing their children are nearby.

If the job you are investigating does not offer any kind of child care or subsidies (which means they pay for a portion of the care and you have a reduced fee because you are a member of the organization), you can always try to get something started later. Chapter 9 explores the different avenues you can follow to make family issues more prevalent in your organization or office.

What Kind of Child Care Is Best for Us?

First Choice: _____

Second Choice: _____

Third Choice: _____

Alternatives/Comments: _____

_____

_____

_____

The Latch-Key Alternative

So you have successfully made it through the baby-sitter and day-care stages. Now you are facing the home-alone stage. Your 12-year-old doesn't want to go to the sitter's house this summer. She's old enough to stay home on her own, she insists. You consider. Is she? What about phone calls, and cooking, and strangers at the door?

It's a big decision. The "ideal" latch-key situation (if there is one) is the one where your 16-year-old is home to watch the 12-year-old during the summer. Yes, they are both kids, but a 16-year-old is better equipped than a 12-year-old to deal with the decisions that come up during the day.

Most parents who rely on latch-key situations insist their children follow a regimented schedule: "As soon as you get off the bus, go right into the house and call me to let me know you're home. Get yourself a snack (I put one in the fridge for you), and get busy on your homework. You can watch TV or play video games until I get home at 5:00. But no friends in, and you can't go out until I get home."

Doesn't sound like a lot of fun. But with proper guidelines, your child will be safe, be proud of taking care of herself, and be able to get homework at least started (with some peripheral dawdling) before you get home.

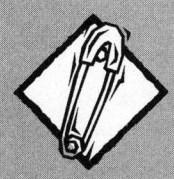 If you let your child stay home alone, make sure you post the phone number of a close relative or friend who can help out in any situation: when your child is frightened, can't get a jar open, has a homework question, or just wants to talk. And of course post emergency numbers and make sure your child knows what to do in case of bad weather or other unexpected happenings.

Did I Tell You About the Time . . . ?

"When our children were first old enough to stay home by themselves, I told them to tell people who called that I was in the shower and couldn't come to the phone. The only problem is that if the caller then asks for my husband, the kids say 'He's in the shower, too!'"
—Mother of two who works part-time

Rules for Staying Home Alone

1. _____
2. _____
3. _____
4. _____
5. _____
6. _____
7. _____

Emergency Numbers:
Police: _____
Fire: _____
Mom at work: _____
Dad at work: _____
Neighbor: _____

Making Day Care Work

Once you get the job, find the child care, and begin moving into a regular routine, what can you do to keep things running smoothly? Here are a few tips that will help you anticipate and maybe bypass problems with your caregiver.

Establish your schedule, and stick to it. Don't vary your drop-off time every day and—especially after a long, harried day—call if you're going to be more than 15 minutes late.

When you think your schedule will change—say you're covering another worker's hours for a two-week period—let your caregiver know as soon as possible. This will enable her to make necessary arrangements to accommodate the change.

If you have a flexible work schedule, give your caregiver a copy of your schedule as soon as you have it. Telling her is okay, but having it in writing lets her refer to it later.

If "drop-ins" are okay with your caregiver and it's possible you might need her services on a stray day here and there, talk to her about it first. Call and ask whether it's okay, preferably a week or so in advance. This helps you know how many children she'll have so you can plan activities for the day.

When you have questions or concerns, express them in a respectful, caring way. If you're upset because Janie said one of the babies bit her, don't call the caregiver up and read her the riot act. When you drop Janie off in the morning, explain what Janie told you and ask the caregiver if she is having a problem with one of the babies biting. Talk about the situation constructively: What's being tried? How can you help? What can you tell Janie to do if it happens again? Look at how you can help the situation, and fight the impulse to explode. (And if your child has been hurt, that impulse is probably there.) Remember that the relationship you establish with your child's caregiver is an important one both for your child and for you, and preserving it with open communication and respect is vital to keeping it healthy.

Ask the caregiver questions to show you're interested in her day. Asking "How are things going?" or "Is there anything you need me to bring?" lets the caregiver know you are interested in how things are working out and are open to hearing about any ways you can improve the situation.

Basic friendliness and appreciation go a long way. Gifts on holidays, thank-you notes, and little expressions of concern and caring for a special caregiver cement her place in your lives as an important part of your family system.

Summary

Sorting through child-care options can be overwhelming: There are a number of options out there, and each is worthy of careful consideration. With your family priorities and mission statement in hand, you should be able to identify the types of child care that are most appropriate for your family. Once you've identified the types of care you'll consider, think about things like the hours you need child care, the age of your children, and the amount of money you can spend.

Being a proactive parent means getting educated and taking steps toward getting what you want for your family. In finding the right care for your children, you ensure a happier balance for everyone and a better working mindset for yourself.

Notes

1. The following percentages are based on interviews a colleague and I conducted in our local area with 65 working parents. Numbers may be different in your area, depending on whether you live in a rural or urban setting and the population size and make-up of the workforce in your area.

2. Eleven percent of interview respondents did not answer the child-care question.

3. Please note that, although I use the pronoun "she" to refer to your potential sitter, I don't mean to discount the possibility of a "he." Both men and women can make good sitters. The "she" simply recognizes that the vast majority of child-care providers are women.

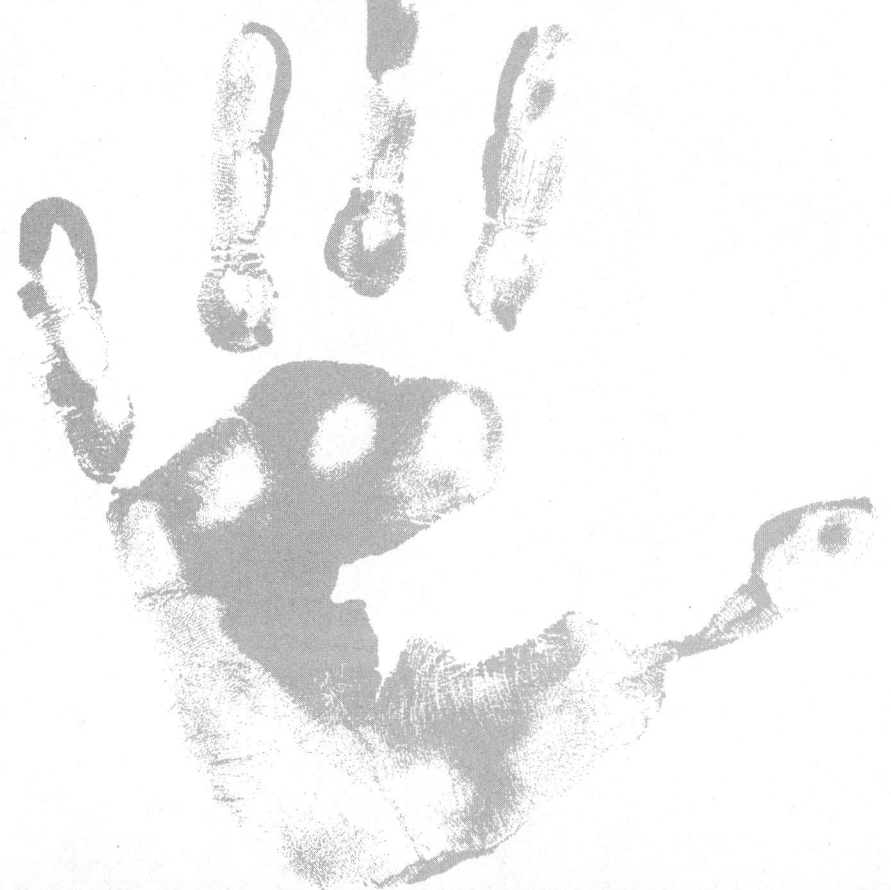

Chapter 4

"Your Sitter Is on Line 1"

*"Big sisters are the crabgrass
in the lawn of life."*
–Charles M. Schultz

Receptionists in large corporations will be the
first to tell you: 3:30 is a busy time at the
switchboard. Calls come in, calls go out. Moms
and dads want to know the kids have made it
home safe. Kids want to know what they can
have for a snack—and is it okay if they play
soccer at Todd's?

As a working parent, don't expect one nice, neat little phone call a day. That may be what you hope for, and that may be what you eventually settle into, but at first you're likely to get several calls a day if your child is at a baby-sitter's or grandma's; fewer—perhaps none—if your child is in a day-care center or at school.

How many phone calls are too many, and how do employers feel about it? Employers know that the parents on their staffs need to check in at home in order to feel comfortable that their children are being well cared for. A parent preoccupied with a child's safety is not going to be a productive employee. Understanding this, most employers won't begrudge you phone contact, although asking about and then adhering to any company policy on personal calls is a smart move. Show your boss that you respect the system, but maintain that your family responsibilities are a priority.

Limit your phone contact to a time that's convenient—for you and for others in your area who are reliant on either the phone or your attention—and then stick to it.

Schedule a time with your child to connect during the day. You might leave it as, "Call me as soon as you get home," or, "Call me right after 'Animaniacs,'" but make sure that your child knows that calling every 5 or 10 minutes is going to be hazardous to both your sanity and your job. If you've got two children at home together—either with a sitter or alone—you might be barraged early on with "he-said/she-said" phone calls, in which each one calls to tell on the other. Set your rules clearly about this kind of behavior and establish what you will and will not accept as a legitimate excuse for a phone call.

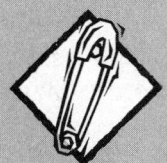

If you don't have the opportunity to talk to your child during the day, you can share a thought instead. I went back to work the same year my daughter started full-day kindergarten. We'd always been together and it was hard on both of us to separate so completely and so suddenly. We agreed to think of each other every day at 11:00 A.M.; and then each night, one of us would invariably ask, "Did you think of me today?" It helped us make the transition and reminded us that even when we're apart, we're not really apart.

Here are a couple of tips for organizing the phone-in, phone-out aspect of your working life:

 Establish a contact time. If you have kids home alone, or kids getting off the bus at a baby-sitter's house, designate a time for them to call you or for you to call them. Make it a quick, pleasant call—not one of those "I-told-you-to-take-out-the-trash-this-morning-and-you-didn't-do-it" calls—and find out how the day went, what homework they've got to do, and so on. A five-minute call that says "I just wanted to make sure you're safe and let you know I love you" is all that's really necessary to set both you and your children at ease.

 Define "callable" events. If your children go to the house of a sitter, friend, or relative during the day, make sure you outline clearly in what situations you do—or do not—want to be called. Do you want your sitter to call and ask you whether Heidi can have a chocolate bunny before lunch? Is a sore throat a problem, or is it okay for you to find out about that at the end of the day? If Tommy swallows a penny, do you want the sitter to call you before or after she picks him up by his feet to see if it falls out on its own? Think about a number of situations—your sitter or other caregiver can help you—and determine whether you think each a callable offense. Make a list for your caregiver—with your work number at the top—so she'll know when and how to call you. Something like this would do the trick:

Call me at 375-5555

1. If Trina begins running a fever.

2. If she gets hurt and is upset for more than five minutes without calming down or being distracted by something else.

3. In any emergency situation; illness, injury, household accidents, etc.

Depending on where you are taking your child for child care, you may want to be notified before any excursions. For example, if you take your daughter to a baby-sitter's house and the sitter doesn't usually take the children anywhere during the day, you might ask to be notified before she takes your child to the park for the afternoon. On the other hand, if field trips are a part of your arrangement—as would be the case with a day-care center—there's no need for the call.

All parents, of course, need to know their children are safe. We need check-in points. We need to know our children and their caregivers have access to us whenever they need us. The trick is to think about and define what you consider a "necessary" phone call. This will keep you from tying up the lines and let you be more productive at work.

These are the best times to contact me in nonemergency situations:

1. _____

2. _____

3. _____

Take Two Aspirins and I'll See You in the Morning

Another home issue that will affect you at work is the health of your children. We've already established that times of change bring on reduced immune systems. Combine that with the germ-ripe environment of a day-care center and, presto—you've got a sick child.

Statistics show that, on average, a working parent misses 1 day every 12 weeks because a child is sick. Bradley misses school, you miss work. It's that simple.

In some areas, sick-child care is available. In these centers, nurses help care for children who are not contagious or seriously ill, those on the mend who are not well enough to be at school. There are plenty of critics of sick-child programs, those who say that a sick child should be at home with a parent, no matter what. But there are just as many working parents who truly need this kind of service in order to continue providing for their families.

Another interesting statistic shows, not surprisingly, that more mothers than fathers stay home with sick children, and that mothers of children under 6 miss more days than do mothers of school-aged children.[1]

What should you do when your child gets sick? Let's break this into two parts: Consider your options, and then decide what you want to do. This is one of those discussions you'll want to have with your spouse or partner, so you can both share in the child-care hospice responsibilities.

Sick-Care Options

When Celia gets sick and needs to stay home from school, what are your options?

The first response to this question is another question: How sick is she? If she's running a fever and throwing up, she needs to be home in bed, not at a sitter's exposing other children or at Grandma's, giving her the flu. If she's got something not infectious, like an ear infection, and feels comfortable drinking juice and watching movies on Grandma's couch, Grandma's house might be an option.

Next, consider what resources are available in your area for child care. If Celia is well enough to go somewhere, where can she go? Do you have a friend or neighbor who could watch her while you get in a few hour's work? Is your mother or father available? Can your spouse come home for a few hours so you can work tag-team style?

Are there partial alternatives you're not considering? In this age of connectivity, can you work at home on your computer and transfer files to the office? Can you run in and get the work you need, then work at home for the afternoon?

Is there a day-care center near your workplace—or perhaps in your workplace—that offers sick-child care? In many larger cities, these options are becoming more and more available.

There may be all sorts of options in your area. The best idea is to check them out and decide what you want before you need them.

These people can watch the kids if they are sick but not contagious:

First Choice

Name: _____

Phone: _____

Second Choice

Name: _____

Phone: _____

Third Choice

Name: _____

Phone: _____

Creating a Sick-Day Plan

Now that you know what your options are, sit down with your spouse or partner and map out a plan of action for that first day you are awakened at 4:30 A.M. by, "Mommy, I'm sick."

BEST & WORST

Best:
"I can't wait to see my kids at the end of the day!"

If both you and your spouse have equal work arrangements (meaning it's equally inconvenient for both of you to take off for a nonsick sick day), you might agree to swap days. If Michael is home from school both Monday and Tuesday, for example, you take Monday off and your spouse handles Tuesday (or vice versa).

If neither of you can comfortably take off an entire day, you might try alternating mornings and afternoons. Sometimes it's easier to get off early or late than it is to miss a whole 8-hour day.

Again, take the time to think about what you want before you need it. Write it down and post it on your information center. Explain to the kids what will happen on sick days before they get sick. Don't tell Trina as you're wrapping her in a blanket and putting her in the van, "You're going to stay at Grandma's while I go in to work for a few hours." A sick child being shuttled here and there is more likely to resist than a well child being shuttled here and there. Have a plan made so, when the sick days come—and they will—all you have to do is follow your prescribed plan.

Sick-Day Plan

If one of the children gets sick during the day, this is how we will handle it:

First Choice

_____

_____

_____

_____

Second Choice

_____

_____

_____

_____

Third Choice

_____

_____

_____

_____

Remember, too, that not all sick days are full-day events. How will you handle it when the school calls and tells you your child is running a fever and needs to go home? Sometimes, this can actually be a blessing—you've been at work for a few hours so you don't feel as guilty as you might missing a whole day's work, and you have the opportunity to grab work to take home.

Will you be the one responsible for picking up your child from school if the nurse calls? Will your spouse do it? What about the baby-sitter or a neighbor? If it's possible that you might not be available, make sure you have a back-up plan in case you can't be reached.

All schools require emergency numbers of friends or relatives they can call when they can't reach you. Make sure you've informed those people— whether it's your mother, your friend, or your sitter—that if the school can't reach you when your child is sick, they are next on the list.

Handling Emergencies

Emergencies come in all shapes and sizes. An emergency might be that Wendy wet her pants and doesn't have any dry ones at day care. Josh falling and breaking his arm on the playground is definitely an emergency.

What kind of emergencies you'll have and how you will respond (and how smoothly you will respond) will depend on your situation. Everyone has them, but we can lessen their likelihood by keeping these factors in mind:

 Accidents happen more often when children are tired or hungry. You've probably noticed the tendency in yourself to be less alert when your resources are depleted. Your children experience the same thing, although they probably won't admit it. They might miss that last step, trip over the toy truck, or just run into something that wasn't there a moment ago.

 Accidents occur more frequently in a new place. If you have just started day care, are visiting at a relative's house, or have recently moved, watch for a higher number of accidents while your child gets used to the new surroundings.

Accidents are more likely if you've recently changed your child's schedule. If you've just returned to work and started dropping your child off at day care or a baby-sitter's house, you've definitely modified your schedule. Watch for increased clumsiness and take a few common-sense precautions to make accidents less likely.

Common-Sense Safety Tips

A little common sense can help you reduce accidents during this transitional time:

 Tie your child's shoes in double-knots so he doesn't trip over the laces

 Dress your child in loose-fitting clothes that she can move freely in.

 If you pack a lunch for your preschooler or toddler, omit anything that is a potential choking hazard: raw carrots in your 3-year-old's lunch when you're not there to watch him is risky: He might be so busy talking to the other kids at his table that he doesn't pay attention to the big chunks he's swallowing.

 Check any toys your child wants to take to day care: Something that is perfectly fine at home can present a problem at school if it has rough edges or a pointed antenna.

 Make sure your child has "action shoes"— shoes made for running, jumping, and climbing. Dressing up is great, and so are dress-up shoes. But if they are slick on the bottom, they will slide on the center's linoleum floors and greatly increase the likelihood that your child will wipe out on a hurried trip to the rest room.

 Make sure your child's clothes are appropriate for the season. Many of us have

been up against the will of a fashion-conscious 4-year-old: It's 30 degrees outside and she's determined to wear her pink sundress and sandals. Remember that she's more likely to have an accident if she's too cold, too warm, too tired, or overstimulated. (That pretty well covers the entire day of a 4-year-old, doesn't it?)

What Is an Emergency?

Webster's defines an emergency as "an unforeseen combination of circumstances or the resulting state that calls for immediate action." That seems to sum it up. In the last section, we discussed some ways you can cut down on the number of "unforeseen circumstances" that might contribute to an emergency. In this section, you'll develop a plan so you can handle the "resulting state that calls for immediate action."

Developing an Emergency Plan

First, define what constitutes an emergency in your family. Is a forgotten lunch an emergency? What about a missed school bus? The big ones you won't need to define: sprained ankles, injuries requiring stitches, or a sudden severe illness that needs Mom's or Dad's attention. It's the little ones you need to determine how you're going to handle. What is an emergency in your family? Toss it out on the table at the family meeting and come up with your own definition.

In our family, these are emergencies:

1. _____
2. _____
3. _____
4. _____
5. _____

Next, consider what actions you will take in an emergency situation. If possible, come up with one procedure you can use for all emergencies. Coming up with the answers to these questions will help you devise your plan:

1. In case of an emergency, do you want the school or day care to call you or your spouse first? The answer to this question is not about who cares the most but, rather, who can get there fastest. If you work on an assembly line and have to call for someone to replace you, you might have a longer wait than a person who can drop everything and go.

2. Who will you use as a back-up if you are unreachable? Is there a neighbor, friend, or relative who will agree to be an emergency stand-in if you can't be reached right away?

3. What hospital is nearest to your child's school, day-care center, or baby-sitter's house?

4. Do both you and your spouse (and any caregiver who might be responsible for taking a child to the emergency room) have current insurance numbers and permissions?

 See "All-Important Permissions" below for information on how give your caregiver written permission to get medical help for your child in case of an emergency.

5. If you are called away to handle an emergency, what will happen to your other children? If you usually pick them up at school, you'll need a back-up plan. Make sure the kids know beforehand—that's part of the plan—who will be picking them up if something out of the ordinary happens. Stress that your absence or the change in routine does not necessarily mean that something horrible has happened— it might mean only that you were kept late in a meeting or had a late appointment. We want our children to be prepared—but not panicked—when they experience a change in the routine.

Code Words

Many families use a code word to signal a child that the adult providing the back-up care was really sent by the parent. In an ideal situation, your mother, your spouse, or your best friend will pick up your children from school when you can't. But if someone outside your normal support group needs to pick up the kids, make sure they know the family code word. Teach your children that it's okay—expected, even—for them to ask the adult what the code word is. If the adult doesn't know the word or forgets it, the children don't go with him or her. It's as simple as that.

Recently in our area, an 8-year-old boy saved himself from abduction at a city park using this very technique. A stranger approached and told the boy his mother wanted him and that she was on the other side of the park. The stranger offered to take the boy to his mother. The boy asked what the code word was. When the man didn't know, the boy threw his bookbag at him and ran in the opposite direction, yelling for the police. The man was apprehended as he tried to leave the park, and the boy made the nightly news two nights in a row, a symbol of smart family protection in the '90s.

Posting Emergency Procedures

Once you come up with the answers to your emergency questions, put them together in a plan that can be easily understood and followed by family members. If you have a child who changes locations during the day—for example, Jimmy is at school from 8:00 to 3:00, then home alone from 3:00 to 5:00—you need two emergency procedures: one for what happens if the school calls with an emergency and one for what happens if Jimmy calls from home in an emergency situation. In the second case, Jimmy needs a set of procedures he can follow until you get home or help arrives. We'll tackle each of these issues separately.

The Family Emergency Procedure

Make sure you've got all the following items included on a family emergency procedure:

 Important phone numbers: Police, fire, poison control center, Mom's work, Dad's work, the closest neighbor or friend.

 Step-by-step listing of what will happen in an emergency. Include an explanation of how each child's schedule will change in an emergency situation. The following list presents an idea of how you could break down the different steps:

1. If Aaron has an emergency at school, the school knows to call me at work. If Elizabeth has an emergency at Linda's house, Linda will call me at work.

2. I will quickly call Dad and tell him what's going on.

3. I will leave work immediately and go get Aaron or Elizabeth.

4. If the situation involves Aaron, Dad will notify Elizabeth's sitter that he will be picking her up at 5:45 instead of me picking her up at 3:30. He will talk to Elizabeth and explain what's happening. If the situation involves Elizabeth, Dad will leave work and pick up Aaron at 3:15 in front of the school building and take him back to the office with him until 5:30.

5. If it is a medical emergency, we will go to Riverview Hospital. If it is not a medical emergency, I will take Aaron or Elizabeth home.

6. Once we get to our destination, I'll call Dad and report progress.

Once you draft your emergency plan, read it aloud to the kids and answer any questions they have. Most likely they'll wonder, "What do I have to do?" Hopefully, the answer will be, "Nothing. We've got it all covered." The idea is to give the adults a specific plan so the lives of the children are disrupted as little as possible. If your children misunderstand a particular step in the plan, consider revising it or adding a step to make it clearer. Knowing they are taken care of and that, no matter what happens, Mom or Dad will be able to handle it is important to kids. They're counting on it.

 Leave a space for "Alternatives" on your emergency plan. Maybe a neighbor could pick up Elizabeth from Linda's house when she picks up her own daughter. Then Elizabeth wouldn't have to stay longer than usual. Or maybe Grandma is willing to pick Aaron up at school if Dad is in a meeting. If you list alternatives on your plan, make sure you have the full names and phone numbers of the alternative support people so they can be contacted easily in a fast-moving situation.

Family Emergency Plan

Important Phone Numbers

Police: _____

Fire: _____

Poison control: _____

Mom's work: _____

Dad's work: _____

Friend: _____

Emergency Procedures

1. _____

   _____

   _____

   _____

2. _____
   _____
   _____
   _____

3. _____
   _____
   _____
   _____

4. _____
   _____
   _____
   _____

5. _____
   _____
   _____
   _____

6. _____
   _____
   _____
   _____

Alternatives: _____
   _____
   _____
   _____

BEST & WORST

Worst: "I missed out on my son's firsts."

The At-Home Emergency Procedure

If your child is home after school by himself, he needs his own set of emergency procedures to follow.

The first step, if you haven't already done so, is to make sure he's clear on what he can and cannot do. Post his after-school rules clearly; they will contribute greatly to his overall safety. Things like, "No cooking on the stove," "Don't answer the front door," and "No swimming," give him guidelines to work with.

Next, devise and discuss a procedure he can follow if he finds himself in an emergency situation. Make sure that he understands what an emergency is and that he knows the most important thing to do in each situation. Here are a few suggestions:

 First aid. Have a first aid kit in a reachable place. Make sure it contains a booklet on simple first-aid procedures (how to treat a burn, what to do for a scrape, etc.).

 Fire. Make sure he knows to get out of the house *first*, and then call 911 (or the number of your local fire department).

 Some families write out a fire plan, with a map of the house and surrounding yard, and even practice "fire drills" once in a while to make sure everyone knows what to do in case of fire. You can make this an adventure and have a fire-training course on one of your family meeting nights. Set a loud timer or alarm, then practice leaving the house and meeting up at your designated "safe place" outside.

 Storms. Write down what your child should do in the event of a severe storm. Should he go to the basement or to an internal hallway? Where is the safest place in your house? Identify it clearly and explain when it's time to head for cover.

 Strangers. Your child needs to know what to do if a stranger calls or comes to the door. What should he do if he feels threatened? Make sure he has the phone numbers he needs to contact the designated person—the closest neighbor, you, or another friend— who can go check on him if he feels frightened or in danger.

Scary News About Scared Kids

A recent news story related this finding: A lot of American children are scared. Results of a survey showed that they are frightened most of gangs, violence, and guns. In the survey of 7- to 10-year-olds, 71 percent worried they might be stabbed or shot at school.[2]

After-School Rules

Complete these sentences with what you want your child to do in each of these situations:

If you get hurt, _____

_____

If there is a fire, _____

_____

If there is bad weather, _____

_____

If a stranger calls, _____

_____

If a stranger comes to the door, _____

_____

If you are frightened, _____

_____

Once you've completed and posted the after-school rules (on your information center bulletin board), you can devise an emergency plan for your at-home child.

At-Home Emergency Plan

Important Phone Numbers

Police: _____

Fire: _____

Poison control: _____

Mom's work: _____

Dad's work: _____

Friend: _____

Emergency Procedures

1. _____

_____

_____

_____

2. _____

_____

_____

_____

3. _____

_____

_____

_____

4. _____

_____

_____

_____

5. _____

_____

_____

_____

6. _____

_____

_____

_____

It's best *not* to include an "Alternatives" section on your child's at-home emergency plan. Options in a time of crisis can be more confusing than helpful. Straightforward, clear instructions— "If this happens, do that"—will be received and followed more easily.

All this talk about emergencies may be unsettling, especially if you're just getting ready to go back to work, or have just started back, and are feeling anxious about the transition. But part of avoiding emergencies is being prepared for them. Your children will feel more secure, and you will feel more at ease knowing that, if something happens, your family has a plan to follow. You will be more relaxed at work knowing you've done everything you can—by way of prevention and education—to avoid those "unforeseen circumstances."

All-Important Permissions

In this day of litigation, giving caregivers permission to get help for your child is an important part of the emergency procedure. If someone else takes care of your child all day, you need to give that person written permission to get medical help for your child in your absence. This doesn't mean you're turning over all your legal rights to someone else. It simply means you give the caregiver the right to authorize emergency medical care as needed until you arrive on the scene. This gives the professionals the legal go-ahead to do whatever is necessary in the case of a dire emergency.

Schools and day-care centers will automatically solicit this kind of permission from you when you enroll your child. If you don't remember signing anything about emergency medical procedures, ask the administrator to be sure.

Write out a simple statement of permission that lists the child's name and age, the caregiver's name, and the date, and sign it at the bottom. It might go something like this:

While _____ is caring for my children (Aaron Amstead, age 7, and Elizabeth Amstead, age 4), I give her permission to authorize emergency medical care in the event that I am unreachable and an accident occurs involving one of my children. I wish to be contacted immediately at _____ in case of such an emergency, but would ask that medical help not be postponed if I am not available.

your signature

You might also list insurance policy numbers, other contact people, or helpful information like allergies or drug sensitivities on the sheet so the attending medical personnel have the information they need about your child.

Summary

In this chapter, you've thought about your expectations and learned about precautions you can take to make your family's transition smoother. You've decided how you want to handle phone calls at work, and mapped out a plan for handling sick days. You've also taken care of basic safety issues and emergency procedures for your family, so everyone is prepared in case an "unforeseen circumstance" appears on your horizon.

Don't let all this "disaster thinking" trouble you. Remember, you're creating these emergency plans to help ensure that emergencies *won't* happen. Once you've got your plan in place, you can sit back and relax. If an emergency ever happens, you'll all know what to do.

Notes

1. Ann Muscari and Wendy Wardell Morrone, *Child Care That Works* (New York: Doubleday, 1989).

2. Matt Lowry, reporting for the "Today Show," December 7, 1995.

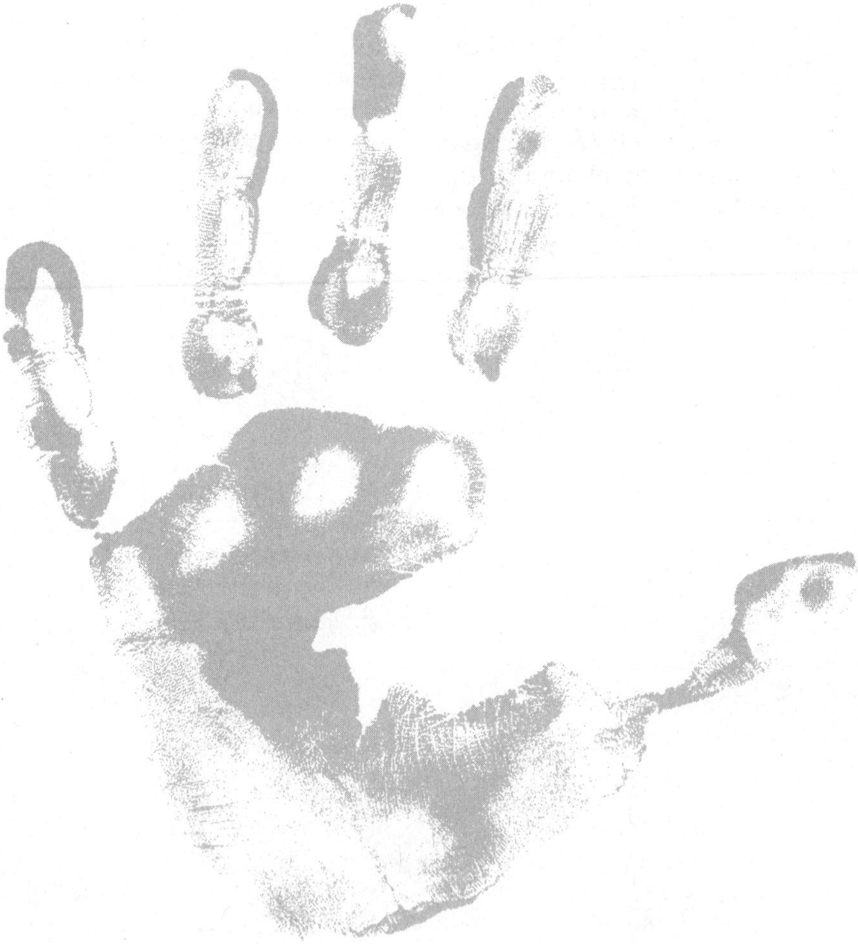

Chapter

5

Inside Looking Out

"By working faithfully eight hours a day you may eventually get to be a boss and work twelve hours a day."
—Robert Frost

So you've found the job of your dreams—or, at least, one that will work for now. It meets as many of your family priorities as possible, you've made child-care arrangements, and you're ready to get yourself organized and back to work. There are quite a few accomplishments wrapped up in that one

sentence: Take the time to be pleased with your family's accomplishments and cooperation.

This chapter deals with life from a different perspective. Instead of looking out at the work world from the welcoming walls of home, we'll be looking at how to handle home issues from the new environment of the office. But first we'll start with a few basics to help you get into the office with as few bumps and bruises as possible.

Great Expectations

You need to take a good long look at your expectations now that your return to work (or job change) is imminent. If you have unrealistic expectations—"Piece of cake!"—you're going to be disappointed or, worse, feel like you've failed. If you have realistic expectations and know that adjustments take time, that your family is going to need some retraining, and that emotions are going to be in an uproar while everyone gets used to the new system, chances are you'll get through the adjustment period faster and with fewer emotional surprises.

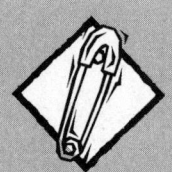

It's easier to steer a ship through a storm when you know the storm is coming and can prepare for it. Anticipating a few storms as you make the big shift from home to work will help you weather them.

Here's a little quiz to test your expectation level.

Back-to-Work Quiz

How difficult do you expect each of the
following things to be as you make your
adjustment back to work? (1 is easy; 10 is difficult)

___ Finding the right wardrobe for the job

___ Getting home organized so the housework and
repairs get done

___ Spending quality time with each child

___ Organizing free time for family events

___ Keeping active in school activities

___ Staying in contact with friends and relatives

___ Finding quiet time for you

When you complete the list, read back through it to
make sure you've been as realistic as possible, and
don't be surprised if you don't have many 1s. You
won't have a whole list of 10s, either—thank
goodness! Some things will be comparatively
simple, and others will be more difficult. The level
of difficulty will vary depending on your
circumstances, the type of job you've taken, the
ages of your children, and so on. The important
thing is this: You should take time to consider what
you're expecting of yourself and of your family and
ask yourself if your expectations are realistic.

What Do You Feel?

Studies show that returning to the workforce after
time at home brings up a number of feelings for
both mothers and fathers. Which of these feelings

do you have? (Remember that having conflicting feelings is par for the course.)

___ Happy		___ Lonely	
___ Sad		___ Eager	
___ Excited		___ Irritated	
___ Insecure		___ Relieved	
___ Contented		___ Anxious	
___ Angry		___ Stronger	
___ Capable		___ Worried	
___ Guilty		___ Proud	

Human animals that we are, we also must anticipate the effects of other situations on our emotions. Being overly tired, for example, makes you more prone to feeling sad. You may feel guilty when you've had to say "No" to room mothering but feel fine later in the week when you haven't had to turn down commitments to balance your work responsibilities. You might be short-tempered at home when there's a big deadline at work; or you might have trouble concentrating at your desk when you're worried about your son's first day at the sitter's.

The key to dealing with back-to-work feelings, experts agree, is to feel them. Some days you'll be thankful to get out of the house. Others you might feel sad or lonely. Sometimes, you might wonder if you can handle the pressure. Especially at first, be willing to hang in there with your emotions. Talk to other employees, your employer, your spouse and family, or a professional, if necessary, but let your emotions be what they are. In any time of transition, emotions are high and can shift easily in any direction. Better to wait until things settle down before you start making additional changes.

Remember that you won't be the
only one at the office with thoughts
other than work on your mind. For
you it may be the kids, but for others
it might be money, a relationship,
graduate work, self-awareness
issues, or other things.

How Do You Feel?

It's an interesting medical phenomenon and a
proven fact: In times of transition, our immune
systems are weakened and we are more likely to
pick up colds, the flu, or anything else floating
around in the environment. This applies to you
and all members of your family. You'll all going
through changes together. As you prepare to
return to work, keep an eye on each of the
following items, which contribute to keeping you
all healthy:

1. **Make sure you're getting the rest you
   need.** Recognize that in times of change—and
   particularly in times of high stress—you need
   more rest than usual.

2. **As much as possible, eat well-balanced,
   healthy meals.** Time for sit-down meals may
   be shorter than it used to be, and you may
   wonder if the local fast food drive-through is
   going to be your standard bill of fare, but try to
   make sure at least one meal a day is well-
   balanced, with produce, protein, dairy—you
   know the scoop. Crock pots and microwaves
   were invented for people like us. For tips on
   creating healthy meals on a working-parent
   schedule, see chapter 8.

3. **Use your supports.** Working parents often
   suffer from "I-can-do-it-myself" syndrome and
   find themselves carrying more responsibility

than they really have to. Ask yourself if you are running errands, washing clothes, drying dishes, or fielding phone calls someone else could really take over. Is there someone ready and willing (or at least enlistable) to take over some of these tasks during your adjustment period?

4. **Keep an eye on your caffeine intake.** Especially when you make a sudden shift from home to office and are struggling with changes in schedule, responsibilities, demands, hours, and expectations, you might notice energy potholes in your day. You were fine a moment ago and now you're tired. Yawn. You've got all kinds of things to do this afternoon, and it's not even 3:00. How can you wake up? A trip to the coffee machine seems like the answer.

   The problem is that too many of those quick trips—or ones to the alternative, the soft-drink machine—will pump quite a bit of caffeine into your system, which will ultimately depress, not increase, your energy level. People often think that candy—in particular, chocolate (that's wishful thinking!)—is a good pick-me-up for the afternoon sleepies. But chocolate puts caffeine in your system for a brief time (hence the pick-me-up feeling) and then causes even more sleepiness because of the release of insulin that floods your bloodstream after a dose of sugar.

   More nutrition news than you ever wanted to know, right? The bottom line is to watch and moderate whatever you're putting into your system. Too much of anything—especially when you're hoping to get a particular reaction ("I've got to wake up!")—can do more harm than good.

5. **Be alert to your body's signals.** Is your neck stiff? You might be carrying the "weight of the world" on your shoulders. Does your head hurt? You might be focusing too intently for

too long without taking a break. Is your child complaining of stomachaches? Nightmares? Fatigue? Our bodies give us signals when we're working too hard, when we're carrying too much stress, and when we're feeling overwhelmed. Tune into yourself on a regular basis and try to take good care of yourself in the midst of all these changes. When you're hungry, eat. When you're tired, sleep. When you've taken work home and you've got 10 pages left to read, but all you really care about is watching the game on TV, watch the game. Being sensitive to your needs is an important key to helping you and your entire family adjust to career changes smoothly.

6. **Take things slow.** One of the hardest expectations we have of ourselves is the one that says we need to have everything handled *now*. Remember that adjusting to work is a process for both you and your family. You'll try a few things in the beginning that just plain won't work. You'll reevaluate and change them. A major task of working parents is assessing what works, weeding out what doesn't, and trying new ideas. It's a rare family that puts a system into place and then maintains it until the kids are grown and the parents retire. Expect your life to be one of continual changing and growing. Every day, you'll make your system a little better. That's a freeing thought: No one says you have to have it all "together" today. You're free to try what works and then change whatever you need to whenever you need to—whether that's this afternoon, next week, or next year.

Expecting the Unexpected

I think the hardest thing for me about returning to work will be: _____

_____

_____

_____

_____

I could make the situation easier by: _____

_____

_____

_____

_____

I'm Late! I'm Late!

One of the first challenges you'll face on a daily basis is the morning routine. Statistics show that working parents have a higher percentage of tardiness than nonparenting workers—both late *to* work and late *leaving* work.[1] In fact, it's estimated that between 40 and 70 percent of working parents wind up adjusting their schedules—at least temporarily—because of home delays and unanticipated crises. ("Where's my lunch box? It was here a minute ago!" "*Mom!* I can't find my other shoe!")

One of the best things about being disorganized is that it teaches you the value of organization. After the third time Scott can't find his homework and it makes you late for a meeting, you're going to insist that he gather his schoolwork in his bookbag and put it by the door every night before he goes to bed.

Learning from our mistakes is valuable—but learning from other's mistakes saves us a lot of frustration. Consider what these parents say about getting out the door in the morning:

* *

"Getting out on time is the hardest thing I face all day. I figure that once I get all three kids up, dressed, fed, and delivered to school and the baby-sitter, I've already succeeded for the day. I go to work feeling great."
—Mother of three who works full-time

* *

"Get school clothes, backpacks, books, and everything you need for the next day ready the night before. This really helps get us out in the morning."
—Mother of three who works part-time

* *

"Get organized! Have things ready the night before. No matter how organized you are, things can pop up and destroy what you've accomplished. My husband travels occasionally and things always break when he's gone: the windows leak on a rainy day, the dog gets hit by a car, our daughter throws up when I'm ready to walk out the door to work. When things get overwhelming, I take a deep breath and say, "Okay, Lord, I can only handle a little more of this!"
—Mother of two who works full-time

In chapter 7, you will learn some ways you can organize your house to spread out household chores and earn yourself a little sanity. Here, the "organization" I'm talking about is really time management. How can you get yourself organized in the morning so you can get out the door on time?

Working Backwards

The first step is to determine how much time you need in order to walk in the door at work every day with a few minutes to spare. Think about how nice that would be—no more rushing through the door, sneaking past the boss's office, or hoping the receptionist didn't notice you're late yet another day this week.

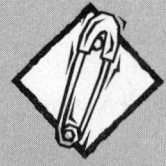

If you make a commitment to yourself to be on time, you're more likely to be on time. If you don't think being punctual on your job is particularly important, chances are you'll continue to scurry in 10 minutes late this day, 20 minutes the next. The choice, of course, is yours. But remember that bosses consider this kind of thing when you ask for additional time off, schedule vacation days, or put in for a promotion.

So, to determine how much time you need to get to work on time, answer these questions:

1. **What time do you need to be at work?** If starting time is 8:00 A.M., plan to be in 10 minutes early. This gives you time to get your coffee, look through your mail, and settle into the day without feeling rushed.

2. **How long is your commute?** If the length of your commute varies depending on the day— for example, you drop Taylor off at day care on Tuesdays and Thursdays, which adds 10 minutes to your trip—figure this out for each day that differs.

3. **How many children do you have?** (If you have to stop and count, you're in trouble!) Whatever number you come up with, leave 5 minutes *per child* for getting-to-the-car-in-one-piece time. If you have three children, leave a 15-minute space to absorb Katie forgetting to brush her teeth, Ian needing to change the brown sock he thought was blue, and Sara running back for her show-and-tell offering.

4. **How long does it take your family to eat breakfast?** Some people eat on the run, others eat in the car. Some don't eat at all. Whatever your breakfast practice is, schedule it and know how long it takes.

5. **How much time does your family need to get ready in the morning?** This might be a hard one to measure and will probably require some observation and perhaps some reorchestration. If your house has two teenagers, two adults, and one bathroom, and you all need to get showers in the morning (not to mention mirror time for things like hair curling and make-up routines), it's going to be hard on your schedule—not to mention your nerves. You may need to think about alternative ways to make sure everybody gets ready on time. Younger children usually don't mind

taking baths or showers at night—in fact, mine prefer it if they think it will delay bedtime—but older kids might feel put off their routine.

 If you suspect there's a better way to orchestrate your "getting ready" time, put the issue on the table at the next family meeting and see what alternatives your family can come up with. You might be surprised at the creative answers you receive.

Once you figure out the time you need for each part of your morning routine, add them up and see what the total tells you. Then subtract the total from the time you need to be at work and you've got the time you need to set your alarm for. The following checklist gives you an example of the basic equation. A blank checklist is provided at the end of this section for you to fill in your own times.

Time I need to be at work: 7:50

Commute:	20 minutes
Time cushion:	15 minutes
Breakfast:	15 minutes
Getting ready:	45 minutes

TOTAL TIME:	**1 hour, 35 minutes**

Time I need to get up: (6:15)

Time Management Checklist

Time I need to be at work: _____

Commute: _____

Time cushion: _____

Breakfast: _____

Getting ready: _____

TOTAL TIME: _____

Time I need to get up: _____

One quick warning: *If you come up with an answer like, "We need three hours to get ready for work and school, and we have to be there by 7:45. That means I need to get up at 4:45!"–then you need to do some reorganizing to reduce the amount of time you need in the morning. The next section will tell you how.*

BEST & WORST

Best: "The kids are more independent— never upset about going to school, etc."

Early Morning Organization

Don't let the heading fool you. What we're talking about here really isn't organization you do in the morning. Rather, it's things you do the night before (or all week) that help you be better organized in the morning.

Most families, no matter how long they've been doing the to-work-and-to-school routine, still have days when they oversleep, the dog doesn't get fed, the kids forget their

homework, and everyone gets stuck in traffic. It's going to happen.

But there are a number of things you can do to get yourself and your family ready for tomorrow morning with fewer hassles and headaches. Consider these:

 Do everything you can the night before. Don't put off until tomorrow what you can do tonight—not if you want to have a smooth exit in the morning. Sign school papers or assignment books, check homework, read through reports, pack swimming gear, make lunches. Whatever it is that eats up your time in the morning, see if you can handle it the night before.

 Have a going-out place. Typically families use one exit regularly—whether it's the door leading to the garage or one leading to the school bus. Wherever your family exits, make sure they've got their belongings there waiting for them. You might even add coat hooks, mitten places, a mat for boots and tennis shoes, and room for other niceties like umbrellas or mufflers, so you can grab everything you need on your way out the door.

> *If you want to save time and energy, teach your kids (and your spouse, if necessary) to be responsible for packing their own things for tomorrow. They can put the bookbags (or briefcases) by the door, get the library books, the swim bags, the show-and-tell items, and have them ready to head out the door.*

 Designate an information center. Hang a bulletin board or reserve counter space by the door for notes that need to be signed, papers that need to be returned, or items that need parental approval. Use this area also for important items you might need to find at a moment's notice: things like your number at work, emergency phone numbers, and your family's activity calendar.

 Be day-ahead clothes conscious. Make sure the next day's clothes (and shoes, socks, and underwear) are set out, ready to be slipped on at a moment's notice.

 Use a color-coded calendar to list family activities. You might want to hang this calendar in your "information center." Use a different color marker for each person in the family. When Sean has swimming on Wednesdays, you'll see the blue ink (when you check Tuesday night) and know you've got to put his swimsuit and towel in a bag by the going-out door. The most important thing about the family calendar, of course, is that you use it regularly, and teach all other family members to do the same. When Steven needs a ride home after the game on Friday, make sure he writes it in (and asks you, too), so he will be picked up when and where he expects to be.

Our Ready List

Things we can have ready each night before bed:

1. _____
2. _____
3. _____
4. _____
5. _____
6. _____

7. _____

8. _____

9. _____

10. _____

The Commute

Ah, you made it. The kids are safely at school or the baby-sitter's, and you are on your way to work. Looks like you'll have plenty of time. Traffic is moving smoothly and there's nothing ominous on the horizon. Now is a good time to leave the morning behind and get ready—mentally—to start your workday.

Depending on the length of your commute and your circumstances—whether you drive alone, carpool, or use public transportation—you can use your commute time to organize your day and priorities, think about creative projects you're looking forward to, or ponder challenges you need creative answers for.

Some people use these few moments of precious quiet as "preparation time" for the day. You might listen to music or inspirational tapes, meditate or pray, or just notice the beauty of the changing sunrise. If you feel you need a few minutes of silence before (or in the midst of) a busy day, don't rob yourself of the opportunity. A few deep breaths, a few moments of quiet thought (or, even better, no thought), and you may be surprised how refreshed and ready you'll feel.

If you have trouble leaving home at home and find yourself worrying about your new baby-sitter, wondering whether you handed John's lunch to Tammy and Tammy's to John, or fretting that you forgot to close the door to the hamster's cage, you might want to try carrying a small notebook—or getting one of those that attach directly to your dashboard—and writing down the item you need to follow up on at home. When you write it down, see yourself mentally putting it out of your mind. There. It's on the paper. Now you don't have to let it crowd your thoughts. You can add it to your "to-do" list once you get to the office, and when you call home to check in later, you can follow up on the things you're concerned about. For now, let it go.

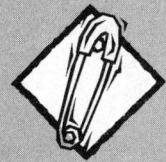

If you find that something keeps bothering you day after day and that writing it down and checking on it later doesn't seem to dispel the worry, take it as a sign that you need to do some further investigating. Maybe something in your system isn't working. If you are worrying about Jessica every morning after you drop her off at day care, take a closer look at what worries you. Is it the look on her face when you leave? Is it the way she interacts with her teachers? Listen to your instincts and follow up on your feelings. Perhaps she needs a few more minutes with you—a slower transition from home to school. Maybe there are some questions you can ask her caregivers that will alleviate your worries. Don't just shrug off concerns that rise to the surface again and again. Chances are, there's something you can learn that will make the situation better for all of you.

> ### Did I Tell You About the Time . . . ?
>
> "When my children were infants, I always
> felt so strongly about their morning feeding.
> That closeness was so important to me to
> start the day. So I'd be dressed and ready for
> work before that feeding. Many times I'd get to
> work and someone would tell me that I had something
> running down my back—it was spit up. I'd walk around
> all day branded, smelling like sour milk!"
> —Mother of two who works full-time

Really at Work

Knowing that your children are safely provided
for—and that procedures are in place to take care
of even the most stressful situations—earns you
peace of mind at work. You can concentrate on
what's before you, which makes you more
productive and ensures your success on the job.

The ability to be "really at work" comes quickly to
some, more slowly to others. It has something to
do with how ready you were to return to work. If
you have changed jobs or returned to the
workforce because you had to, tearing yourself
away from home mentally and emotionally
probably is harder. You might resist the idea of
leaving home behind. If you were eager to get
back into the workforce and felt ready for it, your
power of concentration is apt to be stronger
sooner.

In any case, be gentle with yourself as you adjust
to the working world. These tips might help
compartmentalize thoughts of home during your
transition time so you can be productive and still
feel connected to your family:

**End each work hour with a 5-minute
"family-thought break."** If you're supposed

to be writing a report, and instead find your mind wandering to the cookies you plan to bake with Emily on Saturday morning, remind yourself that it's not "family-thought" time and even make a note, if necessary, to think about the ingredients you need for the cookies at the designated break. No employer will begrudge you 5 minutes of daydreaming an hour if it makes you more productive the other 55 minutes.

 Surround yourself with drawings and pictures the kids have made for your office. Bring in clay sculptures, photographs, or whatever makes you feel more "at home" in your work area.

Did I Tell You About the Time . . . ?

For part of one summer, I took over the management of a retail museum shop. After eight years as a work-at-home mom, I was having a hard time with the adjustment. My then-6-year-old son Christopher had the answer. One morning, while I was making a sad exit to work, he came rushing up with something behind his back. "Here Mom," he said, thrusting a well-loved Ernie doll into my free hand, "Ernie can go to work with you so you won't miss me so much." Ernie did go to work with me, and sat on my desk the rest of the summer. The artists and sales reps who met with me probably thought my taste in "art" was a little weird, but my heart felt better.

 Seek out other working parents. When you are introduced to fellow employees, be alert to pictures of children, comments about kids or pets, or other signs that they might be working parents. At break time or lunch time, start a conversation. Chances are, they've felt just what you're feeling about

starting a new job and balancing home and work. They might be able to give a few pointers that will help make the transition a smoother one, or at least give you an idea of how your employer responds to family adjustments.

 Be proud of your family and your accomplishments. Although the emotional tide is turning, not too long ago we easily adopted an apologetic attitude when discussing our families. The prevalent feeling was that being first-rate parents made us second-rate employees. Today, more and more companies are recognizing the value of hiring employees with a strong sense of family commitment. That commitment can translate to more responsibility, loyalty, and creativity on the job.

 When you are at work, work. Especially when you first make other working-parent friends at work, the temptation might be strong to share the latest cute story, the newest teacher complaint, or the most outrageous Christmas wish. Remember, above all else, that the balance of home and work means you need to be home when you're home and at work when you're at work—physically, emotionally, and mentally. Employers will see even more benefit in hiring employees with family priorities if they are pleased with the return they get on their investment. In short, share kid stories on your own time and when you're at work, work.

Coming Home

In your first few weeks back to work, leaving work at work might not be difficult at all. You may be itching to get out the door and make sure everything is okay with the kids. After a few weeks, you'll fall into a routine. Your basic fears

BEST & **WORST**

Worst: "Not being there when my son gets off the schoolbus."

will have been allayed, you'll see what works and what doesn't, and you'll have made some changes to correct the things that haven't been working the way you expected.

With your system basically in place, your mind will be free to get more invested in your job. Now is when you discover if you're an "after-work worrier" or a "forget-about-it-till-morning" personality type.

You can use the commute home to make the transition between the work world and the happy chaos of incomplete homework, marshmallow squares, and mismatched socks.

How do you let the day go? Deep breathing works. Even in the worst traffic, you can feel the stress subsiding with a few deep breaths. Make a checklist of things you need to follow up on at the office in the morning, if the office keeps intruding on your thoughts. As you write down the notes, consider them "taken care of" and give yourself permission to enjoy your evening with your family. You'll have plenty of time to address work issues again tomorrow, beginning bright and early at 8:00 A.M.

Summary

You've taken a big step—perhaps the biggest step in establishing a home-and-work balance. You've made the transition from home to work by recognizing what a terrific adjustment you're going through and making sure you have the time and resources in place to deal with your changing days.

The next chapter tells you what you can expect once the honeymoon period ends. You can count on some turbulence, but nothing you can't navigate with a little foresight, love, and tenacity.

Notes

1. Ann Muscari and Wendy Wardell Morrone, *Child Care That Works* (New York: Doubleday, 1989).

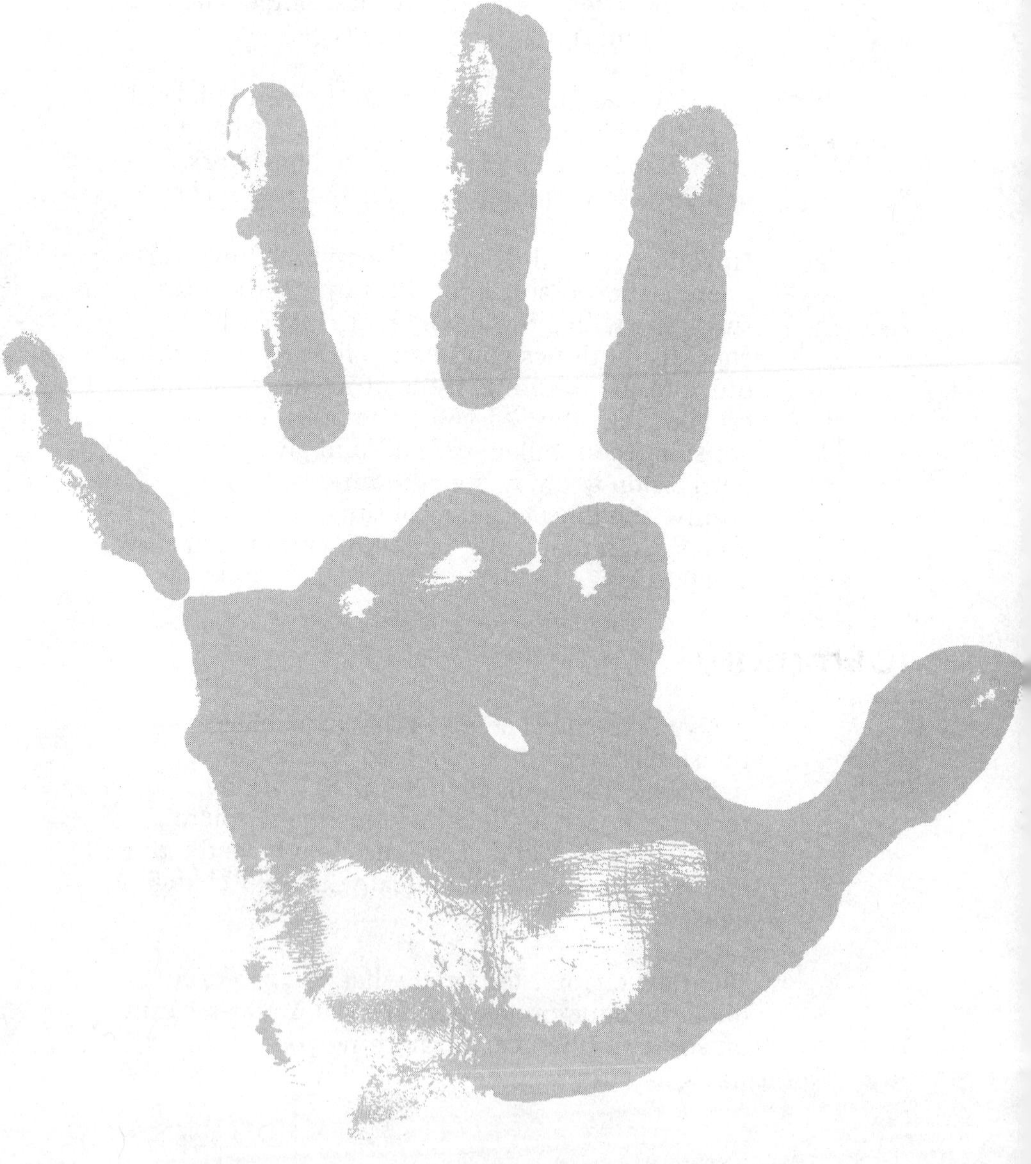

Chapter

6

Post-Parting Blues

"There's no such thing as fun for the entire family."
—Jerry Seinfeld

You may be feeling a little skeptical right now. Sure, family priorities, you're thinking. Yeah, that mission statement *really* helped. How come Kim has started wetting the bed again and Max has been getting in trouble at school? Why isn't the house getting any cleaner? Will there ever be a day when I get to work on time? Will there ever be a morning when I don't have to stand in a cold shower just to get my eyes open? I'm not sure my boss likes me.

I'm not sure my kids like me. I don't think the dog likes me. Come to think of it, even *I'm* not too crazy about me.

The Honeymoon's Over

Let's recap what has happened here. You got your priorities in line and set out to find the job that matched them.

Good.

You found just the right child care and organized with your spouse on getting the kids to and from the caregiver's house, day care, or school.

Terrific. We're really getting somewhere.

Next, you made the big move into the office. You covered all the bases for keeping the lines of communication open and making sure everyone knew the plan for handling emergency situations. You figured out how to leave home at home and, at the end of the day, work at work.

There you were, finally, a working parent. Life was all organized and everyone knew what he or she was supposed to do. A magnificent accomplishment!

For two or three blissful days—or perhaps a week or more, if you were lucky—there was a happy little thought bouncing around in your head: "We can do this! This is working!"

Then it all began to unravel.

What Have I Done?

The unraveling probably started slowly. The dog got sick. Kim threw her first temper tantrum as you dropped her off for day care. Max missed the bus to school.

A deadline at work came and went. You didn't get the report finished on time. Your spouse had to work overtime and you had to leave early to get Kim from child care. Max overflowed the toilet and couldn't find the plunger.

Continue adding up these minor incidents and pretty soon you've got what feels like total meltdown. Combine that with your own fatigue, disappointment, and worry, and you've set yourself up for a bad case of What Have I *DONE*?!

It's Normal

We humans are complex creatures: When we go through periods of change, we are adjusting on several different levels. When you do something as drastic as change jobs or return to work (which ranks right up there with having a baby, losing a loved one, or going through a divorce as a stress-inducer), you are adjusting emotionally, physically, and mentally. All these are interrelated; which means the more you worry, the more tired you are. The more you add to your daily schedule, the more worn down you become. The more you use your brain, the more you need time to rest it.

Being run down—temporarily or continually—has a dramatic effect on you as a complete package: your emotions are more volatile and less consistent; your physical stamina is noticeably lessened; and your mental sharpness blurs into a fog that may really alarm you at work.

The answer? Realize how much you've changed and commit to taking good care of yourself while you adjust. Rest more, eat right. Sleep whenever you can—at least seven and a half hours a night.

When you take better care of you, you'll have more emotional wherewithal to deal with your rebelling children and your angry dog. If you don't take care of yourself, the emotions of everyone

else will flatten you like a steamroller on hot asphalt.

 Chapter 8 is all about finding time for yourself—in both big and small ways—in the midst of a hectic, harried lifestyle. It's possible. I promise.

It's easy to neglect our own needs without even knowing we're doing it. But it's where you need to start rethreading when life begins to unravel. Take this quick quiz to see if you've been caring for yourself:

Self-Care Quiz

How many times this week did you...

____ tell yourself you did a good job?

____ do something you really wanted to do?

____ feel proud of an accomplishment?

____ eat a well-balanced meal?

____ rest in the afternoon?

____ go to bed early just because you felt like it?

____ accept a well-deserved compliment?

____ let someone help you when they offered?

____ do something just for fun?

It's Temporary

This slump you've fallen into is part of the overall adjustment period. It may look like the kids weren't being sincere when they said they'd help with household chores, take messages, get along, and generally cooperate with the changes taking place. But remember, they are going through a pushing-and-testing-and-generally-out-of-sorts phase, too.

You've heard the phrase, "This too shall pass"? It applies here, too.

Know What to Expect

In the last chapter, we talked about expectations: what you expected of yourself and of your family as you made your first steps back into the workforce. What we didn't address there—because it fits here—is the issue of adjustment expectations.

Some of us live life with a "been-there, done-that" philosophy. We think that once we've accomplished something, we should be able to pack it away in our bag of "learned" things. We shouldn't have to learn it all over again.

If we apply this philosophy to ourselves as parents—and, in particular, as working parents—we're never going to measure up to our own expectations. We're not going to accept that learning to be a working parent—to balance home and work successfully—is an ongoing process that takes continual fine-tuning and reassessment. We're going to think, "We should have mastered this by now," and beat ourselves up (or get really upset with our families) when the situation spirals out of our control.

The solution is simple. Especially in this adjustment period, be grateful for the way your family is pulling together, even if they seem to be pulling together in separate directions. Find small things to be thankful for, even if you need a microscope. Notice how the kids are trying and make a lot of noise about that. And correct the rebellions or misunderstandings directly but without a lot of fanfare.

When you see this difficult time as part of the overall adjustment cycle, it becomes easier to weather. As one mother put it,

"Try not to over-focus on failures that are insignificant. Choose your battles wisely—if you choose to engage in a power struggle with your child, make sure it's worth the bloodshed."
—Mother of two who works full-time

Whatever Can Go Wrong, Will

This is an old recast of Murphy's Law, expressing not so much an expectation as a perspective on how we can look at the "wrong" things that happen in our lives.

I'm not suggesting you should expect things to go wrong, but we do have a choice of how we react when they do. If we understand that our system is going to be tested—that things will break down, the kids will fight, this one will miss the car pool, that one will break the rules—maybe we won't overreact when things go wrong. We will see the breakdowns not as something we've failed to orchestrate or control but, rather, as part of the natural process of adjustment that is happening in our families.

Not that enforceable offenses—broken household rules, blatant violations, refused chores—shouldn't be dealt with; they should. But having the proper perspective on the "wrongs" when they happen helps you address the problem clearly.

Looking at Wrong the Right Way

If you look at your back-to-work adjustment as a continual process, you'll see that your system

BEST &
WORST

Best:
"Being away from my children during the day makes me cherish the time that we do have together so much more. It makes me so thankful that I have a wonderful family to go home to."

breaks down only where it needs reinforcement. The "wrongs" then become the weak links that need to be addressed. Each time you find something that doesn't work, you can see it as another way to make your system stronger.

If Patrick isn't calling you after school at the prescribed time, you need to assess why. Consider where the rule is breaking down. Is he simply disregarding your rules? Is it a difficult time for him to get to the phone? Is there another reason you don't know about? Talking with Patrick will help you assess the situation and make any necessary changes or additions.

Challenges at Home

The first place you're likely to be tested is on the home front. Things aren't the way they used to be, and change always causes some resistance. You can save yourself from fighting the resistance effort by thinking about your family rules and deciding which ones you need to keep, which ones need to go, and which ones should be revised.

Family Rules

What are your family rules? Each family is different, but most of us have some rules in common. We have determined what time the kids need to be in bed, whether Joe can watch TV before his homework is done, how long Erica can talk on the phone after dinner, and what kind of snacking we allow between meals. We have set curfews, decided on room cleaning issues, and drawn the lines of responsibility around family chores and allowances.

But do you have the rules in writing? If you already have your family rules written down and posted on the refrigerator, good for you—you're a few steps ahead of the rest of us. Many parents have learned that rules that are simply stated— "Christa, I told you to be in bed by 9:00!"—can be easily bent: "But, Mom, I thought you meant in bed *reading* by 9:00!"

If you have written rules—well-thought-out, clearly written rules—the verbal loopholes won't be open. Your kids won't be able to say, "But Mom, I thought . . . " and knock you off your resolve. Write them down and put them up. It will make the up-front aspect of your communications much clearer. Your kids—and you—will be able to see in black and white what you meant.

If you looked into the home lives of 100 working parents, you'd see a wide range of parenting styles: strict and permissive, liberal and conservative. You'd find people who spank and people who don't. You'd find parents who yell and children who yell back. You'd discover families in which kids are in control, families in which parents are in control, and families in which nobody (except perhaps the dog) is in control. Such is the nature of modern life. It's not a judgment, it's just fact: Whatever works for you, works for you. The main thing is to keep trying. Sooner or later you'll run across the tools, knowledge, insight, and/or experience you need to put together the system that works for you.

Our Family Rules

1. _____
2. _____
3. _____
4. _____
5. _____
6. _____
7. _____
8. _____
9. _____
10. _____

A few tips for creating your rule sheet:

 If you name one child in a rule, name them all (or rewrite the rule to omit names entirely). If Rule #3 is "Erica must wash the dinner dishes before she can talk on the phone," change it to "Phone time is allowed only after the dishes have been done," to avoid singling out one child. Or if this is a rule that applies only to Erica, make sure you've got one that applies only to her brother, as well: "Joe must finish his homework before watching TV."

 Use positive wording. Nobody wants to read a list of don'ts. "Don't raid the refrigerator while Dad and I are at work" becomes "Eat only the snacks I've set out on the counter for you."

 Think about the most important issues and write them into your rules. Which

issues cause you the most consternation? These are the ones you need to be clearest about. A well-written rule can end all the "But, Mom . . . " hassle you've been wrestling with.

Know that your rules will be tested and broken. As you write the rules, be realistic and reasonable. Remember that the primary purpose of making rules is to create guidelines your children will ultimately enforce themselves—not to overload them with standards they can't live up to.

Be ready with consequences for broken rules. The consequence should be logically linked to the crime, and they should be written on the rule sheet so the kids know what they're setting themselves up for before they break the rules.

Expect resistance. If you've never done anything like this before, expect grumbling. If you've got teenagers, you might hear something like, "I suppose you want to control how many times a minute I *breathe* now." With smaller kids, you may get varied reactions, from "Aw, Mom" to a willing attitude, a feeling that this might be "fun," or even some sense of relief.

Information is power, and when your kids know—and see in black and white—what you expect of them, they will be relieved on some level. They won't have to guess where the boundaries are. At first they may think this limits their freedom, but your clarity about family rules will make life easier for everyone.

Rules and Consequences

There's a problem. "We could handle it this way," your spouse says, as you discuss your son's impending punishment. "We could just ground him for a month and that would be the end of it!" you exclaim.

In most cases, rules are actually solutions. A problem pops up and you create a rule to keep it from popping up again. If you've been waiting for an important call and the caller finally contacts you at work and says, "I've tried the last three nights to get through on your home line, but it's always busy," you know you have a problem with phone use.

A rule can solve this. "Your phone time is now 7:00 P.M. to 8:00 P.M., Sandra," you say to the 14-year-old with the phone growing out of her ear. You revise the rule sheet to include the new rule. But simply setting the rule doesn't necessarily mean the battle's over. Rules were made to be—and will be—tested.

Experts tell us that effective rule setting—coupled with the foresight that things will undoubtedly crop up to challenge the rules—makes a tremendous difference in how quickly your family begins pulling together.[1] When you set the rules for your family, follow this three-pronged approach:

Every rule should address a particular problem.

Every rule should have logical consequences.

Every rule should be reviewed on a regular basis.

What's the Problem?

Now that you're back at work, you may need to think about either modifying your existing rules or officially writing them down for the first time.

Start with a list of problems you need to address:

Rules Worksheet, Part I

These are the problems we're having right now:

1. _____

2. _____

3. _____

4. _____

5. _____

Your list might involve problems like these:

1. Derrick has invited friends to the house twice after he's been told no one is allowed in while we're gone.

2. Casey refuses to take naps at the baby-sitter's.

3. Megan is not doing her chores.

4. Ben has missed the bus three times in the last two weeks, making me late for work.

5. Luke has been in trouble for fighting at preschool.

What's the Answer?

Look at each entry on your list and consider how it could be reworded into a rule. For example, the first issue could be made into a rule that reads,

1.   Friends are allowed in the house only when Mom or I are home.

Go through your list, turning the problem statements into solution statements (your new rules).

Rules Worksheet, Part II

These rules address the problems we've been having:

1. _____

2. _____

3. _____

4. _____

5. _____

What's the Consequence?

Now that you've identified what's going wrong in your system (or, more positively, where your opportunities for improvement lie), and turned the problems into rules, you need to think about the consequences that will result when the rules are broken.

The best consequences—the ones that teach cause and effect—are linked to the broken rule in some logical way. When Casey refuses to take a nap at the baby-sitter's, the logical consequence might be an earlier bedtime or a rest time when she gets home at the end of the day.

There are as many potential consequences as there are circumstances. You may need to give quite a bit of thought to the best reaction for the action. In the case of Casey and the refused naps, for example, there could be other things at play. Maybe she doesn't really need the nap. Perhaps the room she's resting in is too noisy. Maybe a quiet time during which she looks at a picture book or listens to music would be enough. Try to look at the entire picture when you define the problem. And know why you've chosen a consequence before you set it up as part of your system.

Rules Worksheet, Part III

If you break this rule: _____

Expect this: _____

If you break this rule: _____

Expect this: _____

If you break this rule: _____

Expect this: _____

If you break this rule: _____

Expect this: _____

If you break this rule: _____

Expect this: _____

The age of your child will determine the rules and consequences he is able to understand and follow. While removing privileges works well for older children, preschoolers are just learning the principle of cause and effect. For the younger set, you might set up consequences like time-out, which stops the negative behavior, sets clear boundaries, and lets the child start again.[2]

When Should You Revise the Rules?

The process of setting family rules is continual. As your children grow, and as your family settles into a routine and gets through the acclimation period, your rules will change as old problems are solved and new ones arise.

You'll soon discover that you have two different kinds of rules: *foundational rules* and *situational rules*. Foundational rules are the basic, no-kidding rules that your family lives by no matter what. These will not change, and you want to be sure your children know they are important to you.

Situational rules you develop in answer to specific problems. Problems like Casey refusing to nap or Sandra's marathon phone conversations are solved with situational rules. When the problem goes away, the rule can go, too. Of course, if the problem returns, the rule can be put back into effect.

The key to knowing when to revise situational rules—to remove one, add another, or edit one you've already got—is simply to be observant. When Casey starts napping again, for example, you'll know the problem is solved, at least for now, and can be removed from the rule list. Removing

situational rules is a good thing. Don't just keep adding to the list until it covers the front of your refrigerator. Better to remove the rules as they are no longer needed. Everyone will understand that the rules are there for a reason—they help the family answer a problem—and that when the problem is solved, the rule is no longer needed. The kids will see rules as solutions to situations, not as an arbitrary form of parental control.

A Final Word

It may seem impossible, but the best way to weather this trying period at home is to (1) expect challenges, (2) prepare solutions, (3) remember that this too shall pass, and (4) keep your sense of humor.

Focusing on the positive things your children are doing to help your back-to-work transition—even if you need to go on a treasure hunt to find them— will encourage the kids to do more. Let the rules take care of the things they *aren't* doing; no more nagging, no more exasperation. If they break the rule, they pay the consequence. This leaves you free to focus on the things they *are* doing well: how well they're doing at school, how straight they're keeping their rooms, how promptly they got off the phone after their phone time, how pleasant they were at dinner.

Being a positive parent is a lot more fun than being a negative parent. Designing and implementing a good set of family rules lets you remove yourself from law enforcement and concentrate on the nurturing, teaching, and loving parts of the job.

Challenges at Work

Having things go haywire at home is bad enough, but things aren't working well on the job, either. You missed your first big deadline. Your boss is looking at you like she thinks she may have made a mistake. The guy in the next cubicle made a comment yesterday about how "sweet" it is that your daughter calls you at work every 15 minutes. Somehow you suspect he doesn't really think it's sweet.

Although the family rule system you're implementing may be new, at least you have a past history to work with. Whether your rules were written and posted on the fridge (or bulletin board) or not, your family had already been working with an established—if only verbal—set of rules.

Work is a different story. You've just gotten this job, so you're not sure what to expect. There are many variables—people, projects, learning curves—and you've somehow got to navigate all of them and still get your work done.

BEST & WORST

Worst:
"The fatigue factor: not much is left at the end of the day."

Great Expectations

First and foremost, accept that you are going through some major adjustments. Allow yourself to feel a little off your game: Don't expect perfection. Chances are, you expect much more of yourself than anyone around you is expecting right now.

What's the Problem?

Next, assess the problem. Where is your new work system breaking down? What are your issues? Get them down on paper where you can see them clearly.

Work Issues

These are the things I'm having trouble with at work:

1. _____

2. _____

3. _____

4. _____

5. _____

Your list might include problems like this:

1. I can't figure out the e-mail system.

2. I don't have time to get all my work done.

3. The deadlines are stressing me out.

4. I feel isolated and alone.

5. I don't know if I'm up to this.

6. My office mate is hard to get along with.

Whatever the issue, know that there is something you can do about it. Sometimes just making the list—getting the problems identified—can help you figure out the answer.

Resolving Work Issues

Now that you've got your list, look carefully at each problem statement, one at a time. Does a solution automatically come to mind? Do you think, "I could try this," or, "Maybe she could help"?

Often when we allow ourselves to brainstorm answers to a situation, many different answers come. Using your "problem statement" list, write a new list, leaving blank space between each entry. Then give yourself 15 or 20 minutes of quiet time (a lunch break, a coffee break, or any other period during which you won't be interrupted) and read through each issue on your list. Read the statement and ask yourself, "What can I do about this?" Then write down any and all answers that come to you. You can weed them out and choose the ones you want to try later.

Resolving Work Issues

Problem: _____

Possible solutions: _____

Problem: _____

Possible solutions: _____

Problem: _____

Possible solutions: _____

From One Parent to Another

"Experience is a great teacher, and your kids will grow up understanding more about your occupation than they will about any other types of jobs. But if you take your children to the office, be sure to do it in age-appropriate chunks. Take your 2-year-old in for a quick appearance while you pick up that file you forgot, for example, or let your 6-year-old sort your colored paper clips while you run off a few copies. But don't take the kids in for hours at a time and expect them to be happy and entertained. It's not their world, and the amusement won't last long."

—Mother of three who works full-time

Once you have a list of possible solutions, you can decide on a plan of action. This involves weeding out the solutions you think are less likely to work, the ones you don't want to try first, or the ones that are totally impractical (like winning the lottery and quitting your job).

What makes a good solution? Only you know the answer to that question. It will depend on what's most important to you, the circumstances surrounding your challenge, and what you're trying to accomplish. The most important thing is to define your problem, know that there is a resolution in there somewhere, and to give yourself the time and space to think creatively and let the answer reveal itself. You can then implement whichever solutions seem to fit the circumstance, whether you need to ask for help, reorganize your work time, communicate more directly with your coworkers or employer, or find friends for support and encouragement.

Balance Is a Verb

If you're like many working parents, there are days you feel like you're walking a tightrope with a baby on your hip and a briefcase in your hand. Beneath you, a hundred feet down, stand all the other people who depend on you: your spouse, your boss, your family, your friends, your clients. You feel all eyes on you. The pressure is tremendous.

The balancing act will continue because many things are important to us and we are continually called to align ourselves with our values and our priorities. Take heart in the knowledge that we're all walking the same rope. The balancing doesn't stop, but it does get easier.

And while we're up here, we might as well have a little fun with it. Finesse is in order. Daring spins and turns will amuse the audience and make your act uniquely yours. In all the pressures and pitfalls of being a working parent, there is something authentically yours about the system you create. Be yourself, have fun with it, and create a system that reflects the best you and your family can do.

Summary

Soon after you begin your job, no matter how perfect everything seems, life begins to unravel. Not only do things start going wrong at home, but the office may seem threatening, as well. But, as this chapter has outlined, there are a number of ways you can assess what's happening and set about making your family system stronger. And you can apply the same problem-solving techniques to figure out your challenges at work and devise a plan to meet them.

The next chapter concentrates on organizing your home so things get done more smoothly with less effort from you. Do less and get more done. Doesn't that sound nice?

Notes

1. Kenneth Kaye, *Family Rules* (New York: St. Martin's Press, 1984), pp. 33-83.

2. The clearest, most helpful book I've found on setting time-out limits is *Time-Out for Toddlers* by Dr. James W. Varni and Donna G. Corwin (New York: Berkley Books, 1991).

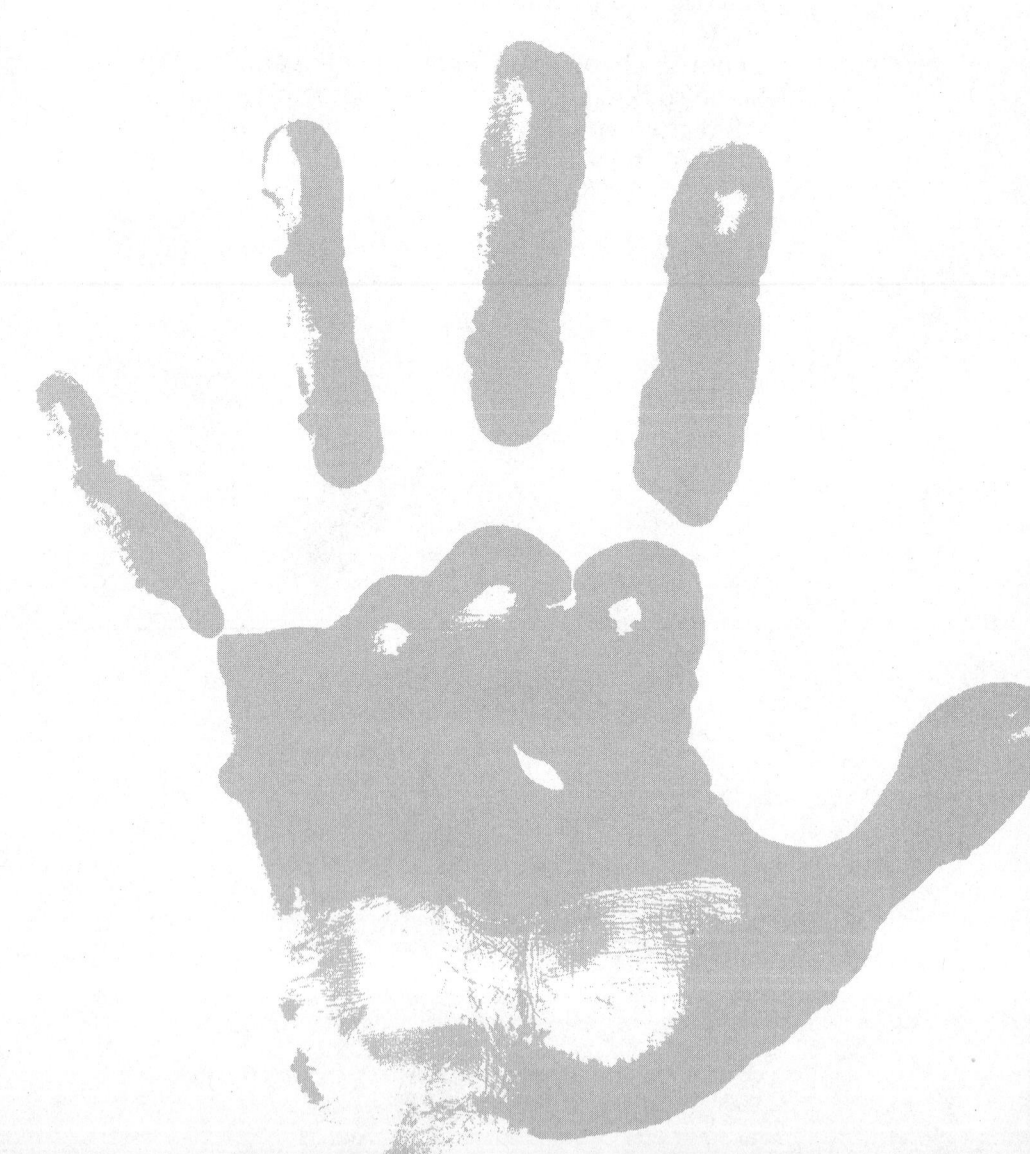

Chapter 7

On the Home Front

"I hate housework! You make the beds, you do the dishes—and six months later you have to start all over again."
—Joan Rivers

Things are on the upswing. Home life is settling down. Life at the office seems more manageable and less overwhelming. The kids are beginning to understand the importance of their willing participation during this adjustment period, and you and your spouse are generally happy with the family priorities you've set. You are working well together to

get everybody where they need to be at the times they need to be there.

Then one day you pull into the driveway and notice a shutter hanging by a single bolt. "I've got to fix that," you say to yourself, making a mental note. A week later, your daughter says, "Did you notice that one of the shutters is falling off the house?" Oops. You forgot. Another week passes, and the shutter is in the bushes. You stand out front and consider your options. "Doesn't look that bad," you think. "Maybe I should just take all the shutters down. Then I don't have to mess with them."

Getting things done around the house is difficult even when life isn't turned up to a frantic pace. Now, more than ever, you need to organize. You need a system to be sure that everything that needs to be done is done and—more importantly— that you don't do it all yourself.

From One Parent to Another

"Get your children to help. If each child does just one thing (puts clothes away, washes the dishes, empties the dishwasher), it makes things so much easier."

—Mother of four who works part-time

The House Is Calling—Loudly

You may have become aware your house needs TLC in a not-so-gentle fashion. Perhaps your son called you at work one day. "Three different lawn care companies called this morning, Mom," he said. "Do you think someone's trying to tell us it's time to cut the grass?"

Or maybe the pastor knocked at the door and you found yourself rushing around the family room, trying frantically to brush the cat hair off the sofa and pick the cracker crumbs off the rug.

Or perhaps your in-laws stopped by unexpectedly, and you began devising ways to keep them out of the kitchen, where dishes were still stacked from dinner the night before.

Life is messy, with or without kids. Everyone has a junk drawer, a monster closet that threatens to spill out into the hallway, or a corner (or room) that just seems to collect broken things. Some of us are more disorganized than others, and some of us don't have a clue how to start digging out.

This chapter helps you come up with practical responses to the practical issues that are bound to crop up as a result of the new demands on your ever-more-precious time. One way to answer household challenges is to enlist help. Another answer is to organize, organize, organize—put a system in place so your house is straight-with-occasional-clutter instead of cluttered-with-occasional-straight-places.

Fire prevention vs. fire-fighting

It's not usually the way the world works, but it's a lot easier to implement a solution to a problem *before* you have the problem. You might even be able to avoid the problem altogether.

Case in point: organizing at home. If you begin organizing after everything explodes and you can't find something you really need, you're organizing in fire fighting mode. ("Things are really a mess! I've got to do something about this!") But if you look around one afternoon and say, "Hmmm. I'll bet there's an easier way to do this," you can begin calmly to organize your life and your house a little at a time. This second approach–fire prevention as opposed to fire fighting–is much gentler and easier to follow through with in the long run.

Basic Housework 101

Chances are, you've been doing housework for years. Soon after your return to work, you'll notice there is dramatically less time for housework than there used to be. You have to let certain things go. And go. And go.

Household Tip #1:
Don't sweat the small stuff.

If you're like most people, you try to fit all your housework into a single weekend session. (Really makes you look forward to the weekend, doesn't it?) Or you try to stay awake long enough to clean the bathrooms after the kids are in bed for the night. Trust me, there are better ways.

Seize the Moment

Time management has a lot to do with how well you keep up with the house. If you try to schedule a huge block of time to do all those things you never get a chance to do, you'll wait a long time for that slot. Instead, you could make the most of those spare moments while Kendra is drying her hair or Roger is walking the dog. While you're waiting, pick up. Get the chicken out of the freezer for dinner. Do a quick refrigerator check and list the things you can pick up from the grocery on your way home. Learn to seize the moment and fit doable tasks into it, and you'll find yourself with less to schedule at the end of the day or week.

What kinds of things can you do in a spare moment or two? Pick up toys, open mail, read notes from teachers, put away dried dishes, plan dinner, fold socks, wipe a countertop, start a load of laundry, make a bed, open curtains, sweep a floor, straighten a cabinet. If you have trouble thinking of things you can do quickly, make a list as they occur to you. Then, when you find yourself standing at the door with your briefcase waiting for Lauren to pack up her science project, you can check the list and knock out one of the items. One working mother of two does it this way:

"Once every couple of days, I walk through the house with a little notebook—something I can keep in my pocket. I make a list of absolutely everything I see that needs to be done. In the morning, before I leave for work, I check the list to see if there's anything I can do. At night, I check it again. All week long I work on that list, and on Fridays I read back through it. I'm amazed at the number of things I can cross off in a week's time! It really makes me feel good to know I do all that I do and I'm still able to accomplish that much at home."

What quick jobs can be done around your house to lighten your "cleaning detail" later? Give some serious thought to the things that drive you crazy because you never seem to get to them. In my house, that includes a loose drawer that needs to be reglued, fingerprints on the door frames, a bowl full of change I want to put into rolls, plants with brown leaves begging to be removed, and probably 20 other things.

Make a list of simple tasks you can do in a "while-you-wait" 10-minute period. Then put the list somewhere easy to find—on the fridge, on the bulletin board—and refer to it when you have a moment to spare.

Sponsor a To-Do competition at your house. Show your kids the To-Do list, and give them a challenge: "Each time you do one of the To-Do chores, cross it off the list and initial it. At the end of the week, whoever has done the greatest number of chores wins." Be specific about what they will win, and about how and when they can collect. You might use allowance bonuses, special movies or privileges, or a long-awaited toy to give incentive to their efforts.

Do a Little at a Time

When it comes to things like keeping the house in tolerable order, you're best off doing a little at a time. Instead of letting things accumulate—not doing the laundry until Saturday, when you will have five loads to do—try to knock them out a little at a time. Do one load of laundry a day—every day, if you need to—and make sure it's washed, dried, and put away *that day*. Don't let it carry over until tomorrow. Then, in the morning, start again. You can start a load almost without thinking—maybe before you leave for work in the morning—then toss the clothes in the dryer later (like when you get home from work). Once you get yourself in the habit, it will almost seem like the laundry is doing itself. (And if you can get the kids to fold and put away, even better!)

One working father uses this spread-it-out approach with household repair projects:

"I work so many hours that I have trouble getting the time to work on the house. So I try to do one fix-it thing a night. Like the faucet dripping. Or putting oil on a squeaky door. I feel like I'm keeping up with things better if I don't let a lot of little things go."

What kinds of things can you manage a little at a time? Think of the things you spend a lot of time on—things you will be doing over and over, no matter what—not one-time projects, like painting the living room or hanging that shutter. Tasks that you do repeatedly will seem much more manageable if you tackle them frequently. Here are a few examples:

 Dishes. We all know the sinking feeling of walking into the kitchen after an exhausting day to face stacks of dirty dishes. Get into the habit of washing them right after you use them, and teach your family to be dish-responsible. They *can* learn to put a glass or dish in the dishwasher when they're finished with it. ("You use it, you load it.")

 Laundry. I'm not sure why laundry has such emotional control over me, but I've been known to stand helpless before piles of dirty clothes with thoughts like, "I just can't keep up. I'll never get this done. I should be a better housekeeper." If the laundry has you feeling powerless, stay on top of it. One load a day keeps that monster mound out of your basement (and may keep the kids from complaining about mismatched socks).

 General straightening. This one gets under my family's skin, but I'm a firm believer in staying on top of clutter. When you're finished in a particular room, make sure it's straight before you leave it. If it was straight when you went in, how much of a mess could you have made? Don't leave it for later, or you'll have to deal with it later. Do it now, clean and simple. Later, when you've got 14 other things to do, you'll be glad you did.

 Organizing bills. If only we could pay bills once and be done with it. But no, they keep coming, accumulating throughout the month until payday rolls around. To keep your stress level low and your coping level high,

have a system to organize and pay your bills. As soon as you get the mail, every day, open it and file it in its proper place. This avoids the stack of bills that grows on the countertop (what a depressing sight!) and keeps you from accidentally misplacing something you really need to act on.

Household Tip #2:
Clean one room a day to avoid spending your whole weekend with the mop.

Who's Job Is It, Anyway?

I knew things had to change at my house when my then 5-year-old son Christopher (who had Napoleonic tendencies anyway) refused to pick up the pajamas he'd thrown on the floor, saying, "What do you think I am, the maid?"

Shocked but not silenced, I asked, "Who do you think the maid is?"

"You are," he said matter-of-factly.

After my blood pressure returned to normal, we established that (1) he didn't know what a maid was (he had heard the line on TV the night before) and (2) it was time to set some *Very Clear Rules About Who Does What Around Here.*

Here are the rules we came up with:

 If you got it out, put it back.

 If you're finished playing with it, put it away.

 If you wore it, hang it up.

 If you spilled it, clean it up.

 If you broke it, admit it.

 If you'll help me, I'll help you.

After we established the rules, we had a long training period. In some families, this might be a "retraining" period. Maybe you established some guidelines early on about household responsibilities and now you need to clarify things a bit. But it does work, and it does help. And having the lines of responsibility drawn helps your kids know what's theirs to do and what isn't. When 15-year-old Adam tells 10-year-old Seth, "Make my bed," Seth glances up from his Batman game and says, "Make it yourself—it's *your* bed." Fair enough.

> **Household Tip #3:**
> *Be willing to let things look less than perfect.*

BEST & WORST

Best: "Teaching children to handle responsibilities"

Organizing Household Tasks

Once you've establish the things you can do in spare moments and the things you can do a little at a time, you can start chipping away at the rest of the tasks you do on a regular basis. Setting up a system to organize household responsibilities may sound like a lot of effort for a little gain— who wants to spend even more time thinking about all the things you have trouble getting to? But in the time you ordinarily spend watching a rerun on TV (don't worry—it will be on again) you can make a schedule that will take a lot of the hassle and headache out of your household chores.

In the next section, you'll learn to identify areas where you need extra help around the house. The extra help might come in the form of chores your kids do or a new way to organize things to make your life easier.

When Does It Get Done?

One of the easiest ways to make sure things get done regularly is to create a housework schedule. Nothing fancy, just a written-down schedule of when the floor gets mopped, when the bathrooms are cleaned, when the sweeper is run, and the like. Once you write it all down, you can stop carrying it around in your head and maybe let yourself relax a while. Your housework schedule might look something like this:

Housework Schedule

To Do	How Often	When?
Clean bathrooms	Once a week	Saturday mornings
Run the sweeper	Twice a week	Tuesday & Friday evenings
Dust the furniture	Once a week	Saturday mornings
Mop the kitchen	Every two weeks	Saturday afternoon
Wipe fingerprints	Once a month	Saturday afternoon
Empty trash cans	Twice a week	Tuesday & Friday evenings

First make a list of all the chores to be done around (inside *and* outside) your house. Then determine how often they should be done. Finally, choose when they will fit into your family's schedule. Don't create the schedule thinking you'll do this all yourself. The idea is to enlist (or, if necessary, draft) other family members into sharing the wealth of work.

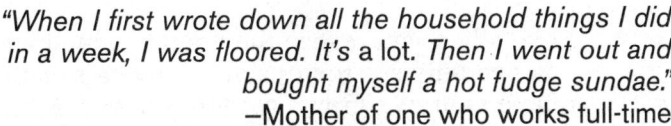

"When I first wrote down all the household things I did in a week, I was floored. It's a lot. Then I went out and bought myself a hot fudge sundae."
—Mother of one who works full-time

Household Tip #4:
Make housework easy on yourself.

Housework Schedule

To Do	How Often?	When?

What Do You Need?

Once you realize you need to try something new to get the house in shape, the question is, "What?"

There are several ways you can respond.

First, when you realize the grass is knee-high and you can only see the tips of bunny ears as they nibble your overgrown garden, ask yourself, "What do I need in order to fix this?" You'll probably hear a number of answers:

 Help!

 A teenager to mow the grass.

 Someone to weed the garden.

 More time so I can weed the garden.

 No garden, so I don't have to weed it.

 Artificial grass, so it doesn't need mowing.

 Cows to graze and keep the yard trimmed. (No, because then we'd need a fence, too.)

The first step in recovering from that overwhelmed feeling is recognizing you are overwhelmed. Then you can begin to think about ways to get the help you need.

Help might come in the form of other people. Maybe a neighbor could help you strip the wax off the kitchen floor (does anybody really do that anymore?) or get those impatiens planted before they wilt. Help might come in the form of time management. Maybe this is one of those things you could do a little at a time (even if you just mow a six-foot-square section of grass every day). Maybe it's something you could delegate to someone else, something you don't need to be doing yourself at all. Do you really have to pick up the dry-cleaning, even though it's 20 minutes out of your way? There might be other options, if you stop to think about them.

Household Tip #5:
*Plan simple meals
for weeknights.*

Let Yourself Think

The second step in determining what you need is
to give yourself time to think about what would
help. Do you need more time? More help? More
resources? More options?

Look at the issue that's giving you trouble. Take
the laundry. (Please!) If it's piling up, consider
why. Get a piece of paper and write the problem
at the top: "Why am I having trouble getting the
laundry done?" Then write down the answers as
they come to you:

1. There's too much of it.

2. I never have enough time to finish it.

3. Someone is always in the shower.

4. The washer is broken.

Within each of these answers are clues to how you
can solve the problem. If there's too much
laundry, ask yourself why. Are the kids throwing
clean clothes in the basket? Are you trying to do it
all at once instead of a little at a time? Is there
another option you haven't let bubble up yet?

Go through your list, item by item, and write
down any other questions, solutions, or options
that come to you. Some answers will be obvious;
others may surprise you. In any event, you won't
be able to get the kind of help you need until you
give yourself time to think of possible solutions.

"I've Always Done It This Way"

One answer you should *never* accept is, "We've always done it this way." If that's the best you can come up with, then it's probably time for a change.

Case in point: For 20 years, every time Diane made a roast beef, she cut the roast into two pieces and cooked them in separate pans. One day, her daughter asked her why she did that (thinking perhaps it made the meat more tender). Diane stopped and said, "I don't know. I've just always done it this way. My mother did it like this."

Intrigued, the daughter called Grandma, who laughingly explained that, when Diane was small, they had lived in a house with a tiny oven. In order to cook a roast big enough for the entire family, she'd had to divide it into two pans and fit them on separate shelves in the oven.

The moral? Whenever you find yourself saying, "I don't know—I've always done it like this," ask yourself whether it fits for you now.

Why am I having trouble with _____

1. _____

2. _____

3. _____

4. _____

5. _____

Ten Ways to Get the Help You Need

1. Have a clear picture of what you need help with.

2. Ask.

3. Be realistic about "when." If you have a situation you need to resolve *now*, do your best to take care of it quickly. But don't put unnecessary pressure on yourself when it's unwarranted.

4. Focus on one task and finish it before moving on to the next.

5. Be willing to be less than perfect. Don't feel bad that you can't finish everything. Reverse your thinking and celebrate because you finish something.

6. Use your resources. If friends or relatives offer help, accept it.

7. Let the people who offer help do it their way. Don't insist that the T-shirts be folded the way you've always done it. If they're folded, they're folded.

8. Focus on the most important things first. Take time to prioritize what you need to spend your time on. You can deal with the less important things later.

9. Don't rule out paid help. If you need a housekeeper, a professional organizer, a lawn service company, or a handyman—even if it's just a one-shot deal—admit it and get help. If it makes your life easier and it's worth the investment, go for it.

10. Think creatively about a solution; don't just settle for the first answer that comes to mind.

Household Tip #6:
Make sure you've got all the tools you need before you start a job.

Designing a Chore List

When you were coming up with your family priorities, mission statement, and rules, you

probably listed who does what around the house. Perhaps your first question, when you noticed the grass overtaking the fire hydrant, was, "Who's job is it to mow the grass?"

What? You don't have a chore list? Oh, your kids are going to *love* this.[1] In fact, studies show that kids respond well to having things written out for them. They like to know what's expected of them, and they are more likely to meet—and exceed— your expectations when they have a good idea of what you want.

Like anything else, you should present the chore list in a family meeting with a "let's-make-this-family-work" kind of attitude. Everyone helps, everyone is important. The only time a chore list doesn't work is when it's uneven or unfair—that is, when one of the kids gets more work than the others, or when you assign all the jobs and don't do anything yourself (and how likely is *that?*)

Daily Chore List

Name: _____

_____

_____

_____

_____

Name: _____

_____

_____

_____

_____

Name: _____

_____

_____

_____

_____

Pick-Up Tip #1:
*Teach your toddler to put away
as part of the game you're playing.
Getting-out and putting-away are the
beginning and ending points of playing
with blocks, puzzles, crayons, trucks,
whatever. The earlier you start, the easier
it will be to enlist your child's help.*

A few suggestions for creating a chore list:

 Bring up the idea at a family meeting.
Explain that you need help with the house
and you're looking for willing volunteers.
Explain that if you don't get willing
volunteers, you'll call in the draft. Ask each
child to come up with three chores he or she
would "like" to do each weekday (you may
want to give them weekends off or have
different Saturday chores). There may be
some haggling ("But I don't want to unload
the dishwasher! I want to feed the dog!"), but,
as much as possible, let the kids work out
who does what. It's your job to act as
secretary and write down the jobs they
finally agree to.

 Set a time limit for the chore roster. You
might say, for example, "Okay, we're going to
try this for a month. Cindy, you'll load the
dishwasher, bring in the mail, and set the
table every day for a month. Kyle, you feed
the dog, make sure the toys are picked up in
the family room, and put the clothes in the
laundry basket. At the end of the month,
we'll see if you want to trade jobs or chose
something else."

 **Include all kids, no matter what their
ages.** Everyone can do something. As soon
as Cameron is old enough to know a spoon
from a fork, he can help set the table. When

Lisa is home from college, she can still take the trash out on Monday nights.

Chore Possibilities

Pick up toys	Set the table
Fold laundry	Make the bed
Run the sweeper	Bring in the newspaper
Take out the trash	Bring in the trash cans
Dust furniture	Get the mail
Let the dog out	Feed pets
Water plants	Clip coupons
Make snacks	Weed the garden
Mow the lawn	Sweep the floors

Household Tip #7:
Don't answer the phone
while you're cleaning.

Teaching Kids About Chores

You may have "chore memories" from your childhood that still haunt you. What were your jobs around the house? I had to bring in the milk. Two glass bottles once a week, left in the stainless steel milkbox on the front porch. (Boy, that really dates me.) I also set the table for dinner, cleaned the upstairs bathroom on Saturdays, and dried dishes every night after supper. (My brother always got to wash. *I* always wanted to wash.)

Your kids learn important things from having chores at home. They learn about teamwork, responsibility, and cause-and-effect. They find out about family responsibility, which helps them grow into a bigger sense of societal and personal responsibility later.

Here are some tips for teaching your children about chores:

 Make it matter-of-fact. Treat the chores as a part of life, not something to be negotiated or candy-coated. The attitude should be, "We all have a part to play, and this is yours." Give the role the respect it deserves: You need each and every member of your household pulling together to make things work. Zach might be helping with little things now, but in a year or two, he'll be able to do much bigger things by himself because you've helped him learn to handle responsibility early.

 Expect grumbling. Who among us would fold laundry if we could whine a little and have someone else do it for us? Don't be shocked, dismayed, or angered when your kids grumble. They will. Just fall back on the matter-of-fact attitude and explain that chores go with the territory.

 Reward performance. Set up a system to reward your kids (and yourself) when they accomplish the goals you've set together. You may want to start allowances, if you haven't already done that. Or use other incentives, like special freedoms, trips to concerts, family excursions, or sleep-over privileges. To encourage team spirit, you could set a family goal: "When we have a week when we all get our chores done without reminders, we'll go to the movies."

Chore Incentive Programs

How you encourage your kids to complete their chores is, of course, up to you. You might simply insist that chores be completed before a favorite activity is allowed:

"Ryan, your bed must be made before you can play video games."

"Maggie, your chores must be finished before you can talk on the phone."

You might want to use an allowance as a motivational factor. If your children perform their chores without any prompting from you for five consecutive days, what's it worth to you? Some parents are comfortable with that. Others feel that chores are simply part of family responsibilities, and that kids should do them without expecting compensation.

A mother of three who works full-time put it this way:

"I started out paying my son Chad for the chores he did, but all of a sudden, every time I saw him, he had his hand out. He'd say. 'Mom, I brought in the trash can for you,' and hold out his hand. Or 'Mom, I let the dog out,' and that hand would go out. I started feeling like he thought I was supposed to pay him for every nice thing he did. So I made a list of 10 things and said, 'These are the things I'll pay you for. Everything else you do is just because you're such a great kid.'"

Whatever your feelings on the subject, you're going to get better results if you reward your children for doing their jobs. Whether that reward is a simple acknowledgment ("Jason, your bed looks great!"), a hug or compliment, a special treat, or some other way you think to say "Good job," letting your children know that you notice and appreciate their help is an important part of making sure they continue it.

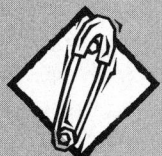

At our house, the old gold-stars-on-the-chart idea worked well for several weeks, until the baby got hold of the stars and stuck them everywhere—on the television, the stereo, the couch, the dog. A simple checklist—or better, a page where kids can add stickers each day they complete their chores—gives you (and them) a visual record of how well they are doing. Hang the chart in your family information area so everyone can see how hard they are working.

Household Tip #8:
When the family helps, let them do it their way—and be appreciative.

Tipping the Allowance Scales

If you decide to go the allowance route, how do you know the going rate? (Better not ask your kids what their friends are getting. You may hear a slightly exaggerated "average.") Should you dole it out a quarter at a time, or make it a lump sum at the end of the week? Should it be tied completely to chores ("If you don't do your chores, you don't get paid"), or should it be given simply on merit? Lots of questions that only you can answer.

Experts suggest, however, that the primary reason to give an allowance is to help your children learn about money, not to coerce their cooperation in family chores. In *Family Rules*, Dr. Kenneth Kaye suggests you protect a portion of the allowance that is irrevocable—in other words, your kids get a certain part of their allowance even if they don't do their chores.[2]

You can make some of the allowance contingent on the completion of chores: This sets up a natural consequence that you can enforce easily and will encourage your children to do their chores. For example, you might tell Jill she loses 50 cents of her allowance each time she forgets to put the dishes in the dishwasher. After a few shortages, she might start remembering the dishes.

So, how much should you pay? The ages of your children have a lot to do with it. Older children might need extra money for things like bus fare or school lunches; younger children need little money in order to learn the spending and responsibility lessons an allowance can teach. Many parents of teenagers feel that kids shouldn't receive an allowance at all—that any spending money above and beyond school expenses the teenager should earn him- or herself, by doing extra chores, mowing lawns, shoveling snow, baby-sitting, or getting an after-school job.

When you know the allowance thing isn't working

A teenager was asked what she does to earn the $10 allowance she gets every week. She looked at the questioner, dumbfounded. "What do you mean, 'What do I *do*?'"

Generally, $1 to $2 a week is more than enough for elementary school children. (Remember, you might want to make one part of the allowance contingent on chores and one part irrevocable.) For junior high students, you might go up a few dollars—to $4 or $5—especially if the student is paying bus fare. High school opens up yet more options, with off-campus lunches, flower sales, candy sales, and other miscellaneous ways your teen will want to spend money. Again, decide for yourself how you feel most comfortable handling the allowance issue and then make the information available to the kids. Another family meeting? You bet.

They'll want to know why some of the kids are "making more" than others. Have your explanations ready. And remember that the most important thing an allowance does is help your child learn how to make money decisions—both how to work for it and how to spend it. Using it solely as something to take away when they don't do their chores teaches them only the effects of irresponsibility, not the rewards of responsibility.

Daily Chore Record

Name: _____

Monday: _____

Tuesday: _____

Wednesday: _____

Thursday: _____

Friday: _____

Pick-Up Tip #2:
Choose a "clean up song" that you play whenever it's time to clean up. Give your preschoolers a five-minute warning ("Okay guys, when I put the song on, you need to start cleaning up."), then put the song on. The song reminds them and gives them something pleasant to sing along with. The room gets clean, and there's no nagging or frustration for you.

Household Tip #9:
Don't redo what others have already done.

Recipe for Harmonious Housework

1 chore list	2 (or more) willing helpers
1 housework schedule	a good serving of patience
resolve to keep trying	realistic expectations
a sense of humor	encouraging words

Gather all ingredients in any order; mix well. Add a heavy sprinkling of encouraging words and keep trying, week after week, until you get it right.

Streamlining Household Efforts

Throughout this section, you've explored different ways to solve some of the issues piling up around you. You can deal with quick things in spare moments. You can spread big jobs out and do a little at a time. You can delegate chores so that everybody is helping.

Something else to think about is streamlining your efforts. By organizing tasks, you can do all of one type at once, thereby lessening the time and effort they require. Case in point: Changing the bedsheets. If you're the one changing all the sheets, do them all at once, every bed, every room. Don't start to strip Brian's bed, then pick up his toys (he should be doing that anyway!), fold his clothes, straighten his closet, and so on. Focus on that one thing and knock it out—for every room in which it applies.

Or you might do all the bathrooms in one fell swoop. You've got the toilet brush, your gloves, the glass cleaner, whatever—now do all the bathrooms at once, while you're in "bathroom mode." When you dust, dust everything. When you sweep, sweep all the floors that need it. Then you'll know you're done, completely, with that task.

Here are a few other time-saving tips for household chores:

 Plan what you're going to tackle before you tackle it. Make sure you've got the tools you need—a mop, the floor wax, a bucket, whatever—before you begin.

 Write out a calendar that shows when you do different tasks. Maybe you mop the downstairs once every two weeks, vacuum the living room twice a week, wipe fingerprints once a month, do windows— when?

Housework Calendar

SUNDAY	MONDAY	TUESDAY	WEDNESDAY	THURSDAY	FRIDAY	SATURDAY
1	2	3	4	5	6	7
8	9	10	11	12	13	14
15	16	17	18	19	20	21
22	23	24	25	26	27	28
29	30	31				

Errands, Errands, Everywhere

How much time do you spend in the car, driving to this store and that, stopping at the post office, running by the bank? With a little forethought, you can organize your errands into stops you can make after work or perhaps on your lunch hour. (Don't try to do them before work unless you're really comfortable with the cushion of time you have in the morning.) Think about what errands fall along your route, when you absolutely need to do them, and what the priorities are. This saves you from running all over town when you'd really rather be home with your family.

Here are a few additional tips to make your errand-running easier:

 Don't do on foot what you can do by phone. If you can accomplish your goals by calling, try that first. It may save you a trip.

 Organize all your errands into a single trip. Think about where you need to go and hit the places in a logical progression.

 Make sure you have everything you need before you leave. If you decide to run an errand on your lunch hour, be sure you've got the sales receipt, the laundry ticket, whatever. (You may want to put these items in the glove compartment of your car so you've always got them.)

 Assemble all the things you need to deliver on your errands in your going-

out place: books going back to the library, laundry to the cleaners, a shirt back to the store, whatever.

Organizing Is Worth the Effort

Many people have mental blocks about organizing. We remember grade-school teachers frowning down at us and saying, "You need to get yourself organized!" More recently, college professors—or perhaps bosses—may have noticed (with displeasure) our avant-garde approach to project management.

What's wrong with being organized?

Some of us think being organized—*really* organized, so we know roughly the balance of our checkbooks and where our car keys are, are sure that our briefcase is where we left it, and have a sense of where each of our children is at this very moment—means being restricted. No freedom. A regimented lifestyle.

But, as Pipi Campbell Peterson points out, "*realistically* planning allows us *more* freedom."[3] When we get organized, we spend less time in a wild panic looking for things we needed 20 minutes ago. We stop moving piles of things from place to place and put them where they go—once and for all. We simply *maintain* the organization once we've created it, which certainly takes a lot less work than dealing with chaos.

If you're a good sorter, you can organize. It's simply a matter of thinking about what goes where and then doing it. The thinking is the key part.

Do You Need to Organize?

We all have different mess-tolerance levels. Plastic building blocks scattered over the family room carpet might not bother you, but (for more than

an hour at a time) they bother me—especially in bare feet! I probably won't notice fingerprints on the windows, but they might drive you crazy.

On a larger scale, you might have a well-designed system for paying bills, getting your car serviced, keeping up with home improvements, and so on. I might just sit here and pray nothing happens that will force me to go hunting for a warranty agreement I know I'll never find.

The level of organization you need to keep your home running smoothly depends on your lifestyle and the needs of your family. Generally, the more complicated your life, the more you need to be organized. There are exceptions, however. Some people write everything down—from the time they intend to call their mother to what they need to thaw for dinner next Tuesday night. Others try to keep everything in their heads—usually with more than a couple of oversights, no matter how good their memories.

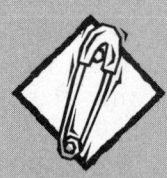 When you find yourself trying to remember too much—this appointment, that password, your deadline, his phone number, her shoe size—start writing things down. Invest 39 cents and get yourself a pocket notebook. When those little bits of information start cluttering your thoughts, write them down and get them off your mind. Your brain will thank you for it.

You know you need to organize things at home when ...

 You leave the house late more than three days in a row.

You can't find socks that match.

 You are looking for a legal document and there are several places it "could be."

 You are always searching for phone numbers on scraps of paper that were "right there a minute ago."

 You spend 10 minutes searching through clothes that don't fit anymore to locate something that does.

 You still have shoes from the '70s.

 You feel you have to know when someone is "stopping by" so you can do a whirlwind clean-up before they arrive.

 You look around at the clutter and feel overwhelmed.

One mother of four, an executive secretary who works 30 hours a week, explained her introduction to organization this way:

"It wasn't until everything started falling apart that I realized, in a panic, that there must be a better way to get things done around the house. We were at each other's throats all the time—each of us blaming the others for everything being a mess, not being able to find the things we needed, etc. So we gave each person a room: Each child is responsible for keeping his or her room clean and has one other room besides. Elizabeth straightens the kitchen and her room; Brandon picks up the living room and his room; Sara is in charge of the bathrooms and her room; and Scott, the youngest, takes care of the dining room (all he has to do is set the table for dinner) and his bedroom. On the weekends, we do the big cleaning, but the house basically stays straight through the week. And if it doesn't, we know whose name to call!"

Where Do You Need to Organize?

Most of us are pretty-well organized in some areas of our lives and not-so-organized in others. You might do a great job organizing your bills, for example, but not have a clue where your appliance manuals and warranties are. Or perhaps you've got laundry down to a science (one load a day, begun in the morning, finished in the evening), but things like storage—what to keep and where to keep it—leave you helpless.

 If you don't have a system for organizing bills and other household papers, see "A Filing System" later in this chapter.

While you're still in the thinking-about-organizing stage, walk around the house with a notebook and do a pre-organizing tour. Make a note of any room, corner, or shelf that is disorganized. You won't necessarily organize all the items you see—and you certainly won't do them all right now—but it will give you an idea of where to begin.

The Pre-Organizing Tour

These places need to be organized:

_____

_____

_____

_____

_____

_____

_____

_____

_____

Planning the Attack

If organizing the house ultimately falls on your shoulders, it behooves you to think about how you can best approach the task. The job may seem formidable, depending on how large a space you've got to arrange and how many other things you've got going on at the same time.

Here are a few guidelines to help you stay grounded in reality:

 Don't expect to get everything done in one afternoon, or even one weekend. If you are organizing files, boxes, closets, rooms, basements, and attics, plan on making "organizing" your new hobby for the next several weeks. Think of it as an extended spring cleaning session. But once you're finished, you'll only need to maintain the organization you've established. Getting organized is the most difficult part—then it's just a matter of _staying_ organized.

 As soon as you get started, the kids will want to help. And if your kids are like mine, "helping" means "going through these

boxes to see if there's anything I want." So 8-year-old Christopher tries to sneak out of the room with an AM radio that hasn't worked in 12 years. "Where are you going with that?" I ask. "I'm gonna' do something with it," he says. Do something with it. That means it will end up in *his* pile of junk, which I'll no doubt be sorting through sometime before the start of the next millennium.

 Careful thought now will keep you on track later. Once you begin organizing, the pull to get sidetracked will be great. You'll discover old memories and new mementos and find things you forgot to resolve years ago. Decide before you begin what it is you want to accomplish in that 30-minute, or 2-hour, or all-afternoon cleaning session. Say your goal out loud. "Before I leave this room, I'm going to finish that filing cabinet." Then stick to it.

 ## Kits for Making Housework Easier

Especially if you delegate jobs to your kids, you can make housecleaning a lot easier by putting together cleaning "kits" that include all the things needed for different jobs. Then, when you say, "John, clean up the soda you just spilled on the carpet," John can go to the cleaning closet (it helps to keep all the cleaning supplies together so you don't hear the inevitable, "I can't find it!"), get the cleaning kit he needs (in this case, the carpet care kit), and get to work. Here are a few kits you could easily create from things you've probably already got around the house:

- Mopping kit: mop, bucket, and floor cleaner
- Dusting kit: spray or oil, duster or cloths
- Spills kit: a roll of paper towels, sponge, small container for water
- Carpet care kit: carpet spot cleaner, a scrub brush, sponge, small container
- Bathroom cleaning kit: sink and tub cleaner, toilet cleaner, gloves, a sponge, toilet brush[4]

Even if you don't organize the items into kits, make sure you have cleaning supplies on hand for routine and emergency jobs. And, if you've got the space, put all the supplies together in one place—this lets you keep an eye on your inventory.

Once you get your cleaning closet organized, take the kids on a tour. Show them what's in there, how they will use the supplies, which supplies *not* to use, and what to do when spills happen, when the dog doesn't make it to the door, when it's their turn to clean the sink in the basement. Take 15 minutes to dole out useful information now, and you may save an hour's worth of consternation later in the week.

Setting Realistic Expectations

Before you start setting goals for yourself, make sure you're thinking realistically. In fact, if you're just beginning to get organized, give yourself the benefit of the doubt and set simple goals. Then, when you meet them, reward yourself. Pat yourself on the back.

If you set your goals too high ("I'm going to get this entire basement organized while the baby sleeps!"), you're setting yourself up for failure. Take it slow and easy. Remember, any organizing is a step in the right direction. You're improving your system, no matter how slowly it seems to be going.

What are realistic expectations?

 For a start, just *think* about organizing your house. Write down a few notes, if you want, but give yourself time to consider what you want to change, how you want it changed, what might make it better, what tools you need, and so on. Then set a date to begin the actual organizing.

 Do one thing the first day. Organize the junk drawer. (That may not be starting small

enough, if your junk drawer is like mine.) Or refold all the towels and separate them from the tablecloths in the linen closet.

 Keep a list. Make a list of all the organizing you need to do. When you finish a task, take a break, cross the item off the list, and celebrate a little.

 Prioritize the jobs. Make sure the tasks you tackle first are the ones that will bring you the biggest benefit. For example, you might want to create your family information center or your going-out place first, because those two items help your whole family stay in step.

Organizing Priorities

These places need to be organized in this order:

_____

_____

_____

_____

_____

_____

_____

_____

_____

_____

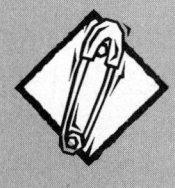 Pipi Campbell Peterson's *Ready, Set, Organize!* is a wonderful workbook that leads you through the process of organizing your entire household system. From basic time management to step-by-step organization of stored items, clothing, papers, and important records, *Ready, Set, Organize!* gives you a road map through—and out of—clutter forever.[5]

Where Should You Start?

Considering all the changes your family is going through and the balancing act you're learning, you should start wherever it will save you the most time. If you hardly ever go into the basement, don't spend your time and effort there. You may want to start with the family information center we talked about in chapter 1.

The Family Information Center

Some families set up their information center on the refrigerator; others create a bulletin board somewhere close to the telephone or in a central area everyone is likely to see. Include these items in your family information center:

 A large monthly calendar with write-in spaces to record all family activities.

 A set of colored markers, so each family member can have his or her own color.

 A list of important phone numbers, including Mom's and Dad's work numbers; the police, fire, and poison control centers; the baby-sitter's; the school; any after-school clubs; and close neighbors.

 Phone numbers of your children's friends, organized by child.

 A pad of paper for "we-need-this-from-the-grocery" items.

 Post-It notes for questions. ("Mom, can I go to Sara's house after school on Thursday?")

 Push-pins for important notices and school permission slips.

 Phone message pads.

Make sure each person in your family old enough to read and write understands the importance of updating his or her own information on the board. If Grant's game is moved from Tuesday to Monday, he needs to change it on the board (and hopefully tell you, too). If someone calls for you during the afternoon and Carrie takes a message, she should write the name, number, and message on the message pad and pin it where you'll see it.

Each night when you get home from work, check the information center to see what has changed. You might want to make a nightly habit of asking if anyone has changes to make (the dinner table is a good place to catch everyone together). The board won't work unless you stay current. With just a few minutes' attention each night, it can dramatically simplify the day-to-day operation of your family.

The Going-Out Place

Another way to help smooth the rough spots is to set up a going-out place. We discussed this in chapter 3, when getting out the door on time was presenting such a challenge.

A going-out place is a spot—usually by the front or back door—where you put all the items you need to grab on your way out. This might include your briefcase, lunches, bookbags, snow boots, car keys, and other necessary tools for the day.

Consider what items your family needs in a going-out place before you choose the site. At our house, we need room for snow boots, bookbags, and extra things like homework projects and swimming bags. Because of the snow boots, we use a heavy-duty floor mat to mark the "place." The bookbags, boots, and other items fit nicely on the 2'-by-3' mat, and it's placed right by the door. The kids just scoop up what they need on their way out to the bus.

Your going-out place might include things like coat and hat hooks, a small basket for keys, a bulletin board for last-minute notes, and/or an umbrella stand. You can probably come up with other items unique to the accessories your family uses.

The trick to the going-out place is using it consistently. With the family information center, you need to keep it updated in order for it to work; with the going-out place, you have to faithfully put everything in its place the night before you need it. Bookbags, boots, and other items should be right there, by the door, before bed the night before. That way, in the morning your out-the-door exit can happen in one smooth motion.

A Filing System

Another mess gathers on the countertops of America: piles of bills and stray papers. Even in this day of ecological consciousness, we receive mounds and mounds of papers—catalogs, bills, letters from friends and companies—and they tend to accumulate on counters and tables, in drawers, or on shelves until we devise some means of dealing with them. Part of "digging out" of household chaos is organizing and filing the papers that are so much a part of our lives.

"My daughter and I were going around about her grades. 'You're just too disorganized,' I said. 'If you'd get your assignments organized, you'd get better grades.' She sighed and asked me what I'd done with her report card. I looked over at the stack of papers on the counter. 'Oh, I don't know,' I said. 'It's somewhere in that mess.'"

—Mother of two who works full-time

What Do You Need to File?

If you've been running a household for any length of time, you know how important it is to be able to find things when you need them. Certain papers you need access to quickly; others you can file away and forget, digging them out only if necessary. Generally, you'll need to create a filing system that helps you organize documents in these categories:

 Family: You need to store birth certificates, immunization records, school records, day-care information, Social Security information, wills, report cards, passports, and other important documents. Don't forget space for special drawings and paintings, names and numbers of back-up sitters, photo IDs, fingerprint records, and pertinent health information and policies.

 Household: You've got bills to track and store and financial information to keep, including investments, bank statements, tax returns, retirement policies, life insurance information; and information on your house, appliances, inventory, and improvements.

 Vehicles: You need to store information on car payments, insurance cards and policies, repair schedules and receipts, and other necessary information.

You need files for legal papers, for medical papers, for information on each of your children. You need files for your bills, preferably sorted according to creditor and organized with some kind of bill-paying calendar. You need someplace to put bills until they are paid, and someplace to put the bill receipts after they are paid. Many people use file folders or accordion files to store these kinds of things. You may want to invest in a filing cabinet and hanging file folders, depending on how much you have to organize.

Show your kids what you're doing—introduce them to your filing system. Let them see that the effort you expend now will save you considerable time and frustration you might otherwise spend looking for misplaced papers.

One mother puts her 7-year-old to work:

"When I have a number of things to file, like right after I pay bills, I have Brock be my assistant. He finds the file the electric bill goes in, for example, and puts the bill receipt away. I pay him 50 cents each time he does it, and he feels like he's done a 'job.' Plus, he's learned about filing papers and getting organized."
—Mother of one who works part-time

Make sure you've got a folder with information about your day-care arrangements, health care, insurance numbers, emergency procedures, and other important information you may need to access quickly. Show your kids where important papers are in case of an emergency, so they can get to any information they need that is not already posted on your family bulletin board.

Keeping Things Straight

Once you get hold of your household system and begin to get organized, how can you ensure that things keep running smoothly? The best possible tool you can use to ensure that life will continue on the upswing is praise. Remember to recognize your family's efforts. Remind them of how well they—and you—are doing. Focus on the teamwork, and reward success.

Especially at first, take failures in stride. People are going to forget—and perhaps flat-out rebel against—the new system. Whenever possible, focus on the positive and you'll get more of it.

Once a week, perhaps on Friday evenings, sit down with your spouse and review the week. What got done and what didn't? Did you wind up meeting more goals than you missed? Discuss what worked well this week and what you might want to change for next week.

Once a month—or sooner if something isn't working smoothly and you think a change is needed—sit down in a family meeting and discuss how things are going. How does the family feel about the system in place? Make sure the discussion is open and honest. Even if you hear considerable grumbling and griping, try to hear what's really being said. Be open to alternatives suggested by other family members. If the suggestion sounds like it might work, try it. (You can vote on it first.) The great thing about establishing a family system is that, once it's established, you can change it easily. Developing a system that works is a process that will grow and change as long as your family does.

Summary

In this chapter, you learned some practical techniques for getting your house and yard back under control. Especially when your priorities change and additional demands are made on your time, things around the house can slip into disarray. Tasks that were once easy to accomplish now regularly get the quick once-over, and you hope your guests won't notice. That's to be expected, especially at first. But with a little help and a few organizational skills, you can get things back under control—and functioning better than ever—in no time.

And once you've gotten the house back in some semblance of order, you're ready to sit back and breathe a little. Chapter 8 helps you protect your most valuable resource during this important time of change: *you*.

Notes

1. Actually, your kids may love it. Different personalities respond to things differently: My 14-year-old looks on most rules as personal affronts to her civil liberties, but my 8-year-old loves having things to do and "check off." And my 2-year-old loves to help, as long as I let him do it "his way," which is often a dangerous endeavor.

2. Kenneth Kaye, *Family Rules* (New York: St. Martins, 1984).

3. Pipi Campbell Peterson, *Ready, Set, Organize!* (Indianapolis: Park Avenue, 1996).

4. Kits that contain caustic or poisonous items—such as toilet cleaner or carpet spot remover—should obviously be kept out of reach of young children.

5. Peterson, *Ready, Set, Organize!*

Chapter 8

Time for You

"No day is so bad it can't be fixed with a nap."
—Carrie Snow

In the Rob Reiner movie *Parenthood*, the main character says to his wife in a moment of exasperation, "My whole *life* is have to!" If you're a working parent, you know what that means. From the time the alarm goes off in the morning to the precious few moments of silence at the end of the day (if you're still

awake to hear them), your life is full of things to think about, plan, solve, orchestrate, and troubleshoot.

Especially in the transitional period when you first return to work, the temptation is great to take care of everyone and everything else first. You want to make sure the kids are okay. You're trying to get the house under control. You're looking for time to spend with your spouse.

But what about you?

Research shows that the more demands we have on our time, the more we need time to ourselves. We need to recuperate, relax, rest. Silence is a rare find of unquestionable medicinal value.

It is possible to find time for ourselves, even in the midst of transition, even in the center of stressful lives. We must make stress-busting a priority, however. Stress, in large doses or small, affects the way we see each other and ourselves. It also can dampen our spirits, make us jumpy or irritable, hamper our ability to make sound decisions with confidence, and generally affect our work performance. Stress, over the long haul, can add to your chances of physical damage, as well—from headaches to high blood pressure to heart attacks.

From One Parent to Another

"Sometimes when I'm feeling really stressed, I take a detour on my way home from work. I drive out in the country where nobody can hear me or see me, pull over to the side of the road, and scream as loud as I can. Usually I laugh at myself afterward, but I sure do feel better."

—Mother of three who works full-time

Stress? What Stress?

Some of us are so busy that we don't even notice the stress we're under. Statistics show that 30 percent of working Americans experience what they consider "high stress" nearly every day. The percentage is even higher for people who say they feel acute stress once or twice a week.

What does "high stress" feel like?

 The moment of panic when you realize the boss is going to ask for your report and it's not finished.

 The knot of anxiety you feel when you're facing a new computer program for the first time.

 The sick-to-your-stomach upset that hangs on after you leave your daughter at day care.

 The tightness in your neck and shoulders when you're stuck in traffic and late for an important meeting.

Your reaction to stress may be to play it down. After all, everyone lives with a certain amount of stress. But in recent years research has shown that stress affects our systems in very negative ways.

When you are under stress—whether it's acute or prolonged stress—your body overproduces adrenaline and other powerful hormones. This, in turn, suppresses the production of T-cells, which are an important part of your immune system.

The result? More colds. More flu. Lower resistance.

There are several things you can do to reduce your stress level and steps you can take toward setting up a self-care system so you don't end up down for the count.

◆ ◆

*"When I know I'm under a lot of stress, I try to make
sure to eat right and take vitamins. Even though I might
be having trouble at work, it won't be compounded by
me getting sick."*
—Father of one who works full-time

◆ ◆

Three Keys to Lessening Stress

No matter what your daily routine is like, you're
bound to deal with stress. Starting a new job is
stressful. Raising kids is stressful. Life in the '90s is
stressful.

How you respond to that stress is something you
decide for yourself. Some people can see stress
coming and neatly side-step it; others get
steamrolled by it. Most of us fall somewhere in
between. But with a little bit of observation, you
can figure out what kinds of things stress you most
and anticipate, avoid, or at least respond
differently to those stresses in the future.

Key #1: Know What Stresses You Out

Before you can really begin to reduce the stress in
your life, or consider ways to deal with it better,
you must be able to recognize it. What really
stresses you out? Talking about money? Giving
presentations to the board? Helping the kids with
their homework? Getting dinner on the table?
We're all different, and what causes me a lot of
anxiety might be laughably easy for you. Figure
out what sets you off and, the next time the
situation comes up, you'll be ready for it.

A major step in lessening stress is to put a real
face on it. Being stressed out about the part of
your job that will involve giving presentations
before the management group is abstract—a kind
of in-the-future fear. As a general situation, you
can't solve that stress in one fell swoop. The
questions Where? When? How? aren't answered.

You're not sure when you will have to give a presentation, where, how, or to whom—but it's stressing you. If you are dealing with this kind of abstract stress, resolve not to worry about it until it's a real event. Give yourself permission to start stressing out when they schedule your first presentation.

If you're anxious about the presentation you have to give next Tuesday, on the other hand, you can put a definite face on the stress. Now it's a real event. *That* you can do something about. You can practice, plan, study, prepare. You can pray that they cancel the meeting. You can make sure your presentation is so unbelievably good that it will knock their socks off. In any case, putting a real face on the stress allows you to take action to resolve it. Being fearful or stressed about a vague circumstance can do nothing but haunt you, until you deal with it in the concrete.

What Stresses You Out?

Here's your chance to make a list of your stressors (and check it twice):

This Stresses Me Out   Abstract or Concrete?

_____   _____

_____   _____

_____   _____

_____   _____

_____   _____

_____   _____

Key #2: Can You Change the Situation?

Some stressful situations you simply have to live with. Your brother-in-law has moved in while he's looking for a job and, well, you're stuck with him till the first of the month. Or you've got to find a fill-in baby-sitter for three days while your regular sitter is out of town. Or you prepared a spreadsheet based on erroneous figures they gave you in accounting, and there's nothing you can do about it now. When your stress is something you can't do anything about, you need to be able to let it go. The only healthy answer is to modify the way you react to the situation.

Look through your list and ask yourself if there is anything you can do about the stress. Stressed about finding the back-up baby-sitter? There are things you can do about that: Ask your current baby-sitter if she can recommend someone; check with area day cares to see if any of them has a drop-in policy; ask your mother if she can help out for those few days.

If the situation is something you can't change, do what you can to take care of yourself in spite of it. Here are a few ideas to help when you're experiencing a stressful situation that you can't change:

 Turn your thoughts to something else — preferably something pleasant.

 Take three or four deep breaths.

 If you can, get outside and go for a walk.

 Change your focus. If you're preparing for a meeting, stop and make a few phone calls or make those copies you were putting off. If you're trying to get the laundry done, put everything down and read your 2-year-old the story she's been wanting to hear.

 Meditate or pray.

Look at the pictures your kids made for your office.

 Listen to music that calms and soothes you.

Whatever your situation—whether the stress happens most at work or at home—you can change the way it affects you, even if you can't completely eliminate it. As you begin reducing the amount of stress you live with on a daily basis, you'll get accustomed to treating yourself better, which results in even less stress. It's a win-win cycle, and all you have to do is ask yourself about the things that stress you and determine to do whatever you can about them.

 I grew up hearing the Serenity Prayer but didn't really understand it—or put it into practice—until I was an adult:

"God, grant me the serenity

to accept the things I cannot change,

the courage to change the things I can,

and the wisdom to know the difference."

Key #3: Take Action

The greatest stress hits us when we feel powerless. Taking action helps us feel back in control, which propels us forward and keeps us from getting stuck in the circumstance.

If you determine that the situation causing you stress is something you can do something about, the next question is, "What?" If you've put a face on the stress and see it as a concrete situation, you can brainstorm possible solutions.

Brainstorming is an easy way to find solutions to stressful situations. Look back at the list of things that cause you stress. Pick the one that causes the most anxiety and write it at the top of a sheet of paper. For example, you might write, "The drive home from work really stresses me out." Then turn the issue into a question: "What can I do to make the drive home less stressful?" Sit back and let the sparks fly. Write down every potential solution that comes to mind—no matter how far-fetched—for the next 5 or 10 minutes. Your list might look something like this:

The drive home really stresses me out.

What can I do to make the drive less stressful?

1. Leave earlier to avoid the traffic
2. Ask Carol if I can carpool with her.
3. Have Dan pick up the kids so I won't be in such a rush.
4. Try a new route home.
5. Get a new car so I'll enjoy the ride.
6. Take my Kenny G. tapes to soothe my nerves.
7. Take the bus.

You may or may not find the perfect answer in your first brainstorming session, but taking action is the key. You begin thinking creatively about how you can reduce your stress, which will eventually translate into a healthier, happier you.

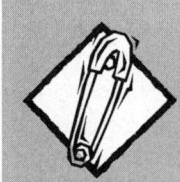

Stress Busters

- Slow down.
- Take deep breaths.
- Meditate.
- Exercise.
- Visualize the situation being resolved the way you want it to be.
- Ask yourself what the situation is teaching you.
- Get outside if you can.

Taming the Dinnertime Crazies

Ask any group of working parents what the most stressful time of day is, and you'll get a surprisingly consistent answer: "arsenic hour," that 60-minute span of eternity that stretches from the time you walk in the door after work to the time everyone sits down to dinner. You may have it better or worse, depending on whether you cook the meals, how many kids you've got (and what their ages are), and whether your spouse shares equally in the pre-dinner challenge.

Why is this time so difficult? Most parents report that they feel pulled in several directions at once. The kids want to tell you all about their days, the dog needs to go out, you're trying to get dinner together, and the phone is ringing off the hook. Mix this with a work project that's hanging on in the back of your mind and a spouse who wants to talk about this weekend's plans, and you're headed for stress overload.

One mother solved this situation by stating forcefully what she needed:

"I'd walk in the door after being on my feet for 10 hours, knowing it would be at least another hour before I could sit down. That bothered me more and more, until I finally told my family, 'We're eating at 7:00, so I can sit down and rest a few minutes before I make dinner. If that's a problem for any of you, you can do the cooking.' Nobody complained, and now I come home, change clothes, and cuddle with the kids on the couch for a few minutes before I start dinner. Our evenings are completely different, and more often than not, the kids help me make and serve the meal. They never did that before."
—Mother of four who works full-time

Lightening the Lunacy

Here are a few ways you can tone down your first hour at home:

 Leave work at work. Even if you commute and have time to review work issues on the way home, don't. Use the drive time to let your workday go and make the mental shift to "person, parent, spouse."

Know what you're walking into. Don't be surprised, day after day, by the frenzied pace of your household in that first hour home. Before it begins, prepare yourself for it. In some cases, a little clear communication can help. "Kevin, when I first get home from work, I really need a few minutes of quiet. Just let me change clothes and wash my face. Then I'd really like to hear all about your day."

 Cut yourself some slack. If you need quiet, ask for it. Let the answering machine get the phone for the first hour. You can answer calls later, when you're not trying to do so much. You can reduce your expectations of yourself in other areas too. Don't try to make gourmet meals on weeknights; dishes don't *have* to be done the minute dinner is over. Sit at the table a few minutes after the kids excuse themselves and talk to your spouse. You'll both feel better for it.

 Look for the good. Resolve that the first thing you say to each child is something positive. "What a great art paper!" Or "You really did a good job picking out your clothes today." It's easy to walk in and see all the things that haven't been done, but the tone of the night—and your own internal stress level—will be better if you affirm rather than attack.

 Grab a few minute's peace. Yes, it's possible—even if it's just while you change your clothes or wash your face. Take a few minutes, slow down your pace, refresh yourself, change into something comfortable, and head out to face the troops as Mom or Dad.

 Remember that there's plenty of time for togetherness. No law says you must have family togetherness time while you're trying to fix dinner, answer phone messages, feed the dog, and look at the mail. Chances are, you're tired, the kids are tired (and probably hungry and grumpy too), and this may not be the most harmonious time for family interplay. If your kids are scattered all over the house doing their own things, let them amuse themselves until dinner. Encourage it with, "I love how you're taking care of yourselves. I can get dinner faster this way." After some alone time, dinnertime might be more peaceful.

BEST & WORST

Best: "Getting out of the house, meeting new people. My job allows me to work with children— which I love."

Kitchen Catch-Ups

Throughout this book, you've no doubt picked up on the theme that organizing makes life easier. Nowhere is this more true than in the kitchen. If you're the one responsible for the family's meals, you'd be amazed to discover how much time you spend planning them, shopping for them, and cooking them. A significant portion of your day is invested in making sure your family is well-fed. Here are some tips to add extra moments to your allotment of "time-for-me."

 Plan your meals for the week, then stick to your plan. If something sounds good on the spur of the moment, right it down for next week's menu. Writing down and then following through on your plan cuts the time you have to spend thinking about what to fix for dinner, which frees up more time for you.

 In the evening, when you're organizing for tomorrow, take a quick look at the menu to see whether you need to defrost, chop, or pick something up from the store on your way home tomorrow.

 Leftovers aren't leftovers if you made too much on purpose. Having chicken on Sunday? Make more than you need and shred the rest for chicken and noodles one night. In the mood for turkey? Buy a pound or two more than you need, and use it for a soup-and-sandwiches night or hot turkey manhattans.

 Who says you have to eat breakfast in the morning? Pancakes, eggs and bacon, and French toast are fast and easy dinners (and you won't hear the kids complain).

 Save your menus and use them again. Instead of spending a lot of time planning meals and then shopping for them, put yourself on a rotating schedule—say a six-week cycle—and you can lighten your planning load.

 Especially if you feel like you spend all your "free time" in the kitchen, make sure it's a pleasant experience. Put on music you particularly like, burn a candle if that's your style, put on your slippers (and maybe your robe, too) and relax as much as possible while you're finishing out the day. Cooking dinner in high heels and fixing supper in slippers are two completely different experiences, I assure you.

 Give yourself a break. Regularly. One night a week, if possible, skip cooking. Eat out or eat in and let someone else fix it. If 7-year-old Patsy just loves to make things with peanut butter, she's sure to invent a masterpiece if you let her. (Be forewarned, though: If she makes it, you'll have to eat it.)

 Have the basics on hand. Think about the things your family just can't do without—staples like macaroni and cheese, chicken breasts, turkey hot dogs, bread, milk, peanut butter, and chocolate-chip cookie dough ice cream (not all at the same meal, of course)—and make sure you've got them on hand. I try to have several different kinds of meats, vegetables, fruits, breads, cereals—you know the routine. Then maybe I can create a menu for the week based on the stuff I've already got and—voilá!—another free hour I don't have to spend at the grocery store.

 Some cooks like help, and some cooks don't. If you're in the kitchen, it's your domain; ask for what you want. If you'd like 30 minutes of quiet while you prepare supper, you're entitled to that. Explain it to the kids, or your spouse, or whoever, and cook in peace. You'll feel rested and more settled when you put dinner on the table.

Make-Ahead Meals

It's amazing what you can do when you start applying "the big picture" to meal planning. That's what they did in the old days, you know, when Pa brought home a deer and Ma and the young'uns ate venison 120 different times until spring brought a fresh crop of rabbits and squirrels.

In this day of fast everything, the idea of buying in bulk may seem foreign. And your budget might limit how much you buy and how often you buy it. But purchasing foods your family really likes, foods you know they'll eat, and having them on hand can save you quite a bit of time in both meal planning and shopping.

With a little thought, you can come up with a pretty hefty list of meals your family really likes. And with a little more thought, you can think of ways to cut down on the time it takes to prepare those meals so there's more time and energy left for you.

Here's an example. At our house, I can always be sure my kids will eat these meals:

 Home-made pizza.

 Spaghetti.

 Chicken, potatoes, and carrots cooked in gravy. (We call it "The Farm Supper.")

 Beef Stroganoff.

 Tuna casserole with peas. (Don't ask me—I have strange kids.)

 Ham, new potatoes, and green beans cooked all day in the slow cooker. (We call it "The Other Farm Supper.")

 Meatballs, mashed potatoes, and gravy.

That's just a sampling of the meals they like. One thing I have discovered as a working mother is that there's a quick way and a slow way to do everything. Each of those meals I just listed has a long form and a short form.

No doubt you've discovered this. Take spaghetti. You can make your own pasta. You can blanche the tomatoes and mush them, and add chopped onion and fresh oregano and basil and parsley, and you can stand over that pot for an hour, stirring faithfully to make a wonderful, aromatic, delightfully spicy spaghetti sauce. Or you can open a jar of store-bought sauce.

You got up at 6:00 A.M., got the kids to day care and school, worked all day, picked up the kids, and are standing there in front of the stove. Which are you going to choose?

Exactly. Me too.

Things like beef Stroganoff have become turkey Stroganoff at our house, with browned ground turkey, mushroom soup, low-fat sour cream (I'm trying to be conscientious), and salt and pepper. Put this over cooked noodles and serve with a vegetable—dinner in 20 minutes, most of it simmering while I change clothes or look through Christopher's school papers.

Favorite Meals ... Faster

What are the meals your family likes, and how can you fix them easier and faster?

Favorite Meals   Faster Version

_____   _____

_____   _____

_____   _____

_____   _____

Make-Ahead Meatballs

Hey, admit it—everybody loves meatballs. If you're not a beef eater, ground turkey can be rolled into meatballs, too. But who wants to stand over a skillet for 45 minutes, turning all those little balls each time one side is brown? (How many sides do those things *have*, anyway?)

Make a bunch of meatballs quickly by mixing up your favorite meatball recipe and pressing the mixture into one large rectangle on a cookie sheet. Cut the mixture in a cross-cross pattern, making a few dozen meatballs. Yes, they're square, but you can bake them at 350 degrees for 35 minutes, cool them, and pack them in freezer bags to keep for two months. Then throw them into soups, subs, spaghetti, Stroganoff, whatever you've got that needs a meatball on top.

 To take part of the rush out of the dinnertime crazies, make up a "kit" with everything you need to set the table—dishes, silverware, napkins, whatever you use. Put it all in a big basket on the table. When it's time to set the table, your "helpers" have everything they need at the table, so they won't be under your feet. After dinner, make sure whoever does the dishes repacks the kit, putting the dishes, silverware, and napkins back in the basket for tomorrow night's dinner. You'll be amazed how much time this can save, and you'll never again have to run back to the kitchen, saying "We forgot the forks!"

And If You Love to Cook ...

There's a time and place for creative cooking too, especially if it's something you really enjoy. If you like to cook new and exciting recipes, and make a great mess doing it, give yourself time to have that pleasure. But consider where and when—and if you'll have the energy to clean up the mess once you've made it. On a work night, something fast, simple, and clean is a lot more appealing. Save your gourmet experiences for weekends and holidays.

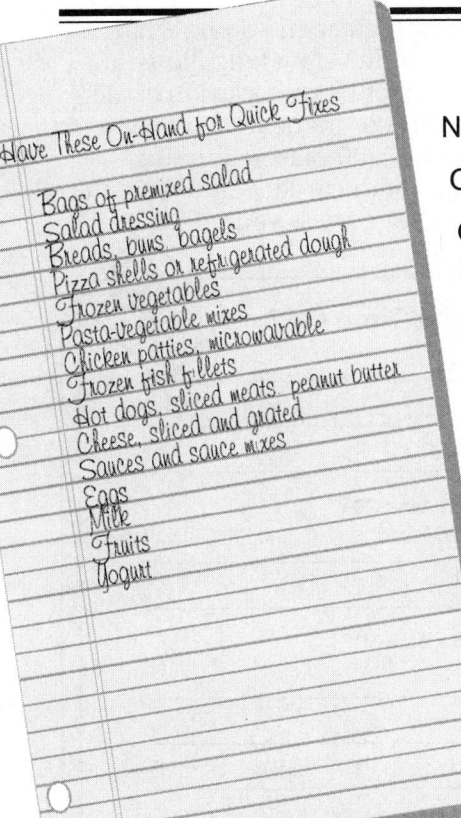

Have These On-Hand for Quick Fixes

Bags of premixed salad
Salad dressing
Breads, buns, bagels
Pizza shells or refrigerated dough
Frozen vegetables
Pasta-vegetable mixes
Chicken patties, microwavable
Frozen fish fillets
Hot dogs, sliced meats, peanut butter
Cheese, sliced and grated
Sauces and sauce mixes
Eggs
Milk
Fruits
Yogurt

Cheater's Lasagna

Nine lasagna noodles, cooked

One jar spaghetti sauce

One large container small curd cottage cheese

Mozzarella slices

Parmesan cheese

Grease a 13"-by-9" baking dish; lay three noodles on the bottom. Top with half of the sauce; top with half of the cottage cheese. Top that with mozzarella slices and 2 tablespoons parmesan cheese. Repeat. Bake for 30 minutes in a 350-degree oven; then let it sit for 10 minutes before cutting. (If you have the time and the inclination, you can add browned sausage, hamburger, or turkey to the sauce.)

Even faster: Prepare the lasagna on the weekend, when you have time, and freeze it until you need it.

Even better: Next time you make lasagna, make two and freeze one.

Where Does the Time Go?

One of the easiest ways to find more time for yourself is to look at how you spend your time now. Do you spend a lot of time and energy on things that aren't important to you? Do you insist on doing things yourself that you could delegate? Put a notebook in your pocket for a few days and keep track of what time you spend doing what. How long is your commute? How long did you spend explaining a policy to a coworker that she could have looked up in the manual? Why were you the one picking up 1,200 plastic building blocks from the living room carpet? (You weren't the one playing with them, were you?)

Where Does the Time Go?

7:00 _____

7:30 _____

8:00 _____

*** Work time ***

12:00 _____

12:30 _____

*** Work time ***

5:00 _____

5:30 _____

6:00 _____

6:30 _____

7:00 _____

7:30 _____

8:00 _____

8:30 _____

9:00 _____

9:30 _____

10:00 _____

From One Parent to Another
*"I believe it's important to give extra
love touches to the children in our
time together at home."*
—Mother of three who works part-time

Making the Moment Count

Once you've logged your time for a few days, take a look at your notes. What stands out? Where could you pick up more time? We all have a certain number of things to do in a day, but you might be able to reorder (or weed out) your To-Do list to get yourself some R&R time. Here are a few suggestions:

Do you drive to work? If you drive, make notes to yourself (get one of those hand-held tape recorders) about things you need to take care of later. Or dictate a letter to someone you need to catch up with. Or work on the report you were planning to do tonight after the kids are in bed. Then, tonight, you can watch a movie, relax in a hot bath, play pool with your spouse, or just cuddle on the couch instead of working.

Do you ride to work? If you commute, you have a block of time when you may be just staring out the window or engaging in idle conversation. While staring out the window and idle conversation are both worthwhile activities in moderation, spending each day in this mode keeps you from having more R&R time for yourself. On the commute, you can catch up with paperwork, balance your checkbook, make your grocery list, write a letter, plan an upcoming birthday party, or do any number of things that might otherwise take up evening time.

What do you do for lunch? Hopefully, eat. But beyond that, you could be using your lunch hour

to get yourself more free time later in the day. Designate one or two days a week as "errand" days, when you do things like pick up the cleaning, shop for the holidays, get the car's oil changed, go to the bank, whatever. On the other three days, of course, go to lunch with friends, coworkers, or your spouse. The social interaction is just as important as the let-down time later. But using one or two lunches a week to get ahead on the "have-tos" in your life can make a big difference in how much time you have left over for yourself.

Do you know when you've done enough?

When I first began keeping a To-Do list, I didn't have the right idea. I'd ask myself each morning, "What do I have to get done today?" I'd make a list of 10 or 12 things I had to get done. Throughout my workday, I'd go at the items, one by one, crossing them off as I finished them.

Fine. I was doing fine.

But then I'd start thinking of other things. "Oh yeah," I'd remember, "I promised to get Kelly's skates sharpened. And those books are due next Tuesday; I could take them back today. And I suppose I could start on chapter 3 and get a jump on my deadline . . . "

Wrong. My To-Do list grew all day long. By the end of the day, I had more things left to do than I had when I started. The list might be 30 or 40 items long. How do you think I felt at the end of the day? The phrase "swimming in quicksand" comes to mind.

If you're going to keep a To-Do list, write down the things you need to get done (be realistic), and when you've crossed them all off, stop. Celebrate. Take that bubble bath. Watch the football game. You decided what you wanted to accomplish today, and you accomplished it. Now it's time to rest.

One of the best gifts you can give another person is the gift of your full attention. As you make an effort to consolidate tasks and get more done with less work, remember to listen carefully and respond to those who need you to be present right now—little kids and big kids alike.

The Art of Simplicity

There's a lot to be said for simplicity. The older we get, the more responsibilities we add, the more complicated our lives seem to get. Especially when you work and you're a parent, there are a lot of things to do, and everything seems important. It takes a fair amount of thought—invested up front—to reduce the number of details in your life so the important things can stand out.

Sometimes we add responsibilities we don't really need. We say, "Okay," when they call us to run the cookie sale. We can't say no to subbing for the first baseman at Thursday night softball. The PTO needs help—and if we don't do it, who will? Randy has to be at play practice three times a week for the next month, and guess who gets to drive him? Life sometimes seems like an endless series of details demanding our attention. As John Lennon put it, "Life is what happens to you while you're making other plans."

Once you've examined where you're spending your time, it might be easy to see where you can eliminate things that aren't worth either the priority or the effort. The suggestions in this section will help get you started thinking about applying the Art of Simplicity to your own life.

Simplify Priorities

When you ask yourself what your personal priorities are, do you come up with a list of 10 or 12 items? A priority is what's most important. If you're carrying around 10 "most important" issues in your life, you may want to think about what's truly *most* important and trim your list accordingly.

Remember in chapter 1, when you and your family came up with a list of family priorities? Those should fit here, as well. When you're looking at your life and your choices with a "time-for-me" perspective, expect your own personal priorities to be slightly different from—but still in line with—your family priorities. There will be times when the priorities of the family come before your personal priorities (for example, you need to fix the furnace when you'd really rather be soaking in a hot tub). And there will be times when your personal priorities come before the family priorities (everyone has a right to be heard, but you really need 10 minutes of quiet).

If you aren't used to thinking about yourself and what's important to you, this may be a difficult task. Sit down with a piece of paper and write your answer to the question, "What's most important to me?" Whether you come up with two or twenty answers, write them all down. Once you see what's in your head, written down in black and white, you can begin the process of weeding out the unimportant things. As you look through your list, one or two items will emerge that are truly important. The rest are just situations to deal with, not issues you must treat with supreme importance. Simply knowing that something is not a matter of "life or death" can make stress evaporate like a puddle on a summer sidewalk.

Just get them down on paper. That's a start.

What's Most Important to Me?

_____

_____

_____

_____

Simplify Time Investments

Some things you simply don't have to do. Do _you_ have to be the one to take Jesse to hockey every other day? Can you arrange to trade off with another parent or with your spouse? Do you _really_ need to make four trips to the grocery every week or, with a little time management and planning, could you consolidate them into one trip? Do you spend more time on the phone than you want to? Would organizing a phone time when you return calls to friends and relatives save some time for you in the long run?

When you examine your priorities and recognize the two or three things you really want to spend your time on, you're free to decide how much time to spend on those things. The time you spend on unimportant things becomes less and less. You begin looking for people to delegate those tasks to. You begin spending more time on the things that really matter to you, the things you need to see through to completion yourself.

What Could I Spend Less Time On?

_____

_____

_____

_____

Simplify Material Possessions

In many ways, we don't really own our possessions—they own us. The more things we have, the more we have to take care of: dusting and polishing, washing and waxing, servicing, repairing, insuring, improving. Don't wait for a garage sale; go through your possessions and ask yourself what you use and what you don't, what you want and what you're ready to let go. Think of your things in terms of how much time, trouble, and money they cost you. Then compare the cost with the pleasure they bring you, the convenience they offer, and so on. The bottom line? If you want it, keep it; but remember, the investment you make in your possessions is more than a monetary one.

Start by making a list of the possessions that take up a lot of your time. If you're spending two hours every Saturday morning fixing the lawn mower, for example, maybe it's time to get a new lawn mower. Once you determine which of your possessions, if any, are possessing you, you can decide what to do about it.

What Things Do I Spend Time On?

_____

_____

_____

_____

_____

_____

Simplify Commitments

Sometimes it's other people—and our reaction to their expectations—that keep us busy with things that aren't priorities. Do you say "Yes" to everything? If you're not sure, watch yourself through the course of a day and see how many times you volunteer for something no one else wants to do, suggest a solution that involves work on your part, or say "Yes" when inside you wish you could say "No." When they ask you to be editor of the historical society's newsletter, you might be honored, but you might also be pressed for time. A clear, "No, thank you," frees you of the responsibility and lets the society look for someone who has the time and inclination for the job.

How can you evaluate which commitments are important and which ones you should pass by? Any commitment you accept should meet these criteria:

 It should fit your time constraints; you shouldn't have to rearrange your life to fulfill it.

 It should be worth what it costs you in effort, investment, and family time.

 It should be fun, challenging, or stretch your creative spirit.

You may not need to relinquish any of the commitments you have now; or you may, after careful thought, decide to keep a few and release those that are taking time you don't want to invest. With the return to work, you need to be more protective of your time, so think carefully about commitments you make in the future.

And, even if you trim back your commitments now, it doesn't mean you will always be "uninvolved." One mother put it this way:

"When I first went back to work, it was all I could do to get the kids to school, work all day, get home, cook dinner, clean a little, and fall into bed at night. On the weekends, I caught up on all the housework I didn't do during the week. I had to give up many outside commitments, because it was all I could do to live my life. After about six months, things got easier, and I started being a room mother again. Then, a few months later, I started teaching Sunday school. Gradually, as my life balanced, I got back into the swing of things."

The moral? Do only what you can do comfortably, and remember that you and your family are all learning how to balance home and work issues.

What Are My Commitments?

_____

_____

_____

_____

_____

Saying no isn't easy, especially when you're not used to doing it. But sidestep the commitment early if you get any of these warnings:

 You know you don't want to do it.

 You feel coerced or guilty.

 People are appealing to you with a "But no one else can take care of this" approach. (If no one else is willing to help, there must be a reason why.)

The clearer you are about your priorities, the easier it is to say no to commitments you don't want. When someone asks you to head the neighborhood task force, check it against your priority list. If it doesn't fit—especially if it will take away from one of your top priorities—just say no.

Simplify Unimportant Jobs

BEST & WORST

Worst: "Missing out on the most valuable time in the children's lives, as they'll be grown before we know it"

The keyword here is *delegate*. Are you still taking out the trash every Tuesday night, even though you've got three teenagers in the house? Do you really have to be the one who washes the dishes morning and night? Do you spend time standing by the copy machine at work when your assistant has nothing to do? If you can release the jobs that don't have to be done by you personally, you free yourself up to get more done in the time you've got. That translates directly to more R&R time at home. Another benefit of delegating is that it gives the kids a chance to contribute to the family, to feel needed, instead of being "guests" in their own home.

Which Jobs Could I Delegate?

Job   To Whom?

_____   _____

_____   _____

_____   _____

_____   _____

_____   _____

Simplify Kids

Ha! If there were some magic formula to this, we'd all be millionaires. But it *is* possible to simplify life with kids if you stay focused on what's important. This, like everything else in parenting, has to be grounded in reality: You can't just sidestep making Tim clean his room because you'd rather do something pleasant. It's a continual process of refocusing on why you're doing what you're doing, and asking yourself whether that's how you need to spend your time and energy right now.

This is a hard issue for me, especially around the holidays. We want to schedule everything. Out for a holiday dinner this night. To a concert that night. Making Christmas cookies today, making candy tomorrow. Pick up the kids at this time, be at Mom's for dinner by that time.

In the hectic pace, people can—and often do—get cranky. Teenagers rebel. Toddlers have tantrums. The rest of us get headaches.

How can we simplify this mess? By focusing on what's important. Is spending time with the kids most important, or is cleaning the kitchen most important? (There is no right answer here; either could be most important in different circumstances.) If you remember to ask yourself the question, "What's most important here?" the answer becomes very clear, and you stop feeling like you've got to accomplish 20 things before bedtime.

See? It's simple. Almost.

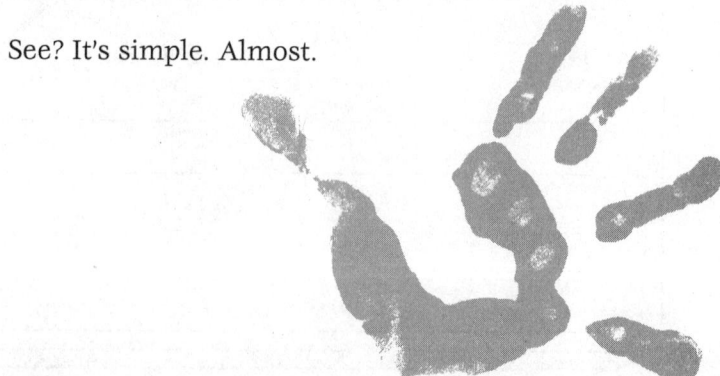

> ### Saving Time
>
> I spend more time than I'd like on _____
>
> _____
>
> _____
>
> _____
>
> I could solve this by _____
>
> _____
>
> _____
>
> _____

What Will You Do with Your Free Time?

Some people don't think about their free time because they don't have any. And if they did, they wouldn't know what to do with it. If you're one of those people, a little daydreaming is in order.

Perhaps we should define "free time." A month-long sabbatical is certainly free time, but that's probably not possible for most of us. Free time, in the context of most working parents, is an occasional spare hour at the end of the day, a few hours on the weekend, perhaps a long weekend getaway.

For best results, especially if you're not used to having any free time at all, start small. Logging how you spend your time (which you did earlier in this chapter) will show you where your time is going. The next logical step is thinking about where you *want* the time to go.

What You Need Is a Hobby!

Can't you just see it—a young mother with a baby on her hip, the chicken she'd meant to thaw for dinner in one hand, her briefcase open by her

feet, the phone cocked on her shoulder, reading from a report while she paces around the kitchen. Tell this woman she needs a hobby, and you'd better duck; frozen poultry hurts!

Unless you had a hobby before your kids were born, it's unlikely you'll have the time or energy to acquire a new hobby while they are small. A hobby is simply something you're interested in, something you do for fun, something that isn't you (1) earning a living, (2) being a parent, (3) being an employee, or (4) being a spouse. A hobby is something you like to do just because you like to do it.

The word "hobby" tends to put a trivial-sounding front on the concept, but it's something you should consider. When you're not being Mom or Dad, Wife or Husband, Daughter or Son, Employee or Employer, what do you like to do? There might be a clue there that could lead you to an enjoyable way to spend your free time.

You might try a hobby that your kids can do with you, like making model cars or planes, arts and crafts, or gourmet cooking. Remember, however, that it should be relaxing and fun—not something that adds to your stress.

What a hobby isn't:

 Something you do with your spouse so you can have more "together" time. (That's your spouse's hobby, not yours.)

 Something you do because it's "good" for you. (If you don't really want to do it, don't do it.)

 Something you "should" do. ("I *should* learn French so I can converse better with our foreign affiliates.")

What Do I Like to Do?

_____

_____

_____

_____

Expand Your Horizons

When you're thinking about what you'd like to do in your downtime, consider taking a class or learning more about something that has always interested you. There doesn't need to be any practical application; just learn it because you want to.

How can you expand your horizons? Here are a few ideas:

 Take a cooking class.

 See a movie that's different from the kind you usually see.

 Go online and chat with computer users across town or across the world.

 Read about an upcoming holiday and learn how other cultures celebrate it.

 Try camping.

 Look through _The New Yorker_ and _MAD Magazine_ in the same afternoon.

 Watch cartoons with your kids.

 Audition for a part in a community theater production.

 Listen to music outside your usual tastes.

 Spend a rainy afternoon at the library.

Horizon Expanders

What would I like to try in my free time?

_____

_____

_____

There's really only one answer to the question, "What should you do with your free time?" The answer is, "Anything you want to." Contrary to popular opinion, free time is not free at all. It comes at a cost. The time and effort you invest in work and family earn you whatever time you can find for yourself. And, chances are, it's less time than you deserve.

The next section lists some ways you can improve yourself and your lifestyle by using your time in healthy ways.

Tips for Self-Rewards

What kinds of things can you do to reward yourself in your free moments? Think about things you really like—activities, foods, experiences, places—and make a list of ways you can pay yourself back for trying so hard and doing such a good job. Make a list of big things and little things.

Little rewards are for things like not blowing up at the dinner table, or getting everybody to school and work on time. A little reward could be a night out, a bubble bath, a new CD, a chocolate eclair, or a night on the couch in your bathrobe.

Save big rewards for longer-term accomplishments: paying off a particular bill, finishing a project, meeting a deadline, making it through your first month of work, handling an important meeting, or resolving a difficult circumstance. A big reward could be an outfit or piece of equipment you've been wanting (even if you put it on layaway), a day in the country, an evening out, a trip to the theater, or something else you've been longing for.

Take Good Care of Yourself

We've talked about the practical issues involved in finding time for yourself and discussed some of the ways people use their free time. The fitness craze is one of America's latest full-blown explosions—and for good reason. Most of us recognize that, in order to get healthy and stay there, we need to take better care of our bodies— and that means what we eat and what kinds of exercise we get. We've seen the statistical and physical link between exercise and health. Researchers have shown that we feel less stress, live longer, and cope better if we exercise on a regular basis. Okay, we're sold. Now it's just a matter of finding the time—and the routine—and sticking with it.

Work Out? When?

Who has time to go to a gym? Not many of us. Unless your company has an on-site workout room or there's a local gym that really is "local" to your home or office, setting a time to work out— and then doing it regularly—is a hard commitment to make.

If you like the contact with other adults and want to participate in a class, most communities offer courses in tennis, racquetball, golf, yoga, or aerobics. Some gyms even offer baby-sitting or classes for the kids, and the extra, outside work contact is a good thing.

But many of us are getting the workout equipment ourselves and setting up our own home gyms. Last

year, Americans spent more than $2.5 billion on home exercise equipment. The most popular pieces of equipment were (in this order) stair climbers, aerobic steps, stationary bikes, ski machines, and treadmills.

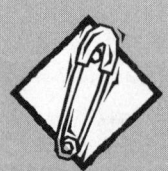 There are workouts for every body type, energy level, and age group. "Workout" doesn't necessarily mean weight-lifting or track-running. Yoga and tai chi are both popular modes of exercise that enable you to work out gently, strengthening and toning your muscles, without the athletic-style training so popular today.

The Basic Workout—Parent Style

Whether you use special equipment or simply do bends, stretches, and toe-touches on your own, moving is the important thing. And it takes less of an investment than you might think.

Experts say that exercising 20 minutes (less time than you spend watching one news show) five times a week will make a difference, especially if your routine is focused and intense.

What kind of exercise should you do? Before you start any new kind of physical regimen, consult your doctor. He or she may have some suggestions about the types of exercise that will best serve your physical needs.

As you think about putting together an exercise program, consider these basic guidelines:

 Start and end with stretching. Every exercise routine needs a warm-up and a cooldown. Slow stretches for your back, legs, and arms prepare your muscles for the coming increase in activity and raise your heart rate gradually. On the other side of your workout, stretching helps your heart rate to return gradually to normal.

When stretching, experts agree that maintaining the longest stretch you can for a moment or two is more helpful and better for you than "bobbing" to a stretch that's hard for you and immediately releasing it. It's not how far you get, it's how well you get there, that counts.

The Home Stretch

One great wake-up stretch is a yoga position that stretches and lengthens the spine. You'll feel lighter and clearer as you stretch all the sleep out of your system:

1. Sit on the floor, in a kneeling position. (If this hurts either your ankles or your knees, put a rolled-up towel across your ankles before you sit back on them.)

2. Lean forward until your forehead touches the floor.

3. Stretch first your right arm, then your left, straight over your head and place your palms down on the floor.

4. Walk your fingers up as far as you can reach. Hold to a count of 10. Remember to breathe slowly and evenly as you stretch.

5. Push up from your kneeling position to straighten your legs. You should now be in a triangle position, with your hands and feet evenly spaced and flat on the floor.

6. Push your hip bones up toward the ceiling and hold to a count of 5. This stretches your spine and releases all the little knots and tight places that accumulated while you slept.

7. Slowly return to the kneeling position; then walk yourself up to sitting using your hands as supports.

8. Take several deep breaths and exhale slowly before standing.

 Do what you like. When you're planning your workout, be sure to include activities you like. If running isn't your thing, try something else. Popular and beneficial exercises you can do at home include knee bends, toe touches, side bends, leg lifts, and jumping jacks.

 Listen to your body. We're all different, and our bodies react to activities differently. Be sure to get advice from your doctor on things you need to consider when designing an exercise program. Aches and pains are not unusual, especially at first, when your body is not used to the exercise. But if you are having chronic pain or feel something sharp and stabbing, like a pulled muscle or some other kind of injury, back off your program until you get professional advice.

Pain in the Back?

A great exercise for relieving simple back pain—caused by standing for too long, lifting something you shouldn't, or carrying too much stress without a break—takes just a minute and enough room to lay down:

1. Lay down on your back on a bed, couch, or the floor.

2. Take a deep breath and exhale slowly.

3. As you exhale, push the small of your back toward the floor.

4. Inhale and allow your back to return to normal.

5. Exhale and press your back to the floor once again.

A simple variation: If your back is feeling tight in addition to being sore, put one hand on the floor at the small of your back; then when you exhale, press your back against your hand. This modified intensity still releases some tension, and the counter-pressure of your hand helps the muscles relax.

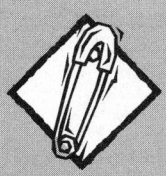

According to Peter Bernstein and Christopher Ma, authors of *The Practical Guide to Practically Everything*, the best exercises for stress reduction are bicycling, cross-country skiing, jogging, running, rowing, canoeing, and walking.[1]

Generally, however, the experts say you should just move. Don't worry too much about the type of aerobic exercise you do. Do it all. Try anything. Just move. They all burn calories, and varying your workout will reduce boredom, which means you will stick with it longer.

An Afternoon Wake-Me-Up

Do you get the 2:00 drag? If you're feeling fuzzy mid-afternoon and need to get the blood circulating back to your brain, you can try this one right at your desk:

1. Take a deep breath; exhale slowly.

2. Nod your head forward as far as you can; repeat three times.

3. Lean your head back as far as you can; repeat three times.

4. Nod your head toward your left shoulder; repeat three times.

5. Nod your head toward your right shoulder; repeat three times.

6. Allow your head to roll forward and then rotate around left, back, right, and straighten.

7. Repeat entire exercise two more times.

Your neck will feel more relaxed, and you'll feel more awake and invigorated.

A few suggestions:

 Stop if anything hurts.

 Especially at first, don't push too hard. Stop as soon as you feel tired or if you become short of breath.

 Do warm-up and cool-down stretching before and after your exercise session.

Concentrate on doing the exercise right rather than quickly. Form is more important than speed. When you're stretching, stretch full out and hold the stretch. It's much better for you than stretching-releasing, stretching-releasing a number of times.

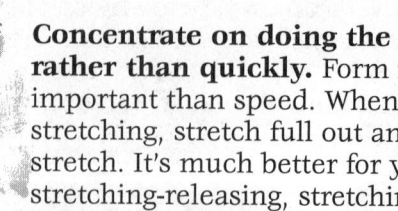

 Increase weight, resistance, and pressure gradually. Build up a little at a time, over many days (or even weeks). Improving your physical condition is a process, not something you can achieve in a few afternoons.

 Be realistic. If you follow a simple exercise plan, you'll see some changes—tightening, toning, strengthening—in 6 to 12 weeks.

 Some families do their exercise together. Try a 30-minute walk after dinner. Or tennis early in the morning, before it gets hot. Or, for the really zealous, a 20-minute wake-up workout is sure to get your family's day off to a rousing start.

Been There, Done That

As a working parent, it's likely you are already exercising more than you realize. Those trips up and down the stairs carrying laundry? That's exercise. Walking to the mailbox? Exercise. Mowing the grass, sweeping, bringing in the trash cans, trimming the bushes? Those all qualify. The trick is to be conscious of what you're doing, use your muscles, and breath. If you've got to be doing it anyway, you might as well get the full physical benefit of the experience.

Exercise, Exercise

This is what I already do for exercise: _____

_____

_____

_____

_____

I'd be willing to try this: _____

_____

_____

_____

_____

The Power of Touch

Have you ever been stressed to the limit when one of your kids, or your spouse, walked up and gave you a hug? It's an amazing phenomenon—your chest lightens, the clenching releases. You probably sighed a great sigh, and allowed yourself to be embraced.

The power of touch is something medical science is exploring more and more, and we have only to see our effects on others—and their effects on us—to know that there's something healing about touching and being touched by someone you care about.

As part of your stress-reducing and self-rewarding plans, consider these ideas:

 Hug your kids more.

 Ask for hugs.

Touch people you care about when you talk to them.

 Hold hands with your spouse.

 Rub your neck when you begin feeling stressed. (Or ask your spouse to do it for you.)

 Cuddle up with your kids when you read to them.

 Learn to give and receive back rubs.

 Read a book on foot reflexology and experiment on yourself or your family.

 When your kids are grumpy or unruly, touch them gently. I learned this with my son when he was 2. When he was on the verge of a tantrum, if I smoothed his hair off his forehead, he would invariably calm down enough that we could avoid a tirade.

Summary

In this chapter, you've thought a little about what you can do for yourself as you adjust to all the life changes going on around you. Finding time for yourself is an important part of staying happy and healthy. If you observe where you are spending your time now, you might be able to find places where you can pick up more free time. You can then decide where you want to invest that free time—whether it's with family and friends, or just for yourself.

Notes

1. Peter Bernstein and Christopher Ma, *The Practical Guide to Practically Everything* (New York: Random House, 1995).

Chapter

9

Creating a Family-Friendly Workplace

"Happiness is having a large, loving, caring, close-knit family in another city."
—George Burns

Family values are getting a great deal of attention in the '90s. In homes all across the country, parents are striving to make the best possible decisions for their children's futures. We seem to have reached an agreement of

some kind: Family values are a critical ingredient to raising happy, healthy children. And parents aren't the only ones raising the family values banner. Teachers are teaching them, preachers are preaching them, and politicians are promising them. And businesses are beginning to understand that creating a family-friendly environment works in the best interest of their employees and in their own best interest, as well: A happy employee is a productive employee.

What Is a Family-Friendly Workplace?

Family-friendly employers come in different shapes and sizes. When you were job hunting, hopefully you found a place that embraces the issues that come with child-raising and that is fairly liberal about things like phone calls from home, flexible scheduling, and pinch-hitting in unexpected circumstances. Not all employers are able to offer such services as on-site day care, child-care subsidies, or schedules that allow you to divide time between home and work. If your company cannot offer these, that does not mean it is not family-friendly or in line with family values.

Family-friendly is an attitude, not a perk. It's not the number of days you can take off for personal time, it's the attitude the company takes toward the needed leave of absence. A company that embraces the family is a family-friendly company. If your company—no matter how small or large it is—understands the importance of the family core and encourages its employees to value their families, you are in a supportive, family-friendly environment.

What You Can Do:
Start a newsletter that includes a parents' Q&A column.

Can One Person Make a Family-Friendly Workplace?

Sue was a great boss. She was pleasant, direct, and challenging, and understood what it was like to raise a family and hold down a full-time career. She had no problem with your getting an afternoon call from the kids or taking a long lunch so you could get Andrew to the dentist, as long as you made up the time or the work during the week. And when Elizabeth had the flu last winter, Sue suggested you take your computer home for a few days and work there. But not long ago, Sue got promoted, and now a new boss has been brought into your department. She's not pleased with the phone calls. And when you asked to take off early Friday afternoon so you could go to Andrew's teacher's conference, she said, "I hope you're not going to make a habit of this."

While it's not unusual to work directly for someone who understands family priorities, one person does not make a family-friendly workplace. Having a boss with a similar understanding of family issues makes life easier, to be sure, but the true mark of a family-friendly workplace is in its personnel policies and can be felt in the hallways. You know when your family is welcome at work—even if only in spirit—and when you're supposed to leave the Mom or Dad part of your heart at home.

Family Realities for Employers—and How You Can Benefit

Whether you are working for a 2-person business or a 2,000-employee corporation, the current steps toward family-friendliness in the workplace are sure to help you balance home and office more easily. Throughout this book, we've focused on the great things you bring to the workplace because of your family core. Your family responsibilities—and the values they represent to you—can make you a strong, capable, insightful, and dedicated employee.

Having children—or, more specifically, having and honoring family responsibilities—is not a liability,

nor should it be considered one. Today's parents are trying hard to balance home and work, providing the best quality care for their families and the highest possible service to their employers. A person who can pull that off must be intelligent, capable, responsible, creative, and determined.

Employers want employees who bring those kinds of qualities to the job. They have less turnover; lower retraining costs; and dedicated, hard-working staffs.

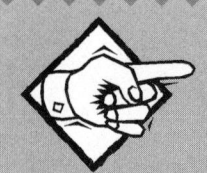

What You Can Do:
Organize a pitch-in picnic for your department and make sure spouses and kids are invited.

But the nature of the workforce is changing. More and more, employers are having to adapt to the worker who is discovering life—perhaps for the first time—outside the walls of the office. That worker could be a young mother who wants to work at home after the birth of a child; a father who wants Thursday afternoons off to coach Little League; a long-distance commuter who wants to work a two-day-in, three-day-out schedule; or a single employee who wants to work and go to grad school at the same time.

 ## Slow Change Is Better Than No Change

Your employer may be going through growing pains as the company evaluates different ways to find and keep good employees and provide them with the flexibility and programs they need to take good care of their families. Watch for these signs that your company is changing:

 More employees with family responsibilities are being hired.

- Better benefit packages are offered.

- A suggestion box goes up in human resources.

- A new company newsletter appears and invites employee participation.

- Leadership and interpersonal communication workshops are held.

- There are new, corporate-sponsored health policies.

Whether you see signs of change or you're still waiting for a glimmer of hope, remember that seeds need time to grow. Companies—especially large ones—can be slow to change and will be sure to investigate every possible angle before implementing new policies that will change peoples' lives and the way they do business. Be patient and supportive of your employer while these changes are being explored (and, hopefully, added), and keep the lines of communication as open as possible so that your opinion is welcomed and valued.

Employers are trying to figure out how to bend enough to allow their employees to grow and be happy while still getting the quality, dedication, and productivity they need to maintain a successful business. It's a tall order, and one that may make your employer more receptive to your ideas on how to balance the work/family issue from both perspectives. How can this "open-mindedness" benefit you as a working parent?

 Businesses are less willing to rely on tradition. "We've never done it that way before" is not a reason to avoid trying it now. More and more, employers are listening to what employees need and want and implementing programs and benefits to address the changing needs of the workforce. Just because your company has never had Family Day before doesn't mean the time isn't ripe now.

Businesses are recognizing that the most successful companies are creative problem-solvers. If you're having trouble with a particular policy or attitude, spend some time thinking about what the problem is and why you're having it. You may be able to come up with a creative response to the situation that no one has thought of yet. If you can propose a "win-win" solution, you may have a shot at solving your own problem and making things better for other employees, as well.

 More businesses are looking into cross-training employees. Especially in large corporations where job-sharing is common, cross-training employees (training employees to do multiple tasks) cuts down on the overall costs of training and allows employers to be more flexible when an employee needs time off for family or personal reasons. If you have a chance to improve your skills or learn new ones on the job, take the opportunity. This might lead to increased flexibility for you and make you a more valuable employee, as well.

Businesses Need to Communicate Policies Clearly

When employers add a new program or benefit, they do well to publish a "how to get involved" sheet and circulate information on what they expect of employees in return (how many days' notice before a leave of absence, sign-up times for day-care programs, how to arrange swing shifts or job-sharing situations, etc.). If your company does not have a document like this, suggest one. Getting policies in black and white will help your employer consider current policies and perhaps begin a discussion for family-friendly additions.

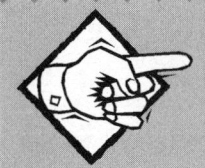

What You Can Do:
Put up a flier advertising your
son's Boy Scout paper drive and
enlist the support of your work group.

More businesses are making employee health their concern. Employers offer health plans to full-time employees; that's nothing new. But today more employers are offering wellness plans—plans that focus on helping employees stay healthy, manage stress, balance responsibilities, feel better about themselves, and work through emotional issues. This wellness approach is a great service to the employee, but it is good for the employer as well. With a small investment of money and time, the employer can ensure that employees are happier, healthier, and more well-adjusted, which translates to a stronger staff for the company. If your company is considering this kind of program, you might want to suggest including family activities—Saturday morning jogs in the park, a lunchtime yoga class—or sponsoring family agencies through participation in walk-a-thons, runs-for-fun, or other community-action projects.

BEST &
WORST

Best:
"Having
a family to
work for
and come
home to."

Employers are realizing that the focus of the workforce is changing. Their real challenge is not to find the employee who will sign on body and soul and then burn out early, but rather to keep their well-rounded, mature employees focused, energized, and inspired. They are recognizing what all working parents know: It's the long-term relationship that blossoms over time. It's simply a matter of envisioning, implementing, and evaluating ways employers, employees, and their families can grow and succeed together.

Helping Your Company Start an On-Site Day Care

Running an on-site day-care facility isn't feasible for many businesses. An employer needs available floor space and—after checking with state requirements—will undoubtedly have to remodel to create a facility that meets with government codes.

If you're thinking of proposing to your employer that he or she start an on-site facility, you'd better do your homework first by answering these questions:

 Is there enough room?

 Is there enough interest? (How many working parents are there in your company? How many of them will use the day care?)

 Are the children involved young enough that creating a facility makes sense? (If most of the children are 8 or older, for example, they won't be needing child care much longer. If your company is continually hiring young families with infants and toddlers, however, the need for continual child care is greater.)

 What building codes and state requirements will you need to look into?

 Approximately how long would it take to get the center open?

 Approximately how much of an investment would be required? (There will be costs of construction and renovation, as well as monthly staffing costs, footage costs, and other overhead expenditures.)

Getting answers to these questions may take quite a bit of phone tag, so don't go scouting until you're fairly sure your employer will be receptive to the idea or, at least, that you have enough of a parental following to sway the interest of the boss.

What does your employer need in order to get started? Once you've got the answers to the basic questions, call your state health and human services department to find out about requirements for on-site day cares. You'll be able to get information on building codes, health issues, teacher-to-child ratios, meal planning, and other items regulated in professional care of children.

To find out more about different types of programs and funding options for day care, check out Laurie Blum's *Free Money for Day Care*.[1]

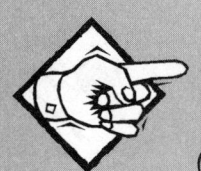

What You Can Do:
Give a talk at your child's school career day about what you do and the service your company offers. (Good for the business, great for the kids!)

Helping Your Company Start a Subsidy Program

Many companies now subsidize the cost of child care for their employees. KinderCare, one of the largest for-profit child-care providers in the

country, offers a corporate sponsoring program called Kindustry. In the program, KinderCare offers a 10 percent discount to employers, who then pay between 20 and 30 percent of the total day-care cost for employees. As an employee of a company that participates in such a program, you may pay only 60 percent of your total child-care costs, which could reduce your bill by $40 or more a week.

If you plan to approach your company about a subsidy program, have the answers to these questions ready:

 How many employees in your company have small children?

 What kinds of problems will a day-care subsidy solve?

 What are the day-care centers in your area? (You might want to call and see if any have subsidy programs already.)

 What costs can the employer expect? Can you show how this will benefit the employer in the long run?

 Who should the employer contact to discuss subsidy arrangements?

Day-Care Information Sheet

Local Day-Care Centers   Contact

_____   _____

_____   _____

_____   _____

_____   _____

_____   _____

Alternative Care Options

Even if your company doesn't offer one of these larger family-friendly options, it may have other programs in place, or the boss may be willing to entertain the idea. Here are a couple of options to look into.

Flexible Work Times

There are several different programs like this throughout the country. Call it flex-time, job-sharing, whatever—you might be able to get the time off you need if you only ask. Some companies, such as IBM, offer employees two-hour flex-time periods in the middle of the day so they can take care of child-care issues, volunteer at school, whatever. Sue leaves her job as a systems administrator on Tuesday afternoons to teach her daughter Kami's computer class at the local elementary school. It's fun for Sue and good for Kami, and fosters good will for Sue's employer. Everybody wins.

Flexible Leave Policies

Congress passed the Family Medical Leave Act (FMLA) in 1993 to ensure short-term guaranteed leave to people who need or want to take care of dependents. FMLA can be used after the birth or adoption of a child or for emergency medical care, and is mandated for companies with more than 50 employees. Your company may have other leave policies in place, including sick day, personal day, and vacation day policies. Be sure to ask about these and other policies, such as extended leave (with or without pay), the option to work at home while caring for a sick child, or half-time or swing-time options that enable you to work fewer hours for a specified period of time.

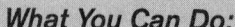

What You Can Do:
*Take your daughter to work
on National Take-Your-Daughter-To-Work Day.*

From One Parent to Another
*"Take your kids to work with you
whenever you can. I work with a
social service agency, so my kids get to
do things like deliver presents to needy
families over the holidays. It's good for them
to see how other people live. They realize
people are different and their homes, values, and
priorities all vary."*
—Mother of two who works part-time

Starting a Discussion with Your Employer

When you've got a suggestion you want your employer to consider, going the extra distance to make sure you've thought it through completely will help get it more than a cursory glance. Here are a few suggestions:

 Put it in writing. In as clear and attractive a form as you can, put your idea on paper. Make sure four things are addressed: (1) what problem will be solved if your idea is implemented; (2) how you plan to do it; (3) what involvement—financial or otherwise— is required of the employer; and (4) what the benefit will be.

 Have other parents review it. Suggestions from more than one or two people give the plan additional force. Having the interest of a number of parents means more to an employer than a single parent wanting a change.

Try to anticipate points of resistance and have alternatives ready. If you think the floor space is the weakest part of your plan, have two or three back-up suggestions to keep the boss thinking.

 At your first meeting, be happy to get an, "I'll think about it." In the corporate world, few suggestions get a go-ahead the first time out. Present your information in such a way that you are merely opening the door, so the discussion can continue in the future.

 ## Yeah, But How Will That Help Us?

If your employer doesn't see how adding family-friendly programs will help the company—whether it's a day-care subsidy or simply allowing a Parents' Q&A bulletin board—use these points to enlighten him or her:

- A happy employee is more likely to be a productive employee.

- A happy employee is likely to stay on the job.

- A happy employee is less likely to be sick, to have problems with tardiness, or to have difficulties with superiors or coworkers.

- A happy employee is one of your best advertisements.

- Sponsoring family-friendly programs spreads good will among employees and in the community.

- Supporting family-friendly programs makes a statement of social responsibility to other area businesses.

- The children being helped in family-friendly programs constitute the next generation of workers. By caring for children today, businesses are investing in their own futures.

BEST & **WORST**

Worst:
"Feeling that I cannot stay home with a sick child if I need to"

A Little Support Can Mean a Lot

Even in a small business, you can set up family-friendly supports. It could be a lunch, an after-work meeting, or a bulletin board, but providing something that enables families to find each other and share concerns and resources is an important asset. This section provides a few suggestions that might start a family feeling at your workplace.

Parents' Lunch Out

One of the first things you'll want to do when you organize a parent's group is have a gathering where working parents can meet one another. With your employer's okay, you can organize a pitch-in on-site or an off-site luncheon at a local restaurant. Give parents the opportunity to get acquainted, and the group may simply form itself.

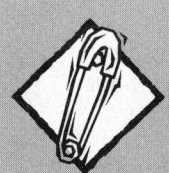

Remember that your employer, while being sensitive to your needs, also must be sensitive to those of other employees who are not parents. Whatever program, group, or support you suggest, make sure you welcome the participation of everyone in your company; don't exclude others based on any perceived differences.

Creating a Parents' Q&A Board

Another idea your employer might go along with is a Parents' Q&A bulletin board, or a section of the existing employee board where parents can set

up carpooling arrangements and post names of back-up baby-sitters, parenting tips, or interesting and helpful articles.

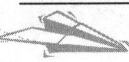 **Things to Put on a Parents' Q&A Board**

- Organizing tips
- Child-care articles
- Names of good baby-sitters
- Notices of special classes
- Carpooling questions
- Schedule changes
- Special products
- Notices of upcoming events

Organizing Co-Ops

Once you know who the other working parents in your company are, you might want to do something like make cooperative child-care arrangements. You can do this yourself, without an employer subsidy.

For example, suppose that you and four other parents in your organization are looking for new child-care arrangements. You hear about a day-care home only two blocks from your office. You talk with the other parents and then approach the day-care provider to arrange for small-group care. You may be able to get a discount, as well as share pick-up and drop-off responsibilities.

Another example of a co-op is one that you actually organize yourself. If you have job-sharing options at your workplace, or if you and other parents work part-time, you could set up a baby-sitting co-op. You watch two or three other

children, along with your own, on your days home; then, when you work, another parent who works a schedule different from yours watches the children. You cut down on child-care costs, know the kids are in homes with people who love them, and make sure the burden of care isn't too great on any one parent.

Possible Co-Op Parents

Parent: _____

Workdays: _____

Children (names and ages): _____

Phone: _____

Comments: _____

_____

Parent: _____

Workdays: _____

Children (names and ages): _____

Phone: _____

Comments: _____

_____

Parent: _____

Workdays: _____

Children (names and ages): _____

Phone: _____

Comments: _____

_____

Setting Up Care Nests for Sick Kids

One of the biggest challenges a working parent faces is that moment when the phone rings and the school nurse tells you your child is sick and needs to go home. Your first reaction, of course, is to want to zoom out of work as fast as you can and care for her. But what will you do tomorrow?

In larger cities, sick-child care is becoming more widely available. In these care centers, a registered nurse is on staff to care for children who are "on the mend"—no longer seriously ill or contagious.

If you don't have a facility like this in your area, or you don't feel comfortable leaving your child in sick-child care, you might want to come up with your own "care nest." Your employer, or your parent group, can approach area home day-care providers—or perhaps a grandma or two in the area—who are willing to take care of children when they aren't quite well enough to go back to school.

Careful screening is important, of course, and you should check out all references before choosing a care provider (as you would for any person responsible for the care of your child). But creating a care nest close to work enables you to check on your child during breaks and lunches and make sure she's getting quiet home care while she recuperates.

From One Parent to Another

"Maintain control of your children from the beginning, but always do it in love. Make the most of the time you have, and don't forget to say 'I love you.' Show it, too."

—Father of two who works full-time

Summary

Today's employers are becoming more aware of the family needs and responsibilities of their employees; a more well-rounded approach to benefits and flexible programs is on the horizon. If your company is not currently offering any family-supportive services—such as subsidized child care, flexible leave policies, or on-site day care—you can do things on your own to start a discussion of possibilities for the future. You can also organize a parents' group by searching out the other working parents in your department or office and coordinating child care; carpooling; or just good, old-fashioned emotional support.

In any case, knowing we're not alone in this balancing act is a comforting thought. People before us and people after us will face the same impossible schedules, the same runny noses, the same mad morning rushes to the car, and the same startled faces when we pull baby bibs from our briefcases. Parents all over the world will worry about the care their children are receiving, fret over the issue of quantity vs. quality time, pray that the educational system is doing its job, and hope that—someday, down the road—they'll know they made the right choices.

One night, as you turn out the light in your kids' room, you'll stop for a moment in the peaceful dark. By the soft glow of the night light, you'll see the kids snuggled down under the covers, the next day's clothing laid out neatly at the foot of their beds, the laundry put away, the toys shelved. In wonder, you'll walk down the stairs, which *don't* have "things to go upstairs" piled on the bottom three steps. You'll walk into the living room and see that the toys are in the toy box and there's not a trace of cat hair on the sofa. As you sit down and pick up the remote control ("You mean I actually have time to watch *television*?"), a quiet little realization washes over you: This can work.

Seem impossible right now? Don't worry—it's coming.

Notes

1. Laurie Blum, *Free Money for Day Care* (St. Louis: Fireside Books, 1992).

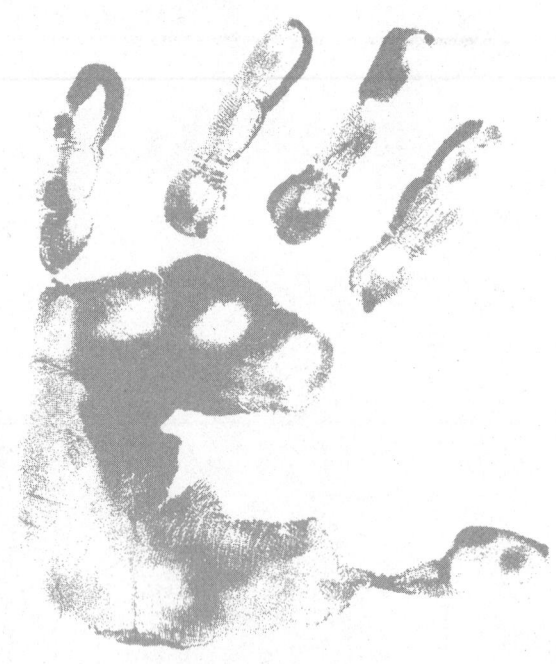

Back-to-Work Checklist

As you and your family prepare for your return to work, use this checklist to make sure you've covered the most important bases:

___ We have determined our family priorities. The most important are:_____

_____

_____

_____

___ We have created a family mission statement:

_____

_____

_____

___ We have discussed the types of jobs that fit our family's needs. They include these: _____

_____

_____

_____

_____

___ We have discussed changing responsibilities with the kids. We've explained that these things will probably change: _____

_____

_____

_____

___ We have investigated different day-care options. We considered: _____

_____

_____

_____

___ We have decided on child care and made arrangements. These are our child-care plans:

_____

_____

_____

_____

___ We have arranged back-up and emergency procedures. In case of emergency: _____

_____

_____

_____

_____

___ We have decided on and posted rules for stay-at-home children. The primary rules are these:

_____

_____

_____

___ We have created and posted a sheet of emergency numbers. These are the most important numbers:

Name   Number

_____   _____

_____   _____

_____   _____

_____   _____

_____   _____

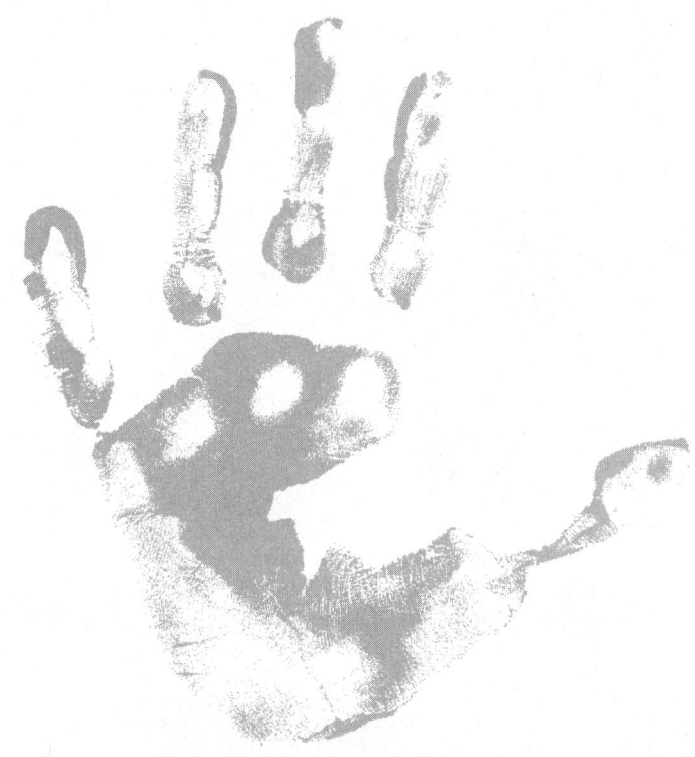

Emergency Numbers for Home and Work

Emergency Numbers for Home

Created __/__/__

Mom's work: _____

Dad's work: _____

Friend: _____

Grandma: _____

Police: _____

Fire: _____

Poison control: _____

Other: _____

Baby-sitter: _____

Preschool: _____

School: _____

After-school care: _____

In case of emergency, when Mom or Dad can't be

reached, call:_____

_____

_____

Emergency Numbers for Work

Created __/__/__

Baby-sitter: _____   Child: _____

_____   _____

Preschool: _____   Child: _____

_____   _____

School: _____   Child: _____

_____   _____

After-school care: _____   Child: _____

_____   _____

Spouse's work: _____

Friend: _____

Police: _____

Fire: _____

Poison control: _____

Other: _____

Special Instructions in Case of Emergency

Child: _____

Instruction: _____

_____

_____

Child: _____

Instruction: _____

_____

_____

Child: _____

Instruction: _____

_____

_____

Appendix

C

Family-Friendly Resources

This appendix lists sources of information on balancing home and work. You'll find basic information on general health, education, and fire prevention as well as the latest on-line offerings for parents and children.

Resources for Parents

American Academy of Pediatrics, Publications Division
141 Northwest Point Blvd.
P.O. Box 927
Elk Grove Village, IL 60009

Child Welfare League of America
440 First St. N.W., Ste. 310
Washington, DC 20001

Children's Defense Fund
25 E St. N.W.
Washington, DC 20001

Commission on Public Health
1411 K St. N.W., 12th Floor
Washington, DC 20005

Council on Family Health
420 Lexington Ave.
New York, NY 10017

La Leche League International
9616 Minneapolis Ave.
P.O. Box 1209
Franklin Park, IL 60131

National Black Child Development Institute
1463 Rhode Island Ave. N.W.
Washington, DC 20005

National Committee for Prevention of Child Abuse
332 S. Michigan Ave., Ste. 1600
Chicago, IL 60604

National Fire Protection Association
Batterymarch Park
Quincy, MA 02269

National Highway Traffic Safety Administration
400 Seventh St. S.W.
Washington, DC 20590

Associations for Children

Boy Scouts of America
1325 Walnut Hill Lane
Irving, TX 64055

Boys' Clubs of America
771 First Ave.
New York, NY 10017

Camp Fire Boys and Girls
4601 Madison Ave.
Kansas City, MO 64112

4-H
U.S. Department of Agriculture
Washington, DC 20250

Girl Scouts of the U.S.A.
420 5th Ave.
New York, NY 10018

Girls' Clubs of America
30 E. 33rd St.
New York, NY 10016

Junior Achievement
1 Education Way
Colorado Springs, CO 80906

On-Line Supports

All of the popular on-line services—America Online, CompuServe, and Microsoft Network— have on-line groups, called forums, specifically related to parenting. You'll find the latest news for parents, games for kids, and "chat rooms" where you can discuss problems or just trade stories with other parents across the country or around the world.

On-line services are also good sources of information. For example, you can access the Internet through America Online[1] (or through other on-line services), and get to the National Parent Information Network, set up and supported by the U.S. Department of Education. You'll find all sorts of information there, including discussions and publications on these topics:

 Assessment and testing

 Child care

 Children and the media

 Children with disabilities

 Children's health and nutrition

 Early childhood

 Gifted children

 Helping children learn at home

Older children, pre-teens, young adolescents

 Parents and families in society

 Parents and schools as partners

 Teens

This is just one example of the information available to you on-line. If you've got a computer equipped with a modem and the necessary software, give it a try.

Notes

1. From the AOL main menu, choose Internet Connection. Then select the Gopher/WAIS search and the Kids category

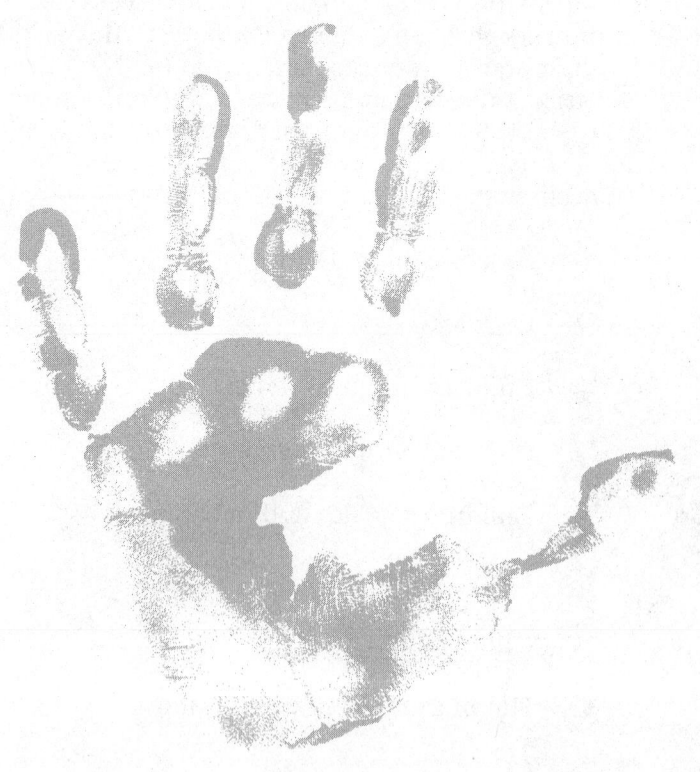

References

Adler, Ronald B., and Neil Towne. *Looking Out, Looking In*. 6th ed. Orlando, FL: Holt, Rinehart & Winston, 1990.

Bair, Diane, and Pamela Wright. "Coping with Five-O-Clock Frenzy." *Woman's Day*, 8 August 1995, 79.

Bernstein, Peter, and Christopher Ma. *The Practical Guide to Practically Everything*. New York: Random House, 1995.

Blum, Laurie. *Free Money for Day Care*. St. Louis: Warren H Green, Fireside Books, 1992.

Canfield, Jack, and Mark Victor Hansen. *The Aladdin Factor*. New York: Berkley Books, 1995.

Chollar, Susan. "Why Are We So Tired?" *Woman's Day*, 10 October 1995, 43.

Collingwood, Harris. "Simplicity Simplified." *Working Woman*, December 1995, 48-49.

Davis, Flora. "Psyching Out Insomnia." *Working Woman*, March 1995, 74.

"Dealing with Downshifters." *Working Woman*, December 1995, 19.

Eshleman, J. Ross. *The Family: An Introduction.* Englewood Cliffs, NJ: Paramount Publishing, Allyn & Bacon, 1974.

Farr, J. Michael. *The Very Quick Job Search.* 2nd ed. Indianapolis: JIST Works, 1996.

Grollman, Earl A., and Gerri L. Sweder. *The Working Parent Dilemma.* Boston: Beacon Press, 1983.

Henricks, Mark. "More Than Words." *Entrepreneur,* August 1995, 54-55.

Houck, Catherine. "Stress!" *Woman's Day,* 4 April 1995.

Kaye, Kenneth. *Family Rules.* New York: St. Martin's Press, 1984.

Krueger, Caryl Waller. *Working Parent—Happy Child.* Nashville, TN: Abingdon Press, 1990.

McGarvey, Robert. "Now or Never." *Entrepreneur,* October 1995.

Miller, Jeanne. *The Perfectly Safe Home.* St. Louis: Warren H Green, Fireside Books, 1991.

"The Minimal Workout." *Working Woman,* June 1995, 61.

Muscari, Ann, and Wenda Wardell Morrone. *Child Care That Works.* New York: Doubleday, 1989.

Peterson, Pipi Campbell. *Ready, Set, Organize!* Indianapolis: JIST Works, Park Avenue, 1996.

Povich, Lynn. "Get a Life." *Working Woman,* December 1995.

"Simple Child-Care Solutions." *Working Woman,* September 1995, 72.

Statistical Abstract of the United States 1995. Washington, DC: U.S. Government Printing Office, 1995.

U.S. Department of Labor. *America's Top 300 Jobs: A Complete Career Handbook*. 4th ed. Indianapolis: JIST Works, 1994.

U.S. Department of Labor. *Occupational Outlook Handbook*. 1994-1995 ed. Indianapolis: JIST Works, 1994.

Varni, James W., and Donna G. Corwin. *Time-Out for Toddlers*. New York: Berkley Books, 1991.

Working Mother Magazine, September 1995.

World Almanac 1995. Mahwah, NJ: Funk & Wagnalls, 1995.

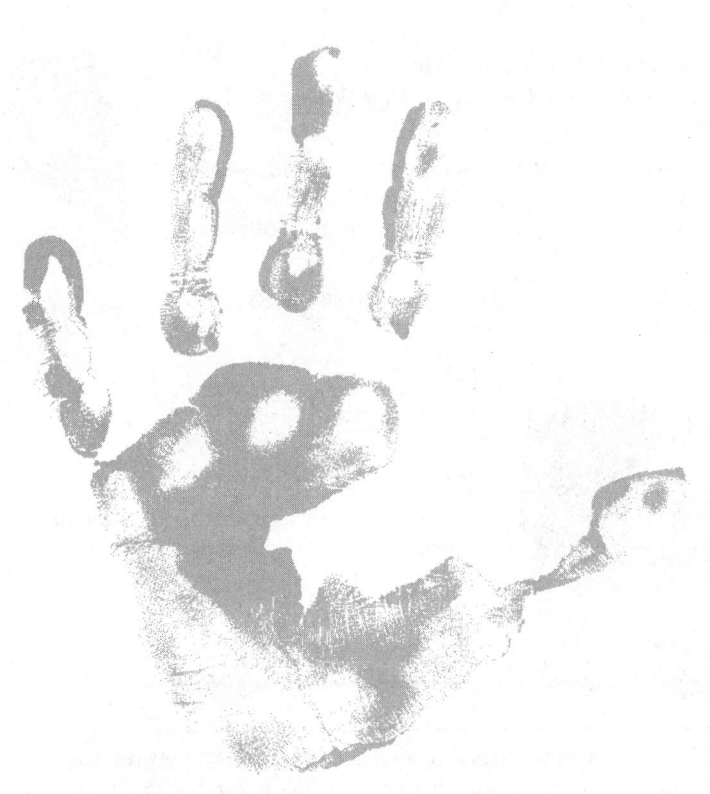

3000 800054 48603
St. Louis Community College

D0680643

Power to Destroy

POWER TO DESTROY

The Political Uses of the IRS from Kennedy to Nixon

John A. Andrew III

Ivan R. Dee

CHICAGO 2002

Library of Congress Cataloging-in-Publication Data:
Andrew, John A.

Power to destroy : the political uses of the IRS from Kennedy to Nixon / John A. Andrew III.

p. cm.

Includes bibliographical references and index.

ISBN 1-56663-452-0 (alk. paper)

1. United States. Internal Revenue Service—History. 2. Tax administration and procedure—United States—History. 3. United States—Politics and government—1945–1989. I. Title.

HJ2361 .A53 2002

336.24'0973'09046—dc21   2002023760

For John,
Love, Roz

Foreword

THE WRITING of history is an exploration in the uncovering of truths. History is the perfect place to hide secrets; historians spend years and lifetimes trying to uncover them.

My father first encountered the Kennedy administration's uses of the IRS against conservative foundations while researching his book *The Other Side of the Sixties: Young Americans for Freedom and the Rise of Conservative Politics* (1997). Even while writing *Lyndon Johnson and the Great Society* (1998) he continued to file Freedom of Information Act (FOIA) petitions requesting IRS documents. With generous support from Franklin & Marshall College, where he taught for twenty-seven years, he traveled to archives across the country to review the papers of IRS commissioners and important political figures involved. He sensed that there was an important untold story in the political uses of the IRS, one that might reveal a profound threat to the personal liberties of all citizens.

Assembling the evidence took sheer tenacity. The IRS had what could best be described as a records mismanagement program, so sometimes discovering what files existed on a particular topic took multiple FOIA submissions. More often than not, when he received a box of files from the IRS, whole reams of paper would be completely or almost entirely redacted—blacked out—even reports and memoranda that were clearly not subject to the IRS's privacy guidelines. He would then file an appeal, and to demonstrate that the overzealous use of the black marker was an attempt to hide IRS actions rather than to protect the privacy of American citizens, he included copies of one or more of the redacted documents that he had found in *another* archive, which clearly justified his claims for access. His research was so unnerving to the IRS that officials could only conclude that someone on the inside (they suspected the

IRS historian, Shelley Davis) must have been pinpointing the documents he should request. They were wrong: my father's determination to find the truth and his skills as a researcher led him to those documents.

My father's sudden and unexpected death in November 2000 left behind an unfinished manuscript and years of research. My mother was determined that his hard work would not be put in a drawer, unpublished. Pulling herself out of her grief, she brought together his colleagues, publisher, and friends in an effort to finish the story. Only my father could have taken his unfinished draft and polished it to perfection. What you are about to read is the product of several people who judiciously sought to put the finishing touches on his manuscript. My family is indebted to their selfless efforts.

On behalf of my father, my family and I would like to thank the many institutions and individuals who made this book possible. We are especially grateful to Shelley Davis, who read the manuscript and offered a number of invaluable suggestions, as did my father's friend Lewis L. Gould. Ivan Dee's faith in this project never wavered: he gently prodded family and friends to complete the manuscript, and he edited the book with sensitivity and skill. Several colleagues at Franklin & Marshall, Associate Librarian for Reference and Instruction Thomas Karel and archivist Ann Upton, as well as Joanna Cheslock and Jana Johnson, Class of 2003, did the research that helped resolve questions that arose during the editing process.

We also wish to thank Franklin & Marshall College for allocating time, money, and people so that work on the book could continue. In particular we appreciate the efforts of Provost Bruce Pipes and former President Dr. Richard Kneedler.

A special thanks goes to my father's colleague and friend David Schuyler. He guided the preparation of the manuscript by being the point man for readers, researchers, and the publisher, writing endless e-mails to keep everyone on schedule, and prodding my family to make decisions to move the book along. Without his dedication this project would not have been completed. We are forever indebted to him

LEA ANDREW FRANDINA

Roxbury, Vermont
June 2002

Contents

The power to tax involves the power to destroy.

—Chief Justice John Marshall,

McCulloch v. Maryland, 1819

Power to Destroy

INTRODUCTION

RESEARCHING
THE IRS

THE INTERNAL REVENUE SERVICE (IRS) remains one of the most understudied of all government agencies. Presidents have used the IRS to settle scores with old rivals, to implement policies, and to enforce moral or political strictures, often through questionable or illegal means. Congressional committees, and even individual congressmen, have used it for much the same purpose. During the 1950s and early 1960s the IRS became a vehicle to target such groups as the Communist Party of the United States (CPUSA), and it successfully delayed CPUSA appeals of its rulings for more than a decade. In a related case, a federal court charged that the IRS was conducting a crusade "to rid our society of unorthodox thinkers and actors by using federal income tax laws and federal courts to put them in the penitentiary."[1] Yet the policies and decisions of the IRS, as well as its application of the Internal Revenue Code, have largely escaped the notice of historians. Its role in law enforcement, as well as tax enforcement, deserves scrutiny. This is particularly true for the years since World War II, when the IRS grew in power and influence. In the words of former IRS Chief Counsel Mitchell Rogovin: ". . . if battle streamers were awarded, Revenue's flag would be resplendent with the silk of past battles. It fought against racketeers and communism in the 1950's; organized crime in the 1960's; and narcotics as well as the enemies of the Nixon administration in the 1970's."[2] What follows is a look at some of those efforts, along with some lesser-known and more suspect activities of the IRS in the years from John Kennedy through Richard Nixon. Historical study of the IRS, however, is not an easy task.

Given the centrality of the IRS to Americans' lives, and often to public policy, why have historians largely neglected it? Researching the IRS presents formidable obstacles that raise questions about the agency and its behavior in our political system. Some of these obstacles demonstrate an inherent contradiction between democracy and secrecy. Others are more mundane, reflecting the ability of a powerful institution to frustrate investigators and go its own way. Several years ago the historian Athan Theoharis noted the difficulties of studying the Federal Bureau of Investigation (FBI). The FBI, he noted, not only denied researchers access to its files, frustrating efforts to study its policies and activities; it continued to do so even after passage of the Freedom of Information Act (FOIA). There was, he concluded, an "in-house coverup."[3] The IRS behaves in much the same way, and when it comes to securing information it has been a tougher adversary than the FBI.

The historian's problem begins with sources. Despite federal law (Title 44 U.S.C. 3101), the IRS has no effective records management or records maintenance programs. A 1995 study by the National Archives and Records Administration (NARA) reported that the "IRS has not conducted a comprehensive records inventory or a complete review of its records control schedules in several years. . . ."[4] While the IRS and the Archivist of the United States have been talking about this problem for some time, little or no progress has been evident. The chief stumbling block is the IRS's enhanced interpretation of the disclosure laws. That is, it refuses to allow NARA personnel—even trained archivists who have dealt with top-secret national security affairs—to examine IRS records, arguing that the records may contain tax-return information. Although a series of congressional hearings that revealed the abuse of power by numerous IRS employees resulted in the 1997 Taxpayer Reform Act, which required the IRS to open its files to NARA, there is little evidence that anything has changed: IRS field offices routinely destroy records after about three years, and many criminal investigation files have been destroyed after ten years. NARA has concluded that an "issue of acute concern to both NARA evaluators and IRS RM [records management] staff is the identification and location of records documenting policy-making within the IRS."

The case of "Operation Snowball" exemplifies this problem. We know that this was a 1968 investigation into companies illegally claiming campaign contributions as tax deductible. Involving more than thirty-one companies in California alone, it spread to almost all the fifty-eight IRS districts across the country. The IRS responded to my Freedom of Information Act request for records, however, with a letter indicating that under IRS policy "case files for a 1968 investigation would have been destroyed." They could find nothing on this operation, even at the agency's Washington, D.C., headquarters, known as the National Office.[5]

Not only are records from various IRS operations apparently missing, there appear to be no procedures in place to prevent high-level IRS officials from taking records with them when they leave office or retire. As the notes to later chapters will reveal, many times I discovered records that the IRS either could not find, partially redacted (blacked out), or denied me in whole, residing in the private papers of former IRS or Treasury officials. These records filled in important gaps in the history of IRS policymaking. They also demonstrated the ability of the IRS to successfully block the release of public information despite the Freedom of Information Act.

Other obstacles compound research problems. The IRS has no finding aids to assist researchers or even to identify records in its possession. Virtually no IRS records, moreover, have been deposited in the National Archives, especially for the past fifty years. The IRS has had only one historian in its entire history, and after only a few years it forced her out and terminated the position. Consequently many IRS records remain unscheduled and may be destroyed at any time. According to NARA, these include key documents from "the Historical Office files of the IRS Commissioner, Criminal Investigative Case Files, Corporate Tax Returns for the period 1909–1919, and records of the Special Service Staff." Compounding this problem is the fact that "few IRS employees are aware of document retention requirements and there is no central depository for IRS records."[6]

Finally, the Freedom of Information Act is not always a useful tool in securing IRS records. There is, first, the problem of adequately describing the records you are seeking in the absence of finding aids or other descriptive information. Too, IRS records are maintained in peculiar ways. For example, there are no files of IRS commissioners' correspondence, even though commissioners clearly write letters and are the only individuals authorized to establish IRS policy. This correspondence, when it still exists, lies scattered in particular projects or operations files. Then there is the disclosure problem, specifically section 6103 of the Internal Revenue Code. Not only are individual tax returns protected under disclosure and privacy legislation, and therefore exempt from FOIA inquiries, so is all "tax-return information." The IRS has interpreted this provision *very* broadly, and the courts to date have generally agreed. To the IRS, "tax-return information" is anything and everything that finds its way into an individual or corporate taxpayer's file, however remotely related to a tax issue or case. It includes not only pertinent financial materials, which we would all agree should be exempt from disclosure, but newspaper clippings, public documents, and even material created for public dissemination by the individual or organization. As one disclosure officer wrote me: "It is immaterial that such return information may be public information in another context." Despite former IRS Commissioner Mortimer Caplin's testimony that "no agency stands to benefit more from a general 'free information' policy than the Internal Revenue Service," IRS records remain extremely difficult to obtain.[7]

My own experience with the IRS, with respect to records involving its operations during the Kennedy administration, illustrates how these obstacles protect the agency from historians' inquiries. I attempted to gain access to all IRS materials regarding the Ideological Organizations Project (more on this later). While I was eventually able to secure many of these records (but, given the lack of finding aids, I don't really know what percentage), the task was difficult and necessitated the help of my local congressman. There was also a persistent problem with IRS secrecy and suspicion of "outsiders." IRS officials tried, arbitrarily, to shift me from an "educational institution requester" to a commercial user, and thereby to deny my fee waiver request. They also sent members of their internal security staff to interview me. On August 9, 1995, Internal Security agents Karen Parker and Steve Raisch came to my office at Franklin & Marshall College, ostensibly to discuss my FOIA submissions. They clearly assumed that I had pinpointed specific documents in my request only because of information that Shelley Davis, then the IRS historian, must have provided. Although I showed Parker and Raisch the public documents that I used as the basis of my request, they were intent on eliminating Davis's position as a step in reducing if not terminating public access to IRS files.[8] The IRS also attempted to deny ownership of IRS materials previously provided. A letter I received from IRS FOIA tax law specialist H. A. Williamson, Jr., is an example of this strategy: "We should point out that page 2 of Document No. 48, which was previously provided to you," Williamson wrote, "appears to have been miscopied. No page in our files resembles the copy you were provided. Please substitute the enclosed Document No. 48 for the copy previously provided." It was the same document, except that it was totally instead of partially redacted![9]

Marcus Farbenblum, formerly chief of the Freedom of Information Branch in the IRS National Office for fifteen years, has noted the tendency of the agency to withhold its records "sometimes in flagrant disregard of laws which require disclosure." Although he remained convinced that the IRS would benefit from making its records more accessible, Farbenblum concluded that the IRS was a "closed society" governed by a "siege mentality" impervious to public demands.[10]

Attorney William A. Dobrovir summed up the problem concisely in a petition to IRS Commissioner Margaret Milner Richardson in 1996: "IRS' extreme position also ignores the legislative history of [section] 6103. The IRS Commissioner at the time . . . never intended NARA to be excluded from examining IRS records. Congress' aim was not to prevent the Archivist of the United States from taking custody of IRS' files of historical value. Rather, Congress was concerned with the very recent events relating to Nixon White House misuse of IRS' records to target those on the infamous 'enemies list,' and with law enforcement agencies' use of IRS tax records in cases involving matters having nothing to do with taxes: both breaches of taxpayers' reasonable expectations of privacy."[11] Clearly, Congress expected that disclosure would be a restraint on such abuses. The problem here is not only a matter of disclosure or even records management; it is a problem of policy. Policymakers should be aware of the issues raised in the past by the use of political pressure on and/or from the IRS to advance partisan or policy interests.

This all adds up to what Athan Theoharis has called a "culture of secrecy." Although Theoharis has focused on the FBI and its activities during the cold war, historians pursuing the IRS and its many operations and intelligence activities encounter the same obstacles. Much like the FBI, the IRS has a bureaucratic culture "hostile to the principle of public access." Secret operations that target segments of the American population, such as Operation Leprechaun, Project Southwest, Operation Snowball, Projects Haven and Tradewinds, the Ideological Organizations Project, the Special Service Staff, and other intelligence and surveillance activities, have largely escaped the scrutiny of historians. Equally obscure are the purposes and results of IRS liaisons with the CIA and FBI. Why were these liaisons established? What information was shared? IRS "antipathy towards public disclosure and accountability" contributes to this culture of secrecy. Excessive and at times promiscuous redaction of released records compounds the problem, as does inadequate staffing at IRS disclosure offices. (I found that each staff person often handled more than three hundred cases and must do his or her own copying.)[12]

To compound matters, the IRS often shared the results of its intelligence gathering with other intelligence agencies, congressional committees, or the White House. Sometimes this was done at its own initiative; other times it stemmed from specific requests or political pressures. In this way, outside agencies used IRS intelligence and operations for nontax-related purposes. Tax-return information became a "generalized government asset." One exhaustive study of the IRS noted that tax returns were a valuable source of information. By looking at Schedule A to the 1040 form, for example, "a reader may learn whether the taxpayer or his family are under medical or psychiatric care. It may also reveal the filer's religious affiliation, the objects and degree of his eleemosynary inclinations, the sources of his borrowed money," as well as such items as union membership, political leanings, and "many other facets of his personal and political life."[13] This is a political as well as a philosophical issue.

One other issue repeatedly surfaces in the various cases that follow: the role of the individual IRS agent. Many years ago Frank Donner noted the functional linkages between IRS intelligence and that of other agencies. This creates a situation whereby "veterans of one agency frequently turn up in another, retaining useful ties to their former employment." They form an "intelligence brotherhood," with personal ties that reach outside of and beyond formal channels of communication. Combined with the "immense discretion" given to IRS agents and the lack of formal restraint on the IRS itself, this has become a recipe for rogue activities. As one IRS agent noted: "I violate laws at all times; it's part of my duties."[14]

The consequences, noted Charles Davenport, former project director of the Administrative Conference of the United States, are serious. Over the years various governmental hearings have clearly established that IRS agents have defied court orders. In addition, agents have illegally picked locks and tapped telephones, stolen records, intercepted personal mail, employed sexual entrapment, and used hidden microphones and two-way mirrors. Some of the operations detailed in this book reflect those consequences. They also indicate that by their actions, individual agents can in effect make policy—despite the fact that policymaking authority resides solely with the IRS commissioner.[15]

Taking its title from Chief Justice John Marshall's famous statement "The power to tax involves the power to destroy," this book investigates how presidents, political appointees, and bureaucrats attempted to use the Internal Revenue Service for nontax-related purposes, often to advance partisan agendas or to punish enemies. The following chapters demonstrate that in the years from John Kennedy's inauguration through the impeachment of Richard Nixon, the IRS was more than a tax collector—that its auditing and investigative functions targeted individuals and organizations not because of real tax liabilities but for ideological and political reasons. The Watergate investigations revealed considerable detail of the Nixon administration's misuse of the IRS, which became the first allegation of the second article of impeachment adopted by the Senate Judiciary Committee: the article charged that Nixon had, "acting personally and through his subordinates and agents, endeavored to obtain from the Internal Revenue Service, in violation of the constitutional rights of citizens, confidential information contained in income tax returns for purposes not authorized by law, and to cause, in violation of the constitutional rights of citizens, income tax audits or other income tax investigations to be initiated or conducted in a discriminatory manner." But the IRS itself undertook actions equally dangerous to the republic. The Special Service Staff conducted one of the most extensive and least-known intelligence-gathering operations in recent American history and used its investigative powers in an attempt to disrupt legitimate dissent and anti-war activity. The politicization of the IRS during these years represented a profound threat to American society.

As the following chapters try to make clear, the Internal Revenue Service alone is not to blame for all of these and other abuses. Political pressure on the IRS is a constant problem. The IRS commissioner is a political appointee. Congressional committees hold the purse strings. Although the public usually thinks of the IRS as a dangerously independent agency—and at times it is—outside political constraints and pressures often push it into positions and policies that do not well serve either the IRS or American taxpayers. The often publicized abuses of the Nixon years brought these issues to public consciousness. Some of them originated with the White House, others with the IRS. There were abuses before Nixon and abuses after Nixon, though it is impossible to determine the extent of illegal activity due to the lack of records. As long as IRS history and policymaking remain shrouded in secrecy, there is little reason to believe that abuses will not continue to plague the IRS and the American public. Congress can hold hearings, and even pass laws, but all too often these are nothing more than reactions to the moment and fail to solve persistent problems. We should not be constrained by the past, but we can learn from it. The challenge for historians is to uncover it.

CHAPTER ONE

THE EARLY 1960S: A NEW ROLE FOR THE IRS?

ON JANUARY 20, 1961, a bitter cold but sunny day in the nation's capital, John F. Kennedy took the oath of office as the thirty-fifth president of the United States. His soaring rhetoric that noon—the promises to "bear any burden" and "pay any price"—led many Americans to believe that a new generation and a new era had arrived, that the reins of power were now in the hands of an idealistic activist interested in exercising power to address social problems. It marked the beginning, many later believed, of Camelot. John Kennedy, however, was a professional politician, more practical than idealistic. His rhetoric often exceeded his intent. He addressed social problems more directly than had Dwight Eisenhower, his predecessor, but he also intended to make government responsive in other ways. With his brother Robert installed as attorney general, one of the powers he sought to mobilize was that of the Internal Revenue Service.

His first move was to use an old colleague and family friend, recently named special consultant to the president, Carmine Bellino, to look inside the IRS. Bellino, undoubtedly the foremost investigative accountant in American history, is perhaps the most important "unknown" in the Kennedy administration. A former agent of the FBI, where he headed the accounting division, Bellino served with Robert Kennedy on the McClellan Committee (Senate Investigations Subcommittee) in the late 1950s. There he was instrumental to the prosecution of labor leaders Dave Beck and Jimmy Hoffa, as well as the Teamsters Union. Bellino later became the Kennedy family's personal accountant, and his

11

cousin (Angela Novello) served as Robert Kennedy's secretary. During his long career in government he held staff positions on many key committees, including service as chief investigator for the Ervin Committee (Senate Select Committee on 1972 Presidential Campaign Activities) during the Watergate hearings, and then later for the Senate Judiciary Committee.[1]

Less than one week after Kennedy's inauguration, Bellino called IRS Commissioner Mortimer Caplin and asked to inspect IRS files on various individuals, including tax data for Teamsters Union boss James R. Hoffa. Hoffa had long been a nemesis of the Kennedys and remained the object of extensive prosecutorial activity throughout Robert Kennedy's tenure at the Justice Department. That same day, January 26, 1961, the attorney general asked the IRS to grant Bellino access to all "files, records, and documents requested by him," presumably to coordinate investigations by the IRS, Justice Department, and other government agencies. Six days later, on February 1, IRS Commissioner Caplin (who had been Robert and Edward Kennedy's law professor at the University of Virginia) authorized Bellino to review the files. Neither the request nor the authorization was in writing.[2]

By then Bellino was not only working as an investigator for the White House but for the Justice Department and for at least one congressional committee. Caplin later recalled that he had "triple credentials." Bellino had offices in the IRS as well as in the White House and the Justice Department. Although Caplin later asserted that the IRS denied the investigator access to much of what he wanted, Bellino was able to scrutinize various tax returns without any written authorization from the president (as the law required). A dozen years later Caplin maintained that "not a single tax return was sent to the White House." Perhaps he is correct; perhaps they went only to the Justice Department. But in a later memo Caplin indicated that the IRS granted Bellino permission to examine returns precisely because he was "the representative of the President."

The record in fact reveals a more disturbing pattern. On January 30, four days after Bellino first appeared at the IRS, Caplin received a written request from Robert (not John) Kennedy asking that Bellino be permitted to review tax returns of various individuals connected with Justice Department investigations. Not until May 23, four months after Bellino first gained access to tax returns, did Caplin write a memorandum to IRS General Counsel Robert Knight formally authorizing Bellino to examine the files. Surprisingly, the IRS had apparently never before addressed this issue.[3]

Bellino was not only looking at tax returns, he intended to photocopy them and keep the copies. Notes from a March 31, 1961, meeting of Treasury Secretary Douglas Dillon's staff reveal that as a White House consultant Bellino was also looking at labor union problems for the McClellan Committee and had requested the returns of labor unions and labor leaders. For some reason he also examined returns from the *New York Times*. Bellino chafed at Treasury regulations, especially the requirement that a full congressional committee must adopt a resolution before its representatives could inspect tax returns. Bellino argued that it was too burdensome to obtain a quorum of the full committee. He also sought to bypass the policy against photocopying returns. Treasury General Counsel Knight advised against changing existing policies, though he admitted that changes could be effected without amending any laws. As later events revealed, these early forays of Bellino heralded the beginning of the Justice Department's organized crime drive.[4]

The organized crime drive (OCD) became one of the first instances in which the Kennedy administration used the IRS for nontax-related purposes. That use of the agency for law enforcement later became controversial as well as a source of trouble for the IRS. The problems stemmed from the fact that when the Justice Department launched the OCD, the IRS also revamped its intelligence organization. A new, more centralized, structure bypassed IRS district directors. The Intelligence Division's national director became responsible for coordinating the OCD program, working with coordinators in the National Office and in each IRS region throughout the country. This was a radical shift in operational authority and contained the seed of future problems.[5] Working with the Treasury Department and the FBI, Attorney General Robert Kennedy coordinated the OCD. Not only did he have the support of his brother, the president; as a senator his brother had served on the McClellan Committee during the 1950s when it "discovered" organized crime in America.

Despite its later reservations, the IRS embraced the task-force approach in large part because Robert Kennedy had secured Caplin's support for these efforts in a pre-appointment screening interview. On January 24, 1961, immediately after Caplin's appointment, the IRS created a special organized crime unit to work with the Justice Department. The attorney general rejected as "specious" arguments that the IRS should not be used to punish the underworld, and organized crime cases moved quickly to the top of tax prosecution case lists. From this emerged the strike force concept, with its extensive efforts to coordinate and exchange intelligence between all government intelligence agencies. These measures not only produced dividends in terms of prosecuting organized crime figures, they created innumerable procedural and legal problems for the IRS. On the organized crime strike forces, IRS agents worked with representatives from other government agencies (especially the FBI and Justice Department) to prosecute organized crime figures, contributing not only their tax expertise but access to tax returns. In the process, however, the IRS lost control over how these returns were used and found it impossible to resist requests to provide additional tax data. In this way the IRS often became an investigative tool in the hands of other agencies, asked to supply tax information to advance nontax law enforcement efforts.[6]

Implementing the OCD also created internal security problems for the IRS. The Treasury Department feared that crime figures under scrutiny would use their financial resources to bribe IRS officials and gain access to confidential files and information. Arnold Sagalyn, director of Law Enforcement Coordination for Treasury, added that "these criminals control highly efficient, ruthless organizations experienced in the successful employment of coercion and violence." Intimidation of officials or their families was likely, as were efforts to frame key officials and quash investigations under way. High-level IRS and Treasury meetings in early November 1961 also targeted internal IRS leaks as a potential problem during the OCD. Some leaks may have already occurred, and the IRS pushed for an enhanced role for its seven-year-old Inspection Service, going so far as to ask that Inspection replace the FBI as the agency designated to investigate IRS corruption. The FBI, however, refused to relinquish that power.[7]

The Organized Crime Section of the Justice Department quickly expanded from seventeen to sixty attorneys. Field units sprang up in major cities around the country. The OCD became a crusade, and indictments soared from 1961 through 1963. Many of these prosecutions for tax crimes, however, were the product of excessive zeal. According to former IRS Chief Counsel Mitchell Rogovin, they often reflected a "significant departure" from the agency's "historic standards." The Justice Department used its own intelligence unit to collect information and refer it to the IRS if it promised a productive tax investigation. LBJ's attorney general Ramsey Clark later noted, however, that Robert Kennedy's conviction that racketeering and political corruption went hand in hand meant that "these procedures also contemplated OCD investigation of public officials." This could be political dynamite. It also led to special appropriations to the IRS National Office for undercover informants and the purchase of information, appropriations that totaled $1.3 million in 1964 alone. So significant was the IRS role that 60 percent of all OCD investigations between 1961 and 1965 were developed by the IRS, and recommended taxes and penalties against OCD subjects totaled more than $200 million.[8]

Donald Alexander, IRS commissioner under Richard Nixon, later criticized the OCD and argued that Robert Kennedy had used the IRS to circumvent the FBI. There is likely some merit to this charge. The relationship between Kennedy and FBI Director J. Edgar Hoover was one of mutual contempt. Hoover had long insisted that there was no organized crime problem in the United States, and the OCD gave Kennedy his own investigative unit. Alexander thought the whole concept was "terrible. I don't think the IRS should be taking orders about who it will investigate and who it will not investigate and how the investigation will be conducted from the political people in the Justice Department." Of course, by then Alexander had his own problems with the politicization of the IRS.[9] In the 1970s the agency found itself under fire for the actions of overzealous agents, an apparent inability to control its own investigations, and its use of tax-return information. In the intervening years, moreover, the IRS developed (and abused) electronic surveillance capabilities and other undercover techniques. These later became the focus of an investigation by Senator Edward Long in the mid-1960s—an investigation aimed as much at freeing Jimmy Hoffa and embarrassing Robert Kennedy as it was at the IRS.

The organized crime drive represented just one aspect of the Kennedy administration's developing tendency to look to the IRS for law enforcement assistance. That many other efforts never developed as fully as the OCD does not diminish their importance. They often heralded efforts to use the IRS to advance social or political objectives.

The escalation of civil rights activists and protests in the spring of 1961 led to one such effort. Robert Kennedy used Burke Marshall of the Justice Department as well as special presidential assistant Harris Wofford and the popular entertainer Harry Belafonte to create a Voter Education Project (VEP) in the South. This sought to bring together various civil rights organizations, such as CORE, SNCC, SCLC, and the NAACP, under the umbrella of the VEP. In this way Kennedy hoped to replace public demonstrations with voter registration, thereby curtailing confrontations and harnessing movements for change to administration agendas, something that SNCC in particular resented. To advance his purposes, Kennedy asked his old law school professor, IRS Commissioner Mortimer Caplin, to issue a tax exemption for the VEP, and helped obtain almost \$1 million in funding from the Taconic, Stern, and Field foundations. This project aroused some dissent from within Treasury. Under Secretary Henry Fowler complained that the IRS should not be used for such efforts unless it was part of a government-wide enforcement campaign involving other agencies such as the FBI. Bertrand Harding, IRS deputy commissioner, added: "I assume that the status of the FBI is not going to be readily resolved and it would be my thought that we side-step this issue."[10]

If politics played some role in the VEP efforts, it loomed much larger in two other areas. One was the desirability of appointing politically responsive individuals to key positions in Treasury and the IRS, long an issue. According to an internal IRS report, it had been a source of considerable controversy during the Truman presidency, so much so that several embarrassing abuses in the early 1950s sparked a campaign to clean up the IRS. During the Eisenhower years a combination of civil service reform groups and Republican party officials led efforts to remove additional incompetents (especially Democrats) and schedule all of the top IRS positions under civil service. Political pressures nonetheless persisted. One district director, for example, had served as campaign manager for Helen Gahagan Douglas in her California Senate campaign against Richard Nixon; Republican loyalists insisted on his removal. (Since the individual was not demonstrably incompetent, IRS Commissioner T. Coleman Andrews, a staunch conservative himself, refused to accede to those demands.) Efforts to place political appointees in the IRS also continued. As Assistant IRS Commissioner for Administration E. F. Preston observed in 1961, at times "it might seem that it would be smart politically to yield to these pressures." But he warned that if those pressures influenced "even one selection, knowledge—or at least suspicion—of this will quickly spread." Ambitious employees would be "tempted to encourage similar intervention on their behalf when future vacancies occur." Influential outsiders would seek greater political influence, exposing the IRS to the abuses of the past.[11]

During the Kennedy years, however, administration officials screened all key IRS appointees for political loyalty. Objections to proposed appointments frequently came directly from the White House, where the screening process was headed by Kenneth P. O'Donnell, special assistant to the president. Being a Democrat was not always sufficient; appointees also had to be loyal to the administration.[12] Part of the concern was not only a desire to shape IRS policy but the issue of "sensitive cases." Sensitive Case files were a feature of every administration. These were IRS files opened when politically important individuals were found to have tax problems. Fearing that public exposure might embarrass a president or an administration, the IRS created Sensitive Case files to monitor those problems and alert the president about particular investigations.

In 1963, for example, the IRS learned of press interest in rumors that Dorothy Davies of the White House staff had failed to file returns for several years, and that other presidential appointees had tax delinquencies. High-ranking IRS officials quietly investigated these charges and moved all confidential information out of the public eye to Sensitive Case files. That same year White House aide Myer Feldman's tax affairs came under investigation. Feldman tried to use his position to have the IRS conclude its investigation quickly, perhaps drawing upon his friendship with the commissioner. Fearing a conflict of interest, however, Caplin asked IRS Deputy Commissioner Bertrand Harding to relieve him of any personal involvement. Harding, together with Assistant Commissioner Donald Bacon, assumed responsibility for the case. More than eighteen months later, the case not only remained unresolved, it had not moved outside the Intelligence Division. A year after President Kennedy's assassination, Feldman was still talking about the case with the IRS, fearing the "possibility of a 'leak' prior to the first of the year." Harding reported that "we had been investigating for over two years and had no problem to date. On the other hand, there is always the possibility of information getting out in a matter as sensitive as this."[13]

The other large question was the use to which an administration might put the IRS to advance its own political objectives. During the 1962 steel crisis, for example, the *Wall Street Journal* as well as Roger Blough of U.S. Steel charged that the administration had used the IRS to initiate tax audits of leading steel officials. Although the president alluded to that possibility at a post-crisis celebratory dinner, both the administration and the IRS denied the charges. A more significant concern, and one that became a dominant theme during the next several years, was the issue of tax-exempt foundations. In early 1962 President Kennedy had written Treasury Secretary Dillon to advocate that the IRS investigate "charity balls in New York which have assumed great proportions and which I believe should be scrutinized." Kennedy then went beyond charity balls to suggest that the IRS also "look into the foundations. . . ." His concerns were not only to capture tax monies that should be going to the federal government, but to crack down on foundations' abuses of their tax exemptions. Mortimer Caplin agreed and asserted that the IRS had begun to investigate "a selected group of foundations." By January 1962 the tax-exempt foundation issue had become a major political concern for the White House.[14]

Central to that concern were the increased prominence and shrill voices of the right wing during the early 1960s, when Robert Welch and the John Birch Society led a growing chorus. Welch's charges that former President Eisenhower was a Communist, together with the expanded membership of the Birch Society, attracted attention from Republicans and Democrats alike. Even archconservatives like Barry Goldwater worried about the problem. Speaking before a joint Washington meeting of the Harvard, Yale, and Princeton clubs, Goldwater lamented that the "idiots are being drawn toward the conservative movement now just as they were attracted to liberalism in the 1930s." Its surging strength, particularly in the South and West, combined with what appeared to be a broader revival of conservatism, led to an increasingly bitter debate between those who found the John Birch Society repulsive and others who defended it as a patriotic organization formed to fight communism.[15]

The inauguration of a massive letter-writing campaign by the Birch Society to impeach Chief Justice Earl Warren provoked Attorney General Robert Kennedy to voice his "concern" about the Society and the expansion of the right wing in general. Publicly the attorney general insisted that the John Birch Society was "ridiculous" and urged Americans to pay little attention to it. Both *Newsweek* and the *Christian Century* ran several stories on the Society. In May 1961 *The Nation* warned that conservatives were trying to build a "movement." When the flamboyant activities of Army Major General Edwin A. Walker and other military officers to indoctrinate their troops with radical-right views led Secretary of Defense Robert McNamara to discipline Walker for violating an assortment of federal laws, the right wing rose to his defense. Attorney General Robert Kennedy assailed the right as a "tremendous danger" to the United States.[16]

During the closing years of the Eisenhower administration, in fact, the FBI had intensified its coverage of right-wing organizations. Although normally drawn to defend virtually all anti-Communist groups, between the late 1950s and 1963 Hoover's FBI tried to move beyond its own conservative bias and identify "rightist or extremist" groups. Between 1960 and 1963, FBI domestic intelligence operations increasingly targeted right-wing and extremist groups. In 1962 *The Nation* warned that these were not isolated extremists but represented "the wedding of fanatics with some of the largest corporations and the most powerful businessmen in the nation. . . . The Respectables have turned the Radicals from freaks into a force."[17]

President Kennedy also lashed out at the right wing. Not only had he received many death threats—thirty-four from people in the state of Texas alone—Kennedy worried that right-wing attacks threatened both his domestic and foreign policy agendas. In mid-November 1961 the president voiced his concern about the growing power of the right, especially groups like the John Birch Society and the Minutemen. Speaking at the hundredth anniversary of the University of Washington, Kennedy warned that the right lacked "confidence in our long-run capacity to survive and succeed. Hating communism, yet they see communism in the long run, perhaps, as the wave of the future. And they want some quick and easy and final and cheap solution—now." While some on the right sought war, others counseled appeasement. Kennedy, who had urged Americans to sacrifice in order to win the cold war, argued that his was the middle path and that the United States should "not negotiate freedom."[18]

Two days later in Los Angeles, Kennedy again attacked fringe groups as a threat to the American spirit in a time of trial. Impatience bred frustration, and frustration spawned simplistic solutions to complex issues. This tension, he argued, was too much for some: "the discordant voices of extremism are once again heard in the land." He warned that "Men who are unwilling to face up to the danger from without are convinced that the real danger is from within." They were suspicious and distrusted their neighbors or their leaders. Seeking instead a "man on horseback," they saw treason everywhere—in the churches, the courts, even in fluoridated water. The president urged listeners to reject these "counsels of fear and suspicion."[19]

The administration was not content with verbal warnings, however, and quickly moved to develop a full-scale plan to attack its right-wing critics. After some conversations with his brother about how to cope with those threats and the growing virulence of right-wing opposition, Robert Kennedy turned to Walter Reuther of the United Auto Workers and liberal attorney Joseph Rauh, Jr., asking them to formulate concrete suggestions for a counterattack. The ensuing memorandum, prepared by Victor and Walter Reuther, together with Rauh, formed the basis for a broad assault on the right wing by the Kennedy administration. It was the first step toward the utilization of the Internal Revenue Service in what became a covert effort to discredit the right and undercut its sources of support.[20]

Delivered on December 19, 1961, to Attorney General Robert Kennedy, the so-called Reuther Memorandum ("The Radical Right in America Today") was a twenty-four-page outline of "possible Administration policies and programs to combat the radical right." Noting that public discussion had produced few programmatic suggestions to deal with the problem, the memorandum warned that *"Speeches without action may well only mobilize the radical right instead of mobilizing the democratic forces within our nation."* Untold millions of Americans subscribed to the doctrine of the radical right, it asserted, ranging from Senator Barry Goldwater on the "left" to Robert Welch on the right. The activists were admittedly much fewer in number, but the "groups are probably stronger and are almost certainly better organized than at any time in recent history." They were well financed, and the memorandum briefly outlined the financial resources available to an array of right-wing organizations. Worthy of particular mention were not only the Birch Society but Fred Schwarz's Christian Anti-Communist Crusade, Billy James Hargis's Christian Crusade, Dr. George Benson's Harding College and National Education Program, and H. L. Hunt's Life Line Foundation. Their growth was likely to continue as cold war tensions and frustrations persisted. "They traffic in fear. Treason in high place is their slogan and slander is their weapon." There was "no question that anybody even slightly to the left of Senator Goldwater is suspect."[21] What was needed was a sweeping counterattack.

The Reuther Memorandum rejected the argument that the radical right was a problem only for the Republican party. It might be an "inconvenience" for the Republicans, but

> it is far worse than that for the Nation and the Democratic Party—for it threatens the President's program at home and abroad. By the use of the twin propaganda weapons of fear and slander, the radical right moves the national political spectrum away from the Administration's proposed liberal programs at home and abroad. By vicious local pressure campaigns against teachers or preachers or any one else who supports anything from negotiation in foreign affairs, to government programs in domestic affairs, they frighten off support for much-needed Administration programs. Pressure tactics on already-timid Congressmen are reinforced with fanaticism and funds.[22]

The question was: what could be done?

Insisting that the struggle against the right was a long-term problem (and by "right" it meant an array of groups to the right of center), the memorandum advocated "deliberate Administration policies and programs to contain the radical right from further expansion" and "to reduce it to its historic role of the impotent lunatic fringe." It also urged private groups and agencies—churches, labor, the press, television, civic and political organizations—to mobilize their resources in the battle, and outlined five actions that the administration should initiate. First, it needed to curb right-wing activities within the armed forces. This was an immediate problem that threatened the "basic American concept of separating military personnel from partisan politics." The attorney general's subversive list aided the radical right, the memorandum asserted, because it focused on the left and omitted the right. "The list today is almost like a Good Housekeeping seal for the radical right." To counter this, the memorandum's second recommendation called for placing several right-wing groups on the subversive list, since many of them clearly met the criteria by which liberal and Communist groups had been judged "subversive." It also urged the attorney general "to announce at this time that he is going to investigate one or more of these organizations with a view to determining whether charges will be filed and hearings held on the question of listing" them as subversive. The "mere act" of investigation would "certainly bring home to many people something they have never considered—the subversive character of these organizations." If it had not already done so, the memorandum recommended that the FBI plant informers inside the right as it had inside the left.[23]

The memorandum's third recommendation, and the one that particularly caught the Kennedys' attention, was to choke off the flow of money to the radical right by challenging groups' tax-exempt status. Arguing that "funds are a source of power to the radical right," Reuther cited several radical right groups—Dr. George Benson's National Education Program, Dr. Fred Schwarz's Christian Anti-Communist Crusade, Billy James Hargis's Christian Crusade, and the William Volker Fund—that enjoyed 501(c)(3) federal tax exemptions. "Prompt revocation in a few cases might scare off a substantial part of the big money now flowing into these tax exempt organizations." Other individuals, such as H. L. Hunt, openly encouraged corporations to use their advertising funds to help the right. The government should ban "certain propaganda ads." Concurrently the administration should use the Federal Communications Commission and the "fairness doctrine" to crack down on radio and television programs that masqueraded as public service programs, which gave right-wing groups free or reduced rates. The memorandum also raised doubts about whether the various right-wing organizations were correctly and legally reporting all their income. Could not the Internal Revenue Service be used to determine if they were complying with the tax laws? Could not the Treasury Department, together with the FBI, utilize undercover agents to probe possible tax violations? The necessary information could only come from "inside . . . these organizations," and the memorandum urged the IRS and the FBI to establish undercover operations if they had not already done so.[24]

The fourth recommendation advocated immediate measures against the Minutemen. Paramilitary guerrilla organizations went far beyond any constitutional mandates for free speech, and the Minutemen represented "a dangerous precedent in our democracy." Reuther suggested that state and federal laws be used to curtail or end their activities. Finally, the memorandum's fifth recommendation urged the administration to place the current domestic Communist problem in proper perspective. The radical right based its appeal largely on an assertion that communism was gaining strength and represented a serious threat of internal subversion. This was fallacious, and exposing this fallacy would undercut much of the right's appeal. That would be difficult, however, for politicians had focused on the threat of communism since the end of World War II, and FBI Director Hoover constantly exaggerated the domestic Communist menace. Although the Communist party might have been strong in the 1930s or 1940s, in the 1960s it had no capacity to threaten the country's internal security. Indeed, the memorandum concluded, the right wing was more of a threat. "It would be the easier course to look the other way and say that the radical right will disappear when we solve our problems at home and abroad. But the radical right may, if it is not contained, make it more difficult, if not impossible, to solve our problems at home and abroad."[25]

An appreciation of the broader issues outlined in the Reuther Memorandum is essential to understanding the administration's determination to exercise federal power and employ federal agencies to undercut the power of the right. Fear that the right wing might become powerful enough to shape the country's political agenda had initially impelled the president and the attorney general to invite Reuther to prepare this memorandum. Although its full contents remained secret for several years, the administration quickly began to implement many of its recommendations. Despite denials from Robert Kennedy's office that he had even read the Reuther Memorandum, and despite Robert Kennedy's assertion in 1964 that neither he nor the president considered the right wing anything more than amusing "pains in the butt," their activities argue otherwise. Indeed, even before Reuther gave the memorandum to the attorney general, the administration had begun to monitor the activities of right-wing organizations. White House staff member Lee White prepared a series of monthly confidential reports on their activities. FBI Director Hoover responded to White House concerns by intensifying FBI coverage of right-wing organizations (although he focused more on the Ku Klux Klan than on these political groups). The Army Intelligence Command at Fort Holabird, Maryland, included right-wing groups in its secret biographic data file. Later investigations revealed that this interest preceded the civil disturbances that led the Holabird system to be computerized. Shortly afterward the CONARC (Continental Army Command) computer system also listed groups on the "political right."[26]

The most far-reaching effort to undercut the power of the right wing, however, involved the Internal Revenue Service. It became known as the Ideological Organizations Project. In late 1961 the IRS launched a program to audit twenty-two "alleged extremist groups." Its purpose was that outlined in the Reuther Memorandum: to investigate whether particular political-action organizations were illegally claiming tax-exempt status or otherwise violating the tax laws. Although the courts had generally permitted some political activity by tax-exempt organizations, that activity was not supposed to be significant with respect to the organizations' purposes. The administration was clearly convinced that these right-wing groups were essentially political in nature, and it believed that virtually any political activity was sufficient to revoke their tax exemptions. But the *targeting* of these groups turned out to be clearly political rather than based on demonstrated tax problems. An internal IRS study obtained through the Freedom of Information Act admitted as much, noting that the "candidates for both the first and second phase were drawn from information received from Members of Congress, complaint letters from the public, publicity in the news media and information contained in the Service's file." The report omitted any reference to White House pressure or guidance, but, as we shall see, the White House was a driving force behind the Ideological Organizations Project. The public remained unaware of this political use of the IRS until more than a decade after the assassination of John Kennedy, when the hearings of the so-called Church Committee (officially the Senate Select Committee on Intelligence Activities) in the mid-1970s revealed the existence of the program and the outlines of its operation.[27]

During the early 1960s the IRS concealed the audit program directed against political activists behind a broader, less political, examination of tax-exempt organizations and foundations. That larger effort stemmed from the insistence of Texas Congressman Wright Patman that tax-exempt foundations gained an unfair competitive advantage in the marketplace. The IRS responded by examining more than 530 foundations named by Patman. Although a later section of this book will examine Patman's efforts in more detail, it is important to note his efforts here briefly for two reasons. In addition to the coincidence of timing that gave the IRS public "cover" for the Ideological Organizations Project, the IRS compartmentalized the projects so as to keep Patman in the dark about its efforts to scrutinize activist organizations. To do so it vigorously fought Patman's demand that it release to him the names of specific individuals involved in some IRS rulings. "Not only would this affect the quality and correctness of our rulings and possibly bring about criticism of the Service," the Exempt Organizations Branch argued, "it would in effect deny taxpayers and organizations their right to a free and impartial judgment of their cases." The White House backed the IRS position. The veil of secrecy was important to both parties.[28]

It is time to lift this veil, to demonstrate how a presumably independent agency like the IRS became politically responsive through a combination of White House pressure and its own desire. The potential for political use of the tax agency certainly did not arise during the Senate confirmation hearings of IRS Commissioner Caplin. They were a virtual love feast. The questioning of Caplin was neither serious nor detailed, and certainly did not explore how the IRS had been or might be used politically. Years later, in his oral history, Caplin insisted that Kennedy pursued a hands-off policy toward the IRS. Conceding that both he and Treasury Under Secretary Henry Fowler were "very sensitive politically," Caplin maintained that while presidential aide Ted Sorensen might call at times on sensitive issues, the president never asked for "favors or anything of the sort." Almost as an afterthought, Caplin acknowledged that Kennedy did inquire about right-wing groups; but he insisted that any ensuing IRS investigation was politically neutral and conducted within the regular organization rather than through a special task force—the strategy that resulted in enormous problems for the IRS during the Nixon administration. More than thirty years after his service as IRS commissioner, in a letter to the *New York Times*, Caplin repeated his assertion that both John and Robert Kennedy "always demonstrated respect for the impartiality and integrity of the agency. We had no enemies list. Tax returns were selected for examination . . . based upon established tax criteria." He rested his defense by noting that the Joint Committee on Taxation found no evidence that either the president or the attorney general "supplied names of organizations to be audited."[29]

A closer look at the Ideological Organizations Project, however, demonstrates the interplay of forces between the White House, the attorney general, and the IRS that sought to exercise federal power and respond to political concerns.

CHAPTER TWO

THE IDEOLOGICAL ORGANIZATIONS PROJECT

THE IDEOLOGICAL ORGANIZATIONS PROJECT (IOP), launched in secret during the late fall of 1961, revealed the complex interplay between politics and taxes. Its specific origin is difficult to pin down, but in essence it sprang from three impulses. President Kennedy's speeches against the right wing that October alerted both the administration and the IRS to his concerns. The Reuther Memorandum in December highlighted several possible avenues of attack. Meanwhile the IRS, sensitive to the political winds, initiated its own actions in response to the president's remarks. By 1962 these three initiatives had merged to form the IOP. Piecing together the background and history of the Ideological Organizations Project reveals continuing political relationships between the IRS and the White House as well as the uncertainty of the IRS as it ventured into politically and ideologically charged territory. It also highlights both a major development in postwar American culture—the explosion of tax-exempt organizations—and how ill-suited existing IRS policy was to evaluate these organizations. Finally, it raises serious questions about the suitability or advisability of the IRS to respond to nontax-related concerns by means of tax enforcement.

On November 16, 1961, John Seigenthaler, assistant to Attorney General Robert Kennedy, called Mitchell Rogovin, assistant to IRS Commissioner Mortimer Caplin, to inquire about the tax-exempt status of four or five right-wing organizations. Seigenthaler later disputed the exact date but admitted that he had had several telephone conversations with Rogovin between November 13 and December 1 on tax issues.

Two weeks later, in a November 29 press conference, President Kennedy once again raised the issue of tax exemption with respect to right-wing groups. Questioned about his West Coast speeches, the president admitted that the federal government could not interfere with the activities of such groups so "long as they meet the requirements of the tax laws. I'm sure," he said, that "the Internal Revenue Service examines that." If it didn't, it soon would.

The very next day, November 30, Assistant IRS Commissioner (Compliance) William Loeb wrote a memorandum to the director of the IRS Audit Division, Dean Barron. Attaching a clipping of the president's remarks, Loeb warned, "I think it behooves us to be certain that we know whether the organizations are complying with the tax laws as a matter of fact." He had already asked Rogovin to supply a list of names to be used for a sample check. Now he instructed Barron to contact Rogovin so that "appropriate audits may be made." On December 20, Barron received a list of eighteen organizations from Rogovin, largely drawn from articles in the December 4 and 8 issues of *Time* and *Newsweek*. With that act of self-protection, the IRS initiated the Ideological Organizations Project under the watchful guidance of Mitchell Rogovin. As IRS Commissioner Mortimer Caplin later recalled: "I assigned Mitch to keep his eye on that whole program. There are a lot of papers in the IRS with his fingerprints all over them on this issue."[1]

At the time there were few meaningful statutes limiting the authority of the Internal Revenue Service to gather this sort of intelligence and provide it either to the president or to members of his administration. Later, during the Nixon administration, similar IRS actions led to the creation of the Special Service Staff (SSS) and well-publicized attempts by the White House to use the IRS for overtly political purposes. But in the early 1960s Americans still retained a basic confidence and trust in their government. The existence of a covert effort like the Ideological Organizations Project would not have occurred to most people, even though the IRS later planned to expand dramatically its initial list of eighteen right-wing organizations. At the time this was a closely held secret. Even presidential adviser Arthur Schlesinger, Jr., apparently remained unaware of the existence of the IOP as late as June 1963.[2] Once under way, the Ideological Organizations Project quickly became integrated into the normal bureaucratic structure of the IRS.

By January 1962 a nineteenth organization had been added—the left-wing Fair Play for Cuba Committee (FPCC). Since the CIA and the FBI were already pursuing the FPCC, this was a safe selection. It also demonstrated the firmly established interagency intelligence linkages at the federal level. Mitchell Rogovin's career gave further evidence of these intelligence ties. Rogovin had worked with the CIA since joining the IRS in the late 1950s, a liaison he maintained while serving as an assistant to his cousin Mortimer Caplin, the IRS commissioner. The FPCC, a pro-Castro organization later associated with Lee Harvey Oswald, had drawn the attention of the CIA ever since its formation in 1960. Indeed, in violation of its charter the CIA had launched a domestic counterintelligence operation against it under the direction of James McCord. Although the CIA apparently terminated its interest in the FPCC in 1961, the FBI quickly stepped in to launch its own intelligence operation through disinformation and break-ins. With the addition of the FPCC to the IOP list in early 1962, the IRS also moved into the picture. Audits began almost immediately on some of these organizations and related individuals. By January 1962 the IRS had also requested tax audits of six large corporate taxpayers in New York and San Francisco as well as of three right-wing groups in the San Francisco area. This effort soon spread to other regions.[3]

Despite the cover of tax audits, the IRS was certainly aware that ideology and political activities rather than tax liabilities had singled out these organizations as targets. In fact, by 1961 the IRS rarely audited such groups because the examinations were difficult to complete, very time consuming, and rarely produced much additional tax revenue. In a summary memorandum for White House aide Myer Feldman, Mitchell Rogovin observed that the audit program defined "ideological organization" as one "seeking to 'educate' the public in currently controversial fields. More specifically," he noted, "in addition to gathering and disseminating information they appear to direct their efforts toward influencing the beliefs or actions of others with reference to certain predetermined governmental, social or economic ends." Another key factor determining the selection of groups to be audited was "their use of mass media to 'educate the public' with reference to certain governmental, social or economic concepts, activities, or ideologies." The IRS assumed, moreover, "that the ideological activities of many of the organizations under study were not appropriate for exempt organizations. . . ." More than thirty years later the IRS remained sensitive to this targeting, redacting the words "mass media" from documents provided through the Freedom of Information Act.[4]

By March 1962 the IRS had substituted the words "political action organizations" for "right-wing organizations" to "avoid giving the impression that the Service is giving special attention to returns filed by taxpayers or organizations with a particular political ideology." This was only a cover, however, and Rogovin "offered to furnish the names of other political action organizations in the future."[5] Even official IRS reports avoided any mention of the IOP. Its Manual Supplement on "Programs and Objectives" for fiscal year 1962, for example, omitted any reference to the IOP, stating instead that overall IRS objectives would be shifted from "enforcement production to the achievement of maximum voluntary compliance."

Only later, in a September 1962 press release, did the IRS allude to an enforcement drive in the exempt organizations area. Even then, it noted only a generalized commitment to expanded audit coverage of exempt organizations, indicating that the IRS planned to examine "all types of exempt organizations, including foundations." To support this effort, Commissioner Caplin established a special advisory group of outside professionals to help identify issues in this area. By the late spring of 1962 the outline of an expanded audit program was referred to field offices for comment. None of this, however, had anything to do with the IOP; indeed, this broader effort in effect provided cover for the examination of "political" organizations.[6]

IRS plans for the examination of ideological organizations called for the investigation of both exempt and nonexempt groups. Despite the addition of some left-wing groups for "balance," the IRS clearly intended to target the right. Commissioner Caplin wrote Under Secretary of the Treasury Henry Fowler:

> The activities of so-called extremist right-wing political action organizations have recently been given a great amount of publicity by magazines, newspapers and television programs. This publicity, however, has made little mention of the tax status of these organizations or their supporters. Nevertheless, the alleged activities of these groups are such that we plan to determine the extent of their compliance with Federal tax laws. In addition, we propose to ascertain whether contributors to these organizations are deducting their contributions from taxable income.

Caplin further revealed that the IRS was essentially targeting these groups because of their political ideology and activities. "Inasmuch as we are not certain any of these organizations or their benefactors are failing to comply with the tax laws," he admitted to Fowler, "we believe it prudent to avoid any possible charges that the Service is giving special attention to a group with a particular ideology. In furtherance of this goal, we are planning to examine the returns of a representative group of alleged left-wing organizations."[7]

This was supposed to be a test study for the IRS, to determine the procedures and difficulties of auditing political-action organizations. But it was more than that, as the targeting indicated. A March 9, 1962, memo to Compliance listed the groups to be pursued first and the IRS district offices responsible for each effort: the National Indignation Convention, Dallas District; the Conservative Society of America, New Orleans District; Americans for Constitutional Government, Austin District; the John Birch Society and Robert Welch, Inc., Boston District; the Life Line Foundation, Dallas District; the National Education Program of Harding College, Little Rock District; and The Conservatives, Aberdeen District. The IRS presumed these to be "the largest and most publicized extremist groups." The memo also noted that magazine articles had extensively covered the financial activities of the Christian Anti-Communist Crusade. Both the Birch Society and Robert Welch, Inc., moreover, had been examined for 1960, but the IRS had been unable to uncover significant problems. They were included for 1961 "because of the widespread interest in the activities of these organizations and because of the allegations made with respect to the large amount of funds received as dues payments in 1961."[8]

Quite apart from the ideological targeting, there were genuine problems with some of these groups. A letter from Robert Welch of the John Birch Society to the head of one foundation illustrates the way some nonexempt organizations were instructing donors on ruses to permit them to claim tax exemptions for their donations. In response to a query, Welch wrote: "to refresh your mind about tax exemption possibilities, I would feel that I was falling short of my responsibility to the cause if I didn't do so." The plan, in brief, was for donors to contribute funds to an exempt organization, the American Council of Christian Laymen of Madison, Wisconsin. The Birch Society had a "long-standing arrangement" with that group, so that 90 percent of the money would "come back to us with instructions from them to spend it, in whatever way seems best to us, in carrying out the purposes of their own charter and organization."

Welch noted that the Birch Society had developed "quite a number of such connections, as one category of sources for the financing of this operation." He cited Dr. Carl McIntire's Twentieth Century Reformation Hour (on radio) as one of the "best such connections." Billy James Hargis was another with whom Welch worked. Welch also used these other groups as conduits through which to mail Birch Society literature without cost, or even at a profit. These groups purchased the literature from Welch, then mailed it along with their own literature and secured large numbers of voluntary contributions from the recipients, contributions that more than covered their costs for the brochures, inserts, and mailings. Citing the example of one such endeavor, Welch wrote:

> The brochures, with their inserts, will be used the same as before. Checks to make up the funds for this purpose can be made out either to Bible Presbyterian Church, which automatically has tax exemption because of being a well-established part of their service; or they can be made out to CHRISTIAN BEACON, which is the name of the organization that publishes Dr. McIntire's paper and also distributes literature for him, and CHRISTIAN BEACON having had the tax deductibility status for many years, is so listed in the Cumulative Index of the Treasury Department. About half the checks which come to us for this purpose are made out to Bible Presbyterian Church, and about half of them to CHRISTIAN BEACON.

Welch's only complaint about this process was that McIntire insisted on purchasing Birch Society publications at the lowest possible wholesale price, thereby cutting into the Society's profits. A more profitable scheme, he noted, came from an arrangement with Freedom Clubs, Inc., of Los Angeles, a tax-exempt organization. Welch concluded by asking that the letter be kept confidential, though he asserted that everything about these activities was "proper, ethical, and legal."[9]

Welch's scheme underscored one of the problems for the Internal Revenue Service. While there was a definite need to examine the conduct of tax-exempt organizations, the targeting of these groups according to their political activities and ideology violated IRS policy and risked public exposure. Exposure would further politicize the IRS, trigger public condemnation, and increase partisan sniping. The duality so evident here would haunt the IRS for decades to come. Indeed, there is little evidence that it has yet run its course.

In May, IRS Commissioner Caplin sent a list of organizations that the agency was auditing to Attorney General Robert Kennedy. By then the IOP audit program embraced twelve right-wing organizations and ten left-wing groups, some exempt and others nonexempt. From the right wing the IRS had selected for audit the National Indignation Convention, the Conservative Society of America, Americans for Constitutional Government (though a handwritten note indicated that the IRS had found it to be "defunct"), the John Birch Society, Robert Welch, Inc., the Christian Crusaders (another handwritten note said "Mistake: should have been Billy Hargis' 'Christian Crusade' "), the All American Society, the Christian Anti-Communist Crusade (revocation already recommended), the Life Line Foundation (revocation already recommended), the National Education Program of Harding College, The Conservatives, and the Christian Echoes Ministry of Sapulpa, Oklahoma. The letter also indicated that the IRS had recommended revocation of the tax exemption for Edgar Bundy's Church League of America.[10]

The balanced audit program that Rogovin had been so concerned about had also produced a list of left-wing groups, drawn chiefly from FBI files because none had received sufficient publicity to come to the attention of the IRS. They included the Fair Play for Cuba Committee, the American Veterans Committee, the League for Labor Palestine (handwritten note indicates "defunct"), the Anti-Defamation League of B'nai B'rith, the Bressler Foundation, the Common Council for American Unity, the Zionist Organization of America, the Kenderland Colony Association, the League for Industrial Democracy, and the Gilbert Freeman Charitable Foundation.[11]

Yet even as the IRS pursued its test audit program of so-called extremist organizations, it felt other political pressures. Not only were there constant demands from Congressman Wright Patman's subcommittee (as a subsequent chapter will detail), other politicians and agencies sought favors. Arkansas Senator J. William Fulbright queried the IRS about the tax status of several groups—the Birch Society, the Conservative League of America, the Manion Forum, and the National Education Program—all of which were conservative. Fulbright was specifically concerned about requests for tax exemption and was told that only the National Education Program was tax exempt. Virginia Senator Harry Byrd pressured the IRS to investigate the NAACP for illegal political activities, which the IRS resisted to Byrd's dismay. The IRS also investigated church groups, following distribution of anti-Catholic literature by the National Association of Evangelicals, but dropped the investigation without any prosecutions, concluding that it could not restrict political activity by some tax-exempt organizations and not others. Carmine Bellino, special consultant to the president, called to inquire about his sister's tax returns. The IRS in this instance responded promptly. Finally, the FBI asked the IRS to audit returns of various groups and individuals "to disrupt their activities." The Network FBI office was particularly interested in the Socialist Workers party for "internal security" reasons.[12]

All of these instances—and there were undoubtedly more—reflected demands for political responsiveness and revealed the dangers of inaction as well as action. What was the IRS to do? Clearly the safest political course was to be as responsive as possible, and the agency generally adopted that approach. In the hands of certain public officials the information contained in tax returns made them valuable tools in the pursuit of nontax-related investigations and even for political purposes. Only belatedly did the implications of these activities appear to have troubled IRS Commissioner Caplin. When Carmine Bellino had requested permission to examine IRS files eighteen months earlier, Caplin had granted his request even though he had no written authorization from the president. The mere presumption that he was acting on orders from the president seemed sufficient. In late 1962, however, Caplin asked the IRS chief counsel for a legal opinion about his "authority to disclose information to the President of the United States." Crane Houser, the chief counsel, replied that Caplin's authority was "unrestricted." Since the executive power was constitutionally vested in the president, he was "entitled to his control over the executive branch."[13] Caplin's earlier presumption about Bellino apparently remained intact. The audit program moved forward.

In early February 1963, Assistant Commissioner (Compliance) Donald Bacon reported to Caplin the results of several IRS test audits conducted as part of the IOP. Although the IRS had added the Fund for Social Analysis to the initial list of left-wing organizations, Bacon's report revealed that almost 75 percent of the audits completed were of right-wing groups. Nine had been audited, and the agency recommended revocation of tax exemptions for two, the Life Line Foundation and the Christian Anti-Communist Crusade. Meanwhile the IRS had audited only four of the left-wing groups, making no recommendations for exemption changes. Although a parallel investigation "found no evidence that taxpayers are claiming deductions for contributions to nonexempt political action organizations," the IRS continued to pursue this question. Bacon concluded that the still incomplete test program was a success and recommended that it concentrate on exempt organizations. Later, after all the test groups had been audited, the IRS planned to "determine the need for increasing audit activity of political action organizations" under an "accelerated exempt organization enforcement program."[14]

By late May the IRS had almost completed its test audit program, and Caplin forwarded Bacon's February conclusions to his superiors in Treasury. Reviewed by at least six other IRS officials, this memorandum reported that these audits differed significantly from the usual IRS audit activity. Not only did they need to be more comprehensive, "to determine if a substantial part of [an organization's] activities is the carrying on of propaganda," but IRS agents needed to examine the "operations and publications" as well as the financial records of these groups. In short, as the demands on agents moved beyond financial accounting, IRS field offices could not really handle this type of audit program.[15]

Caplin provided detailed Internal Revenue assessments for each of the audited groups. One of the two recommended for revocation, the Life Line Foundation, had run into problems with the IRS because "approximately 50 percent" of its publications were "in the nature of propaganda. These releases discussed only one side of an issue and were not consistent with the purposes of an exempt educational organization." Caplin's report was more detailed for the other group recommended for revocation, the Christian Anti-Communist Crusade. Unlike the recommendation on the Life Line Foundation, this one dealt almost entirely with the financial transactions of the organization. The IRS cited numerous instances in which the organization's director, Dr. Fred Schwarz, and his wife had used the Crusade for personal financial gain or to avoid tax liabilities.[16]

None of the other right-wing organizations drew IRS criticism in this memo. Among the left-wing groups that were audited, the American Veterans Committee and the Fair Play for Cuba Committee were apparently examined most closely. In neither case did the IRS find irregularities. In the latter case it found that all donations were in small amounts from individuals, with the exception of one donation from the Cuban government, but failed to discover any noncompliance with the tax laws. Indeed, perhaps the most revealing feature of these other audits, either for right-wing or left-wing organizations, was that the Internal Revenue Service knew very little about the groups on its tax-exempt list. In some instances it was not even aware that particular organizations no longer existed.[17]

Caplin sent a similar confidential report to White House aide Myer Feldman on July 11, 1963, a week after Feldman had requested an update on IRS activities involving "extremist groups." By summer, nine of the ten left-wing groups had been audited, with only one of them (the Zionist Organization of America) requiring further study. Caplin noted that the IRS was troubled by the amount of time consumed by these audits. Not only did they need to be comprehensive, with agents examining materials such as publications or speeches that they were ill-equipped to judge, but organizations could legally resist IRS conclusions through various avenues of appeal. Caplin cited the Church League of America as an example. The IRS audit of the Church League actually predated establishment of the IOP, beginning in 1958, yet the organization remained tax exempt because of the appeals process. A letter from Myers Lowman of the Circuit Riders, following a 1965 IRS audit that proposed to revoke that group's tax exemption, further revealed the agency's difficulties. "No tax deductible political action cause group," Lowman wrote supporters, "will stay out of investigation in and out of court procedure if we are discriminated against." Caplin observed that some legislative changes might be necessary to clarify and limit the political actions of exempt organizations as well as eliminate some deductions to extremist causes. There was also congressional interest. On the Senate floor, Democratic senators Maurine Neuberger of Oregon and Joseph Clark of Pennsylvania attacked the misuse of tax exemptions by the right wing, and at least two congressional committees held hearings on exempt organizations' political activities.[18]

The White House was delighted with the results. This detailed review of these organizations' financial and written records promised to meet the objectives outlined in the Reuther Memorandum and fulfill hopes the president had articulated in his speeches and press conferences. President Kennedy called Caplin on July 23, 1963, urging him to go ahead with an "aggressive program—on both sides of center," and indicated that Democratic Senator Ralph Yarborough of Texas had scheduled hearings on the problem for January 19, 1964. Three days later an IRS task force on "political organizations" launched a second phase of the IOP, and three days after that, on July 29, Caplin met with Feldman at the White House to review the audit program. Although investigations later found no evidence linking either the White House or the attorney general to requests that specific organizations be audited, they did reveal that at least one member of the White House staff had reviewed the proposed targets for the second-phase program and recommended the deletion of two organizations. This second phase, which projected an expansion of the Ideological Organizations Project to ten thousand organizations, ran from late 1963 until 1966 or 1967, encompassing both the remainder of John Kennedy's presidency and much of Lyndon Johnson's tenure in the White House.[19]

Despite IRS hopes, the plan to audit ten thousand organizations never came to fruition. Instead the agency selected twenty-four groups for audit in the second phase of the Ideological Organizations Project. While headlines in papers like the *Newark Star-Ledger* screamed that "Taxpayers Subsidize Political Propaganda," the IRS task force conducting the second-phase audit program began by examining right-wing groups and absorbed the first-phase cases into the new effort. The list was drawn from IRS files as well as from publications of Group Research, a labor organization that served as a watchdog of right-wing groups. According to Frank Chapper, technical adviser to the director of the Tax Rulings Division, the criteria for selecting an organization for audit included "whether the organization was trying to influence the legislative process, and also the publicity the organization was getting." Rogovin warned agents that this was not a drive against tax-exempt organizations but "an honest attempt to come to grips with a very complex problem—and to enforce the law." He instructed them to "go up the middle" and examine both extremes. The objective was to be sure "that tax-exempt money is not being used for political purposes." Most IRS employees working on the project apparently knew nothing about the White House interest in their efforts.[20]

But that interest was ever present, and this looked like all-out war on the right wing. On July 29 and August 21, after the task force had compiled a list of organizations with "probable cause" for IRS examination, Rogovin met with Myer Feldman at the White House to review the new program. Feldman made available to Rogovin an extensive confidential memorandum on both exempt and nonexempt right-wing groups that he had drawn up for President Kennedy. He also suggested that the IRS delete the Daughters of the American Revolution and the Zionist Organization of America from the project. Feldman requested IRS materials on the second-phase organizations for a meeting the following week with Robert Kennedy, Commissioner Caplin, Rogovin, and the chairman of the Federal Communications Commission. Finally, Feldman asked that the second phase be completed by October 1. Rogovin said they would try, but he frankly doubted that the IRS could finish its audits by then. In a final request, Feldman asked that the IRS "not take any action regarding these organizations, but merely hold the information in abeyance." This puzzled Rogovin, though he did not respond. Did the White House have some larger political purpose in mind?[21]

On August 20, Rogovin met with Attorney General Robert Kennedy to brief him on the new program. Kennedy requested an expedited audit on one right-wing group (the Life Line Foundation) at that time, and Rogovin promised to complete the case within six weeks. Kennedy also suggested that Rogovin contact Louis Oberdorfer of the Justice Department so that it "could properly defend any action growing out of our revocations," and asked to be kept "personally advised" of his progress.[22]

Assistant Commissioner (Compliance) Donald Bacon issued guidelines for the new program to all IRS regional commissioners. Noting that the earlier test audit had revealed a "serious lack of sufficient information" on whether or not these organizations were compliant with federal tax laws, Bacon outlined the second-phase effort. The IRS National Office tried to direct its regional and district offices carefully, and asked that they forward all materials collected to headquarters for evaluation. Bacon warned:

> In undertaking this difficult project, we are mindful of the competing political philosophies expressed by many of these organizations. Nevertheless our program has but one standard—an even handed administration of the existing law. We must make it clear that any personal preference or bias by any Service employee has no place in tax examinations. Anything short of this would be the creation of a double standard, inimicable [sic] to the administrative process.[23]

Bacon provided one example of what was needed, with respect to the auditing of the Christian Freedom Foundation. The investigation should focus on the "published and broadcast materials or substantial expenditures" that might "promote particular political, economic or sociological philosophies." Agents were to obtain "*all* promotional literature circulated" as well as publications, contributors, conferences, and correspondence.[24]

A late-August memorandum from Mitchell Rogovin to the regional IRS commissioners further highlighted the difficulty and time-consuming nature of the Ideological Organizations Project, as well as the IRS's intent. The examinations, Rogovin noted, "require reorientation of the agent's thinking and place him into areas fraught with interpretative difficulties." Agents had to collect and analyze books, pamphlets, telecasts, broadcasts, and speeches distributed by the organizations and its members. Because of that, the "true purpose of the test audit program was not satisfactorily completed, *i.e.*, a detailed analysis of the actual activities of the organizations." Rogovin noted that hereafter field agents were to gather facts and materials, then submit them to the National Office. There a small group of individuals would evaluate that evidence, make recommendations concerning the group's tax status, and submit a technical advice memorandum to agents in the field.[25]

This centralization of review attempted to make the effort more efficient and at the same time allowed the National Office to respond to political considerations or White House influence. It also reflected an appreciation of the difficulties and dangers facing the IRS as it conducted these audits. While ostensibly focusing on tax-related matters, the IRS was moving into the realm of political ideologies and philosophies, something for which it was unprepared. One purpose of the annual IRS regional commissioners' conference in 1963 was to discuss these difficulties. Rogovin also admitted that the IRS would actually lose money in this venture, estimating that the losses would amount to "$175,000 for every man year spent on such examinations, as opposed to 'otherwise productive' income tax audits."[26]

In early September, Rogovin forwarded a list of 109 organizations to Commissioner Caplin, from which the 24 to be audited immediately had been drawn. Because these groups were "engaged in more pronounced activities of a 'political' nature—a 'probable cause standard' was developed." He also included a shorter list of 20 organizations that had applications pending for tax exemption. The purpose of this second list was not clear, but these groups apparently were potential targets for the Ideological Organizations Project. The next day Rogovin submitted much the same list to the director of the IRS Collection Division and asked that he be notified of any "request to inspect or disclose" information on any listed organization.[27]

The assassination of President Kennedy in November 1963 caused no delay in the IRS program. By December field agents had completed investigative reports on nineteen of the twenty-four organizations and sent the results to headquarters. Within two months the National Office had analyzed eighteen of them. Although this was a covert operation, rumors of its existence had provoked some congressional inquiries. Arkansas Senator Wilbur Mills, for instance, had found out about the investigations of the National Education Program, Harding College, and Dr. George Benson in his home state. Mills asked the IRS to keep him abreast of the review, and the IRS promised to do so. A few supporters of the organizations under investigation also discovered the IOP's existence and protested. A follower of Carl McIntire wrote Delaware Republican Senator John Williams, a longtime critic of the IRS, demanding that he "stop this coercion of free men before it is too late." This crusade against the right, he argued, represented "outright subversion and collusion between evil and Socialistic forces in the U.S.A. and the IRS today."[28]

An early-December IRS staff meeting was devoted entirely to a discussion of the Ideological Organizations Project, under the title of "Political Action Survey." Those in attendance saw a need to move quickly. Stanley Surrey of Treasury suggested the need for legislation to deal with the problem of organizations furthering their political views with tax-free dollars. Rogovin indicated that "intense interest" in the issue "existed on the Hill" but claimed that the IRS suffered from a shortage of space and manpower to move very quickly. It needed equipment— movie projectors, tape recorders, slide projectors, and record players—

before it could examine some of the material obtained during the field audits. The biggest dilemma, however, was that the IRS had no sense of what the Treasury Department considered the appropriate basis for allowable deductions to so-called political-action organizations.

In the attempt to establish a framework for evaluating whether a group's political or ideological activities were at odds with the tax code's charitable or educational purposes, Rogovin outlined a profile of what such an organization might look like. The salient characteristics included the use of a single spokesman, use of the mass media, a broad dissemination of information, efforts to mold public opinion rather than mere education, a concern with current issues, and an intent to be educational or religious. These factors might serve, he noted, as the basis for future legislation. For now they provided some guidelines, but the problem remained that "current regulations were designed to let these ideological outfits in under the tax exemption tent unless they were clearly 'action' groups." IRS staff agreed that their best hope was to complete a few audits quickly on those organizations where the issues seemed relatively clear-cut, then use these cases as the basis for legislation by early 1964. Under Secretary of the Treasury Henry Fowler warned that "a very difficult question of civil liberties was involved here and that the policy questions here covered a good deal more than the tax issues." He concluded that a tough audit policy might force these organizations to modify their activities so as to qualify for continued tax exemptions.[29]

A month later, on January 4, 1964, another meeting on the IOP was held in the main Treasury building. At this time, searching for criteria by which to evaluate exempt organizations, the staff discussed a proposal to judge all exempt groups according to their educational methods. Perhaps revealing their wariness of ideological determinations, they spent considerable time arguing whether exemption should be determined by an organization's methods or by its purpose. In the course of a far-ranging discussion, IRS and Treasury staff discovered to their surprise that agency regulations did not define "religious." This was a problem, particularly when one moved beyond major church groups. Also problematic was the issue of organizations that engaged in personal or group attacks, often under the cover of patriotism or anticommunism. Not only did personal biases threaten to influence the decision-making process, the IRS had to negotiate the treacherous waters of censorship. Specifically citing the example of CORE (the Congress of Racial Equality), the staff wondered if "charity" included the use of physical or economic coercion, such as picketing or boycotts. Treasury official Stanley Surrey revealed that the IRS had "never before explored the problem whether the use of a particular method of operation could disqualify an organization" and asked for further discussion at a future meeting. Before adjourning, staff members agreed to circulate a proposed draft of an amendment to IRS regulations and to have the IRS analyze the twenty-four cases then under audit to indicate the "approaches we will take in applying present rules to problems presented." Treasury Department officials said they would not welcome new regulations until the current educational regulations had been judicially tested. In short, the IRS had uncovered a host of new problems but resolved nothing.[30]

Momentum begot momentum, and the Ideological Organizations Project continued without objection from Kennedy's successor, Lyndon Johnson. Mitchell Rogovin served as the IRS–White House contact during these years. In the White House, Myer Feldman continued his investigation of the right wing. On March 23, 1964, Rogovin sent a status report on the second phase of the IOP to Feldman, describing what had been done and the procedures used. Although Feldman told the Joint Committee on Internal Revenue Taxation in 1974 that the Johnson administration expressed no further interest in the project, the Joint Committee found that additional reports were given to various Treasury officials on August 17, September 30, and December 24, 1964, and February 8 and March 8, 1965.[31]

In an August 17 memo to Treasury, Acting IRS Commissioner Donald Bacon characterized the groups under scrutiny and noted that nineteen of the twenty-four were conservative, with twelve comprising "the anti-communist complex or radical right as it is sometimes known." He admitted that this group, which he also labeled the "ultras," was distinct from other right-wing organizations. It was characterized by opposition to "foreign aid, Supreme Court, National Council of Churches, United Nations and the Federal government." The "ultras" considered all of these to be part of an international Communist conspiracy. The IRS list of "ultras" included the American Council of Christian Laymen, America's Future Inc., the Cardinal Mindszenty Foundation, the Christian Beacon, the Christian Anti-Communist Crusade, the Christian Echoes Ministry, the Church League of America, the Circuit Riders, the Four Freedoms Study Group, the Life Line Foundation, the National Education Program, and the National Society of the Daughters of the American Revolution. The second listing of right-wing organizations, which the IRS characterized in terms of their opposition to "labor unions, government regulation of business, unbalanced budget, Keynesian economics, progressive taxation and support of states' rights, right to work laws, free market economy and 'libertarianism,' " included the American Economic Foundation, the American Enterprise Institute for Public Policy Research, the American Good Government Society, the Christian Freedom Foundation, the Foundation for Economic Education, the Freedoms Foundation at Valley Forge, and the Intercollegiate Society of Individualists.[32]

Bacon's other two categories were much smaller. Under left-wing groups he included only the League for Industrial Democracy. The rest, listed as "unclassified," included the American Council for Nationalities Service, the Council on Foreign Relations, the Oxford Group (Moral Rearmament), and Protestants and Other Americans United for Separation of Church and State. Only the information for the Christian Beacon and the Daughters of the American Revolution was incomplete. The "ultras" appeared to "provide the strongest case for revocation," but the IRS task force had recommended revocation for "several other organizations because of lobbying activity." Those revocations, however, were awaiting "the developments of the Hargis file." This was "more or less a test case in this study" because it contained "all the legal and factual elements necessary for a judicial affirmation of our position." IRS "success in the whole political action area, without recourse to new legislation or regulations, will be measured by this case." The agency hoped to proceed by the end of August.[33]

By the fall of 1964 the second-phase audit program was rolling along. A twenty-fifth organization—the National Council for Civic Responsibility of the Public Affairs Institute—was added to the study during that fall's presidential campaign. The group had taken out newspaper ads and sought deductible contributions for anti-extremist radio broadcasts. Although the organization remained under investigation into 1965, the IRS had concluded that it was a covert operation of the Democratic National Committee, clearly designed for electoral purposes. That fall the IOP also received its first public notice when Congressman Wright Patman's Foundation Subcommittee obtained information on the audit work done to date. The IRS at first refused to release a list of the groups under review, but changed its mind by the end of October.[34]

A late-September memorandum to Treasury Secretary Douglas Dillon further updated the status of the IOP audit program. Five case analyses remained incomplete, but the IRS hoped to have them finished by mid-October. At least three of them had the potential for revocation. The agency recommended no exemption changes for nine of the groups, although that conclusion would be reviewed in the Tax Rulings Division. It recommended revocation for the other ten organizations. Legal reviews of five of them posed "substantive problems," however, and those reviews were continuing. All were expected to be completed by the end of the year, with an exemption denial to be issued within thirty days if the review supported revocation. These groups included Protestants and Other Americans United for the Separation of Church and State, America's Future Inc., the Cardinal Mindszenty Foundation, the Christian Anti-Communist Crusade, and the Foundation for Economic Education. Final legal reviews had concurred in revocation for the Christian Echoes Ministry, the Life Line Foundation, the American Enterprise Institute for Public Policy Research, and the Church League of America. The Circuit Riders had already been notified that the IRS contemplated denial of its tax exemption.[35]

All of this contradicted what the IRS told Texas Democrat Wright Patman when it provided him with the list of groups under study. In that letter the IRS cast the Ideological Organizations Project as an experimental study of exempt organizations' problems. Use of mass media was a common denominator for all of them, the IRS admitted, but it also claimed that the selection rested on the organizations' espousal of "diverse ideologies and objectives" as well as their pursuit of "diverse methods and activities." This had the ring of truth. What rang false, however, was the IRS claim that it was "highly unlikely that the exempt status of all or perhaps even a majority will be affected by our study." It also asserted that organizations with "extreme or controversial ideologies" were not the sole target of the study, though some of those were included. The IRS warned Patman that public disclosure of those organizations "at this stage of our inquiry" would be prejudicial to the groups involved. Later, when a list of some of these groups appeared in the *New York World-Telegram and Sun*, the IRS suspected that Patman had leaked the information but could not prove it.[36]

As noted, the IRS had already proposed revocation of several groups' tax exemptions. In October, Acting Commissioner Bertrand Harding had briefed IRS regional commissioners on progress during a meeting in Washington. Why, then, deny the same to Patman? The answer lies not only in the fact that Patman was outside the IRS, but in the politically charged nature of the IOP.

The case of the National Council for Civic Responsibility of the Public Affairs Institute highlights the IRS's dilemma. The IRS had examined this group's tax exemption a few years earlier and determined that it should be revoked. But then the group spun off its most activist (political) efforts to a separate organization, thereby retaining its exemption. During the 1964 campaign it took out full-page newspaper advertisements in the *Washington Post* and the *New York Times* opposing extremism and soliciting tax-deductible contributions. These ads once again brought the group to the attention of the IRS.

In fact, Mitchell Rogovin had received a telegram in August inquiring how one might secure an immediate tax exemption for an organization to combat extremism. As Rogovin later noted, he was more concerned at the time with the practical rather than substantive problems of securing an exemption almost overnight. More troubling for the IRS by the fall, however, was a statement from Wright Patman which the IRS found in the file of the Public Affairs Institute, endorsing its efforts. Not only did Patman's name appear in the file, so did that of former commissioner Mortimer Caplin along with Senators Douglas, Clark, Engle, Jackson, Kefauver, Bible, McCarthy, McNamara, and Mansfield, and Congressman James Roosevelt. This was an impressive array of political power, and the IRS was wary, even though Rogovin admitted that the Institute was "engaged in activities not too far out of line with our ideological study." At the same time Billy James Hargis of the Christian Echoes Ministry, a group whose tax exemption the IRS had threatened to revoke, made clear his outrage at the Institute's newspaper ads. Rogovin warned that the IRS could expect more public comment as the "Council for Civic Responsibility becomes more active—and we revoke the exempt status of organizations the Council focuses upon." Finally, at an October 13 meeting in Harding's office, a select group of top IRS officials agreed to invite representatives of the Council into the National Office "for a conference."[37]

Clearly the Ideological Organizations Project faced increasing delicacy. The IRS had backed away from recommending remedial legislation for some of the problems it had encountered, despite interest from Treasury Secretary Dillon, largely because it feared that legislative proposals at this stage might be construed "as an admission that we could not touch the exemptions of the organizations involved under present statute." That threatened to "jeopardize any proposed adverse actions we might want to take" as a consequence of the IOP. Determined to move forward and assert its authority, the IRS decided to accelerate the process. If a prima facie case for exemption existed, rather than wait for extensive legal reviews the IRS would immediately route those cases through the protest and conference procedures. Although the agency embraced this approach chiefly to meet its target dates, one side effect would be to put all such organizations on notice that IRS scrutiny was likely. That might provoke behavioral changes by some of these "action" groups and achieve IRS objectives by other means.

Even for those cases where auditors had already determined that there was no reason to change the exempt status, the IRS determined to contact the organizations, let them know that certain of their activities had raised questions "as to their right to continued exemption," and ask them to explain. The organizations themselves, of course, did not yet know that the IRS did *not* plan to revoke their tax exemptions, so this was a powerful threat. This new face of regulation was most apparent in the case of Billy James Hargis's Christian Echoes Ministry.

> The status of Christian Echoes Ministry was discussed. . . . a transmittal to the field had been drafted as a joint Technical-Compliance effort and . . . the case was ready to go to the field as soon as we got the files from Chief Counsel. It was generally agreed that it would not be advisable to send a legal memorandum on the "educational" and "religious" aspects of the case to the field. . . . The field would be further cautioned not to be evasive if probed by Hargis or the press. In such situations it would be best to acknowledge the fact that the case was considered preliminarily by the National Office. The file would be returned at once by Chief Counsel and referred to the field for issuance of the proposal to revoke. It was indicated that both the Technical organization and Chief Counsel concurred in the proposal to revoke.[38]

With the election approaching, the IRS remained cautious about proceeding. Indeed, though it made public its move against the Life Line Foundation before the election, it did not initiate action against the Christian Crusade until afterward. The timing, according to one IRS official, "was 'no coincidence.' "[39]

The experimental nature of the IOP kept the IRS uncertain as to how it should initially detail the actions of any organization that prompted a revocation decision. To complicate matters, columnist Jack Anderson exposed the political liabilities of the IOP in early March, just as the IRS was starting proceedings against these right-wing groups. Anderson noted that the Democrats had used the National Council for Civic Responsibility to receive undercover contributions during the election campaign of 1964, including donations from such high-profile contributors as Arthur Larson, former adviser to President Eisenhower, Marion Folsom of Eisenhower's cabinet, former Army Chief of Staff

General J. Lawton Collins, and Erwin Griswold, dean of the Harvard Law School, as well as $50,000 from the Democratic National Committee's "Book Fund."[40]

This alarmed the IRS because Anderson linked the National Council for Civic Responsibility to the activities of right-wing groups that had tried to smear President Johnson during the campaign as well as to the issue of tax-exempt organizations. While Anderson concluded that it was perhaps a public service to challenge the distortions of the "hate propagandists," he also noted that it violated federal law for exempt groups to engage in political activities. "This law was introduced in 1954," he observed, "by none other than Lyndon B. Johnson, then a Senator." Not content to stop there, Anderson went on to note that the IRS had already begun to crack down on "extremist outfits" which had engaged in political activities despite holding tax-exempt status, with notices already issued to the Life Line Foundation, the Christian Echoes Ministry, and the Circuit Riders. The Circuit Riders had already sent out a mass mailing for large donations before their tax exemption expired. Anderson's column made the IRS uneasy because it threatened not only to expose the IOP's apparent bias against right-wing groups but to intensify an already politicized situation, especially with the Public Policy Institute now under IRS review.[41]

With Sheldon Cohen as the new commissioner of Internal Revenue under President Johnson, the IOP continued on its course. Cohen provided regular updates to Treasury. IRS Chief Counsel Mitchell Rogovin reported the agency's decisions to revoke tax exemptions to Stanley Surrey, assistant secretary of the Treasury. In April 1965, Rogovin indicated that his office had issued several General Counsel Memoranda (GCM) affirming IRS decisions either to revoke some exemptions or to request additional information from specific organizations before proceeding further. A March GCM concluded that there was no prima facie case for revocation with respect to the Foundation for Economic Education, and Rogovin's office issued a GCM to the Christian Echoes Ministry setting out in some detail the reasons for the proposed revocation. Eight cases remained active in the chief counsel's office, but progress was slow because of the need to "make a fairly careful study of the materials actually disseminated by each organization."[42] With the issuance of various GCM in the last months of 1964 and throughout 1965, the time had come for the IRS to conduct an internal assessment of the Ideological Organizations Project.

CHAPTER THREE

PRIME TARGET:
BILLY JAMES HARGIS
AND THE
CHRISTIAN CRUSADE

PRESIDENT KENNEDY'S speeches in the fall of 1961, together with the Reuther Memorandum, highlighted a growing administration concern about right-wing power in American politics during the early 1960s. Not only was the John Birch Society in full cry against administration policies; other radical right and ideologically conservative organizations and individuals added their voices in a chorus of criticism, attacking Kennedy's policies, attempts to moderate the cold war, and new efforts in civil rights. For many on the right, even the Republican party was too moderate. The right wing had attacked Dwight Eisenhower's "modern Republicanism" and was lining up behind Senator Barry Goldwater for the 1964 Republican presidential nomination. That resurgent political activism, together with the growing number of groups on the right, had triggered the Ideological Organizations Project.

While most of the organizations the project investigated were small operations with limited funds, one stood out. Billy James Hargis's Christian Echoes Ministry had access to extensive financial resources and had assembled a mass media network. The controversy between the IRS and the Christian Echoes Ministry is a story of two powerful forces in conflict. It is also a tale of determination on both sides, as well as one of confusion. How closely could religion and politics mix? Could the

IRS scrutinize a tax-exempt ideological organization without itself becoming ideological?[1]

Billy James Hargis hailed from Texarkana, Texas, and was ordained in 1943 at the age of seventeen in the Disciples of Christ. After receiving a clerical exemption from military service during World War II, he served as pastor to churches in Sallisaw and Sapulpa, Oklahoma, and Granby, Missouri. In 1950 he resigned to devote his energies to directing a network of anti-Communist activities. Although he used the title "Doctor," this was largely a self-initiated honorary designation. Hargis had received a doctor of divinity degree in 1954 from Defender Seminary in Puerto Rico, two years before he received a bachelor of arts degree. He later accepted honorary doctor of laws degrees from Belin Memorial University in Missouri and Bob Jones University in South Carolina. His education, in many respects, was a product of so-called diploma mills. But they provided him with claims to religious authenticity.[2]

More important, perhaps, was his energy. Despite weighing more than 260 pounds, he was, according to one critic, an "engine of energy" who had "mastered the art of moving crowds who want to be freed of the burden of thinking." He participated in a seemingly endless round of meetings and revivals, sold Bibles, and operated a mobile radio station. Often speaking for as long as two hours at a time, Hargis attacked the National Council of Churches, communism, liberalism, federal aid to education, medical care for the aged, Eleanor Roosevelt, disarmament, and civil rights activity. "I'm a radio preacher," he told one reporter, "fighting liberalism and communism. What we are doing is creating a climate of conservatism." Liberals were part of the Communist conspiracy, in his view, and liberal economic policies were socialistic. Linking religion, liberalism, and communism, Hargis proclaimed that he "got into this in 1948 because I saw apostasy growing in our churches. Liberals were discouraging belief in the virgin birth. The end of liberalism will be to destroy the church." The message of one Hargis pamphlet, "The National Council of Churches Indicts Itself on 50 Counts of Treason to God and Country," even found its way into a 1960 Air Force training manual on security, a manual that the Air Force eventually withdrew.[3]

This mixture of religion and politics was the core of Hargis's message and the source of his troubles with the IRS. In 1961 his tax-exempt Christian Crusade raked in almost $1 million from more than 100,000 contributors. The center of his empire was his Christian Echoes National Ministry, which he incorporated in Sapulpa, Oklahoma. It received tax-exempt status from the IRS in 1952 as an educational and religious organization. At that time the enterprise was just beginning. By 1961, however, his Christian Crusade, centered in Tulsa, Oklahoma, had fifty staff members and a budget of $75,000 per month. A year later the monthly budget had climbed to $90,000. Hargis recorded anti-Communist radio programs and mailed 250,000 pieces of literature each month to contributors. In 1962 he purchased an old resort hotel in Manitou Springs, Colorado, where he started a retreat and an "anti-communism summer college." His activities attracted "earnest, deeply troubled people." According to one observer:

> Many were ministers fearful of modernism in the churches. Many were students, revolting against the liberalism of their teachers. Some were mothers, worried about nuclear war and the future of their sons. Some were small-business men, troubled about taxes. A few were farmers, frustrated and angered by the fact they could survive only by Government subsidy.

Hargis's answer to all of them was a simple moral absolutism: communism was the source of their anxieties and problems. Yet, throughout all his activities, Hargis claimed that his political and religious operations were entirely separate. Group Research, which monitored the right wing, agreed, concluding in a 1962 special report that Hargis went to "considerable lengths to maintain a distinction between his political and religious operations."[4]

The Internal Revenue Service did not agree. Hargis seemed to be using religion as a cover for politics. Given the president's concern about right-wing political activity, and Hargis's public promotion of unity and coordination among right-wing groups throughout the country, Hargis and his operations were a prime target for the Ideological Organizations Project. In April 1962, agent John S. Donovan of the Tulsa IRS office conducted an extensive examination of the Christian Echoes Ministry. After spending almost a hundred hours reviewing its activities for 1959–1961, Donovan filed a "No Change Report" with the National Office. He concluded that "for all practical purposes" Hargis's operations were the same as they had been when the IRS granted Christian Crusade a tax exemption in the 1950s. A few weeks later the National Office directed Donovan to conduct another review, and in November 1962 Donovan submitted a second "No Change Order" to his superiors. During the spring of 1963 the IRS returned the case file for further audit, arguing that "additional facts need to be secured and questions answered." This led to a third field examination, but the report that IRS agents Donovan and Harry Riggs filed in July reached the same conclusion: Christian Echoes Ministry was entitled to its exemption.[5]

In a memo for the file on September 16, 1963, Albert F. Schrempp, chief of the Audit Division in the Oklahoma IRS district office, noted that the IRS National Office in Washington had sent Dallas regional office director Larry Stewart a letter indicating "more particular interest in this case than has previously been evidenced . . . [the] National Office are asking for copies of specific publications of Hargis and other information." Two days later, in a telephone conversation with Stewart, Schrempp revealed that a June 1962 National Office memorandum expressed a "particular interest in this case from the political action standpoint." That reflected the *modus operandi* of the Ideological Organizations Project.

This prompted the fourth examination of the Christian Echoes Ministry in barely a year. Agents were instructed this time, however, not to close the file before both the IRS regional office in Dallas and the National Office in Washington had looked at it. Less than two weeks later Stewart, the assistant regional commissioner (Audit), called Schrempp again. Stewart directed him to tell Hargis, *if* he asked, that the IRS had no "drive" against exempt organizations, but that it was "in the process of making more examinations of this type organization throughout the country." The new examination, moreover, would not be limited to "the financial operations but also [would include] the types of activities which the organizations are conducting." In addition, the "information and documents which we are asking for" would be sent to the National Office, and "we won't close the case until the National Office has had an opportunity to study these documents." By late October the Oklahoma City district office had collected the documents. The Christian Echoes Ministry was "under active examination" and was listed as a Sensitive Case Report.

In mid-November 1963 a new report with accompanying documents was forwarded to the National Office. Agent Riggs reported that he had found no radio speeches "where a listener was urged to vote for a certain candidate or where certain legislation was advocated." In his final report that December, Riggs concluded that as "far as can be determined the organization operates within the exemption letter as a religious and educational organization." On December 20, 1963, the Oklahoma City district office requested technical advice from the National Office regarding the status of the Christian Echoes Ministry.[6]

It heard eleven months later. On November 6, 1964, the IRS recommended revocation of the Christian Echoes Ministry's tax exemption. From the National Office, Assistant Commissioner (Compliance) Singleton Wolfe placed a conference call to the IRS regional office in Dallas and the district office in Oklahoma City, as well as to some other staff members. Wolfe not only notified staff at those offices of a proposed letter to be sent to Hargis revoking the Christian Echoes Ministry's tax exemption and instructed them to mail the letter no later than November 13; he also conveyed a series of points that the IRS declined to put in print. Wolfe's most important essentials were that the promise of a legal memorandum would remain unfulfilled, at least for the moment; that there should be no effort to cover up the involvement of the National Office in this particular examination, should Hargis ask; and that none of the material developed by the National Office should be shown to Hargis. These were directives rather than technical advice. That same day the IRS forwarded its administrative file on the Christian Echoes Ministry, along with additional material, to the Oklahoma City district office. This triggered a protracted battle between Hargis and the IRS.[7]

As directed, the Oklahoma City district director, Clyde Bickerstaff, advised Hargis on November 13, 1964, of the IRS proposal to revoke his tax exemption. Three days later Hargis called a press conference to criticize the action. He also threatened a lawsuit to force the IRS to deny tax-exempt status to left-wing groups that had engaged in similar activities. At the same time Hargis sought support from others on the right. The *Fort Lauderdale News* editorialized that the IRS was unfairly targeting right-wing groups, insisting that the "quickest route to a liberal dictatorship in this nation is through the silencing of all opposition in just the way the Reuther memorandum has proposed." Hargis's files bulge with similar articles from newspapers around the country. "The trouble with policing tax-exempt organizations," the conservative columnist William Buckley wrote, "is that it simply cannot be done with justice." Buckley suggested that if the IRS intended to behave in this manner, it should investigate the National Student Association or the Public Affairs Institute. He warned that it "was never more clear that the 'power to tax is the power to destroy.'"[8]

Representative Thomas Curtis, Missouri Republican, also defended Hargis. In December 1964 he asked the IRS to explain its actions. The IRS sent him a fact sheet, explaining that it had received "numerous inquiries" about the case. Some of Curtis's constituents also asked him to intervene. They argued that this was part of a "left-wing" Reuther-LBJ-Democratic attack on anyone who opposed liberal views. The press and news media had become one-sided, in their view, and anyone who disagreed with them risked losing their tax exemption. Curtis promised to "look into this as soon as possible."[9]

Colleagues on the right also gave Hargis a platform as he fought back against the IRS. Perhaps the most striking was a 1965 newspaper on "Religious Discrimination" sponsored by the Christian Beacon of Collingswood, New Jersey. Distributed by the Reverend Carl McIntire, it carried the full text of the Reuther Memorandum as well as a front-page letter from Hargis. Underscoring all his comments for emphasis, Hargis railed against the IRS and liberals.

> Since no announced action has been taken against those left wing groups, educational and religious, which definitely violated Internal Revenue Code 501, and in light of the letter we have received proposing to revoke our tax-exempt status, although we did not endorse or oppose any candidate, and taking cognizance of the date of their action (only ten days after the election of Mr. Johnson), I have come to the conclusion that this may well be evidence of a beginning [of a] reign of harassment and persecution for those who hold opposite views to the Administration in Washington. Freedom of speech is on trial. Only under an absolute dictatorship are opposing opinions prohibited. Will the Administration now take official "dictatorial-like action" against those spokesmen of Christian orthodoxy and conservatism in an effort to silence their opposing views? Will the "Great Society" now become the "Great Stick" to crush those who may disagree with the Administration in power? For liberty's sake, I sincerely hope not.[10]

This tirade revealed the fundamental question behind the Ideological Organizations Project. Was it really aimed at tax-exempt organizations that had violated the Internal Revenue Code? Or was it an effort that used any pretext to crack down on right-wing organizations in order to muzzle their opposition to government policies? Hargis was convinced it was the latter; the IRS maintained it was the former.

In a lengthy letter to a law firm retained by Hargis, Clyde Bickerstaff, IRS district director in Oklahoma City, detailed the rationale behind the agency's recommendation for revocation in November 1964. Reviewing Hargis's activities from 1961 to 1963, the IRS cited three reasons for its action. All were interrelated and involved political activities. The Christian Echoes Ministry was not, the IRS believed, "operated exclusively for religious, educational and charitable purposes." Second, many of its activities focused on trying to "influence legislation." Finally, the IRS charged that Hargis had directly and indirectly intervened in "political campaigns on behalf of candidates for public office." Also important was the revelation that this was the first complete IRS review of the organization's activities since it had acquired tax-exempt status in 1953. Not only did this reveal lax IRS enforcement of tax-exemption laws, it also provided ammunition for Hargis to argue that the examination was politically motivated.[11]

The primary problem, according to the IRS, was that it found almost no evidence to substantiate the Christian Echoes Ministry's operation as a religious organization. The IRS had scrutinized various materials submitted by Hargis, including his chief periodicals, *Christian Crusade* magazine and *Weekly Crusader*, as well as radio and television broadcasts. Aside from publication of a Bible study series and an occasional broadcast or article, these materials appeared to be "concerned essentially with secular matters, largely of a political nature." There was little evidence that nonpolitical religious, educational, or charitable activities were at the heart of the organization's operation. The IRS concluded that not only was the Ministry "not engaged exclusively in religious activities or advancement of religion," but "such materials failed to establish that any of the major activities of the organization so qualified." There was, consequently, no basis for continuing its tax exemption. Hargis, of course, claimed otherwise. The core of his defense was that he was essentially presenting conservative religious views on important public issues that impacted religion. The private sphere and the public sphere, the religious and the secular, could not really be divorced from one all-encompassing worldview.

As Hargis contested the IRS's conclusion, the case demonstrated why examinations of ideologically charged tax-exempt organizations created political ripples of their own. Not only was this a relatively new exercise for the IRS, it occurred in a politically contentious environment and, given the intent and operation of the organization in question, took place under the full exposure of the mass media. After all, Hargis's activities had existed for a decade or more, so the timing as well as the substance of the IRS's action raised serious questions about its motivation. The determination of what represented a "substantial part" of an organization's activities was a judgment call, and the IRS itself was unclear about the guidelines for such a conclusion. This was crucial to the case because, as the IRS noted in its letter, if "any substantial part of an organization's activities" did not qualify, its exemption would be invalid even though some of its activities qualified.[12]

Not surprisingly, the IRS emphasized Hargis's "advocacy" of a "political viewpoint" on a range of topics that included agricultural, hospitalization, and education legislation, medical care for the aged, mental health, urban renewal, the income tax, U.S. participation in the United Nations, foreign aid, the McCarran Immigration Act, and the Supreme Court. All of this indicated clearly to the IRS that the Christian Echoes Ministry's "major purpose and objective" was to influence legislation in these areas. At the very least they represented a "substantial part" of the organization's activities. The IRS cited specific issues of the *Weekly Crusader* and other Hargis publications that addressed this legislation. Finally the IRS concluded with a third charge, that the organization had "urged public and voter support of candidates whose views paralleled those of the organization," as well as the defeat of candidates "not conforming to its views."

> It is the position of this office that the foregoing and similar activities in question were directly designed to enlist and solicit voter support and voter opposition in regard to particular candidates and a particular class of candidates, and in the particular circumstances constituted participation and intervention in political campaigns on behalf of candidates for public office.[13]

Ultimately, the IRS noted, the burden of proof rested on the organization. The Christian Echoes Ministry had to demonstrate to the IRS that it deserved its tax exemption. The IRS documented its charges by listing three pages of publications it had examined to reach its conclusion to revoke the exemption. These included two books, forty-three pamphlets, the two periodicals, transcripts of several radio broadcasts, several speeches, and miscellaneous petitions. With few exceptions, titles of the books and pamphlets all addressed foreign policy concerns (chiefly communism), race, and labor. The religious connection, if there was one, was not evident.[14]

Hargis rallied the right wing, sending a letter to supporters detailing the IRS actions. Bob Jones, president of Bob Jones University in Greenville, South Carolina, wrote South Carolina Senator Strom Thurmond asking for his support. Jones railed that this was a "tyrannical attempt on the part of the Johnson Administration to exact vengeance. CHRISTIAN CRUSADE takes a Scriptural stand, and the Scriptural stand is always Conservative." He emphasized that the National Council of Churches and other liberal tax-exempt organizations promoted the United Nations, endorsed "social agitation" and "labor activities," but retained their exemptions. Republican Congressman Howard "Bo"

Callaway of Georgia, who wrote the IRS to protest its action, raised similar concerns.[15]

Despite these efforts of the Christian Echoes Ministry to mobilize other religious conservatives to support its appeal of the proposed revocation, the IRS resolutely defended its actions. On occasion the agency implicitly acknowledged that it was operating on new ground. In a letter to Kentucky Republican Congressman Charles Farnsley, the chief of the IRS Exempt Organizations Branch asserted that the revocation proposal was "consistent" with the IRS's "long standing and recently stepped up audit and review procedure for all exempt organizations." By 1965, when this letter was written, the IRS had indeed increased its examinations of tax-exempt organizations. Nowhere, however, did the letter reveal that this particular case was part of an earlier, more ideologically targeted operation. After a conference that July with attorneys from the Christian Echoes Ministry, the IRS sustained its revocation decision. The only path left for Hargis was to request a formal hearing in the National Office.[16]

In the meantime he turned his editorial pen to the attack. A "Special Report" on the battle appeared in the August-September 1965 issue of *Christian Crusade* magazine. Hargis editorialized:

> If Christian Echoes National Ministry, Inc., (Christian Crusade) loses its fight to retain our tax-exempt status, it will be positive proof that the present Administration in Washington is an absolute dictatorship that uses the various Departments of Government to harass its enemies, and persecute its opponents. "Fair Play" and "Justice" will become shallow words, without meaning in Twentieth Century America.

Noting that the IRS had moved against Christian Crusade ten days after LBJ's election, Hargis cited this as further evidence of an administration plot.[17]

IRS Commissioner Sheldon Cohen explained to Congressman Thomas Curtis that, even after a conference with Christian Crusade representatives, the IRS district office remained convinced that its recommendations were warranted. Curtis asked Cohen to send him the IRS's operating guidelines for exempt organization reviews as well as details about how the IRS initiated such inquiries. Hargis later wrote Curtis to complain that justice had become a "one-edged sword," employed only against opposing viewpoints.

> Whether you are liberal, conservative, Republican or Democrat is irrelevant and beside the point. The important thing is this—will ministers

be allowed freedom of speech in the future, regardless of their viewpoints, theologically or philosophically, or will only those ministers friendly to the reigning administration be allowed such freedom?

Howard Callaway warned Curtis that, despite IRS assurances that foundations "need have no fear about testifying," he had found that "a number of the foundations that I talked to do have such a fear." Congressman John Byrnes, Republican from Wisconsin, requested a list of Treasury actions against foundations for the past five years, and questioned how these Treasury activities were promoting the public interest.[18]

Sheldon Cohen kept in close contact with Curtis, clearly hoping to head off congressional support for Hargis. In April 1966, Cohen patiently outlined IRS procedures and the provisions of the tax code that governed operations of tax-exempt organizations. Admitting that these involved "discretionary judgment" by the IRS, Cohen explained that "judicial precedents have failed to yield any mathematical method" for making such determinations. In addition, Cohen pointed out that disseminating "unsupported opinion" was not an educational activity. He could not provide the data Curtis had requested on IRS activity in this area, he said, because the IRS had never maintained any such records. In fact, it had no information about the number of exempt educational organizations in existence, though it was beginning to compile a master file of all taxpayers as part of its early efforts to computerize tax processing.[19]

Two months later, after two members of Cohen's staff had personally talked with Curtis, Cohen noted Curtis's continuing interest in IRS actions as they related to "organizations of diverse socio-economic and political ideologies." He referred Curtis to testimony before Wright Patman's subcommittee on foundations, making only oblique references to the Ideological Organizations Project that had been under way for several years. When he did so, he referred only to efforts that had been conducted before 1962, attempting to disassociate the IRS examination of the Christian Crusade from the IOP. Those earlier efforts, he told Curtis, had led the IRS to launch a special study of guidelines for exempt organizations and the difficulties associated with reviewing their operations. The IRS was now nearing completion of that study and had a "much clearer understanding of the activities of those organizations which use mass media to influence public opinion and thinking." In short, Cohen believed that the IRS examination of the Christian Crusade was the result not only of a careful examination of its work and publications but also of lengthy study of diverse organizations in the same field. It was neither targeted nor biased.[20]

During the next few years the battle between Hargis and the Internal Revenue Service raged. Conservative congressmen queried the IRS about its decision. They asked for detailed reports and complained that organizations supporting the administration remained untouched. Some of them also questioned tax exemptions for groups like the NAACP, which had passed a resolution at its 1964 convention denouncing Goldwater yet apparently had escaped IRS scrutiny. At the same time, however, they conveniently overlooked Hargis's use of the Christian Crusade's computer expertise to train several George Wallace staffers to develop their own direct-mail fund-raising campaign. Conservatives became even more exercised when the IRS denied a tax exemption to the World Youth Crusade for Freedom, particularly when the agency rested much of its decision on a conclusion that "Fostering and participating in the creation of groups to oppose Communism in the United States and abroad, while possibly having broad educational aspects, are not, basically, educational purposes or operations as the term is defined in the regulations." Both sides to the controversy seemed to take an ideological approach to the issue.[21]

In early January 1968, while Hargis and his attorneys were waiting to go into yet another conference with the IRS, the agency assessed Christian Crusade more than $45,000 for Social Security taxes that had not been taken from the employees' payroll between 1961 and 1965. The Crusade immediately appealed to supporters for funds, sending out what it called the "most important—the most urgent—letter you have ever received from Christian Crusade." Hargis intended to appeal this assessment, of course, and attacked the IRS as "dictatorial and un-American." Noting that a Moscow radio broadcast had recently attacked the Christian Crusade as the chief enemy of communism in the United States, Hargis asked: "*Is it merely a coincidence that the Internal Revenue Service of the Johnson Administration moves to put Christian Crusade out of business just after this declaration of war against Christian Crusade by Moscow?*"[22]

In mid-January attorneys and accountants for the Christian Crusade met with IRS officials in Oklahoma City to discuss the new assessment and the revocation of its exemption. Knowing that the IRS usually granted a six- to eighteen-month delay if requested, they asked for a postponement. But the IRS granted them only an additional forty-eight hours, and on January 17, 1968, the two sides met, ostensibly to present their case. The speed with which the IRS was moving shocked some of the participants. Not only was the IRS pushing the case faster than usual, indeed, faster than anyone had ever seen, but there really was no conference. According to Christian Crusade officials, they were unable to present their side of the case. What was clear, as subsequent memos revealed, was that the entire affair was being orchestrated from the National Office in Washington. A Christian Echoes Ministry memo cast the case in nearly apocalyptic terms: "This case, which will forever affect every fundamental church and every Bible-believing Christian in America . . . will decide once and for all if the Supreme Court has the power to interpret religion. . . ." Could the IRS make its rulings and assessments stand up in court?[23]

Hargis attacked the IRS in the Christian Echoes Ministry's March newsletter. *"Without question,"* he warned readers, *"Christian Crusade has been singled out as the initial target, the opening wedge, in the fight to separate a Christian ministry from government tax-exempt privileges."* The IRS, he argued, "is the most frightening agency in government." It had assessed penalties of more than $60,000 against the Christian Echoes Ministry and was apparently not through yet. *"God is using you and me in this way,"* he told readers, *"to preserve freedom of worship in the U.S.A."*[24]

The Christian Echoes Ministry took its battle with the IRS to the courts, and on June 24, 1971, Judge Allen E. Barrow, chief judge of the U.S. District Court, Northern District of Oklahoma, ruled that the organization *was* entitled to a tax exemption, overruling the decisions of the IRS. Although the IRS appealed, Hargis believed that he had won his case and that his argument linking religion and anti-communism had prevailed. In its finding of fact, the court concluded:

> Plaintiff believes the threat of Communism is a direct threat against the Christian religion and that plaintiff's Anti-Communist activities are representative of a dedication toward its religious activities. Churches and religious organizations cannot be isolated or insulated from the outstanding issues of the day and religious organizations should encourage their members and participants to take active stands and get involved as far as their religious beliefs are concerned and to fight against those things they believe to be anti-religious.

This led the court to conclude that the Christian Echoes Ministry was "organized and operated exclusively for religious and educational purposes."[25]

The court seemed to rest its decision on a conclusion that Hargis was sincere in his beliefs, and that denial of Christian Echoes's tax exemption deprived Hargis of his First Amendment rights. But sincerity was something the IRS had never questioned. The issue, to the IRS, was not sincerity but the tax laws. While various appeals followed, and the courts eventually overturned the district court's decision, the central issues for the IRS persisted. What procedures were appropriate for the examination of tax-exempt organizations? How was the IRS to distinguish between educational and noneducational activities? Could an organization successfully put all its activities, religious or secular, under a religious or charitable umbrella? IRS recognition of witchcraft as a religion, and its grant of a tax exemption to the Church and School of Wicca in 1973 and to the Church of Scientology twenty years later, indicated that the IRS faced a continuing dilemma. The agency pondered these issues as it sought to develop guidelines for its agents and scrutinize the activities of tax-exempt organizations and foundations. At the same time it faced political pressures from the White House and Congress. The lessons of the Ideological Organizations Project were not always clear-cut.[26]

CHAPTER FOUR

THE IDEOLOGICAL ORGANIZATIONS PROJECT: LESSONS LEARNED

During 1965 the IRS moved to complete the second phase of the IOP. By December it had also produced a lengthy analysis of the project. This study, reviewed by the Exempt Organizations Branch during 1966, summarized the actions taken by the IRS to date and proposed legislation and tax rulings for tighter control of the activities of exempt organizations. Whether or not these changes would resolve the question of political pressures on the IRS, however, remained unclear. Meanwhile, throughout the year the IRS concentrated on determining whether or not to recommend revocation of tax exemptions for groups targeted in the Ideological Organizations Project, forwarding those recommendations to the chief counsel's office and then to the affected organizations for response. That office then issued a series of General Counsel Memoranda. Designed chiefly to guide IRS policy, these documents illustrate the sensitivity of the IRS toward political as well as tax-related issues surrounding activist organizations.

The IRS summaries of how it had disposed of the test-audit cases reveal not only the fate of the individual organizations but the procedures, thinking, and dilemmas of Internal Revenue with respect to ideological and activist organizations. They also expose the minimal experience of the IRS in dealing with these types of tax-exempt activities, and often how little the agency knew about the organizations involved. The efforts of the American Council of Christian Laymen to funnel money to the John Birch Society for a 10 percent commission, for example, led the IRS to propose revocation of the Council's tax exemption. By the time that recommendation reached the chief counsel's office in October 1964, however, the case was moot. The Council had been a one-man operation and had dissolved upon the death of that individual.[1]

In several cases the IRS determined, for various reasons, that there should be no change in an organization's exempt status. The American Council for Nationalities Service had been included in the test-audit study because it engaged in some legislative activities. But the IRS concluded that those activities were inconsequential and its own efforts "misdirected." Although it raised questions about the impartiality of the American Economic Foundation, the IRS also recommended no change in that organization's exempt status. This was an economic foundation without an economist on its staff, "merely a group of industrious conservatives turning out a great mass of material having little real scholarship." But, the IRS concluded, "educational purpose" did not demand scholarship. The "level of intelligence of the audience or the advocate" was not relevant. Sources of income also were apparently a factor in IRS decision-making, for it decided not to recommend a change in the tax status of the American Good Government Society after discovering that it had no regular source of income and engaged in insubstantial activities. Other organizations investigated as part of the IOP for which the IRS recommended no change in exempt status included the Christian Freedom Foundation, the Council on Foreign Relations, the Freedoms Foundation at Valley Forge, the Intercollegiate Society of Individualists, the League for Industrial Democracy, and Moral Rearmament.

The case of the American Enterprise Institute for Policy Research, however, presented a different concern. Although the IRS recommended revocation, the chief counsel's office concluded that the "ideological aspects" of the case provided "no basis for revocation." Internal Revenue persisted, arguing that since its intended audience was Congress, the Institute might be "engaging in a very sophisticated form of attempting to influence legislation," and it requested further field examinations. The connection of the Institute's chief executive officer, William J. Baroody, with the Goldwater campaign also elicited IRS concern about its political activities. The IRS found another organization, America's Future Inc., to be even more "conservative and controversial." It recommended revocation and noted complaints from members of Congress about its operations, which included distribution of John Stormer's anti-Communist tract *None Dare Call It Treason*. The IRS was embarrassed by its own inconsistencies in evaluating this organization. It discovered that it had recommended revocation of the group's exempt status in 1958, then given America's Future Inc. a clean bill of health in 1961, even though its activities had not changed over three years. The 1961 action, it confessed, was "improper."

The disposition of other cases revealed further problems facing the IRS as it sought to complete the Ideological Organizations Project. The parameters of activism were unclear. The Cardinal Mindszenty Foundation, for instance, had clearly engaged in noneducational activities—and the IRS recommended revocation. But whether those activities were really "substantial" was less clear to the chief counsel's office. The Christian Anti-Communist Crusade presented a related problem. Were its foreign operations sufficient to provide grounds for revocation, despite its extensive domestic activities? Problematic in a different sense was the case of the Christian Beacon. It sponsored religious broadcasts by Reverend Carl McIntire on more than five hundred radio stations nationwide, broadcasts that were highly conservative and often political in nature. A recommendation for revocation currently sat in the chief counsel's office. But the IRS was anxious about the political impact of such a ruling. Although McIntire ran many such corporations, each one susceptible to revocation, they were all church controlled or church related, and the IRS feared that it could not

> survive the criticism which might result from adverse action. While there might be support voiced from some "liberal" elements in society, it would hardly be the equal of the exacerbic [sic] commentary from other quarters that the Service was seeking to (a) require churches or ministers conform their political views, (b) hamper the free exercise of religion, or (c) punish hostile organizations. This case requires intensive consideration, more than any other in the study.

Ironically, as the preceding chapter revealed, Internal Revenue had not been so hesitant in revoking the tax exemption of another church-related organization—Billy James Hargis's Christian Echoes Ministry—and the chief counsel's office concurred. The IRS had concluded that that organization attacked "nearly all prevailing government policies and the government leaders, the civil rights and labor movements and their leaders," as well as other moderate or liberal groups and individuals. Noting that even though Hargis himself had personal tax problems, the IRS admitted that revocation would "probably not diminish the organization."

The educational regulations developed by the IRS to support the Internal Revenue Code were as ill-defined as the religious tests, often providing more questions than answers. Enforcement was inconsistent. For instance, could an organization (such as the Church League of America) disseminate derogatory information about the loyalty or political philosophy of private institutions (the National Council of Churches) and remain "educational"? The National Office didn't think so, and recommended revocation in this case, but it moved very slowly. Interpretation of the educational regulations also led the IRS to back away from recommendations to revoke tax exemptions for the Foundation for Economic Education, the Four Freedoms Study Group, and the National Education Program of Harding College. In addition, while both the Daughters of the American Revolution (DAR) and Protestants and Other Americans United for Separation of Church and State (POUA) had come under IRS scrutiny for attempting to influence legislation, what seemed more important to the IRS were their methods and ideology rather than their lobbying activities. The DAR was cited for having a "very conservative theme on social, economic and political matters," while the POUA drew IRS ire for its attacks on Roman Catholics.

The General Counsel Memoranda (GCM) provide more details about some of these cases. They open a window into IRS operations throughout the Ideological Organizations Project and into IRS assessment of activist exempt organizations. In instances such as the IOP, when the IRS was operating in uncharted and politically sensitive territory, these memoranda reveal how ultimate policies and courses of action developed. A group of them, some sent to the Tax Rulings Division and others to the Exempt Organization and Pension Trust Division from IRS chief counsels Sheldon Cohen and Mitchell Rogovin, are particularly revealing.

Each GCM provided an informal opinion about proposed IRS action in cases where the agency hoped to establish probable cause for revoking a tax exemption. By explicitly stating that they were informal, and not official policy, the memoranda allowed the IRS to develop its policies, respond to protests, and perhaps even change its mind. A November GCM with respect to Protestants and Other Americans United for Separation of Church and State highlighted the difficulties facing the IRS as it sought to complete the IOP. It summarized the operational methodology of the POUA and concluded that revocation might be premature. Instead it suggested advising the organization "that it is engaging in activities considered questionable by the Service" and to request further information about those activities. Acknowledging that the POUA engaged in legislative activities that violated its exempt status, the IRS confessed that it was "uncertain whether such involvement constitutes a substantial portion of the organization's total activities." This was a "difficult determination," and the IRS sought the organization's views. There was also doubt whether POUA's dissemination of information was wholly educational; indeed, the IRS believed that its litigation activities were definitely not educational. If the organization argued that its litigation was charitable in nature, moreover, its attacks on the Catholic church would jeopardize its entire tax exemption. This was, the IRS admitted, "largely an unexplored area," and it was reluctant to move quickly.[2]

A November 1964 memorandum on the Circuit Riders highlighted another continuing problem. Even though the IRS found substantial grounds for revoking the organization's tax exemption for failing to meet the "educational" tests as legally defined—and it detailed those failures—the IRS worried about the impact of such a decision in the highly charged political atmosphere of the country at the time. Chief Counsel Sheldon Cohen warned that in "view of the sensitive nature of this and similar cases and the importance of avoiding any misunderstanding of the position of the Service, we believe extreme care should be used in drafting the letter notifying the organization of the proposed revocation of its exempt status."[3]

In providing some of these documents through the Freedom of Information Act, more than thirty years after they had been written, the IRS carefully redacted references to anything remotely political. In its memorandum on the American Enterprise Institute (AEI), for instance, the words "Members of Congress" were redacted, solely to obscure recipients of AEI reports and analyses—the purpose for which it was founded. This particular memo also reveals, as do the others, that the IRS had carefully scrutinized the organization's publications both for content and for audience. Yet, despite the AEI's admitted pro-business bias, the IRS concluded that even with further examination by experts it could not revoke its tax exemption "under existing regulations." Although the AEI did not seek to educate the general public directly, and apparently sought to influence legislation, the IRS tentatively concluded that it should rule in its favor. The question, the memorandum observed, was "a subtle one and, so far as we are aware, without controlling Service precedent." Nonetheless, it left the door open for reconsideration.[4]

The purpose of the Ideological Organizations Project was never more clearly reflected than in a February 1965 GCM relating to the National Education Program of Harding College (NEP). Chief Counsel Mitchell Rogovin recommended that a "no change" letter be sent to the organization, though he raised several substantive questions. More important, however, was the memorandum's revelation that the IRS had carefully scrutinized the organization's publications and films for ideological content. The NEP was formed to educate Americans about the dangers of communism, and the IRS remained skeptical that its presentations were balanced with respect to "educational method." In particular, the IRS cited the "controversial" film *Communism on the Map.* The agency admitted that "because of the subtlety of the possible distortion, it would be extremely difficult to prove the existence of bias or misleading factual development in the film" so as to disqualify it as educational. This clearly reflected how the IRS had moved beyond financial accounting to make ideological and political judgments as it scrutinized tax-exempt organizations. In addition, the NEP memorandum reflected both the unwillingness of the IRS to test the limits of educational or charitable exemptions through the courts and its difficulty in interpreting those exemptions. A major deterrent, as Rogovin noted in his remarks on the NEP's publication program, was that "an assertion of lack of qualification of this phase of the organization's program would involve a relatively advanced refinement of legal position in terms of present judicial development in the area. Loss of this case in court would be a real possibility, and could seriously affect the success of Service's present efforts to develop judicial precedent."[5]

Quite apart from pressures brought by the White House or members of Congress, the IRS felt pressures of its own. As it reviewed tax-exempt organizations, whether under the Ideological Organizations Project or as part of a broader review, Internal Revenue found itself at odds internally as it tried to define such apparently innocuous terms as "educational" and "religious." Despite the intensity in the early years of the IOP, the IRS now moved slowly.

The case of the Foundation for Economic Education (FEE) illustrated this posture. In a lengthy GCM in March 1965, Chief Counsel Rogovin noted that his office "felt the question whether the organization is 'educational' is extremely close." The FEE had been chartered in 1946 to advocate particular philosophies about economics and government, and had been included in the IOP. Conservative in nature, with corporate executives dominating its board of trustees, the FEE was funded by large donations from businesses across the country and advocated free-market economics and limited government. Rogovin concluded that even though the FEE failed to present contending points of view, that should not be fatal to its exempt status as long as it presented the facts fairly. Particularly revealing was Rogovin's assertion that the absence of "rancor, irresponsible assertions, innuendo, [or] appeals to emotion rather than intellect" were as important as the facts an organization presented. Apparently, for the IRS, style of presentation was as significant as content. Given the circumstances of this case, the agency concluded that it had no argument for revocation.[6]

Nowhere were the pressures from Congress on the IRS with respect to ideology more evident than in its investigation of Dr. Fred Schwarz's Christian Anti-Communist Crusade (CACC). Internal Revenue launched a comprehensive investigation of the CACC but concluded that its domestic activities did not provide evidence for revocation. Although the organization's operations in foreign countries furnished evidence to revoke its exemption, the chief counsel argued that the IRS should not do so until the CACC had had an opportunity to comment on the propriety of its actions. This was a reversal from the original IRS judgment, which cited numerous examples of illegal domestic activities that merited revocation. Several inquiries from "congressional sources" had triggered the initial field investigation in 1961, and extensive reports from agents were received in 1962 and 1963. The General Counsel Memorandum on this case reads like a history of the organization's finances, publications, activities, and methodology. Despite its forceful presentation of opinion, its publications also presented sufficient factual material to qualify the CACC for an educational exemption.

What troubled the IRS most were the group's operations abroad. The CACC sent significant contributions to various foreign countries—especially India, British Guiana, and Australia—to subsidize anti-Communist activities and publications and to support anti-Communist candidates. This latter effort led the IRS to conclude that revocation was possible. The agency believed that the prohibition against participation in domestic political campaigns also applied to foreign elections. What was perhaps most important about Internal Revenue's analysis in this case was its conclusion that merely supporting anti-communism was insufficient grounds for the removal of a tax exemption. The decision not to immediately revoke the Crusade's tax exemption was significant in that the CACC had been one of the first organizations targeted following President Kennedy's speeches and the administration's receipt of the Reuther Memorandum in late 1961. As those events receded into the past, the IRS became more deliberate in its proceedings.[7]

The same caution was evident in the treatment of the Four Freedoms Study Group (FFSG). Although concluding that many of the organization's activities did not meet the criteria of the educational regulations, the IRS decided not to recommend revocation solely because the FFSG had a "close relationship" with the Christian Anti-Communist Crusade. Since the IRS had decided not to challenge the CACC's domestic activities, it also decided not to challenge those of the FFSG. And since this latter group had no overseas activities, the IRS concluded that it had no grounds for revocation—though the FFSG should be "warned that certain of its activities are not considered to be educational." The IRS also moved away from its earlier standard that style of presentation was significant, failing to act even though it concluded that material in *The Tocsin*, the FFSG's "principal publication," contained "misleading and inflammatory statements, unsupported conclusions and incomplete facts." Arguing that this newsletter accounted for only a small portion of the organization's revenues, the IRS asserted that it did not represent a "substantial part" of the FFSG's activities. Internal Revenue continued to monitor the organization but did not move to revoke its tax-exempt status at this time.[8]

In a final case from the Ideological Organizations Project, that of the Cardinal Mindszenty Foundation, the IRS also reversed an earlier conclusion that the revocation of its tax exemption was warranted because the foundation's activities and publications did not conform to the educational regulations of the Internal Revenue Code. In this case, as in the two noted immediately above, the IRS relied on the foundation's similarity to other organizations to reach a decision that no prima facie case existed. The agency concluded not only that this foundation represented a Catholic counterpart to the Christian Anti-Communist Crusade but that the case resembled that of the Four Freedoms Study Group, in that it involved anti-Communist activities. The IRS came to this conclusion despite finding that materials published in "The Mindszenty Report" failed to qualify as educational. Rather than revoke its exemption, however, it decided to issue a warning that the foundation stood to lose its exemption "if this activity is continued."[9]

These General Counsel Memoranda reflect the extensive investigations undertaken by the IRS as the Ideological Organizations Project unfolded in the years after 1961. Several agents in the field, as well as various personnel in the National Office, had requested a wide array of records from the targeted organizations. Not only did they pore over financial statements, they also scrutinized publications, speeches, films, methods of operation, and a variety of other internal operations. The ultimate purpose of this activity was to determine whether or not the organizations met the "educational" or "religious" tests of the Internal Revenue Code. What the IRS discovered, however, was that these tests were rather murky and the standards uncertain; that conclusions often rested on individuals' personal judgments; and that any decision would involve the IRS in political and ideological wrangling. The agency also moved away from accepting the implied premise of the Reuther Memorandum—that right-wing anti-Communist groups were almost by definition violating their exempt status. That premise had largely been responsible for initiating the Ideological Organizations Project and clearly had been the source of White House pressure. By 1965 the IRS had reconsidered its preliminary decisions to revoke the tax exemptions of many of these so-called activist groups. Whether or not this reflected a belief that the resounding defeat of Barry Goldwater in the 1964 presidential election had discredited such right-wing groups is unclear, but the timing was coincidental.

At the close of 1965 the IRS assessed what it had discovered in the course of the Ideological Organizations Project. At the time the assessment was prepared, the IRS had recommended the revocation of exemption for fifteen of the twenty-five organizations in the study. Nine others had escaped with "no change" conclusions, and one case remained in the field because of a late start. All the revocation cases had gone to the chief counsel's office, and four remained there in the review process. The remaining eleven had been reviewed, and the General Counsel Memoranda discussed above reflected the policy decisions of the IRS in the most important of these. The IRS concluded that another year might pass before all twenty-five cases were resolved, chiefly because some of the organizations would appeal. Noting that the organizations involved in the project shared a "corporate ideology on social, economic and political topics capable of being disseminated to the public through the mass media," the IRS believed it had made "sufficient progress" to recommend legislation, revenue rulings, and developmental guidelines for the future.[10]

The IRS assessment provided a brief history of the IOP, noting that it was separate from a concurrent investigation of "communist dominated labor unions" and that the IRS had experienced some difficulty in finding enough "left-wing" organizations to scrutinize. Congressional investigations in the 1950s had so depleted groups on the left that "only two or three were in fact sufficiently dissident to warrant the manpower expenditure." This was an important conclusion. Not only did it highlight the suppressive success of the anti-Communist crusade, it revealed that dissidence, not evidence of tax violations, determined the targeting in both phases of the Ideological Organizations Project.

The study also noted that a thorough examination of these exempt organizations imposed a tremendous burden on the IRS. There was, in fact, so much information to review that referrals to the chief counsel's office could elicit only informal opinions. Only those cases with revocation recommendations were forwarded to the chief counsel, despite earlier plans to send all cases for review. The project also led the IRS to produce a series of informal reference documents to guide its operations. These included a lengthy study of the educational exemption, a discussion of political activities by exempt organizations, an analysis of social welfare organizations and political activities, and criteria for determining educational and religious exemptions for ideological organizations.[11]

The IRS assessment featured the conclusions of the chief counsel's office about criteria for granting an educational exemption to ideological organizations. Despite earlier arguments of the Reuther Memorandum, the IRS concluded that "an admittedly predetermined point of view" was not fatal to such an exemption, provided there was a "sufficiently full and fair exposition of pertinent fact" to allow a reader to form an "opinion independent of that offered by the advocate." But what constituted "full and fair"? Four criteria emerged from the test cases. The material should be prepared by individuals "reasonably qualified" to discuss the subject; it should possess "sufficient integrity and competence" to improve the understanding of those who read it; it should be "moderate in tone and responsible in nature"; and it should appeal to intellect rather than emotion, avoiding "rancor" and "irresponsible assertions." These criteria provided some guidelines for the IRS but did not preclude politically inspired decisions nor remove suspicions that its decisions were politically driven. The underlying problem was, what constituted a "substantial body" of an organization's publications?[12]

As if to emphasize this, the IRS found "overt political activity" relatively easy to define: it comprised directing the public whom to vote for or distributing voter questionnaires that asked candidates about their political philosophy. The case of the Christian Echoes Ministry reflected IRS conclusions in this area. At the same time, however, Internal Revenue admitted that the criteria for determining "educational purpose" remained vague and subject to individual interpretation. A January 23, 1965, memorandum emphasized that the IRS had found no "magic words, no precise formula and, in short, no definition" to apply uniformly to exempt organizations. "At best," the IRS concluded, it was the "ascertainment of the presence or absence of factors which, when taken in their entirety, and applied to a given factual situation, argue for a particular result." The "factual basis" necessary for any presentation to "improve understanding," moreover, would "vary greatly with the subject matter being discussed. . . ."

How would the IRS make that determination in the case of activist organizations while avoiding arbitrary political decisions? It concluded that educational presentations should substantially "conform" to the methodology employed by established educational institutions, and that any group should present its viewpoints through "traditionally accepted methods of education." Only that would provide society with "adequate safeguards." But what was the IRS safeguarding? Its specific charge was to monitor the requirements for tax exemptions. By attempting to normalize methodologies, the suspicion emerged that it was also trying to normalize the content of presentations.

Compounding that suspicion was the IRS argument that subject matter which "engenders partisan controversy and strong emotional feelings" often indicated a failure to "utilize an educational method." Use of the mass communications media, the lack of "special qualifications" by individuals preparing the material, the absence of a dialogue with opponents, and an "extensive concern" with political issues also signaled the absence of an educational method. Experience demonstrated, the study argued, that in those instances organizations should be investigated and exemptions challenged. After such an investigation, moreover, the organization should be watched closely and examined again in three to five years. With this, the agency appeared more intent on following particular target groups than conducting random examinations. The study also highlighted the continuing sensitivity of the IRS to political pressures, warning that there had been no significant effort to "assure that complaint letters or Congressional letters" were maintained in the files of specific organizations to which they related. That should change, the study concluded, because information in those letters "could well affect the exempt status of the organization cited."

Many of the study's remaining recommendations focused on IRS procedures and applied to all exempt organizations, not just ideological organizations. They revealed how inattentive the IRS had been to these groups in the past. There were, for instance, no existing procedures for the IRS to issue information notices about deductibility issues quickly. Any organization could solicit contributions and claim they were deductible without IRS scrutiny, even though the IRS may have had serious doubts about their legality. Indeed, the IRS even failed to maintain records listing organizations whose exempt status had been revoked! The agency hoped that revising its forms would improve its records on exempt organizations. Finally, the study concluded that the IRS not only lacked a clear definition of "religious purpose" but was vague in its classification of many exempt groups and frequently misclassified them. As important as it was to examine these ideological organizations "to determine whether their individual operations comport with the statute and regulations governing exemption," it was more important for the IRS to "extrapolate a body of interpretative decisions into an area with confusing, conflicting decisional law."

Many of these observations indicated that the IRS was becoming more interested in examining the broader issue of exempt organizations than in continuing its study of ideological or activist groups. This would remove Internal Revenue from a politically sensitive area, and it reflected the study's observation that "the education-ideology-propaganda area is not susceptible to statutory policing." Despite this admission, however, the IRS had defined a new principle as a result of its test audits. Expressed only as an aside in General Counsel Memoranda 32897 (Foundation for Economic Education) and 32982 (National Education Program), this principle argued that attacks on "the character, integrity, or loyalty of individuals or institutions" were "incompatible with a 'charitable' or 'educational' exemption." If enforced, this would go a long way toward fulfilling the objectives of the Reuther Memorandum by muting right-wing attacks on the president and his policies.

Admitting that much work remained to be done, William Lehrfeld, senior tax law specialist in the Exempt Organizations and Pension Trust Division, who prepared the study, warned that the IRS must continue to be "vigilant in policing exempt organizations." Abuses would continue as tax-exempt groups, particularly "extremist groups," sought new ways to secure tax-free monies. Only three of the original twenty-five cases had been closed. The IRS had not yet implemented recommendations by the chief counsel's office for the disposition of the other twenty-two cases. Appeals and requests for explanations persisted for several months, and new evidence of improper activities surfaced in several of those outstanding cases.

Looking to the long term, the study proposed remedial legislation to clarify existing laws. One of the IRS's goals was to eliminate the term "propaganda" in these definitions. It was too polemical and provided "no measurable assistance in the administration of the [attempting to influence] legislation clause." Congressional intent, the IRS believed, was to ban exempt organizations from influencing legislation regardless of their motives. At the same time, however, the IRS proposed changes to allow churches full participation in the legislative processes. Arguing that the "temporal and the spiritual are not easily distinguished," the IRS was willing to permit "established religious organizations" to publicize the "religious or moral implications of federal and state legislation." This change appeared to permit political activities by religious organizations, albeit only "established" ones, and threatened, in the words of one judge, to "'place the Lord on the side of the heaviest money-bags.'"[13] The IRS proposed to articulate publicly its legal position and then seek "judicial affirmation."

The study also proposed prohibiting any activities that attempted to "influence the violation of any Federal law." This section was added specifically to deny exempt status to any "pacifist groups advocating draft card burnings or noncompliance with the draft laws, or civil rights groups advocating breach of Federal court orders or other Federal legislation." It was, the study insisted, merely a refusal to allow tax exemptions for "activities contrary to the sovereign's criminal and civil policies." The IRS did not elaborate on its use of the word "sovereign" but asserted that it was not "aimed at limiting free speech." The study also suggested that the IRS might apply the section "profitably" to labor unions for "illegal boycotts or subversive activities or trade associations for anti-trust violations." Fearing that an articulation of these additional "benefits" endangered passage of any changes, the study recommended only the broader language quoted above. This interest in pacifist and civil rights organizations clearly reflected an intent to normalize behaviors and enforce social as well as legal conformity.[14]

To fulfill the objectives of the test-audit program, and to speed the resolution of existing cases, the study proposed a series of revenue rulings. Admitting that they would be controversial, it urged their publication.

> Doubtless there are levels of review which will find particular terms and statements inflammatory or injudicious, especially when reciting that certain organizations are denied exemption for the manner in which they "combat communism." That is to be expected. The Internal Revenue Service, and its grandmother, the Treasury Department, have not been noted for induration when dealing with exempt organization matters. Too frequently each is the first to sound retreat, the last to call the charge.

The proposed five rulings were drawn from several sources: the test-audit program, nonideological exempt organizations' issues in New York and Chicago, and two that were unrelated to any specific cases. The IRS argued that the rulings should constitute a "package" for "greater impact." They were designed to clarify problems encountered in the Ideological Organizations Project and to make IRS determination of exempt status easier, more clear-cut, and less susceptible to successful appeals.

Proposed Revenue Ruling #1, drawn from problems with the National Council of Churches, grappled with the thorny issue of "attempts to influence legislation." The IRS noted that this was not a ban on *any* legislative activity, and the proposed ruling suggested a quantitative test of an organization's charitable activities and expenditures to determine compliance. Proposed Revenue Ruling #2 dealt with the question of religious organizations participating in political campaigns. This stemmed from efforts in Chicago by the Christian Century Foundation. The IRS found that many editorials in its weekly magazine crossed the boundary between charitable and political activity, and concluded that political activity of this nature constituted "participation and intervention in a political campaign." This would be sufficient, therefore, to revoke the foundation's tax exemption.

Proposed Revenue Rulings #3 and #4 reflected IRS efforts to clarify issues encountered in its test-audit program. Although they did not relate to specific cases then before the IRS, they clearly reflected the dilemmas of evaluating some groups in the Ideological Organizations Project. The rulings sought to clarify whether or not organizations formed to educate the public on patriotic, civil, or political matters, or which conducted a "freedom forum" where speakers addressed such issues as the political or economic system, qualified for exempt status. Proposed ruling #3 dealt specifically with the question of anti-communism and was drawn from a composite of groups then active in that field. The IRS argued that instruction should reflect "recognized educational methods" by providing a "full and fair exposition" of the facts to the public. It noted, moreover, that "insinuations or allegations relating to the character, loyalty or integrity of private individuals or institutions" were not encompassed by those criteria. Personal attacks or harassment of individuals would disqualify an organization for exemption. This would resolve any IRS hesitation to revoke the tax exemptions of many organizations in the IOP. Proposed ruling #4 paralleled #3, concluding that a freedom forum devoted to the discussion of public issues did not endanger an organization's tax exemption as long as it did not select its speakers to "champion a particular political philosophy, party or cause."

To close another loophole evident from the test-audit program, particularly in the case of the Circuit Riders, the IRS proposed Revenue

Ruling #5. This dealt specifically with the issue of publications by tax-exempt organizations that contained derogatory information about individuals, even if they were part of a larger effort to combat communism, socialism, or some other political philosophy. The impression conveyed to the reader of these publications, the IRS asserted, was that the individuals named were of "questionable national loyalty" and might be involved in some "political conspiracy." This was not instruction; it was not primarily educational. That sort of information controverted the "alleged religious and educational purpose of the organization." Any such organization, therefore, would fail to qualify for a tax exemption.

Finally, the assessment of the Ideological Organizations Project recommended various measures to ease the development of information on tax-exempt groups by Internal Revenue. Throughout the Project this had been the agency's most persistent problem. It had not kept careful track of exempt organizations' activities or funding once it granted an exemption. The numbers of exempt organizations had grown significantly, and the activities of some had become controversial and attracted public, congressional, and White House attention. Even guidelines issued to agents only two years earlier had proved inadequate.

But while the IRS sought systematically to gather specific data on exempt organizations, it failed to divorce that effort from the collection of information not essential to the determination of exempt status. Indeed, the report admitted that other agencies frequently called on the IRS to supply information because they found it "useful for other purposes," and the agency suggested twenty-eight pages of guidelines for the collection of data. Not only did it propose to collect basic information on the operation and leadership of exempt organizations, it asked agents to examine "thoroughly" the correspondence files of these individuals as well as external and internal office reports. It instructed agents that the "existence of a single nonexempt purpose or activity, if substantial," would "defeat qualification for exemption regardless of the nature or extent of other truly charitable, educational or religious purposes or activities." While this appeared to resolve some of the dilemmas expressed in the General Counsel Memoranda, the inclusion of "substantial" perpetuated an interpretive minefield.

While most of the other guidelines asked IRS agents to perform specific functions—to examine publications, speeches, recordings, movies, and the like—the sum total of these demands virtually guaranteed that few exempt organizations could ever be examined in any single year. The examination requirements, particularly for a large or active organization, were simply too formidable. As with the Organized Crime

Drive, these guidelines also reflected yet another reduction in the accounting training needed by special agents, substituting instead a content analysis of literature and other types of publications as well as an evaluation of ideological and political activities. From another perspective, record-keeping requirements for the organizations themselves were enormous. In many respects, however, these groups had brought on themselves many of these demands. As the IRS study concluded, some had "received funds from national political committees to carry on political work quietly and the names of such donees have been disguised." Others, the IRS determined, had funneled "tax deductible contributions to nonexempt organizations (for a fee)." Overall, the lengthy list of suggested guidelines sought to respond not only to problems uncovered in the Ideological Organizations Project but to a broader study of exempt organizations conducted by Texas Congressman Wright Patman, who attacked the IRS on another front.

The study's proposals looked more toward the future than the present. Despite the arrival of Sheldon Cohen to replace Mortimer Caplin as IRS commissioner, the Ideological Organizations Project continued apparently of its own momentum. Meanwhile the IRS decided not to refer its remaining cases to the chief counsel's office unless there was "substantial doubt" about its actions. Chief Counsel Mitchell Rogovin nonetheless asked that the Technical Division review them anyway. Noting that the IRS had committed a "very substantial amount of time and energy in study and analysis in this general area," Rogovin thought it would be "fruitful" for the IRS to review activities that "seem questionable." In the spring of 1966, Commissioner Cohen approved that recommendation.[15]

Throughout 1966 and 1967, Cohen received periodic updates as the IRS attempted to wrap up its test-audit program. The November 1967 status report indicated that it had fulfilled the major purposes of the IOP more than eighteen months earlier, with the promulgation of guidelines for handling activist organizations. One Revenue Ruling had been published, and two more rulings and one Revenue Procedure were in process. A few cases remained to be resolved, but the project now ended. Later examinations would proceed through normal channels. When the Joint Committee on Internal Revenue Taxation interviewed Cohen in the course of its 1975 investigation of the IRS, he told them that "after he became Commissioner there was a decision to wind down the project." Where that command originated remains unclear. President Lyndon Johnson made several public statements about proper IRS activity but used the agency for his own purposes anyway. Cohen himself may have given the order to terminate the IOP, a legacy of the Kennedy years.

Its termination, however, did not end political pressures on the IRS. Critics of IRS activities, such as Republican Senator John J. Williams of Delaware, requested confidential information. But by 1968, when he received Williams's request, Cohen replied simply that the law precluded him from furnishing such confidential information.[16] Indeed, by then the IRS was more concerned about intrusions from Congress than from the White House. Representative Wright Patman of Texas and Senator Edward Long of Missouri had launched attacks on the IRS that raised serious issues and attracted attention from both the public and Congress.

The internal IRS assessment of the IOP failed to address the fact that the White House had stimulated both phases of the project. It failed, therefore, to propose safeguards to prevent such pressures from erupting again. Not only had policy directions emanated from the White House, so had suggestions about the groups to be investigated. Those communications did not flow through prescribed official channels; indeed, there appeared to be no such prescription. White House requests were often not formalized, nor were they recorded in any systematic way. By the late 1960s the failure to provide such safeguards would permit unprecedented White House pressures on the IRS; Internal Revenue responded to these pressures by creating the Special Service Staff (SSS). The SSS ushered in a far more sinister and comprehensive crackdown against individuals and organizations than the IOP had ever proposed.[17]

CHAPTER FIVE

FOUNDATIONS, POLITICS, AND WRIGHT PATMAN

THE CONJUNCTION of power, politics, and IRS policy was sharply etched in the 1960s crusade of Texas Congressman Wright Patman to investigate tax-exempt foundations. Patman's efforts led to major clashes, not only with various foundations but with the IRS as well. Because the IRS had only sporadically examined tax-exempt organizations, the Texas Democrat called the agency to task. The IRS, in turn, resented Patman's oversight and feared his political power. The foundations found their normal routines interrupted, their activities scrutinized, and often their tax exemptions challenged. In the course of his investigations Patman also uncovered some cozy relationships between the IRS and the CIA, where tax-exempt foundations served as CIA "fronts." By the end of his efforts, many foundations found Patman's insistence that he did "not seek to destroy the foundations, but to reform them" difficult to believe. His own actions and recommendations appeared to contradict that assertion, especially when he argued that philanthropy had been "perverted into a vehicle for institutionalized deliberate evasion of fiscal and moral responsibility to the Nation."[1]

During his investigations, which continued throughout the decade and beyond, Patman raised serious questions not only about the behavior of tax-exempt foundations and their directors, but about the policies, oversight, and enforcement mechanisms of the Internal Revenue Service. The underlying question, as the historian Nancy Beck Young has argued, was whether foundations represented elite privilege or served as social benefactors for the country. Was their primary purpose to protect family or business assets from taxation, to implement governmental policies through the private sector, or to engage in and support activities that the government either did not choose to undertake or that it assigned a lower priority? Was the purpose of tax-exempt foundations, in short, to serve as agents of public policy? And should they continue to enjoy tax-exempt status only as long as they did so? What if foundations' objectives contradicted those of the government? These were important questions largely unaddressed in public before Wright Patman launched his crusade. While the IRS was examining the tax-exempt status of many right-wing organizations under its Ideological Organizations Project, that effort had been motivated largely by the White House and was politically driven. Despite the rapid proliferation of tax-exempt organizations, the IRS had paid scant attention to the revenue aspects of the issue before Patman forced it on them. This led Patman and others to question whether the IRS was a tax collector or a policy-making arm of the government.[2]

Wright Patman was a Democrat and a flinty populist from Texas who had first been elected to Congress just before the 1929 stock market crash. He served there continuously for forty-seven years, until his death in 1976. His populist streak led him to challenge entrenched economic interests and pursue economic justice. He generally assumed that private wealth abused public power, and in the case of tax-exempt foundations, that they represented a fraudulent attempt by men of means to hide their money from taxation while using it for their personal benefit. This imposed, he argued, an extra burden of taxation on everyone else. The public, in effect, subsidized the lifestyles of the rich and famous. To cite examples of this problem, Patman had to look no farther than the Ford Foundation. Created by Henry Ford in the 1930s to escape inheritance taxes while still maintaining family control of its automobile company, the Ford Foundation was the recipient of 90 percent of the family's Ford Motor Company stock holdings. The power of the IRS to grant or refuse tax-exempt status thus enabled the agency to wield a powerful influence on American life. The conflict between Billy James Hargis and the IRS noted earlier demonstrated how politically charged this power could be.[3]

Congress had investigated the role and performance of tax-exempt foundations in the mid-1950s. The so-called Reece Committee, chaired by Tennessee Republican B. Carroll Reece, was created in July 1953 by a House resolution. Although the Reece Committee was charged to investigate educational and philanthropic foundations to determine if their activities reflected the purposes for which they had been founded, its actual agenda more closely reflected the preoccupation of the times with communism. The committee specifically focused on whether these organizations were using their resources for "un-American and subversive activities." Perhaps for this reason, the committee did not really investigate all foundations, narrowing its examination to those in the social sciences. It found these foundations to be powerful and generally a force for good, but concluded that grave abuses existed. In an address at the University of Chicago, the committee's general counsel sketched the danger. These organizations could become, he warned,

> Frankensteins, though perhaps benevolent ones. It is possible that, in fifty or a hundred years, a great part of American industry will be controlled by pension and profit-sharing trusts and foundations and a large part of the balance by insurance companies and labor unions. What eventual repercussions may come from such a development, one can only guess. It may be that we will in this manner reach some form of society similar to socialism, without consciously intending it.[4]

The Reece Committee worried especially about social science research. It was, they concluded, "almost wholly in the control" of these foundations and their "obedient satellites," and that research played a "key part in the evolution of our society." Although most of these foundations had not supported communism, the committee charged that they "actively supported attacks upon our social and governmental system and financed the promotion of socialism and collectivist ideas." And their growth had been fueled by tax planning rather than charity. The committee believed that the IRS was not adequately staffed to oversee these organizations.[5]

A minority report from the committee charged that the Reece Committee had failed to execute its congressional mandate. The committee had wasted public funds in trying to link foundations to subversion, and its results were therefore "of no value to the Congress." Since the organizations in question were not given a chance to testify at public hearings, and their documented responses were not incorporated into the committee's report, the charges against foundations remained largely unsubstantiated.[6]

In the late 1950s the IRS finally began to examine tax-exempt foundations with greater care. By 1958 the Treasury Department was more aggressively enforcing the prohibition against political activity by foundations. Almost fifty organizations lost their exempt status, and applicants for tax exemption faced closer scrutiny of their charters and proposed programs. In short, though the definition of permissible activities remained broad, the *actions* of foundations became more significant as a qualification for tax exemption. This new emphasis led the IRS to label the targets of many early 1960s investigations "activist" organizations. The 1960s, however, ushered in a period of increased activism by virtually all segments of society. The Internal Revenue Service, as we have seen with the Ideological Organizations Project, found it difficult to distinguish between activism and ideology as a stimulus for investigation.[7]

On May 2, 1961, when Wright Patman rose to deliver the first of his many speeches attacking tax-exempt foundations, a new era began for these organizations. Since the report of the Reece Committee, the number of foundations had almost quadrupled to more than 45,000. Patman worried about this growth, but he was chiefly concerned about the effect of removing more than $11 billion in wealth from taxation. Patman's remarks that day were temperate. During the next several months he became much less restrained, however, following up the May 2 speech with other speeches on May 3, 4, and 8, and then two more in August and September. He demanded that foundations provide him with massive amounts of data about their finances and activities, called for the Treasury Department to initiate a new study of foundations, and insisted that the Internal Revenue Service grant him access to tax-return information from more than 500 foundations.[8]

Patman's requests set off a debate within the IRS that had to do as much with power as with policy. Should Internal Revenue provide him with the data he requested? At a July 1961 staff meeting, Treasury Secretary Douglas Dillon insisted that if the only obstacle was IRS regulations, not the law, then the regulations should be changed so that the IRS could provide Patman with photostats of foundations' tax returns. At the same time, however, the IRS hoped to contain Patman's probe and sought to head off a list of thirty-nine questions he had prepared. In mid-August, convinced that the IRS was not being fully responsive, Patman used his authority as chairman of the House Select Committee on Small Business to ask for extensive tax-return information directly from the five hundred largest foundations. His sweeping requests included "all tax exemption paperwork, foundation charter and administration documents, data on income and expenditures, all Internal Revenue Service forms, annual reports, biographical information on trustees including their occupations, and an accounting of securities holdings and investment counselors." His was a one-man crusade. Only in September did Patman obtain approval from the House Select Committee on Small Business for his actions.[9]

The staff of the Joint Committee on Internal Revenue Taxation (JCIRT), a bipartisan congressional committee, complained that Patman was poaching in areas that were its province or that of the House Ways and Means Committee. While this had a ring of truth to it, it also reflected a fear that Patman might be hostile and uncontrollable. He had subpoena power and threatened to use it. Colin Stam, chief of staff for the JCIRT, was in a quandary. On the one hand he was reluctant to take Patman's demands to the Joint Committee and perhaps trigger an internal struggle for power; on the other hand he believed that the IRS "had gone farther than necessary in dealing with [his] requests and recommendations."[10]

Reaction from the foundations was mixed at first, perhaps because some of them believed that nominal cooperation would best serve their interests and pacify Patman. One foundation president wrote Patman that his study was long overdue and would be of "great value to the country." But this executive was sorely mistaken if he believed his response would blunt the investigations. A more typical reply was that the government had all the data it (and Patman) needed, and that the inquiry was "entirely unnecessary." In his letters to foundation executives, Patman made clear his belief that any organization enjoying a tax exemption owed a public accounting to the people. As Patman forged ahead, it became clear that most of the problems he cited were real and that his goals were ambitious. The IRS grew more concerned and resisted the congressman's recommendations for change. IRS Commissioner Mortimer Caplin tried to be politically responsive and conciliatory, but IRS staff members insisted that their existing system "serves our purpose."[11]

Finally, in January 1962, the House Select Committee on Small Business formally authorized a study of the impact of tax-exempt foundations on the American economy. Somewhat belatedly, this gave Patman the authority to proceed. By then he had already launched his crusade, but the timing of the resolution reflected the unorthodox nature of his efforts. Not only was it to be a one-man effort, other members of the subcommittee rarely participated in its proceedings. Foundations were placed under scrutiny but were not called to testify at hearings.[12]

In a July 23, 1962, House speech, Patman outlined his agenda and released a portion of a three-phased report of his subcommittee to his

Select Committee on Small Business and to the House. The agenda contained fifteen very broad topics. They included foundations' business activities and moneylending activities, their relationships with donors, conflicts of interest, activities that channeled funds so as to hurt competitors, and their contributions, self-dealing, and favoritism. "Foundations today," Patman argued, "bear a frightening resemblance to the bank holding companies that were invented by the champions of monopoly and combination in the early 1900s." Control of "our industrial and commercial enterprises" was passing into the hands of these foundations. They had unlimited powers, with no apparent public duties or responsibilities. Patman argued that his study

> revolves around the possible exploitation of the people's respect and admiration for charitable acts and gifts. Are foundations being used as a cloak and a vehicle for crippling competition and accelerating concentration of economic power? Are foundations being used to facilitate the use of economic power, disguised as charity, to attain ends never intended by the people or the Congress—ends such as taking control of commercial enterprises?

The IRS, he charged, had failed to enforce the tax exemption regulations, and he hoped to provide suggestions for improvement. Indeed, he noted, the Treasury Department had already decided to make "more information on foundations available to the public."[13]

Patman doubted that this represented a significant change, chiefly because the IRS lacked adequate information on foundations and their activities. When he went directly to the foundations himself for information, he often found them uncooperative and even arrogant. "They appear," he reported, "to have adopted the attitude that tax exemption is their birthright. . . ." One foundation executive responded that he was "unaware" of any Internal Revenue Code provision or regulation that required him to report stock ownership in companies. Patman quickly responded with the citation, and the foundation complied. But the fact that it was unaware of the requirement revealed the failure of the IRS to enforce its own regulations. More typically, foundations responded that they had never had an IRS audit, often from the inception of their tax exemption. The Internal Revenue Service, of course, *had* audited some tax-exempt foundations. But a shortage of trained personnel, together with the rapid growth of these organizations and other agency priorities, had led to an enforcement gap. Patman exploited that gap vigorously.[14]

Patman's findings led him to call for an immediate moratorium on new tax exemptions until Congress could adopt new laws to "fit present-day economic circumstances and needs." To justify his demand, Patman cited the IRS for being lax and irresponsible in its supervision of foundations. Too little information and inadequate supervision meant that the IRS in effect exercised almost no oversight of foundations and their activities, and Patman's inquiries to foundations revealed a widespread disregard of Treasury regulations on their part. They had amassed huge accumulations of income rather than spend it for charitable needs. They had used these untaxed funds to speculate in the stock market. Some even operated for-profit businesses with tax-exempt monies. This not only deprived the public of tax revenues, it represented an unfair competitive advantage. In response, the IRS called Patman's request outdated, noting that Commissioner Caplin had called for stepped-up auditing activity five months earlier.[15]

The IRS response, however, was a bit disingenuous. It had indeed been studying the problem for eighteen months—a reaction to White House pressure—but had yet to issue any guidelines to the field. Its internal discussions, moreover, revealed that the IRS sought to limit its exposure to Patman's inquiries. The agency's immediate response was simply to state that it was studying Patman's report—nothing more. The IRS was in fact trying to walk a thin line. On the one hand, as Treasury Under Secretary Henry Fowler cautioned, they did not wish to be too defensive. On the other hand they had little concrete progress to report. They believed, moreover, that Patman was aware of their internal study, largely because he cut off his inquiries at 1960, a year before the IRS study began.[16]

The IRS appeared more concerned about what Patman might find. Patman "didn't know what he was getting into," Assistant Secretary of the Treasury Stanley Surrey warned. "There were many sophisticated questions involved." Fowler tried to focus any response on the enforcement of existing laws rather than broader IRS policy or recommendations for change, insisting that the "broader questions of policy we don't have to get into." But, as Surrey noted, existing law, IRS policy, and recommendations for change were intimately related. The staff finally agreed to draft a letter for the commissioner in the next week or ten days. After that they would decide whether or not to send the letter. The IRS remained cautious and defensive, moving a half-step at a time.[17]

On August 20, 1962, Patman released another installment of his report on the floor of the House. Whereas his July report had concerned the income and abuses of foundations, the August report focused on foundations' assets and how they used them. He concluded that foundations had "assumed functions, in some cases, wholly foreign to the object for which they were granted tax exemption and, in my opinion, at variance with the public interest." They had also competed with private businesses and challenged government policies. And yet they remained largely unregulated. Concluding that an "agonizing reappraisal is overdue," Patman argued that tax-exempt organizations had a responsibility to behave "in accordance with public policy." Complaints that Patman had bypassed his committee and violated customs of the House failed to slow his charge.[18]

The IRS counterattacked, finally sending Patman a letter outlining recent initiatives that, it claimed, preceded his investigation. Patman had asked for a list of IRS reforms in the tax-exempt area, undoubtedly hoping to publicize the lack of oversight and concern. Although Commissioner Caplin admitted that the IRS had lacked sufficient manpower to examine tax-exempt organizations and had chosen to focus on returns "known to be productive of revenue," he asserted that this situation changed when he became commissioner and began a program to improve voluntary compliance with the tax laws. Caplin claimed that "extensive studies in the exempt organization area" began in April 1961, and the following October the IRS had issued a letter on revised programs and objectives to field personnel that promised more audit coverage for exempt organizations. IRS regional commissioners had discussed the issue at their December meeting, and in February 1962 Caplin had announced "intensified examinations of a greater number of exempt organizations" in a speech before the Southwestern Legal Foundation in Dallas, Texas. Tests of the project had begun in two IRS districts in March 1962. That same month Caplin had discussed formation of a special advisory group, the Exempt Organization Council. Additional steps were taken throughout the spring of 1962. Caplin conceded that he would take Patman's advice and revise Form 990-A, on which foundations reported their assets and activities, but he conceded little else. He also failed to mention anything about the ongoing Ideological Organizations Project. Indeed, as noted earlier, the IRS actually hid that project behind its broader scrutiny of exempt organizations.[19]

Although an IRS press release a few weeks later tried to pacify Patman by citing his reports as valuable in helping correct existing abuses in the exempt area, Internal Revenue staff vigorously attempted to resist any political pressures that Patman's reports might generate. They also sought to deny him access to IRS files. The central line of defense was the question of disclosure. Patman had requested the names of Internal

Revenue employees who had participated in several exemption rulings. The IRS refused to provide them, arguing that disclosure would "interfere with the exercise of sound judgment in this difficult area." The release of employees' names would "hurt morale" and provide a precedent for future requests. According to the IRS, the Exempt Organization Division was the most difficult to staff, had many vacancies and a huge backlog of cases, was politically sensitive, and carried the heaviest workload of any division of the Internal Revenue Service. The White House supported the IRS position against disclosure even as IRS and White House officials met regularly to discuss tax-exempt foundations. Ironically, Attorney General Robert Kennedy was skeptical of the IRS position. According to Treasury staff notes, Justice almost gave them "a bad opinion on this but we have argued with them about it," and the agency hoped to receive an opinion that "we are not obliged to give him [Patman] the files."[20] As the IRS came under closer scrutiny, this question of disclosure became fundamental. While disclosure laws did limit responses to certain types of requests, the IRS often used those laws simply to avoid providing information it chose not to make public. Indeed, the somewhat vague and untested disclosure provisions of the Internal Revenue Code became another tool, often the most important one, in the arsenal of weapons the IRS employed to escape scrutiny, even from those vested with oversight of the tax agency.

At the end of the year Patman printed a full report outlining his activities. "Unquestionably," he claimed, "the economic life of our Nation has become so intertwined with foundations that unless something is done about it they will hold a dominant position in every phase of American life." He attacked the IRS for "laxness and irresponsibility" and criticized foundations for violating Treasury regulations, withdrawing at least $7 billion from taxation and fostering a rapid concentration of economic power. Of 570,000 exempt organization tax returns filed between January 1958 and June 1960, the IRS had audited only 5,300 (fewer than 1 percent).[21]

To emphasize his point that tax-exempt organizations were unfairly competing with small businessmen and the private sector, both of whom *were* taxed, Patman cited several examples. Three foundations in St. Paul, Minnesota, for example, had purchased gasoline service stations and other commercial buildings and then leased them back to the sellers. These sales and lease-back arrangements essentially provided those companies with "instant capital with which they can accelerate their growth in competition with independent service station operators, and small retailers." These foundations—the Louis W. & Maud Hill Family

Foundation, the Amherst R. Wilder Foundation, and the Tozer Foundation—were engaging in activities irrelevant to their charters. Another example was that of Gulf Oil Corporation. It had created a company foundation, the Gulf Oil Foundation of Houston, which filed for tax-exempt status in May 1961. Two months later the IRS granted the exemption. Then the parent corporation turned over to the foundation 100 percent of the voting common stock in Pontiac Refining Corporation of Corpus Christi, Texas, worth $32 million. Dividends paid by Pontiac Refining, once taxable, now went to a tax-exempt foundation which, in turn, had disbursed only 50 percent of its income. This was, Patman insisted, a new version of the old industrial trust.[22]

The Treasury Department remained indecisive about a course of action. Treasury Under Secretary Henry Fowler observed that "we must decide whether we are basically for or against foundations." Secretary Douglas Dillon proposed that they should be for foundations but against abuses. This indecision revealed how far both Treasury and the IRS had to go before they could satisfactorily respond to Patman's charges and demands.

Meanwhile a lengthy article by Fred Cook in *The Nation* called attention to the connection between foundations and politics. Cook focused largely on foundations' support for right-wing causes, delineating how foundations had used tax-exempt funds to propagandize. Whether or not these foundations knowingly violated the law, Cook pointed out that they had nonetheless done so. As Patman had noted, "Uneducated sharecroppers are presumed to know the law, but many of the foundations . . . and their well-paid, well-educated advisers are apparently exempt from this ancient presumption. . . ."[23]

Cook cited the case of the National Foundation for Education in American Citizenship (NFEAC) as an example. The NFEAC was closely tied to *Human Events*, a right-wing newspaper. According to Cook, that opened a "window on a whole nest of ultra-Right activities" largely financed with "tax-exempt, foundation funds." Felix Morley, an early director of NFEAC, was a former president of *Human Events* and now served as secretary for the Americans for Constitutional Action, which published a *Voting Rights Index* that had become the "bible of the radical Right." That index, in turn, was compiled and distributed by *Human Events*. The newspaper was also linked to H. L. Hunt's Life Line Foundation, and the two shared a Washington office. These "cross-ties and proliferating bequests that water right-wing propaganda causes," Cook argued, "are obviously a far cry from the law's definition of a tax-exempt charity. . . ." Even though it knew as early as 1951 that 40 percent of contributions to the NFEAC were going to *Human Events*, not until 1962 did Internal Revenue staff move—and then only after several congressmen questioned the propriety of these activities. On October 10, 1962, when the IRS finally announced the revocation of NFEAC's tax exemption, it did so quietly and refused to make public any penalties it might levy.[24]

Cook also outlined Patman's case against the Howard Hughes Medical Institute, incorporated in 1953 for the purpose of engaging "primarily" (rather than "exclusively" as the law required) in the "promotion of medical research." That same day Howard Hughes had incorporated Hughes Aircraft, with the Hughes Medical Institute as its only stockholder. Hughes's original corporation, Toolco, gave the Medical Institute all its patents and trademarks. The Institute then "subleased" them to Hughes Aircraft, and Toolco took a tax deduction of $2 million. Yet, as Cook reported, "as a matter of hard cash it is difficult to discern how a single screaming nickel had escaped from the control of Howard Hughes." The IRS agreed in 1953, denying an exemption to the Institute, but reversed itself in 1957 when Hughes protested. Both Patman and Cook concluded that Hughes, with the complicity of the IRS, had essentially placed his entire operation beyond the reach of the tax collector.[25]

One of the most revealing, and complicated, examples of foundation abuse and IRS failure was the case of the Baird Foundation—actually three Baird foundations: the Winfield Baird Foundation, the David, Josephine, and Winfield Baird Foundation, and the Lansing Foundation. David Baird visited Patman in September 1962, praising the work of the subcommittee and telling the congressman that "we have found the Internal Revenue Service most thorough in the supervision of our charitable foundations." Patman's chief investigator, Harry Olsher, reported that the IRS had once suggested revocation of the Baird Foundation's tax exemption. It had reviewed the foundation's operations from 1951 to 1959 and cited five problems. But when Baird protested, IRS Commissioner Caplin overrode his district director's recommendation in October 1962, and the foundation retained its tax exemption for the years under question.[26]

While the IRS reached a fairly amicable agreement with the Lansing Foundation, whereby the foundation agreed to disperse its assets by December 1965 (an arrangement contingent on securing agreements with the other Baird foundations), Patman was frustrated in his efforts to secure information from the Baird foundations. David Baird claimed that the records were sufficient for the foundation's purposes, even though

Patman found them inadequate and inefficient. Baird asserted that there was no tax avoidance, but Patman complained that Baird furnished mountains of useless information, professing cooperation but creating "thick smokescreens." In June 1963, Patman asked the U.S. marshal in New York City to serve Baird with a subpoena for "books and records, including ledgers and correspondence," relating to the three foundations. Indeed, by this time Patman's Select Committee on Small Business had an inventory almost a hundred pages long of records it had subpoenaed.[27]

When in October Patman issued a report that focused largely on the Baird foundations and severely criticized the failure of Internal Revenue to audit foundations, the IRS temporized, even though some of Patman's claims were demonstrably wrong. Assistant Commissioner Harold Swartz told Treasury Secretary Dillon that the IRS had indeed performed a solid audit on the Baird foundations and had entered into a closing agreement. Stanley Surrey urged that the agency "take advantage and respond to the criticism." But Under Secretary Fowler hesitated, urging caution to the point of inaction. IRS behavior, he warned, "might not be equally satisfactory with respect to the other foundations." Other staff members feared that this might not be "the time" to disclose "a new audit program in this area." In the end, the IRS decided to do nothing except review Patman's report and then prepare a press release. Whether or not it would issue that release, however, was another question altogether and would require additional meetings.[28]

Acting IRS Commissioner Bertrand Harding's assessment of Patman's October report reviewed IRS actions with respect to the six specific foundations Patman had cited. The IRS had audited the Baird and Lansing foundations, and agreements were pending with all of them. The Lansing Foundation had an unreasonable accumulation of income and would lose its exemption for 1952 and 1953. The three Baird foundations would be forced to discontinue various questionable activities and "disgorge income and corpus to other charitable organizations" by December 31, 1965. The IRS had not yet examined tax returns of either the Helmsley Foundation or the Noyes Foundation, both cited by Patman, but they had been assigned for audit. IRS examination of the Wien Foundation had found no basis for revocation, but in light of Patman's findings, staff determined to take another look. Harding concluded that there was room for improvement in the exempt organizations area, but he vigorously denied that IRS performance had been a "complete, dismal failure," as Patman charged. Finally, Harding argued against issuing a press release in response to Patman's report: an adequate response might violate disclosure laws and "might give more impetus to the report and result in a continuing public debate between Mr. Patman and the Service." In that case, he worried that disclosure provisions would handicap the IRS in clearly "presenting its side of the matter."[29]

The case of the Baird foundations was instructive for several reasons. Not only did it reveal IRS caution about getting into debates with political figures, it also revealed how existing disclosure laws could be used as a pretext for IRS refusal to divulge information or as a constraint on its efforts to do so. That the IRS had notified the Winfield Baird Foundation in May 1959 about its decision to revoke its tax exemption failed to slow Patman's attack on both the foundation and Internal Revenue. He aimed to shine light in dark corners of the tax-exempt world and to achieve greater oversight by both the IRS and the Congress. Foundations clearly engaged in much more than charitable activities, becoming securities dealers, business brokers, finders of credit as well as trading mortgages and supplanting banks as a source of loans to affiliated companies and business associates.[30]

Publication of Patman's year-end report also revealed his pique at IRS Commissioner Mortimer Caplin. Much of the subcommittee's efforts he attributed to Caplin's failure to provide the committee with data. Not only did he conclude that the IRS record on foundations was a "dud, a dismal failure," he rated Caplin's performance no better. The IRS, he complained, touted its progress in the tax-exempt area, but there were "no recognizable signs of progress. . . ." Indeed, Patman complained, the IRS would never be able to meet its responsibilities merely by issuing "ringing statements" by the commissioner or other "public relations gimmickry." He wanted fewer speeches from IRS leadership and more productive work from staff.[31]

Patman then documented the IRS field-audit experience he had uncovered. The IRS had performed no field audits for 433 of the foundations he had examined, including the 10 largest. No field audits were evident for the 115 foundations with assets of $10 million or more, and 11 Rockefeller-controlled foundations (out of 14) had no field audits. None of the Carnegie foundations had undergone field audits, and 8 (of 9) Ford-controlled foundations, 4 (of 6) Mellon-controlled foundations, and 6 (of 9) DuPont-controlled foundations had also escaped audits. Not only had the IRS failed to perform audits on most foundations, when it had acted it had been "incompetent." Among the 113 foundations that had experienced one or more field audits during the years Patman studied, he found that more than one-third had failed to file required schedules and continued to ignore Treasury regulations even after the audits. And the IRS had done nothing.

Treasury officials, according to Patman, "lacked the zeal for reform and the know-how necessary" to supervise tax-exempt foundations. "There is," Patman concluded, "considerable evidence that the Treasury is sweetly oblivious to what is going on in the foundation business." This had led to abuse of the tax-exempt privilege. As the Baird foundations had illustrated, that abuse had allowed foundations "boundless opportunity" to lavish favors on "business associates and friends" while escaping not only the tax collector but accountability to the public.

Although much of what he said was true, Patman overstated his case. The IRS had indeed been lax, but since 1960 it had initiated audits on many of the foundations that Patman surveyed. By December 1963 it had received preliminary reports on 496 of the 530 foundations named by Patman and had completed audits on 218 of them. Eighty-one others were currently under audit or assigned for examination. Of the 218 completed, the IRS had recommended revocation of exempt status in 12 cases. More important, perhaps, was the revelation that the IRS was responding to Patman's political pressure. Commissioner Caplin noted that, to "assure proper attention to Mr. Patman's allegations," he had directed field offices to "immediately examine all foundations named which have not been subjected to audit since the release of the first Patman report." What motivated these audits? The IRS appeared to have been blindsided by Patman's aggressive actions and responded primarily for political reasons.[32]

For example, the IRS initiated a new audit of the Baird foundations following the release of Patman's critical report. This time it audited returns for 1960 through 1963, and did so with great efficiency. To get the information required for the audit, however, the IRS had to request the foundations' files from Congressman Patman. In the spring of 1964, Patman reported to the foundations' lawyers, who needed to send the files to the IRS, that they were available. The files were so voluminous that the IRS had to send a car to pick them up. During summer hearings of Patman's subcommittee, the congressman questioned Mortimer Caplin and Bertrand Harding at length about the Baird foundations' activities and the ongoing audit. Finally, a year later, the IRS levied a $5.5 million fine against the Winfield Baird Foundation and the David, Josephine and Winfield Baird Foundation for tax deficiency.[33]

In his remarks to district directors and regional commissioners in February 1964, IRS Commissioner Caplin outlined some of the difficulties facing the IRS in the exempt organizations area. Insisting that the

IRS was "committed" to securing compliance in this area, Caplin cited "broad Congressional interest" in the question and interest from the Treasury in legislative remedies. Unfortunately, he admitted, these were "low yield examinations," and motivating revenue agents was "difficult." Nonetheless the IRS hoped to complete ten thousand examinations in fiscal year 1964. That included examining every single organization "cited by Congressman Patman" that had not been audited before 1962. This was a bold projection, and Caplin expected assistance from the newly formed Exempt Organization Council chaired by his cousin Mitchell Rogovin. Formation of this fourteen-man advisory council, however, seemed to be more window dressing than substance. Ten of the members were in some way affiliated with foundations.[34]

In testimony before Patman's committee in July 1964, Caplin defended IRS actions and tried to draw a line between the jurisdiction of Congress and that of the IRS. He asserted that Congress, not the IRS, determined the "social and economic justifications behind the statutory grant of exemptions," that Congress had established the criteria of qualification for exempt status and the standards for revocation of an exemption. Conveniently failing to mention that the IRS writes the regulations that, in most cases, have great impact on the administration of the laws, Caplin portrayed Internal Revenue as an impartial agency carrying out congressional will. The IRS only administered the laws passed by Congress. Since many of those laws were imprecise, Congress made the agency's job difficult. Caplin testified that he had established the Exempt Organizations Council to "help remove these impediments" and to develop "workable principles." As a consequence, the IRS had allocated sufficient audit manpower to examine ten thousand exempt organizations a year, and it had decided that these audits would be of the "same scope and depth as income tax audits." Moreover, the IRS had already examined more than nine thousand exempt organizations in the past fifteen months and had discovered that most of them "were in substantial compliance with the law" despite "extremely light audit coverage" in the past. Caplin claimed, in short, that the problem was not as severe as Patman had argued.[35]

Yet, as Bertrand Harding testified before Patman's committee, the IRS had been unable to determine how many exempt organizations existed in 1964. Consequently the agency had decided to create a master file of such groups on electronic tape, a project it hoped to complete within a year. Commissioner Caplin himself guessed that in 1960 there had been more than one million exempt organizations in existence. Many were churches or cooperatives, not foundations. If the IRS examined these groups, it did so only with an eye to their compliance with exemption laws. It had never checked to determine if they engaged in trade practices that violated federal laws. Indeed, IRS agents were not sufficiently trained to recognize violators of those laws, unless they were flagrant. Yet on occasion the IRS had in fact secretly checked with other government agencies to see if some exempt organizations' operations conflicted with "public policy, private diplomacy or criminal statutes." A case in point was the Tractors for Freedom case, which involved discussions with the Castro government to free Cuban prisoners from the aborted Bay of Pigs invasion. In that case the IRS had contacted the CIA, the State Department, and the Justice Department to "determine their interest or position." Briefing papers for testimony before Patman's committee, however, warned that "for policy reasons, our liaisons with certain government agencies should not be disclosed to Mr. Patman or the public." The IRS was intentionally withholding vital information from Congress and citizens alike.[36]

Thus despite what appeared to be candid testimony, Caplin and other Treasury witnesses were cautious about what they revealed. While Caplin did not attempt to contradict Patman directly, insisting instead that there was another, less ominous, side to the story, briefing papers for these officials' appearances before the committee document their intent to conceal more than they revealed. In response to a question about whether and how the IRS shared nontax information with other government agencies, for instance, Treasury Secretary Dillon was provided with a suggested reply that did little more than recite the disclosure laws. The IRS maintained that it could not disclose any information to Patman without a written request, following issuance of an executive order. In his testimony Dillon portrayed Internal Revenue as playing a passive role, responding only to authorized requests. But that answer was simply not true. Dillon's briefing paper also included an option: "IF PRESSED" he was to note a procedure, authorized in July 1961, whereby the IRS "voluntarily advised the Attorney General" whenever it came across information that anyone had violated U.S. law, "even though the indicated offenses are not violations of the Internal Revenue laws." The attorney general would then formally request the relevant IRS files ("returns and related data and other information in possession of the Service"), thereby providing a cover for Internal Revenue should it leak to the press that a government agency was using nontax information gathered by the IRS. This was a quite different story from Dillon's prepared testimony. The IRS was in fact not a passive recipient of requests for information; on its initiative it passed information to other government agencies. The IRS, moreover, had issued a Manual Supplement on July 17, 1961, that outlined such procedures. When combined with IRS audit procedures for exempt organizations, exemplified in the Ideological Organizations Project which examined a "myriad of materials," this was a potent weapon.[37]

Perhaps the underlying disagreement between Congressman Patman and the Internal Revenue Service with respect to foundations was the role of the IRS itself. Patman clearly believed that the Internal Revenue Service bore responsibility for policing virtually every aspect of a foundation's behavior, and that it was in fact the only federal agency with regulatory responsibility for exempt organizations. In his 1964 report he listed eighteen failures of the IRS with respect to foundations. He charged IRS officials with covering up the "propaganda peddling of the elite bureaucrats of the large foundations, their gravy trains, and their inefficiencies." The IRS, Patman insisted, had abdicated its public responsibilities.[38]

Bertrand Harding refused to plead guilty. The IRS, he argued, was not the "general policeman of all activities of charitable foundations." It was neither the IRS's role nor its responsibility. Under further questioning, Harding suggested that this was something for the executive and legislative branches to work out. At the same time, however—and in direct contrast to Harding's claims—when the IRS listed thirty-two organizations to which it had denied exempt status, it indicated that the denials were based on the nature of their activities rather than on narrow questions of taxation. The difference was that in these cases the IRS *presumed* to work within the exemption statutes. But as the Ideological Organizations Project revealed—and this ran concurrently with Patman's investigations but out of his sight—those decisions often rested more on ideological than statutory or tax-related conclusions. At a time when the president was Catholic, the IRS determined that the distribution of anti-Catholic political material was a partisan ideological activity.[39]

By the fall of 1964 the IRS had begun to consider some of these issues. In October, Stanley Surrey questioned whether foundations should be able to own operating businesses. Previously the IRS had assumed that any unrelated business activity would generate taxable income, but now, he noted, there was "considerable feeling" that the ownership of operating businesses by tax-exempt organizations should not be permitted. A lengthy Treasury Department report on foundations later that month found four types of problems: restrictions against dealings between a foundation and its major contributors were inadequate; private parties used foundations to gain tax benefits without relinquishing control over their wealth; foundations intervened between donors and charities to usurp benefits or assets; and foundations increasingly operated commercial enterprises. Legislative solutions, not IRS action, Surrey emphasized, were necessary to clarify all of these situations.[40]

While Surrey was correct, his analysis obscured the operational role of the IRS in the exempt organizations area. Once the IRS decided whether or not to review an organization's exempt status, it was omnipotent—and at times arrogant. Internal Revenue wielded near-absolute power once it initiated a tax investigation. And audits could be triggered by nothing more than an agent's opposition to a group's beliefs, or a congressman's political inclinations, a situation that placed unprecedented power in the hands of individual and often low-level government employees. Selection criteria knew no checks or bounds. The IRS concluded, for example, that the goals of the Fellowship of Reconciliation could be achieved only through legislation, and withdrew the group's tax exemption. Senator Gaylord Nelson objected in a letter to Commissioner Caplin, asking how on earth legislation could secure world peace. But, as one legal scholar noted, given the IRS's approach, any "continuance or withdrawal of exempt status is a matter of conclusory characterization: the organization's ultimate goal will be emphasized where exemption will continue; the means it adopts or must adopt for achievement, if withdrawal is the intended result."[41] On two major issues Wright Patman and the Internal Revenue Service would clash over just this argument over ends and means.

CHAPTER SIX

ROBBER BARONS
AND SPIES

As WRIGHT PATMAN'S investigation into founda-
tions' activities deepened, two profiles emerged—one stark, the other
shadowy. Patman found each of them shocking, and he used both to attack the activities of Internal Revenue and its oversight of exempt
organizations. The first involved H. L. Hunt and his Life Line Foundation; the second was the revelation of cozy relationships between foundations, the IRS, and the Central Intelligence Agency. In the case of
H. L. Hunt, Patman and the IRS fought over the tax-exemption issue
and the implications of Hunt's activities. The White House, meanwhile,
quietly but forcefully took a third position, one that had as much to do
with ideology as it did with taxes. With respect to the CIA and foundations, however, Patman exposed and then attacked the IRS for complic-
ity and deception. The White House, in turn, maintained the lowest
possible profile but solidly supported the IRS.

Haroldson LaFayette Hunt was a modern-day robber baron. There
is simply no better characterization of the ideas and activities of this
very wealthy man and strong advocate of plutocracy. Described as "the
richest man in the world (and a bigamist as well, managing to juggle
three wives and families and a bevy of young mistresses)," he had six
children by his first wife, Lydia. When she died, he married Ruth Ray,
his secretary, who had already borne four of his children. Together both
branches built a huge family empire. In 1957 Hunt's wealth was estimated at $3 billion. During the 1950s he spent up to $1 million a year to
support two radical right anti-Communist radio programs, Facts Forum
and LIFE LINE. The latter was a revival of Facts Forum, a revival that
sprang from Hunt's discovery of religion, which in turn stimulated his

renewed anti-communism. Each fifteen-minute LIFE LINE program, broadcast six or seven days every week, presented a small selection of hymns, sermons, and Christian fundamentalism but focused its real message on political issues of the day. Through this program Hunt lobbied for the oil-depletion allowance and reform of the Electoral College while attacking the United Nations, the State Department, the Supreme Court, unions, urban renewal, and almost all Kennedy administration programs. It was, in essence, a political broadcast with a veneer of religion, and reached millions of listeners in forty-two states and the District of Columbia.[1]

That mixture of religion and politics was reflected in LIFE LINE's personnel. Wayne Poucher, a Church of Christ minister, essentially developed and ran the program. Poucher's ministerial credentials were thin. He had been pastor of Owen's Chapel Church in Franklin, Tennessee, for one year, and had also served as a part-time preacher for churches in suburban Washington. More important were his political credentials. Poucher had run unsuccessfully for the South Carolina legislature and had served as campaign manager for Strom Thurmond's victorious write-in campaign for the U.S. Senate. Working with Poucher was James Dobbs, who also bragged of conservative religious affiliations and had been an unsuccessful candidate in a Texas congressional race. Both men drew upon the almost unlimited financial resources of the Hunt oil and food empire, and Hunt spent about $100,000 per month to finance LIFE LINE's programs.[2]

Patriotism proved more profitable than food. Hunt's food company, HLH Products, apparently lost money steadily but continued to underwrite LIFE LINE, which in turn prospered. By 1963 the program reported a gross income of more than $500,000. This discrepancy cried out for examination. In the words of one investigator, "LIFE LINE continued to masquerade as a nonpolitical, 'educational and religious' organization [that] qualified for tax-exempt status. . . . A donor could do a favor for H. L. Hunt, strike a blow against communism, and claim a tax deduction all at the same time." That meant, in effect, that "LIFE LINE's real financial backers—willingly or not—were America's taxpayers."[3] Life Line Foundation, Hunt's parent organization, supported an array of activities that collected tax-free funds. These included not only the LIFE LINE radio program but a LIFE LINE television program broadcast five days per week; LIFE LINE LINKS, a book club that distributed right-wing publications; a LIFE LINE essay contest that solicited "patriotic" writings; and LIFE LINE Seminars, a separate corporation that conducted three-day meetings promoting radical conservative views and anti-communism in cities around the country. Hunt also published *Lifelines*, a newspaper that at the height of its popularity in 1962 had 35,000 subscribers.[4]

By the early 1960s Hunt had three major problems: the White House, Congressman Wright Patman, and the Internal Revenue Service. The Kennedy White House was after the IRS to crack down on right-wing organizations, and Hunt's activities became part of the Ideological Organizations Project. Congressman Wright Patman was an implacable foe, charging that foundations like Hunt's used tax loopholes to pursue noncharitable purposes and undercut small businesses. The IRS, which had investigated Hunt's tax-exempt enterprises for some time, not only came under pressure from the White House and Patman to take action but initiated its own stepped-up enforcement of exempt organizations. Hunt was caught in the middle. Although these three forces did not always operate in concert with one another, at least theoretically they pursued similar goals. One of Patman's difficulties with the IRS stemmed from the existence of the Ideological Organizations Project. This was still a secret operation, and the IRS had no intention of divulging it, even to a United States congressman or a congressional committee. Patman's criticism of the IRS increased when he discovered that it had investigated LIFE LINE's predecessor, Facts Forum, in the 1950s.[5]

When President John F. Kennedy attacked the political activities of right-wing groups in the fall of 1961, LIFE LINE was one of his targets. Later, when Kennedy aide Myer Feldman prepared his long memorandum on right-wing groups for the president in the summer of 1963, he used H. L. Hunt as a model of radical right organizing, noting that Hunt alone had access to more than five hundred radio stations. Together with his colleagues on the radical right, Hunt believed that the United States faced a Communist conspiracy at home that was "softening the country up" for a Communist takeover. Hunt, Feldman noted, had access to the funds necessary to broadcast this message. He used Hunt food company funds to underwrite his program, then took those costs as business deductions even though his company might "sell no food whatsoever within 1,000 miles of the place of the broadcast." Contributions to the Life Line Foundation, moreover, were tax exempt, even though the foundation used the funds for "purely right-wing propaganda purposes."[6]

By the time Wright Patman locked onto Hunt and the Life Line Foundation as a target for investigation, an IRS field audit had already proposed (on September 28, 1962) revocation of its tax exemption. A conference between representatives of the foundation and the IRS in

November revealed that the examining agent had based his revocation recommendation on radio scripts which he considered one-sided (conservative) and which required legislation to implement their suggestions. Life Line received permission to file a brief by January 31, 1963, to argue against revocation of its tax exemption.[7]

The foundation did not dispute that its radio programs advocated conservative positions and views. It contended instead that revocation of its tax exemption violated its constitutional rights of free speech and the right to petition. It also argued that its messages were educational, despite their avowedly conservative content. Finally, perhaps with an eye toward the Ideological Organizations Project, Life Line asserted that it was not an "action organization." When the Ideological Organizations Project expanded in 1963, the IRS added the Life Line Foundation to the study. The foundation underwent another IRS examination in 1963. Once again an IRS task force recommended revocation of the foundation's tax exemption. The chief counsel's office concurred, and, after an administrative appeal, the IRS issued a final revocation letter on March 23, 1965. That did not deter the foundation; it promptly filed another exemption application.[8]

The IRS actions also did not deter Patman. In May 1963, Ohio Democratic Congressman Wayne Hays, for one, urged Patman to investigate. Patman readily agreed (he had already collected some information) but cautioned that he had to clear it with others first lest he be "accused of getting outside of my proclaimed program on foundations." Patman even suggested that organizations such as Hunt's should be "listed as subversive by the Attorney General." He assigned his chief investigator, Harry Olsher, to the case. Olsher requested help from J. S. Seidman, a certified public accountant in New York. Seidman outlined what Olsher needed to investigate the Life Line Foundation and push for revocation of its exempt status. He also provided Olsher with a three-page list of probing questions which reflected Seidman's scrutiny of the foundation's finances. Seidman clearly believed that many of its transactions violated IRS regulations, and his questions were designed to challenge Hunt on several fronts. Their significance, he told Olsher, was that Hunt contributed (and probably deducted) "$4,000,000, and other people and organizations primarily in the oil field likewise took deductions in substantial amounts." Loss of the foundation's exemption would disqualify those deductions. Patman's belief that the IRS was dragging its feet, despite its 1962 revocation letter, further energized him in 1963 and 1964.[9]

White House hostility toward Hunt also intensified. In October

1963, President Kennedy complained once again about the tax exemptions of far-right organizations. Oregon Democratic Senator Maurine Neuberger delivered a blistering speech on the floor of Congress urging the IRS to investigate these groups and their propaganda activities and attacking their tax subsidies. Indeed, money was an avenue of attack, just as the Reuther Memorandum had suggested back in the fall of 1961. It was the tax-exempt status granted by the IRS that allowed contributors to deduct their contributions to organizations such as LIFE LINE. Perhaps as a result, LIFE LINE seemed to float on a "sea of funny money." It reported more money for subscriptions than it claimed for the circulation of its publications. As Senator Neuberger concluded, there was probably nobody who got "more right-wing propaganda for his tax dollar" than H. L. Hunt.[10]

Hunt counterattacked. In the weeks before President Kennedy's assassination, his radio programs blasted the administration and its policies. They warned that it was "tyrannical," bypassing Congress to follow a line enunciated from Moscow. It was a time, LIFE LINE broadcasts cried, for "extreme patriotism." In a lengthy article, prepared in part with information from Patman's chief investigator, Robert Sherrill concluded that the most important legal feature of the Life Line Foundation was the "underlying duplicity of its creation." It failed to complete required IRS forms, yet, inexplicably, the IRS kept giving it another chance. In a letter to Olsher, Sherrill also noted that Wayne Poucher was then suing Hunt and could be an important source of information. Poucher had resisted Hunt's attempts to muzzle his criticism of "hate groups," and he rebelled at Hunt's request that he huckster Life Line Bibles. Sherrill also forwarded the contents of a "Dear Karl" letter from Hunt to Republican Senator Karl Mundt of South Dakota. In it Hunt wrote, "you will indeed throw out the Life Line and Life Line will get the Electoral College broadcast under way. They will also need an additional script on the subject every eight or ten days until it becomes law. This is the advantage of Life Line." Sherrill charged, incorrectly, that the IRS had failed to investigate anything. In fact, the problem within the IRS was not a failure to investigate but a failure to follow its investigators' recommendations. The war of words between the administration and Hunt was so venomous that, after Kennedy's death, charges surfaced that Hunt had been behind the assassination.[11]

Patman attacked the Life Line Foundation during his 1964 hearings on tax-exempt foundations, grilling both Bertrand Harding and Mitchell Rogovin of the IRS about the foundation's adherence to the Internal Revenue Code. After presenting reams of financial information from the foundation's records, Patman asked about the IRS revocation of its exemption. Harding replied that, despite the revocation recommendations, the IRS had not yet made a decision. It needed more information, and Harding carefully avoided giving direct answers to Patman's questions about the foundation's behavior. IRS Chief Counsel Rogovin defined what constituted improper behavior for a tax-exempt organization but refused to go beyond that. Such determinations were difficult, he insisted, and the law was vague. In short, despite the recommendation by field examiners, the IRS National Office remained unwilling to revoke Life Line's exemption. This enraged Patman, and he lectured the agency about what sorts of investigations it should conduct.[12]

He also quizzed Harding about why the IRS was acting so slowly. Wouldn't revocation of a tax exemption immediately disqualify donors from taking further deductions for contributions? Harding agreed that it would. Then, asked Patman, why the delay? Isn't it "more of a challenge to the IRS to be on the alert and make sure that you quickly end a tax exemption when you are justified in doing so?" Harding agreed in principle but refused to budge, even though prompt action would not put Hunt out of business. As Patman sarcastically noted, even without tax-deductible contributions Hunt would not suffer from an absence of funds to carry on his crusade. He was a very wealthy man and could still escape taxes by taking advantage of the oil-depletion allowance as well as personal contributions to his foundations. Patman did get Harding to agree that by October 12, 1964, the IRS would submit to his subcommittee a written report on its findings and recommendations with respect to the Life Line Foundation. When that date arrived, however, all the IRS provided was a brief summary of its actions, which Patman already knew, and a concluding statement announcing that Harding was not in a "position at this time to report to you on the issues and findings in this case." Patman must have been furious.[13]

What the exchange between Patman and Harding revealed, essentially, was that Patman had acquired much more specific information about the operations of Life Line Foundation than had the IRS. It also revealed that the congressman was probing every conceivable aspect of the foundation's operations to determine if its tax exemption was justified. The IRS, on the other hand, was focusing on the broader issue of the foundation's educational nature and its activist orientation. Harding argued that the IRS simply did not have the money or the manpower to investigate whether all the foundation's donors took proper or improper deductions, or to look into the fact that dollar figures for its subscriptions did not coincide with the number of subscriptions. This sort of microanalysis fueled Patman's crusade against both the foundation and the IRS. Throughout the exchange, Harding seemed determined to reveal as little as possible about IRS operations to Patman. The congressman, in turn, appeared most interested in putting information on record and gaining publicity. The case of the Life Line Foundation served as a case study for Patman, revealing not only how individuals could exploit tax exemptions to protect their wealth but how they could subvert the intent of the law to advance political agendas. He believed that it reflected a massive failure on the part of the Internal Revenue Service to enforce the law and monitor tax-exempt organizations.[14]

The AFL-CIO urged Patman to persevere, insisting that Hunt and other conservative foundations were the "brain trust" for Goldwater, their publications nothing more than propaganda. Hunt also struck back, sending counterattacks to his contributors and asking that they distribute them. Patman, he argued, was part of a national socialist conspiracy that sought to terminate the First Amendment rights of "patriotic foundations." Letters from Hunt's minions to Patman reflected LIFE LINE's broader political agenda. One, typical of the responses, agreed that LIFE LINE opposed the United Nations; she did too. If LIFE LINE was against integration, so was the writer. "What can miscegenation do for either race except make mules?" These letters, perhaps unwittingly, revealed that Patman was right—the foundation did broadcast essentially political propaganda. Only by believing that politics and charity were the same thing could an observer conclude that the foundation deserved its tax-exempt status. The IRS eventually came to the same conclusion.[15]

The agency finally revoked Life Line Foundation's tax exemption in March 1965, along with the exemptions of almost 150 other foundations. Because of constant inquiries from Patman and his staff, IRS Director of Information Joseph Rosapepe sent Patman a copy of its public information fact sheet. At that point the IRS admitted that LIFE LINE's programming did not constitute "instruction of the public" within Internal Revenue Code guidelines. The IRS found that LIFE LINE's broadcasts had indeed advocated a "particular point of view" on such issues as "government expenditures, public welfare policies, federal educational programs, congressional appropriations policies, foreign aid, foreign policy, and the policies of the United Nations." A few broadcasts might have been educational, but most were "essentially political commentary consisting largely of unsupported opinion and conclusions."[16]

Still the fight continued. Not only did H. L. Hunt appeal and continue to file for tax-exempt status, other conservative spokesmen rallied to his cause. William F. Buckley's *National Review* attacked the IRS crackdown and asked the agency for a list of left-wing organizations whose tax exemptions had been revoked. The *National Review* reported being told that the IRS did not keep such a list, but critics could look through its master list of sixty thousand tax exempts and "make their own comparisons." The editors declined, expressing doubt that those organizations had ever had their exemptions revoked.[17]

The case of H. L. Hunt's Life Line Foundation was indicative of the broader problem that Wright Patman sought to address. Where was IRS oversight of tax-exempt organizations? How many organizations were even filing the required forms and data? Why had the IRS been so negligent? Patman reiterated recommendations first outlined in his 1962 subcommittee report, including an immediate moratorium on the granting of exemptions. If ordinary citizens flouted the tax laws as foundations did, Patman argued, the IRS would pursue them "in force."[18] The IRS reiterated that it lacked both the manpower and funds to fulfill its legal obligations toward tax-exempt organizations. It also made clear that its energies were concentrated in those areas where it stood to recover the greatest amount of income from back taxes or fines and penalties. Tax-exempt foundations did not represent one of those areas. For the moment Patman failed to recommend remedial legislation, turning his attention instead to making public the shadowy links between the IRS and the CIA.

The connections between the Internal Revenue Service, the Central Intelligence Agency, and certain tax-exempt foundations first surfaced in August 1964, in a series of whispered asides during testimony by IRS Chief Counsel Mitchell Rogovin before Patman's subcommittee investigating tax-exempt foundations. The committee's chief counsel, Harry Olsher, who despised foundations as much as Patman did, had asked Rogovin why a particular foundation had retained its tax exemption despite IRS findings that it was guilty of profiteering. Walking to the subcommittee stand and calling Patman and Olsher aside, Rogovin whispered that certain CIA connections prevented further discussion of the case. Rogovin, unbeknownst to Olsher or Patman, was the IRS liaison to the CIA and knew many such secrets. But that secrecy, or any invocation of national security issues, failed to deter Patman or Olsher from making public CIA involvement with tax-exempt foundations.[19]

This was sensational news, but it was only the tip of the proverbial iceberg. In the early 1960s, CIA money was hidden in nearly half of all international foundation grants. Between 1963 and 1966, 164 foundations awarded 700 grants of $10,000 or more; 108 of these grants, and nearly 50 percent of those for international activities, involved some CIA funding. Even Waldemar Nielsen, Ford Foundation staff director, was a CIA agent. Through Rogovin, the IRS worked to conceal this fact from the Congress as well as from the public. The writer Taylor Branch later reported the dimensions of this involvement in just one case. Citing Rogovin as his source, Branch revealed that in the case of drug companies' donations of medical supplies to Fidel Castro to ransom the Bay of Pigs prisoners, more than $16 million of CIA money was "buried in the ransom."[20]

News of CIA links to foundations had surfaced as early as 1961 but attracted little interest. That year the *Washington Post* uncovered CIA support for a wide range of student and youth groups through a network of foundations. These included the Intercontinental Research Company, which worked in Latin America, as well as a wide variety of foundations that ran international programs in the areas of journalism, law, and labor. Among the foundations, some of which had university connections, were the Pan American Foundation (University of Miami) and the International Marketing Institute (Harvard Business School). Also on the list were the American Society for African Culture, the American Friends of the Middle East in Washington, the International Development Foundation of New York, the United States National Student Association, the Independent Research Service, and the United States Youth Council of New York. Several other large foundations also had CIA links, according to the *Post*, including the Catherwood Foundation of Bryn Mawr, Pennsylvania; the San Jacinto Foundation of Houston, Texas; the Independence Foundation of Boston; the Sidney and Esther Rabb Foundation of New York; the J. Frederick Brown Foundation of Boston; the Borden Fund of Philadelphia; the Price Fund of New York; the Beacon Fund of Boston; the Kentfield Fund of Dallas; and the Edsel Fund of San Francisco.[21]

Patman smelled publicity. Once he began to investigate IRS-CIA-foundation links he unraveled, at least partially, a complex series of relationships designed to hide these connections. He began with the J. M. Kaplan Fund, a foundation he was investigating even before Rogovin's whispered asides accelerated his efforts. The Kaplan Fund was one of those tax-exempt organizations from which Patman had requested financial data. It donated chiefly to liberal and Jewish causes, such as the Highlander Folk Center and the Southern Student Organizing Committee. Its treasurer informed Patman in 1963 that the foundation had undergone detailed IRS examinations for the years 1952 through 1960, and that the agency had reaffirmed its tax-exempt status.

After Rogovin's revelation, Patman changed course. Now he concentrated on the CIA aspects of the foundation's activities. This was more exciting than dry financial data, and it attracted television cameras and press interest. Not that Patman wasn't serious about his pursuit of other foundations' activities, but as with the Hunt investigation he really sought to find symbolic examples of IRS failures to dramatize publicly his investigations and the problems they exposed. He discovered that a CIA-Kaplan arrangement had begun as early as 1959, but he could not find out why the CIA had selected the Kaplan Foundation and who had made this decision. Rogovin further tantalized Patman when he revealed that the CIA was "known to use existing foundations and on occasion to set up its own foundations in order to conduct certain of its intelligence gathering activities." What he failed to say was that Kaplan, who was president of the Welch Grape Juice Company, had approached the CIA in 1956 to offer assistance in the Eisenhower administration's efforts against communism. The Hungarian Revolution had just failed, and the United States appeared impotent before an aggressive Soviet enemy. CIA Director Allen Dulles arranged a CIA appointment with Kaplan, and the link was established.[22]

When Bertrand Harding of the IRS testified before Patman's subcommittee in August 1964, much of the discussion focused on the Kaplan Fund and its CIA involvement. Harding admitted not only that Internal Revenue staff had investigated the fund's activities but that it had recommended revocation of its exemption in 1957 because it did not seem to be organized chiefly for charitable, religious, or educational activities. Appeals in the case dragged on for years, but the fund's attorney told Patman that there had been no conferences with the IRS for the past two years, since July 1962. Had the IRS Exempt Organizations Branch belatedly discovered that the foundation was a CIA front? In his testimony, Harding insisted that the IRS was vigorously investigating the Kaplan Fund and promised Patman a full report within a "reasonable" time. Harding left the hearing room believing that the discussion had convinced the subcommittee that it had no interest in the CIA connection.[23] Harding's appearance was punctuated by Patman's decision to release to the public Rogovin's earlier private aside, which Patman did in a rather curious manner. He noted first that public exposure of the Kaplan Fund as a CIA conduit would serve the public interest, but then recognized that Harding "would rather not discuss the matter for the public record" and did not probe further. Patman also revealed that the

"Fund's operations with the CIA was the reason for the lack of action on the part of the IRS."[24] What lay behind this procedure—a sudden revelation followed by an apparent decision to close the door on further investigation? Was Patman finally intimidated by the national security question, even though none had yet been raised? Patman then pressed Harding for the complete IRS file on the Kaplan Fund, but Harding had not brought the file and insisted that he could not properly comment on its contents while the case was still under investigation.[25]

That again aroused Patman's ire, and he returned to questioning both Harding and Rogovin about the CIA connection with the case. Harding denied "personal knowledge" of that connection, but Rogovin admitted that he had "limited knowledge" of it. Responding to questions, Rogovin revealed that the CIA had not asked the IRS about using the Kaplan Fund as a conduit through which to channel CIA funds. Patman was incredulous that Harding, an eleven-year veteran of the IRS and acting commissioner, knew nothing about the CIA involvement. Indeed, throughout his testimony Harding was unable or refused to answer any but the most mundane questions. Only when Patman turned to Rogovin did he get even vague answers. Harding told Patman only that the IRS and the CIA had "an arrangement," and under that arrangement Rogovin "represented the Commissioner in all dealings with the CIA for our office." When pressed, Rogovin admitted that the IRS learned of the CIA interest in the Kaplan Fund only in late 1961 when the CIA had intervened to stop an IRS audit of the fund. "They were concerned," he told Patman, "as to whether or not their interest in the Fund would be made public and whether . . . [it] would to any degree jeopardize the status of the Foundation."[26] By that Rogovin clearly meant not only its tax-exempt status but its role as a conduit for CIA funds.

Rogovin later changed his testimony, insisting that, while the issue was a sensitive one, there was "no arrangement between the Revenue Service and the CIA dealing with the Kaplan Fund." That, of course, was not true. Reluctant to reveal any further information, Rogovin conceded that the IRS had told the CIA in 1961 about its investigation of the fund, but he refused to tell Patman why the CIA had chosen the Kaplan Fund for its conduit. If Patman wanted to know more about CIA relationships with that fund or any other, he should ask the CIA. Even if the IRS had such information—and both Rogovin and Harding were deliberately vague on that point—Internal Revenue would feel "a little delicate" in giving it to the subcommittee. Both Harding and Rogovin refused to discuss details in a public hearing. And if Patman intended to

pursue the matter in private hearings, Harding insisted that CIA representatives be present. "I am a little concerned," he told Patman, "that
the Revenue Service divulge information even to this Committee which
has been given to us in confidence by the agency." Finally, Rogovin revealed that his CIA contact was Milan Miskovsky in their general counsel's office, and that in 1961 he and Miskovsky had engaged in a series of
conversations about IRS interest in the Kaplan Fund. Rogovin also testified that, while he had talked with other IRS officials about the case,
he had found "no need" to discuss the CIA connection with anyone
working on the case in the IRS. From the beginning, Rogovin had handled it himself. Harding and Rogovin both testified that they had no
knowledge whatsoever about when the Kaplan Fund first began using
CIA funds.[27]

Yet the arrangement continued even as the two men testified. Rogovin admitted that he had brought Patman's interest in the fund's CIA
connections to the attention of Miskovsky and the CIA's general counsel, Lawrence Houston. Under close questioning from Patman, Harding conceded that the IRS had never examined the Kaplan Fund to see if
it actually disbursed the CIA monies. Rogovin did admit that "during
the audit examination one of the items of the examination for determination was as to what fund went where." If those funds appeared as receipts of the foundation, then the IRS would trace them "through to
determine what projects it supported." The basic problem in tracing
this link, Rogovin told Patman, was that the IRS examiners did not
know of the CIA's connection to the foundation. Neither he nor the
CIA nor the Kaplan Fund had told them. The result, as Rogovin admitted, was that the IRS investigators were "not aware of the significance of
one set of dollars as compared to another set."[28]

In a dramatic gesture, Patman then produced the tax returns of the
J. M. Kaplan Fund for 1961 through 1963. Handing them to Rogovin
and Harding, Patman called for a fifteen-minute recess. Upon return he
asked Harding to indicate where he found the CIA funds. Harding
replied that "as you might expect" he had found "no indications of any
CIA money on the returns." Only then did Rogovin return to the hearing room. Patman then sprang his trap. He told both men how, after the
August 10 hearings, George Cary, an assistant legislative counsel of the
CIA, had called on him and revealed details of the IRS–CIA–Kaplan
Fund arrangement. But Cary had insisted that the arrangement had
begun only in 1960 and had ended in 1962. When he was pressed for
more details, Cary admitted that the arrangement had begun in 1959
and had not ended until 1964. Cary also indicated that there were three

CIA contacts in the IRS who had handled the original arrangement, Rogovin, Dunlap, and Worley. (The last two were no longer with the IRS.)

All this seemed a bit strange to Patman, and he asked Rogovin who Cary was. Although Rogovin admitted talking with Cary on one occasion, he failed to shed further light on Cary's duties with the CIA. He also denied knowing anything about Dunlap's or Worley's involvement. He admitted, however, that he had talked with Miskovsky about Patman's questioning in their last session, conveying Patman's interest in hearing from a CIA representative. That was probably what had triggered Cary's visit. But Patman complained that he still did not have the information he wanted from the CIA, and he argued that the "purported or alleged CIA–Kaplan Fund arrangement" was "being used as a gimmick or diversionary tactic for the purpose of attempting to stop this Subcommittee from proceeding further on the subject of the Kaplan Fund." He was not at all convinced that this episode should be shrouded in secrecy. In the subcommittee's report, Patman wrote:

> Additionally, our study of the J. M. Kaplan Fund's operations indicates a large possible tax liability as well as violations of Treasury regulations and abuse of its public trust, including self-dealing to the detriment of the Fund's stated charitable purposes. Moreover, the Congress provides the funds for CIA operations and has the responsibility to see that the funds are properly disbursed and adequately supervised. I, personally, have the conviction that the expenditure of public funds is the public's business.[29]

Patman then pressed Harding for information on several other tax-exempt foundations that he suspected had CIA connections. These included the Gotham Foundation, the Michigan Fund, the Andrew Hamilton Fund, the Borden Trust, the Price Fund, the Edsel Fund, the Beacon Fund, and the Kentfield Fund. He demanded that the IRS produce not only current addresses for all officers, directors, and trustees but copies of their tax exemptions and their tax returns. He also wanted a list of years, beginning in 1952, when the IRS had audited any of these foundations and what taxes it had assessed. At a closed-door meeting following this session, subcommittee members met with CIA and IRS officials. They later told newsmen that they had decided not to pursue the CIA connections to the Kaplan Fund.[30]

By then, not surprisingly, the press had seized the issue. The *New York Times* attacked the IRS-CIA-Kaplan arrangement on the grounds that it allowed Communists to charge that "American scholars, scientists and writers going abroad on grants from foundations are cover agents or spies for the CIA." Using government intelligence funds in this manner, moreover, was a "distortion of CIA's mission on gathering and evaluating information." It introduced "governmental direction into cultural and scientific spheres where it does not belong—at least not in a democracy like ours." The *Pittsburgh Post Gazette & Sun Telegraph* was even stronger in its condemnation of CIA behavior, arguing that CIA "intrusion into policy-making" was dangerous in a democracy. The arrangement with the Kaplan Fund also raised the larger question of how citizens could have confidence in the integrity of any foundation. Despite Patman's willingness to halt his investigation, the paper called for creation of a "watchdog committee to keep an eye on the CIA's devious operations."[31]

Other evidence indicates that Patman may have been snookered by Harding and Rogovin. In a letter to White House aide Myer Feldman that November, Harding reported on a recent meeting with Patman. He indicated that, despite Patman's pressure, he remained adamant about not giving him the "exchange of correspondence on the Kaplan case," resting his refusal on "Executive privilege." In an internal IRS memo, however, Harding reminded Treasury Secretary Douglas Dillon that the IRS was "coordinated with CIA." Dillon instructed Harding to take a "hardline . . . in future dealings." John Warner of the CIA also worked on Patman. He arranged a private meeting, without any IRS representatives, in early October. This was partly a charade, because he agreed in advance to report the results as well as provide minutes of the meeting to Bertrand Harding. Warner apparently convinced Patman that the CIA information would not interest him.[32]

Nevertheless, what Patman had uncovered went far beyond the J. M. Kaplan Fund. The CIA had provided secret government funds to dozens of private foundations, which in turn had funneled those funds to other foundations. These conduits then channeled the funds to individuals and institutes in the United States and around the globe, some of whom also received funds from foundations not connected with the CIA. Some of these foundations were engaged in a variety of projects, only a few of which were CIA-related. Others, however, were nothing more than CIA fronts. A vast CIA pipeline had been created through the manipulation of tax-exempt foundations. Over the years some of these connections have become public. The Ford Foundation, for example, underwrote with CIA funds the Congress for Cultural Freedom. Ford Foundation director John McCloy established a permanent liaison with the CIA to "manage" the foundation's "cover for CIA projects."

One example of persistent CIA funding involved the Committee of

Correspondence, a private voluntary organization. The CIA secretly funded the group beginning in 1952 and continued to do so until it disbanded in 1969. The Committee of Correspondence was established to cultivate women leaders in countries around the globe, and drew most of its support from the J. Frederick Brown Foundation of Boston and the Dearborn Foundation. Both foundations were CIA conduits; the Dearborn Foundation was not listed in the Foundation Directory and apparently had no tax records. As Helen Laville has noted, CIA support of the Committee of Correspondence provided a key insight into "the relationship between the private/voluntary sphere and the public/government sphere in Cold War America." Since the Committee was staunchly anti-Communist, it well suited the CIA's purpose. The CIA funded eight of its international conferences between 1956 and 1963, conferences that targeted women in Third World countries and promoted democracy. The Committee's monthly bulletin reached more than 5,000 women in 140 countries and was published in 8 different languages. Revelations about the Committee's CIA connection surfaced in 1967, and (as had happened with the National Student Association) prompted a flurry of concerned activity within the group as to who was a witting accomplice to the secret funding and who was not. A CIA spokesman tried to assure the women that they had not been a propaganda cover, but without continued CIA funding the Committee faded into obscurity.[33]

The CIA also used private research institutes to conceal its activities. In one 1956 case, it provided $1 million to Hadley Cantril and Lloyd Free to gather intelligence "on popular attitudes in countries of interest to the agency." The Rockefeller Foundation apparently served as a conduit for these funds. Throughout the 1950s the CIA spent "tens of millions of dollars" on various communication research projects, indirectly underwriting such groups as the Bureau of Applied Social Research at Columbia University, the Institute for International Social Research at Princeton, and the Center for International Studies (CENIS) at MIT through grants to such conduits as the RAND Corporation or the Human Ecology Fund. The Human Ecology Fund was later tied to the CIA's MKULTRA program for mind-control and behavioral analysis, which secretly experimented with LSD and other drugs. The CIA also funded work by Carl Rogers and B. F. Skinner. Linked to MKULTRA as CIA conduits were the Josiah Macy, Jr., Foundation and the Geschickter Fund for Medical Research, a family foundation. CENIS, in turn, not only received CIA funds for its own work but served as a conduit for the transfer of funds to other institutions, such as the Center for Russian

Research at Harvard University. MIT faculty such as Walt Rostow and James Killian (later president of MIT), together with visitors like Robert Lovett and McGeorge Bundy, were aware of CIA funding. Indeed, MIT's Max Millikan, former assistant director of the CIA, remarked that there was "some continuing ambiguity as to whether we were creatures of the CIA or whether CIA was acting as an administrative office for other agencies." According to papers uncovered by the historian Bruce Cumings, the CIA even had a hand in CENIS's hiring policies. The Bureau of Scientific Research at American University, another grantee, pioneered in studies for the CIA on the use of "drugs, electroshock, and other forms of torture in [the] interrogation of prisoners."[34]

Foundation conduits were spread across the country, from Boston to Dallas and San Francisco. Perhaps ironically, they were often some of the same foundations about which Patman had requested additional information from Bertrand Harding in his 1964 hearings: Borden, Price, Beacon, Kentfield, and Edsel. Sol Stern later exposed the establishment connections undergirding these arrangements in *Ramparts* magazine.

> Two foundations that have supported the international programs of NSA—the J. Frederick Brown Foundation and the Independence Foundation—have received regular contributions from four of these CIA-linked Funds: Price, Borden, Kentfield, and Edsel. Both the J. Frederick Brown and the Independence Foundation list the same address, 60 State Street, Boston, which is also the address of the prestigious law firm of Hale and Dorr. Paul F. Hellmuth, a well-known Boston attorney and a member of Hale and Dorr, and David B. Stone, a Boston businessman and philanthropist, are the trustees of the Independence Foundation. Hellmuth alone is the trustee of the J. Frederick Brown Foundation.

These revelations prompted the IRS secretly to furnish the CIA with tax-exempt information on the National Student Association as well as the tax returns of *Ramparts* magazine.[35]

When Delaware Senator John Williams tried to determine if the connections Patman had uncovered in 1964 still existed two years later, he met much the same response from the CIA as Patman had. Letters to IRS Commissioner Sheldon Cohen produced some information, but the State Department refused to cooperate. Although information about the National Student Association had already become public, a presidential review committee reported that "no useful purpose would be served by detailing any other CIA programs of assistance to private

American voluntary organizations." CIA funding would remain secret, although the committee did report that such funding was supposed to end as soon as possible. When Williams persisted in efforts to secure a list of CIA contributions to the Kaplan Fund, even anonymously, he was told that the State Department did not have the information and was unable to obtain it from the CIA. Perhaps, just perhaps, if Williams called the agency a CIA representative might come to his office and talk with him privately. The ghost of George Cary lived on, and there the matter died.[36]

During the next two years, building on Patman's efforts, investigative reporters penetrated the secrecy shrouding CIA relationships with foundations. Writing in *The Nation*, Robert Sherrill reported that at least seven foundations whose CIA connections Patman had uncovered had been providing money to Christianform and/or the American Friends of the Middle East. They had laundered these contributions through the Brown Foundation, the Jones-O'Donnell Fund, and the Marshall Foundation. Christianform had created the Cuban Freedom Committee as well as established three radio stations to broadcast propaganda throughout Latin America. Most of its active board members were right-wingers, such as Donald Bruce, Peter O'Donnell, George Schuyler, and John B. McClatchy. Through former General Albert Wedemeyer, they also had ties to H. L. Hunt's Life Line Foundation.[37]

By 1967 various revelations had exposed a CIA network of front foundations that had served as conduits for anywhere from $15 million to hundreds of millions of dollars. The Foundation for Youth and Student Affairs, one of whose directors was Francis T. P. Plimpton, former U.S. deputy representative to the United Nations, gave more than $1.6 million to the National Student Association alone from 1959 to 1965. That foundation, however, was a CIA front. The funds really came from the Houghton Foundation, whose president, Arthur Armory Houghton, Jr., was also president of the Metropolitan Museum of Art. The columnist Drew Pearson reported that there were "no public tax records available for the Foundation," and the IRS indicated that the foundation did not file the required 990A exemption form. The IRS, however, had not investigated. Within a week after Sol Stern's NSA *Ramparts* exposé, the CIA's "sugar daddy" role was revealed to have included the American Newspaper Guild, the Retail Clerks International Association, the International Confederation of Free Trade Unions of Brussels, the National Education Association, the Institute of Public Administration, the American Fund for Free Jurists, the Foreign Policy Research Institute of the University of Pennsylvania, and Operations and Policy Research, a Washington think tank for the comparative study of political systems.[38]

In February 1967 the *Washington Post* published a chart detailing how the CIA's covert funding system worked. Some connections were disingenuous as well as covert. The Inter-American Affairs project in British Guiana, for instance, received funding from the American Federation of State, County & Municipal Employees (AFSCME). But AFSCME was really only a conduit for the Gotham Foundation, itself a conduit for the CIA. The "virtue" of such an operation was that the final link in the pipeline was sufficiently removed from the CIA so as to thoroughly disguise the original source of the funds and in effect conceal the entire pipeline. In another approach, several funds served simultaneously as CIA conduits to yet another tax-exempt group, which in turn funded national or international projects. The International Development Foundation, for example, received funds from nine separate tax-exempt foundations. It then funded numerous international programs.[39]

As this information became public, it triggered still more discoveries. Richard Harwood reported in the *Washington Post* that "the decision to fight the cold war covertly through private groups was no whimsical, unilateral decision by the men who have run the CIA for the past 20 years." Under Secretary of State Nicholas Katzenbach reported to President Johnson that the CIA had acted "in accordance with national policies established by the National Security Council in 1952 through 1954." But explanation was not justification, and the public became appalled at the extent of the CIA's covert domestic network. Wall Street investment firms and prestigious New York law firms had provided cover for CIA agents and funds. The San Jacinto Foundation represented yet another aspect of this network, serving as one of several dummy foundations established by the CIA to launder its distribution of funds. While a few of the ultimate recipients of this largesse were not always aware of its original source, most of the conduits were willing and knowledgeable participants. Waldemar Nielsen of the African-American Institute, for instance, indicated that he was aware that the CIA had subsidized the organization from 1953 until 1961, even though he recognized the "'inherent imprudence and impropriety' of the arrangement." Since he had earlier been a CIA agent, this was not surprising![40]

The American Institute for Free Labor Development (AIFLD) had been founded in 1961 by the American Federation of Labor with the cooperation of more than sixty U.S. corporations with large investments in Latin America. It too received secret CIA funding through conduit foundations which the IRS either had not scrutinized or whose undercover operations the agency had deliberately ignored. Between 1961 and 1963 the AIFLD received most of its funding from the Alliance for Progress for work in Latin America, but it also received at least $1 million from the J. M. Kaplan Fund and the Gotham Foundation. The Gotham Foundation, which also funded CIA activity in British Guiana against President Cheddi Jagan, appears to have been almost solely designed as a CIA conduit for cold war undercover activities. As in British Guiana, CIA funds helped the AIFLD organize labor in countries like Brazil to promote liberal unionism and counter left-wing or Castroite activities as well as to provide cover for CIA agents operating in Latin American countries.[41]

Wright Patman's exposés had harvested reams of publicity, but now action was needed. Pennsylvania Republican Senator Hugh Scott complained to President Johnson in March 1967 that the CIA had supported the American Friends of the Middle East (AFME) through at least nine foundations. Scott detailed the amounts channeled through each one, and warned that the AFME was a pro-Arab, anti-Israel organization that opposed U.S. Middle East policy. He asked Johnson to direct the IRS to "begin an immediate investigation into the tax exempt status of the foundations that have provided funds for this organization." Johnson did not seem terribly interested in exposing more problems, particularly since he was preoccupied with the war in Vietnam. But one week later he did issue a policy statement that "No federal agency shall provide any covert financial assistance or support, direct or indirect, to any of the nation's educational or private voluntary organizations." Critics quickly noted that this left considerable room for covert activities, especially given the failures of the IRS to scrutinize foundations' tax-exempt activities, as the Kaplan case had revealed.[42]

Patman himself attacked the continuing cover-up of the full CIA-IRS relationship. "How great a share of the receipts of some of these foundations came from the Central Intelligence Agency probably will never be known to the public, or even to most members of Congress," he observed. "But the CIA undoubtedly conveyed millions of dollars of taxpayers' money through foundation pipelines to organizations and individuals in this country and overseas that the CIA counted on to support the agency's objectives." Since the foundations remained essentially unregulated, Patman complained, a state of "permissive anarchy" existed. He lamented what he labeled the IRS's "non-virginal knowledge" of these operations. The Kaplan Fund, a "notorious 'crossroads' of secret CIA funds" in the 1950s, represented a symbol of the future. Despite years of investigation by the IRS, the fund still "perks along as always, still available for secret payoffs."[43] Change would clearly be difficult. Only if Patman pursued reform rather than exposé did there appear to be a chance for change. Clearly the IRS would not initiate change on its own.

Not until congressional investigations of intelligence abuses in 1975 was any serious action taken. Then, under pressure from the Pike Committee in the House and the Church Committee in the Senate, and with the revelations of the Rockefeller Report on CIA activities in the United States, Treasury Secretary William Simon suggested reforms. Although he organized a Treasury Department task force to consider the Rockefeller Commission report, which reviewed IRS sharing of tax-return information with the CIA as well as reports of thirty-two domestic wiretaps and a dozen break-ins associated with that relationship, Simon was chiefly concerned with CIA access to tax-return information that did not follow established procedures. He demonstrated little interest in CIA use of foundations as conduits for the covert funding of private organizations.[44]

In September 1975, Simon ordered his special assistant for national security to review those arrangements, to consult with the Treasury's general counsel, and to report "all such arrangements to me on a continuing basis." All agreements with the CIA were to be reduced to writing and extensively reviewed before adoption. In an important exclusion, however, Simon noted that the "directive does not apply to the routine exchange between the intelligence community and Treasury of substantive intelligence information and reports on a continuing basis."[45] More work remained to be done.

CHAPTER SEVEN

FOUNDATIONS: THE CONTINUING STRUGGLE

Despite the CIA revelations and the publicity generated by Congressman Wright Patman's exposés of IRS behavior toward tax-exempt organizations, there were few signs that the IRS intended to reform its practices. Arguing that "I do not seek to destroy the foundations, but to reform them," Patman turned to legislative solutions. Conservatives joined liberals in sharp criticism of IRS oversight in the tax-exempt arena, adding impetus to Patman's long-standing efforts. This led, eventually, to the Tax Reform Act of 1969. That act, however, failed to resolve all the issues. During the Nixon years, foundations' activities continued to attract attention from politicians who implored the IRS to take action. IRS actions, in turn, were often themselves contentious. As the foundation problem persisted, the IRS remained embroiled in political controversy.

During the late 1960s, when tax-exempt organizations attacked major social problems, controversy swirled around many foundations' activities. By 1970 at least sixty-five foundations had awarded more than three hundred grants to social movements. The Ford Foundation, to cite one example, sought to improve conditions in Mexican-American communities in the Southwest through a series of grants to the Mexican-American Youth Organizations (MAYO). Attacked from the left as too moderate, from the right as partisan, and by sitting politicians as subversive, the foundation was besieged. Much of this criticism was simply a product of the times, which themselves were turbulent. The Ford Foundation had awarded grants to various Mexican-American organiza-

tions since 1963 in an effort to advance civil rights and rural development where legal processes had failed. Controversy erupted because the
foundation had defined a "social objective" and had the money to pursue it. It disturbed and threatened vested interests, raising the question
of whether foundations' activities should promote change or merely
support the existing political and social order. That question attracted
legislative attention and became overtly political after McGeorge Bundy
moved from the White House to the Ford Foundation in 1966 and the
foundation became more activist.[1]

The efforts of Ford and other foundations to underwrite grants to
explore change in sensitive political areas drew steady fire from critics
and the Congress. Foundation-backed voter registration efforts in both
the South and the North, for example, promised structural change and
endangered established politicians' privileged positions. Purveyors of
power, liberal as well as conservative, joined forces to call for regulation
of tax exempts' activities. Conservatives were particularly outraged.
They complained that groups like COFO (the Council of Federated Organizations) channeled foundation grants to voter registration efforts in
the South. In the North, conservatives attacked the IRS for granting tax
exemptions to organizations cited by the House Un-American Activities
Committee for subversive activities, such as the Metropolitan Music
School of New York City. The IRS reminded critics that it maintained a
"continuous program of audit and review" of tax-exempt organizations,
but this failed to stem the criticism.[2]

The case of the Sierra Club highlighted the broad question of tax-
exempt organizations' permissible activities. On June 9, 1966, the Sierra
Club ran full-page advertisements in the *New York Times* and the *Washington Post* attacking federal legislation permitting the construction of
two dams in the Grand Canyon. A day later the San Francisco IRS district director advised the group that the IRS would terminate its practice of assuring in advance that contributions to the Sierra Club were tax
deductible. Three weeks later the IRS initiated an investigation into the
club's tax exemption. By mid-December, after a whirlwind investigation,
Internal Revenue staff concluded that the Sierra Club should lose its tax
exemption. Most observers believed that political forces, perhaps ema-
nating from the White House, had mobilized the IRS in an unprecedented response. The IRS had never before given advance notice that
contributions to a tax-exempt organization might no longer be deductible, and had rarely moved with such startling speed to terminate a
tax exemption. IRS actions also contradicted its policy that revocation of
a tax exemption would precede the denial of tax-deductible contribu-

tions. After December 1966 the Sierra Club remained tax-exempt as a social welfare organization, but contributions were no longer deductible. Thanks to the precipitous IRS action, which publicized the threat to the Grand Canyon, public sentiment supported the club, membership increased dramatically, and contributions multiplied.[3]

Speakers at a conference on charitable foundations the following year raised additional questions about the political activities of tax-exempt organizations. Former IRS Commissioner Mortimer Caplin outlined what he understood to be the limitations on such activity. Although he did not refer to the IRS's Ideological Organizations Project, begun during his tenure as commissioner, Caplin listed the types of activities that classified a group as an "action organization" not entitled to tax exemption. With specific reference to the Fellowship of Reconciliation and the Sierra Club, Caplin noted that revocation of a tax exemption would be warranted if there were any participation in a political campaign on behalf of or in opposition to any candidate, advocacy of legislation to achieve the organization's objectives, or if any "substantial part" of an organization's activities attempted to influence legislation. Although the Fellowship of Reconciliation had changed its organizational papers following an IRS audit, thereby avoiding revocation of its tax exemption, Caplin argued that the case of the Sierra Club "will be of interest to all exempt organizations which, from time to time, find it essential to engage in some form of political activity."[4]

The underlying problem, as the Ideological Organizations Project had revealed, was that there was no "rule-of-thumb of 'substantiality' of political activities." All such tests were relative and therefore open to political influence and the likes and dislikes of the IRS staff reviewing exempt organizations. "In close cases," Caplin acknowledged, "the human factor might well come into play; and a revenue agent understandably might be swayed by the merit of the organization's political activities." In theory, however, the substantiality doctrine should prevail. Caplin, whose detailed recounting of the Sierra Club case revealed that he had likely been carefully briefed by his successor in the commissioner's office, defended the IRS actions. An intensive audit had found that the club had advocated or opposed various legislative proposals on conservation from 1964 through 1966, and that these activities represented a "substantial part" of the club's activities. Caplin tried to present the IRS as a neutral arbiter in these matters, but he admitted that its final determination often rested on the "good judgment" used by the "leaders and membership" in carrying out an organization's program.[5]

The heart of the problem was that different groups organized for similar purposes seemed to be covered in different ways. A "charity," for instance, could advocate "social or civic changes" and present "opinion on controversial issues," even if its intent was to shape public opinion or create "public sentiment." The only restriction was that it could not be an "action organization." A nonprofit educational organization, on the other hand, could advocate a "particular position" only so long as it presented "full and fair exposition of facts" to enable the public "to form an independent conclusion." To many observers the intent of the two groups seemed similar, yet the restrictions differed. The essential distinction appeared to rest more in the eyes of the beholder (or regulator) than in the operation of the organization.[6]

A Treasury Department report in 1965 confronted many of these problems and eventually became a springboard to reform in 1969. Driven in large part by Wright Patman's investigations into foundations' activities, and at the specific request of the Senate Finance Committee and the House Ways and Means Committee, the Treasury Department produced a detailed report on private foundations. Responding to critics' charges that foundations represented a "dangerous concentration of uncontrolled economic and social power," the report concluded that while most foundations operated without abuses, six specific problems merited legislative attention: self-dealing, delays in benefits to charities, involvement in business, family use of foundations to control corporations, financial activities that were unrelated to charitable functions, and a need to broaden foundation management. Few of these issues were new; most dated at least to 1950 when the House had considered amendments to the Internal Revenue Code .[7]

Each of these recommendations also addressed problems that Patman and his subcommittee had identified earlier. Taken together, the six problems identified by the Treasury report appeared to reinforce one another. The self-dealing issue was one that particularly sparked Patman's populist ardor, for it allowed donors privileged use of foundations' assets—assets they had supposedly pledged to charitable uses in return for tax advantages. Coupled with that, at least in Patman's mind, was the obvious failure of many foundations to expend their funds in a timely manner. Instead they accumulated income that was supposed to advance charitable purposes. Foundations' continued involvement in active, for-profit businesses also seemed to betray their purpose and aroused Patman's suspicion that foundations too often represented tax evasion rather than tax avoidance. That many of them were family foundations, where tax deductions often preceded charitable activities, aroused further suspicion, as did the failure of many foundations to broaden their management circle beyond the immediate donors. The use of foundations' assets for noncharitable functions also contradicted the intent of Congress in allowing tax exemptions for charitable purposes. Treasury's report was important, particularly in light of the fact that a 1962 comprehensive survey had identified fifteen thousand private foundations, most of which had emerged since 1959.[8]

Although the report rejected Patman's argument that foundations should be seriously curtailed or eliminated, it refused to sweep complaints under the rug. It recognized that foundations were "uniquely qualified to initiate thought and action, experiment with new and untried ventures, dissent from prevailing attitudes, and act quickly and flexibly." Even if Congress adopted the report's recommendations, therefore, foundation activities were likely to remain politically controversial.

The immediate response of the IRS was defensive. Commissioner Sheldon Cohen insisted that the aggressive examination of exempt foundations was the "key to improved compliance." At the close of 1965 the IRS reported auditing 12,406 returns of tax-exempt organizations, 21 percent more than in 1964, and proposed revoking exemptions on 123 cases. The IRS also published and distributed tax-audit guidelines for exempt organizations to its examiners, and conducted specialized exempt organization training classes for 188 trainees in its regions.[9]

In the wake of the Treasury report, the agency also moved to head off future controversies. Thomas Terry, assistant to the commissioner, asked for advice from the Commissioner's Advisory Group about formalized procedures to prevent recurrence of the controversy caused by the Sierra Club case and to keep the IRS out of political crossfires. An IRS staff report recommended changes in existing practice to normalize IRS actions in the Sierra Club case, terminating exemptions even while audits were ongoing and before the IRS had made any final determination to revoke a group's exempt status. Even President Lyndon Johnson jumped into the debate. In his 1967 Economic Report to the nation, Johnson urged reforms to deal with abuses by tax-exempt private foundations. But the problem remained a difficult one for the IRS. Commissioner Cohen admitted that the agency needed to improve the quality of its audits and its operational methods. Perhaps the biggest stumbling block, however, was the belief of many examiners that auditing exempt organizations was an exercise in futility. Cohen admitted that this perception was a problem, noting that the IRS had difficulty "retaining the services of competent agents in this specialized area. Since approximately 98% of exempt organizations audited are found to be nontaxable," it was difficult to "generate interest of district management in this non-revenue producing activity." Many agents therefore believed "that permanent assignment to the Exempt Organization Program may have an adverse effect on their promotional opportunities."[10]

Seeking to overcome this and other obstacles, in 1965 the IRS established an Exempt Organization Master File (EOMF). Using computer technology, it sought to create comprehensive files on the mushrooming number of tax-exempt foundations, files that would be indispensable to the process of selecting organizations for audit. Two years after its creation, however, problems remained. Too many foundations, together with inadequate statutory provisions, limited manpower, and unproductive audits left the IRS vulnerable to criticism even though the number of Revenue Rulings on exempt organizations had increased sharply. Perhaps the underlying cause for many of these problems was that most audits of exempt organizations were initially activity audits rather than financial audits. Agents still were not well trained for that type of examination, nor did they bear much relation to agents' work elsewhere in the IRS. Growing budgetary pressures presented an additional problem, especially in the audit and collection areas. Reductions and cuts rather than budgetary expansion were the order of the day, despite protests from IRS and Treasury officials. Internal Revenue also came under public fire, with articles in *Reader's Digest* in 1967 and 1968 attacking IRS procedures and its handling of individual cases.[11]

The chief question for the IRS was, what should it do? Was greater regulation needed, as both Patman and the 1965 Treasury report argued? Or should the activities of foundations remain free from additional regulation? Throughout 1969, Wright Patman pressed for greater oversight and legislation. Even former IRS Commissioner Mortimer Caplin testified that foundations' activities represented "unfair business competition." Too often they sheltered commercial activities, and the average taxpayer essentially subsidized those activities. Churches distributed phonograph records, at least one church had acquired seven clothing businesses, another manufactured mobile homes and ran a drilling business. Still others were involved in real estate or manufacturing activities. Foundations, of course, considered the criticism unfair and defended their tax breaks against government regulation, arguing that greater regulation endangered the pluralistic nature of American society. In an effort to solve some of its problems, the IRS decided in 1969 that all tax-exempt organizations' returns were to be processed at a single center by a specially trained staff. It also intensified efforts to improve the Exempt Organization Master File, increasing the scope of that file to embrace 416,291 organizations. All this was to be a prelude to an "intensified exempt organizations enforcement effort."[12]

Wright Patman quickly tested this new commitment, requesting IRS cooperation with his continuing investigations of foundations. The IRS resisted, despite its promises of cooperation. Commissioner Randolph Thrower assigned Deputy Commissioner William Smith and the new special assistant to the commissioner, Roger Barth, to meet with Patman's staff and work out details. But Patman's pleas for cooperation fell on deaf ears. Smith and Barth argued that providing Patman's subcommittee with the relevant information would be too expensive, and refused to develop detailed information on privately controlled foundations unless it had direct benefit to the IRS. Internal Revenue, in short, was not interested in maintaining this information solely for the benefit of Congress. Howard Greenberg reported back to Patman that, "although both gentlemen were courteous, I got the impression I was being given the rush, since Mr. Smith kept looking at his watch with an impatient air, as if he wished that I would leave." An exchange of correspondence between Patman and Thrower failed to improve the situation. Thrower insisted that the IRS lacked the resources even to process regular tax returns in a timely manner, and it considered the tax-exempt area "unproductive of tax revenues." Patman reported to his subcommittee that they could not depend on the IRS to cooperate. He recommended asking for tax information directly by sending individual letters to each of the thirty thousand foundations.[13]

This launched Patman into yet another crusade against foundations and IRS handling of tax-exempt organizations. He sought to mandate reforms, asserting that we "have built a Frankenstein monster, which together with high interest rates, the big greedy banks and big corporations will continue to choke economically our average taxpayer and small businessman." Although critics accused Patman of "taking a baseball bat to kill a gnat," he forged ahead. When more than a thousand of his letters to foundations were returned because of incorrect addresses, he complained that the IRS Exempt Organizations Master File was full of errors. Yet Patman amassed a huge quantity of data, so much in fact that by the fall of 1969 the IRS itself asked to inspect his files on selected foundations. Now that Patman had successfully collected reams of tax data directly from foundations, Internal Revenue suddenly became more cooperative. In a dramatic turnaround, the IRS conceded that it might be able to produce reports for Patman "on their own computers without cost."[14]

Patman's zeal infected other members of Congress, and House Ways and Means Committee hearings exposed additional problems. The case that perhaps pushed Wright Patman and the Congress into finding a legislative solution to the foundation issue was that of Americans Building Constitutionally (ABC). In 1967, Patman's committee had discovered that this Barrington, Illinois, organization had concocted a scheme whereby individuals could operate their businesses and even their homes as tax-exempt foundations. For revealing its secret, ABC received hefty fees. IRS audits in 1968 convinced many of these so-called foundations to relinquish their claims for charitable deductions and tax-exempt status. But the case prompted Patman to press for legislation to control tax-exempt foundations and charitable trusts. The Treasury Department, he charged, had failed either to supervise or to regulate them, and the IRS audited only a small fraction of known foundations in any one year. ABC executives' testimony that they had practiced tax avoidance rather than tax evasion failed to mollify Patman. Worse still, most ABC trustees invoked the Fifth Amendment and refused to testify at all.[15]

In January 1967, ABC spokesmen had outlined how their scheme worked to a group of life insurance executives. That plan, which they called a "constitutional trust," revealed some glaring flaws in the existing regulations of foundations. The ABC plan argued that individuals could turn their home as well as all their income into a tax-free lifestyle. The ramifications were mind-boggling.

> They stated that the home, as well as his transportation, his vacation—along with his family—and all his other major needs are supplied in the form of fringe benefits from this Foundation. Further, they stated that he would have the right, as Executive Director of the Foundation, to endow his children's college education. In fact, they stated that the Foundation would supply all the needs of himself and his family, excluding only the most personal items, such as food, clothing, cigarettes and liquor.[16]

Despite its promises, many of the executives in attendance expressed skepticism about the legality of such a plan.

Following his hearings about ABC, Patman barraged IRS Commissioner Sheldon Cohen with requests for copies of 990-A forms that foundations were required to file. With respect to ABC, Cohen reported that despite an eight-month investigation, the IRS had been unable to identify any foundation established under the ABC plan, nor did it have any record of ABC filing a request for exempt status. Patman asked postal inspectors to place a mail cover on ABC, suggesting the "possibility of serious and widespread violations of tax statutes and of the mail fraud statute." He was incensed over the failure of the IRS to pursue the matter, and a series of articles in the *Wall Street Journal* outlining such tax-dodging devices further enraged him. He promised additional investigations, warning that without action, tax-exempt foundations would be as "commonplace in this country as bath-tub distilleries were during the Prohibition Era."[17]

The ABC affair had a long life, slowly winding down during the next two years. IRS field agents were alerted to the scheme, and the National Office provided them with criteria for identifying such organizations. All suspected cases went directly to the IRS National Office. By the spring of 1970 the IRS had identified more than six hundred participants in "'ABC' type activities." Internal Revenue staff examined every one of them, recovering more than $450,000 in taxes. In 1969 a California grand jury indicted ABC's primary promoters for conspiring to commit grand theft. Patman welcomed these efforts but remained determined to enact reforms that would prevent such adventures in the future.[18]

IRS procedures with respect to foundations continued to trouble Patman and his colleagues in Congress. Leaving aside overt political targeting, as in the Ideological Organizations Project, even normal Internal Revenue procedure appeared weighted toward political considerations. Before pushing a case too far, a field agent sounded out the National Office, which was acutely sensitive to the publicity potential or political ramifications of tax-exempt revocations in important cases. The papers of former IRS commissioners reflect this oversight. In 1967, to cite one example, Commissioner Sheldon Cohen asked to be kept "informed on progress of Radical Education Project tax exemption request." In all such cases the National Office and its legal staff then carried the ball, though affected organizations usually remained unaware of this fact. Should an organization appeal revocation of its exempt status, the same individuals who framed the letter of revocation heard the appeal. Under those circumstances, appellants did not really appear to have a chance, since a clean review of the case seemed unlikely. Too, IRS commissioners were often inconsistent. In the words of one investigator of the situation, the "Commissioner's need to collect taxes has seen him adopt contrary positions respecting the status of foundations and their controlling parties and the membership certificates issued to such parties."[19]

During the late 1960s conservative as well as liberal activists asked the IRS to play politics with respect to tax-exempt organizations. These requests raised legitimate questions about IRS definitions of tax-exempt status and its policies toward those organizations. Conservative critics such as the newspaperman Ralph de Toledano argued that the IRS operated with a double standard: "Liberal, *si!* Anti-Communist, *no!*" It rejected petitions for tax exemption from the World Youth Crusade for Freedom, headed by Tom Charles Huston, but supported the exemption of the Center for the Study of Democratic Institutions, which de Toledano insisted bankrolled black power groups and the "Communist–'Black Power'–dominated National Conference for New Politics."

More sweeping was an April 1969 report issued by the American Conservative Union (ACU). Titled "The Financiers of Revolution," the report attacked tax exemptions as privileged sanctuaries that promoted liberal political beliefs to the point of "national scandal." Although the ACU supported the concept of tax exemption, it complained that there was no "systematic method of legislative oversight" to prevent tax-exempt foundations from lobbying. The crux of its attack focused on the activities of groups that received foundation funds. The ACU objected to organizations that supported "Negroes . . . for state and federal offices," or groups that "showed sexually explicit movies," pushed for school decentralization, or advocated school integration and voter registration. Attacking foundations (which unbeknownst to them were CIA conduits) for funding the National Student Association and other liberal groups, it insisted that definitions of exempt activities be tightened and that tax-exempt foundations not be permitted to act as "fronts for government action." The report ended with a complaint about the liberal bias of foundations, pleading that "all political ideologies should have the same right to compete within the framework of our constitutional system." A writer in the *Tulsa Daily World* echoed this view, complaining that foundations had become the establishment, untouchable elite power centers. Several foundations supported ERAP (Economic Research and Action Projects) efforts sponsored by Students for a Democratic Society (SDS). Billy James Hargis noted that even the ACLU had secured exempt status for some of its activities.[20]

Liberals also complained. New York Democrat Richard D. McCarthy asked the IRS to review the tax exemption of the National Rifle Association, which Internal Revenue had classified as a "social welfare organization." George Rucker of Group Research wrote Harry Olsher, Patman's chief investigator, to call his attention to Steven Shadegg's book *What Happened to Goldwater*. "It seems to me," Rucker wrote, that the book made a "*prima facie* case of staggering proportions" to revoke the exempt status of the American Enterprise Institute for Public Policy Research. Its director, William Baroody, had actively participated in the Goldwater campaign for two years, as had other AEI employees.[21]

These outbursts, and others like them, focused congressional attention on the question of foundations' political activities and then on the broader issue of foundations' behavior and their regulation. When some critics urged a forty-year limit on foundations' existence, foundations themselves joined the debate in an effort to temper the political heat. Their defenders warned that excessive reforms would cripple valuable institutions. But the sheer magnitude of the wealth controlled by foundations aroused concern. The James Irvine Foundations, for instance, owned more than 53 percent of the Irvine Company, which in turn owned one-sixth of the land in Orange County, California. This begged for attention. Wright Patman testified before the House Ways and Means Committee that foundations spent too much of that wealth abroad rather than in the United States. The real question, however, was not so much where they spent their money as how they spent it and the freedom they possessed to make those decisions. Wisconsin's John Bymes complained that "anything that anybody can conceive of can be said to be educational. We must develop some guidelines."[22]

As Congress moved toward tax reform, foundations examined their own activities. In 1968, John D. Rockefeller III, developing a suggestion made earlier by Alan Pifer, president of the Carnegie Corporation, formed a Commission on Foundations and Private Philanthropy. Known popularly as the Peterson Commission, after its chair Peter G. Peterson, it sought to curb abuses through voluntary guidelines in hopes of preempting congressional action. It concentrated on long-term analysis and public recommendations rather than legislative matters, and its operation and final report overlapped with congressional consideration of the 1969 Tax Reform Act. The Peterson Commission hoped to deliver a public report before final congressional action in December 1969.[23]

The Commission on Foundations quickly identified a series of key issues or questions, most of which paralleled concerns raised either by Patman or by other foundation critics. How could one define where "innovative social reform ends and [undesirable] political activity begins?" Should foundations have guidelines for activity in sensitive areas that differed from "non-foundation activities in these same areas?" The commission proposed to review questions about so-called "controversial activities." It also raised a series of questions about future roles for foundations and the allocation of foundation resources in a changing society.

A third concern of the study evaluated foundations as "Philanthropic Middlemen." Did foundations "represent undesirable aggregations of power through their grant making?" Other issues were the relations between donors and foundations, the existing tax-incentive system and its societal benefits, and the extent to which the IRS effectively supervised foundations.[24]

A year later, in May 1969, Robert Caulkins, vice chancellor of the University of California, Santa Cruz, and a former officer of several foundations, offered a strong defense of foundations in a Cosmos Club Award address. Outlining "The Role of the Philanthropic Foundation," Caulkins traced the history of foundations and reviewed their role in a rapidly changing society. There had been, he observed, four congressional investigations of foundations since 1952. Without mentioning Patman by name, he complained that recent hearings had "aroused public interest and created considerable confusion as to whether foundations have violated their public trust, and as to the proper role of foundations in these times." Recent congressional investigations had produced too much misinformation, too many sensational charges, and too many errors by "careless or politically motivated staff work." In his review of philanthropic foundations, Caulkins found "little to suggest" that they were anything but a benefit to society. He warned that in its haste to regulate or tax foundations and curb abuses, Congress risked overlooking the "role of foundations in advancing the public good." Foundations were not subversive. They had advanced creativity and innovation, which often led to social change. "If the social costs are to be measured against the social benefits, the record is clearly on the side of the benefits."[25]

The conservative critic Jeffrey Hart was not so sure. In a lengthy article titled "The New Class War," Hart threw his support behind Patman's efforts and dismissed the Peterson Commission's defense as an exercise by "neophytes." Tax-exempt foundations, he charged, were instruments of the liberal establishment. Some were tax dodges, others were "frivolous to the point of kookery." But the real issue, Hart argued, was the enormous power held by unelected boards with no public accountability. As foundations had moved into the public sphere with their grant-making, they had become a political force—"a kind of shadow government." The careers of men like John J. McCloy, Robert McNamara, and Dean Rusk proved that liberal foundations were a "kind of farm club to the executive branch of government." Hart's attack was, in many respects, disingenuous. He complained chiefly about the ideological bent of foundations' grants and the fact that few went to conservative groups. He charged, in brief, that an "upper-middle and upper-class governing elite is attempting to carry out a social revolution under forced draft at the expense of the middle and lower-middle classes—who it is safe to say, won't put up with it, and don't have to." One gets the clear impression that if more grants had gone to conservative causes, Hart's article would have remained in his typewriter. It revealed that much of the struggle was chiefly over who got what and the purposes to which they applied it: ideology over principle.[26]

In October the Peterson Commission delivered a series of recommendations to the Senate Finance Committee. They were aggressive as well as conciliatory. The commission defined its aims as increasing the funds "actively devoted to philanthropy," directing those funds to "legitimate charitable purposes," and increasing private-sector diversity. In short, the commission wanted to expand foundations' activities while maintaining their tax exemptions. To do so it acceded to some of the critics' demands, embracing higher payouts, greater reporting and disclosure, prohibitions against self-dealing, more IRS audits, and penalties for violators. But the report opposed any restrictions on foundation contacts with legislators. This was healthy, it insisted, and it was "impossible to draw any line of demarcation between the foundations' fields of interest and those of governments." To protect those activities from future criticism and legislative interference, the report recommended that

> foundation funds should not be used for grass roots campaigns designed to bring pressure on legislators. We believe that the only proper role of foundations in the political process is an educational one. When the objective is political pressure rather than dissemination of ideas, foundation involvement becomes improper. We recognize, of course, that this principle is more easily stated than it is applied in practice. However, the fact that there may be some difficult borderline case is no reason for ignoring the underlying principle. We would encourage foundations to seek advanced rulings before venturing into questionable areas. This should not be a legislative requirement.[27]

Tax-reform fury swirled in Congress in the early Nixon years, but the Treasury Department was unprepared to respond to congressional critics, and the administration had yet to adopt a firm position on the question of tax reform. Assistant Treasury Secretary Edwin Cohen was strongly anti-foundation while other administration officials moved to defend foundations against the wrath of Congress. The House and Senate quarreled over foundation reforms to be included in new legislation, with the Senate proposing adoption of the forty-year limit on foundations' existence. This in turn mobilized foundation executives to testify to the value of their enterprise. Although the proposed limitation was eventually dropped, congressional debates reflected division and confusion over the question. Some liberals defended foundations and their work in progressive causes; others attacked them as representatives of vested interests that became rich through tax breaks. Finally, on December 23, 1969, Congress passed the Tax Reform Act.[28]

Almost one-third of the bill focused on the question of foundations, and it imposed a series of new restrictions on their operation. By and large it addressed the major problems outlined in the 1965 Treasury report, instituting comprehensive definitions and a scale of penalties. It discouraged speculative investments, more clearly defined self-dealing, forced foundations to distribute more of their income to charity, mandated that they use their assets only for activities that accorded with their tax-exemption privilege, sought to limit foundations' control of private businesses, and required annual public reports. The bill dramatically widened the distinctions between types of foundations. Not only were foundations now to be different from other 501(c)(3) organizations, but Congress defined three different types: private foundations, publicly supported foundations, and operating foundations. Private foundations received their support from a wide array of donors. The other two spent most of their income "directly for the active conduct of their own programs." The significance, as one observer noted, was that "the 'private' foundation is . . . accorded markedly inferior tax treatment in comparison to the other two."[29]

Perhaps the most significant feature of the Tax Reform Act was its elimination of the rule of substantiality. Judging the percentage of a foundation's activities that might be political in nature had proved to be difficult. The new law prohibited *any* "political and propaganda activity" or other efforts to influence legislation. Ostensibly this blanket ban on political activity made the regulatory task of the IRS easier. But the same law also required foundations to spend their funds only for specific purposes in accord with the foundation's mission. In effect, while the law removed the IRS from judging foundations' political activities, it made Internal Revenue responsible for monitoring the substance of virtually all foundation activity. It took, one critic complained, a "blunderbuss approach to regulating private foundations," requiring the IRS not only to "examine every reported expenditure for political overtones" but to "identify individual violations without reference to the foundation's other activities."[30] In the effort to cripple some foundations' activities,

Congress enacted a law that failed to address the very source of many past abuses.

Congressional critics were so intent on disabling a few foundations' activities in controversial areas, particularly grassroots organizing, that they failed to adopt comprehensive reforms. In the words of one observer, they had

> singled out for attack those few foundations in the United States that had been attempting to deal with such controversial problems as race relations, the urban crisis, and governmental inadequacies. Conversely, [the bill] had allowed the orthodox, conservative foundations—however inert—and the foundations that shelter themselves in the safe areas of science and medicine to get off scot-free.[31]

Why had Congress finally acted? Clearly it had responded to rising public concern about the activities of some foundations and the inequities of the tax burden that Wright Patman had harped on. But perhaps a more important explanation lay in a series of unrelated events that sparked controversy. Three examples illustrate. First, during the fall of 1968, revelations about a cozy relationship between Supreme Court Justice Abe Fortas and the Wolfson Family Foundation had leaked to the press. Wolfson was then under federal indictment, and Fortas had accepted a $20,000 annual consultant's fee from the foundation ever since he had been appointed to the Supreme Court. Although he resigned from the foundation a year later, in 1966, he did not repay the money for another six months. Second, in 1967 the Ford Foundation had given a grant to the Congress of Racial Equality (CORE) for voter registration in Cleveland; shortly thereafter Carl Stokes became the city's first black mayor. Third, many members of Robert Kennedy's campaign staff had received Ford Foundation grants soon after the senator's assassination in 1968. The *Wall Street Journal* reported complaints from Republicans that Ford Foundation officials believed they had a "blank check to form a little government of their own." The 1969 Tax Reform Act, in short, passed largely because a congressional majority believed that foundations represented a concentration of power that had betrayed their public trust by acting independently, establishing questionable political relationships, and fostering change—and because the IRS had failed to do anything about it.[32]

Tax reform did not halt efforts by the Commission on Foundations and Private Philanthropy to defend foundations' operations and resist unwanted government oversight. The commission worried that while ideologically motivated attacks were not new, they had taken on a dangerous tone. Critics had long attacked foundations as "tools of capitalism," but now they denounced them as "promoters of 'creeping socialism.'" Such distortions threatened to cast foundations as essentially un-American. Commission members feared that the IRS would become overzealous and hamstring foundation-financed studies of public policy. They worried that it would use provisions of the 1969 Tax Reform Act prohibiting "legislative activities" by foundations to curtail their public policy efforts. A year later, in a response to Patman, commission chairman Peter Peterson observed that only 4 percent of all foundation grants went to community action projects. Patman replied that while he agreed with many of the commission's recommendations, he was disappointed in its support of a federal tax policy that encouraged the "continued growth and expansion of government subsidized entities" with almost no consideration for the cost of "lost tax revenues measured against the benefits." In essence, Patman rejected the fundamental premises that underlay the commission's report, insisting that foundations remained "vehicles for the control of corporate wealth" and not for the "social and economic betterment of less fortunate Americans."[33]

Three years later, in 1972, Patman queried twenty-four tax-exempt foundations to see if the IRS was enforcing the provisions of the 1969 act. He discovered that it had not yet issued final regulations, and reform remained an illusion. Many of these larger foundations had not even been audited, even though the 1969 act levied a 4 percent excise tax on the annual net income of foundations specifically to fund additional audits. A year later, testifying before the House Ways and Means Committee, IRS Commissioner Randolph Thrower complained about this tax. He noted that it was raising more than twice as much money as the IRS needed to administer the entire exempt organizations field. He called it a "tax upon private charity itself." The Treasury Department, which had opposed the tax in 1969, supported a reduction from 4 percent to 2 percent, arguing that this would be more than sufficient to cover the costs of an enhanced audit program.[34]

Political controversies about IRS policies toward tax-exempt organizations did not disappear after passage of the 1969 Tax Reform Act. If anything they intensified, not so much from failure of the 1969 legislation as from the arrival of the Nixon administration in Washington. Determined that federal agencies should help implement the administration's policies, Nixon administration officials sought to enlist the IRS in efforts to undermine the Civil Rights Act of 1964. The issue was whether or not to grant tax-exempt status to segregated private schools. It had first arisen during the Johnson administration. In 1965 the IRS chief counsel's office began to assess what impact discrimination by tax-exempt organizations on the "basis of race, color or creed" might have on exempt status under Section 501 of the Internal Revenue Code. During the course of this review, between 1965 and 1967, the IRS stopped considering applications for tax exemption from racially discriminatory schools. An August 1967 press release from the chief counsel's office noted that "private, nonprofit schools which are not involved with the state in a way that would make their operation unconstitutional," or violate any laws, would continue to "be exempt even though they may serve groups restricted as to race, religion, or nationality." IRS Commissioner Sheldon Cohen had sought to deny recognition under any circumstances, but congressional pressure (and perhaps some from the White House) led him to back off. When Randolph Thrower succeeded Cohen as IRS commissioner, he found that this was " 'the baby left on the doorstep.' I knew that the problem would not go away," he later said, "and that it would have to be resolved by the IRS, or the Courts, or both." For the short term, the IRS would investigate racial policies of Southern schools only upon complaints. This was, Senator Walter Mondale complained, "palpably ridiculous."[35]

In fact the Supreme Court had already forced the issue with its 1968 decision in *Green v. School Board of New Kent County*. The Court declared that freedom-of-choice plans for desegregation were unconstitutional. The Johnson administration then set a deadline of January 29, 1969, for the desegregation of five Southern school districts, and a September deadline for all other districts to desegregate. The Nixon administration, despite its Southern strategy, at first announced support for the law. This prompted Georgia Republican "Bo" Callaway to complain that Nixon had promised to change that law. "The time has come," he warned, "for Nixon to bite the bullet, with real change and none of this communicating bullshit."[36] The administration reversed course and sought to gut the 1964 Civil Rights Act.

In 1970 several African-American residents of Mississippi, charging violations of the 1964 Civil Rights Act, filed a class-action lawsuit to prohibit the federal government from allowing tax exemptions for Mississippi schools that practiced racial discrimination. By then more than two hundred segregated academies had been established throughout the South. In *Green v. Kennedy*, a three-judge district court issued a preliminary injunction that prevented the IRS from granting tax exemptions to any additional racially segregated Mississippi private schools. In June the courts suspended the deductibility of contributions for forty-one Mississippi private schools that had previously received favorable rulings. This decision caused political problems for the Nixon administration, which was busy courting Southerners and implementing a broad Southern strategy whose success rested in large part on the administration's ability to slow enforcement of the civil rights laws. A central issue in the Mississippi case was the extent to which the IRS was an agent for implementing or frustrating public policy. Caught in the middle again was the Internal Revenue Service, especially where the new public policy conflicted with existing law. The IRS believed that Congress meant to deny tax exemptions to organizations that violated public policy. One critic, however, later challenged that idea, arguing that the statute contained no language "supporting such a conclusion."[37]

For the next four months the Nixon White House struggled to find a way out of its dilemma. The IRS had changed its sixty-year-old policy, and though it had begun making rulings once again, it still intended to deny tax exemptions to private segregated schools "when its involvement with the state makes its operation unconstitutional." In early April 1970, Nixon aides complained that despite ruling on several cases, the Supreme Court had not clearly defined "*what* state involvement makes a segregated private school's operation unconstitutional." The law was uncertain, and so was administration policy. Also uncertain was the extent to which the administration should involve itself in the issue. Finally, Lamar Alexander, a White House aide, recommended that the Treasury Department adopt a policy providing that the IRS grant exemptions despite discriminatory admissions policies, "except where state support of the school is predominant." President Nixon, however, wanted to take a neutral position by maintaining the former policy and letting the courts decide "in what circumstances racial discrimination in private schools is unconstitutional." This would keep the administration out of the line of fire, he hoped, and yet permit attacks on unfavorable rulings should they become politically valuable. The problem, however, was that this would make the IRS the final arbiter of defining what constituted an "unconstitutional operation of a racially discriminatory private school." Treasury preferred a policy that would grant exemptions only to schools with nondiscriminatory admissions policies. Nixon, however, refused to support that policy.[38]

Finally, at an April 17 session, Nixon strategists decided to recommend that Attorney General John Mitchell review the *Green* case settlement to make "*sure*" that it "explicitly did not indicate Administration policy that tax exemption for segregated schools without any government support was illegal." They also decided to outline to Nixon the fact that the law was likely to equate tax exemptions with government grants. If this meant an end to exemptions for religious and other private schools, a constitutional amendment should be prepared to change that. Special counsel to the president Harry Dent warned in mid-May that the administration should just let the Supreme Court "do its thing," no matter what happened. Then it could choose a course of action, and the onus would be on the courts rather than on the administration. After almost two months of wrangling, a memorandum for Nixon was finally ready by early June. It outlined various options and summarized previous discussions, but it failed to recommend a single course of action. The administration continued to look for a way out of a political dilemma caused, it believed, by the IRS.[39]

Politics, policy, and taxes created a complicated conflict. The debate within the Nixon administration was intense. One day after the district court's preliminary injunction in *Green v. Kennedy*, on January 13, 1970, the IRS responded to the comments of Robert Finch, Secretary of Health, Education and Welfare, that the Treasury Department should eliminate the tax-exempt status of all private schools. The IRS noted that law, not the discretion of the IRS commissioner or political pressure, should determine exempt status. Eight days later the court allowed parents supporting schools with exclusively white enrollment to intervene in the case. In June 1970 the court ordered the IRS to suspend any advance assurances of deductibility for contributions to schools operated on a racially segregated basis. Finally, on July 10, 1970, the IRS ruled that racially discriminatory private schools would no longer receive tax exemptions and that donations to those schools would not be tax deductible. It also agreed, pursuant to an earlier court order, to require tax-exempt schools to publish a policy of nondiscrimination and provide the IRS with their admissions data.

Defenders of segregated schools in Congress complained loudly, and opponents of those schools expressed fear that the IRS was in effect granting segregated schools a second chance. Again, the IRS found itself in the middle of a political controversy. Although Congress eventually endorsed the IRS position, the issue did not go away. Commissioner Randolph Thrower insisted that it should be resolved by the IRS, not the courts. From his perspective the policy was obvious: activities that conflicted with public policy should not be deemed charitable. "It was clear," he noted later, "that pervasive segregation in an educational organization based on race was against the well-established policy of the United States and should not receive the imprimatur of 'charitable' from an agency of the United States Government." In September 1971 the Supreme Court affirmed, without opinion, Thrower's position as well as the decision of the district court in *Green*.[40]

In the White House, meanwhile, debate raged. Political and economic adviser Peter Flanigan collected arguments and convened meetings as the White House feared attacks from religious conservatives and outraged Southerners. Senator Strom Thurmond of South Carolina led the charge, blasting the administration. Presidential aide John Ehrlichman reported to Nixon that this was to be expected, and was essential to Thurmond's political position, but that Southern anger would "simmer down" if Commissioner Thrower followed his instructions and IRS enforcement was evenhanded. Thrower's conduct would determine whether or not this became a "continuing problem with lasting political effects in the South." Speaking to Nixon's concern that he was now on the wrong side of the issue, Ehrlichman suggested that Nixon meet with Treasury officials and have Treasury Secretary George Shultz monitor IRS conduct. Fred LaRue, White House staffer and a prominent Mississippi Republican, should also be dispatched to talk with every Southern senator, congressman, and governor about the issue in order to demonstrate Nixon's concern and to reassure them that the IRS would "not engage in punitive enforcement." Supported by presidential advisers Bryce Harlow and Leonard Garment, Flanigan concluded that the White House had to make a choice. It could not force public schools in the South to desegregate while at the same time permitting private schools to segregate. Nixon eventually endorsed that view.

What had happened? The White House had been pressing the IRS to leave the issue to the courts. Now it suddenly reversed that position and moved to keep the question out of the courts. IRS Commissioner Randolph Thrower implied that the reversal was sudden and politically motivated.

> A few months later, after a White House conference between the President and the Black Congressional Caucus, I was asked to move posthaste to withdraw recognition from segregated private schools. The next few months were spent in the development of drafts that circulated through the IRS, the Treasury, the Department of Justice and the White House. The words "pervasively segregated" were inserted by me to avoid complaints based on isolated incidents.[41]

The private school issue did not die, however. Within a year it had returned in the case of Bob Jones University. Once again the administration feared that IRS rulings would undermine its political agenda. In that case, Commissioner Thrower recommended that the IRS grant tax-exempt status to Bob Jones University if it admitted "blacks and other minority groups even though they admit them on condition that there be no interracial mixing of the sexes." John Nolan, assistant secretary for tax policy, agreed, but reminded Treasury Secretary John Connally that this was a very sensitive issue and that the administration would be publicly criticized. Connally also agreed. Bob Jones University officials, however, did not change their admissions policy but instead challenged the IRS ruling, and several years of litigation ensued. In 1975 the university was finally ready to change, but by then the IRS considered its response inadequate. The issue of tax exemptions for segregated schools persisted. Four years later IRS Commissioner Donald Alexander urged the Treasury Department to review earlier decisions that had limited to a single state, Mississippi, the revocation of tax-exempt status because of segregation. This was, he insisted, legally questionable. He proposed that the IRS adopt a Revenue Procedure that would give all private schools uniform guidelines in such cases. Much the same problem surfaced later in the Reagan years, but the issue then was that of religious schools, and it galvanized evangelicals into political action.[42]

Political controversies in the late 1960s had brought the issue of foundations and IRS policy into the public consciousness. It would not soon go away. Foundations now supported, and at times opposed, public policy. Foundations operating overtly in the arena of public policy were something new in American politics. They became, throughout the latter years of the sixties and into the seventies, an adjunct to liberalism. As political divisions heated up in Congress, as a backlash set in against the policies of the Great Society and advances in civil rights, and especially when Republicans recaptured the White House in 1968, foundations' policies increasingly came under fire. Opposition to public policy now endangered their tax exemptions. Writing in *Science*, the historians Irving and Ruth Horowitz warned:

> While foundation responses to criticism have been both cautious and vigorously self-defensive, the foundations' peculiar position between business and government has left them vulnerable and searching for formulas for survival. A liberal orientation and collaboration with government agencies to liberalize policy have helped them. But these trends have led to more criticism from both the right and the left. A major increase in the impact of either type of critic would precipitate a crisis.[43]

IRS Commissioner Randolph Thrower agreed. In a speech to the American Society of Association Executives in August 1970, he warned that there was "trouble" ahead for the IRS on the issue of tax-exempt organizations. Thrower admitted that Internal Revenue had given little priority to exempt organizations; both Congress and the foundations themselves complained about the unpreparedness of the IRS. Neither would tolerate excuses in the future. Nevertheless, Thrower noted that the IRS did not intend to be the "dominating force in examining or reviewing the activities of the thousands of exempt organizations in this country."[44]

This disclaimer led Wright Patman's staff to conclude that an independent agency with oversight responsibility for private tax-exempt foundations and charitable trusts—what he called a Private Foundation Control Commission—was needed more than ever. Thrower defended his efforts as commissioner to implement provisions of the Tax Reform Act of 1969, but the congressman's staff worried that the IRS would "slip back" into a "passive" or "ineffective" role with respect to tax-exempt organizations. Supporters of foundations, on the other hand, warned of a "new kind of administrative McCarthyism" that had emerged in the "guise of enforcement of the tax laws." In their efforts to enforce provisions of the 1969 Tax Reform Act, IRS agents had examined not only financial data but confidential memoranda about applicant organizations and grantees. "In some cases," warned one critic, "quantities of documents containing information about individual student organizers, academic specialists, and labor, black, and Mexican-American leaders who had been involved in foundation projects were Xeroxed and shipped to government files in Washington."[45]

Patman failed to get his independent agency. In the short term that failure probably made little difference either to the public or to tax-exempt organizations, chiefly because the political turbulence of the late 1960s and early 1970s, combined with the suspicions of the Nixon administration, made almost all ventures by those organizations politically suspect in the eyes of their critics. Randolph Thrower's remaining months as IRS commissioner witnessed a steady stream of controversy as the IRS was pressured from all sides to crack down on exempt organizations' activities. Patman continued his close scrutiny of IRS actions, and complaints about action or inaction filled mailboxes at the IRS National Office and at Patman's congressional office. Conservative critics complained that the liberal foundations—Rockefeller, Ford, Mellon, Carnegie, and others—were financing "socialist revolution." Members of the Senate Internal Security Subcommittee agreed, warning that foundations promoted "subversion, communism, anti-American causes" in an effort to undermine the "security of the United States." In the aftermath of the 1969 Tax Reform Act, IRS critics both challenged and supported the ban on lobbying by tax-exempt foundations. Most of them seemed motivated by political considerations.[46]

Three controversies illustrate that motivation: college students' political activity, the Jerry Rubin Foundation, and the tax-exempt status of public-interest law firms. Significantly, all challenged the existing political and social order, and all opposed policies of the Nixon administration. The issues of political activity on college campuses and the Rubin Foundation were sharply focused; the question of public-interest law firms was much broader.

The issue of political activity by college students, faculty, and staff surfaced at the time of the 1970 election. The U.S. invasion of Cambodia the previous spring had rocked campuses across the country, and hundreds of institutions had ended their semester early when demonstrations against that invasion effectively closed them down. In the fall the IRS began to interpret Section 501(c)(3) of the tax code as prohibiting political activities on the campus. Central to the issue was the decision by Princeton University, under the so-called Princeton Plan, to provide an academic recess for two weeks before the fall elections so its students could participate in political activity. At the same time the IRS threatened to revoke the tax-exempt status of *The Spectator*, the seventy-three-year-old undergraduate newspaper at Columbia University, apparently on the basis that it "refused to agree in advance not to endorse candidates for public office." Fearing additional IRS action, Columbia President William McGill warned that activities by campus organizations aimed at off-campus issues could not be conducted on the campus. Various congressional committees threatened investigations of IRS behavior, but the issue passed as campus political activity declined sharply on its own.[47]

The issue of the Rubin Foundation grabbed instant headlines, chiefly because Jerry Rubin, founder of the Yippie Movement, was a media figure who for several years had artfully used the press to express opposition to government policies. In October 1970, Wright Patman, apparently prompted by a constituent's letter, queried the IRS about how and why Rubin had been given tax-exempt status for his foundation. The foundation was established in 1969 essentially as a tax shelter for profits from his book *Do It!*, and was presumed to distribute those funds to leftist causes. Republican Congressman William J. Sherele of Iowa, who had called for revocation, insisted that "We should not be forced to subsidize our own destruction with our own taxes." Thrower's response indicated that once the matter had appeared in the press, Internal Revenue had received numerous letters critical of its action. The IRS defensively issued a "fact sheet," arguing that the foundation (officially titled the Social Education Foundation) was legally entitled to an exemption. In the face of strong criticism, however, the IRS proposed to revoke the exemption a few months later. The Rubin case demonstrated the degree to which political considerations rather than a sound policy determined how the IRS treated some foundations.[48]

The final issue, that of public-interest law firms, brewed a firestorm of political controversy. Looking back on it, IRS Commissioner Randolph Thrower admitted that he was "surprised and disappointed" that the agency had granted exemptions to public-interest law firms without "any definition of standards that would have to be met by such an organization." In the fall of 1970 the IRS announced that it was reconsidering its policy, and reaction was swift—what Thrower labeled a "hornet's nest." Former commissioners Mortimer Caplin and Sheldon Cohen, "who had client interests in the field," along with Larry O'Brien, chairman of the Democratic National Committee, wrote blistering letters of complaint. Critics feared that the IRS was responding to political pressure from the Nixon administration to block attacks against Nixon's friends and policies. Patman's staff noted that although the issue was relatively small, the IRS action was a startling contrast to its "years of inertia in supervising private foundations generally." In addition, they feared that any restrictive ruling would "impair one of the more useful recent activities of foundations, channeling important social issues into the judicial system rather than into potentially violent or disruptive forms of protest." After a sixty-day study, the IRS established guidelines for such firms to obtain favorable rulings, and Thrower assured the Senate Subcommittee on Employment, Manpower and Poverty that Internal Revenue staff would interpret those guidelines liberally in the future.

> It is the availability of this type of representation that is being deemed charitable rather than the particular cause being served, provided, of course, that the cause is wholly a public one, not tainted by any substantial private interest, that it is a serious one and not frivolous, and that it is not illegal or otherwise without possibility of social benefit.

Mortimer Caplin, for one, sighed with relief and testified that he supported the guidelines. They would not restrict his client, the National Resources Defense Council, and had amicably settled "an issue of extreme national importance." The *New York Times* was not so sure, however, and warned of future consequences. Private interests would still get their tax breaks while public-interest organizations lived in "uneasy apprehension that the IRS may swoop down on them if they are suspected of lobbying." The IRS would still decide the issue on a case-by-case basis.[49]

The Nixon White House was upset with Thrower's handling of this and other problems, especially that of tax exemptions for segregated private schools. More than two years of political controversy finally took its toll, and in January 1971 Randolph Thrower resigned as commissioner of Internal Revenue.[50] Political pressures remained an ever-present fact of life for the IRS. Indeed, as later chapters will indicate, they increased dramatically during the Nixon years as the administration sought to use the Internal Revenue Service for political purposes in ways previously unimagined—to reward friends and punish enemies. Still, the question of tax-exempt foundations remained at the forefront of these political pressures.

CHAPTER EIGHT

POLITICS, TWO-WAY MIRRORS, AND WIRETAPS IN THE JOHNSON YEARS

THE RELATIONSHIP between the White House and the Internal Revenue Service is much more difficult to uncover under Lyndon Johnson than during the Kennedy years. On one hand the president's memos available at the LBJ Library, in the words of a biographer, "bristle with indignation" about wiretaps and bugging. He not only feared control by others who held information gathered through wiretapping and bugging, he also sought to protect his own operations from scrutiny. Yet as president, LBJ used manually operated recording devices for the secret taping of more than ten thousand hours of conversations with other individuals. In addition, the volume of requests from the White House to the IRS for tax reviews rose steadily during the Johnson years. In 1968, with his presidency beleaguered, they rose by 60 percent.[1] Finally, LBJ was a highly secretive individual who preferred to use the telephone rather than the typewriter to conduct business, convey opinions, and instruct subordinates. For such an active president, the hand of Lyndon Johnson is often invisible.

When he entered the presidency, Johnson seemed intent on exercising White House direction over some IRS operations. Although LBJ professed no interest in pursuing Kennedy's Ideological Organizations Project, it nonetheless continued for the first several years of his administration. During his first two years in office he also retained the services of Myer Feldman, who had compiled extensive dossiers on the right wing for Kennedy. In addition, LBJ appointed Robert L. Phinney, an old friend, to be district director of Internal Revenue for the South Texas District. This was the district that "oversaw" his own Johnson Foundation's tax-exempt status. For Internal Revenue commissioner he appointed Sheldon Cohen, who had at one time been a tax lawyer for Lady Bird Johnson and a partner at Arnold, Fortas & Porter with close Johnson friend Abe Fortas. Cohen's tenure at IRS is difficult to evaluate. The Senate confirmation hearing for both Cohen and his chief counsel, Mitchell Rogovin, was a love feast. Later, in the mid-1970s when the IRS was under much closer congressional scrutiny during investigations into intelligence agency abuses, Cohen resolutely insisted that during his four years as IRS commissioner neither the president nor any member of his staff ever saw any tax return. No document was "allowed out of the building, nor were any of those officials allowed inside the building to review them." William Kolar, former director of the IRS Intelligence Division, also testified that during the Johnson years no demand had ever been made on him "personally by the White House."[2]

Despite these careful assurances that the IRS provided no tax returns to the Johnson White House, the record is less clear. What Lyndon Johnson appears to have done is simply use more indirect methods, keeping himself clear while others did his work. During his struggle for the Democratic nomination in 1960, for instance, LBJ used his friend and aide Bobby Baker to court Pennsylvania convention delegates with the promises of help with the IRS. According to Baker, after Albert Greenfield (a wealthy Pennsylvanian) delivered a handful of votes, the IRS later dropped a demand for $10 million in back taxes. Efforts to woo Congressman Bill Green of Philadelphia also turned on promises of influence with the IRS. Because of the large Catholic vote in Philadelphia, Green was committed to JFK on the first ballot. But Johnson promised to let him choose the next Treasury secretary if Green switched other delegates on later ballots. Kennedy's first-ballot victory at the convention rendered that promise moot. Later, after he became president, Johnson had aide Marvin Watson ask Cartha "Deke" De-Loach of the FBI to check with the IRS about Robert Kennedy's approval of ELSUR (electronic surveillance) in tax cases. Clearly hoping to dig up dirt on Bobby Kennedy in anticipation of a challenge for the Democratic nomination in 1968, Johnson was careful to hide his fingerprints. Watson made clear to the FBI that LBJ was only suggesting, not instructing the Bureau to inquire. Johnson also disguised his use of the IRS to run tax reviews in 1968 on members of the California and Texas delegations to the Democratic National Convention. To do so he by-passed the Compliance Division and went directly through the "front office." IRS Commissioner Cohen ordered the California operation canceled, but tax information was used to prevent the appointment of some individuals to the Texas delegation.[3]

Two other features of the Johnson years that linked the president to the IRS—though once again often at some distance—were the issues of tax-exempt foundations and Sensitive Case files. As earlier chapters have indicated, Wright Patman pressed his investigation of tax-exempt foundations without respect to who sat in the White House. Johnson expressed concern at the abuse of exempt status by several foundations but worried that his fellow Texan's populist impulses might lead him too close to his own tax-exempt interests. He therefore tried to rein in Patman, even as he pushed for tax reform in 1965. But when that legislation failed, LBJ refused to resubmit reform legislation in 1967. Instead he turned to Sheldon Cohen and the IRS for stricter enforcement of tax laws governing charitable foundations. Cohen reported, however, that even increased IRS efforts were not likely "to yield satisfactory results." The laws themselves were too much of a hindrance and needed to be changed. Cohen asked the Treasury Department to begin an overhaul of the tax-exempt area, but no final legislative recommendations emerged until after Johnson had left office.[4]

As president, Lyndon Johnson followed the lead of his predecessors and granted various congressional committees access to tax returns. Most notable, because of its overtly political character, was his grant of access to inspect "any income, excess profit, estate or gift tax return for the years 1948 to 1967 inclusive" to the House Un-American Activities Committee (HUAC). Although HUAC had been the recipient of similar executive orders in the past, scrutiny of tax returns was usually limited to committees that were directly involved in fiscal policy. HUAC was not.[5]

The relationship between the White House and the IRS developed more decisively in the area of Sensitive Cases. This was an IRS program apparently begun during the Eisenhower years and then retained during the Kennedy presidency. It was designed to protect both the IRS and the White House from possible embarrassment. Now, under Acting Commissioner Bertrand Harding, who served before the confirmation of Sheldon Cohen as commissioner, the IRS Sensitive Case program expanded. A September 8, 1964, directive revised the timing of Sensitive Case reports to the National Office from monthly to "immediately after a significant change" had occurred in any Sensitive Case. A second directive in November revealed the political ramifications of the change. Any IRS office or agent who received an "inquiry or information evidencing interest being shown in a case by the White House, Treasury Department, [or] Members of Congress" was instructed to notify the National Office immediately. A year later, after Sheldon Cohen became IRS commissioner, another classified memorandum to all assistant regional commissioners of collection further expanded the program by directing "advance notice of any enforcement collection action planned in Sensitive Cases." The Treasury Department prepared a card file on all Sensitive Cases and then sent these cards to the White House, which maintained a geographic file to "forewarn the President during the campaign about individuals who may be under investigation by the Service." The White House, in turn, channeled its inquiries about particular cases through Commissioner Cohen.[6]

Before LBJ left office, a new twelve-page internal directive in February 1968 once again expanded and revised the Sensitive Case procedures. This time the IRS created special reporting forms—Form 4341, Sensitive Case Report, and Form 4341-A, Sensitive Case Report Continuation Sheet—along with a special transmittal letter. The IRS then required periodic reports on all existing Sensitive Cases. The program expanded to include not only major political figures (such as local, state, or federal officeholders) but also "prominent" party officials, their family members, or close personal friends. Other targets for Sensitive Case reports were nationally or internationally known businessmen, racketeers, union officials, religious figures, entertainers, or sports figures; any "organization of national scope"; all national or major metropolitan mass media; a "club with a large influential membership"; and any person who had received attention because they had criticized the IRS or the tax system. Finally, the IRS would open a Sensitive Case file on *any* taxpayer if a "major political figure" showed "substantial" interest in that individual's dealings with the IRS. In all instances, any "urgent" developments were to be telephoned immediately to the appropriate assistant regional commissioner. In essence, the IRS had unlimited authority to investigate anyone it wanted under the auspices of the Sensitive Case program.[7]

The ramifications of this program become evident when one realizes that by 1968 the IRS was conducting more than 130 investigations, involving more than 1,000 cases, into political corruption and the deduction of illegal campaign contributions. Investigations were active in almost every one of the 58 IRS districts, but most centered in California. In Los Angeles alone the IRS had launched "Operation Snowball," an investigation into more than 31 companies for double billing and fictitious invoices to make campaign contributions appear deductible. IRS agent Caesar Cantu observed that he had been told to "proceed cautiously" because political figures were involved. Despite federal requirements to preserve the record of its activities, the IRS later destroyed all documents related to "Operation Snowball."[8]

During the Johnson years the Internal Revenue Service also demonstrated an increasingly avid interest in dissident groups. As such it became both a collector of intelligence information and an interagency intelligence resource. The FBI obtained tax returns and other tax information directly from the IRS Intelligence Division. Although the IRS Disclosure Branch labeled this "illegal" in 1968, there is little evidence that it ceased. In fact, almost no documentary evidence of pre-1968 procedures still exists today: all IRS records of disclosures to the FBI before 1968 were destroyed in 1972 in a "space-saving drive"—yet another euphemism for the violation of federal law. Congressional investigations in 1976 did, however, document the existence of such cozy interagency relationships, with both the FBI and the CIA using (or misusing) IRS information. Even after the IRS realized in 1968 that other agencies were violating its procedures, the CIA retained its ability to receive tax-return information without filing requests. Later, from 1968 through at least 1974, this IRS conduit became an important component of the FBI's Counter-Intelligence Program (COINTELPRO) operations against dissident groups.[9]

IRS information also became increasingly important to the Justice Department. Information provided by Internal Revenue had previously been central to the department's Organized Crime Drive, beginning in the Kennedy years. Then, in 1967, the Justice Department created a secret intelligence unit—the Interdivision Information Unit (IDIU)—to analyze FBI information on targeted individuals and groups in urban ghettos. Its purpose was to focus on individuals involved in civil disorders, and it asked several agencies, including the IRS, to funnel information to it for review. The IDIU sought to turn a variety of other sources, including poverty programs, the Neighborhood Legal Services Program, Labor Department programs, and the Community Relations Service, into sources of intelligence information. It also established contact with the CIA, though that agency was prohibited by its charter from operating within the United States. By 1970 IDIU computer tapes included as many as twenty thousand entries on "antiwar activists and other dissidents." These were turned over to the CIA and the IRS during the Nixon years. At the same time the FBI launched its "key activists" program to target dissidents, particularly those in the New Left and anti–Vietnam War groups. Although the IRS required the FBI to make formal requests for tax information, it never questioned Justice Department assertions that such information was essential to pursue "official matters" involving "internal security." Bureau misuse of tax information became a problem, such as when the FBI led the IRS to audit a New Left–oriented professor at a Midwestern college who was planning to attend the 1968 Democratic National Convention. IRS demands, the FBI noted, "may be a source of distraction during the critical period when he is engaged in meetings and plans for disruption" at the convention. "Any drain upon the [professor's] time and concentration . . . can only accrue to the benefit of the Government and general public."[10]

President Johnson and FBI Director J. Edgar Hoover had a long relationship, and Hoover willingly used the FBI for him. During Johnson's feud with Robert Kennedy, the FBI engaged the IRS in a probe of Joseph Dolan, longtime Kennedy friend and Justice Department official, as well as other Justice Department personnel who had gone to work for Kennedy. Cooperation between the FBI and the IRS, according to a note from Commissioner Cohen to Hoover in early 1965, was "at an all time high." These ties solidified further when the Bureau began to penetrate the ranks of anti-war activists, including the Liberation News Service. It regularly forwarded reports to the IRS as well as to other government intelligence agencies. IRS Deputy Assistant Commissioner for Compliance Leon Green recalled, "I do not think we ever questioned their need for a tax return." President Johnson's Executive Order 11396 in 1968, urging the IRS to cooperate with other agencies in the investigation of organized crime and corruption, further strengthened those ties.[11]

This relationship became central to FBI investigations of various groups and activities. In December 1963 the Bureau decided to investigate the Southern Christian Leadership Conference (SCLC) and Martin Luther King, Jr. By January 1964, FBI supervisor Seymour Phillips had requested copies of tax returns from the IRS. Although the IRS reported that its examinations failed to reveal any tax violations, Hoover refused to believe the agency, scrawling "what a farce" on the memo. Designating the SCLC as a "Black Nationalist–Hate Type Organization," the Bureau obtained "all available information" on King and the SCLC from the IRS. This included tax returns as well as IRS investigative files and audits. At that time the SCLC was a tax-exempt organization, but since contributions to it were not tax deductible it was required to disclose the names of contributors. The FBI decided to create phony correspondence on official SCLC stationery to inform contributors that the IRS was investigating its tax records. The Bureau hoped that this would strike fear into contributors, and that contributions would cease. The FBI also intended to investigate King himself for tax avoidance. To aid their investigation, they planted accountant James Harrison inside the SCLC as an FBI informant.[12]

The IRS was active on other racial battlegrounds as well. President Johnson complained that Robert Kennedy had "*demanded*" that he send IRS agents into Mississippi in 1964 to help curtail white extremists. More significant, and in many ways more troubling, were IRS efforts to use its intelligence capabilities in other racial situations. Because the IRS failed to maintain its records, only limited evidence exists about these efforts, but that evidence is intriguing. In September 1965, IRS Commissioner Sheldon Cohen informed Ramsey Clark of the Justice Department that "We are proceeding in the Detroit area with caution and tact in potentially explosive racial areas." Seven months later, in April 1966, Cohen forwarded to Presidential Special Assistant Marvin Watson a report on the situation in Watts. "I am sure," Cohen wrote, "you will be interested in forwarding this comprehensive report of one of our undercover men." He warned Watson that distribution of the report should remain limited "in order to protect our undercover man." What was the IRS doing in both of these situations? Were there active tax investigations that targeted racially troubled areas? Or was the IRS using its intelligence capabilities for other purposes? Given the manifest deficiencies in the IRS records management program, we will likely never know the full story.[13]

The FBI also used IRS records in its efforts to penetrate and neutralize the Ku Klux Klan during the mid-1960s. The Bureau's COINTELPRO–White Hate program secured the tax records of several Klan officials, and the FBI employed informants to uncover possible tax abuses. In 1965, for example, it discovered that one KKK member had not paid taxes on a veteran's pension and so informed the IRS. Its larger effort, however, was to use tax data to discredit or embarrass the United Klans of America. Birmingham FBI agents urged the IRS to investigate the United Klans of Alabama, hoping that IRS attention would not only disrupt the organization's operations but also dry up its contributions. The IRS willingly cooperated, though it lost control over the FBI's use of the returns. It provided such records at least through 1970, and perhaps beyond. When the KKK organized a defense fund, the FBI asked the IRS to audit selected KKK officials to see if the fund was being used to launder money. The Bureau used similar tactics in Louisiana, where an FBI agent in New Orleans reported that the local Klan leader was a nervous wreck because he expected "a prison sentence due to the IRS inquiries." In none of these cases did the IRS find evidence of tax avoidance or evasion. What was questionable, however, was the use of IRS intelligence capabilities as a handmaiden to FBI investigations even though prior evidence of tax liabilities did not exist. The IRS had become much more than a tax collector.[14]

This pursuit of legitimate objectives through questionable activities took other forms as well during the Johnson years. From January to May 1968 the IRS ran a mail cover program through the New York post office. It sought to compile lists of all individuals and companies doing business with Swiss banks. Using the postage meter markings on return envelopes to the banks, the IRS matched meter numbers with specific Swiss banks. The IRS did not open the mail but photographed 128,000 envelopes from almost 75,000 individuals. By summer the IRS had compiled a printout of 8,500 taxpayers whose returns it could select for audit. Between the fall of 1968 and early 1972 the IRS audited 168 taxpayers identified from a list of 800 individuals it had targeted for possible examination. During the Nixon years the IRS would run two other mail covers, but apparently it did not initiate audits from those efforts.[15]

In 1961 the IRS had initiated a procedure to voluntarily inform the attorney general when it found evidence of offenses against the government, even though they did not violate any revenue laws. This became the framework for subsequent IRS intelligence sharing. The primary problem for the IRS during the Johnson years, however, was one in which jurisdiction was not an issue. When the insertion of U.S. ground troops into Vietnam in 1965 expanded protests against the war, the administration quietly began using the IRS to harass dissenters. A growing number of dissidents urged taxpayers to withhold tax payments as a protest against the war. In response, the IRS announced that it would vigorously enforce the income tax laws, and that after the 1966 filing deadline it would "pursue several of the organizers of the conspiracy on a selective basis" and take action "as quickly as possible." Following publication of a protest ad in the *Washington Post* on April 14, 1966, signed by about 360 individuals, the IRS acted. It targeted each one of them, intending to collect all amounts owed in excess of one dollar. "Our general policy," the IRS told Treasury Secretary Henry Fowler, was to collect taxes due "without publicity which would further the cause of the group."[16] Internal Revenue staff remained concerned about tax protests for the next several years.

It also targeted dissidents for other, less legitimate, reasons. Retired

General James Gavin, for example, insisted that LBJ had arranged an extensive IRS audit of his tax returns in 1966, after he had testified against the war. By the time Lyndon Johnson left the White House, the IRS had joined the FBI, CIA, and even the U.S. military in conducting intelligence operations against war protesters and sharing that information with other government agencies. Although no available evidence indicates that the IRS worked with army intelligence, its loose sharing of tax information with the FBI and CIA allowed that information to circulate within several agencies. Once information left the hands of the IRS, the agency no longer had effective control over its dissemination or use.

When the IRS created a formal National Security Case procedure in April 1968, it established a system that made tax returns and return information on political organizations and individuals widely available to other agencies. Under the FBI's "key activists" program, the Bureau requested tax information on dozens of individuals between 1966 and 1968. In no case did the Bureau indicate, or the IRS inquire, what use might be made of this information. Not until February 1969 did the Bureau reveal its methods.

> We have caused a survey to be made by Internal Revenue Service (IRS) concerning Key Activists. We have found a number where no record exists for payment of taxes in 1966, 1967. Included in this group are [names redacted]. IRS has initiated appropriate investigations as a result of our inquiries. It is anticipated the IRS inquiry will cause these individuals considerable consternation, possibly jail sentences eventually. We have now sent requests on 35 Key Activists to IRS and anticipate many will have filed no returns. This action is consistent with our efforts to obtain prosecution of any kind against Key Activists to remove them from the movement.[17]

The Bureau also used IRS information against organizations, as did the CIA. A case in point is the IRS audit of Students for a Democratic Society (SDS), initiated in 1968 in both New York and Chicago at the FBI's request. Congressional investigators found the audit to be appropriate because the IRS had denied SDS a tax exemption, but they also noted that the IRS had passed lists of SDS contributors to the FBI and to the White House to use as they saw fit.[18]

More complicated, and illegal, were IRS links with the CIA. This issue surfaced with the revelations in *Ramparts* magazine about CIA funding for the National Student Association. The White House quickly denied that President Johnson knew anything about student involvement with the CIA. This proved difficult to believe, however, since as senator he had served on the watchdog committee that oversaw CIA activities. Johnson's close friend and mentor, Senator Richard Russell of Georgia, later confirmed that the watchdog committee had known about the CIA financial support from the beginning. NSA officials had also met with Vice President Hubert Humphrey and presidential assistant Douglass Cater in July 1966 to explore ways to break those financial ties. That Johnson did not know of these meetings, particularly since he kept a tight rein on the activities of his vice president, seems inconceivable. Wright Patman's revelations about links between the CIA and various foundations also exposed the president's involvement with domestic CIA-IRS activities. Some of those key conduits were run by old Texas friends of the president. A trustee of the Hoblitzelle Foundation, one such conduit, was federal judge Sarah Hughes, a longtime political ally of LBJ and the person who administered the oath of office to him on the plane following John F. Kennedy's assassination in Dallas. A trustee of the M. D. Anderson Foundation of Houston, also a CIA conduit, was another old friend, attorney Leon Jaworski (later of Watergate fame). The Hobby Foundation, created specifically as a CIA conduit, was established by Houston publisher Oveta Culp Hobby, former commander of the Women's Army Corps during World War II, who had been close to LBJ since the 1930s.[19]

When the *Ramparts* story broke, the CIA quickly turned to the informal IRS channel it had opened in 1957. On February 1, 1967, a CIA counterintelligence agent met with Thomas Terry, an assistant to the IRS commissioner and the half-brother of Deputy Commissioner Bertrand Harding, and requested an audit of *Ramparts'* corporate tax returns, and then follow-ups to be conducted on individuals' returns. The CIA quickly provided the IRS with "detailed informant information" on the magazine's supporters, and by August the spy agency had compiled a computerized listing of several hundred Americans, with substantive files on at least fifty of them. By mid-February the CIA had obtained the tax return of Edward Keating, owner of *Ramparts*. The IRS also audited Robert Scheer, a reporter for the magazine. Meanwhile the White House quickly decided on a press line about the affair. It would volunteer nothing and not respond to newspaper allegations or statements by individuals. All diplomatic posts were to refer questions to Washington as well as provide the White House with any information available about federal assistance to student programs operating in their area. It would deflect any other questions with a statement that Nicholas Katzenbach was "undertaking an immediate and full survey and study of the problems involved in this matter. . . ."[20]

Even as the White House set this spin control in motion, it sought to determine how the CIA-NSA ties had become public. White House aide Walt Rostow reported to the president that they were "100% sure" that Patman was the source of the leak. "With a few clues," Rostow said, "it is apparently easy to sort out which foundations are CIA-linked." Douglass Cater told LBJ that Education Secretary John Gardner had earlier protested to CIA directors Allen Dulles and Richard Helms about CIA activities in the education community. Gardner was reluctant to serve on a review panel for the affair because he could not deny these activities, but the White House hoped he would be more circumspect in the future. Zbigniew Brzezinski, professor of government at Columbia University and later Jimmy Carter's national security adviser, called the White House to complain that no one had yet stood up for the NSA and the service those students had performed for the nation. He complained about "phony muckrakers in the press and in Congress" who were making this an "unsavory business." President Johnson eventually prohibited CIA support of foundations, but the Agency merely transferred its funding to private companies and the relationships continued. For the IRS, the *Ramparts* affair demonstrated "the dangers of informal exchanges of information" with intelligence agencies. They encouraged illegal disclosure of tax information and provided those agencies with "a lever by which to manipulate or persuade the IRS into action directed against certain taxpayers for reasons having no bearing upon compliance with the tax laws." Ironically, had the CIA followed legal procedures, IRS disclosure of tax information to the Agency would have been legal under existing law.[21]

All of these events paled before two others involving the Internal Revenue Service and the Johnson White House. The first involved a tax investigation, and later a criminal investigation, into LBJ aide and longtime friend Bobby Baker. The second concerned IRS use of electronic surveillance.

The Baker case began as an IRS tax investigation. It quickly devolved into a grand jury probe and later became the focus of congressional investigations. Johnson's critics saw the Baker affair as a way to discredit the president and undermine his ability to pursue Great Society legislation. The president quickly called the IRS for copies of Baker's income tax returns and also requested his FBI files to see if Baker was vulnerable to criminal prosecution. The Baker affair was intensely complicated, and the available evidence often thin. Oral testimony, however, revealed Baker's convoluted ties to a Teamsters Union loan for Florida land deals as well as links and ownership interests in an assortment of vending machine companies and a speculative motel deal in Ocean City, Maryland. Baker's role in Washington was to open doors and lobby congressmen. He did both with a flair, providing gifts and women as his currency of exchange. In the course of these efforts Baker had accumulated a net worth of more than $2 million which, as one senator noted, "didn't happen just by clever operation."[22]

In the Baker affair, Lyndon Johnson relied on his political instincts rather than his long ties of friendship to set his course of action. He quickly distanced himself from his friend and aide, seeking to insulate himself from any political fallout even while he secretly tried to help Baker. He granted the Senate investigating committee access to Baker's tax returns. At the same time he used indirect channels to find out what was going on, instructing Deputy Secretary of Defense Cyrus Vance to "call Sheldon Cohen . . . he's our man." LBJ's friend, attorney Abe Fortas, also received confidential IRS documents about Baker's tax problems in the form of an IRS Sensitive Case file. At the same time the president used the FBI to determine if Robert Kennedy might be behind Baker's exposure.[23]

During his appearance before the Senate investigating committee, Baker refused to answer questions about an IRS reversal of an unfavorable tax ruling on one of his stock deals. He also refused to produce evidence that the committee had requested, insisting that this was a judicial and not a legislative matter. Committee efforts to force others to testify about Baker's tax liabilities also failed, in part because of revelations about telephone taps placed by the FBI. Lester Stein, special assistant to IRS Chief Counsel Mitchell Rogovin, warned the committee that it was illegal for them to ask witnesses about material that came from a tax return that was not their own. Republican Senator John J. Williams of Delaware testified that he had already spent considerable time investigating Baker, though he did not indicate why. Williams, however, had long been concerned about the IRS and was an inveterate opponent of Lyndon Johnson and the Great Society.[24]

The investigating committee was divided, generally along partisan lines. Republicans wanted to explore widely and call a long list of witnesses; Democrats refused, and their votes carried the day. Particularly nasty was the discussion over whether or not to call LBJ friend and aide Walter Jenkins as a witness. In frustration, Pennsylvania Republican Senator Hugh Scott insisted that there was "something suspicious" going on. He believed that additional witnesses would reveal a connection between the running of what he called "hot money" from gamblers and underworld characters and Bobby Baker. According to Scott, Washington, D.C., lobbyist Fred Black was the linchpin of the entire operation. The Supreme Court later learned that the FBI had wiretapped Black, who had been convicted of income tax violations. Since Black and Baker were close business associates, many of their daily conversations were recorded on the taps. The entire Baker affair eventually ended up in what one writer called a "wiretap war." The Justice Department and the FBI sought to shift responsibility for the bugging and blamed each other for it. Members of Congress, together with FBI Director Hoover, tried to blame Robert Kennedy. RFK, in turn, released his own documents to cast blame on Hoover. It was a messy affair and fed into a wide-ranging and highly politicized investigation led by Senator Edward V. Long of Missouri.[25]

The Long Committee investigation represented both a problem and an opportunity for Lyndon Johnson. It focused initially on the problem of electronic eavesdropping, illegal electronic surveillance, and personal privacy, but eventually expanded to raise questions about Robert Kennedy, Lyndon Johnson, the Mafia, and even Jimmy Hoffa. The immediate issue involved wiretapping and bugging carried on during Robert Kennedy's tenure as attorney general. The distinction between the two activities was critical. Federal law prohibited wiretapping unless authorized by the Justice Department, but there was no federal prohibition of bugging, or eavesdropping.[26]

Senator Edward Long had come up through Democratic political ranks in Missouri. Beginning in the mid-1930s he had held a number of offices, including a stint as prosecuting attorney for Pike County, state senator, lieutenant governor, and since 1960 as a United States senator when he won a special election to fill the unexpired term of Thomas C. Hennings, Jr. Long had then been elected to a full six-year term in 1962. He had long been interested in privacy issues. In 1961 he had opposed a wiretapping bill in Congress, backed by Attorney General Robert Kennedy, because it was not restrictive enough. In 1962 he had written an article tracing the history of wiretapping since a 1929 Supreme Court decision that First Amendment protection did not extend to the "tapping of telephone conversations." Wiretapping was a "comprehensive form of espionage," Long warned, that could put the "policeman's ear into 74 million homes and offices in the United States."[27]

During 1963 hearings on the Freedom of Information Act, Treasury

Department General Counsel G. d'Andelot Belin submitted a list of objections to the act almost fifty pages long. Although Belin tried to sugarcoat his remarks with a statement supporting the bill's principles, in fact Treasury opposed all disclosure. Access to government files was important, he conceded, but not when it clashed with "good government" or with the public's right to privacy. During those same hearings, moreover, Massachusetts Senator Edward Kennedy wrung a concession out of an IRS spokesman that the public had "no idea of what kind of information the Revenue Service is sticking into a file on or about 180 million of us." Later, in a September 1964 press release, Long revealed that he had quietly been investigating government snooping. "The further we dig," he said, "the more disturbing information we uncover."[28]

At this time Long chaired the Senate Judiciary Committee's Subcommittee on Administrative Practices and Procedures, and in the fall of 1964 he sent a questionnaire to all government agencies asking about possible invasions of privacy. On February 18, 1965, even before all the questionnaires were returned, the committee began hearings into government agencies' invasions of citizens' privacy. The IRS was particularly slow to respond, claiming that it took time to gather information from its far-flung field offices. Long charged that it was stalling, and he concentrated on the IRS Intelligence Division, the unit responsible for investigating organized crime during the Kennedy years. Long's real objectives quickly became apparent. He had always opposed the organized crime drive. Critics suggested that this was because he had political ties to the Teamsters Union and Jimmy Hoffa, and because he was also a friend of Roy Cohn. But there was more to it. As Johnson aide Bill Moyers told Richard Goodwin, "He is out to get Bobby" and "Johnson's egging him on." The FBI also encouraged Long, chiefly because Long shared J. Edgar Hoover's dislike for Robert Kennedy and might turn up information that could be used against him.[29]

The IRS was not caught flatfooted. In mid-December 1964, Acting IRS Commissioner Bertrand Harding spent several hours with IRS personnel in Intelligence, Alcohol and Tobacco Tax, and Inspection discussing their "equipment and technique" for electronic surveillance. Harding pronounced himself "completely satisfied" that they were following the law "as they understand it." Just to be safe, however, he asked Treasury General Counsel Belin for an opinion on the legality of IRS eavesdropping devices and procedures. "I am convinced," Belin concluded, that "other than in rare instances of employee failure to follow instructions, the *legal* devices used are being used *legally*," a guarded conclusion that did not really reflect much confidence. Then, in late

February 1965, Harding asked Vernon Acree and Donald Bacon of the IRS to review a Long Committee report on the agency's use of two-way mirrors.[30]

The more the IRS looked into its own operations, the more it discovered facts that it believed should be concealed from the Long Committee and the public. In April 1965 the IRS defied the committee by refusing to turn over diaries of IRS agents who had engaged in wiretapping and eavesdropping. Claiming that the documents were privileged, Cohen, still chief counsel, clashed directly with Senator Long. He also announced that, contrary to the subcommittee's expectations, no IRS employee would be prosecuted for any violation of state or federal eavesdropping laws. Having just learned that an IRS wiretap in a Miami apartment picked up conversations of more than a thousand individuals in 1962 and 1963, and that a Michigan parolee from a federal prison had placed a transmitter in one of his boots (with batteries in the other boot) to collect information for the IRS, Senator Long was outraged. The government began a quiet counterattack against Long, suggesting that his real objective was to free Jimmy Hoffa, who was serving a prison sentence for jury tampering and who claimed that the government's case against him rested on illegal eavesdropping. Although Long quickly denied the allegation, it had a ring of truth about it and refused to die.[31]

To cover its flanks, in April 1965 the IRS issued instructions to all special agents and criminal investigators on the "Proper Use of Investigative Techniques." In his foreword, Assistant Commissioner for Compliance Donald Bacon warned that, while agents should vigorously pursue tax violators, "the illegal use of investigative techniques and equipment" was "strictly and unconditionally prohibited." Sheldon Cohen had told Acting Commissioner Bertrand Harding in early January that IRS use of mail covers, wiretaps, telephone toll slips, desk searches, special observation equipment, telephone monitoring or interception, and the use of electronic listening, recording, or transmitting devices was not prohibited by federal law. But Cohen had warned that those devices should not be installed or operated so as to invade an individual's constitutional rights. The IRS instructions, Document No. 5596 (4-65), were cautionary rather than proscriptive.[32]

Far more troubling, both to the Long Committee and to the IRS, were revelations that the Treasury Department operated a secret school for undercover agents. In addition to being plied with liquor and women to see if they could resist blowing their cover, agents at the Treasury's Technical Investigative Aids School received instruction in such subjects as electronics, room security, photography, microphone installation, counterintelligence, and the installation of transmitters on people and in cars. All agents received a set of lock picks at graduation. Now commissioner, Sheldon Cohen assured the Long Committee that IRS agents would no longer attend the school until the curriculum was changed, and the Treasury Department later replaced it with a Federal Law Enforcement Training Center. Even more troubling was the school's relationship with the Army Intelligence School at Fort Holabird, Maryland. All agents spent eight hours at Fort Holabird, which by the late 1960s had compiled massive data files on thousands of American citizens.[33]

These revelations spurred Treasury officials into frenzied activity, and they scrambled to head off public hearings. Under Secretary Joseph Barr admitted that Treasury had given Senator Long false reports, especially on IRS operations in Pittsburgh. Although the IRS believed that most violations had occurred in the organized crime drive, it launched its own internal investigation to discover the extent of wiretapping by Internal Revenue staff, hoping to prevent the entire tax collection system from being discredited. Barr personally confided that he would happily "yield the criminal area back to the FBI." The Justice Department, on the other hand, believed IRS participation in the organized crime drive to be essential. At least 60 percent of its cases in the past four years had involved the IRS and taxes. Its crackdown on gambling operations in Pittsburgh was a case in point. Following information provided by the IRS Intelligence Division, the Justice Department had broken up numbers operations run by Tony Grosso, Meyer Sigal, and Henry Katz, each of whom grossed between $2.2 million and $13 million annually. In mid-June, however, Cohen met with Senator Long and admitted that the IRS had provided false information about its investigative methods. Investigations in Pittsburgh alone had uncovered thirty-eight cases of IRS wiretapping used in federal criminal cases. The agency feared that it had discovered only the tip of the iceberg.[34]

The IRS seemed to be out of control. Even Commissioner Cohen recognized that, and he launched efforts to protect IRS effectiveness and prestige and shield it from criticism. The IRS hoped to convince the public that wiretapping and other excesses were confined to the organized crime drive and not used in noncriminal cases against taxpaying citizens. Even though public disclosure would seriously impede the OCD, as well as federal-state cooperation, both the Treasury secretary and the attorney general recommended to President Johnson that Cohen go before the Long Committee and testify in public hearings. Treasury would also assure Long that it would cease improper practices and appoint a special assistant to the secretary for law enforcement. The attorney general intended to inform Long that he would circulate federal guidelines for wiretapping, and that the IRS would no longer use illegal techniques in the OCD. These concessions, they hoped, would lead Long to cancel the hearings in Pittsburgh and other cities. Fowler and Katzenbach also warned LBJ that committee requests for information would certainly raise the question of executive privilege, such as requests for agents' diaries and for names of organized crime subjects. In response, President Johnson prohibited wiretapping except in national security cases, and told Cohen to cease immediately all use of electronic eavesdropping.[35]

The IRS and the Justice Department feared that these measures would not deter Senator Long. Events quickly proved them correct. Bernard Fensterwald, committee counsel, asked the IRS for all equipment logs and diaries maintained by the Pittsburgh Intelligence Division. Cohen forwarded the logs but refused to provide the diaries. The IRS argued that reports of its activities had been blown out of proportion, insisting that it owned only eighty-three pieces of electronic equipment. Long persisted and asked for more information, including the names of individuals forwarded to the IRS by the Justice Department for a "special tax investigation."

The diaries provoked the greatest concern. Although President Johnson did not see why Internal Revenue could not provide the diaries, he instructed aide Lee White to contact attorney (and confidante) Abe Fortas for an opinion. Cohen, on the other hand, urged noncompliance. The diaries identified confidential IRS informants. They also contained names of taxpayers who had not been prosecuted. Releasing that information would damage reputations and perhaps endanger lives. The IRS drafted guidelines for its employees who might be called to testify before the Long Committee, warning that they could not reveal tax returns or tax-return information without violating federal privacy law. Finally, IRS Chief Counsel Mitchell Rogovin warned that agency employees might have to seek private counsel to defend themselves against a Pennsylvania law that prohibited eavesdropping. The diaries were to remain confidential.[36]

Meanwhile the Justice Department worried about its own exposure. In July it prepared a memorandum outlining its defense and attempting to shift blame wholly to the IRS. It claimed that until early June no Justice Department official in western Pennsylvania had "any knowledge that agents of the Internal Revenue Service were engaging in illegal wire tap activities or were presenting cases based on illegal state or local activity." Protesting that the IRS had assured Justice "repeatedly" that "such charges were without substance," the memorandum insisted that not until a conference with IRS officials on June 11 did Justice officials learn that this was not true. They conceded that "from time to time" the department had received FBI intelligence reports that "we suspected might come from wire tap sources," but the FBI had never revealed its sources. The Bureau, meanwhile, worried that revelations of its extensive microphone surveillance would "play into the hands of such groups as the Long Committee." Justice Department officials then cited a series of cases, largely gambling cases, where wiretaps apparently played some role in securing convictions. It began a review of those cases.[37]

All of this further inflamed Senator Long and his staff, and he opened public hearings in Pittsburgh. As late as March, he complained, Treasury Secretary Douglas Dillon had sat in his office and assured him that IRS wiretapping was "absolutely banned." Although Long believed Dillon to be ignorant of IRS wiretap practices, he insisted that there "appears to be a festering infection in IRS which must and shall be corrected. This correction can be accomplished in part by exposure to sunlight, and in part by legislation." He did not believe the IRS capable of self-correction.

IRS Commissioner Sheldon Cohen was his prime witness. Cohen refused to provide the committee with copies of agents' affidavits about wiretapping, though he agreed to discuss them. The commissioner tried to strike a pose of cooperation with Long and the subcommittee, insisting that he had only recently learned of these activities and intended to expose wrongdoing and terminate illegal wiretaps. Perhaps because of this, Cohen and Long got along fairly well at first, and Cohen was able to admit a few problems while at the same time protect the IRS. The problems stemmed, he insisted, from agents' zealous enthusiasm for the organized crime drive and not from any effort to subvert taxpaying citizens' constitutional rights. He provided the committee with copies of his new instructions to agents and a new definition of IRS policy. All wiretaps, he told Long, would end. They were improper if not illegal. In addition, the Justice Department would abandon cases where evidence resulted from the installation of illegal wiretaps.[38]

Responding to charges that the IRS had also secretly opened first-class mail, Cohen admitted that mail covers were controversial, but he defended their use and opposed any blanket prohibition of them. They were, he maintained, a "valuable investigative technique" and had been crucial in several criminal cases. Although the courts had found them to be legal and the IRS had used them chiefly in criminal investigations, they would no longer be used in audit cases or the collection of delinquent accounts. On April 12, 1965, Cohen had issued instructions to that effect, and the Post Office had adopted a new policy of tighter controls.

The commissioner also revealed that he had terminated the use of bugged conference rooms and asked for removal of the two-way mirrors used in Pittsburgh, where one had even been placed behind a picture of the Statue of Liberty. Other two-way mirrors, in New York, Baltimore, Detroit, Montgomery, Alexandria, Brooklyn, Kansas City, and Greenville, South Carolina, would also be removed. Senator Long demanded that bugs installed in public phone booths in the lobby of the IRS building be removed. In his testimony, Cohen admitted that several divisions of the Internal Revenue Service had engaged in these activities since 1958. Not only had the Intelligence Division used two-way mirrors and placed concealed microphones in conference rooms, so had the Alcohol and Tobacco Tax Division (A&TT), which was part of the IRS until 1972, as well as the Internal Security Division. Altogether IRS conference rooms in more than twenty cities had been wired for electronic surveillance.[39]

IRS agents testified that they were unaware of Pennsylvania laws prohibiting wiretapping. "I was very enthusiastic about my job," agent William Marsh told the committee, "and I believed at the time that there was implied authority to do this because of the equipment and services furnished by the national office." Senator Long sympathized with the agents, believing they were not always to blame. The Treasury Department had banned the use of wiretapping since 1938, he observed, but "which of us would not believe that the regulation was made purely for show, to be winked at, but not obeyed." Another factor in the lack of control over IRS agents, the committee heard, was the decentralization of the agency implemented during the 1950s after serious National Office scandals. Cohen recognized, however, that even if IRS officials did not know about the actions of individual agents, they were nonetheless responsible. Consequently he replaced H. Alan Long as director of the Intelligence Division with William Kolar, former director of the IRS Internal Security Division, and shuffled other personnel.[40] Cohen assured the Long Committee that

> The commissioner's guidelines for agents' activities were explicit. A highly important part of administration of the Internal Revenue laws is the bringing to justice of willful offenders of those laws. *Of equal importance in the administration of these laws is the observance of the highest level of*

integrity by Service personnel in carrying out their duties. The constitutional rights and other legal rights of all persons will be fully respected and observed. . . . The use of wiretaps is unconditionally prohibited, as is a deliberate making of an unreasonable search or seizure.[41]

He conceded that implementation would be difficult among all sixty thousand employees of the IRS.

While Cohen insisted that cases of illegal activity were "relatively isolated," the *Wall Street Journal* reported that the commissioner's crackdown on wiretapping was much more sweeping than his actions with respect to other forms of surveillance. In response to a *Washington Post* editorial that fall, the commissioner defended his testimony and actions. Insisting that he was personally and officially committed to "constitutional principles and safeguards," he explained his revelations of IRS wrongdoing as an effort to "quarantine the damage already done" and eliminate doubt about IRS activities in taxpayers' minds. At stake was the integrity not only of the IRS but of the entire "self-assessment tax system" of the United States. This was too vital for him or anyone else to conceal illegal activities.[42]

By that fall, with morale in the IRS Intelligence Division slipping, Commissioner Cohen concluded that Senator Long was more interested in publicity than in reform. "On reflection," he told Senator John Williams of Delaware, "perhaps I should not be too surprised at some of the confusion that seems to exist." The Long Committee hearings had "so interwoven wiretapping with other investigative techniques which are not illegal, that it is difficult for anyone to be certain of the present situation." To defend itself, the IRS distributed press releases to newsmen in cities where the subcommittee was about to hold hearings. By doing so, Long charged, it was harassing the committee. In retaliation, Long and subcommittee chief counsel Bernard Fensterwald pestered IRS Director of Information Joseph Rosapepe to admit that he knew about the wiretapping and had concealed it. Rosapepe stoutly denied everything. Long also called IRS intelligence agents to testify, hoping to uncover more details. But he was unable to get them to admit they had bugged anyone—until agent Lawrence Bennett confessed that he had set up a bugging operation as part of the OCD in Kansas City during the early 1960s. The issue, Long now insisted, was the "great power placed in the hands of the Internal Revenue agents" and its potential to ruin lives and reputations.[43]

In December, Long attacked a letter of complaint he had received from Cohen as "extraordinary." The problem lay, he insisted, with the

IRS and not with the committee. The IRS had refused to answer the committee's questionnaire. It had also refused access to key documents requested by the committee, to turn over agents' diaries, or to supply a list of persons tried and convicted of tax charges under the OCD. What, he asked Cohen, are you trying to hide? "Could it be that the much vaunted IRS drive against organized crime has been one huge failure?" Long charged that Cohen's complaints about a trial by press were "about as cynical as anything I have seen of late." The commissioner seemed interested only in wiretapping whereas the committee was interested in broad legislation against eavesdropping, where no federal legislation existed, and in the harassment of taxpayers. Two years later, in January 1967, the Justice Department finally formed an Electronic Surveillance Committee to examine departmental policy in cases where problems might exist. Examinations would occur, but only on a case-by-case basis.[44]

In defense, in January 1966 the IRS sent a copy of its own internal report to Senator Long. This "Report of Investigation of the Improper Use of Electronic Devices and Investigative Techniques in the Intelligence Operation of the Internal Revenue Service" was little short of a whitewash: it concluded that between 1961 and 1965, of 18,234 investigations, there had only been 39 cases of attempted wiretapping and 12 cases of attempted bugging. All of them had occurred during investigations of suspected tax evasion by racketeers or other subjects of the OCD. While the report praised the Long Committee for investigating the problem, it asserted that well before any committee interest the IRS itself had initiated steps to address the issue and insisted that it had cooperated with the committee. "Under the circumstances," the report concluded, "the extent of IRS cooperation constitutes a remarkable chapter" in the history of legislative-executive relations. All evidence made public by the committee, the report argued, came from the IRS. Transcripts of the hearings filled eleven volumes by the end of 1965.[45]

The IRS investigation concluded that blame for the agency's illegal activities fell completely on the OCD. This operation had altered the traditional role of the IRS and had led the commissioner and deputy commissioner to accept an "unusual organizations arrangement." In prohibiting regular line officers from "active participation in and supervision of our OCD activities," the arrangement had "impaired control of the operation and influenced its tone." Under the OCD, the IRS had sacrificed control for security. Establishment of the position of assistant chief of intelligence operations coordination branch within the IRS National Office created a "network of positions" that "functioned outside the basic fabric of the operation." IRS district directors, the chief of the Intelligence Division, and the assistant regional commissioner for intelligence played nominal roles as OCD operations bypassed "normal supervisory channels." Even then, the report insisted, many of the transgressions were only of the "hairline variety."[46]

Arguing that IRS personnel attached to the OCD were influenced by other government agencies' use of wiretapping, the report blamed the setting for IRS purchase of surveillance equipment. Incredible though it might seem, the report maintained that the IRS had acquired the equipment only for "defensive purposes," though it did not explain why this was necessary. Given all these pressures, the report concluded, the only surprise was the limited number of "transgressions in the form of wiretaps, illegal entry, and use of spike mikes."[47]

These findings appeared designed to exonerate the IRS as much as possible from any wrongdoing. The investigations board found that IRS field personnel could not *justifiably be held administratively accountable for transgressions.*" It also concluded that no field employee in the IRS intelligence operation was at all accountable for any *"unauthorized or proscribed actions that have been reported in OCD cases."* Even a reprimand, therefore, would have a damaging ripple effect throughout IRS intelligence and hurt morale. The report claimed that only two National Office employees knew about illegal uses of these electronic devices. Both testified before the Long Committee and had since been reassigned.

The report also insisted that no justification existed for *"taking any administrative action against any regional officials."* Even though bugs and two-way mirrors had been discovered, investigators concluded that they were not illegal. In a rather dramatic shift of focus, they claimed that industry and educational institutions routinely used them to record meetings and conferences, implying that IRS use was no different. "Obviously there was no question of invasion of privacy," the report argued, "since the suspected evader and his representative knew who they were talking to and why they were asked to come to the IRS offices." Not only did this beg the question, it implicitly acknowledged that suspects' attorneys had come under illegal surveillance even while the IRS insisted that there was no evidence of any invasion of privacy. No one currently in jail for a tax crime, according to the chief counsel's office, was there because of tainted evidence. The report also claimed that two-way mirrors were found in only ten cities, usually in federal courthouses rather than in IRS offices. The IRS claimed that, despite the presence and use of two-way mirrors, the constitutional rights of no taxpayer had ever been violated or his or her privacy invaded. In short, the IRS took a hard stand, arguing that despite some "hairline" violations of the law, it had engaged in no illegal activities. The courts would eventually find otherwise.[48]

Despite these professions of innocence, the investigation board recommended numerous changes in IRS intelligence operations. Not only should Internal Revenue refuse to engage in illegal activities, its employees should not pay attention to the techniques and behavior of other agencies. It should quickly eliminate special organizational arrangements created for the OCD, and restore control over all IRS employees to the National Office. The IRS should reevaluate the technical training school. In a remarkable denial of individual accountability, the board urged that the National Office take no disciplinary action against any IRS field employee. They were only doing what they believed their employer wanted them to do. Yet even when the report criticized National Office personnel for improper activities, it praised their accomplishments and blamed only "errors in judgment." It placed full blame on the "combination of pressures, existing organizational structure of the Service as a whole, unclear laws, and misunderstood directives."[49]

The report then attacked the Long Committee. Despite cataloging the electronic and other surveillance devices owned by the IRS (which included omnidirectional electrovoice microphones and infrared binoculars), it charged that committee allegations of IRS wrongdoing were contrary to the facts. Indeed, it insisted that the only evidence of wiretapping came from the IRS's own investigations, not those of the Long Committee (a claim that ignored evidence presented in the series of trials in Pittsburgh and Miami). In essence, the six-month internal investigation reflected the arguments made earlier by Commissioner Cohen and recommended actions he had already initiated. Perhaps more was not to be expected from an investigative board that included no individuals outside the IRS.[50]

Senator Long, meanwhile, continued his investigation and hearings. He indicated to Justice Department officials that he would persist as long as Commissioner Cohen refused to acknowledge illegal IRS actions "for the public" and to announce what the agency had done and intended to do. The IRS should allow the subcommittee to examine its records, particularly diaries and affidavits, so it could verify agents' testimony. After a lunch meeting in early February, Robert Spatz, an IRS employee who worked closely with Cohen monitoring the activities of field agents, sent a memo to Cohen maintaining that the "ultimate target of the Subcommittee is Robert Kennedy. This factor, together with our course of real or professed cooperation from here on in, will effect [sic] the nature and extent of future IRS road-shows before the climax in Washington." Spatz also noted that Senator Long had turned to him at lunch and said, "You'd never guess who put me on to Bobby [Kennedy] signing the order that got this whole business started." The unanswered question was whether Lyndon Johnson or J. Edgar Hoover had leaked information. Both hated Robert Kennedy.[51]

Long also prepared a report attacking IRS tactics and warning about intrusions by "Big Brother." The senator charged that leading Treasury and IRS officials had professed ignorance, that they were "inclined to lie" and were "clever" in using diversions to divide and "smear" the committee by implying that it opposed efforts against organized crime. He also charged IRS officials with unethical conduct and concluded they could not be trusted to tell the truth or take remedial action because they were "stubborn" and "sneaky." In the end, he warned, the IRS was "contemptuous of authority" and protected its own. Both Bertrand Harding and H. Alan Long had been promoted, not disciplined. The "key to Killing Big Brother," Senator Long said, was to keep him in the spotlight, alert the public about the threat to individual liberties, and pass legislation to curb IRS powers. In June, speaking before the Suffolk Law School Alumni Association in Boston about invasions of privacy, Senator Long recited his committee's accomplishments and warned that though the information they found was "frightening," they had only "scratched the surface."[52]

Long, complaining that the "antipathy" of the IRS had slowed his investigation, told the lawyers that in Boston alone IRS agents had used "snooperscopes, mail covers, insurance checks, breaking and entry, illegal seizure of records and saturation surveillance." Suggesting that the "Orwellian society of 1984 is almost upon us," he expressed alarm at federal agencies' apparent lack of concern. Despite Commissioner Cohen's order to remove the two-way mirrors and illegal bugs, Long supported legislation to make all wiretapping and eavesdropping illegal.

For his part, Cohen tried to keep channels of communication to the senator open, insisting that his own measures would solve the problems. But he also warned LBJ's special assistants Bill Moyers and Marvin Watson about reports that Long was "out to get the IRS" and that "high officials" needed to fight back. Meanwhile Long broadened his investigation, sending detailed questionnaires to all federal departments and agencies to determine what information they maintained on individuals and how they used it.[53]

Senator Long also wrote an article for *Playboy* magazine that warned against the intrusion of "big brother" in the United States. IRS officials, he warned, had "developed an attitude that makes me wonder if they have lost sight of who is the master and who is the servant." They were arrogant and oppressive. Long provided yet another version of how his investigation began, and heralded his efforts to protect Americans' privacy. IRS replies to his queries, he complained, had been "deliberately evasive and misleading." He revealed that the agency had used two-way mirrors to film individuals. The Treasury Department secured a copy of the article, and in the margins an official noted that this was not true and was "technically impossible." Treasury officials annotated Long's remarks to indicate misstatements—and there were many. Long celebrated his defense of privacy to an audience that would appreciate his efforts. He complained that the IRS had tried to smear the subcommittee and cast it as the villain that protected organized crime.[54]

By this time Treasury Secretary Henry Fowler was concerned that the IRS might go too far in its efforts to uncover improper use of investigative techniques before Cohen's June 1965 order. Cohen also defended himself and the IRS against attacks made by Senator Long in the *Playboy* article. They were, he told Fowler, "blatant exaggerations and misstatements." Only a complete rewrite could correct all the errors, and he warned Fowler that "as with all demagogues, there is some substance to this piece, but it goes well beyond reasonable insinuation." Long and the IRS were in open warfare.

To further exploit personal animosities, Long announced plans to call both Robert Kennedy and J. Edgar Hoover to testify. A December 1966 article in *U.S. News & World Report* revealed the outbreak of a war of letters and files, a war with deep personal malice. Long was determined to prove that Kennedy had approved all wiretaps, while both Kennedy and Hoover continued to try to shift the blame to each other. The IRS worked with the Justice Department to compile a complete record of its use of wiretaps and other surveillance techniques.

> In order that the National Office can have immediate knowledge of all instances of electronic surveillance, each A&TT criminal investigator, special agent, intelligence and A&TT supervisor, division or branch chief, and OCD coordinator, including any employee who has held one of these positions at any time since January 1, 1957, will submit an immediate report.

Assurances to IRS agents that no disciplinary action would be taken for honest responses, however, did not seem terribly reassuring in this poisoned atmosphere. Agents feared reprisals.[55]

Looking back on the affair, IRS Chief Counsel Mitchell Rogovin characterized the IRS-Long confrontation as a "traumatic situation." Although at the time IRS Intelligence denied any wiretapping, Rogovin later admitted that this was a lie. It was indeed a "pervasive practice" in Pittsburgh and throughout the country. Only at the last minute, Rogovin noted, did Internal Revenue staff tell Cohen and himself that earlier denials were untrue. In an oral interview years later, Rogovin said he just could not "believe that they were all so virginal." They weren't. The impressive record of convictions in Pittsburgh had stemmed largely from the extensive use of wiretaps and other surveillance techniques. Some in Treasury, Rogovin admitted, wanted to "terminate the practice, but not to publicize that it had taken place." LBJ refused to support Treasury's position that it be buried, and Long got his exposure. The Fred Black case and its impact on the Baker investigation made things even worse for the IRS. Not only did it reveal direct evidence of a conviction based on wiretapping, it exposed further rifts between the FBI and the Justice Department, with the IRS caught in the middle. "The memoranda writing that was going on in the spring of 1966," Rogovin recalled, "was intense, fierce, and made for a very, very wide gulf between the FBI, a subordinate unit of the Department of Justice, and the Attorney General." Worse still, Black was acquitted in a new trial.[56]

The administration struck back. It not only sought to contain Senator Long's investigation, it began an investigation of Long himself. As Long's inquiry widened, the Technical Services Staff of the CIA became concerned that the Agency's dealings with the Narcotics Bureau and its system of safehouses might be compromised. The CIA solution was simple: it lied to the Treasury Department about the safehouses and how they were used. Meanwhile, in an effort to discredit Long, Senator John Stennis, who chaired the Select Committee on Standards and Conduct, requested a series of tax returns from the IRS. He particularly asked for the returns of Senator Long, his chief counsel Bernard Fensterwald, Jr., and those of mob attorney and Long friend Morris Shenker, Jimmy Hoffa, and H. Gordon Homme, Jr. Senator Stennis designated Carmine Bellino, who had snooped through tax returns for President Kennedy in the Ideological Organizations Project and was now staff consultant to the Stennis Committee, to inspect the returns. Between December 1967 and February 1968, Bellino and two colleagues scrutinized the returns, making "detailed analyses on columnar pads." They seemed particularly interested in substantial increases in dividends and capital gains, as well as some individual investments made by Shenker. Meanwhile Cohen held staff meetings to discuss improper efforts by a subcommittee investigator to harass a lawyer for the IRS chief counsel.[57]

Long complained to the IRS that he was upset by an agent auditing his income tax records, and he tried to get Commissioner Cohen to intervene. Cohen refused to become involved in a personal audit. But Long persisted in his attempt to publicize what he considered IRS invasions of privacy. One of his aides suggested that he take some of the "snooping devices" with him to New York to "spice up the TV show appearances." The aide selected several smaller devices and put them in the senator's briefcase for the trip. Long also continued to speak out on the need to protect privacy, describing the IRS as having produced a "sordid series of cases." Cohen, meanwhile, found he had to defend IRS operations to his superiors at Treasury. "The important thing," he told Under Secretary Barr, "is that we are now doing the right thing and have reported to the Department of Justice all cases in which we might have our possible problems."[58]

In the spring of 1967, Long held a series of hearings on a Right of Privacy Act. Once again Cohen was the chief witness, and once again Cohen asserted that the IRS had halted all "illegal and improper eavesdropping" two years earlier. Long was not satisfied; he wanted a wider investigation as well as *all* eavesdropping stopped. Cohen said that he had already sent a teletype to all agents to elicit in writing "all known or reasonably suspected instances of or attempts at electronic surveillance." But he continued to insist that whatever blame existed fell on the IRS as an institution, not on any of its individual agents. He also resisted Long's efforts to prohibit all eavesdropping, arguing that Fensterwald and other members of Long's staff appeared "excessive in their zeal to uncover real or imagined problems."[59]

To forestall further revelations, the Department of Justice and the IRS continued to crack down on all electronic surveillance, even its legal use. They now authorized eavesdropping only in cases where someone's life or safety was endangered, and then only through legal means. The IRS tried to conform to the attorney general's guidelines. But Internal Revenue also fought implementation of the Freedom of Information Act, passed a year earlier, which took effect on July 1, 1967. In an effort to inhibit the public release of any information, the IRS created a "multi-level process" to review requests. And the agency continued to drag its feet in providing information to Senator Long's committee, unless the existence of the information in question had somehow already become public knowledge. Thus in July, Commissioner Cohen sent the committee a tabulation of all electronic surveillance equipment installed from July 1958 through June 1966 but refused to admit that they were either legal or illegal, claiming that the law remained unclear. "We believe it essential to recognize," Cohen told Long, "that the overwhelming bulk of the installations . . . were not considered illegal by the agents at the time, and, in fact, cannot today be considered clearly illegal in the presently unsettled posture of the law."[60] Each side had dug in its heels.

CHAPTER NINE

JIMMY HOFFA, SENATOR LONG, AND THE IRS

Every story needs at least one thread that binds the central characters to one another. In the case of the IRS and political activity from the Kennedy administration through the Nixon years, Jimmy Hoffa was that thread. Hoffa and his activities connect webs of intrigue. He not only is a central character in IRS activities but provides links to Robert Kennedy, the organized crime drive, John Kennedy, Lyndon Johnson, Richard Nixon, Edward Long, and an assortment of mob figures who themselves were often enmeshed in several strands of this web. Throughout the 1960s and 1970s, intriguing connections emerged between Senator Long, Hoffa, attorney Roy Cohn, mob lawyers, and other individuals of dubious character. Those ties are difficult to unravel. Evidence is often circumstantial and in short supply. Not only do we have no Hoffa body, we have no Hoffa papers. Most of his associates, moreover, did not keep their papers or even commit many deals to writing. Fortunately a few of the principals did, and that enables us to piece together at least the outline of these chains of association. The Long investigation of wiretapping, privacy, and the IRS became a focal point for these links.

By the spring of 1967 the subjects of Senator Edward Long's attacks, including the IRS, began to retaliate. Reports appeared linking Long with Teamsters boss Jimmy Hoffa and the Mafia. Newspaper reporters roamed the country interviewing dozens of individuals, attempting to substantiate circumstantial evidence. Information surfaced in surprising places, and from unattributed sources. Efforts to discredit Long's investigations and their findings multiplied, especially after he introduced wiretapping legislation (the Right of Privacy Act) in 1967. Concerned, Long questioned Sheldon Cohen about leaks at the IRS, leaks that he believed had provided information for an article scheduled in *Life* magazine that linked him to Hoffa. Reporters had learned about fees Long had received from Morris Shenker, a friend and noted mob attorney, and the senator believed that information could only have come from the IRS. Cohen claimed he had refused interviews with reporters trying to "dig up dirt" on Long, and had counseled other IRS officials not to grant interviews. Although Long came to believe that Cohen was not involved, he was certain that the Internal Revenue Service had leaked information. It turned out that he was probably correct, but the IRS was not willing to cooperate. It used its own Internal Security Division to investigate the leaks but kept its findings to itself. In the words of Raymond Kieley, director of IRS Internal Security at the time, "Long caused us grief—on past cases—on wiretapping." Sheldon Cohen wrote IRS Assistant Commissioner Donald Bacon later that year: "I have had an idle thought—Did Edward V. Long file a self-employment tax schedule?"[1]

The circumstantial evidence that cast doubt on the motives for Long's investigations and linked him to a nefarious cast of characters is complicated but essential to an understanding of the relationships involved and their implications. Senator Long did not like Bobby Kennedy. Neither did FBI Director J. Edgar Hoover, who was always willing to help Long in any dispute with Kennedy. The conflicting Kennedy-Hoover testimony and public statements about who had authorized wiretaps was a prime example of this. In addition, Bobby Kennedy's persistent efforts to convict Jimmy Hoffa of almost anything had fueled opposition not only from Hoffa but from his Teamsters Union as well. Kennedy's crusade joined at times with the organized crime drive, which sought to convict key mob figures and curtail Mafia operations in the United States. The OCD, in turn, inflamed Hoover, who stoutly refused to admit that the Mafia existed in the United States and who adamantly opposed employing FBI assets in Justice Department efforts to attack it. Hoover also criticized former agents who went to work for Kennedy's Justice Department, calling them "runners" and "stooges."

Another piece of the puzzle was LBJ protégé Bobby Baker, who had his own difficulties. Baker was a business associate of individuals such as Edward Levinson, who had large loans from the Teamsters Union. These loans concerned enterprises in Las Vegas and in the vending machine business, both known or suspected arenas of mob activity. And if Robert Kennedy and the Justice Department were to go after Bobby Baker, they would tread perilously close to Vice President Lyndon Johnson. In addition, Senator Long owed his appointment to the Senate Judiciary Committee to Bobby Baker. Baker had told the Democratic steering committee that the two senators ahead of Long for the appointment did not want it, though in fact they did. Judiciary Committee chairman James Eastland subsequently appointed Long to head the subcommittee on Administrative Practice and Procedures. Finally, Baker's attorney in 1963 was Abe Fortas, the longtime Johnson friend whom LBJ later appointed to the Supreme Court. A more tortuous and complex series of relationships was difficult to imagine.[2]

After Johnson became president, he terminated the Las Vegas OCD investigations, and in February 1964 testimony before a Senate investigating committee, Bobby Baker repeatedly took the Fifth Amendment when questioned about his involvement. The committee was loaded with LBJ supporters, and with the 1964 elections ahead chose not to probe very deeply. Meanwhile, however, Senator Long's subcommittee began to review RFK's practices as attorney general in the area of eavesdropping and wiretapping. Supporters of Jimmy Hoffa welcomed this effort, as did attorney Roy Cohn, whom Chicago columnist Mike Royko called "the prince of darkness." Like Hoffa, Cohn also believed that he was the target of a Kennedy vendetta, despite his recent acquittal for perjury and obstruction of justice. In fact, it was during Cohn's trial that Senator Eastland, a close friend of Cohn's from the Joseph McCarthy days and a staunch opponent of the Justice Department's support for civil rights, urged Long to launch an investigation of Robert Kennedy. Cohn and Long were apparently close; the senator had recently saluted Cohn for "distinguished service." Long called Cohn to testify, and Cohn complained that Kennedy's Justice Department had violated his civil rights as well as those of Hoffa. Long's chief counsel, Bernard Fensterwald, scoured government sources for reports of Justice Department activities, particularly the OCD, during the time RFK had been attorney general. What he found, however, consisted largely of digests of information printed in the *New York Times*.[3]

While Long focused his attention on Robert Kennedy, others scrutinized Senator Long. His Hoffa connection was particularly intriguing. Its tentacles and ramifications seemed everywhere. To many Teamsters, Jimmy Hoffa was the man who had given them power. Hoffa was one of them. His father had died when Jimmy was only seven, and his early years were poverty-stricken. He had dropped out of school, worked in

Detroit warehouses, and organized his own union by the time he was eighteen years old. He also had an extensive police record. By the time he was twenty-four he was president of Teamsters Local 299, and three years later he became chairman of the central states negotiating committee. His power base quickly spread throughout the country. The IRS had investigated union spending in the 1950s, and government committees had uncovered relationships between Hoffa, Paul Dorfman, and his son Allen. Paul Dorfman was, in the words of one reporter, the "Capone-connected boss" of a Chicago union. In the late 1950s the McClellan Committee (the Select Committee on Improper Activities in the Labor or Management Field) had investigated Hoffa. Robert Kennedy was chief counsel for the committee and later wrote a book on its efforts—*The Enemy Within.*[4]

Hoffa had been active in the 1960 political campaign, hoping to prevent John Kennedy's nomination by supporting first Hubert Humphrey and later Lyndon Johnson. At a secret meeting with LBJ insider John Connally, arranged by Washington public relations specialist I. Irving Davidson at the Democratic National Convention in Los Angeles, Hoffa agreed to back Johnson should he wrest the nomination from Kennedy. Hoffa had also been friendly with Bobby Baker, but after Kennedy secured the nomination Hoffa threw his support to Richard Nixon. He used the *International Teamster* magazine as a platform to attack the Kennedys, characterizing Robert Kennedy as a "young, dimwitted, curly-headed smart aleck" and his brother John "unworthy of the trust to be President of the United States." During the remainder of the campaign Hoffa worked closely with his executive vice president, Harold J. Gibbons, to rally support for Nixon. He also secured $1 million in cash (presumably unreported) for the Nixon campaign, half from Louisiana crime boss Carlos Marcello and the other half from mob bosses in Florida and New Jersey. In return, Nixon intervened before the election to delay Attorney General William Rogers's indictment of Hoffa in Orlando, Florida, until after the election. Nixon's later efforts to convince Rogers to drop the entire matter failed, however. Efforts to prosecute Hoffa multiplied when Robert Kennedy became attorney general.[5]

Hoffa's ties to Nixon would again surface in the early 1970s, although the full extent of those connections was not always apparent. Had it been, Nixon's dark past and long ties to organized crime would have become public during the 1972 presidential campaign. During Nixon's first administration, aide Clark Mollenhoff maintained a Hoffa file at the White House. In his quest for Teamsters support, President

Nixon arranged a deal to parole Hoffa. One of his behind-the-scenes organizers was longtime political "hit man" Murray Chotiner. Chotiner had long-standing ties to bookmakers and hoodlums, including Carlos Marcello of Louisiana, and had been the link that secured substantial funding for Nixon's 1946 House campaign from Los Angeles mobster Mickey Cohen. In December 1971, hoping to secure Teamsters support, Nixon pardoned Hoffa despite the U.S. Parole Board's rejection of Hoffa's parole application. This came after several meetings between Chotiner and James Hoffa, Jr., during the summer of 1971.[6]

While Nixon was willing to pardon Hoffa, he was unwilling to see Hoffa displace Frank Fitzsimmons, a strong Nixon supporter, as Teamsters president. Accordingly a requirement of Hoffa's parole was that he not engage in politics nor in any labor organization management until 1980. Reports later surfaced that in return for this restriction, Fitzsimmons and the mob secretly gave Nixon more than $1 million in cash. The White House also put Hoffa under surveillance after he left Lewisburg Prison. Using the code name "Chapman's Friend," Chotiner provided secret reports on Hoffa to Attorney General John Mitchell and presidential aide H. R. Haldeman. Nixon aide Chuck Colson was so concerned about Hoffa's potential political involvement that he suggested at one point that his parole be revoked. Nixon also paroled several mob figures with ties to Hoffa. In 1972 the White House expedited the release from prison of Angelo "Gyp" DeCarlo, a captain in the Genovese crime family, and DeCarlo resumed his control of the New Jersey mob. Spurred by Chuck Colson's advice to "do all possible," the White House intervened in the case of Daniel F. Gagliardi of the Teamsters only a week after he was indicted for extortion. The case was dropped. A week after Hoffa's pardon, Nixon's friend George Smathers of Florida called the White House to request parole for Calvin Kovens. Kovens, a Florida Teamsters official and real estate speculator who was in prison for defrauding the union's pension fund, had secretly contributed $30,000 in cash to Nixon's campaign. Smathers said he had talked with Nixon confidante Charles "Bebe" Rebozo, and that Kovens was "the most popular Jew in Dade County, South Florida." Colson wrote John Dean that this was "much too hot for me to handle" and sent him a transcript of his recorded conversation with Smathers. Eight days later, supposedly for medical reasons, Kovens was released. Later, just before Nixon resigned, General Alexander Haig reportedly ordered the Army's Criminal Investigation Command secretly to investigate Nixon's possible ties to organized crime.[7]

During the early 1960s the paths of Jimmy Hoffa and Senator Long crossed several times. In 1962, Long praised Hoffa in a speech at a St. Louis Teamsters conference, which later passed a resolution condemning Robert Kennedy. He was also invited to Teamsters receptions. The Teamsters were a powerful presence in Missouri, especially in St. Louis, where Harold J. Gibbons had handled their affairs since the early 1950s. Gibbons had long been involved in the St. Louis labor movement and had turned to Hoffa for help when the St. Louis mob tried to move in on his operation. By the time Hoffa gained control of the Central States Conference, Gibbons was his second in command. For many years Gibbons maintained contact with the St. Louis underworld through Robert "Barney" Baker, a three-hundred-pound fighter who had been a strong-arm man for numerous mob-controlled businesses in New York, Florida, and Las Vegas, including "Bugsy" Siegel's Flamingo Hotel. Gibbons became a political ally of Long's. Teamster votes were important in St. Louis politics, and Long needed those votes. At a March 1965 meeting, the Teamsters unanimously passed a resolution of "high commendation" of Long for his investigations into electronic surveillance.[8]

The prospect of Robert Kennedy challenging Lyndon Johnson for the Democratic party nomination in 1964 brought many of these individuals together in common cause. Paul Demos, administrative assistant to New Mexico Senator Joseph Montoya, set up a meeting between Senator Daniel Brewster of Maryland and Jimmy Hoffa. Hoffa asked Brewster to act as a middleman in the transmission of $100,000 to President Lyndon Johnson through Johnson's friend Cliff Carter. Brewster agreed to be the go-between, and Sid Zagri, the Teamsters Legislative Representative, delivered a tan suitcase bulging with bills to Brewster's office. Another individual, Jack Sullivan, then drove Brewster to Carter's office at the Democratic National Committee where he made the delivery. Zagri, meanwhile, urged the Republican party to issue a scathing indictment of Kennedy in its national platform.[9]

Sidney Zagri was also close to Senator Long, and he fed Long information in hopes that he would use it against Kennedy and to help Hoffa. In April, Zagri sent Long a copy of a forthcoming article in *The Nation* on the trial of Jimmy Hoffa. The article, written by the investigative reporter Fred J. Cook, provided a lengthy account of Justice Department efforts to prosecute Hoffa for jury-rigging. Cook detailed issues of informers, wiretapping, and eavesdropping, reporting that Hoffa was convinced he was under FBI surveillance and had been bugged. At stake, Cook argued, were the "root principles of American justice—and American democracy." Hoffa's conviction through the use of these techniques, he concluded, called for a congressional investigation into Justice Department activities. After LBJ's sweeping victory in the November 1964 elections, however, any incentive to proceed with that investigation died.[10]

Hoffa used the August 1964 issue of the *International Teamster* to attack Kennedy, insisting that Kennedy had planted an informer within Teamster ranks to leak information and secret documents. This "fiendish and sinister plot," according to the article, was evident in secret memos surreptitiously obtained from *Life* magazine's Washington bureau. The story detailed how reporter Hank Suydam had been "led down back corridors at the Justice Department, sworn to secrecy," and then taken on a "round-about route to a home in Virginia" for a meeting with the informer, Sam Baron, former field director for the Teamsters National Warehouse Division and friend of Harold Gibbons. Baron later told Senator Long that he had suggested publication of an article on Hoffa's corruption in *Life* to Bobby Kennedy—"a decision I made despite the obvious danger to me and my family." He hoped that it would create a "maximum impact in making the American people aware of the threat." Jimmy Hoffa's reaction was to place an advertisement in Teamsters newspapers offering a $25,000 reward to any individual who furnished information about the use of electronic surveillance in his case.[11]

The Internal Revenue Service was not entirely a passive observer in the Hoffa investigation. The IRS monitored examinations of the use of tax-exempt funds for subversive purposes by the Teamsters Union and the Mine, Mill and Smelter Workers. It released to Carmine Bellino the tax files of several key figures in these matters, including Jimmy Hoffa and Morris Shenker. Bellino also examined the returns of Senator Long, his chief counsel Bernard Fensterwald, and H. Gordon Homme, a subcommittee staff member. Bellino, who had probed income tax returns for the Ideological Organizations Project during the Kennedy administration, now did the same thing for Robert Kennedy as he pursued Hoffa.[12]

In 1966, after the Supreme Court turned down Jimmy Hoffa's appeal, Senator Long renewed his investigation into electronic surveillance. This time he branched out to call FBI agents. Claiming that he had not done so earlier for fear of harming the OCD or impinging on national security concerns, Long now sought to exploit the Hoover-Kennedy feud. Assistant FBI Director J. H. Gale visited Long to explain why the Bureau had bugged Fred Black in its investigation of Bobby Baker. Clearly an effort to preempt public revelations of the bugging, Gale's briefing was designed to protect the FBI from Long's investigations. Baker had been indicted for tax evasion and fraud, and much of the damaging information had come from the bugging of his associate, Fred Black. To counter this, Black himself called Long for an appointment.

Long planned to resume hearings on electronic eavesdropping in March 1967. Two days after he announced the upcoming hearings, however, he asked the IRS to produce police sergeant William DePugh for an emergency Sunday morning hearing. DePugh had supposedly supervised the wiretapping of Teamster official William Bufalino. Bufalino was an attorney and a union boss. His jurisdiction extended to jukeboxes, automobile wash racks, parking lots, and garages. He was married to the niece of Angelo Meli, a Mafia chieftain in Detroit whose cousin, Vincent Meli, ran an association of jukebox owners that had a contract with the Teamsters. When DePugh arrived for the hearing, he found only subcommittee counsel Bernard Fensterwald and one staff member, H. Gordon Homme, present. They questioned DePugh about eavesdropping and wiretapping in Detroit. "It was becoming very obvious," a Justice Department investigator later wrote, "that Senator Long's committee was being used in a last-ditch effort to bail out Hoffa."[13]

Meanwhile the nature of Senator Long's involvement with Morris Shenker became more apparent. Shenker was Hoffa's chief attorney, had represented leading St. Louis racketeers, and traveled among the elite in the state's Democratic party. He stayed in close contact with Long, though he tried to hide this connection by urging the senator not to return his calls "on your number." He also paid "referral fees" to Long, though the senator had done nothing to earn them. Ironically, Shenker later chaired the St. Louis Commission on Crime and Law Enforcement, a testament to his political importance in the city. Justice Department investigators later charged that Shenker made millions in fees from the Teamsters Pension Funds in dealings the courts had prohibited in 1964. For his part, Senator Long denied that he had a close relationship with Hoffa, insisting that he had met Hoffa only three or four times in the past twenty years. He also denied that he was using his subcommittee to help Hoffa.[14]

Publication of an article in the May 26, 1967, issue of *Life* magazine detailing the Long-Hoffa links undercut Long's denials. The article was a result of a three-month investigation by reporter William Lambert. Lambert related that the senator had spoken at the 1966 Teamsters convention about wiretapping and eavesdropping, and had described Hoffa as "your dynamic and fighting president." Long admitted that he had first met Hoffa when Long was lieutenant governor of Missouri in the late 1950s. At the time, he said, Hoffa was "a hot article" and "I was the only state official that had the audacity to show up." Lambert concluded that friends in the Teamsters' hierarchy had prevailed on Long to investigate federal wiretapping, that the hearings had impaired the OCD by discrediting the IRS, that he had misused his subcommittee by trying to free Jimmy Hoffa, and that he had received at least $48,000 (later revealed to have been $160,000) in referral fees from Morris Shenker in 1963 and 1964, despite the fact that he had not practiced law in those years.[15]

Lambert also detailed the relationships between Long, Hoffa, Roy Cohn, and Sidney Zagri. Zagri had been "shopping" for several years to find a friendly committee to investigate Hoffa's prosecutors. He had "combined forces" with Roy Cohn, then under surveillance and in trouble with the IRS. Zagri found a friendly face in his old Missouri friend, Senator Edward Long. Apparently, however, Long's senatorial colleagues were not aware of his relationships with Hoffa, the Teamsters, or other organized crime figures. Moreover, Long's chief counsel, Bernard Fensterwald, once close to the Kennedys, had come to despise Robert Kennedy after he had donated $5,000 to his brother's campaign but failed to land a job in the State Department. Fensterwald and Long had found their chief target in the IRS. Not only had the IRS gone after Roy Cohn, it had pursued other Long friends for tax evasion. Former Mayor William Sermon of Independence, Missouri, for example, a longtime political ally of Long's, was convicted of tax evasion. Long attacked the IRS for this and defended Sermon in public, despite the fact that Sermon had pleaded no contest to evading $225,000 in taxes over a five-year period. Lambert claimed that Long had played loose with the facts of several cases in efforts to discredit the IRS. In his Sunday morning questioning of William DePugh, Fensterwald had tried to link the Detroit police, the IRS, and the Justice Department's Organized Crime and Racketeering Section to wiretaps on Jimmy Hoffa. DePugh was later called to testify before the committee, as were IRS intelligence agents. Long denied everything, but at the same time he blamed the IRS for leaking information about his referral fees.[16]

Senator Long soon encountered still greater difficulties. Even though his aides reported that the general public seemed unconcerned with the charges against him, largely considering them a smear by the IRS, Delaware Republican Senator John Williams began to probe the motivations behind Long's investigation. Williams uncovered evidence that he believed pointed to a concerted effort by the Teamsters and the mob to discredit the use of wiretapping in order to protect themselves and to free Jimmy Hoffa. Having failed to interest any House committees in launching an investigation, they had turned to the Senate and Edward V. Long. "From reliable sources," Williams recorded, he understood that Long would "receive payments which were to be channeled through Morris Shenker and that such payments were to be in proportion to what he was able to do" if he investigated wiretapping. *Life* had apparently reported some of these, but Williams understood that they continued and had grown larger. Williams also heard from John Barron of *Reader's Digest* that the *New York Times* had assigned five reporters to investigate Long's financial affairs and political ties. Barron's information had come from *St. Louis Globe-Democrat* reporter Danny Walsh, who had assisted William Lambert in preparation of the *Life* article. Walsh also indicated that the IRS was auditing Long for additional payments he had received in 1965 and 1966.[17]

In late July 1967, Senator Long struck back. In a speech on the floor of the Senate he attacked his critics, particularly William Lambert's article in *Life*. Neither Jimmy Hoffa nor the mob had influenced the investigation, Long argued, and its conclusions were not made "at the suggestion of the Teamsters Union." Long admitted only that *Time* magazine had been a catalyst for his investigation into wiretapping when it had published a March 1964 article entitled "Bug Thy Neighbor." Although Long had earlier opposed any authorization of police wiretapping, revelations that the federal government spent $20 million a year on bugging equipment (exclusive of the CIA) spurred him to action. He then detailed for the Senate the course of his investigations and the obstacles his subcommittee had encountered from government agencies, particularly the IRS, when it sought information on eavesdropping and wiretapping. "We were shocked," he said, when his subcommittee began to have problems with the IRS and other agencies. He complained about delays, noting that it took the IRS thirty months to complete a questionnaire from the subcommittee. "This attitude," he complained, "has marked our relations with IRS from the beginning." Even as he spoke, he told senators, he had not received the results of an IRS investigation into its own eavesdropping, and "there is no indication yet when we shall receive it."[18]

In saying this, Long not only ignored the fact that IRS Commissioner Sheldon Cohen had sent him a copy of the internal report in 1966, he also revealed that Cohen had provided the subcommittee with a record of all installations of electronic surveillance equipment. In a letter to Long, which the senator inserted into his remarks, Cohen had noted that he was sending along the results of the IRS investigation into "instances of possible improper uses of electronic surveillance equipment by Service personnel." Cohen went on to admit:

> The board's findings confirm the matters developed before the Subcommittee. The board found that Service personnel in fact participated in improper uses of electronic surveillance equipment as stated above, and that such participation peaked in 1963. The board attributed the occurrences to misunderstanding of applicable directives and instructions; departures from the Service's normal line management direction and control; and overzealousness on the part of certain personnel engaged in the investigation of the criminal element.

Cohen then repeated his earlier assurance that new IRS "proscriptions on investigative techniques" had halted these activities.[19]

To compound Long's problems, the Senate Committee on Standards and Conduct looked into his relationship with Morris Shenker and his conduct of the subcommittee's investigation. Thanks to the testimony of Clayton, Missouri, financier Max Lubin, the committee exonerated Long. But the ethics committee investigation revealed additional ties between Long and organized crime. Not only was he linked to Morris Shenker but to insurance salesman John "The Bug" Schiavarelli, "one of the top ten ranking members in the Chicago Syndicate once controlled by Al Capone." Stories in the *St. Louis Post-Dispatch* challenged the ethics committee's vindication of Long, and its St. Louis bureau chief sent Senator John Williams clips of those stories with a plea that the truth be known. Williams also received letters indicating that Long had several conflicts of interest with respect to lawyers' fees and bank charters in Missouri. The *Post-Dispatch* looked into charges of conflict of interest in several Anheuser-Busch anti-trust suits between 1961 and 1965, and tracked Long's continued relationships with Morris Shenker, Harold Gibbons, and the Teamsters Union. Although the truth of these allegations remained unclear, a letter to Long from one of his St. Louis allies hinted at what it might be: "even if it could be demonstrated that your clients are or were associated with the Teamsters or Steamfitters or with organized crime they are still entitled to legal representation. . . . How is it possible to tell what is in a senator's mind when he sponsors or votes on a bill?"[20]

In the end, these investigations did not help Senator Long retain his office. Not only had he been associated with organized crime figures and exposed in a national magazine, he had the Internal Revenue Service after him. IRS Commissioner Sheldon Cohen had long stopped working with the senator, convinced that cooperation would not help the IRS nor satisfy Long's inquiries. Then, in November 1967, Cohen had raised the self-employment tax issue. The next year, with Long up for reelection, someone at IRS leaked his tax returns to *Life* magazine. They indicated numerous irregularities. Not only was Long asked to justify thousands of dollars of deductions for 1964 through 1967, the subcommittee's chief counsel Bernard Fensterwald had his tax returns for 1966 and 1967 audited as well. Fortunately Fensterwald had taken the precaution of having a well-known accounting firm prepare his returns. Although an exhaustive investigation and audit eventually exonerated Long, the voters rejected him in the Democratic primary in favor of Thomas Eagleton. Eagleton was then elected that November. Following Long's primary defeat, Sheldon Cohen called *Life* writer William Lambert to congratulate him on his investigative reporting. The subcommittee's chief counsel, Fensterwald, later commented that "Senators and Congressmen not scared of looking into the IRS have to be crazy, because the IRS will just ruin your career."[21]

Over the years that fear had not prevented Senator Long from probing IRS practices. Had he been victorious in the primary and then in the November elections, the senator intended to launch a series of even more sensational investigations into bugging and wiretapping during the Johnson administration. A central focus was to be the " 'secret electronics eavesdropping laboratory' located in a suite of offices formerly occupied by Deputy Assistant Secretary of State for Security Joseph Reilly, a close friend of Senator Robert Kennedy." Reilly was by that time at the Federal Communications Commission, after a Senate committee had accused him of lying. This "secret laboratory" was supposedly used by CIA and State Department officials to eavesdrop on various government officials and newspaper reporters during the Kennedy and Johnson administrations.[22]

By this time the IRS had expanded its organized crime drive within the Intelligence Division, following a May 1966 speech by President Johnson attacking crime in the United States. Commissioner Sheldon Cohen later testified that he had opposed efforts to use the Internal Revenue Service to prosecute organized crime figures, whose real crimes often lay outside IRS purview. He preferred prosecution for "the crime he committed rather than a tax crime" because he believed that was the way the "laws were designed." He also feared that it would result in a "different standard of prosecutorial judgment." But Cohen agreed that "if it need be, he ought to be prosecuted for the tax crime." A few years later *Life* magazine reported that the new St. Louis mayor,

Alfonso Juan Cervantes, and his new crime commissioner, Morris Shenker, were under investigation for their mob connections and criminal operations that began at least as early as 1964. For years the IRS had assigned a team of agents and auditors to unravel Shenker's financial operations and manipulations, but without success. "Every gangster case," Sheldon Cohen had noted earlier, "has political overtones."[23]

Long's hearings had exposed serious breaches of American citizens' right to privacy but were effectively shut down by the IRS's manipulation of the press and public opinion through the selective leaking of information. By 1967 the Freedom of Information Act (FOIA) had become law over the strenuous objection of the IRS. FOIA promised increased government accountability by offering citizens greater access to government-controlled information. Despite the fact that the act offered several exceptions for IRS operations, the Internal Revenue Service created its own task force to study what information it was obliged to make available to the public. Tax returns and all "taxpayer information" were to remain confidential—another example of the IRS's use of privacy guidelines to protect its own interests—but IRS rulings and procedures were not so protected. In response to Long's investigations, and perhaps in recognition of the Freedom of Information Act, the IRS attempted to curtail agents' use of electronic surveillance. Singleton Wolfe, assistant IRS commissioner for compliance in the mid-1970s, told a congressional committee in 1975 that ever since his involvement in the Long hearings, "I don't think there has been a year since 1965 that we have not put out some documents advising the field of the proper use of all investigative techniques." The IRS developed a manual designed for the training of all special agents. As later chapters will reveal, however, the agency was not always effective in curbing abuses. The Nixon years would demonstrate that problems with and for the IRS persisted. In retrospect, Senator Long's investigations paled before the abuses of the Nixon era, when freedom of information and privacy often became scarce commodities.[24]

CHAPTER TEN

THE NIXON YEARS: TAWDRY TALES AND TATTERED PRINCIPLES

THE OCTOBER 15, 1973, issue of *Newsweek* announced that a "new scandal" was "about to break over the Nixon Administration, involving manipulation of the Internal Revenue Service for political ends."[1] This scandal quickly led to the discovery of other misuses of the IRS by the Nixon White House. Altogether they epitomized a pattern of abuse of power as characteristic of Richard Nixon's presidency as was the Watergate break-in and cover-up that later led directly to his resignation. Various investigations exposed Nixon's use of the IRS to punish enemies and reward friends, as well as the placement of an informer within the IRS to report on the ideological and political positions of Internal Revenue personnel and to act as a conduit for White House requests for action.

The most revealing of these investigations was one that never attracted much publicity, that carried out by the Watergate Special Prosecution Force (WSPF). The WSPF investigated White House abuses of the IRS under Nixon, but Congress never held extensive public hearings based upon the information uncovered. Watergate prosecutors ultimately decided that they had sufficient evidence to prosecute Richard Nixon for impeachable offenses without the IRS materials. They also believed that public hearings on Internal Revenue Service matters would not draw much public attention. By the time the Watergate hearings concluded, therefore, only a tiny percentage of their business focused on abuses of the IRS. What investigators found, however, is both revealing and frightening.

President Richard Nixon wanted the White House to control the Internal Revenue Service and use it for his own political purposes. He directed his appointments and policies toward that end. The president's earliest relationships with the IRS reveal this intent to politicize the organization. Before we explore some of his major and (eventually) most publicized efforts, most notably the infamous "Enemies List" and the lesser-known Special Service Staff (SSS), an examination of a few smaller but specific episodes will illustrate how tattered his principles were. What is perhaps most remarkable about these episodes, in hindsight, is that Nixon's approach was so awkward and bumbling. Despite the president's determination, several of his appointees proved to be more independent than he intended. In the end, unfortunately, that did not deter him from misusing the tax system as well as intelligence agencies to hound enemies and opponents as well as reward friends.

Attempts to politicize the IRS began almost as soon as Nixon took the oath of office. His first objective was to find a compliant individual for the office of IRS commissioner. Politics and ideology were his chief concerns, and he asked his chief of staff, H. R. "Bob" Haldeman, to search out prospective candidates. Haldeman believed that finding a good political appointment was more important than finding someone who might be a "great" commissioner, but in this respect the search was bungled. It soon focused on Randolph Thrower, an Atlanta attorney and former Republican party chairman for the Fifth District of Georgia. Thrower was well qualified and was reputed to be a "good tax man," but his nomination and eventual appointment upset Republican conservatives in Georgia. They warned Nixon that Thrower represented the liberal faction of the party, and they were outraged that his nomination bypassed such state Republican leaders as Howard "Bo" Callaway. Despite these concerns, and despite Nixon's apparent doubts about his "loyalty," Randolph Thrower became Richard Nixon's first commissioner of Internal Revenue on April 1, 1969. Ironically, given Nixon's intentions, Thrower indicated during the WSPF investigations that he spoke with no one in the White House about his appointment, though several individuals in the Treasury Department had approached him about the position. The only concern voiced to Thrower seemed to be, since he was a Southerner, what his racial views were. Even then there was little evidence of any independent inquiry by either Treasury or the White House.[2]

Nixon also established a formal liaison with the IRS, appointing the investigative reporter Clark Mollenhoff in July 1969 as his special counsel—for much the same reason that John Kennedy had appointed

Carmine Bellino to a similar post in 1961. In fact, however, Mollenhoff really served as deputy counsel under presidential aide John Ehrlichman, and the promise of direct access to the president never was fulfilled. Mollenhoff had worked with Delaware Senator John Williams and Assistant IRS Commissioner Vernon "Mike" Acree on Internal Revenue Service affairs. In the mid-1950s he had investigated allegations that Nixon crony Murray Chotiner had arranged favors for some defendants in white-slave activity cases, and accordingly he was wary of Nixon's intentions with respect to the IRS. But Nixon assured him that he was "disassociating himself from Chotiner," so Mollenhoff accepted the appointment. Since Mollenhoff was aware of previous abuses by IRS officials in New York and New Jersey, he came to the position determined to eliminate cheating or fixing in tax cases. Given Nixon's priorities, Mollenhoff's appointment, like that of Thrower, was a bit odd. On the one hand, Mollenhoff intended to prevent the sort of tax scandals that had plagued the Truman administration, when politically appointed IRS officials accepted bribes and fixed tax cases to please local political leaders. But he also sought access to tax returns on behalf of the Nixon White House, and that access later raised doubts about his motives. Was he another Carmine Bellino, doing the bidding of the White House and gathering information from the IRS to use for political purposes? Did Nixon intend to use him as "cover" for his efforts to politicize the IRS?

Mollenhoff's experience provides a case study of Richard Nixon's intentions to use the IRS for political advantage as well as his rather inept procedures and ill-considered judgments. The journalist apparently was appointed to seek access to individuals' income tax returns on behalf of the White House, providing copies to White House staff while giving the president plausible deniability as to his involvement in any harassment that might follow. In September 1969, Mollenhoff made an oral request to Thrower for that access. Thrower replied by suggesting that every time Mollenhoff wished to "inspect a tax return, application for exemption, or other Internal Revenue file," he send him a "memorandum briefly setting forth the nature of the request. Naturally," Thrower wrote, "we will infer in every case that the request is either at the direction of, or in the interest of, the President." In essence, therefore, the IRS would consider *all* requests from Mollenhoff to be from the president without any validation whatsoever. Pandora's box was open. Roger Barth, the White House "plant" within the IRS, later told WSPF investigators that he passed requests to Donald Bacon of IRS who then sent the returns to Mollenhoff at the White House. The president apparently never signed anything.[3]

What later sparked controversy was Mollenhoff's March 1970 admission that he had requested tax returns for several individuals. Apparently acting on behalf of Haldeman or Ehrlichman (at least that was the conclusion of Watergate investigators), Mollenhoff sent two lists of individuals to the IRS and requested that audits be started. There was some indication that those individuals may have been guilty of underreporting their income, and Mollenhoff was a small fish compared with the President of the United States, so subsequent investigations did not attribute much blame to the special counsel. Indeed, during his approximately nine months in office, Mollenhoff requested less than a dozen returns. There is, furthermore, no evidence that he spent his days snooping through IRS files in fishing expeditions. But even Mollenhoff's modest request apparently caused some concern in IRS, for only two weeks later he wrote Nixon to warn that "there is a strong possibility" that Commissioner Thrower was going to "cut off my access to federal tax returns." He argued that continued access was "vital to my operation" and asked the president for "public affirmation" of that fact. Not only did Nixon decline his request, he refused to meet personally with Mollenhoff.[4]

Later, when White House interest in the tax returns of Democratic National Chairman Lawrence O'Brien surfaced, Mollenhoff's earlier requests took on a more sinister character.* After he left his position, however, Mollenhoff defended his role and criticized the administration. He insisted that he had requested tax returns in only nine cases, largely involving improper activities by judges, and that information from those returns was not leaked. When later Nixon IRS abuses were revealed, however, Mollenhoff's position and his access to tax returns raised eyebrows and elicited concern that the White House had used him to circumvent disclosure laws.[5]

But it was Richard Nixon, not Clark Mollenhoff, who schemed to politicize the IRS. Nixon was initially interested in an "alleged exempt list of individuals maintained by the Revenue Service" who should not be audited. He was convinced that such a list existed and was determined to discover who was on it. Already concerned that his recent appointee as IRS commissioner, Randolph Thrower, might "not be the most reliable source of information on this subject," he had John Ehrlichman send a personal memorandum on the matter to Treasury

---

*This White House interest, which is linked to issues involving Howard Hughes, Charles "Bebe" Rebozo, and a host of other characters, will be examined in some detail in the next chapter.

Secretary David Kennedy. Kennedy apparently turned the matter over to Treasury General Counsel Paul Eggers, who relied heavily on Mike Acree at IRS. Acree, according to Eggers, was "a Republican and absolutely trustworthy." But after a three-week investigation the IRS reported that it could not find any such "exempt" list, though it did not rule out the possibility that one might have previously existed. Nixon remained convinced that the Kennedy administration had compiled one and that several prominent citizens (probably Democrats) had been on it, but further IRS investigations failed to uncover any evidence. This would not be the last time that Nixon initiated actions with the conviction that the Democrats had done worse and were plotting to control his administration and frustrate his policies.[6]

Nixon's overall objective was to gain "control" of the IRS, and here is where Mollenhoff's experience is revealing. Whether or not he was a witting participant in White House schemes remains unclear, but in late February or early March 1970, Haldeman asked him (ostensibly on behalf of the president) to look into the IRS tax investigation of George Wallace's brother Gerald. Mollenhoff thought this was because Nixon sought to have the case prosecuted expeditiously, and responded to Haldeman that requests for "one or more of the tax returns" might "make the investigation more diligent." Despite his background as a top investigative reporter, Mollenhoff seemed naive in his belief that secret scrutiny of Wallace's tax returns was justified on the grounds that Nixon suspected corruption among Wallace appointees working in Alabama IRS offices. He could not get copies of tax returns, since the case was then in the field, but he did procure a summary prepared by Donald Bacon of the IRS. He quickly forwarded a copy to Haldeman. Murray Chotiner, who had a well-known reputation as a hatchet man for Richard Nixon and was then serving as a White House special counsel, also requested a copy. When Mollenhoff refused, Haldeman pressured him to comply, arguing that Nixon wanted Chotiner to have a copy. Mollenhoff responded that if that was true, Haldeman could supply the copy. Within days the *Wall Street Journal* ran a story on Mollenhoff's access to tax returns, and that led to a complaint from Lawrence O'Brien about Mollenhoff's arrangement with the IRS. Chotiner quickly leaked details to columnist Jack Anderson, and an April 13, 1970, story on the affair by Anderson further fueled the flames of controversy. Leaks abounded as high administration officials sought cover by pointing fingers at Mollenhoff and others.[7]

The Wallace case raised some important issues. Although the so-called "Alabama Project" had started in the Johnson administration, without question the White House request was politically motivated. Nixon undoubtedly hoped to remove Wallace as a threat in the 1972 presidential campaign. He sought leverage to keep him out of that race either by dangling the possibility of his intervention to terminate the IRS investigation, or by orchestrating his defeat in his 1970 Alabama gubernatorial primary race against Albert Brewer (a likely possibility, since agents of the White House secretly contributed $400,000 to Brewer). It was, according to Mollenhoff's memo to Haldeman, a "large case" and possibly a "rather large criminal case." When questioned later by Thrower, Mollenhoff denied leaking any tax returns, insisting that the information came from "very high above me." Together with IRS Chief Counsel Martin Worthy, Thrower met with Ehrlichman and Haldeman to express his concern about the leak. He later told WSPF investigators that both men indicated that "they took the meeting seriously but they did not acknowledge their responsibility." Thrower also wrote Nixon to express his conviction that Mollenhoff was innocent, and that he had handled tax-return information "consistent with our general arrangements for providing information on your behalf." The leak must have come from the White House staff, Thrower innocently told Nixon. Indeed it had, and Murray Chotiner was the culprit. The IRS and the Justice Department later dropped the investigation for lack of sufficient evidence to convict, and out of fear that Wallace would claim persecution if tried and exonerated.[8]

Among the broader issues raised by the Wallace case was the question of access to individual tax returns. Thrower asked K. Martin Worthy, IRS chief counsel, for his opinion as to whether the commissioner (or anyone else) could disclose income tax returns to members of the president's "immediate staff." Worthy replied that the president had an unquestioned right to examine tax returns, and to designate a member of his staff to examine them. Thus if Mollenhoff had been acting on "behalf of the President," he had a lawful right to examine returns. Then Worthy went further, concluding that "even in the case of heads of departments and other officers of the Government, *of lesser stature than the President*, they may authorize inspections of returns by their subordinates acting for them." This opinion, in effect, meant that an almost unlimited number of government officials could examine individuals' income tax returns merely by claiming that they were acting on orders from the president. Moreover, referring to limits on disclosure expressed in Section 6103 of the Internal Revenue Code, Worthy argued that it was "inconceivable that the President should be bound by such rules and regulations." Given this interpretation, it appears that perhaps Richard Nixon was right when he later characterized himself as "the sovereign."[9]

Whatever Thrower or any IRS commissioner thought about presidential requests to examine tax returns, their hands were tied, according to the IRS chief counsel. The law only defined the "manner in which returns may be made available," not the right of the president to request and examine them. Worthy also noted that until the 1961 Bellino incident, the chief counsel's office had never addressed the issue. Although there had been no formal ruling in the Bellino case, the fact that he did examine returns with the permission of IRS Commissioner Mortimer Caplin created a precedent. A subsequent memo on this question by Chief Counsel Crane Houser had supported Caplin, arguing that the president was entitled to "all information relative to his control over the executive branch." Later, after the assassination of President Kennedy, the IRS had provided copies of income tax returns to the Warren Commission, "presumably on the basis of the foregoing opinion." Worthy's ruling opened the floodgates for unlimited White House requests for individuals' income tax returns and revealed a serious flaw in the disclosure laws.[10]

Worthy's own recollections of his term in office (1969–1972) revealed just how widespread such requests became. He remembered phone calls from private individuals as well as from the White House about tax-exempt nonprofit organizations, calls from senators and congressmen about campus newspapers, meetings with White House staff about private segregated schools and public law firms. Lines of communication became murky, particularly when Roger Barth joined the IRS as a Nixon appointee and inside informant. Commissioner Thrower became increasingly concerned about these inquiries and eventually asked Barth to keep written records of all White House requests as well as to channel the requests through the IRS bureaucracy. This not only failed to curtail inquiries, it also failed to prevent the White House's political use of the agency and its intelligence resources.[11]

From the perspective of the White House, however, even the creation of a paper trail for all requests was an unprecedented imposition. In his testimony before the Senate Watergate Committee, John Ehrlichman complained that the Kennedy administration was not required to follow similar rules. In response to a complaint from Kennedy White House staffer Lawrence O'Brien, then chairman of the Democratic National Committee, about illegal snooping in tax returns (especially his own), the Nixon administration blithely responded that it welcomed the "strictest kind of scrutiny." If a problem existed, the administration argued, it did so because of "previous Democratic adminis-trations." President Nixon was only defending "the body politic from official corruption." O'Brien responded that Mollenhoff's entire opera-tion was illegal because it violated the confidentiality of tax returns, and he called upon Nixon to terminate it immediately. To support his posi-tion, O'Brien attached a legal opinion from former IRS officials Mor-timer Caplin, Sheldon Cohen, and Mitchell Rogovin. Noting that Mollenhoff had requested returns without a written request from the president, they insisted that no theory of law supported such a position and that it was "specifically rejected by the very language of the regula-tion."[12]

A few days later, Senate Republican John Williams of Delaware de-fended Mollenhoff, pointed to the Bellino experience during the Kennedy years, and attacked critics of the administration for engaging in "gutter politics." Those critics, he complained, had "tried to give the impression throughout the country that these tax returns under the Nixon administration have been used indiscriminately. They have not, and that is the point." While Williams was correct with respect to the Mollenhoff affair, his confidence in the administration's propriety was misplaced. The next few years would be a learning experience for every-one. Thinking back on his tenure as IRS commissioner, Randolph Thrower later recognized the mistakes made by the IRS and the warn-ing signs he had failed to heed. His appointment of Roger Barth as his special assistant was one misgiving. Although Thrower insisted that the White House did not pressure him into making the appointment, he re-gretted that he had not hired a young lawyer from his Atlanta firm in-stead. Barth proved too "combative" during discussions of controversial matters, and Thrower became concerned about Barth's close relation-ship with members of the White House staff. This led him to gradually distance himself from Barth, although Barth retained his position throughout Thrower's tenure as commissioner of Internal Revenue.[13]

The other key issue revealed by the Mollenhoff-Wallace tax return affair was the handling of Sensitive Case Reports (SCRs) by the Nixon administration. The IRS Sensitive Case Report system, designed to pre-vent embarrassment for the administration, had long been subject to political pressure and misuse. For instance, a March 6, 1970, memoran-dum from Mollenhoff to Nixon reported the tax problem of Republican Arch Moore, governor of West Virginia. Nixon then canceled plans to name Moore to the National Defense Civil Advisory Board. But hand-written notes on the memo reveal that Nixon wanted the IRS to "get an audit on all Democratic governors." Murray Chotiner was contacted to "order audits."[14]

Thrower later told WSPF investigators that Treasury did inform the White House of Sensitive Cases on a "need to know" basis, though that decision was made by the secretary of the Treasury, a political appointee. About twenty to twenty-five cases per month were sent to the IRS commissioner and chief counsel. The commissioner's office then forwarded a copy to Treasury, who presumably forwarded it to the White House. After John Connally became Treasury secretary, interest in SCRs became "keener." Roger Barth played an increasingly important role here as well, personally carrying SCRs to John Connally and George Shultz (then chairman of the Office of Management and Budget), who reviewed them. Barth also relayed some of this information to the White House, chiefly through John Ehrlichman but occasionally to White House counsel John Dean, and followed up White House requests for more information. Although copies of SCRs were normally maintained in the files of the commissioner, the chief counsel, and the Compliance Division, Barth also retained copies in his own files. In November 1972, after Johnnie Walters became IRS commissioner, Barth was scheduled to be removed from such a central role in the handling of SCRs. Plans for his removal, however, were never implemented.[15]

Nixon tried to use reorganization to gain control over the Internal Revenue Service, to attack what speechwriter Patrick Buchanan called a "well known" conviction that the IRS "was politically controlled by Democrats." The year after taking office the president pushed reorganization efforts to create opportunities for Republican appointments and to remove Democrats from positions of power within the agency. His appointment of Clark Mollenhoff was the first step in that process. In addition to gaining access to tax returns, Mollenhoff was to investigate departmental and interdepartmental wrongdoing, locate anti-administration personnel in various agencies, and seek solutions to problems that administration officials believed existed within the IRS. John Dean told Haldeman that to "solve the problems at IRS it will be necessary to make major changes from top to bottom. Accordingly, I recommend that there be a total reorganization of IRS—in the name of improving tax collection operations, etc." Haldeman responded: "Right on!" The administration had set its course.[16]

John Dean assigned Jack Caulfield to devise a White House proposal for agency-wide cooperation. In September 1970, Caulfield reported his plan to Dean. The centerpiece of the proposal was the establishment of an "independent, White House contact" within each agency, including the IRS, to be selected by the agency head. These contacts should be of "unquestioned Republican loyalty" and have broad knowledge of all agency issues that might affect the White House. They should also be able to act independently to initiate inquiries, identify issues before they became problems, and prepare option papers for their solution. Any "unnecessary delay between problem identification and White House notification shall be frowned upon." Although ostensibly under the control of agency heads, in fact these individuals would operate under a direct line of command from the White House. As such, the White House should reserve a "proficiency option" that would enable it to review constantly the individuals' performance. Caulfield proposed that "any White House decision to replace the designee" not "be subject to veto by the agency head."[17]

With respect to reorganization of the IRS, the White House focused first on removing Democrats. Nixon adviser Peter Flanigan reported that a reorganization before the end of the year could create three deputy commissioners who would be presidential appointments. That alone would solve most of the problems with respect to gaining control of IRS intelligence and enforcement operations. By early October the administration had developed a confidential document entitled "Organizational Concepts for IRS," secretly prepared by an insider at the agency. According to John Dean, the administration intended to "make a case for reorganization of IRS in the name of more efficient and effective tax collection!" But Dean told Tom Charles Huston, "we need more political appointees placed within IRS" instead. Although the avowed purpose of this reorganization was to enhance IRS criminal law enforcement efforts and to centralize them within the agency, the Nixon administration planned to turn the IRS to political advantage through the appointment of an assistant commissioner (Law Enforcement) who would operate "completely independent of the voluntary compliance and balanced enforcement oriented activities."[18]

The White House chafed at its inability to move faster. That November, John Dean told Assistant Attorney General William Rehnquist that Thrower knew about the White House plans. Dean complained not only about the administration's failure to make any supergrade appointments in IRS but also about the grant of tax exemptions to organizations hostile to the administration. By December the White House was finally ready to move. Further study of the secret reorganization plan had led to a proposal to create four top-level noncareer positions, to be filled only after clearance from the White House.

Once the fall 1970 congressional elections were over, Haldeman directed Dean to implement reforms. Fred Malek, who in the fall of 1970 had studied and ultimately rejected potential strategies for increasing White House control of the IRS, reported to Haldeman that Commissioner Thrower was making progress in "gaining control of the IRS," and that Treasury Under Secretary Charls Walker urged his retention. The real problem was the need to restructure the IRS to allow new appointments in top management. Dean and Walker had agreed on a plan to freeze all supergrade actions immediately. Malek was meeting with Treasury Secretary David Kennedy in a few days to "arrange actions on Thrower to be effected next week, preferably in a quiet way." At that time he would also propose organizational changes. Within the week an outline of the new scheme would be in place and the search for new appointees under way. Malek would coordinate all of this with Secretary Kennedy, Dean, Egil "Bud" Krogh, and other White House staffers. John Ehrlichman had signed off on most of these actions, but Malek wanted to talk privately with Haldeman about other aspects of his thinking.[19]

A few days later, however, John Dean surprisingly warned Haldeman that such a reorganization of IRS was "neither necessary nor wise." He had talked with individuals inside and outside the government, including officials in the Justice Department, and had concluded that there was a "serious problem in politicizing the IRS or taking action that would give the appearance of politicizing the IRS." Malek's scheme might work, Dean admitted, but it would have to be done carefully. Clearly the creation of a few new management positions, whose occupants would be presidential appointees, was preferable to politicizing existing departments and functions within the agency. The IRS was unique among federal agencies in having only one political appointee in a bureaucracy of sixty thousand employees, which the Nixon administration clearly deemed insufficient. A week later Malek forwarded a new action plan to Haldeman along the lines Dean had indicated.[20]

Malek's proposal had a whiff of subterfuge about it. It intended to address his earlier criteria and make the IRS responsive without overtly politicizing the agency. The appointment of new supergrade officials was designed to make the IRS "sensitive and responsive to White House and Treasury policy in its tax rulings and in its priorities of enforcement"; but at the same time the IRS was to retain its nonpolitical, objective tradition. These changes within the IRS were to be implemented so as to minimize "negative public relations." This was important not only for public perceptions but because the IRS seemed more responsive to

Congress (particularly the House Ways and Means Committee) than it was to the White House. The four new special assistants to the commissioner would not have line authority but would be responsible for policy coordination, liaison with the White House, and public relations. "They should assist the Commissioner reflect Administration policy on tax rules, other IRS operations, and priority utilization of resources."[21]

Malek also addressed four problems: the lack of IRS responsiveness and the resulting political embarrassment to the White House; poor public relations when the IRS acted independently of the White House (especially with respect to tax-exempt organizations); poor White House liaison with the IRS; and the agency's failure to maximize revenue collection. His attention to these issues reflected a belief that the problems were essentially structural. In a nutshell, Malek reported, there was "no system of management information and control to force information from within IRS to the top in a timely and systematic manner." Unless dramatic action was taken, he argued, the situation would only worsen. Reform was essential "if the Administration wants to avoid further problems with the IRS, relieve some of the pressure current trends are building within the IRS, and capitalize on a strong Administration-oriented IRS in 1972. . . ." The four new special assistants would help. The plans also called for greater centralization of authority under the IRS commissioner, the selection of a new deputy commissioner when the current one retired in January (with consultation from "appropriate White House and Treasury staff"), and the installation of a new "top management information and control system." The administration had charted the retirement dates of top-level IRS officials and was delighted to discover that more than half were due to retire within the year. This opened opportunities for new appointments without the appearance of a wholesale housecleaning that might excite opposition and trigger negative publicity.[22]

As the White House pondered ways of placing allies in high-level civil service positions within the IRS, another opportunity to extend the political influence of the White House presented itself. This concerned the division of Alcohol, Tobacco and Firearms (ATF), then a division of Internal Revenue that dealt with narcotics trafficking, law enforcement intelligence activities, gun control, and wiretapping. During the Nixon years it became heavily involved in political intelligence. The administration apparently hoped to use ATF to clamp down on sixties protesters and radical movements. By the summer of 1970 there was a vacancy in the Enforcement Section of ATF as well as a need to appoint a new ATF director. Jack Caulfield and Gordon Liddy sought these posts, and the White House saw an opportunity to remove ATF from "Democratic control." IRS Commissioner Thrower later recalled that he received "strong pressure" from the White House to make the appointments. He managed to convince Gordon Liddy, who wanted to become ATF director because he was interested in the firearms aspect of the position, to withdraw his name. Liddy apparently lost interest when Thrower indicated that the position was almost entirely administrative, but ATF personnel also had no confidence in him. Jack Caulfield, head of personal security at the White House and (as later revealed) a political operative, then sought the position. Nixon strongly endorsed his application, indicating that Caulfield should report directly to Thrower and not through regular IRS reporting channels. John Dean also called Thrower about hiring Caulfield. Thrower objected, fearing that his real reporting would be to the White House, and that objection apparently sealed his own fate as IRS commissioner. But the struggle over the Caulfield appointment was a long, often devious, and tawdry tale. Because it reveals so much about the intentions and operations of the Nixon White House with respect to the IRS, it is worth following in some detail.[23]

Caulfield lobbied heavily for the ATF appointment, sending a barrage of letters and memos to such key White House staffers as John Dean, John Ehrlichman, and Bob Haldeman. He cast himself as under attack from Democrats and argued that his appointment was crucial to White House control over a piece of the IRS. Caulfield insisted that Democratic appointees within the IRS, such as Donald Bacon, opposed his appointment for political and ideological reasons. Bacon, he complained, "has been most effective in manipulating Thrower and, in effect, blunting the Administration's interests in many key areas." Two of Bacon's subordinates, moreover, were under instructions to do whatever was "necessary" to block the Caulfield appointment. Caulfield cannily played to the administration's fears and self-interest.

> There is much more at stake in the ATFD position, in my judgement, than appears on the surface. In the face of strong White House endorsement entrenched Democrats are exhibiting a willingness to blatantly challenge our interest in placing our candidate in a sensitive federal law enforcement position. You are aware that below Thrower there is but one member of IRS in a position to be trusted by the White House. Considering Thrower's performance, I am not sure that we have only ONE person in all of IRS (65,000 employees!) who can be trusted to perform with the Administration's interests at heart.[24]

There was more. Pushing all of Ehrlichman's buttons, Caulfield observed that ATF was a "key federal law enforcment unit" with "significant tools" to combat "the revolutionary terrorist activity accelerating across the country." The current IRS executive structure, he complained, was too "tax oriented" and insufficiently concerned with law enforcement. He argued that under his direction ATF would play a "dominant law enforcement role" which was critical for the "security of this nation." To do this it was essential that he report directly to the IRS commissioner or to the assistant secretary of the Treasury for enforcement, not to IRS regional tax commissioners or Donald Bacon. After he received Caulfield's lengthy memo, Ehrlichman called Under Secretary of the Treasury Charls Walker to urge his appointment. When IRS personnel interviewed Caulfield, however, they found he was simply not qualified for the position. His candidacy had moved forward solely because of his loyalty to the administration and Ehrlichman's patronage.[25]

Walker had initially been supportive, but now he backtracked. He based his reversal on his discovery that the ATF position was not entirely a law enforcement position, as well as the difficulties of appointing a noncareer individual to a career Civil Service position. That would require a restructuring of the job, which would be "difficult to pull off" and might "cause considerable difficulties within IRS" and the press. Walker tried to interest Caulfield in one of the new high-level positions to be created within IRS, but he was interested only in the ATF position. Caulfield did agree to step aside if Ehrlichman concurred and if the enforcement arm of ATF might in the future be pulled out of the IRS and given a direct line to Treasury. Walker indicated that such a move was "conceivable."[26]

Caulfield was not really stepping aside, however. He immediately wrote Ehrlichman to denounce the IRS for influencing Walker with a specially prepared nine-page job description for the ATF position. Even the attorney general could not have fulfilled all the responsibilities it outlined, Caulfield complained. He also suggested that Walker himself was not to be trusted. "I did not feel it appropriate," Caulfield warned Ehrlichman, "to discuss with Walker . . . the important political questions inherent in the function of this organization." He then outlined them for his patron. Of primary importance was the gun question, which he believed was "of key political significance" for the 1972 election. The administration needed a "proper and credible gun control position" to attract the forty million gun enthusiasts and gun manufacturers. There were also "significant political contributions" at "stake with respect to the Alcohol, Tobacco and Firearms industries." He concluded by noting that he was meeting with John Dean and Bud Krogh in four days to address the matter.[27]

Ehrlichman quickly pressed Walker to follow through on the Caulfield appointment, noting that both he and the president were counting on him. Since the president supported Caulfield, he warned Walker, there was "really no room in this matter for a question of qualifications." Ehrlichman's persistence apparently stalled the appointment of anyone else for the moment. Twelve days later Caulfield complained to Ehrlichman that none of this would have occurred if Walker had "properly finessed the IRS bureaucracy." Treasury Secretary David Kennedy now tried to involve the White House more openly, primarily so it would take some of the heat from the media should Caulfield's appointment go through. At the same time Caulfield again lobbied for the removal of ATF enforcement responsibilities from the IRS, enclosing excerpts from a confidential IRS document prepared earlier in the year as well as a 1950 reorganization plan that suggested just such a move. He added: "We should not overlook the media advantage inherent in a Presidential announcement indicating that the President considers the explosive and gun control responsibilities (vis a vis militants) so important that he has assigned one of his personal staff to head up the organization and make it directly responsive to the Secretary of the Treasury!"[28] Here lay revealed the real attraction for Caulfield's appointment: the White House would use him and ATF to launch an all-out attack on militant protesters who objected not only to the war in Vietnam but to the Nixon presidency.

Less than two weeks later, Caulfield was at it again, writing Ehrlichman to complain about the "latest Thrower instigated ploy" to neutralize "White House interest in my candidacy." The IRS now planned, he said, to reorganize ATF and place its separate functions within the Internal Revenue bureaucracy. This would diffuse its power, and Caulfield's appointment would be to a "meaningless entity." Together with Randolph Thrower, Donald Bacon was a "co-conspirator" in this plan. Caulfield urged Ehrlichman to defuse this "conspiracy" quickly and recommended that the administration require any reorganization to be signed off at the "White House level." Caulfield's fears were not totally misplaced. Thrower prepared a memo for Walker that proposed roughly what Caulfield conveyed to Ehrlichman, but even then Assistant Commissioner (Compliance) Donald Bacon and Deputy Assistant Commissioner (Compliance) Leon Green urged Thrower to circumscribe the duties of an appointee more clearly, warning him that the position might be "misinterpreted" and "have greater authority and responsibilities than you envision." After reading their comments, Thrower noted at the bottom of the memo: "Job Description to Walker will be inflated." Both sides could play the political game.[29]

During the next two days Walker and Thrower discussed a new directive from Secretary Kennedy that Caulfield be appointed ATF director. According to Caulfield, Thrower flatly refused to do so, indicating that he considered Caulfield unqualified for the position. "There is no question in my mind," Caulfield wrote Ehrlichman, "that Mr. Thrower is aware that he is challenging the will of the White House in this matter." Caulfield was convinced that Thrower considered him solely a political appointee, given his White House experience as a member of both Ehrlichman's and Haldeman's staff. As such, Thrower deemed him unsuitable to be director of ATF. For his part, Caulfield adamantly refused to accept a "subordinate role manufactured by hostile career officials with a view towards winning this battle." He then played for bigger stakes.

> I am aware that the removal of Thrower has been under consideration here for some time. Further, that Bob Haldeman has in hand a compilation of documented incidents similar to this which tend to support the concept of removal. Should this now be considered a positive eventuality, we might wish to time my arrival at IRS to coincide with the arrival of the new Commissioner. This tack, I feel, would minimize any attempt by Thrower and/or the career hostiles to make my candidacy an excuse for derogatory media advantage.

The White House, however, backed off and withdrew Caulfield's name from consideration.[30]

Randolph Thrower was a casualty of the struggle over ATF. As early as the winter of 1970, as part of a midterm assessment of all Nixon's appointees, Haldeman had noted that Thrower should be tested to see if he "is our man—with guts; if not—he's out." Before leaving as secretary of the Treasury, David Kennedy had told Thrower that Nixon wanted a new commissioner. Barth had been reporting to Ehrlichman that Thrower was uncooperative with White House requests and plans. According to Jack Caulfield, the White House hated Thrower as did Roger Barth. After appointing John Connally as his Treasury secretary in 1971, Nixon wrote him to "reiterate for the record" that he wanted Thrower "removed at the earliest feasible opportunity and replaced with someone mutually acceptable to you and me." Thrower discussed the matter with other administration officials, including the attorney general, but Nixon refused his request for a personal meeting. Clearly his effectiveness as an IRS commissioner who was part of the administration team was over. Thrower submitted his resignation a few weeks later but agreed to a request from newly appointed Treasury Secretary Connally to delay his departure until his successor was in place. Six months later Thrower gave way to Johnnie Walters as IRS commissioner, a victim of White House efforts to politicize the Internal Revenue Service. In late 1972, Caulfield finally became an assistant director of ATF after undergoing a Civil Service review. By that time, however, he did not have access to IRS files or to the narcotics trafficker tax files because ATF had become an independent agency.[31]

The Caulfield affair did not end promptly or tidily. Nor did it mark the close of White House efforts to control the IRS through top-management appointments. Later, during the Watergate investigations, Thrower told the House Judiciary Committee that he had resigned because he was "very much concerned about the potential for a personal police force which would not have the protection and insulation of the career staff." He also must have been concerned about increased activity from his assistant, Roger Barth. By late 1970, Barth was in almost constant contact with the White House, and he alerted Nixon's staff to what he believed was a growing pattern of political intervention by Democratic appointees at IRS, especially Donald Bacon. For this and other favors, the White House perceived Barth as their only "really loyal guy" at IRS.[32]

While the White House searched for Thrower's replacement, Caulfield warned Ehrlichman in February 1971 that IRS bureaucrats wanted someone as hard-nosed as Thrower, and to screen potential nominees very carefully. As Albert Hunt reported in the *Wall Street Journal*, sociology as much as taxes guided the search. Quoting sources who characterized Thrower as "too straight and too apolitical," Hunt wrote that the political and social climate would define the role of the new commissioner. The IRS, he noted, was "at a crossroads." Its "deepening involvement" in social issues "has prompted charges that the IRS could become an instrument of political oppression." According to an anonymous Washington lawyer, it was "hard not to believe the main intent is on serving the political interests of Richard Nixon." Although Treasury Under Secretary Charls Walker labeled these fears "untrue," he was not very convincing. The fact was that the IRS was increasingly involved in controversial social and political issues that roiled political waters.

Of particular concern to the administration was the proliferation of organizations seeking tax-exempt status (particularly those that opposed Nixon's policies), public-interest law firms, and social research groups that addressed contemporary issues. The investigations of Wright Patman and the passage of the 1969 Tax Reform Act had focused public attention on abuses of tax-exempt privileges. Foundation officials reported a "genuine fear" that the "government could clamp down anytime." The IRS itself was the central player in these issues, investigating tax exemptions for public-interest law firms, conservation groups, segregated private schools, and social action organizations. Any policies that the agency adopted could embroil the administration in controversy, and Nixon wanted to control IRS actions. For their part, IRS officials denied that they had "singled out any groups for review because of political overtones," but they did admit that they were examining more closely all types of exempt organizations' activities. For all of these groups, as well as for the public and the administration, political considerations appeared paramount.[33]

Later chapters will explore the Enemies List and the Special Service Staff, both manifestations of this politicized atmosphere. But even while those two efforts went forward, internal White House memos reveal a persistent fixation on politics and ideology as the defining characteristics for IRS appointees as well as for assessments of the agency's activities. Nixon's replacement of Randolph Thrower with Johnnie M. Walters was one effort to resolve this question in favor of the administration. Even before the Walters appointment was final, Roger Barth had gone to Walters to request that he be appointed his deputy. Walters refused, and the next morning he received a call from John Ehrlichman. Apparently as a test of Walters's loyalty, Ehrlichman asked if Walters planned to get rid of Barth after he became commissioner. He then warned that Barth was a "man that tracks the President well and is generally helpful." The White House quickly set up a meeting between Walters and Fred Malek to discuss the issue. From Walters's perspective, the problem was that Barth was perceived as a "White House spy," and he refused to take the job if such a position was essential. The White House, however, told Walters that without an agreement on the retention of Barth, his nomination "papers just wouldn't move." Malek eventually suggested that Barth be retained but not be a White House spy. Walters agreed, though he must have realized that neither the behavior of Barth nor the White House was likely to change. Walters later told an interviewer that he retained Barth in part because he believed Barth was looking for another position and soon would be gone. Walters did end the practice of taking minutes at the commissioner's staff meetings, and excluded everyone except top staff from those meetings. Both policy changes upset Barth, particularly his exclusion from close contact with the commissioner. But White House pressures, as we shall see later, did not cease.[34]

The White House regarded Walters as a Nixon loyalist, though it had preferred conservative Washington tax lawyer George Webster, who ran into opposition because he opposed granting tax-exempt status to labor unions or civil rights organizations. (Webster later loaned Chuck Colson $5,000 for a confidential operation; this turned out to be the burglary of Daniel Ellsberg's psychiatrist's office.) The White House then turned to Walters, a Republican from Greenville, South Carolina. Walters had served in the IRS chief counsel's office from 1949 to 1953, and then had left to join the tax department of Texaco. His contact there with John Alexander of the Mudge Rose law firm—Nixon and Mitchell's firm—later brought him to the attention of the administration. He then became assistant attorney general under John Mitchell. Walters accepted the IRS appointment but intended to leave government service by January 1973 at the latest. He eventually would leave office on April 30, 1973. Soon after he became commissioner, Walters received a memorandum from his predecessor, Thrower, addressed to "Successor," which outlined some problems in the office.[35]

At least throughout 1971 the White House continued to believe that Walters was their man and would do their bidding. It continued to worry about the appointment of liberal Democrats from inside IRS to vacancies at the top management level, and to fret about the possibility that Roger Barth was being boxed out at the agency. Walters had established a working relationship with Charls Walker in Treasury, and Gordon Liddy alerted Bud Krogh that Walters had sources of information that warned him about White House plotting. Immediately after Barth had tried to block the promotion of one liberal Democrat within IRS, for example, Walker had warned Walters that Barth was "probably going around your back to the White House." Walters immediately called Barth on the carpet, warning him that he alone would handle White House contacts, concluding that "we are trying to operate nonpolitically around here." The White House, moreover, had begun to use the IRS not only to reward friends and punish enemies but to check on supposedly loyal members of the administration itself. In September 1971, for instance, Haldeman instructed Larry Higby to begin an IRS file on John Dean.[36]

Walters never received the full confidence of the White House. As early as the spring of 1971, Haldeman questioned Walters's loyalty: "is he ruthless—do what he's told—go after our enemies—show us any re-turn?" Or would he be a "lawyer to tell us how to do things—like Kldst [Kleindienst]?" Haldeman's correspondence clearly indicated that he ex-pected the IRS to be "politically responsive in order that Dean will have access to political infor. within the IRS and in particular, audits, tax ex-emptions and selected returns." By November 1971 the administration had prepared a talking paper and memorandum to make the IRS more politically responsive. The problem, as they saw it, was a "lack of guts and effort." They wanted to crack down on left-wing tax-exempt foun-dations, obtain information on their political enemies, stimulate audits on demand, and place Nixon supporters in the IRS bureaucracy. Wal-ters, the document indicated, "*must* be more responsive" with respect to "personnel and political actions." From the White House perspective, Walters had failed to exercise leadership—meaning, of course, that he had not implemented the administration's plans. He should simply be instructed to act, to know that "discreet political actions and investiga-tions on behalf of the Administration are a firm requirement and re-sponsibility on his part."

Despite its best efforts, the Nixon White House never managed to gain complete control of the IRS. One sign of that failure was the ap-pointment of William Loeb, not Roger Barth, as deputy IRS commis-sioner in August 1971. Loeb was a career IRS employee and most recently had been assistant regional commissioner in the Southeast Re-gion (Atlanta). He had joined the agency in 1942 and worked his way up the management ladder. With Loeb's appointment, the White House suffered three blows. He was not Roger Barth, he was a Democrat, and he was a careerist. He represented, in short, exactly the kind of person the White House had attempted to eliminate from IRS policymaking. Barth quickly advised Gordon Liddy that Loeb had completely "sub-verted" the IRS Narcotics Project by assigning investigative responsibil-ities to individuals within the normal IRS reporting channels. Liddy had wanted "hundreds of additional agents" working as a special team out-side the regular bureaucracy. It was not to be.[37]

Despite this setback, Nixon did not give up his grand scheme of politicizing the IRS. In January 1973 he told Haldeman, in Haldeman's words, that "the government must act when we speak, therefore it is better to have a dumb loyalist than a bright neuter. For IRS, a loyal Jew would be good." In March 1973, Nixon sent Haldeman an "Eyes Only" memo asking, "What happened to the suggestion that the IRS should run audits on all members of the Congress?" Nixon then vacillated as he tried to justify the request, at first admitting that it would upset friends as well as enemies and insisting that there must be an "even-handed approach." Then he did an about-face and devised a cover story that he wanted a routine check of individuals who usually were not checked because "of their special position." In the end, neither effort apparently proved very convincing, for Nixon told Haldeman that he wanted only an "oral report" and reminded him that the request was "highly confidential." He left a note for his longtime private secretary, Rosemary Woods, that she should make only one copy for his private file and deliver the original to him personally.[38]

More sweeping, and more public, was Nixon's issuance of an executive order permitting the Agriculture Department to inspect farmers' tax returns. A later congressional investigation revealed no apparent indication that Agriculture officials had requested such authority, nor any rationale for Nixon's order. When the president's proposed 1974 budget eliminated all funding for a farm census that year, the request became even more puzzling. By then, of course, Nixon's actions were highly suspect regardless of their actual intent. Investigation soon revealed that the Agriculture order was a prototype for similar orders for other departments, whereby many other tax returns would receive scrutiny. Missouri Democratic Congressman Jerry Litton was outraged and alerted the public to what he perceived to be a blanket snooping into the tax returns of more than three million farmers. By the time Congress fully investigated the affair, in 1976, issues such as the Enemies List and government intrusion into private lives through the examination of tax returns had become widely known. But in 1973 many of those activities were still rumors. Operating on the assumption that this order was designed to develop statistical data, Litton introduced legislation to provide alternatives and plug loopholes. He warned:

> Today, we allow the Department of Agriculture to inspect farmers' tax returns for "statistical purposes only," as contended by the Internal Revenue Service; tomorrow the Commerce Department will be examining the tax records of businessmen, HEW will be examining the records of doctors and HUD the data of homeowners. And, who can guarantee that the inspections will be for the harmless project of compiling statistics—statistics which in most cases, can be obtained from other, less sensitive sources?[39]

Protection for individual privacy was essential.

A subsequent Treasury Department study of Executive Order 11697 concluded that it was drafted more broadly than necessary. The study insisted that this was because the order was designed as a prototype, but warned that it was dangerous. The information Agriculture sought was actually fairly limited—names, addresses, identification numbers, and type of farming activity—and designed for statistical compilation. In retrospect this executive order revealed the dangers of trying to politicize the IRS. Announced by Richard Nixon and published in the *Federal Register*, it actually was the product of cooperation between the Treasury Department, the Agriculture Department, and the Joint Committee on Internal Revenue Taxation. But because of the highly politicized atmosphere of distrust, and because it followed four years of Nixon administration efforts to make the IRS politically responsive, few saw the announcement as anything more than another move to use the IRS to ferret out politically useful information from individuals' tax returns and invade personal privacy. The fact that it authorized the direct inspection of tax returns when the information was available by other means only heightened suspicion.[40]

This affair proved Clark Mollenhoff's later charge that the "Nixon White House created a milieu in which the insidious poison of secrecy permeated virtually all departments and agencies of the federal government." Power and control guided White House relations with other government agencies, and top White House staff sought out and found "subservient and pliant sycophants" as assistants to do their bidding.[41] Development of the Enemies List and the targeting of both individuals and organizations for action by the Internal Revenue Service between 1969 and 1973 would demonstrate how concentrated and effective these efforts were.

CHAPTER ELEVEN

THE ENEMIES LIST

RICHARD NIXON had a lot of enemies. To exact revenge against them, as well as against political opponents and organizations that simply disagreed with his policies, Nixon created the Enemies List. Established with substantial input and assistance from the White House staff, the Enemies List remains as perhaps the most shocking violation of Americans' constitutional liberties by any president or individual within the government. It went well beyond other 1960s efforts to turn the intelligence capabilities of the federal government against its own citizens. Many of these federal efforts had originated with specific government agencies, such as the FBI's Counter-Intelligence Program (COINTELPRO), but the Enemies List was more personal. It was, moreover, part of an even broader program to make partisan use of the Internal Revenue Service. The decentralized operation of the IRS left institutional fissures where compliant individuals could operate. One might have expected that, through careful leaks and its own cultivation of political allies, the IRS would have found ways to sabotage Nixon's efforts and prevent their implementation. It did not, and even now many questions remain.

The Enemies List and its operation were part of a pattern of White House behavior between 1969 and 1973 that pressured the IRS to initiate tax audits and otherwise harass opponents of the administration or its policies. These opponents, some ideological and others who simply differed on politics or policies, Richard Nixon labeled "enemies." In doing so, he demonized his political opposition, turning differences of opinion into matters of state security. His purpose, in the words of White House aide Jeb Magruder, was to bring about "ideological conformity." Nixon used sensitive information and individuals' tax data for partisan purposes. He sought to have the IRS initiate audits of individuals who criticized his friends as well as to discourage tax audits of his friends. The IRS often tried to resist this White House pressure, but was not always successful and eventually succumbed to pressures of its own.[1]

Ironically, the Enemies Program was under way for almost two years before the administration articulated a formal structure and rationale. Not until August 16, 1971, when John Dean prepared a memorandum, "Dealing with Our Political Enemies," did the program acquire its name. According to Dean, anyone who gave the administration a "hard time" should be targeted. "This memorandum," Dean wrote, "addresses the matter of how we can maximize the fact of our incumbency in dealing with persons known to be active in their opposition to our Administration. Stated a bit more bluntly—how we can use the available federal machinery to screw our political enemies." Later, in testimony before the Senate Watergate Committee, Dean portrayed the Watergate break-in as an "inevitable outgrowth" of excessive concern by the White House about political opposition, together with "an insatiable appetite for political intelligence." The Enemies Program fused these two concerns. It was not, as Dean insisted, an "accident of fate" but a deliberate attempt to stifle dissent and discredit opponents. Dean recalled that

> the information regarding demonstrators—or rather lack of information showing connections between the demonstration leaders and foreign governments or major political figures—was often reported to a disbelieving and complaining White House staff that felt the entire system for gathering such intelligence was worthless. . . . This attitude toward the intelligence gathering capability of the Government regarding demonstrations prevailed through my tenure at the Justice Department and the White House, and I was hearing complaints from the President personally as late as March 12 of this year [1973].[2]

Although Dean insisted throughout his Watergate testimony that "99 out of a 100 times" requests for IRS action against "enemies" only went into his file, and that he never had a "political enemies project that was in any way operational," a careful study of the Enemies Lists (there were eventually several) indicates that this was simply not true. H. R. Haldeman, Tom Charles Huston, and Chuck Colson, among others on the White House staff, compiled lists of enemies and labored to make the project work. Within the IRS, Barth provided access to tax information, and the White House constantly pressured the commissioner of Internal Revenue to cooperate with its demands. The administration was dedicated and diligent in its efforts to discredit and undercut political opponents. The scope of its activities was calculated and comprehensive. "What we cannot do in a courtroom," one White House memo said, the "IRS could do by administrative action."[3]

Efforts to manipulate the IRS began at least as early as June 1969, though Nixon had expressed an interest in using the IRS to review "ideological organizations" almost as soon as he took the oath of office in January of that year. On June 16, Arthur Burns and Tom Huston met with IRS Commissioner Randolph Thrower to discuss targeted tax enforcement. Although Burns later denied any memory of the meeting, Thrower took notes and prepared a memorandum for his files outlining the discussion. Two days later, Thrower and Burns discussed names of individuals who might be appointed to an Exempt Organizations Advisory Committee that would target "activist" groups. Haldeman aide Jeb Magruder later likened this to Kennedy's efforts to use the FBI against steel executives when the administration had opposed hikes in the price of steel. Magruder told Haldeman that they should use the IRS to scrutinize "various organizations that we are most concerned about," because "even the threat of an IRS investigation will probably turn their approach." Magruder was apparently unaware of Kennedy's efforts to use the IRS against right-wing groups in the early 1960s, but his intent was more far-reaching: the administration should "use the power at hand to achieve our long term goals which is eight years of a Republican Administration." In late July, H. R. Haldeman noted in his diary that "we haven't used the power of the White House, to reward and punish."[4] That quickly changed. This first initiative led the IRS to establish the Activist Organizations Group (later renamed the Special Service Staff), which will be examined in later chapters. This effort was separate from the Enemies Lists, which originated with the White House and chiefly targeted individuals. Throughout the Activist Organizations Group's existence, however, the White House remained dissatisfied with IRS efforts. Perhaps not trusting the IRS to do his bidding, Richard Nixon wanted a program more directly responsive to his wishes. He intended to operate that effort out of the White House.

Clark Mollenhoff's request for tax returns in the fall of 1969 appears to have been an early foray into IRS files for political purposes. Mollenhoff later attacked the administration for its activities and stoutly defended his requests as fully justified and separate from later "enemies" efforts. He may well have been correct, but his request marks the first exploration of how the administration might turn the IRS to political advantage. Some of Mollenhoff's requests also caused concern in the IRS commissioner's office. Randolph Thrower worried that such audits might attract attention, and he hesitated to approve them. He did write Mollenhoff, however, that they should talk about it. Mollenhoff's subsequent departure allowed Nixon to appoint someone less principled. At that time Roger Barth became a key player, though Barth later tried to convince Watergate prosecutors that he was "totally unaware of anything like an enemies list."[5]

Nixon's determination led to a series of Enemies Lists, one with about twenty names, others with hundreds of names, as well as separate queries about particular individuals. Lists were constantly updated and revised. Eventually more than seven hundred individuals found their way onto one Enemies List or another. The importance of the targeting of enemies to the Nixon presidency is reflected in its scope and attention to detail. By the time of Watergate, finding one's name on an Enemies List had become a source of pride.[6]

Nixon moved quickly to use the IRS against his enemies. By the end of 1969 the White House had requested tax audits on an assortment of individuals, from the columnist Tom Braden to the Polaroid inventor Edwin Land to the Chicago educator George Fischer. It also made a series of requests to the FBI for name checks. Although the practice of name checks was a routine part of the federal appointment process— running someone's name through the FBI computer system—when Watergate investigators provided the FBI with lists of individuals drawn from the various Enemies Lists, they discovered that the White House had requested name checks on many of them. The WSPF list of names included organizations such as the Institute for Policy Studies as well as individuals like Harvard President Derek Bok, the entertainer Bill Cosby, Kennedy staffer Mary Jo Kopechne, several newsmen (including David Brinkley, Sander Vanocur, Marvin Kalb, and Seymour Hersh), the activists Bayard Rustin and I. F. Stone, and establishment figures like Robert McNamara and Clark Clifford, to name but a few. The entire list is lengthy and consists largely of individuals who clearly were not serious candidates for a Nixon administration appointment. That most of the requests originated from key White House staffers—John Ehrlichman, Egil Krogh, and Alexander Butterfield—reveals the administration's effort to dig up dirt on political opponents. That spirit fueled the Enemies Lists.[7]

While John Dean's 1971 memo provided the rationale and structure for the program, Chuck Colson was the individual who originated the idea. Colson was a rogue force in the administration. Nixon once noted that Colson would "do anything," that he had "the balls of a brass monkey." His ideas not only outran those of others, they outran the law, moral principles, and common sense. Lyn Nofziger was his accomplice. Nofziger's job at the White House "was to screw the enemies."[8]

Nixon speechwriter Patrick Buchanan was also a dynamic presence in efforts to utilize the IRS for political purposes. In March 1970, Buchanan prepared a memorandum, at Nixon's request, outlining "how to combat the institutionalized power of the left concentrated in the foundations, that succor the Democratic Party." Buchanan outlined a series of steps to provide some short-term corrections. He proposed the formation of a study group to examine the top twenty-five foundations in the country and determine which were for and which against the administration. Those deemed "potentially friendly" could be "co-opted" to support administration projects. Essentially Buchanan urged that all foundations be given an ideological litmus test. Those that failed should not only be shunned; "anti-administration foundations should be cut off without a dime."[9]

The administration's political objectives could best be served, according to Buchanan, by the creation of a new conservative foundation, perhaps called the MacArthur Institute. It would be a home for conservative Republican intellectuals and a "parking place" for administration officials when they left office. It could also stockpile names of conservative intellectuals and create a "talent bank" for future Republican administrations, as well as offer fellowships to underwrite conservatives who would prepare articles or books on major policy questions. To do this, Buchanan argued, required a "strong fellow running the Internal Revenue Division" as well as a "friendly fellow" in the tax-exempt office. "Am not sure we have this right now," he told Nixon. In addition to these overt programs, the foundation should engage in several covert activities. Part of "the essential objective of the Institute would have to be blurred," Buchanan warned Nixon, "even buried, in all sorts of other activity . . . that would provide the cover for the more important efforts." At the same time the IRS could "engage in combat with some of these lesser anti-Administration institutions like the Stern Foundation."[10]

Buchanan argued that the political process was "unbalanced." He had studied the Ford Foundation and the Brookings Institution in some detail, and was convinced that they operated almost as an arm of the Democratic party. Together with other liberal foundations, they were "quasi-political operations" which played an important role in the governance structure by undertaking studies for the government and suggesting policy alternatives. It was time to balance the equation with a conservative foundation.

During his testimony before the Senate Watergate Committee, Buchanan stoutly defended his recommendations, insisting that they violated no law and that Democratic administrations had hounded conservative foundations by threatening their tax-exempt status. Buchanan skirted the question of the administration's use of the IRS in this effort, insisting that all his information came from public documents filed by the foundations themselves. While technically true, it did not address questions about political abuse of the IRS to advance Buchanan's goals. When pressed, he reminded senators that he had urged cutting off the flow of federal funds to liberal foundations, not the termination of their tax exemptions.

Buchanan's testimony is not only fascinating, it drew ideological and political battle lines that characterized the Nixon years. Liberal foundations, he argued, together with Eastern media, the major networks, and leading public policy institutes, constituted not only the liberal wing of the Democratic party but the political establishment of the country. Against this imposing array of power stood "Mr. Nixon and his middle American constituency." Buchanan's innovative proposal later came to fruition, fueling and then feeding off the revival of conservatism in the 1980s. By the end of 1970, however, Buchanan had gone further and called for the termination of liberal organizations' tax exemptions. In a memo to Haldeman he complained about a mailing he had received from Martin Luther King's Southern Christian Leadership Conference, claiming that it was wholly political in nature. He asked if "we can at least see to it that the head of the IRS jerks the tax-exemption of these people." It would be a warning, and despite the fact that there would be "considerable howling from blacks and liberals," action was essential if "we are not simply going to roll over and play dead."[11]

Buchanan's suggestions found their way into pieces of the administration's targeting of its enemies. Chuck Colson enlisted the American Enterprise Institute (AEI) to study whether or not campus political activities violated the tax-exempt status of colleges and universities. He complained that the American Council of Education had circulated a "very liberal interpretation" of the tax code and had even cleared it beforehand with the IRS. He anticipated that the AEI would reach much different, much more conservative, conclusions. Colson found "considerable evidence" to indicate that threats to revoke institutions' tax exemptions would prompt college administrators to "rigidly restrict campus political activity." This would be an "effective technique for curbing the 'peace/new left movement.'" Nixon himself was determined to undertake an "all-out hatchet job on the Democrat leaders, through IRS." He proposed auditing all Democratic senators running for reelection in 1970.[12]

During the summer of 1970 the administration requested a Justice Department report on the Urban Coalition, a Washington, D.C., corporation. This recalled Buchanan's spring memo; the group was funded with $100,000 in seed money from the Ford Foundation. The administration was concerned that the organization engaged in political activities in violation of its tax-exempt status. Johnnie Walters, then an assistant attorney general in the Justice Department's Tax Division, advised John Dean that he did not know what "activities the Urban Coalition has been engaged in since its organization." He then suggested avenues of investigation to determine whether or not it had violated the Internal Revenue Code, but "responsible complaints" were needed before the IRS would launch an investigation. Nine days later, John Dean admitted that insufficient evidence existed to pursue the matter, but he asked if the activities of related groups could jeopardize the Urban Coalition's exemption. The IRS had not studied that issue. In particular, Dean wanted to document ties between the Urban Coalition and the Urban Coalition Action Council, a separate organization (later renamed Common Cause) headed by John Gardner. Walters warned Dean that the effort to do so was potentially dangerous. Before going that route, he observed, "we should discuss carefully the possible consequences and ramifications of the project."[13]

In early September, Haldeman pressed his aides to begin creating income tax problems or launching tax investigations of Democrats. Senator Vance Hartke of Indiana was a particular target, and Haldeman aide Larry Higby insisted that the Democrats were doing the same thing to Republicans. Murray Chotiner replied that the matter was in the "hands of the proper person" who would handle it. Lyn Nofziger, meanwhile, explored the tax status of the Jerry Rubin Foundation, a tax-exempt organization established to shelter royalties from the radical activist's writings. Later, IRS Commissioner Thrower denied that the White House had pressured him to suspend tax exemptions of any organizations. There was, he told reporters for the *Washington Post*, "an overreaction." The fact was, however, that the IRS considered withdrawing tax exemptions from groups that filed environmental lawsuits. William Ruckelshaus, the new director of the Environmental Protection Agency, and even Republican Congressman Gerald Ford opposed such a step.[14]

Colson, meanwhile, enlisted a tax-exempt group to campaign against liberal Democrats, particularly Senators Kennedy, Gore, Muskie, Fulbright, Goodell, McGovern, Yarborough, and Cranston. Using the American Security Council, he launched "Operation Alert." The American Security Council was a nonprofit organization in Illinois, with offices in Washington, D.C. During the 1970 campaigns it spent money on conservative candidates and used its postal permit to mail political materials. Colson distributed "Operation Alert" voting material through a September White House memorandum. The appeal was essentially an anti-Communist one, telling voters that the targeted candidates opposed the president's Vietnam policy and missile-defense proposals. Before the campaign was over it targeted not only senators up for reelection but most senatorial opponents of the president. It eventually attracted the attention of Wright Patman, then studying the Internal Revenue Service's failure to examine tax-exempt organizations. Unlike the case of environmental groups, however, there appears to be no evidence that the IRS took any action against the American Security Council.[15]

By the end of the year the administration had further broadened its efforts to collect political intelligence. Robert Mardian of the Justice Department's Internal Security Division met with FBI Director J. Edgar Hoover to revitalize interdepartmental intelligence activities. Whether or not Mardian was aware of the FBI's COINTELPRO efforts is unclear, but he embraced Hoover's argument for Justice Department action based on the results of FBI reports. Using the Internal Security Division as a cover for his real intent, Mardian developed an independent intelligence operation to assist in illegal wiretapping and mail openings as well as to prosecute radical protesters. The CIA apparently cooperated for a while but then backed out. The IRS, however, did not. By the fall of 1970, Alcohol, Tobacco and Firearms—at that time still a division of Internal Revenue—was working "hand in glove" with Mardian, operating like an organized crime strike force. Watergate investigators later concluded that this effort was an "unholy marriage between young Turks and those pseudo-superpatriots that every law enforcement agency spawns." It was, in effect, implementation of the Huston Plan through the use of an Intelligence Evaluation Committee. Mardian also planned to have the IRS investigate whether dissident speakers on college campuses correctly reported their honoraria. Developed almost simultaneously with the enemies program, Mardian's intelligence network complemented White House efforts.[16]

Attempts to foster ideological conformity, however, focused chiefly on the targeting of the administration's enemies. During 1971 it developed from a series of almost random efforts directed at specific individuals and groups into an organized structure to identify opponents systematically and make the IRS politically responsive. Between June 1971 and the end of the year, a steady stream of memoranda on the topic flowed between almost a dozen White House aides. Bob Haldeman and his staff oversaw the operation, but several layers of deniability emerged. John Dean was to be the most direct liaison with the White House, but Dean himself developed his own liaisons to run the program. In March, George Bell of Colson's staff was assigned to keep a book of the president's supporters and opponents, an assignment that came to Bell from Nixon and Haldeman through Colson. In theory the lists were to provide guidance for invitations to White House functions, but they were quickly used for other purposes. Rosemary Woods, Nixon's private secretary, kept the social list along with Marge Acker, while Pat Buchanan researched political opponents and maintained the Republican National Committee files. Colson handled the more obvious political targeting. Colson later charged that Dean was the individual who confused the two purposes and lists, and who deceived him. After they assembled the evidence, Watergate investigators found that explanation to be unbelievable.[17]

John Dean was the linchpin of the operation, and it was he who responded to Pat Buchanan's inquiry about the tax exemption of the Southern Christian Leadership Conference. He had received the material from Buchanan through Haldeman, and Tom Huston had checked it out with Roger Barth at the IRS. Dean reported that, unfortunately, the activity was not illegal—though other White House aides disagreed. Hopefully, Dean told Buchanan, changes at the IRS would correct such problems. Huston was more direct in his memo to Dean. Since Thrower had not acceded to White House requests in 1969 to move against the National Student Association, he surely would not move against the SCLC and "the ghost of Martin Luther King." Huston recommended that "we wait and see if we get a new commissioner." Then they could bring the matter to the IRS "along with half a dozen similar situations that require attention."[18]

White House identification and investigation of "enemies" was helter-skelter. Apparently almost anyone could suggest a target, and requests were channeled from Haldeman to Dean to Jack Caulfield and back again. By December 1970 the White House had launched a three-month investigation of Jack Anderson. Concerned that columns reflected access to intelligence memos and other inside sources, the White House attempted to locate and intimidate or fire his sources. The intent was not to uncover illegal activity but to erect a wall of secrecy around the operations of the administration. Anderson later reported that an "entire section of Henry Kissinger's staff was disbanded" on the suspicion that Anderson "had a source in that area." Robert Mardian also turned the Internal Security Division and the FBI against the columnist, tailing not only Anderson but his wife and nine children. The effort was impressive and frightening, but not fruitful.[19]

Once under way, the Enemies List grew like Topsy and included groups as well as individuals. Chuck Colson had assembled an initial list by mid-March 1971. Haldeman urged that it be the basis for a concerted attack against all the groups on the list. Colson should "take them on" and not wait to react to their actions, monitor their activities, and "place someone on the inside if possible." Colson assured him that those actions had begun and that he had a "good system for determining contributors to the campaigns of potential Democratic opponents." By spring 1971 pressures mounted to have the IRS investigate the tax-exempt status of the Fund for Investigative Journalism (because it had funded Seymour Hersh's investigation of the My Lai incident), Citizens for a New Prosperity, the Amendment to End the War Committee, and the National Education Association. In mid-May, Nixon began outlining his requirements for a new IRS commissioner to succeed Randolph Thrower. "I want to be sure," Nixon told Haldeman and Ehrlichman, "he is a ruthless son of a bitch, that he will do what he's told, that every income-tax return I want to see I see, that he will go after our enemies and not go after our friends." Otherwise "he doesn't get the job."[20] He eventually settled on Johnnie Walters, who apparently was not expecting the volume or intensity of White House demands on his services.

By June 1971, Larry Higby had a thirteen-page list of opponents, along with a seventeen-page list of contributors to Edmund Muskie's fledgling campaign for the Democratic presidential nomination—all to be investigated. A probe of the National Education Association had failed to provide much hope that the administration could induce the IRS to revoke its tax exemption, and Dean tried to rein in Colson by warning him not to challenge the IRS in that case unless the evidence of wrongdoing was "strong." Colson, meanwhile, constantly updated his lists. Nixon also wanted Roger Barth to pull Clark Clifford's IRS file as well as files on "all of the top supporters of the doves" and have the IRS launch "a full field audit." Then the administration could "see what we can make of it on analysis." This was a fishing expedition. John Dean was to coordinate all these intelligence operations. Pat Buchanan, meanwhile, urged Ehrlichman to advance "Project Ellsberg"—an investigation of the Pentagon Papers publication. It would, he wrote, "be psychologically satisfying to cut the innards from Ellsberg and his clique in a major book exposé of what they attempted to do, and what they did." Buchanan admitted, however, that aside from its psychological benefits it might not do anything for Richard Nixon. He then advocated launching "a major public attack" on the Brookings Institution.

> No one in the country knows what the thing is. We could have it attacked, discredited in the eyes of millions of people, and suspect in the eyes of millions of others—thus, tainting every single anti-Nixon paper that came out of there, subsequent. This is what we have in the works right now; we have the West Wing approval, and VP enthusiasm.[21]

The Brookings project began almost immediately.

Dean instructed Caulfield to obtain Brookings' tax returns, seeking ways to "turn off money" or initiate measures against individuals involved with the organization. In July he sent that information to Ehrlichman's aide Egil Krogh, linking Brookings with the Ford Foundation as key enemies of the administration. "It is clear," Dean wrote, "that the financial wealth and influence" of both groups, "when used to engage in either direct or indirect political activity represents formidable opposition to the best interests of this Administration." The administration should pressure the IRS to "strictly enforce" tax-exemption laws as well as "promulgate regulations designed to threaten the tax exempt status" of both organizations. The IRS had yet to complete a 1969 audit of the Ford Foundation, and Dean complained that "purposeful delay appears to be the chosen bureaucratic tack." According to Dean, Commissioner Walters had failed to exercise the "firm leadership expected at the time of his appointment" and appeared reluctant to "make discreetly politically oriented decisions and to effect major appointments based upon Administration loyalty considerations." Walters had surrounded himself with Democrats and appeared to be trying to ease Roger Barth out of the agency. In addition, he had it decreed that all tax-exempt matters should flow through William Connett, his special assistant for tax-exempt organizations—and a Democrat.[22]

Prompt action was essential, and Dean suggested that Treasury Secretary John Connally speak out against political abuses by tax-exempt foundations. The administration should create a new position in Treasury, such as a Deputy Under Secretary for Taxation, to represent the administration's interests and oversee IRS tax administration and policy. It should also advocate restrictive legislation and instruct Senator Bob Dole to make this a key issue for the 1972 campaign. Driving the campaign against Brookings, at least in part, were rumors that it was preparing a Vietnam study based on current documents to be released in the fall as part of a new series of foreign policy studies funded largely by the Ford Foundation. The administration also planned a break-in at Brookings to obtain papers from Leslie Gelb's office. Gelb, who had headed the secretary of defense's Vietnam task force in 1967–1968, was then a senior fellow at Brookings. Chuck Colson suggested setting a fire as a diversion and cover to the operation. It was a fanciful scheme that revealed the administration's desperation and determination, but it proved not to be an isolated incident.[23]

Numerous other foundations and organizations found their tax-exempt status challenged by the administration, chiefly because of their funding patterns and policy stances. The Institute for Policy Studies (IPS), for instance, attracted interest from the administration soon after Nixon took office. By 1970 the IRS had conducted an audit of the IPS's tax-exempt status in its Baltimore District, and the revenue agent there recommended revocation of the group's tax exemption. During the next eighteen months Internal Revenue staff conducted reviews of IPS in other districts as well. It also opened a Sensitive Case Report on IPS. In mid-1971 the new IRS commissioner, Johnnie Walters, asked Roger Barth to see why this case remained unresolved. Yet in 1972, Treasury Secretary John Connally still complained about the lack of action. A Compliance review, however, turned up serious deficiencies in the proposed revocation, and Barth turned the case over to June Norris, an assistant in the Miscellaneous and Special Provisions Tax Division. By December 1973, four years after the initial IRS examination, the case remained incomplete despite repeated White House pressure to revoke the Institute's exemption.[24]

Throughout this extended scrutiny, IPS officials complained about government harassment. When Institute directors Marcus Raskin and Richard Barnett, together with their attorneys Mitchell Rogovin, the former IRS official, and Richard Hubbard, met with Watergate investigators in October 1973, they detailed this harassment and presented their version of events. They indicated that in 1968 the IPS had undergone a regular audit of its tax returns for 1964–1966, and that the IRS had made no adverse recommendations. Then, in 1969, IPS received notice of a new audit, which began in January 1970. The Institute was also subpoenaed by the Internal Security Committee for its bank records, a subpoena that IPS successfully fought. But the new audit continued, examining tax returns not only for 1967–1969 but also for 1970 and 1971 as it dragged on seemingly without end. Finally, in October 1972, the IRS recommended revocation based on three books written by IPS fellows that the IRS believed represented political activity prohibited by the Institute's exempt status. Efforts to resolve the matter stalled, in part because the IRS lost part of its own report. Rogovin, who had been at the very heart of IRS activity against right-wing groups throughout the early 1960s, proved a powerful presence. He argued that not only were the audits unreasonable but that the IRS had used a secret Special Services Group to investigate IPS, and that the FBI had gained access to the Institute's bank records, even after the IRS investigation had ended.[25]

Both Raskin and Barnett were also wiretapped, apparently as part of this same "unrelenting audit." During the Watergate inquiry, Rogovin wrote Senator Sam Ervin, asking to testify before the Senate Select Committee on Presidential Campaign Activities and to set the record straight about IRS abuses with respect to the Institute for Policy Studies. He objected to Pat Buchanan's earlier testimony, which claimed that IPS had supported a "radical underground newspaper" (*Quicksilver Times*). Rogovin said that IPS testimony would reveal "how the Nixon Administration has applied the power of the federal government in a coordinated program of harassment against one of its enemies." He also complained about illegal surveillance as well as breaking and entering by the FBI. IPS had been selected, Rogovin argued, because it presented "viewpoints differing sharply from those of the Administration."[26]

The Nixon administration also sought to block the granting of tax exemptions to groups that it considered opponents, as well as to prevent existing exempt groups from creating nonexempt entities while maintaining exempt status for a portion of their activities. When Republicans compromised on this latter point, Pat Buchanan attacked his own party.

> This is a foolish position which our people have taken on the Hill. What it guarantees is that all the left-wing church groups, environmental extremists, and the like will now be able to use tax-exempt dollars to lobby against our policies and in favor of anti-war, anti-business policies and the like. Most of these "public interest" outfits are hard against the President—some of them should never have been granted tax exemptions in any case—let alone now granting them the right to use a portion of their funds lobbying for legislation. We are just cutting our own throats by making huge political concessions to our adversaries like this. If these groups are tax-exempt, they should stay the hell out of public policy.

Buchanan had earlier pleaded with Haldeman to gather materials "on all these anti-Nixon tax exempt organizations and lay the boom on them at once, and throw in a few right wing political fronts for spice."[27] In at least one case the administration tried to heed his advice.

When the Center for Corporate Responsibility applied for exempt status, the White House intervened to stall the application process and force a denial. The Center was a public-interest group that had brought proxy contests against several major corporations, launched "Campaign GM," and studied the conditions of migrants working for the Coca-Cola Company. Run by former JFK speechwriter Ted Sorensen's younger brother Phil, its board included "enemies" like Fred Harris, Edmund Muskie, and Walter Mondale. After two and a half years of waiting for the IRS to approve its application for exemption, and with its funds depleted, the Center sued Treasury Secretary George Shultz and IRS Commissioner Donald Alexander for deliberate delays. As part of its suit, the Center presented a photocopy of its application which had a handwritten note, "pressure from the White House," scrawled in the margin. The Center's attorneys noted that the Rulings Section of the IRS had prepared a favorable report in October 1972, that the Conference and Review Section of the Exempt Organizations Branch had given the application a favorable comment in January 1973, and that the IRS chief counsel's office had issued a favorable ruling on February 20, 1973. At that time the file went to Roger Barth, the White House operative within Internal Revenue. Barth had June Norris of the Rulings Division prepare an eighty-page adverse ruling, which she did at home and on her own time. Only after the case went to court did the IRS turn down the Center's application for exemption, on May 16, 1973. Finally, in July 1973, Judge Charles Richey of the U.S. Court for the District of Columbia ordered the IRS to grant a tax exemption to the Center.[28]

Nixon also used the IRS to attack ethnic groups that he believed opposed him. In particular, he blamed many of his problems on Jews. He believed, for example, that there was a "Jewish cabal" at the Bureau of Labor Statistics that cast the effects of the administration's economic policies in an unfavorable light. Haldeman ordered aide Fred Malek to do an " 'ethnic' survey of the BLS." Twenty-five of the top thirty-five officials, Malek reported, were Democrats, and thirteen of the thirty-five were Jewish. Nixon's White House tapes reveal that he pushed for IRS tax audits of wealthy Jews who contributed to Democrats. "Could we please investigate some of the cocksuckers," he directed Haldeman. Even individuals who sought to work on Nixon's reelection campaign, such as Lawrence Goldberg, were investigated on the suspicion that their Jewish ties made them covert opponents of the president. Vernon "Mike" Acree, IRS assistant commissioner for inspections, provided the

White House not only with information on Goldberg's taxes but with copies of his actual tax returns.[29]

During the summer and early fall of 1971, these "enemies" activities accelerated. Almost everyone in the White House seemed to play some role, although, as it sought to locate accountability during its investigation of the Plumbers and abuse of the IRS, the Watergate Special Prosecution Force encountered layers of conflicting testimony from all the participants. Once the matter was out in the open, everyone blamed everyone else, or claimed that what they had done had been naively done in all innocence. Investigators, to put it mildly, were skeptical, and what they uncovered justified their skepticism.

In mid-August 1971 various Haldeman aides met to develop "oral recommendations for political intelligence and covert activities." Attorney General John Mitchell was to contact the IRS about the exempt status of the National Movement for the Student Vote, an anti-Nixon group. He apparently did so, because in March 1972, Mike Acree of the IRS sent Dean a two-page report on the organization as well as a listing of its national advisory board. On the basis of a complaint, the IRS had investigated the organization in late 1971 but found in its favor. By this time Murray Chotiner had provided at least two different lists of individuals to be audited. Dean initially suggested that they develop a list of ten enemies for Lyn Nofziger to target for IRS scrutiny rather than undertake "any elaborate plan or system because of ineffectiveness and risk of discovery." But clearly this initial list was a trial run. "We can learn more about how to operate such an activity," Dean noted, "if we start small and build."[30]

Momentum built quickly, however. By early fall several lists were in preparation. At one point Jack Caulfield met Mike Acree in Caulfield's office in the Executive Office Building. They walked to John Dean's office, where the three men discussed how to initiate audits on a list of about twenty individuals that Dean handed Acree. According to Watergate investigators, "Acree indicated that he could not initiate audits on all of the names on the list," and the men agreed that he would "commence audits on four of the names which were checked off by Dean." Acree wrote the names on a piece of paper and left the room with Caulfield. This entire transaction took about ten minutes. After returning to Caulfield's office, Acree expressed concern that Dean's request was "dynamite."[31]

That one effort quickly blossomed into a major campaign. In early September, Nixon complained to Ehrlichman that "we have the power but are we using it to investigate contributors to Hubert Humphrey;

contributors to Muskie, the Jews, you know, that are stealing every [deleted]?" The next day Colson sent Dean a list of political opponents, with "top priority opponents" marked in blue. Less than a week later Dean forwarded to Haldeman aide Larry Higby a list of names Higby had requested. Most were the same names provided earlier by Colson. Dean also received additional lists from Higby and Haldeman aide Gordon Strachan, as well as a list of McGovern supporters prepared at Ehrlichman's direction by Murray Chotiner. A few weeks later Erhlichman aide David Young indicated that Dean had sent the names to Johnnie Walters for review.

Colson also pressured Dean to investigate the tax exemption of the Urban League, complaining that recent remarks by the League's Vernon Jordan were political in nature. Dean's aide David Wilson prepared a memorandum on the matter, concluding that action was not advisable. Any IRS investigation would entail not only the League's activities but the context in which they occurred. It would, therefore, run the risk of a leak. At the moment, political prudence indicated that this be avoided. Civil rights groups were certain to scrutinize the two pending Supreme Court nominations, and "any hint of possible Administration pressure against what is one of the most conservative civil rights organizations would be disastrous."[32]

The administration then turned its attention to filmmaker Emile de Antonio, who had recently produced "Millhouse: A White Comedy," a satirical film derogatory to the president. Caulfield suggested to Dean that the administration immediately attack the film by discrediting its producer, arguing that the Democratic National Committee was interested in a massive distribution of "Millhouse" starting in January 1972. Warning that any action "should be weighed carefully and well hidden," Caulfield proposed IRS audits of de Antonio as well as film distributor Daniel Talbot and New Yorker Films, and urged the release of derogatory FBI information on de Antonio. Fred Fielding cautioned Dean that, while the Democrats might use the film "quite effectively to garner the 18–21 yr old vote" against Nixon, leaking information and initiating IRS audits "doesn't seem to be a solution that will help us." It would likely "send de Antonio flying into the arms of the DNC" and give the film greater publicity. This became one of many ongoing political intelligence projects under John Dean's supervision. Dean advised Strachan that his staff would "monitor the situation and try to do anything we can to deal with it."[33]

But Strachan, whom his secretary later characterized as "completely loyal to Haldeman" and a person who would "never express any opinion" of his own, complained that "covert complicated intelligence" was "simply not being done." In a longer memo to Haldeman that accompanied an IRS "talking paper," Strachan enumerated four problems. The administration had been "unable to crack down on the multitude of tax exempt foundations that feed left-wing political causes," unable to obtain information "in possession of IRS re. our political enemies," failed to "stimulate audits" of individuals who "should be audited," and failed to place Nixon supporters "in the IRS bureaucracy." The purpose of the talking paper was to give Dean greater access to "political info within the IRS," especially through examining selected tax returns, to give Malek personal authority to "replace entrenched democratic bureaucrats," and to get rid of Johnnie Walters's deputy commissioner William Loeb, who the administration believed (probably through Roger Barth) had exerted his "Democratic credentials" to thwart administration requests for action. This use of the IRS, attorney John Doar later reported, was an "abuse of the powers granted to the President by the Constitution to superintend the agencies of the executive branch" and a "challenge to the integrity of the tax system."[34]

By the close of 1971 the administration had asked for IRS information on several other individuals and organizations. The Joint Fall Peace Fund was added to the opponents list in mid-November, based on a newspaper advertisement it sponsored. Roger Barth asked the IRS for information about the Association of Student Governments as well as copies of its tax returns. Bayard Rustin, executive director of the A. Philip Randolph Educational Fund, complained that the fund was subjected to two IRS audits, though neither led to any government action. Rustin also charged that he was personally under surveillance and was convinced that his telephone was tapped. Paranoia struck deep, but it was often warranted.[35]

Haldeman, Fred Malek, and John Connally all spearheaded efforts to make the IRS more responsive in advance of the 1972 election. It was a key source for political intelligence, but they were convinced that it remained underutilized despite efforts on the Enemies Lists. The White House eagerly sought the tax returns of all potential Democratic presidential contenders, hoping to dig up tax troubles for them as well as to compile lists of contributors for the IRS to target. To do this the White House had in place a network of individuals committed to violating individuals' privacy and securing tax data. Jack Caulfield, described by one Watergate witness as the "White House gumshoe," sought IRS audit reports, often working through Mike Acree. According to attorney Bernard Fensterwald, former chief investigator for Senator Edward

Long, when Assistant Commissioner Donald Bacon insisted on written requests he was forced to retire. Acree and Caulfield met with Roger Barth, the three men brought together by Myles Ambrose (whom Acree later succeeded as commissioner of customs). Roy Kinsey, a member of White House counsel John Dean's staff, later testified that Barth was the "person I normally dealt with in the Internal Revenue Service," particularly on "politically sensitive matters." A later Senate investigation revealed that about half the people targeted in the Enemies Program were audited. Involvement in these "enemies" activities was apparently a pathway to promotion. Gordon Liddy later told attorney Douglas Caddy that he broke into the DNC headquarters at the Watergate because, if successful, he would then demand to be appointed assistant secretary of the Treasury. He believed that the administration "owed it to me."[36]

When the Watergate Special Prosecution Force later assembled its evidence, it related the procedures through which this system of harassment worked. Ambrose, an assistant attorney general, and Caulfield met frequently with Acree, carrying requests for income tax information that they said had come from presidential counsel John Dean. Acree requested the returns, and others analyzed them for potential tax problems. Anonymous complaints were then prepared—what the IRS called "squeals"—and these served as justification for forwarding requests for tax audits against those persons designated by Dean, Caulfield, and Ambrose. Although Acree later testified that he had never requested similar name checks during any of the three previous administrations, he was able to implement them during the Nixon years without the knowledge or authorization of the IRS commissioner. So long as there were no leaks, everyone was protected. During 1972, requests for these audits proliferated.[37]

An examination of White House requests reveals the breadth of the administration's efforts. Chuck Colson sent John Dean a steady stream of names, asking for audits on such groups as Common Cause, Vietnam Veterans Against the War, and the National Council of Senior Citizens. Other White House aides added to the Enemies List the names of all individuals involved with the National Committee for the Impeachment of the President. The White House asked the FBI to investigate leaders of this group, in addition to having the IRS probe its tax status. This request accompanied a list of dozens of individuals that Watergate prosecutors later believed to have been the subject of FBI investigations, at the request of the White House, for purely political purposes. The list included members of Congress and the media. After Watergate, enemies seemed to be everywhere; Haldeman and Nixon asked Dean to keep a list of people who attacked the administration in the press so that they could "give them trouble after the election." They targeted war protesters as potential tax resisters, along with individuals such as Doris Day, Frank Sinatra, Armand Hammer, and groups like the Church of Scientology, the Gay Liberation Front, sponsors of a "salute to Walter Reuther," the Concerned Veterans of Vietnam, the American Indian Movement, and the Black Panther party.[38]

The administration seemed particularly interested in the Black Panthers. The FBI was investigating and attempting to destabilize the Panthers; now the White House wanted the IRS to ferret out the organization's funding, plans, and operations. The IRS might be able to trace its sources of funding, and the administration could then initiate tax audits against Panther supporters. The Panthers, according to the White House, represented the "most serious long-range security threat to the country," and it demanded "more and better hard intelligence about their operations." The White House also believed that almost "every revolutionary organization" operating in the country was in "violation of some section of the Internal Revenue Code," and complained that IRS cooperation with other federal investigatory agencies had been "inadequate." It urged the IRS to implement the strike force concept, to work with the FBI and other agencies in "a full scale effort" against "revolutionary organizations." But, aides complained, the IRS lacked a "leadership team" that was "disposed to cooperate in these areas." That would have to change. Until it did, however, greater efforts should "be made to enlist what support we can get from the IRS."[39]

As the 1972 fall campaign season approached, Nixon's demands for domestic intelligence became almost insatiable. In a diary entry for August 3, H. R. Haldeman noted that Nixon and Ehrlichman had discussed the need "to get some action on tax and other matters involving people supporting the opposition." The Nixon tapes are more explicit. "Are we looking over McGovern's [the Democratic nominee] financial contributors?" Nixon asked. "Are we running their income tax returns?" "We have all this power," Nixon complained to Ehrlichman, "and we aren't using it." At the moment, Ehrlichman replied, nothing was being done. That changed quickly, and ten days later Nixon emphasized the need to run tax checks on McGovern's contributors once again as well as determine if they had links to the left wing or the Mafia. Nixon and John Connally agreed that "we now have to pour on the coal in following up any investigations of the top Democratic officials which might yield some pay dirt." Connally believed that the "dirt" was there, and

Nixon instructed that either Haldeman or Ehrlichman assume "personal responsibility" for getting several specific files "within the next 24 hours." Experts should comb them carefully and construct criminal cases or release derogatory information.[40]

This pre-election push actually began at least as early as June, when Chuck Colson wrote an "Eyes Only" memo to John Dean reporting a tip he had received that Harold Gibbons, a liberal Teamsters Union vice president who had endorsed George McGovern for president, had income tax discrepancies. Gibbons, according to Colson, was "an all out enemy, a McGovernite, ardently anti-Nixon." Colson demanded an immediate investigation and asked if there were an "informer's fee," promising to donate it to a "good cause."[41] By August anti-McGovern efforts were in high gear. Prompted by Nixon, Ehrlichman directed Murray Chotiner to prepare lists of major McGovern contributors and prominent McGovern staff members. Chotiner called presidential assistant William Timmons and asked him to check with the House Internal Security Committee to see if he could secure records of "subversive activities by a known list of McGovern supporters." Timmons discovered that this was possible, and Chotiner promptly sent him a list of two hundred names. A few weeks later the list came back with annotations. Chotiner also compiled the larger McGovern lists, one that included approximately five hundred names of contributors and another with seventy McGovern staff people on it. He gave them to John Dean, who presented them to IRS Commissioner Johnnie Walters at a September 11, 1972, meeting in Dean's White House office with instructions to commence investigations or audits. There was no evidence, however, that any of these individuals had any tax problems, nor did Dean suggest this to Walters. Walters said later that he warned Dean: "If you really want pie on our face, I will do it; but this will make Watergate look like a Sunday school picnic."[42]

The White House attempted to do all of this, of course, without publicity. Dean requested IRS action that would not "cause ripples." He pressed Walters, but no evidence ever surfaced that the IRS acted upon Ehrlichman's and Dean's requests. Walters discussed the matter with Treasury Secretary George Shultz on at least two occasions, and both men agreed that action was not warranted. Walters then apparently locked the lists in his office safe. Dean, Tod Hullin (Ehrlichman's administrative assistant), and Larry Higby (Haldeman's administrative assistant) discussed the issue, as did Chotiner and Ehrlichman, and possibly Haldeman. Meanwhile, Maurice Stans, Nixon's chief fundraiser, pressed liberal Republicans in Connecticut about their failure to contribute to Nixon. After indicating their intention not to do so, each received notice of an IRS audit. The coincidence was striking! Despite the apparent refusal of the IRS to take action, Watergate investigators concluded that the attempt itself constituted a violation of law. It represented, they argued, a conspiracy to defraud the United States, a civil rights conspiracy, and an "attempted interference with the due administration of internal revenue laws." The failure of Walters and Shultz to inform the Justice Department about these White House efforts also constituted "questionable conduct." The attack on the McGovern campaign, moreover, was part of a larger White House effort to initiate "counter-actions" against negative Watergate publicity.[43]

Walters's refusal to act set the stage for his forced departure as IRS commissioner. White House tapes reveal that during a September 15 meeting in the oval office, Nixon asked about IRS action on the list. For more than a quarter-hour Nixon, Dean, and Haldeman talked about the problems of conducting audits, with Nixon complaining that Shultz had not been sufficiently responsive to White House requests. Nixon insisted that the Treasury secretary "should be made to understand the political significance of the IRS." The discussion also focused on administration personnel to be removed after the fall election. Johnnie Walters's name headed the list. Nixon intended to turn Chuck Colson loose while distancing him somewhat from the White House. In Haldeman's words: "You let him go ruthless until you kill these people."[44]

The September 15 meeting tapes reveal Nixon's anticipation of a time when he would have the Justice Department and the IRS "totally under our control" so he could oust all Democrats and use both agencies to his advantage. Until the election was over, however, the White House had to deal cautiously with the IRS. "We have to do it artfully," Nixon said, "so that we don't create an issue by abusing the IRS politically." He then noted that "there are ways to do it. God damn it, sneak in the middle of the night." Dean agreed, noting that Acree had obtained information for him without going "through Walters or anyone else." But now Acree was commissioner of the customs and Walters was an obstacle who, according to Dean, was a "disappointment." He would be out, Nixon said, as of November 8 if not earlier. Get the tax information, Nixon ranted, "even if we've got to kick Walters' ass out first and get a man in there."[45]

Ten days later Dean queried Walters about his progress on the lists. Walters replied that there had been none, and told Dean that he and Shultz had agreed that the "project should not be undertaken." Dean then asked for tax checks or audits on even fifty or sixty or seventy of the names. Walters replied that they "can't do anything on this list" but promised to advise Shultz of their conversation. Shultz agreed to handle future inquires, but apparently there were none. When Walters left office in April 1973 he took a copy of the lists with him. Nixon was upset at the lack of progress, and later discussions between Nixon and Haldeman revealed their determination to pursue the matter. They would use the IRS to go after foundations to "scare the shit out of them," in Haldeman's words—as well as to target individual opponents such as Katharine Graham of the *Washington Post*. Whether or not the IRS ever found any tax problems was secondary to the effort itself. Both men believed that the investigations alone would mute their opposition and keep them too preoccupied to bother the administration.[46]

During 1971 and 1972 the Nixon White House sought to protect friends as well as target enemies. Not surprisingly, the "friends" list was much shorter than the Enemies Lists. As early as October 1969 the administration had intervened with the IRS to secure a favorable tax ruling for International Telephone and Telegraph (ITT). The White House staff, apparently at the request of Alexander Haig, also asked the IRS to check on the status of a tax exemption for the University Centers for Rational Alternatives (a group of faculty, organized by Sidney Hook of New York University, that sought to defend academic freedom and opposed student violence). Roger Barth set up a meeting between representatives of the group and the IRS in December 1969, and indicated that the exemption would be forthcoming. The administration also suppressed charges of tax evasion and security violations by Manufacturers Hanover Trust Company, where the father of White House aide Peter Flanigan was chairman of the board. South Carolina Republican state chairman Harry Dent complained that special agents of the IRS had demanded a list of individuals who had contributed $1,000 or more to the South Carolina Republican Committee from 1966 through 1969. Roger Barth promptly wrote Ehrlichman and Haldeman about the matter, hoping to curtail any investigations.[47]

The real concerns of the White House focused on individuals closer to the president. In 1971, Ehrlichman complained to IRS Commissioner Thrower that the agency was harassing Donald Nixon, the president's brother. Noting that Donald Nixon was a "potential source of embarrassment," Ehrlichman asked Thrower to intervene. The commissioner looked into the matter and discovered that personal issues as well as a potential criminal fraud investigation had piqued IRS interest. The investigation continued.

More dangerous was the C. Arnholt Smith case which, Thrower was told, would "send tremors through the Administration." He never specified exactly what he meant, but it likely referred to a case being put together by an organized crime strike force in Southern California against Smith for conspiracy and violation of the Corrupt Practices Act. In short, Smith had used a company he controlled as an illegal conduit for money to defray some of Nixon's 1968 campaign expenses. (Documents connected with this case later disappeared in 1972.) Smith had long been a leading Nixon patron. He had raised millions of dollars to support Nixon's political career and had ties to the Del Charro Hotel in La Jolla, California, as well as the La Costa resort development south of San Clemente. Both projects had ties to various gangsters as well as the Teamsters.

Smith's banking interests were linked to the gambling activities of John Alessio. Alessio, also from San Diego, had extensive bookmaking and banking operations in Mexico, and Smith had been his mentor. Although Alessio had been named "Mr. San Diego" in 1964, he was later jailed for not reporting to the IRS $1.2 million he skimmed from his racetrack operations.

Despite the warning, Commissioner Thrower told the district director to pursue the matter. Roger Barth later called Tod Hullin's office to pass along the information that the columnist Jack Anderson was probing for evidence linking President Nixon and Smith with John Alessio. As the next chapter will relate, even more serious IRS problems surfaced in the exposure of links between Nixon, Bebe Rebozo, Howard Hughes, and Lawrence O'Brien. In all of these cases John Ehrlichman was the principal figure, largely because of his ties to Roger Barth.[48]

Meanwhile Nixon instructed White House aides to head off IRS tax investigations into several of his friends, including the evangelist Billy Graham and the actor John Wayne. In August 1971, Haldeman received a memo about the Wayne case from Dean, through Higby. Roger Barth examined the Sensitive Case Report on Graham, found what he thought were discrepancies, and went to Mike Acree, IRS assistant commissioner for inspection, to learn more about the case. The Nixon tapes reveal that at a September 13 oval office meeting, Nixon complained to Haldeman that Internal Revenue's pursuit of Graham had not been terminated, and that the IRS was "battering the shit out of him." Nixon sought to counterattack by having the IRS investigate wealthy liberals, Democratic celebrities, and Jews. In late September, however, Jack Caulfield reported to Dean that Billy Graham was under IRS audit for his 1965, 1966, 1969, and 1970 returns. The IRS was concerned that he had not declared various gifts he had received as taxable income and had received free construction and decorator work. Caulfield's efforts to track the source of the audit revealed only that it probably stemmed from an "anonymous telephone call." He warned Dean that as IRS investigators contacted several of the donors, the issue might "surface in the media." Caulfield suggested that Walters simply terminate the audit. In response to Higby's query about what could be done, Haldeman replied that it was "already covered."[49]

The Wayne complaint, Caulfield told Dean, did not seem worth pursuing. In a detailed memo dated October 6, 1971, Caulfield provided Dean with data on audit examinations of various individuals in the entertainment industry, including Richard Boone, Sammy Davis, Jr., Jerry Lewis, Peter Lawford, Fred MacMurray, Gary Morton, Lucille Ball, Ronald Reagan, and Frank Sinatra. Caulfield indicated that this was a response to a request from Dean a week earlier, and that he had chosen individuals who had been politically active in prior elections. In sum, he said, John Wayne's experience was similar to theirs. All of his information, Caulfield later testified, came from Mike Acree at IRS, though Acree later professed to remember nothing about the matter.[50] By that time, moreover, the White House was much more worried about IRS probes into the affairs of Nixon intimate Bebe Rebozo, his links to Howard Hughes, and the connection between Hughes and Democratic National Committee chairman Larry O'Brien. White House staff feared that multiple tangled webs might unravel and expose Nixon on several fronts.

CHAPTER TWELVE

DANGEROUS RELATIONSHIPS: THE REBOZO-HUGHES-O'BRIEN CONNECTION

W HEN PRESIDENT RICHARD NIXON sought to use the Internal Revenue Service to punish enemies and to go lightly on his friends, he ran into a dilemma. Some of the enemies were linked to some of the friends, in a web so tangled that protecting one person and punishing another seemed impossible. So central was use of the IRS to Nixon's political agenda, however, that he tried nonetheless. The most important of these relationships, and undoubtedly the most involved, were those between his good friend Charles "Bebe" Rebozo, the reclusive yet powerful Howard Hughes, and Democratic National Committee chairman and archenemy Lawrence O'Brien. Connections between these three individuals also linked Nixon to an assortment of shady financial dealings, questionable real estate transactions, and an array of underworld characters and mobsters. With respect to Rebozo, Hughes, and O'Brien, investigations by the news media and the IRS threatened to reveal covert linkages and money transfers that underlay Richard Nixon's entire political career. Nixon feared that revelations about these individuals' activities would reveal his own dark past, and he used the power of his office in an effort to prevent investigations and conceal that past. There is reason to believe, in fact, that Nixon's concern and the dilemma it caused led directly to the Watergate break-in.

These dangerous relationships were often convoluted and not always direct. Most dangerous for the president was the Rebozo-Hughes connection, which threatened to expose a long trail of corruption involving Nixon. To make matters worse, Richard Nixon's brother Donald had a financial connection to Hughes that was troubling. Larry O'Brien, in turn, was a sworn "enemy" of Nixon's, and his close ties to Howard Hughes threatened to expose Nixon's affairs on another, more dangerous flank. As head of the Democratic National Committee and supporter of George McGovern, O'Brien might have his own motives for action. An IRS investigation of the O'Brien-Hughes relationship threatened to involve Nixon. Not surprisingly, therefore, Nixon was anxious to target O'Brien and muzzle him for the duration of the 1972 campaign. In each of these instances a politically responsive IRS was crucial to investigate and intimidate, thereby to prevent Nixon's presidency from unraveling.

Let's begin with a friend, Charles "Bebe" Rebozo, who had long-standing ties to Richard Nixon. Rebozo was a wealthy Cuban-American with extensive real estate and banking operations in South Florida. Born in poverty, he started with a Shell gas station in the 1930s, then during World War II went into the tire recapping business. It became profitable when wartime tire rationing made reuse essential. By the end of the war Rebozo had become the largest tire recapper in South Florida and had developed ties to three men who served on the state's tire allocation board. Frank Smathers, father of later Rebozo and Nixon friend George Smathers, served on the board, as did Lucien Renuart, who had loaned Rebozo the money to expand his business, as well as C. W. Chase, Jr., who hired Margaret Barker, Rebozo's sister, to work in his Chase Savings and Loan Association. This bank later was the source of capital for Rebozo's real estate purchases. Smathers helped get a ruling from the Office of Price Administration (OPA) about the legality of bringing tires into the United States from Cuba. Working in the interpretations unit of the OPA during the war, coincidentally, was Richard Nixon.[1]

Rebozo met Nixon sometime in the 1940s. George Smathers, a fellow Congressman (though a Democrat), and Richard Danner arranged for Nixon to visit South Florida. Danner, who had been Smathers's campaign manager, headed the FBI's Miami office in the early 1940s and then served as city manager of Miami Beach from 1946 to 1948, a time that one publication called "the heyday of mob rule." The Miami city council dismissed him after he was caught brokering local gangsters' efforts to control the Miami police force. Later Danner went to work for Howard Hughes, courtesy of former FBI agent Robert Maheu (who was later employed by General Motors to spy on Ralph Nader in the mid-1960s). Rebozo was intimately involved with anti-revolutionary Cuban exiles who became active in the branch of the Lansky-Trafficante mob in Florida and the Bahamas.[2]

By the 1960s Rebozo had created a financial empire, establishing the Key Biscayne National Bank as the only bank on Key Biscayne Island. The first person to open a savings account was Richard Nixon. By 1968, Rebozo and the bank were in trouble with the Securities and Exchange Commission for receiving stolen stock from underworld figures. None of this was generally known at the time, and neither Rebozo nor Nixon wanted it public. The bank later became a repository for Nixon slush-fund deposits from Howard Hughes, and may have been the center for campaign money laundering as well. Rebozo used his bank and his connections with George Smathers and Richard Nixon to become very wealthy. He also secured several guaranteed loans from the Small Business Administration without fully disclosing his business dealings. He built a Miami shopping center with one of the loans, hiring Alfredo "Big Al" Polizzi as his contractor. "Big Al" was an underworld figure with convictions for tax evasion, smuggling, and black marketeering who had ties to Meyer Lansky and other Mafia figures. To manage the project Rebozo hired Edgardo Buttari, a former mayor of Havana under Cuban dictator Fulgencio Batista. Buttari later ran the Cubans for Nixon effort in 1968, and claimed to be close friends with Rebozo and Nixon. One of the shopping center's early tenants was Manuel Artime, a CIA-supported military commander in the 1961 Bay of Pigs invasion who was later a financial conduit for the Watergate burglars. Imprisoned on the Isle of Pines until ransomed by Robert Kennedy, by 1963 Artime was running a CIA-backed naval guerrilla base in Guatemala to train recruits for a second invasion of Cuba. He also headed the MRR (Insurrectional Movement for the Recovery of the Revolution). Later evidence surfaced that placed Artime close to former CIA agent and Watergate figure E. Howard Hunt as well as Bernard Barker (Rebozo's brother-in-law).[3]

In the early 1960s Richard Nixon invested in Florida land through a "secretive investment syndicate headed by Bebe Rebozo," which bought Fisher Island off the southern tip of Miami Beach. Nixon eventually owned more than 185,000 shares of the enterprise, and doubled his investment when he sold the shares in 1969. This was a speculative venture; the investors hoped that construction of a causeway linking Fisher Island to the Florida mainland would escalate land values on the island. The prospects for financial gain attracted individuals such as Leonard

Bursten to work with Rebozo. Bursten, a Milwaukee attorney, had worked for Senator Joseph McCarthy in Washington and had later helped secure asylum in the United States for Cuban dictator Batista. He was a friend of Jimmy Hoffa and was later convicted for income tax evasion. Nathan Ratner, whose father was a Cleveland builder, arranged for the sale of Fisher Island to Rebozo's syndicate and oversaw plans for its development. He also owned more than 3,000 shares in the Bank of Miami Beach, a bank formed in 1955 to "service organized crime based in the Havana gambling empire" and controlled at one time by mobster Samuel Cohen. Cohen, together with Morris Lansburgh, owned the Flamingo Hotel in Las Vegas, for which they reputedly paid a finder's fee of $200,000 to Meyer Lansky. They purchased the hotel from Albert Parvin, who leveraged loans from the Teamsters into the construction of several Las Vegas hotels and casinos, contracting with mobster Bugsy Siegel for decorations and furnishings. In 1960, Parvin formed the Albert Parvin Foundation, apparently from Flamingo Hotel stock. This was sinister company.

These ties led to others. Ratner was involved in various Key Biscayne land deals as a broker for Keyes Realty. Both Rebozo and Nixon had close ties to Keyes Realty executives, and Keyes Realty was an "investment funnel for the hundreds of millions of dollars that syndicate figures and freebooting Cuban politicians hauled out of Batista's Cuba." By 1971, Eugenio Martinez, later a Watergate burglar, was a vice president in Keyes Realty. Together with Bernard Barker (also of Watergate infamy), Martinez formed another real estate firm, Ameritas, that served as "a cover for the principals of the Watergate break-in." Watergate special prosecutors later pursued these links between various Cubans, Rebozo, Nixon, and Smathers, trying to flesh out details of any "disclosed or undisclosed interests Rebozo may have in corporations which are literally holding companies for other enterprises." They were also concerned about Rebozo's dealings in pre-Castro Cuba as well as his ties to Resorts International and Worldwide Realty.[4] Needless to say, Nixon did not want his ties to these individuals and organizations made public.

There was more. During the 1960s, Rebozo was a partner with Donald Berg in another real estate company. Berg had a dark past and was a former friend to associates of Meyer Lansky as well as Richard Nixon. Berg, Rebozo, and Nixon became involved in the purchase of land in Key Biscayne that one investigative reporter revealed had been "owned for twenty years by various fronts of organized crime" and by former Cuban dictator Fulgencio Batista. After Nixon became president, the Secret Service asked him not to eat at Berg's Key Biscayne restaurant because of Berg's unsavory connections. Another individual interested in Key Biscayne land was Arthur Desser, a friend of Jimmy Hoffa, whose Teamsters Union loan helped Desser purchase the land. Desser's real estate company then became connected with the Miami National Bank, which the Teamsters controlled and which had connections to mobster Meyer Lansky. Nixon later bought this land but concealed his investment for several years, until after Arthur Desser's mortgage was paid. During this same time Richard Nixon served as a director of the Miami National Bank, together with Desser (a front man for Jimmy Hoffa) and Lou Poller (a front man for Meyer Lansky).[5]

Another potential problem for Nixon that he feared an IRS investigation would reveal was the activities of the American National Insurance Company (ANICO) of Galveston, Texas. ANICO had close ties to John Connally, who served as secretary of the Treasury under Nixon, and to former Assistant Attorney General Will Wilson (later one of the targets in the IRS's Southwest Project). It had loaned millions of dollars to Las Vegas gambling casinos, to mob attorney (and friend of Missouri Senator Edward V. Long) Morris Shenker, as well as to the Mary Carter Paint Company (which became Resorts International) and a Worldwide Realty subsidiary. The latter two firms had links to bookmaking in the Bahamas. The head of Resorts International, James Crosby, was suspected of running a skimming operation and depositing the funds in Rebozo's bank. Crosby had ties to the Meyer Lansky syndicate through his casino in the Bahamas. His deputy director of security, James Golden, had been Nixon's staff security chief as well as security director for both the Republican National Convention in Miami and the 1969 inauguration. Intertel, a subsidiary of Resorts International, was hired to spy on the columnist Jack Anderson by ITT after Anderson had reported "curious cash flows" from Rebozo's bank to the Cosmos Bank in Switzerland. Intertel was a private operation organized by veterans of the Secret Service, CIA, FBI, and Justice Department. It was headed by Robert Peloquin and was on retainer with Howard Hughes. Peloquin was a former organized-crime investigator in the Justice Department who left to become an officer in a new gambling casino on Paradise Island in the Bahamas, a casino that hosted Richard Nixon at its opening gala in January 1968.[6]

An important aside to the Intertel question was that it spawned a crash effort by the administration to form its own intelligence service. In the summer of 1971, Jack Caulfield proposed creation of "Sandwedge," a private political intelligence security organization designed to be the Republican counterpart to Intertel. At various meetings with

Mike Acree of the IRS, Roger Barth, and Joe Woods (a Cook County, Illinois, commissioner, former FBI agent, and brother of Nixon's confidential secretary Rosemary Woods), first in the Black Steer Bar on 17th Street in Washington and later at Caulfield's home in Fairfax, Virginia, the men developed a proposal. By mid-October, at the direction of Attorney General John Mitchell, Nixon's personal attorney Herbert Kalmbach had given Caulfield $50,000 for the operation. A month later, however, a talking paper for Mitchell questioned if they were "really developing the capability needed?" Another $100,000 to $300,000 was needed for political surveillance. By December the idea was apparently dead and the White House had turned to Gordon Liddy. But Caulfield persisted, and by June 1972 he had prepared a lengthy prospectus. Acree was expected to provide IRS input (something he later denied). The effort was essential, Caulfield argued, because the "Kennedy mafia" dominated the political intelligence field, and Larry O'Brien's presence as DNC chairman guaranteed an extensive Democratic covert intelligence effort during the campaign. Aimed at creating greater intelligence capabilities for the 1972 campaign, Sandwedge would be "surfacely disassociated from the Administration by virtue of an established business cover." Caulfield noted:

> The offensive involvement outlined above would be supported, *supervised* and programmed by the principals, but *completely disassociated* (separate foolproof financing) from the corporate structure and located in New York City in extreme clandestine fashion. My source would be charged with setting up and supervising this operation. In other words, he would not surface.[7]

It was to be extra insurance to protect Nixon's secrets.

Given all of these nefarious and secret links between Richard Nixon, his close friend Bebe Rebozo, and a host of organized crime figures and their conduits, both Rebozo and the White House became acutely anxious in early 1971 when rumors surfaced that a Long Island newspaper, *Newsday*, was investigating Rebozo, Nixon, Smathers, and banking and real estate dealings in South Florida. Rebozo first heard about the investigation in February 1971. *Newsday* investigative reporters combed through Rebozo's 1949 divorce as well as every one of Rebozo's land purchases and transactions. They also conducted more than four hundred interviews. Worried about what they might uncover, Rebozo talked with White House staff about the impending stories and how to block them.[8]

Newsday editor Robert Greene headed the investigation. Greene, who had been an investigator for the McClellan Committee in the late 1950s, tried repeatedly (and without success) to interview Rebozo. Before Greene went to Florida in March 1971, he talked with a special agent in the Internal Revenue Service's Mineola, New York, office about the Fisher Island Corporation. The agent became a liaison to Greene and prepared a standard item of information form about Greene's comments. In a move clearly designed to keep this information out of normal bureaucratic channels, his supervisor, Vince Clayton, instructed him to draft a handwritten memo rather than use the standard form. This was sent to Howard McHenry, chief of intelligence at the IRS Brooklyn District office (and later North Atlantic regional commissioner for intelligence) in a double-sealed envelope. The agent, codenamed "Zip," raised tax questions about the Fisher Island Corporation with respect to Nixon and George Smathers. McHenry instructed Zip to stay in touch with Greene and to let him (McHenry) know when the series was to be published. When he learned this information, Zip called McHenry, who in turn instructed him to call Leon Green in Washington and to identify himself. He was to refer to "Operation Greenhouse." At the time, Leon Green was deputy to the assistant IRS commissioner of compliance.[9]

Greene's team of *Newsday* reporters spent three months at the Key Biscayne Hotel and attracted considerable attention. Greene later told Watergate investigators that Secret Service agents visited them in Key Biscayne, and that he believed a woman from the Dade County clerk's office was reporting on the team's work to Rebozo. The FBI conducted a series of interviews with local residents about the *Newsday* investigation, though no criminal activity had been alleged, and the White House detailed Jack Caulfield to investigate the newspaper. Caulfield forwarded a summary of the FBI interviews to the White House, where several aides, including Haldeman, Gordon Strachan, and Fred Fielding, read the memorandum. White House counsel John Dean also talked with Rebozo about the investigation. Greene later requested an interview with President Nixon about his Key Biscayne holdings, but was denied. Greene then submitted fifty-three questions to Nixon. Acting through Dean, the White House refused to reply. By late July 1971 the White House had decided to move beyond harassment and to retaliate. A memorandum of July 26 stated that "we need the IRS program for looking at the people involved in the *Newsday* investigation. . . . We need a plan that covers all the things that can be done to utilize the assets available while we have that opportunity."[10]

Haldeman gave Dean two assignments to launch the retaliation. He was to explore the possibility of having the Justice Department file an anti-trust suit against the *Los Angeles Times*, which owned *Newsday*, and also have the IRS begin tax audits on reporters working on the story as well as on Otis Chandler, the *Times'* publisher. Dean asked Caulfield to arrange the audits. Although former IRS Commissioner Randolph Thrower did not believe the system would allow Caulfield to initiate audits, the wily White House employee found ways to circumvent the system. He reported to Dean that he had contacted a "knowledgeable source at the IRS" (Mike Acree) and posed a hypothetical situation of a White House request for tax audits on individuals. He discovered, however, that IRS procedures required such requests to go through Assistant Commissioner Donald Bacon. Bacon, Caulfield complained to Dean, was "a liberal Democratic holdover who had been continually identified with anti-Nixon intrigues at IRS within the past two years." That avenue would not work. Acree suggested, however, that Caulfield target members of the group who lived in New York, because "such target could discreetly be made subject to IRS audit without the clear hazard for a leak traceable to the White House." Later, during Watergate, Nixon attorney James St. Clair argued that it was "ridiculous" to "suggest that the administration was able to manipulate the Internal Revenue Service," citing the use of anonymous letters for evidence.[11]

Throughout August 1971, Caulfield and Dean worked on the problem of the upcoming *Newsday* articles. Haldeman instructed Dean to discuss the matter with John Connally and Johnnie Walters, though Walters later said that he did not discuss the matter with anyone at the White House. Dean also forwarded material about the reporters' activities to Attorney General John Mitchell, following a conversation between the two men. Caulfield reported regularly to Dean, and in mid-September Haldeman discussed efforts to get something on Greene with President Nixon. Leon Green of the IRS furnished a copy of the Service's Sensitive Case Report on the *Newsday* investigation to Roger Barth, who likely forwarded it to the White House. White House efforts apparently knew no bounds.[12]

On October 6, 1971, the first article in the *Newsday* series appeared, with five subsequent articles published over the next week. The investigative team had collected thousands of documents, and both Rebozo and Nixon were alarmed at what might be revealed. As soon as the first article hit the newsstands, Rebozo called Attorney General John Mitchell to see if he should file a libel suit, an idea suggested by Nixon. Mitchell, who later claimed that the call was nothing more than one friend calling another, told Rebozo that a libel suit was not a good idea.

Coincidentally, George Smathers called another attorney in Mitchell's office with the same question. He received the same answer. In the White House, Fred Fielding reviewed each of the articles and took extensive notes on them. Fielding sent the notes to Dean and Ehrlichman for review, and Ehrlichman forwarded them to Rebozo so they could discuss each incident cited and Ehrlichman could get Rebozo's version. Haldeman instructed Dean that at least one of the authors of the articles, preferably Greene, should "have some problems." Caulfield again went to Acree, who suggested that a nontraceable audit could be triggered by using an anonymous letter of complaint against Greene. Douglas Lea of the ACLU later reported that the audit of Greene was "laundered through the New York State tax agency," a fact confirmed in a later investigation by the Joint Committee on Internal Revenue Taxation (JCIRT). The JCIRT claimed that this audit was unrelated to Enemies List activities. Later investigation by the Watergate Special Prosecution Force, however, uncovered evidence not only that Greene *was* audited in the fall of 1971 but that the White House also pushed for an audit of David Laventhol, editor of *Newsday*.[13]

White House efforts in this case were extensive. Haldeman led the charge for an audit of Otis Chandler and kept pressure on John Dean to get the audit started and generate results. In mid-October, Dean reported to Haldeman aide Larry Higby that an audit was under way. By then the White House had enlisted not only its own agent, Jack Caulfield, and the efforts of several White House staff, but also the Secret Service, the IRS, and the FBI in its attempt to derail publication of the *Newsday* series and create tax troubles for key individuals at the newspaper. Later testimony revealed that this intense interest stemmed not only from a concern that the articles might reveal pieces of Nixon's past and connections to questionable individuals that he wanted concealed, but also from a conviction that the entire effort had originated with the Kennedy family. Rebozo was convinced that the Kennedy Foundation had funded the investigation, largely because some of the key figures behind it were Kennedy loyalists. John Dean admitted to Caulfield, however, that the connection would be difficult to prove. Whether or not Rebozo actually believed it or simply used it, knowing Nixon's paranoia about the Kennedys, to trigger White House efforts to prevent publication of the story or discredit the authors remains unclear. (Nixon had already placed Senator Edward Kennedy under surveillance.) But associates of President Nixon hired private investigators to attack the series. James N. Juliana Associates of Washington, D.C., hired John Doermer Associates to gather information on the motivation behind the articles and details about the sale of *Newsday* to the *Los Angeles Times*, and to conduct complete background investigations on all the individuals on the investigative team. That investigation also raised the possibility of a Kennedy connection, citing the fact that some of the participants knew Carmine Bellino.[14]

As the *Newsday* articles detailed the backgrounds of Rebozo, Smathers, Nixon, and their associates in Florida and the Bahamas, there was reason to fear that these revelations would spark additional investigations by other news media. Perhaps because of this anxiety, at the request of Nixon Rebozo sent John Ehrlichman several documents (at least six) in early November 1971. He told Ehrlichman that "you alone should read the attached and retain in your confidential file or destroy any items you are not sure you will need later." He did not indicate the nature of the documents, and they appear to have since disappeared.

Later IRS intelligence operations—Operation Tradewinds and Project Haven—uncovered tax-evasion and money-laundering efforts in the Bahamas. They linked casino gambling to organized crime and international traffic in cocaine and marijuana, and Resorts International was a focal point of the investigations. Richard Nixon's name again surfaced, as it did in the mysterious "Project 3." Apparently an effort to examine some Watergate-related matters and their tax consequences, Project 3 was linked to Richard Jaffe, a special IRS agent in Miami. Jaffe claimed that a computer printout from Operation Tradewinds contained the name of Richard Nixon, and cited additional problems linked to Bebe Rebozo. Nixon apparently had been a client of Castle Trust, a Bahamian bank the IRS believed was being used by wealthy Americans to avoid U.S. taxes. The three-year undercover operation using private investigator Norman Casper, who operated as agent TW-24, was later terminated in a controversial move by IRS Commissioner Donald Alexander, a Nixon appointee.[15]

With the *Newsday* investigation unfolding, Nixon must have panicked when rumors surfaced in the summer of 1971 about $100,000, reportedly skimmed from Howard Hughes's Silver Slipper casino in Las Vegas, that had been passed to Rebozo (at Nixon's request) for the president's use. During their Watergate investigations about Nixon's abuse of the IRS, prosecutors explored this transaction and its accompanying links. Their files include a long study of skimming and how it was done, paying particular attention to "Skimming Methods Employed by Nevada Gambling Casinos" and various IRS efforts to counter those methods. The prosecution force encountered conflicting stories and found that the transaction involved Hank Greenspun, former owner of the Desert Inn Hotel and Casino in Las Vegas, Jimmy Hoffa and Harold Gibbons of the Teamsters, Bebe Rebozo, and Richard Danner. Greenspun had told the IRS, under oath, that Danner carried "two $50,000 cash contributions to Rebozo in 1970." One was delivered by Danner and Robert Maheu in Key Biscayne, the other by Danner alone to San Clemente. Maheu approved both, Greenspun said, and the money came from Howard Hughes's Silver Slipper casino. Soon after, Hughes received permission from the Justice Department to purchase the Dunes Hotel. Danner confirmed the transactions, revealing that he conveyed the first to Rebozo on July 3, 1970, at Nixon's San Clemente residence, and the second to Rebozo in his Bank of Key Biscayne office in mid-August. He insisted that the money was for the 1970 congressional campaign. Rebozo, however, testified that the funds were for the 1972 campaign and that the contributions were kept secret from the campaign committee. He later told the IRS in 1973 that he still had the money in his safe deposit box.[16] This prompted IRS Commissioner Donald Alexander to write William Simon, deputy secretary of the Treasury:

> The reason for the joint investigation (Audit and Intelligence) is that there has been a transfer of a substantial amount of cash and, we are advised, a retention of such cash, undisclosed by BBR [Rebozo]. Conflicting statements have been made, thus far, about the purpose of the transfer and the receipt of this cash. Funds transferred from one person to another for a particular purpose but not used by the transferee for such purpose generally constitute income, for tax purposes, to the transferee unless the transferee can prove otherwise. The additional aspect of nondisclosure is significant. In a situation involving a transfer of a substantial amount of cash and the retention of such cash by the transferee, IRS calls upon the transferee to prove that he has not received taxable income. If funds are embezzled or converted by a transferee for his own use, they constitute income for taxable purposes.[17]

Bebe was worried.

The IRS launched an investigation out of its Jacksonville office, joining it with an existing investigation of Howard Hughes. But, perhaps fearing Rebozo's political clout, it moved slowly. Although the IRS uncovered the transaction in May 1972, Commissioner Johnnie Walters refused permission for agents to interview Rebozo, claiming that a high-level decision had been made "not to interview sensitive political figures during the campaign year." Not until May 1973 did IRS agents contact Rebozo, and even then the IRS and the White House gave him advance notice through Roger Barth. Walters reported to Treasury Secretary George Shultz, moreover, that he did "not see the interview with Mr. Rebozo as leading to any action against him." The IRS seemed very reluctant to pursue money-laundering charges against Richard Nixon's close friend.[18]

Watergate prosecutors later found the Walters to Shultz memo particularly significant. Not only did Shultz discuss it with White House aide John Ehrlichman, the document outlined facts that would have given Rebozo advance warning about the IRS agents' line of questioning. As we shall see, it also represented a dramatic contrast to IRS behavior with respect to Larry O'Brien. Then, when the IRS finally received permission from the White House to interview Rebozo (an astonishing procedure in itself), it also reopened its investigation of O'Brien. Through all of this Shultz steadfastly insisted that he had done nothing wrong and that he knew little about the investigation, later telling Watergate investigators that they should ask the IRS why the process unfolded as it did. He claimed to have talked about the issue only with Walters and White House aide Alexander Haig.[19]

Deputy Secretary of the Treasury William Simon, however, contacted White House counsel Leonard Garment about Rebozo's tax problems in May 1973. Then, in August, FBI Director Clarence Kelley reported to IRS Commissioner Donald Alexander that a Bureau investigation had discovered that the $100,000 was delivered to Rebozo in packets of $100 bills. Alexander asked the FBI to try to determine how long the money had been in Rebozo's safe deposit box. Rebozo told the FBI that he had intended to give the money to the Republican party chairman, but then, suddenly, Hughes, Danner, and Maheu had become embroiled in a fight for control of the Hughes financial empire and attracted national publicity. Rebozo claimed that he had then decided not to pass the money along, and that he had asked Danner how he should return the funds. Danner told him, according to Kelley, that Hughes not only intended that the Republicans keep the money, but he had given a like amount to the Democrats. Rebozo blamed Danner for leaking the transaction to the IRS and for implying that Rebozo intended to keep the $100,000.[20]

As part of their Hughes investigation, IRS agents moved to interview Donald Nixon, the president's brother, but Walters checked first with Treasury Secretary George Shultz "in view of the sensitivity" of the issue. Shultz approved, but Ehrlichman warned both Donald and Richard Nixon about IRS plans. Donald Nixon was a potential source of embarrassment for the president, who had kept his brother under electronic surveillance. Anthony Ulasewicz had already traveled to California once to "rescue Donald from a hippie commune." But the Hughes connection posed greater dangers for the president. In 1956, Richard Nixon had arranged "a secret and laundered" loan of $205,000 from Hughes to his brother Donald. According to one report, when Donald defaulted the Nixon family became "a cool $150,000 richer." The Kennedy Justice Department investigated the circumstances of the loan but decided not to prosecute for political reasons, even though it believed the case to be solid. There was also another somewhat mysterious loan of $140,000 from Hughes.[21]

John Meier, a Hughes executive, had swindled millions from Hughes, and Donald Nixon had worked closely with Meier. The IRS had established a Sensitive Case Report on Meier. That report, Roger Barth discovered, revealed not only Meier's ties to Donald Nixon but associations with Vice President Hubert Humphrey and several United States senators. Meier had been employed by Robert A. Maheu and Associates, and had acquired mining claims for the Hughes Tool Company. He had later run for the U.S. Senate from New Mexico but lost the election. The IRS had been investigating him since June 1970, but their efforts to interview Meier had been unsuccessful. The agency claimed that Rebozo had "allegedly instructed" Meier "not to be available for interview" because of his "alleged association with Donald Nixon in regard to the acquisition of mining claims." The IRS discovered, however, that Meier and Donald Nixon, together with their wives, had traveled together to consult with Richard Nixon on November 21, 1968, in Washington. In addition, Meier had subsidized the vacation of Donald Nixon and his wife at the Kahala Hilton Hotel in Honolulu, Hawaii, in the fall of 1970. Agents also found a payment of $190,000 from the Hughes Tool Company to Lawrence F. O'Brien and Associates in 1970. The relationships intrigued the IRS. A 1972 interview of Donald Nixon by an informant also revealed that he had negotiated "unknown deals" with Aristotle Onassis and was currently negotiating a large loan from the Teamsters pension fund.[22]

The IRS had been interested in Hughes and the Hughes Tool Company for some time. Howard Hughes, of course, was an extraordinarily wealthy and eccentric individual who shrouded his life and financial empire in secrecy. He had long been linked to the CIA, and had hired Robert Maheu as his right-hand man. Hughes's income from noncompetitive and secret CIA contracts was reported to be in the neighborhood of $6 billion. Maheu had been a contract employee of the CIA since the mid-1950s and had recruited mobster Johnny Roselli to assassinate Fidel Castro. Roselli, together with Teamsters president Jimmy Hoffa, was later involved in Hughes's 1967 purchase of the Desert Inn in Las Vegas. To compound the administration's problem, Maheu had hired Lawrence O'Brien's consulting firm to represent the Hughes Tool Company, an arrangement that apparently terminated in November 1970 when Maheu was fired and replaced by Robert Bennett. O'Brien's retainer had disturbed Chuck Colson, who was White House liaison to the Hughes company. Colson feared that, with O'Brien on retainer to Hughes at the same time that he chaired the Democratic National Committee, O'Brien might check into Donald Nixon's affairs, including some shadowy activities with Maheu in the Dominican Republic. The IRS had audited Hughes Tool and found no improprieties. The IRS report, however, contained information about Rebozo, O'Brien, and Hughes. According to IRS Commissioner Johnnie Walters, the investigation produced sufficient evidence against Donald Nixon that led Walters to recommend further study.[23]

The IRS was interested in Howard Hughes for a variety of reasons, and apparently Donald Nixon just got caught in the agency's investigative web. Internal Revenue had a Hughes Project under way and had coordinated investigations with the FBI about alleged kickbacks by entertainers at Hughes's casinos. The FBI was pursuing possible extortion charges while the IRS wondered if the kickbacks had been reported as income. The IRS had also detailed an elite team of investigators and attorneys to Las Vegas to investigate Hughes's investments in Nevada. The IRS had Hughes under surveillance and had requested a personal interview with him about "political contributions which were funneled through your various businesses." Among them, according to Paul Laxalt of Nevada, were contributions from Hughes's Silver Slipper casino to state political campaigns in Nevada. This was the same source for the funds that had gone to Rebozo, and apparently the source of other contributions to Nixon in 1969 and 1970. Nixon sought to terminate the investigation, but aide Al Haig told him that there was "no way you can turn it off."[24]

In July 1971, Robert Bennett called John Dean's attention to a related problem. Bennett noted that in 1953 the Hughes Aircraft Company had created the Howard Hughes Medical Institute (HHMI) as a nonprofit organization. It had transferred the entire value of Hughes Aircraft stock to the Medical Institute, thereby avoiding all tax liabilities even though the Hughes empire retained control of the stock. Congress had since passed the Tax Reform Act of 1969, which promulgated harsher rules for the behavior of private foundations like HHMI. The

Treasury Department had subsequently passed new regulations pertaining to medical research organizations, insisting that they pay out annually sums equivalent to 4 percent of the fair market value of their endowment. This would require, Bennett told Dean, defense contractor Hughes Aircraft to pay HHMI (its sole stockholder) as much as $5.5 million per year. Could Congress "grandfather" HHMI? Without saying so directly, Bennett hoped Dean would convey the problem to the president and Hughes would be exempted from the new rules. Dean moved quickly, forwarding Bennett's letter to Under Secretary of the Treasury Charls Walker five days later and asking Walker to send him an "appropriate draft response to Mr. Bennett."[25]

Walker responded that Treasury was giving the HHMI issue "careful attention." He had met with its representatives, and he noted that Treasury had not made a final decision about whether to change the proposed regulations so as to exempt HHMI from their provisions. Walker then defended Treasury's regulations, arguing that they were fair and that the problem with Hughes from Treasury's perspective was that Hughes Aircraft had given only part of its assets to HHMI. In a series of complex transactions, the remainder was "sold" to HHMI and could be used for debt service on the purchase price. The debt, moreover, could even be forgiven—a fact that Dean underlined in his copy of Walker's letter. The consequence of all this was that if HHMI was exempt, "100 percent of the stock of Hughes Aircraft can remain lodged forever in the Institute, which is using only a part of the dividends for charitable (medical research) purposes." As Wright Patman's investigations had earlier revealed, this was just the sort of corporate behavior that brought tax-exempt foundations into disrepute. Walker also told Dean that the Hughes group was aware of this problem when Congress was considering the 1969 act, but "either they were unable to obtain relief at that time or they chose to take the risk that we would issue regulations that would cover them."[26]

Despite this setback, the White House continued to pursue the matter. In late January 1972, John Ehrlichman asked Dean to "discreetly determine the date of the Institute's original tax exempt status," and Dean contacted Roger Barth at IRS for this information. Shortly thereafter Leo Rosenberg, news director at radio station KMET in Los Angeles, called for a congressional inquiry, citing a "remarkable series of coincidences" between the 1956 IRS grant of tax-exempt status to HHMI (thereby protecting the earnings of Hughes Aircraft) and a $205,000 Hughes loan to Donald Nixon three months later. Congressman Wright Patman, stunned at the news, also investigated, requesting all

IRS documents relating to proposed regulations about medical research foundations and the tax treatment of HHMI. The IRS resisted, noting that Patman's request raised "the fundamental question of whether we must turn over all documents, including internal Treasury memoranda, to any Congressional committee which asks for them." Patman spent the next several months trying to get detailed information from Treasury Secretary George Shultz. Finally, in October 1973, Patman wrote Shultz that his failure to respond "can only be interpreted as another indication of the lack of independence and the politicization of the Internal Revenue Service."[27]

Perhaps goaded by Patman's letter, in late October 1973 Shultz's office finally responded. Blaming "obstacles" in gathering information, it apologized for the delay. Shultz sent Patman copies of correspondence on the subject of medical research organizations as well as a list of IRS personnel who participated in decision-making. But he refused to supply any internal memoranda, claiming that they were confidential and that their release would intimidate subordinate officials in the future from recording their detailed and candid analyses and opinions. The documents disclosed, perhaps ironically, that the White House actually had a fairly minimal role in HHMI efforts to secure further tax breaks worth potentially $24 to $36 million per year. Shultz's response, however, failed to mollify Patman, who demanded the internal memoranda. During the next several months Patman and Assistant Secretary of the Treasury Fred Hickman engaged in a lengthy exchange on the issue. Patman insisted that there was "no statutory basis" for withholding the memoranda. Watergate special prosecutors later found evidence that Roger Barth furnished information on the HHMI to Bob Haldeman and Larry Higby, as well as evidence of serious White House concern about the matter, but failed to uncover evidence of efforts beyond that.[28]

The White House moved quickly, however, to press the IRS for tax audits on Larry O'Brien. Richard Nixon launched "Operation O'Brien" in early 1970, fearing that O'Brien's appointment as DNC chairman signaled that Edward Kennedy was back in control of the Democratic party and loomed as an adversary in the 1972 election. O'Brien attacked the administration in April 1970 for giving Clark Mollenhoff access to his returns. In defense of Mollenhoff's efforts, Republican Senator John J. Williams of Delaware labeled O'Brien's argument as phony. During the Kennedy years, he noted, Carmine Bellino had done the same thing. Why should Democrats complain now, as Mortimer Caplin and Mitchell Rogovin (both central to the Bellino efforts) did, that giving

Mollenhoff access to tax records without written authorization from the president violated the Internal Revenue Code?[29]

Aware of O'Brien's ties to Hughes, Richard Nixon argued in a January 14, 1971, memo to Haldeman that "it would seem the time is approaching when Larry O'Brien is held accountable for his retainer with Hughes." Throughout 1971, Haldeman and other White House staffers compiled more information about that relationship, assigning Jack Caulfield to the investigation. The White House was cautious, however, fearing that a public pursuit of O'Brien would reveal relationships and transactions between Rebozo, Donald Nixon, and Hughes. Any efforts to embarrass O'Brien publicly could backfire and embarrass the president. To complicate matters, independent IRS investigations and audits of various Hughes businesses in late 1971 and early 1972 revealed a pattern of kickbacks, which in turn led the IRS to designate their Hughes investigations as a criminal case. The IRS called in special agents of its Intelligence Division in the spring of 1972 and created a special reporting system of "status reports" from Assistant Commissioner (Compliance) John Hanlon to Commissioner Walters. This system remained in place from May through September 1972. In the process of its investigation, the IRS discovered that Rebozo had counseled several Hughes officers "not to be candid in talking with IRS agents." This, of course, represented criminal activity. Yet the IRS did not interview Rebozo until more than a year later.[30]

Despite the danger of revealing connections among Nixon, Hughes, and O'Brien, the approach of the 1972 election accelerated White House efforts against O'Brien. Roger Barth told Ehrlichman that he had noticed O'Brien's name on a Hughes Tool Company Sensitive Case Report, indicating that Hughes had paid more than $100,000 to O'Brien or his consulting firm. Ehrlichman asked if that was a political contribution or income, laying the basis for a tax-audit request. Since Barth considered this a legitimate inquiry, in early July 1972 he went to either Mike Acree or Frank Geibel in the IRS Inspection Division to get O'Brien's tax returns for 1969 and 1970, as well as those of his partner and the partnership consulting firm. Barth told Watergate investigators that he later reported to Ehrlichman that everything seemed legitimate. He claimed not to be aware of "O'Brien's tax returns having been brought down to Washington by plane," nor to have any knowledge about "who the inspector was who had requested the tax returns which he had asked Inspection to requisition." In fact, O'Brien's 1969 tax return was audited by the IRS in 1970–1971, and his 1970 return was audited in 1971. Both audits stemmed from O'Brien's large income and not from political considerations. Later the 1969 audit was reopened and completed in early 1973. O'Brien complained that this represented a White House vendetta. After a brief investigation, IRS Commissioner Donald Alexander advised O'Brien that "it had all been a mistake." Notations on at least one IRS document, however, revealed that the agency had coordinated its response with the White House.[31]

Nixon quickly joined his concern about Hughes with his worry about O'Brien. During an April 3, 1972, meeting in the Executive Office Building, he told John Ehrlichman that "if they bring up that Goddamn Hughes loan again, we ought to break this over O'Brien's head." Ehrlichman replied that O'Brien would "get the word" that he was going to be audited. All the White House wanted was for O'Brien "to quit sleeping nights." Aware of Nixon's concern that George Shultz was not going to "play politics with IRS," Ehrlichman reassured him that "Roger Barth is over there and we've been wanting him to be deputy general counsel of IRS because he'd be in a position to do a lot more." He believed that Barth would do their bidding. The White House also pressured IRS Commissioner Johnnie Walters to move on the case. Walters discussed the Hughes-O'Brien connection with Treasury Secretary Shultz, then asked Assistant Commissioner (Compliance) John Hanlon to look into the matter. Hanlon reported back that an O'Brien audit had revealed no indication of fraud. Walters called Ehrlichman with the information in late August, but Ehrlichman was not pacified. He angrily lashed out at Walters: "God damn it Walters, you had better stop dragging."[32]

While all this was going on, throughout late July and early August agents from the IRS Intelligence Division were anxiously trying to interview O'Brien. This hot pursuit of O'Brien by the IRS during the 1972 campaign directly contradicted Walters's earlier statement with respect to Bebe Rebozo that Internal Revenue agents would not interview prominent political figures until after the fall election. The administration, of course, considered O'Brien an enemy, whereas Rebozo was a close friend of the president. In his affidavit before the House Judiciary Committee in June 1974, moreover, Walters admitted that an exception to the "no interview" policy was made for O'Brien because of the White House inquiries.

A summary report by the Watergate Special Prosecution Force reveals more detail. Following a series of coast-to-coast telephone calls, on August 14, 1972, IRS intelligence agents were called from Washington by Dan Bonomi, a high-ranking Intelligence Division official.

Bonomi told them to arrange an interview with O'Brien and to "report back to Washington within the hour as to their progress in so doing." The agents argued that there was "no legitimate purpose" for this action and worried about charges of "political harassment," but Bonomi indicated that his orders came from the commissioner. The agents followed orders. Not only was this in striking contrast to the IRS's treatment of Rebozo, it also contrasted sharply with its treatment of Donald Nixon. At a mid-August meeting, in fact, Walters asked if the IRS pursuit of Donald Nixon could wait until after the election. "I'm not really telling you to hold off," Walters allegedly said, "but if it can't let me tell you about it so I can start running."[33]

Throughout August and September the White House doubled its efforts to intimidate or harass O'Brien through IRS audits. At one point Bebe Rebozo met with former Johnson aide Bobby Baker in an effort to dig up dirt on O'Brien. Soon after that meeting, Baker had a call from Herbert Kalmbach, who grilled him for information. Baker later characterized both men as disappointed and desperate. Nixon told Ehrlichman in early August to "scare the shit out of them. Now, there are some Jews with the Mafia that are involved in this all, too." O'Brien later recalled:

> I was an arrogant wise guy in their view. I had caused them real concern. I had hit sensitive areas which I didn't recognize to be as sensitive as they turned out to be. So with that I was subjected to a series of audits in 1971 and 1972 that gave me pause only because this seemed to be somewhat unusual.

O'Brien also insisted that "for me the stunning manipulation of the power of the IRS can be considered the most shocking phase of the Watergate scandal." What he once considered the product of a "stuck computer" he soon came to see as "political espionage" and "political sabotage." Much of the impetus for the IRS pressure certainly came from Richard Nixon, but both John Ehrlichman and Bob Haldeman (as well as other White House aides) urged the president on, as did John Connally.[34]

Following his testy telephone conversation with Ehrlichman from Shultz's office on August 29, 1972, Walters met with J. G. McGowan, deputy assistant commissioner (Compliance). He ordered Compliance to put all copies of O'Brien Associates tax returns, as well as returns filed by Larry O'Brien, Sr. and Jr., and his two associates, Napolitan and De-Sauteles, in his hands within two days. He also requested extensive background information on Napolitan and DeSauteles, including "who they are, what they are, what they do, where they are at the present time and so forth." Hughes had paid a $12,000-per-month retainer to Napolitan, and Walters wanted more information on that. He also discussed possible issues with respect to "lobbying expenses, or conduit payments passing through the individuals or corporation involved." Walters stressed the need for the "high degree of confidentiality involved in this matter," warning that "any field contact should not result in any initial or overreaction with respect to any of these cases." The IRS would not go public, he insisted, until it could "PROVE" any misconduct. Clearly Walters was not convinced that he had seen the end of White House pressure, and he intended to be prepared.[35]

In a September 8 conversation in the oval office, still hoping to put O'Brien in jail, Ehrlichman detailed for the president specific figures from O'Brien's tax returns. A week later, in what became a fateful meeting, John Dean reported the progress of the IRS investigation of O'Brien to Nixon. At that time the president explicitly directed Dean to use the IRS to deal with political enemies through audits or other devices. Everything was recorded on tape. If the president's direct involvement in using the IRS for political purposes had ever been in doubt before, no doubt remained after the September 15 meeting. White House aides, led by Haldeman, Ehrlichman, and Dean, were certainly complicit, as apparently was Attorney General John Mitchell, but Richard Nixon was the hub of the inquisition's wheel. Several months later Nixon tried to assure his attorney Fred Buzhardt that the September 15 meeting only dealt with "things you would normally discuss in a campaign." And later, in Nixon's defense during Watergate, the minority counsel insisted that the president's actions were something done in the "heat of politics" and represented only an "error of the heart" rather than a "gross abuse of power." But it was too late for the spin doctors.[36]

By 1973 Richard Nixon was under fire from several quarters for efforts to cover up responsibility for the Watergate break-in and his abuse of the IRS with respect to his political enemies. Despite that, and despite his fears about what might emerge from IRS probes into Bebe Rebozo, Howard Hughes, or Larry O'Brien, Nixon persisted in his efforts to use the IRS for political purposes. In March 1973, worried about the increasingly anti-administration stance of Connecticut Senator Lowell Weicker (a Republican), he told Haldeman to "get the goods" on Weicker and check his income tax returns. He hoped that the installation of "our man" (Donald Alexander) as IRS commissioner would be an avenue to exploit. At the same time he worried about an IRS investigation of the Enemies List, telling Alexander Haig that it was "important that we not let the IRS drag out their investigation." Defying reality, Nixon tried to put a positive spin on some of his administration's notorious activities.

> In fact, what we have here if we combine the facts that we know are true with regard to our limited use of the FBI is a very positive story rather than a negative one. This Administration has never used the FBI for purely political purposes—both Kennedy and Johnson did. This Administration discontinued the use of the Armed Services in domestic intelligence and if our IRS study turns out as we hope and expect it to this Administration has not used the IRS for political partisan purposes.[37]

This was pure fantasy. As Donald Bacon of the IRS later said: ". . . At first I thought they were smart and arrogant. Later, it turned out they were stupid and arrogant."[38]

Following publication in June 1973 of a White House Enemies List with 216 names on it, the IRS examined its files and audit activity on each of them. Assistant Commissioner for Compliance John Hanlon reported in a 42-page document to Commissioner Alexander in July that more than half the individuals on that list had not been audited at all between 1968 and 1971. A second project, concerning an additional list of 551 names, was under way. Hanlon indicated that to date the IRS had evidence of audit activity on only about a quarter of those individuals. He did not address, however, why the IRS seemed caught by surprise at the revelations of Enemies Lists and efforts to use the IRS for political purposes.[39]

In fact the IRS was defensive in the face of investigations by the Watergate Special Prosecutor. Its own investigation seemed designed primarily to clear Internal Revenue of any wrongdoing, and was initiated in response to the negative publicity. The IRS also worried about the investigations of the Special Prosecutor, Archibald Cox. During the fall an exchange of memos between new IRS Commissioner Donald Alexander and Cox revealed the agency's concern. Alexander worried that Cox would try to criminalize the behavior of IRS agents who acted on informants' information. That interpretation, Alexander told Cox, raised "serious questions about the propriety of IRS investigations based upon a wide variety of informant materials" which had traditionally been the catalyst for IRS investigations of taxpayers. Attempting to preserve traditional IRS operations and to keep covert intelligence-gathering operations from public scrutiny, Alexander argued that Cox's concern rested on a "theory" of criminal behavior that required IRS agents to be aware of informants' motives. "Such a development," he warned, "would seriously impair, if not preclude, the Service's ability to act upon informant materials."[40]

Archibald Cox assured Alexander that prosecutors were only trying to investigate efforts by White House staff to initiate IRS audits of individuals "solely because of the political affiliation or political sentiments of those individuals rather than because of information suggesting possible tax delinquencies." He failed to see how anything his staff was doing threatened the IRS use of informants, so long as the IRS evaluated the information before taking action. No agent would face criminal liability for past actions if they were undertaken in good faith and "without criminal intent." When Leon Jaworski replaced Cox, he also assured Alexander that he was not about to do anything that "would adversely interfere with the IRS' long standing reliance on the use of informants for developing tax cases."[41]

These assurances failed to reassure the IRS, however. Chief Counsel Meade Whitaker sent copies of the entire exchange to Assistant Attorney General Henry Petersen of the Justice Department's Criminal Division. He requested clarification of guidelines for IRS use of informants in light of the special prosecutors' investigation. The IRS could not understand, he wrote, why efforts by third parties (such as the White House staff) to have IRS personnel initiate audits was illegal, so long as no documents were falsified. Present practices, he insisted, prevented audits based only on unsubstantiated assertions by third parties, but Whitaker insisted that "the typical informant is not altruistically motivated." Initiation of an audit, he asserted, was a "discretionary act," and IRS employees should be immune from civil and criminal actions "when acting on informant information." Whitaker asked for Justice Department assistance in drafting new policies with respect to informants.[42]

The other side of this argument, raised by an ACLU study, was that of personal privacy. Led by Douglas Lea, the ACLU launched a Project on Privacy and Data Collection, surveying individuals named by the Senate Watergate Committee as White House enemies. Almost two hundred individuals received questionnaires, and more than one hundred were returned. The ACLU published an interim report in January 1974, after secretly sharing the responses with the Watergate Special Prosecution Force. IRS audit activity received considerable attention, and 27 percent of the respondents reported being audited, often more than once. The report made clear that these rates were far in excess of normal audit rates for any income brackets. The ACLU report took sharp issue with a parallel investigation by the Joint Committee on Internal Revenue Taxation (JCIRT).[43]

During 1973, reacting to charges that the White House had abused the IRS by demanding tax audits on its enemies, the JCIRT investigated IRS treatment of individuals on the Enemies Lists. It reviewed IRS files on individuals named on the various lists, and compared audit rates for those individuals with national audit rates. The JCIRT found that individuals on the Enemies Lists had indeed been audited more frequently than normal, although perhaps not more often than a narrow spectrum of taxpayers in similar income and expense brackets. It also concluded that no evidence existed that IRS actions had been harsher than usual, nor that any of these individuals had been targeted because of their political views. With respect to Nixon's friends, the JCIRT study was more ambiguous. Although it claimed that it could not substantiate firm conclusions, the study found sufficient evidence of favoritism to conclude that White House pressure on the IRS for favorable action was a possibility. What the JCIRT largely looked at, however, was IRS tax-collection efforts rather than the use of the IRS for purposes of harassment. Critics concluded that the JCIRT study was little more than a whitewash designed to protect the IRS and its constituency and represented a failure of congressional oversight. In 1975, Tom Jarriel reported that the JCIRT study was completed without ever holding "a hearing on Internal Revenue Service practices or procedures."[44]

The Watergate Special Prosecution Force uncovered much more convincing evidence of political pressure with respect to both enemies and friends. Conflicting testimony, memory lapses, and legal problems with respect to participants, however, led the WSPF to conclude that criminal charges would be difficult to prove. But in later hearings on the topic of privacy, IRS targeting of individuals on the Enemies Lists remained a sore point. Despite the assertions of Edward Schmults, general counsel of the Treasury Department, that the JCIRT study exonerated the IRS and its behavior, critics charged that there was more to the story. In one exchange with Schmults, Congresswoman Bella Abzug, a target of Nixon's Enemies List, argued that the IRS "reviewed information and they proceeded on that information for no authorized reason." Individuals' names were "committed to the Internal Revenue Service for an investigation totally without cause." Although Schmults steadfastly defended the JCIRT study, he admitted that White House pressures during the Nixon years had revealed persistent problems with privacy and access to tax returns. The House Judiciary Committee agreed, finding "clear and convincing evidence" that Richard Nixon and members of the White House staff sought to invade individuals' privacy because they opposed the administration. In the end, the central issue became who determined what was private information and what was not. Later, during hearings held by the Senate Select Committee on Intelligence, the IRS question surfaced again. By then, however, too many of the committee's members envisioned themselves as presidential or vice presidential candidates. Looking for headlines, they decided that "hearings on the IRS didn't promise to be very 'sexy'" and canceled all but one day of the scheduled sessions.[45]

All of these investigations revealed one persistent and glaring problem with respect to the use and misuse of the Internal Revenue Service. That was the issue of the disclosure, or privacy, of individuals' tax returns. During the Watergate investigations the IRS raised the question in an effort to limit access to and the dissemination of tax information. The IRS tried to walk a narrow line between cooperation, observance of disclosure laws, and self-protection. The agency placed no obstacles in the path of Watergate investigators but did express a "strong preference" that IRS files be used only in IRS offices. Working through Assistant to the Commissioner Burke Willsey, the IRS expressed concern that the prosecutors might investigate every allegation of wrongdoing with the same intensity as it did the O'Brien incident. The intent of prosecutors, however, was chiefly to determine how the IRS could conclude that "no audits were commenced at the direction of the White House." Special prosecutors were determined not to repeat the performance of the House Judiciary Committee, which had produced a 440-page volume of evidence about political uses of the IRS without ever making an investigation of its own.[46]

The privacy issue remained at center stage for the next several years. Although the IRS claimed that the Watergate investigations did not reveal "any extraordinary political abuse of the IRS" during the Nixon years—citing as evidence the fact that no officials had been indicted for misuse of tax information—it remained defensive. Congressmen, senators, and the public all clamored for greater privacy protection for individuals' tax returns. IRS Commissioner Donald Alexander, testifying in hearings on surveillance and privacy in 1975, issued a ringing defense of privacy in his efforts to maintain traditional IRS operational methods and techniques—which would maintain IRS control over access to tax returns and information. But other revelations about IRS misuse of tax information undercut Alexander's efforts. Evidence surfaced that even while the White House pressured the IRS to go easy on friends and punish enemies, the IRS itself had launched a massive effort to use tax data as a weapon against dissent. Senator Howard Baker of Tennessee later remarked that the "great tragedy is, under the most tumultuous civil strife we have ever known except during the time of the Civil War, our institutions failed us."[47] The IRS's own creation, the Special Services Staff, was a prime example.

CHAPTER THIRTEEN

THE SPECIAL
SERVICE STAFF:
AN IRS ENEMIES LIST

By EARLY 1969, FBI agent Robert Wall had spent two years investigating SNCC in order to pin charges on black militants. When he tried to close the case for lack of evidence, he discovered that the IRS had asked the Identification Division of the FBI for the arrest record of a former Student Nonviolent Coordinating Committee member. "When I went to the IRS," Wall later wrote, "I found it had secretly set up a special squad of men to investigate the tax records of 'known militants and activists,' and that the FBI was supplying the names of the persons for the IRS to include in this list." Conversations with several IRS officials eventually led him to a "locked soundproofed room in the basement of the IRS headquarters in Washington where I found a file on my subject, among hundreds of others piled on a long table."[1] Robert Wall had discovered the Special Service Staff.

Although the Nixon Enemies List attracted considerable press attention, connected as it was to the President of the United States, the Special Service Staff (SSS) was far more extensive and intrusive yet received virtually no coverage in the national media. The SSS was a creation of the Internal Revenue Service to gather intelligence on a wide array of individuals and groups who advocated social and political reform, or who simply objected to the policies of the Nixon administration. In part a defensive reaction to the administration's complaints about a failure to curb dissident activity, the Special Service Staff was also a forerunner of a systematic Intelligence Gathering and Retrieval System (IGRS) that the IRS would have in place by 1973. More than any other IRS program, the SSS exemplified an abuse of the income tax system. It focused more on intelligence gathering than it did on enforcement of the Internal Revenue Code. Its files ran to thousands of pages. And, despite its termination in 1973, SSS records indicate that material was added to those files at least through 1990. Former IRS historian Shelley Davis labeled the SSS the "most controversial episode" in recent IRS history. Operating in conjunction with the FBI's Counter-Intelligence Program (COINTELPRO) as well as programs operated by Army Intelligence and the CIA, the SSS represented one of the most extensive and least known intelligence-gathering operations in American history.[2]

Although the SSS formally came into existence during the summer of 1969, its roots lay deeper. During the mid-1960s both the FBI and the CIA had attempted to use IRS tax information against critics and dissidents as well as against organized crime. In 1964, for instance, the IRS supplied the FBI with a list of contributors to Martin Luther King's Southern Christian Leadership Conference. The FBI then proposed sending a forged letter to those contributors in an effort to curtail future contributions. Probably the most famous incident involved CIA pressure on the IRS to investigate *Ramparts'* financial supporters in retaliation for the magazine's exposé of CIA funding of the National Student Association. At a February 1967 meeting with Thomas Terry, assistant commissioner for compliance; Leon Green, his executive assistant; and John Barber, chief of rulings, Exempt Organizations Branch, the CIA pressed the IRS to examine the corporate tax returns of *Ramparts*. A February 15 CIA memo indicated that the agency did obtain access to tax returns of individuals bankrolling *Ramparts*. All this was done quietly because of the potential political repercussions, and IRS officials later denied any recollection of either the meeting or the event.[3]

By 1968 the IRS Intelligence Division had established a process for handling requests for tax information from the FBI and other government agencies. It had a formal liaison with the FBI, to whom the Bureau directed its requests for tax returns. The returns were copied and then provided to the FBI without any written responses. The procedure was efficient but illegal. Only the commissioner or assistant commissioner had the legal power to release returns, and no one in the Intelligence Division had the authority to sign either of their names. Donald Virdin, chief of the IRS Disclosure staff, warned that recent court decisions had required the FBI to reveal bugging records and their sources of information. If the IRS link with its illegal disclosures became public, it would "embarrass" the IRS. All future requests should be in writing,

Virdin recommended, because if "Intelligence is actually giving copies of returns to the FBI without these procedures, they are violating the law." Since the IRS was already being accused of harassing SDS and other militant groups, Virdin's fears were well placed.[4]

Pressure on the IRS to release tax information increased when the McClellan Committee (the Permanent Subcommittee on Investigations, Senate Committee on Government Operations) held hearings in 1968 and early 1969 to investigate militant groups and individuals that might hold tax-exempt status or receive tax-exempt contributions. Philip Manuel, an investigator with the committee (and formerly with the House Un-American Activities Committee), met with IRS officials in September 1968 to establish procedures for committee access to IRS files on militants. Senator McClellan formally requested files on twenty-two organizations in late September, and the IRS commissioner instructed district directors to cooperate with committee investigators. Since the FBI had refused to release any information to the committee that was not already public, the committee had turned to the IRS when other investigatory avenues failed. Once again, IRS files were being used for nontax-related matters. Since Congress adjourned before action could be taken, in early 1969 the committee repeated its request.[5]

McClellan's requests and the hearings provoked the IRS into considering the establishment of an Activist Organization project. By this time, moreover, the FBI was in almost daily contact with the IRS Intelligence Division and maintained regular contact with the IRS Division of Alcohol, Tobacco and Firearms. In January 1969, IRS employees Paul DeLong, Chuck Hulberg, and Paul Wright met to discuss the proposed project. Its purpose was to insure that targeted activists and militant groups were in strict tax compliance, and it submitted biweekly status reports to the IRS commissioner and then transmitted them "directly to the White House." In the long term the IRS hoped to use data processing techniques to systematize the effort. SSS files are unclear about how much this project actually developed before mid-1969, and the fact sheet later released by the IRS on the SSS failed to mention the project.[6]

Senator McClellan's renewed request for IRS files in late March 1969 triggered the first broad IRS response. This time the IRS apparently heeded Donald Virdin's earlier warnings and tried to establish a paper trail and limit its response. The Audit Division refused to provide any data unless it was specifically requested. Assistant Commissioner for Compliance Donald Bacon warned regional commissioners that many of the twenty-two organizations named by McClellan were controversial, and that a few apparently had not filed tax returns. Bacon specifically requested that regional commissioners provide a detailed memorandum on each group in their region. Virdin cautioned that investigations should "not be initiated solely because of this memorandum nor should contacts be made with Police Departments, the FBI, or any external sources to obtain information for the report." If a region had no information in its files on specific groups, it should simply file a negative report. As another IRS official wrote Virdin: "I've never seen so much fuss over what I thought was a clear, uncomplicated request for a report." Yet handwritten notes in SSS files on the investigations reveal that the IRS did contact the FBI as well as explore Sensitive Case Reports. By 1970 voluminous files existed on several of the organizations.[7]

The McClellan Committee's request also prompted a defensive reaction from the IRS. Now the agency initiated plans for a more systematic investigation of controversial individuals and groups so as not to be caught napping by Congress. A later congressional investigation reported that this new effort differed from previous IRS intelligence operations in that its "sole objective" was to gather general intelligence rather than support specific tax investigations. It began in Los Angeles under the direction of the chief of the IRS Intelligence Division. Later the Los Angeles project became a nationwide effort. Robert Lund, former director of the IRS Intelligence Division, maintained that its files were separate from those of the SSS, but this proved to be a distinction without a difference.[8]

IRS response to the McClellan Committee's request was initially confined to the twenty-two organizations, but the search for violations encompassed all operations of Internal Revenue. In early May it reported a list of those groups "whose activities have created or caused an atmosphere of violence in the United States," breaking them down into four categories: black power groups, "White radical groups and groups which advocate and employ civil disobedience," Communist groups, and "White supremacy and extremist groups." By mid-May the IRS had compiled a special report for the Senate committee that it labeled "Sensitive" and to be handled with "appropriate security measures." The report not only identified specific individuals within each of the groups, it also indicated other groups that these individuals were associated with, even though they were not included on the committee's list of twenty-two. The report warned, however, that individuals who "are members of the organizations" should not be confused with individuals, "especially negroes, who have sincere, legitimate aspirations." The IRS in effect defined what constituted legitimate as opposed to illegitimate protest.[9]

The IRS report on black power groups and their tendency toward "armed insurrection" focused particularly on their cultural characteristics. The intent, as the following passage reveals, appears to have been not only to describe those characteristics but to imply that they were un-American.

> Most members of the black power groups manifest a natural "African bush" type haircut or style in which the hair is allowed to grow long, and is not treated with pomade or processing. The result is characteristic. Coupled with this may be a Chinese mandarin-type moustache which tends to droop around the mouth. Goatees are also much in vogue. Some of the more extroverted may, at times, wear Central African-type raiments consisting of flowing colorful robes, and truncated cloth hats of matching cloth. An African amulet is usually worn around the neck on a leather thong. It may consist of a medallion, wooden figure or an animal tooth. The "Bible" for them is the Autobiography of Malcolm X.

According to the IRS, these individuals often wore black clothing to emphasize the "'black is beautiful' philosophy."[10]

But the IRS investigations did not yield much data. What information they discovered usually came from FBI reports and metropolitan police departments, particularly those in Cincinnati, Cleveland, and Detroit. The IRS expressed concern that many of the organizations violated firearms laws and built "destructive devices," and it reported seven active investigations of its own into these groups. Perhaps most revealing was the IRS admission that it had identified many other militant groups and had cross-indexed each one by the name of the individual or organization and any known aliases. "Upon request," the IRS told the committee, "we can readily tell if any particular individual or group is mentioned in our file(s) and in which file(s)." It had twelve thousand case folders from Los Angeles alone.[11] This was an open invitation to the McClellan Committee to expand its investigation.

Despite this information, Senator McClellan was upset that the IRS had apparently done nothing about these organizations, and insisted that IRS Commissioner Randolph Thrower take an active role. Committee investigator Philip Manuel also asked the IRS to investigate foundations that may have transferred funds to militant organizations, specifically citing the Fund for Education and Legal Defense, the Medical Committee for Human Rights, and the Artists Civil Rights Foundation. He also wanted tax returns for the Louis M. Rabinowitz Foundation, the Edgar Stern Foundation, and the Glickenhaus Foundation. Assistant Commissioner Donald Bacon, however, warned the IRS chief counsel about several legal issues that might arise if IRS personnel were to investigate federal matters where there was no federal tax interest. He feared charges of unauthorized use of IRS appropriations, the liability of IRS agents, or potential physical injury when agents acted outside the perimeter of their official duties, as well as questions of deceit and other legal ramifications when agents showed their credentials during nontax investigations. The SSS records do not reveal if the chief counsel's office took action on Bacon's warning, but his memo reveals that at least some high-ranking IRS officials were aware of the dangers and illegalities of such an operation.[12]

In June 1969 the McClellan committee opened hearings, focusing on Students for a Democratic Society (SDS), the Student Nonviolent Coordinating Committee (SNCC), and the Black Panthers, hoping to discover that the organizations or their financial supporters had violated provisions of the income tax code. McClellan focused on the tax-exempt status of the Black Panthers because they engaged in political activities (which, of course, he did not like). This was an extremely "sensitive point" for the IRS, and Donald Virdin warned that McClellan was likely to ask why the Panthers had not filed returns, why the IRS considered it a political organization and how it made such a determination, and what types of returns political organizations had to file. To examine the political aspects of an organization, Virdin noted, would raise questions about "both the Democratic and Republican parties" and open up a "sensitive and potentially explosive area." IRS officials immediately met for a strategy session to determine their response.[13]

On June 16, the same day the hearings began, Commissioner Thrower, presidential counselor Arthur Burns, and Nixon aide Tom Charles Huston met at the White House. The administration pressed the IRS to supply more information on activist groups. This pressure stemmed from an informal group of conservative White House staffers, known as the "Committee of Six," who met occasionally at the request of President Nixon and made policy recommendations. On June 16 they recommended that the IRS examine "exempt left-wing organizations to determine if they were complying with the tax laws," a recommendation prepared by Patrick Buchanan. Two days later Huston wrote President Nixon that the IRS was to take a "close look at activities of left-wing organizations which are operating with tax-exempt funds."[14] This White House involvement was important but apparently not crucial in the creation of the SSS.

Senator McClellan had asked IRS officials to testify in executive session about SNCC and the Black Panthers, and on June 20 Commissioner Thrower granted permission. After a former Panther, Jean Powell, testified that the Panthers had never filed an income tax return and had never been audited, Senator Karl Mundt, the ranking Republican on the McClellan Committee, charged the IRS with favoritism and demanded that the IRS immediately conduct an audit. The IRS was embarrassed. It became even more chagrined during the executive session held on June 25. Internal Revenue officials argued that Assistant Attorney General Mitchell Rogovin was responsible for failing to enforce IRS summonses for these organizations' records so that IRS staff could determine their tax liability, but agency officials refused to agree with the assertion that this represented "favoritism." The IRS also refused to allow the committee to release publicly information that SNCC had received more than $4 million in funds but had filed an income tax return for only one year, 1967.

Deputy Assistant Commissioner (Compliance) Leon Green was so severely criticized during his testimony that he immediately recommended the establishment of a system to follow up information and complete the audits on exempt organizations. The Patman inquiries years earlier had raised the same issue, but the IRS had failed to act in any comprehensive way. Now it was not only embarrassed, the question had become very sensitive and highly politicized. That same day the IRS laid the foundation for what became the SSS. Assistant Commissioner (Compliance) Donald Bacon wrote the directors of the Alcohol, Tobacco and Firearms Division, the Audit Division, the Collection Division, and the Intelligence Division, asking that they "prepare a list of the ideological organizations—left or right—which we have examined in recent years or for which we have other information." He was "particularly interested" in the "source of funds, notorious persons or organizations with which [they] associated directly or indirectly, whether or not the organizations are exempt, the kind of exemption or whether a request for exemption was denied." Bacon also asked for information on five specific organizations: the National Student Association, the Black Panther party, Students for a Democratic Society, the Progressive Labor party, and the Louis M. Rabinowitz Foundation. He asked that the information be provided "*as promptly as possible.*" Within two days he began to receive replies.[15]

Ever since the Watergate investigations there has been confusion about the origin of the SSS. Did it stem from White House pressure, or was it an effort by the IRS to protect itself against further congressional criticism? As Green's actions indicate, agency self-defense was the driving force. But White House pressure persisted for the IRS to do more about tax-exempt organizations that criticized administration policies. On July 1, 1969, Assistant to the President Tom Charles Huston called Roger Barth, special assistant to the IRS commissioner and the White House "plant" within IRS, to ask how the IRS had responded to President Nixon's earlier demand for action against left-wing organizations. This was a coincidence that later led even congressional investigators to connect formation of the SSS with White House pressures. But in the case of the SSS, unlike that of the Enemies Lists, the IRS took the lead.[16]

On June 30 (some records indicate July 1), ATF special agent Eddie D. Hughes, an expert on militant organizations, arrived in Washington, recalled from his Atlanta office. Hughes spent a full day briefing Donald Bacon's staff on those organizations, then worked with Bernard Meehan of Bacon's staff to prepare a report for the White House. SSS files reveal that Hughes's trip was a direct result of White House pressure on the IRS for action against those groups. He brought with him most of his records to use in the preparation of his report. On July 1 the Hughes-Meehan memo was sent to Roger Barth under Assistant Commissioner (Compliance) Bacon's name. It outlined IRS actions and listed specific groups against which enforcement activity was under way.[17]

The Bacon memo recognized the "recent high level interest" in "Ideological Organizations" and asserted that the IRS was on top of the problem. The Compliance Division, it declared, had already initiated action against the Black Panther party, Students for a Democratic Society, the Progressive Labor party, the Louis H. Rabinowitz Foundation, and the Interreligious Foundation for Community Organization. Action was planned against the National Student Association. In addition, the Alcohol, Tobacco and Firearms Division had investigated other groups and their officers and members: the Minutemen, the United Klans of America, the Neighborhood Organized Workers (NOW), the Black Power Unity Movement (BPUM), the Wilmington Youth Emergency Action Council, the Republic of New Africa, the Confederation of Free City States, the Student Nonviolent Coordinating Committee, the Black Liberations, the Black Liberation Front, and the North Ward Citizens Committee.[18]

The IRS was coordinating these investigations with the Department of Justice Internal Security Division and the FBI. FBI reports were relayed directly to the IRS Intelligence and Compliance divisions. The IRS had also used ATF undercover agents, and those agents had arrested several members of the targeted groups. Attached to the Bacon report was an even longer list of organizations then under examination by the IRS. Among the more prominent were the Americans for Democratic Action, the Christian Echoes Ministry, the Church League of America, the Fund for the Republic, the Life Line Foundation, the National Council of Churches of Christ, SDS, and the Southern Student Organizing Committee. The list was a bit deceptive, since some of these groups had been part of the Ideological Organizations Project during the Kennedy years.[19]

The very next day, July 2, 1969, six IRS officials held a 10 a.m. meeting in Bernard Meehan's office at IRS headquarters to discuss the subject of ideological organizations. They hoped to coordinate the examination of organizations that fell under this classification, although members of the group did not define what they meant by "ideological organizations." That was to be left to the task force chairman, who would decide what organizations would be investigated, the types of investigations undertaken, and how all field activities would be coordinated. The chairman would establish relationships with the Internal Security Division in the Department of Justice, and the overall structure was to resemble the IRS strike forces in the organized crime drive of the Kennedy era. The task force, to be called the Activist Organizations Committee, would operate out of the IRS National Office. A memorandum to IRS field offices would request information on various groups—much the same as Donald Bacon had done on March 25—and the task force would reconvene on July 8 to assemble that information and establish files on every organization. Data processing would key punch it into a database. "The basic use of this task force initially," according to minutes of the meeting, "will be as an intelligence gathering operation and a promoter of coordination between the several field activities."[20]

Selection criteria for the Special Service Staff—which grew out of the Activist Organizations Committee—thus were not random and were not necessarily tax related. To some extent the SSS would be a captive of its sources. Any name sent along by the Internal Security Division of the Justice Department, the FBI, or any other agency would be entered into the SSS database. Ultimately the SSS compiled almost 12,000 files on more than 8,500 individuals and almost 3,000 organizations. One SSS employee later recalled that FBI reports were coming in like "Niagara Falls," by the " 'armload' and by the 'pound.' " Despite its scope, this was to be a secret unit of the IRS. "We do not want the news media to be alerted to what we are attempting to do or how we are operating," one SSS document noted, "because the disclosure of such information might embarrass the Administration or adversely affect the Service operations in this area or those of other Federal agencies or congressional committees."[21]

Originally the SSS was to be a small committee, with representatives from the Compliance, Audit, Collection, and Intelligence divisions as well as from Alcohol, Tobacco and Firearms. It was to report to Leon Green, the assistant commissioner (Compliance), who would supervise its operations. The group established a "need to know" restriction because it feared that many younger IRS employees were sympathetic to many of the activist organizations. IRS officials also believed that organizations under investigation should not know of SSS's existence. The problem with this approach was the question of accountability. Exacerbating that problem was the continuing failure to define "ideological organizations." At the July 8 meeting the group could only conclude that the term meant "different things to different people." Because different definitions might lead to misinterpretations in the field, they decided that future memoranda would be titled "Request for Information Concerning Various Organizations."[22]

By then the operation had expanded beyond what Leon Green had envisioned. Paul Wright, from Harold Snyder's staff in the Collection Division, now became chairman of the new intelligence-gathering group. There was a staff of eight, plus the five permanent members from the various IRS divisions. Wright forwarded to the FBI a list of fifty-five organizations generated by the Collection Division to all FBI files on those groups. Intelligence gathering, not tax enforcement, seemed paramount. Wright's case procedure instructions required preparation of a narrative report for each SSS case at least once every three months. These reports from the field would be double-sealed and sent to Wright at a post office box in Washington. Each report was to include a summary of major actions proposed or completed, plans for future actions, copies of any referral reports to another division, copies of any delinquent returns secured, and any results if a case was closed at a district office. At about the same time Donald Bacon requested FBI Director J. Edgar Hoover to place the SSS on the FBI's dissemination list for "the types of organizations mentioned above and people associated with them." He then listed three pages of organizations.[23]

At the moment this was still no more than a working group, but it did not stay that way for long. The director of the Collection Division, Harold Snyder, prodded Meehan on July 9 that he should not wait to hear from the Justice Department about the organizations before acting. "That might be some time away," Snyder concluded. On July 14, Donald Bacon sent another memorandum to all regional commissioners, requesting additional information on the twenty-two organizations cited in his March 25 memo as well as asking for information on the fifty-five groups for which the SSS had requested FBI files. He received an immediate reply from revenue agent Robert Handley of the Los Angeles District Office, who had been investigating many of the organizations for several months. Handley reported that they obtained their funding chiefly from the federal government, religious organizations, and tax-exempt foundations. Because Handley had so much information, Donald Virdin revealed to him the existence of the Activist Organizations Committee but warned that this was not to be publicized even within the IRS.[24]

Eventually the IRS audited a number of these fifty-five organizations, including the Americans for Democratic Action, Breakthrough, the Christian Beacon, the Christian Echoes Ministry, the Church League of America, the Citywide Citizens Action Committee, the Conservative Vice-Lords, the Fund for the Republic, the Institute for American Democracy, the Institute for the Study of Black Unity, the Life Line Foundation, the National Council of Churches of Christ, the National Student Association, the Patriotic party, the Peace Foundation, Protestants and Other Americans United for Separation of Church and State, the Republic of New Africa, the Southern Student Organizing Committee, and the United Black Community Organization.[25]

SSS files reveal that throughout this formative period the IRS remained in touch with the White House about the program. Patrick Putnam, the FBI liaison with the IRS, reported to Donald Virdin that White House aide Tom Huston had read the various IRS memoranda and was pleased that Internal Revenue was finally taking action against many of these groups. Copies of Bacon's memoranda as well as minutes of the early SSS meetings had gone to Roger Barth, who had given them to Huston.[26]

On July 18, 1969, the IRS formally established the Special Service Staff. It was designed to "coordinate activities in all Compliance Divisions involving ideological, militant, subversive, radical, and similar type organizations; to collect basic intelligence data; and to insure that the requirements of the Internal Revenue Code concerning such organizations have been complied with." The new committee was to "function indefinitely." It would target organizations (and individuals too) based on their ideas, tactics, and objectives rather than on violations of the tax code. Not only was this mandate broad, it duplicated in many ways FBI COINTELPRO efforts currently under way. The SSS committee believed that some of the organizations under investigation "may be a threat to the security of the United States," and intended to investigate "the sources of their funds, the names of contributors, whether the contributions given to the organizations have been deducted as charitable contributions, [and] what we can generally find out about the funds of these organizations." Paul Wright, chairman of this new group, planned an organizational meeting for July 24; full-time operation would begin August 1, 1969.[27]

A July 22 memo outlined the group's operational method: "what we will attempt to do is to gather intelligence data on the organizations in which we are interested and to use a strike force concept. . . ." In preparation for the July 24 meeting, Donald Virdin prepared a more detailed "talking paper." He indicated that the current activism was an "extremely important and sensitive matter" that had attracted interest from the "highest levels of Government." By that, he later explained, he meant the FBI, the Department of Justice Criminal Division and Internal Security Division, military intelligence activities of the Defense Department, and several congressional committees. The problem of defining "ideological" or "activist" remained, however, and Virdin admitted that the SSS group had a "general idea" but "no fixed limits." The seventy-seven organizations for which the committee had requested FBI files were presumably representative of future SSS targets. The IRS would try to determine their source of funds, and data processing would run filing checks on all individuals. But, Virdin warned, they had to be very careful. Many of the groups considered themselves to be political organizations, a sensitive issue where the committee would need guidance from the IRS chief counsel. "We certainly must not open the door to widespread notoriety that would embarrass the Administration or any elected official," he wrote. Finally, and perhaps most revealing, Virdin concluded:

> From a strictly revenue standpoint, we may have little reason for establishing this Committee or for expending the time and effort which may be necessary, but we must do it. We have gotten too much adverse publicity about exempt organizations and, even though these may not be considered exempt, they are nonbusiness organizations of a completely different character.[28]

This was a stunning admission. The IRS was targeting groups because it feared embarrassment when they exercised their First Amendment rights under the Constitution.

Minutes of the July 24 meeting, marked "Disclose on a need to know basis only," indicate that the group adopted Virdin's talking paper virtually without change. The committee again failed to define what it meant by activist organizations, and merely referred to the lists of seventy-seven organizations already sent to field offices for investigation. In a confidential report on the SSS prepared a few years later, the IRS admitted that it never really developed any definition for its targets. Claiming that it examined organizations and individuals "without regard" to their "philosophy or political posture," the IRS revealed that its efforts were "directed to the notoriety of the individual or organization and the probability that publicity might result from their activities and the likelihood that this notoriety would lead to inquiries regarding their tax status." In other words, the SSS was to provide cover for the IRS with Congress and the media.[29]

The principal function of the SSS would be to analyze data that came in to the National Office, then disseminate that information to the "appropriate Compliance activity" for field investigations. Although full-time committee members would have top-secret clearance, the SSS itself would not conduct investigations or assume any Compliance functions. The danger of this operation was that the "tentacles of some of these organizations are so far reaching that it would take an exorbitant amount of our resources if we did everything that could be done." With "limited resources in money and manpower," SSS could only "hit the high spots." This sounded very much like selective enforcement.[30]

Five days later the group met again, together with Philip Manuel and two other representatives from the McClellan Committee, chiefly to deal with the disclosure problems and to enlist the committee's help. While all requests for disclosure were to go through "regular channels and the Disclosure and Liaison Branch," Paul Wright made clear his determination that *everything* else would run through him. This was, as events quickly made clear, a move for greater control and power. As such, it irritated some SSS members such as Bernard Meehan and Donald Virdin. The group also brainstormed ways to jump-start the SSS. Virdin suggested close liaison with the FBI and subscriptions to "all underground militant and revolutionary newspapers," and the group reviewed individuals and organizations that contributed to SNCC. Their chief purpose, Virdin reported, was to "insure that all IRS laws have been complied with, that all income tax returns and payroll tax returns have been filed, that regular information returns have been filed, [and] that any income is reported properly." All the SSS needed to launch its operation was office space.[31]

Within days it was fully operational, and reports on a wide range of organizations and individuals poured into the IRS National Office from the regional commissioners. Some of the reports clearly concerned organizations that represented no security threat but merely challenged the status quo, such as the Denver War on Poverty. Each report included not only the tax return filing and payment history but the names and addresses of the organizers and present officers along with an assortment of other information. The Los Angeles Intelligence Division reported, for example, that churches were subsidizing "militant organizations," and that a "maze of interlacing individuals and organizations ... are bent on destroying the economic, political, and military powers of the United States Government." They later added a thought, "not as yet developed," that perhaps wealthy individuals were donating funds to tax-exempt organizations, who in turn financed militant groups. This was the only tax implication they could concoct.[32]

It was sufficient for SSS supporters, however. The FBI was ecstatic about the new IRS operation, believing it was "long overdue" and would seriously cripple dissident organizations. On August 5 three FBI special agents met with the SSS and agreed to provide everything the group wanted and more. The Bureau supplied a broad range of reports, selecting them on political and ideological criteria rather than on potential tax liabilities. It included, for instance, a list of 2,300 "Old Left," "New Left," and "Right Wing" organizations. The SSS also received folders and index cards relating to national security cases. All of this further shifted the IRS's focus from tax enforcement to intelligence gathering.[33]

In August 10 remarks before the American Bar Association in Dallas, IRS Commissioner Randolph Thrower noted that it "should come as no surprise" that the IRS was having "some difficulty in determining the outer limits of the traditional concepts of charity as they relate to current efforts to improve the status of under-privileged persons or minority groups within our inner cities." While he admitted that the purposes of the organizations in question fell within traditional definitions of education, religion, or charity, he spoke instead on the relationship of their activities to their tax exemption. "What are the consequences," he asked, "of such activities as coercive picketing, sit-ins, lie-ins, mill-ins, forceful occupation of university buildings, demonstrations that evolve into disorderly conduct, economic boycotts or the concerted nonpayment of debts?" He failed to indicate, however, how and why these activities raised tax-exemption questions; he was more concerned about the political tone of their message than anything else. If the "scope of education" extended to "scholarly dissertations on the allegedly historical inevitability of revolution," he asked, "would it also extend to instruction in guerrilla warfare techniques? How about instruction in draft evasion?"[34]

A few days later Paul Wright told Donald Bacon to expect "an extreme proliferation of our files." Within thirty days he expected to have amassed between five hundred and eight hundred files, and this was just the beginning. The SSS had arranged for a "drop box" and had developed a pseudonym to subscribe to nine "militant and revolutionary communist endorsed newspapers." Those papers would provide leads to other organizations and individuals. Committee members clipped articles furiously from various newspapers, magazines, and the *Congressional Record*. Although only nine days had passed since its formal operations had begun, Wright reported the discovery that few organizations in their files had complied with Internal Revenue laws. Wright also revealed important philosophical and political biases, lamenting the "sorry state of affairs" whereby many "extremist, dissident, militant or revolutionary organizations" had received federal funding or funding through religious organizations. His report freely mixed a combination of fact and editorial comment. The SSS effort, he wrote Leon Green, would "over a period of time represent a massive central intelligence file for use in initiating and facilitating IRS actions." That effort clearly targeted organizations and individuals based on intelligence dealing with nontax activities. Boasting to Green about the group's efforts after only two weeks, Wright reported that the committee was "dealing with over 700 organization or individual names where there is ample evidence of activities involving arson, fire-bombing, civil disorders, accumulation of illegal firearms, stores of ammunition, printing and distribution of publications advocating revolution against the government of this country."[35]

Wright was particularly drawn to the Black Panther party because of its internal structure as well as its perceived threat. He enumerated the leadership structure by position, noted the spread of chapters throughout the country, and concluded that its " 'soldiers' apparently number into the thousands." Less than three weeks after becoming operational, the SSS had amassed more than 500 files identifying Black Panther members. A week later this figure had grown to 950 files, and by late October to 1,750. Proliferation indeed! In late August the SSS also received from the Justice Department a computer printout of 10,000 individuals involved in civil disturbances. Again, the IRS had no evidence that any one of these 10,000 had tax problems. It used the list to create targets of opportunity, hoping to discover individuals with tax problems, no matter how minor, in a broader effort to disrupt dissident activity in the United States. Other files arrived from congressional committees, local law enforcement officials in California, the Naval Investigation Service, and Air Force Intelligence. Bob Handley of the Los Angeles District Office promised large charts on three militant organizations prepared by the Los Angeles Police Department. Senator John Williams of Delaware, upset at the anti-poverty program and seeking ways to harass it, asked the IRS to investigate community-action agencies in his state. The IRS declined Williams's request, claiming that cost considerations prevented it from investigating every agency and taxpayer delinquency. This was a surprising response, considering Wright's zeal and the approach the SSS had already taken. As Wright himself later admitted in one of his biweekly reports, "tax considerations were not always paramount in SSS decisions to refer cases to the field." There were instances, he noted, "where enforcement against flagrant law violators would have some salutary effect in this overall battle against persons bent on destruction of this government."[36]

By this time the Justice Department was generating weekly computer printouts of individuals involved in civil disturbances as well as creating three 5x8 cards for each individual cited. It also printed organization data listings as well as an incident data listing, the latter broken down by region, state, and city and in chronological order. In early October 1969 the SSS asked for copies of all these files. SSS officials also contacted Army Intelligence and borrowed copies of the army's counterintelligence *Compendium*, a listing of dissident individuals and organizations. It established liaison with Air Force Counterintelligence, although it is not clear if the SSS received any files from the air force. The Secret Service provided files on more than 25,000 individuals, but the SSS apparently did not draw significant information from those files. Later, in a response to a query from Senator Sam Ervin, IRS Commissioner Donald Alexander denied that the IRS had ever received the Secret Service master tape. SSS records seem to indicate otherwise. Finally, SSS investigators made extensive use of the *Guide to the American Left* and the *Guide to the American Right*, listings of more than 5,000 individuals and organizations. SSS copies of these guides were dog-eared and color coded.[37]

Perhaps the most revealing data that the SSS received was a guide to the identification of potential insurgency, which it requested from the army following an October 7 telephone call to establish liaison. This lengthy guide outlined "indicators for insurgency"—political, social, economic, and military. It also included a section on "Operations against the infrastructure," which seemed directed chiefly at potential communist takeovers and social pressure exerted against the government. It noted that dissident organizations were vulnerable to attacks against "either the causes or the leaders in order to choke off support before it becomes widespread." SSS targeting and operations would reflect that judgment. Overall the army document was oriented toward foreign threats and operations. But the SSS took to heart its admonition that the "force with the most effective intelligence operation will have a crucial advantage over the other side which may well mean the difference between defeat and victory." SSS officials also met with a criminal investigator and firearms enforcement officer from the Army Institute for Military Assistance at Fort Bragg, North Carolina. In addition, they evaluated Special Forces training classes "relating to insurgent indicators and organizational structure of insurgent forces." Leon Green concluded that "this training would be very beneficial to investigative personnel working hard core extremists."[38]

In early October, Donald Bacon sent a third letter to IRS regional commissioners, asking for information on twenty-two additional organizations. Committee files were proliferating rapidly, and Bacon wanted data on "substructures" and "splinter groups" in SSS files. In addition to tax-return information, he requested the organization's financial status and source of funds as well as a narrative statement that provided an "overall picture of the organization, its motives, its activities, its attitude, its size, and its impact on the general public." Bacon's new list again focused on organizations that challenged the status quo and administration policies, and was heavily weighted toward the black community and its activists. About this same time the IRS requested permission from Congressman Wright Patman to examine files of his Subcommittee on Foundations. Patman agreed to cooperate, but the SSS seems to have made little use of his documents.[39]

By late October, Paul Wright reported that his investigators had compiled 1,750 files, each of which "represents potential for worthwhile IRS field effort." But staffing was short. The original list of 77 organizations was considered insufficient; it should be expanded to include all individuals linked to those groups and others. One FBI report Wright had reviewed, for example, "clearly identified 27 individuals and 3 organizations for which files should be established as the information was pertinent and vital to our mission." Wright admitted that many of the organizations were "insolvent," but without more staffing the SSS could do no more than "skim the top off" what it already had. Organizations continued to proliferate; they were "springing up all over the country, each bringing in a new crop of individuals identified with them and their operation." Even as Wright lamented manpower shortages, however, the SSS expanded its liaisons by meeting with representatives of the Immigration and Naturalization Service and the Bureau of Narcotics and Dangerous Drugs. It also made almost 3,000 requests for Social Security numbers and hundreds of requests for wage information from the Social Security Administration. The director of Naval Intelligence provided two of its publications on the Vietnam protest movement and radical movements in general, and Air Force Intelligence furnished information on four anti-war organizations' solicitation of funds.[40]

With its voracious and apparently unlimited appetite for investigations, liaisons, and files, the SSS needed more than manpower additions. SSS officials explored the creation of a computerized master file for all individuals and organizations in its files and in the files of cooperating agencies. At a meeting in early October, the Justice Department's Civil Disturbance Group agreed to cooperate. With this information computerized, the SSS could merge FBI reports as well as reports from the Bureau of Narcotics and Dangerous Drugs, the Alcohol, Tobacco and Firearms Division of IRS, the Army Operations Center, the United States Attorney's office, newspaper clippings, and various local publications. Before the month was out the assistant IRS commissioners for compliance and data processing had prepared a formal proposal for a Compliance master file tape system. This was essential, they argued, "to ensure that certain individuals and organizations are adhering to their tax filing responsibilities in order to minimize any criticism or embarrassment upon the Commissioner and the Service." It would include the names of at least two thousand organizations and more than thirty thousand individuals. Each quarter "certain tax information" would be extracted from the business master file and the individual master file and added to this new file.[41]

SSS officials justified this request not only by citing the growth of their files but by asserting that investigations to date had revealed a "high rate of delinquency" with respect to these organizations' tax returns. They did not claim, however, that any of the organizations owed significant sums of money, and the report's focus on groups that financed "militant and revolutionary activities" revealed the ideological slant to the project. Computerization was essential, they argued, but a "primary factor that should be considered is the reaction to this type of system, computer or manual, from the mass media." With thirty thousand names in the file, innocent individuals would inevitably find their names included in the computerized files, particularly because the SSS intended to draw names provided by the Church League of America, a private right-wing group. When complete, the system would generate biweekly statistical data; other listings could be generated "periodically dependent upon need and demand."[42]

With SSS intelligence coverage now widespread, operations moved into high gear. Extensive reports from IRS regional offices on anti-Vietnam War demonstrations that November were sent both to the SSS and to the White House. By mid-November the regional commissioners were forwarding information on Bacon's most recent list of twenty-two organizations. Paul Wright reported that an IBM 360 computer was about to be moved to the IRS National Office and could be used for the computerization project. Donald Bacon asked Air Force Colonel Heston C. Cole, chief of the Army Counterintelligence Division, that the SSS be placed on his dissemination list of extremist organizations. Donald Virdin screened incoming Sensitive Case Reports to determine whether copies should be forwarded to Wright for use by the SSS.[43]

The SSS files for 1970 are filled with reports from other agencies and congressional committees, particularly from the House Committee on Internal Security. Staffers from those committees used SSS files in the IRS basement for their own investigations. Prints and investigative materials from congressional committees appear to have routinely migrated to SSS files. Efforts to complete the computerization project the previous fall had failed, and SSS staff members were still exploring ways to create a Compliance master file. Although one staffer reported that the "genesis of this project is purported to be from the Commissioner," others questioned if this was a project the IRS should undertake since it would take months just to program the data. Could Internal Revenue afford the loss of personnel to staff the new system? Was the potential return worth the effort? The administration expressed a keen interest, and Paul Wright forwarded lists of specific organizations and individuals under investigation to Roger Barth, who transmitted them to the White House. Student, anti-war, and racial groups received particular attention, in part because Wright knew the White House would be interested and in part because Wright was upset at their challenges to the status quo.[44]

The SSS investigation of the Black Panthers raised not only the issue of militancy and possible tax violations but the troubling question of what constituted a political party. The White House and the House Internal Security Committee were both interested. But in many respects the IRS in 1969 was no further along than it had been in 1962 during the Ideological Organizations Project, when it failed to arrive at a workable definition of what constituted impermissible behavior for exempt organizations. The IRS had never defined what constituted a political party for tax purposes, and individual regions often used different definitions. Alternatives to the Democratic and Republican parties had always experienced difficulty becoming part of the political system in the United States, and the controversies surrounding the Panthers drew particular attention to them.

During October 1970 the IRS did investigate the issue, concluding only that political parties were not taxable. It admitted, however, that not only had it never published a position on the issue but that that information had never been "divulged outside of the Service." Political parties occupied a "no-man's land in the world of taxation." They were neither exempt organizations nor did they pay income taxes. Despite the fact that no one had "ever come up with any consistent rationale to explain why this is so," it was the "longstanding Service position in the matter." Congress had not previously expressed a desire either to tax parties or to exempt them. That left the IRS to make its own administrative decisions, and the Exempt Organizations Branch provided a chronology drawn from a series of General Counsel Memoranda between 1957 and 1965. A Technical Study Project in 1968 had failed to deal with the issue, concluding only that contributions to parties were not taxable income. The IRS was reluctant to tax political parties because it feared that taxing them

> will lead to charges the tax laws are being used for partisan political purposes, especially where an effort is made to tax parties other than those in power. This would be particularly true in the case of minority groups which cannot realistically expect to obtain elective offices for their candidates.

After intense discussion, the IRS decided not to disclose its practices regarding political parties to the House Internal Security Committee. Commissioner Thrower eventually responded only that the IRS had an investigation under way.[45] In short, the IRS had considered the problem seriously but done nothing and revealed nothing.

If "political party" was a term reserved for an established or establishment party, the Panthers were clearly something different. But there was no justification for such a definition, and merely because Republicans and Democrats opposed the Panthers should not have affected the Panthers' tax status. Despite that, an investigator for the House Internal Security Committee forwarded to the SSS a list of Black Panther party bank deposits, arguing that "this is no longer a political party." What was the IRS doing about it? At least one regional counsel asked the National Office to prepare a position paper on the question to assure uniformity, and in March 1970 the assistant commissioner (Compliance) instructed agents not to seek income tax returns from the Black Panther party "pending the establishment of a uniform Service position concerning political parties." Two years later nothing had been done. The IRS was outwardly concerned that whatever guidelines it created would invoke the ire of both Republicans and Democrats; it undoubtedly also feared that serious inquiries from either major party would result in the exposure of IRS methods and investigative techniques. Pressure from the House Internal Security Committee for action against the Panthers only made IRS inaction more untenable. Donald Virdin reminded Assistant Commissioner (Compliance) Donald Bacon that the "Service may get into another embarrassing situation unless some action is taken promptly in this matter."[46]

The SSS faced other difficulties. It eagerly exchanged files with the House Internal Security Committee but in the process lost control over its own files. Donald Virdin of the Disclosure Branch asked the SSS not only for tax returns but for FBI reports, special agent reports, and other confidential IRS information on a wide range of organizations in which the committee had expressed interest. At the same time, however, questions surfaced about the FBI furnishing IRS materials to the White House. Some files apparently bypassed the IRS Disclosure staff, and as the SSS withdrew files from the IRS Intelligence Division the situation worsened. At one point, when dealing with matters involving Students for a Democratic Society, Disclosure staff found themselves having to open safes housing SSS files to see what was there. Meanwhile the White House demanded lists of contributors to various militant organizations, and the IRS eventually authorized the FBI to transmit any IRS information in its possession to the White House. The intelligence and political communities had become highly interactive; as the intelligence network expanded, the IRS was failing to protect the confidentiality of tax returns.[47]

All of these matters came to a head when the IRS tried to determine the exempt status of particular groups. The Patman hearings in the early and mid-1960s had revealed the failure of the IRS to scrutinize exempt organizations; by the end of the decade the multiplication of activist organizations, many with tax-exempt status or funding from tax-exempt groups, had aggravated the situation. A "discussion draft" prepared by the IRS outlined the basic problem: to "what extent should we use confidential information relative to certain notorious individuals to refuse to rule on an organization's exempt application?" The Internal Revenue Code did not provide for an examination or consideration of individuals' backgrounds when organizations applied for exempt status. But the IRS feared criticism if it granted exempt status to groups who had officers or directors with "flagrant criminal records or notoriously anti-social backgrounds." (It did not define the latter.) These were Sensitive Cases and attracted congressional attention. The IRS apparently failed to make any decision in the short term, but by 1972 the Exempt Organizations Branch was sending all cases that involved "ideological, militant, subversive or radical elements" to the SSS for audit. The word "activist" was now so loaded that Donald Bacon discontinued use of the title Activist Organizations Committee. In May 1970 the group officially adopted the title of Special Service Group (later changed to Special Service Staff).[48]

After the spring of 1970 the SSS became increasingly concerned about war tax resisters, which it defined as any individual or organization that refused to pay federal income or excise taxes as a protest against the Vietnam War. During the next two years it accumulated more than 800 files, largely from the FBI, and acquired copies of tax-resistance publications as well as a list of underground newspapers and their editors. The SSS used these to compile a list of individuals and organizations active in the resistance movement. After a long delay it referred at least 550 to the field in 1972 and 1973 for further investigation. The SSS also stepped up its surveillance of "national security" cases and revoked the exempt status of groups such as the United States Servicemen's Fund that provided minimal support to GI coffeehouses and underground newspapers. IRS agents also testified before congressional committees investigating radical activity. In one case, in Fall River, Massachusetts, agents actively aided FBI investigations of the National Conference for New Politics and the Venceremos Brigade, and received biweekly intelligence digests from informants. The SSS was also suspected of receiving documents stolen from the homes of dissidents by state officials or the FBI. The SSS had created an intelligence octopus.[49]

As White House interest in dissident organizations continued to sharpen, President Nixon requested a full review of all intelligence collection practices involving domestic dissenters. Nixon wanted an operation run out of the White House, and presidential assistant Tom Huston proposed the so-called Huston Plan. Huston's proposal was even more far-reaching than SSS efforts, although the two overlapped at times. His plan, which FBI Director Hoover opposed (calling Huston a "hippie intellectual"), never became operational, but Huston did not give up easily. On August 14, 1970, he wrote Roger Barth to ask what progress the IRS Compliance Division had made with respect to ideological organizations since the first expression of White House interest a year earlier. On September 19, IRS Commissioner Randolph Thrower responded, sending Huston a copy of a status report on the Special Service Staff. Emphasizing that "knowledge of the existence and operations of this Group should be carefully limited," the report did not really say much. It noted that some "extremist groups" posed a tax-liability problem for the IRS, and outlined in general terms the history of the SSS and its interests. Perhaps most significant, though somewhat buried in the report, was the admission that data on only twenty-six organizations and forty-three individuals had been "referred to the field for enforcement action." It was too early, Thrower argued, for the IRS to have completed many field investigations. But he defended the effort as "necessary to avoid allegations that extremist organizations ignore taxing statutes with immunity [sic]."[50]

Thrower claimed that the SSS identified organizations and individuals without regard to their philosophy or "political posture," emphasizing instead that notoriety and the "probability of publicity" determined SSS targets. Although he cited the possibility that these groups might deliberately avoid their tax responsibilities, public relations rather than tax concerns predominated. His notation that the group's name had been changed from the Activist Organizations Committee to the Special Service Group in May 1970 to avoid "possible criticism and embarrassment to the Service" further emphasized this point. It now investigated any "organization or individual that may cause discredit or embarrassment to the Service." Files had increased dramatically, and Thrower foresaw steady increases well into the future since "extremist, militant and revolutionary groups" were "coming into existence all over the country in unabated profusion." He concluded by warning that

> tax exempt money had been directed into politics, civil disorders, criminal activities involving organized burglary, arson, fire-bombing, "shakedowns," purchase of firearms, stores of ammunition, and the printing of revolutionary publications, all aimed at destroying the economic, administrative, political and military powers of the United States Government.[51]

It was war, and the IRS was on the front lines.

Huston apparently was less than impressed, noting to Bob Haldeman that Thrower's report was "long on words and short on substance." IRS intelligence operations still held promise, he insisted, and he argued that Internal Revenue could take action against left-wing groups that "we cannot do in a courtroom via criminal prosecutions." Field audits would turn up intelligence information, but the IRS needed to be more vigorous. In 1975, Huston testified that neither Haldeman nor anyone else in the White House responded to his memorandum and that he had no subsequent contact with the IRS and had never asked for information on any organization from the IRS. Huston implied, however, that the SSS was the IRS reaction to earlier White House requests for information on exempt organizations, and that it "was rooting around in a thousand different organizations" but had never provided any specific responses. Senator Barry Goldwater rose to Huston's defense, characterizing the IRS as a "rattlesnake sliding along in the grass" and warning that the IRS would protect "any organization in this country they feel like protecting."[52]

During the next three years, as SSS operations reached their peak, both liberals and conservatives expressed outrage at IRS actions. Liberals attacked its intrusiveness and raised privacy concerns while conservatives wanted harsher measures against radical groups. But neither political faction knew that the Special Service Staff even existed. Ironically, an effort by the Internal Revenue Service to inoculate itself from political pressures and criticism had embroiled it in a political crossfire as radical activities increased in the United States along with demands that the government suppress them.

CHAPTER FOURTEEN

THE SSS:
IN THE TRENCHES
AND UNDER FIRE

DURING THE NEXT THREE YEARS the Special Service Staff accelerated its investigations of tax-exempt activist groups opposed to administration policies. It developed smooth working relationships with the FBI, the House Internal Security Committee, and the Internal Security Division of the Department of Justice, sharing the tax returns of many organizations and their officers, including Students for a Democratic Society, the Black Panther party, the New Mobilization Committee to End the War in Vietnam, and the Progressive Labor party. Senator John McClellan's Committee on Government Operations also obtained tax returns as it investigated riots and campus disturbances. Although disclosure laws required the congressional committees to keep this income tax information confidential, they found a loophole in the law. When a committee reported to Congress, it could legally publish reports and release tax information, thereby skirting confidentiality laws. During this same time the FBI intensified its harassment of dissident groups, often breaking into their offices and checking their income tax records. Income tax information was pivotal to the Bureau's Key Black Extremist Program, established in December 1970 as part of the FBI's counterintelligence program. The IRS cooperated without hesitation with at least seventy-two of the ninety FBI requests for tax returns.[1] Then, in 1973, IRS Commissioner Donald Alexander suddenly abolished the SSS. Two years later, in the aftermath of Watergate, the IRS and the SSS were under investigation from congressional committees and Watergate prosecutors.

Between 1970 and 1973 two targets were paramount: black organizations and anti-war groups. Forty-one percent of the groups the Special Service Staff investigated were black. It compiled large clipping files on such individuals as Bayard Rustin, Roy Wilkins, and Vernon Jordan, files that included materials with no apparent connection to tax issues. It also targeted war tax resisters. Staff members clipped newspapers and reviewed the activities of peace activists based chiefly on press reports. Between 1969 and 1972 the FBI sent eleven thousand investigative reports to the SSS, and the group regularly received FBI COINTELPRO files. Even though the SSS occasionally found tax violations, politics was the driving force behind this intelligence activity. On occasion these investigations leaked to the press. The IRS quickly sought to locate and seal the leaks, but disclosures failed to curb SSS zeal for investigating anti-war organizations. The American Friends Service Committee (AFSC) attracted particular attention because it opposed the war in Vietnam and provided funds to other anti-war organizations. The IRS characterized the AFSC as "long associated with radical, militant, and subversive groups," charging that it had taken a leadership role in anti-war activities. That role, not known tax problems, made it a target for challenges to its exempt status. The SSS used the same tactic against the Vietnam Moratorium Committee, insisting that the organization was liable for taxes and eventually placing a lien against officials of the organization for $17,500 in employment taxes. In this case, however, Sam Brown of the Moratorium Committee admitted that the group "legitimately owe[d] the taxes" and was working to pay them. Brown even praised the IRS for being "pretty decent about it."[2]

The Special Service Staff's relationship with the Justice Department's Internal Security Division (ISD) was particularly important. At a meeting on March 26, 1971, officials from the ISD and the SSS met to discuss a new unit formed by Assistant Attorney General Robert C. Mardian, known as the Analysis and Evaluation Section. It had two components, an Intelligence Analysis Unit and a Legal Evaluation Unit, which together employed about 46 technicians and attorneys. Their purpose was to obtain information from the FBI, IRS, and other federal agencies on "subversive" organizations. The Justice Department had compiled a computerized listing of 18,000 individuals and organizations, along with a list of laws each one might have violated. SSS chairman Paul Wright revealed that his group had a list of 1,500 organizations and 5,500 individuals, and hoped that the ISD could aid IRS intelligence efforts against all of them by merging the lists. Chief of the Analysis and Evaluation Section of the ISD, R. Richards Rolapp, assured Wright that his group would provide "whatever cooperation was needed" and hoped the SSS would reciprocate.[3]

ISD reports could address Paul Wright's complaint that FBI reports received by the SSS provided good leads but lacked specific data bearing on tax liability or compliance. The ISD was a direct recipient of FBI reports on civil disorders as well as "subversives" and "extremists," and Rolapp promised that he would be "happy to obtain amplifying information from the FBI" whenever SSS investigators requested it. The disclosure issue remained a stumbling block for full SSS cooperation, however, and Wright considered a definite commitment from the IRS to be premature. For their part, ISD officials wanted to establish informal lines of communication so they could request information on IRS tax investigations without going through formal disclosure procedures. Wright was eager to cooperate, and Donald Virdin indicated that "something could be worked out along a more informal basis" so as not to involve the IRS commissioner at every point. Both organizations agreed to exchange listings of organizations and individuals of primary interest to each of them, and Wright arranged to provide, "on an informal basis," IRS guidelines for the investigation of tax-exempt organizations.[4]

The extent of interaction between these two groups is a bit unclear. IRS historian Shelley Davis claimed that the entire effort was nothing more than a "smoke-and-mirrors monstrosity" that provided the illusion of activity. The SSS itself later asserted that arrangements with the ISD were never implemented. Investigations by congressional committees, however, tell a different story, characterizing the SSS as the "effective intelligence arm" of the IRS and developing evidence that the SSS furnished copies of tax returns and written reports of cases that involved nontax violations to the ISD. A Subcommittee on Constitutional Rights, chaired by Senator Sam Ervin, later discovered that informal arrangements *were* implemented, and were then followed by formal requests to the IRS for disclosure of information that the ISD had already received informally, and which it considered relevant to ongoing investigations. In other words, ISD first looked at IRS information informally, then, if it decided to take action, it formally requested the same information so as to appear in conformity with disclosure laws.

The SSS also implemented exchanges with the FBI. In one 60-day period the SSS received 581 FBI files. Apparently this was not unusual, for Senator Ervin discovered that by "prearrangement FBI knew SSS would be interested in certain individuals and organizations." During the FBI's investigation of the Black Panther party, Director J. Edgar Hoover requested SSS updates of its investigations of the Panthers. Although the SSS denied that it was collecting information on anyone because they opposed administration policies, it privately admitted that in 1971 and 1972 "changing social, political and economical trends and uneasiness about our ability to gain general agreement on the rightness of maintaining files on 'extremists' had something to do" with a shift of emphasis to tax resistance.[5]

Most of the traffic in intelligence appears to have flowed to the SSS rather than from it to other agencies. The Joint Committee on Internal Revenue Taxation, which tended to exonerate the SSS of all transgressions, concluded that no list was ever passed to the ISD. Bountiful evidence exists, on the other hand, of FBI and ISD reports becoming part of SSS files. In addition, the ISD provided SSS with a computerized list of individuals "considered to have a potential for civil disturbance"—the Subject Data list. SSS clerks systematically combed this list, preparing a file on every individual for whom the SSS did not already have one. The SSS sent the names and birth dates for listed individuals to the Division of Reporting and Accounting Methods in the Social Security Administration, requesting their Social Security numbers. It then tracked each individual, in a fishing expedition, to see if they had complied with Internal Revenue laws. It also sent a list of the individuals and their Social Security numbers to the IRS National Computer Center in Martinsburg, West Virginia, to secure a printout from the Individual Master File and determine whether an audit was needed. Audit information referred to IRS field offices, moreover, contained excerpts from FBI reports, though the SSS did not identify the source of the information. There is no evidence that the Subject Data list had anything whatsoever to do with tax violations. The SSS also received requests for tax information from the ISD—ninety-nine between 1969 and 1972—and it sent at least eighteen of these to the field for investigation.[6] Since these totals do not seem very large given the scope of its effort, the SSS seems to have been more committed to intelligence gathering and the compilation of files than it was to action.

SSS officials nonetheless were pleased. Anticipating the arrival of a new commissioner following Randolph Thrower's resignation in January 1971, Donald Bacon took stock of the SSS. Concluding that "we have gotten good mileage out of the group," he proposed that operations continue until the IRS was reorganized under the new commissioner. And they did. Bacon sought information from Army Intelligence about anti-war operations around military bases, and reported to Roger Barth about IRS audits of radical organizations as a consequence of SSS intelligence gathering.[7]

The case of the Cummins Engine Foundation of Indiana exemplified these SSS operations. In December 1971 the ISD Analysis and Evaluation Section developed a "Preliminary Analysis" of the foundation, which claimed that it supported various dissident groups, including "Black Revolutionary Groups." The SSS then provided its own evaluation as part of its review of philanthropic foundations to determine if their activities were consistent with their announced purpose. The report revealed the close working relationship between ISD and the SSS, as well as evidence that they exchanged files on Cummins. The IRS admitted that the foundation was a "legitimate philanthropic enterprise," but believed that it served as a "conduit for funds to support black militants and other organizations" that were "known to consistently promote racial revolutionary activities." Much of the IRS's information clearly came from the FBI, and records in SSS files described Cummins's chairman as part of the "avant garde of the civil rights movement." Among the charges against the foundation: it gave money to organizations that recruited black activists to participate in revolutionary training in Communist China; it contributed money to the Institute for Policy Studies (where the foundation's Washington Program Director Ivanhoe Donaldson was a resident fellow); it provided funds for printing equipment to organizations "advocating revolutionary social change"; it had close relations with "certain Marxist-Leninist organizations"; one of its program directors (Walter Lively) had been indicted for inciting a riot in 1970, and the same individual had used Cummins funds to purchase a farm for use as a youth camp "to train children in self-defense and in African culture."[8]

The report cited the Cummins Engine Foundation for providing funds to the National Association of Black Students in 1971 and for giving at least $5,000 to the Frantz Fanon Institute. It criticized Lively's establishment of the Liberation House Press and Liberation Bookstore in Baltimore, as well as his intent to create a SOUL school on the farm in Bedford, Pennsylvania. The ISD also reported that its survey of organizations "involved in the CEF [Cummins] financial web" found "consistent efforts to disseminate revolutionary materials and information." Two facets of the report are striking. Not only does it reveal a web of intelligence linkages between the ISD, the FBI, and the IRS, it also demonstrates that these agencies targeted groups because of their political philosophies and activities rather than because they had committed any illegal acts or violated provisions of the tax code. Once targeted, the groups then came under close scrutiny as all three intelligence operations sought to uncover violations of law that would justify action.[9]

To advance its own intelligence-gathering capacity, the SSS (and apparently the ISD as well) subscribed to the *TUPART Monthly Reports on the Underground Press*, published in Washington, D.C., by National Media Analysis. This publication contained reports and summaries of stories in the underground press as well as independent commentary, and in 1971 it reported that underground newspapers claimed a readership of twenty million. Typical of its reports was the assertion that the underground press not only sought peace in Vietnam but used the desire for peace to further "violent REVOLUTION." The reports also called attention to war tax resistance. Apparently the market for *TUPART* was not large, however, and it ceased publication in September 1971. To replace it, the SSS obtained copies of the Liberation News Service's "Radical Publications and Organizations List." It tried to attack these papers by examining their corporate tax returns but discovered that since expenses usually surpassed deposits, most of the papers made no money and thus were not liable for corporate income tax. It then turned to the Social Security Administration, hoping to discover that employers had not reported wages and withheld the proper Social Security taxes. It sent the Social Security Administration lists of employers and possible employees, requesting tax information for 1969, 1970, and 1971. That approach did not prove fruitful either, since most employees were students with little income. Examinations of bank records and other facets of these individuals' lives also turned up nothing. One district director, while insisting that these people were "armed and dangerous," concluded that the results did not justify the effort. Full-scale audits would be a waste of time and money. The fact remained, however, that the groups were targeted by a variety of federal intelligence agencies solely because they published anti-government opinions that were not popular.[10]

Throughout 1971 and 1972 the SSS became extremely interested in war tax resistance. Because it believed the underground press was crucial to investigations of the tax resistance movement, SSS interest in these papers persisted. They were a "conduit" for the movement, according to the SSS, and many articles detailed ways to confuse IRS operations. The SSS compiled files on 148 underground papers, launched investigations of the two major sources of articles for them, and infiltrated a May 1971 meeting of "underground press personalities" in Austin, Texas. Unlike many earlier targets, tax resistance raised a legitimate issue of tax compliance, but politics still determined the targeting. The war tax resistance movement was chiefly the work of individuals, many of whom had little income and owed little if any tax in the first place. They were driven by conscience, not by any conviction that the funds they withheld were monetarily important to the IRS. The SSS, however, saw an opportunity to send a message that no one should be able to escape taxes except under IRS guidelines for deductions.[11]

To catch resisters, the SSS infiltrated national committee meetings of tax protesters; reports for 1971 and 1972 are in SSS files. The 1971 report outlined strategies of tax resistance, particularly efforts to expand and advocate other places to deposit tax monies (such as People's Life Funds) as opposition to the Vietnam War mounted among the middle class. Tax resisters also wanted to expand their recruitment of IRS employees "to help with internal sabotage of the system." IRS informers took an active role in these meetings, even providing advice to resisters about how to cheat on their taxes. Concealing income attracted attention, one informer noted, but inflating deductions did not. "That's going to be our game," declared the resisters, "bloating up the deductions." This led resisters to believe that many IRS employees were sympathetic to their movement, and they welcomed informers who presented them with plans to "screw up the Establishment's works." The idea was to send in ten to twelve thousand phony 1040 forms and have them fed into the computers, as well as phony W-2 forms asking for refunds. Other resisters believed that the Internal Revenue Code itself was unconstitutional. Informers in one region warned that some protesters might turn violent due to a "combination of environment, heredity, religion and an unusual class of people that inhabit the area."[12]

Testifying later before a congressional committee, IRS Commissioner Randolph Thrower insisted that Internal Revenue staff gave minimal special attention to groups who "openingly and notoriously" advocated "nonfiling of tax returns or nonpayment of certain taxes" because "we could not ignore them." There were few prosecutions, and most individuals paid taxes (like the telephone tax*) when asked. Thrower may have been correct, but SSS files tell a different story. In fact, after 1971 the commissioner's office pressed the SSS to limit its files to tax resisters. At the same time the SSS itself had decided that "more and more of our indexes should be directed toward tax protes-

---

*First enacted in 1898 to raise money for the Spanish-American War, the telephone tax had been revived in every twentieth-century war. The Korean War tax was set to expire in 1966, but in the aftermath of the Gulf of Tonkin incident, Congress extended the tax. It became a target of war resisters during the Vietnam era.

tors." By January 1971 it had initiated field investigations of at least two groups that it considered leaders in the war resistance movement, both of which were 501(c)(4) social welfare organizations to which contributions were generally not tax deductible. Other cases had been referred to the field for investigation. SSS efforts apparently were well targeted, for Paul Wright reported that all the individuals listed in an article on war tax resistance in the November 28, 1971, *Washington Post* were already in SSS files and had been the subject of SSS tax investigations. When that article came to the attention of new commissioner Johnnie Walters, he directed the IRS to intensify its activity in this area. Within a short time the SSS had compiled 800 files and referred 550 cases to the field, 397 on individuals and 153 on organizations. The final 230 cases were sent to the field in December 1973, four months *after* IRS Commissioner Donald Alexander disbanded the Special Service Staff— a telling reminder that while the IRS may have disavowed the SSS, it did nothing to prevent the agency or rogue employees from continuing to undertake actions like those of the SSS.[13]

In the midst of its pursuit of war tax resisters, the SSS became formalized within the IRS and received commendations from leading IRS officials. Deputy Commissioner William Loeb thanked Paul Wright for "performing a fine service in helping to identify those who would avoid, evade, or defeat our tax system.... Keep on Keeping On!" In January 1972, Wright complained that the SSS still did not officially exist on paper and lacked program guidance and evaluation. Not only did too many IRS employees not take it seriously, they often considered an SSS assignment to be a dead-end job which threatened opportunities for promotion. Wright urged his superiors to incorporate the SSS formally into the IRS bureaucratic structure, insisting that its data accumulation methods had been successful by providing an "area of non-compliance detection otherwise unavailable." Commissioner Johnnie Walters, apparently learning about the SSS for the first time, agreed, ordering the SSS into new facilities on the sixth floor of the National Office and transferring its operations to the Collection Division. In April 1972, the IRS finally disclosed the existence of the SSS in its Internal Revenue Manual, ending three years of secrecy. Even then, however, there was no mention of its focus on activist individuals and organizations.[14]

Formal acknowledgment of the SSS did not slow its energetic pursuit of tax resisters. By spring 1972 it had sent to all districts a war tax resister package consisting of a brochure listing centers and individuals identified as advocating tax noncompliance, examples of "propaganda" used by the resistance movement, and names of known resisters in each district. Meanwhile the SSS continued to update its resister files as fast as it could identify individuals and organizations, prepared supplements for the districts, and warned that the movement appeared to be "growing by alarming dimensions." Paul Wright revealed that *WIN* magazine in New York City and *Tax Talk*, published by the War Tax Resistance in New York City, had obtained and published an internal IRS memorandum warning that resisters were illegally claiming a "War Crime Deduction" on their tax returns as well as filing various forms to bring the system down. The law firm of Egnal and Egnal, it reported, was counseling clients to "use the 'War Crimes Deduction' as a vehicle to protest the conflict in Vietnam." The IRS launched an internal investigation to find the source of the memorandum leak.[15]

The issue of war tax resistance was a primary topic at a November 1972 IRS conference for assistant and regional commissioners in Charlottesville, Virginia. The National Office warned:

> The proliferation of highly organized groups attempting to accomplish massive tax rebellion actions is moving into epidemic proportions and ultimately could erode the very roots of our tax system. There is an increasing degree of sophistication in the methods used by these groups. The Service must take the offensive and bring together all of its resources in order to combat this movement.

The IRS actually went further, warning that classified SSS documents revealed the transfer of "large amounts of money" into the country from abroad to fund organizations that sought to overthrow the government. It listed Cuba, North Vietnam, Algeria, and the "Iron Curtain" as sources for those funds.[16]

The conference focused on "extremist" organizations and their propensity for tax resistance. The National Office warned that tax-exempt organizations were taking actions outside their charters, not filing required taxable returns, and fighting proposed revocations of their exemptions. Telephone Tax and Air Fare Tax movements were also multiplying, and the IRS expressed concern about a "General Tax Strike Movement." It worried about its inability to obtain a "good fix" on several organizations that expressed "anti-establishment views," and feared that some had infiltrated as employees into the IRS to learn its system, disseminate information, conduct sabotage, and cause various internal security problems. It urged regional commissioners to provide the SSS with more specific information from the field. "We are dealing with a more sophisticated type of individual," it warned.[17]

The document also served as a talking paper for the commissioner, who hoped to persuade the Treasury secretary to establish a strike force. In doing so it revealed SSS methods: using pseudonyms to become members of suspect groups and receive their literature, making small contributions to these groups under pseudonyms to obtain information and names, and subscribing under false names to publications from which SSS maintained a clipping service for its files. Finally, it listed the categories of protest groups that evoked concern.

> Radical groups; Campus groups, Extremists on Right; Extremists—Religious; Telephone tax resisters; General tax resisters—purporting by legal means; General tax strikers—activists, subversives proposing general strike to kill system; Ideological groups we don't know too much about; Radical telephone tax groups are moving rapidly to [General tax strikers]; Black Militants; Ethnic militants; Extremist EO [Exempt Organization] groups operating under cloak of religious, charitable or do-goody (welfare, etc.) auspices; Para military groups; Identified subversive groups; Organizations and groups identified as supported and directed by *extreme liberal elected officials* [my emphasis]; Violent groups not well publicized—many individuals identified by FBI; Org. alleged non-violent military based groups; Underground newspapers for all kinds of protesters; [one category redacted]; Citizen Action Groups with *questionable motives—anti-establishment* [my emphasis]; Anti-War Groups.

Not only was the list extensive, selection appeared based more often on political criteria than tax criteria. The SSS admitted that it knew little about some of the organizations listed but included them because of a belief that they threatened the established system.[18]

A more formal memorandum prepared for the Charlottesville conference broadened the SSS mission well beyond concerns about tax compliance. Although it began with a sentence recognizing the right to "legally and peacefully protest," it quickly moved to complain about those who would tear down the current system or who made "unreasonable demands." Citing incidences of May Day demonstrations, destruction of draft cards and Selective Service records, and rock festivals that attracted "youth and narcotics," the National Office advised field personnel to be "alert to criminal violations other than those involving the tax statutes." All such violations should be reported to the SSS, which would "coordinate with the appropriate agency" and provide access to its voluminous files.[19]

The reach of the SSS apparently recognized no limits and seemed out of control. It now saw every sort of protest as a move against the tax system, and believed that only a massive counterintelligence effort could prevent an insidious and massive attack on the American economy.

To drive the point home, as if more evidence was needed, the IRS also provided regional commissioners with a package of exhibits focusing on war tax resistance, including internal documents of the resistance movement. These reveal that resisters' plans were grand but participation minimal—quite the opposite of what the SSS had implied. One document, from the Charlottesville, Virginia, conference that concentrated on the War Tax Resistance movement, outlined an impressive list of activities and protests the group had undertaken, from demonstrating against the Vietnam War by holding up posters of the My Lai massacre to passing out leaflets and participating in guerrilla theatre skits. It revealed, however, that the group consisted of only about twenty-five people and admitted that its effectiveness was "hard to measure." The SSS apparently was alarmed by its activities, no matter how puny, as well as by pamphlets that characterized the IRS as "tyrannical." The SSS underlined every name mentioned and in all likelihood opened a case file on each one. But this was not the coming of the Revolution, no matter how much both sides hoped or believed it was.[20]

During the next year or so the SSS created sets of profiles on organizations that it believed "might attempt to infiltrate our organization or otherwise breach our personnel security," making them available to regional inspectors. An August 1973 IRS Manual Supplement highlighted the agency's concern for tax resistance and laid bare its uncertainty about what was happening. The IRS seemed worried chiefly about the publicity that tax noncompliance attracted, fearing it would erode public confidence in the tax system and damage voluntary compliance. It admitted, however, that there were "no reliable estimates" of how many people resisted by failing to comply with the tax laws. The problem, as the IRS saw it, was not that only a handful of people refused to pay taxes, but that "there may be a sizable number" who "would engage in serious tax violations as a means of protest" if they believed they could escape criminal penalties. The major pocket of tax resistance appeared to be in the Western Region, but the SSS feared it would spread. Consequently it outlined a series of objectives in the Manual Supplement. Claiming that it did not intend to "suppress dissent" or "persecute individuals" simply because they criticized the system or government policies, it concluded that "a selective approach" rather than a large national effort would be most effective. The purpose, in short, was to publicize the intent to crack down on resisters, not to pursue each and every one.

The IRS hoped that extensive news coverage would deter others.[21] This meant, of course, a further expansion of SSS files.

To gain control of its proliferating files, which had ballooned from seventy-seven to eleven thousand, the IRS launched a computerization project. Following an internal audit of the SSS, which concluded that it offered "high potential as a deterrent in coping with widespread tax violations sponsored by activist groups," the IRS concluded that its agents could do only so much on their own. Help was needed. This raised the question of privacy and possible violations of constitutional rights, and Senator Ervin's subcommittee investigating computers, privacy, and constitutional rights queried the IRS about its plans. After citing IRS files that would be automated, filmed, or computerized, Commissioner Walters revealed to Ervin that a "manual enforcement oriented file" existed that linked activism to the likelihood of tax or firearms violations, but that it was "limited entirely" to those activities. He cited the War Tax Resistance Movement as an example, noting that the problem ranged through "all economic, racial and social levels" and included professionals as well as blue- and white-collar workers. IRS replies to the committee carefully avoided any references to its investigation of activists and its targeting of underground newspapers on college and high school campuses, even while it defended those efforts in internal memoranda.[22]

Ron Pickering, an IRS employee, conducted the computerization study, under instructions from the outset that the result was to be a memorandum to IRS officials arguing that computerization of SSS files was essential. He was not, however, to submit cost estimates with the recommendation. Pickering found disagreement within the IRS about the capabilities of a mechanized system, but he concluded that his job was to provide Paul Wright with a system (defined by Wright and the SSS) that embodied "as many capabilities as possible" and that could be operational within six months. The system Wright had in mind was massive, to "convert to tape *all* data necessary for evaluation of referral potential." Pickering estimated that, conservatively, this would produce a printout of more than fifteen thousand pages, and evaluations of individuals' profiles would be "subject to initial interpretation of various source documents previously abstracted by another party." The printout would be the sole source of field referrals. It seemed unwieldy and dangerous.[23]

But Pickering labored diligently, recommending two systems for computerizing the files that would generate a composite picture of every subject with detailed notes on their activities, historical and financial data, and filing history as well as abstracts of "all relevant documents." He recommended, in short, a massive Intelligence Gathering and Retrieval System (IGRS). Pickering reported that SSS files were so large that "orderly evaluation and dissemination" without computerization was impossible. Internal Audit had taken no action on 70 percent of the individuals and organizations in the files, and there was massive duplication. Not only was the SSS staff behind in its file maintenance but sources for "potential noncompliance information" remained untapped, such as the twenty-five volumes of published hearings into urban riots by the Senate Committee on Government Operations. Pickering reported that about "40,000 activists, individuals and organizations have been identified through various intelligence sources," and most of that was backlog. He estimated a "growth factor of 10,000" during the next year. Computerization would remedy that.[24]

Aside from privacy concerns, the problem with this proposal was that it would computerize records of minimal value to tax enforcement. Senator Ervin later asserted that two-thirds of all SSS files did not relate to tax compliance, and an internal IRS memorandum in August 1972 revealed that its own review of SSS files found that about 37 percent of them "were not worthy of Staff consideration." SSS compliance enforcement in 2,700 cases since August 1969 had resulted in only 182 being referred to the field for investigation. By the summer of 1972, 103 of those had been closed, 52 without "productive results." The other 51 cases had resulted in total tax liabilities of only $56,000 and audit deficiencies of $50,000 (and refunds of $3,900!).

Despite the privacy invaded, the surveillance activities that drew the IRS far from its statutory purposes of tax collection and enforcement, and the money spent to achieve this sorry record, Internal Revenue blamed the meager results on staffing limitations and argued that the answer was more effective utilization of SSS files rather than termination of the project. To accomplish this, the IRS added postcompliance monitoring to SSS responsibilities, hoping to ensure that individuals and organizations would not revert to noncompliance once an IRS investigation had been completed. It would also refer to the field for investigation cases in which individuals or organizations failed to file tax returns, even though there was no apparent tax liability. This reflected previous failures of the SSS to follow up recommendations for action. Field action had been slight. Between August 1969 and June 1972 the Audit Division had revoked the exempt status of only one organization and recommended deficiencies in only six cases. The Collection Division, which handled most of the cases, had not done much better (probably worse in percentage terms), securing tax returns in only thirty-four cases. In three years SSS-targeted enforcement had resulted in the collection of $104,700, not even enough to cover its office expenses.[25]

Computerization planning was complete by late fall. Now SSS index cards had to be converted to a tape record, a card register and index created, and classified and unclassified documents as well as congressional records converted to a tape record. These would be matched and merged with the card register, and additional registers created. The IRS would extract from its Master File information on any individual or organization with an identifying number (Social Security number or Employment Information number) and add all new information to the file. The second phase entailed a system to monitor cases referred to the field, and the IRS revised its Automatic Data Processing Handbook to provide instructions about tax protest cases. Twice a year a special Vietnam Protest Coordination Function would prepare reports for the National Office on these activities.[26]

Commissioner Walters signed off on the computer feasibility study in March 1973, whereupon the SSS began computerizing files from published congressional hearings. It did not go smoothly. There were problems with the data; some of it was more than six years old, and several organizations no longer existed. Editing was needed to eliminate innocent witnesses, and since the hearings had no index, data processors would have to extract data laboriously, page by page. Alert to problems, Wright warned about a need to "introduce effective self corrective measures" to tighten SSS practices that "might be susceptible to infringement of rights." But his solution was simply to be selective in the input of names, and that selectivity was questionable. Any group or individual that SSS staffers believed might disrupt "the orderly process" or "attempt to embarrass the government" would still be added to the data base. In effect, there was no change. The SSS still targeted groups and individuals based on their philosophy as well as their actions. Tax resistance, Deputy Commissioner Ray Harless noted in June, was "simply an additional factor to weigh in arriving at a judgement." The project was never completed.[27]

The SSS continued to emphasize that its role was to gather intelligence on all individuals and organizations that were violent or advocated violence, as well as on nonviolent groups whose demonstrations might lead to violence. A revealing memo in December 1972 from John Flynn, regional commissioner for the North Atlantic Region, outlined these SSS priorities. Repeating much of the IRS memorandum distributed at the Charlottesville conference, Flynn added that field personnel "should be alert to criminal violations other than those involving the *Tax Statutes*," including "any indication of acts of violence, falsification of official documents and threats against Government officials or offices." Despite recent efforts to focus on tax resistance, apparently the original mission of the Special Service Staff remained intact. Worried about internal sabotage, the IRS beefed up security at its service centers and asked Wright to review SSS files to see if service center employees had ties to activist organizations.[28]

The leak of Flynn's memo to *Time* magazine resulted in a dramatic change in IRS activities. One day after Donald Alexander was sworn in as IRS commissioner in May 1973, he restricted SSS operations to tax resisters; three months later he announced that the SSS would terminate all activities. But it was too late to avoid unwanted publicity; congressional investigators had just launched probes of the SSS. Senator Sam Ervin, chairman of the Constitutional Rights Subcommittee, led the charge, noting in May that he had just learned about the SSS from an anonymous letter and wanted to know more. He requested complete information about the group's mission, staffing, files, and operations, noting that the organization was not listed in the Treasury's response to his survey of federal data banks. Ervin's request agitated IRS executives. Treasury's general counsel, Samuel Pierce, Jr., asked various Treasury officials for a response; they in turn bucked it to IRS commissioner Alexander and asked him to respond to Ervin.[29]

Alexander's response ruffled Ervin's constitutional scruples. The commissioner not only provided little information about the SSS, he also indicated that the IRS was about to purge its files. Ervin immediately intervened to prevent that, and by July Alexander had agreed to retain the files and to cooperate with Ervin's investigation as well as another being conducted by the Joint Committee on Internal Revenue Taxation. But he refused to grant Ervin's committee access to SSS files themselves or provide the names of individuals and organizations in them. Further riled, Ervin claimed that since SSS materials were clearly *not* tax related, the subcommittee should have complete access. He sent Alexander a list of forty-seven interrogatories. Alexander prepared responses but still refused to grant access. The question of access to SSS files remained a point of contention between Ervin and Alexander for almost a year. Not until April 1974 was the subcommittee staff granted access to the SSS card index. By that time Senator Lowell Weicker had raised other questions about the SSS and tax returns in testimony during hearings on warrantless wiretapping and electronic surveillance. Exasperated, Ervin subpoenaed the IRS for SSS files. He finally obtained not only a list of the individuals and organizations who were in the files, but permission for subcommittee counsel to review the files. This proved to be less than met the eye, however. In June 1974, IRS and FBI officials met with the majority and minority counsels of the subcommittee in a walk-in vault at IRS headquarters in Washington. For the next three weeks counsel reviewed a sample of the SSS files according to the strict requirements imposed by the IRS. The process was convoluted, with counsel selecting "a file subject, a former [SSS] staff employee physically getting the file, another IRS representative screening the file for tax return data, a representative of the [FBI] screening the FBI data, and finally review by Subcommittee counsel."[30]

This procedure dragged on in part because the IRS was slow to respond to Senator Ervin. Drafts of proposed responses circulated well into June 1973, largely because the IRS tried to word its reply so as to indicate that it pursued only tax resisters and similar groups. IRS officials debated, in essence, about how and how much to deceive Senator Ervin. At least one urged his colleagues to write "candidly" to Ervin about the organization's past and its present plans to narrow its focus and automate its records. Efforts to deceive were not successful; one IRS official observed that the response gave the impression that "we have files on the whole extremist universe." That impression was correct. Underlying this debate within Internal Revenue was a parallel discussion about how to retain certain files and maintain an operational unit like the SSS should it have to be abandoned.[31]

In the spring of 1973, Commissioner Alexander had wanted to restrict, not abolish, the SSS. His assistant, Burke Willsey, informally investigated the SSS at Alexander's request, recommending maintenance of a "functional unit" to liaison with law enforcement agencies on tax compliance issues. Willsey questioned why the IRS maintained files from other investigative agencies and investigated draft-card burners or anti-establishment groups, even if they might be expected to challenge the tax system. He recommended that the IRS modify SSS activities and that Paul Wright be instructed to meet those directives. In his report, curiously enough, Willsey did not emphasize SSS's lack of action, even though it had referred only 234 cases to the field for investigation and made only 18 intelligence referrals between August 1969 and June 30, 1973, and had revoked the exempt status of just three organizations. It had referred 320 tax-resistance cases to the field for disposition, yet another 446 remained to be referred. About 300 other tax-protest cases were under review, but the SSS had not yet even sampled the income tax records of the thousands of known telephone tax resisters.[32]

Alexander responded to Ervin's demand that SSS files be preserved with an announcement that he had already begun an investigation of the IRS and domestic intelligence, as had the Joint Committee on Internal Revenue Taxation. The Joint Committee, Alexander assured Ervin, would surely advise his subcommittee of its findings. But the senator from North Carolina was not about to play second fiddle to other investigators, especially when he sensed massive violations of constitutional rights. He quickly posed a series of supplementary questions to Alexander about the nature of SSS files, what had been purged from them, and the chain of command. Watergate was heating up, and Ervin also wanted information on all relations between the White House and the SSS. He was not convinced by Alexander's earlier inference that the SSS was essentially a passive group which merely summarized information for various IRS divisions. In addition, Alexander professed to know nothing about the SSS, but SSS chairman Paul Wright reminded him that he had met at least three times with the commissioner to discuss the operation. Then, perhaps feeling the heat from Congress or perhaps interested in protecting the IRS from further controversy and attack, on August 9, 1973, Commissioner Alexander abolished the Special Service Staff following what he claimed was a "two-month study" (there is no surviving evidence to indicate that this study was actually undertaken). His announcement came only a few days after a *Time* magazine article on the group. With anti-IRS feeling running high in Congress, it was time to run for cover.[33]

By the time Alexander terminated the SSS it had reviewed only slightly more than half its lists of individuals and organizations. Yet it had established thousands of files—8,585 on individuals and 2,873 on organizations, including files on prominent individuals identified in Inter-Divisional Information Unit printouts as useful to help quell (not incite) civil disturbances in particular localities. Its reach was indiscriminate. The IRS immediately began transition planning, but the SSS continued to operate as before. It received, logged, and filed FBI reports; retained a liaison with the House Internal Security Committee; and maintained contacts and received information from the Senate Committee on Government Operations as well as the Subcommittee on Internal Security. Wright chaired a task force to recommend how SSS files could be phased into regular IRS files, as well as what other SSS functions the IRS would continue. The IRS would retain many SSS materials, such as files on the Black Panther party and the Ku Klux Klan. The SSS continued to accumulate "tax resister material under present pseudonym procedures during phase-out." Abolition apparently did not really abolish anything.[34]

The task force charged with dismantling the SSS spent much of its time in August and September 1973 discussing where the IRS might house SSS operations that it wished to retain. It concluded that continuing scrutiny of tax-resistance groups was important, and decided to place information gathering in the Intelligence Division while the Audit and Collection divisions would be on the dissemination list. Paul Wright reminded his colleagues that maintenance of internal SSS operations was essential. Data from FBI files and other intelligence sources had to be extracted and analyzed, then expanded into solid leads through Master File searches or Social Security checks before it was disseminated to the field. Existing SSS files with no revenue significance or potential would be selected out, and all classified and unclassified material in these files would be destroyed pending approval from the commissioner. The SSS itself would disappear, but its functions and centralizing influence would remain largely intact through Intelligence Division operations. Covert operations to uncover possible tax resisters would continue. By late September the task force had selected for retention about 25 percent of all SSS files, about 90 percent of which involved tax resisters. Curtailment of SSS operations was well under way, though the structure in place allowed abuses to reappear in the future.[35]

By now the IRS was under scrutiny not only from congressional committees but from the Watergate Special Prosecution Force (WSPF) as well. The IRS was on the defensive. Besieged IRS officials worried about the WSPF investigations, complaining that they were going beyond background information and inquiring about who handled SSS files, especially the Sensitive Case files, and how much was reported to the White House. Assistant to the Commissioner Burke Willsey told WSPF investigators that the IRS "was totally chaotic" because of the many requests for information and because private individuals were filing suit to see if the SSS had files on them. The most pointed questions, however, came from Senator Ervin. In late September 1973, Commissioner Alexander responded to a long list of subcommittee questions, claiming that the "principal characteristic" of individuals or organizations in SSS files was their "inclination to use violent methods" to adversely affect the tax laws, or their "intention to ignore or willfully violate tax or firearms statutes." He explained that SSS files had been omitted from the federal data bank survey response because they had not been automated, and generally argued that he now had a handle on the files and would purge all information extraneous to tax enforcement. Alexander insisted that the SSS had never received a request for tax information from the White House, nor had the White House suggested names for investigation. There were, however, SSS files on several individuals who also appeared on the Enemies Lists. This was only a coincidence, Alexander claimed, and stemmed from SSS interests and not White House interests. (An internal IRS memo providing background for Alexander as he drafted his response to Ervin indicated that in at least four cases the SSS did in fact initiate or provide investigative assistance for the Enemies List.) Alexander also insisted, contrary to fact, that the SSS had not requested information from the Social Security Administration. His letter, which ran to fifteen pages, was, in short, an explanation and defense of a purely IRS operation. He received in return another list of interrogatories from Senator Ervin's subcommittee.[36]

By this time the IRS was in full protective mode. Alexander worried that the *New York Times* would report that the Joint Committee was "accepting everything IRS says and is going to whitewash IRS," and demanded to know who had been talking to reporters. In addition, an IRS official accompanied Eileen Shanahan and Dave Rosenbaum of the *Times* when they interviewed Roger Barth, reporting its content afterward to the IRS's public affairs office. The reporters focused on Barth's political role at IRS, and the IRS worried that the paper was "going to do a job on Roger and it's going to be hard for us to disassociate IRS." By the end of 1973, with a full public relations spin under way, Paul Wright discontinued the post office box that the SSS had used to obtain information on tax-resistance groups under a pseudonym, and then retired on December 31. The IRS changed the combination to the vault door where SSS records were stored, and closed the vault with files intact until it could reach a decision about their disposition or destruction. Despite this apparent care, IRS historian Shelley Davis later reported that the SSS files she viewed as the IRS historian "were woefully incomplete, considering the enormity of Paul Wright's covert efforts."[37]

Throughout 1974 the IRS found itself under constant pressure to respond to congressional inquiries. Senator Ervin warned Alexander that the greatest threat to the IRS was not his subcommittee but that the IRS might come to "be regarded as a governmental weapon to be employed against the political beliefs and expressions of American citizens." While Ervin agreed that the IRS had appeared to resist White House pressures for tax audits, he remained convinced that SSS activity rested more on disagreements with individuals' political beliefs than their tax liabilities. He characterized IRS refusal to grant his subcommittee access to SSS files as "paradoxical" and "ridiculous." The IRS insisted that it did not target dissidents because of their beliefs and that its interest in "extremists" stemmed solely from a belief that "they were prone to avoid or violate Federal tax laws." In many respects, the agency argued, the SSS was "nothing but the extension of routine procedures." Yet Jack Anderson reported that the IRS had revoked and then reinstated a tax exemption for one individual's "favorite charity" because it did not want to reveal "how she and her friends were tailed, [wire]tapped and spied upon." The IRS was not having much luck persuading foes or making friends.[38]

IRS problems stemmed not only from attacks on its operations but from the contents of the SSS files once they were revealed. One file, on a group known as The Conspiracy, included about fifty newspaper clippings, confidential FBI reports, solicitation letters, a case review discussing its bank account and recipients of funds, memos from various IRS divisions and district directors, and an evaluation of its returns. Other files were opened on religious leaders of all faiths, hosts and hostesses of cocktail parties that raised money for radicals, contributors to defense funds for protesters, individuals connected to "women's lib," actors and actresses who publicly expressed political views, habitués of certain bookstores, a convicted political assassin, and various civil rights leaders and elected officials. The IRS feared that if it provided a listing of these topics to the Ervin Committee, Senator Ervin would contact the taxpayers and get them to waive their confidentiality, enabling him to examine their full SSS files. Taking the position that all the information was gathered for tax administration purposes, an internal IRS memo warned that Internal Revenue personnel "cannot for a moment allow ourselves the luxury of determining that some of this information might not fall within that classification and possibly not be subject to the penalties for unauthorized disclosure of tax information." This implied that opening SSS files would undermine claims that everything in them was tax related.[39]

By May, however, the IRS was sharing lists of file subjects and memoranda with Ervin's subcommittee. More important, Burke Willsey had revealed how the SSS files were constructed. The "mere existence" of a file did not mean that any investigation or audit activity ever took place. The SSS often created files based on "nothing more" than newspaper clippings connecting an individual or organization with "another person or organization that was of interest to the Staff." In essence the SSS operated like a giant dragnet, scooping up everything in its path. IRS responses rarely pleased the Ervin Committee, and it kept coming back for missing items. Citing the "third agency rule"—which meant that an agency that received information from another agency would not divulge that information to a third agency without permission from the originating agency—the IRS refused to supply ISD printouts on which many SSS files were based. That rule, subcommittee counsel complained, was used by agencies "to circumvent or avoid Congressional oversight." The IRS also refused to turn over Paul Wright's administrative files, claiming that they constituted taxpayer information and were exempt from disclosure under Section 6103 of the Internal Revenue Code. Subcommittee counsel recommended that it issue a subpoena for them, arguing that IRS arguments were "specious at best" and that the information was vital. A day later the IRS not only agreed to purge some identifying information from Paul Wright's files and provide them to the subcommittee, it also asked the Justice Department to grant the subcommittee access to FBI files and the ISD lists.[40]

During the next two years several Senate committees continued their investigations of the Special Service Staff, concentrating on issues ranging from constitutional rights and privacy to intelligence gathering and foundations. The history of these investigations is a topic unto itself and is beyond the scope of this book. But one of the effects of these probes was not only that the IRS felt besieged but that it took steps to control future access to tax returns by the White House. Commissioner Alexander reasserted the oversight that resided in his office but that had been ignored in recent years: he established written procedures that required all requests to be in writing and to be channeled through the commissioner's office. The commissioner would evaluate the request and instruct officials how to respond. A second effect, less salutary, was that the IRS persisted in denying access to its files. When the General Accounting Office requested audit reports on taxpayers referred to the field by the SSS, Burke Willsey, in an internal IRS memorandum, responded that he "positively did not want any information from the Special Service Staff disclosed to GAO, even though they were acting as an arm of the Joint Committee on Internal Revenue Taxation." The IRS eventually provided the GAO with a list of case names and districts but redacted names of all organizations. Despite this protective reaction, in late 1974 the *New York Times* published a list of ninety-nine organizations that the SSS had targeted.[41]

The IRS took some solace from a preliminary report from the Joint

Committee on Internal Revenue Taxation which found "no evidence" that the IRS treated individuals referred from the SSS any more harshly than other taxpayers, though the committee admitted that it had "not had access to the Special Service Staff files." IRS efforts to control damage to its reputation, however, were undercut by its decentralized structure. As the outside investigations unfolded, and as the IRS both responded to inquiries and launched its own internal investigations, it discovered that information about SSS activities was so compartmentalized that almost no one really could provide comprehensive answers. It had to gather information from its various divisions and frequently did not know what it was looking for or where to find it. Some searches, even in 1974, discovered that files had been destroyed, even files in the director of the Collection Division's office. They had been destroyed, moreover, despite federal laws that clearly made such an act illegal. Consequently, officials not involved in SSS operations but now responsible for drafting replies to investigative queries could not answer such questions as why the SSS collected "information on 'non-violent groups' if they were not advocating revolution or stated tax resisters." They even had to admit to Senator Vance Hartke that the "extent to which former Commissioners of Internal Revenue were kept informed" of SSS activities was "unclear."[42]

To make matters worse, some SSS targets filed a class-action lawsuit against the IRS and its officials. Claiming that SSS activities were "undertaken not for legitimate tax enforcement purposes but rather for the purpose of punishing, harassing, and burdening individuals and organizations whose political beliefs, activities and associations were disapproved," they asked for permanent court injunctions against further activity of this nature and demanded that the IRS produce all files it had collected on these organizations. The IRS response claimed that Commissioner Alexander had ordered an investigation of the SSS in July 1973, an investigation undertaken by William C. Rankin, Jr., director of the Internal Audit Division in the office of the assistant commissioner (Inspection). Although no copy of such a study appears to exist, in an affidavit Rankin stated that he had investigated more than eight hundred cases, conducting interviews and examining all returns and supporting documents as well as IRS Intelligence and Collection files. He prepared written analyses on each case, sharing this information with the Joint Committee. Rankin admitted that he found cases in which the IRS had erroneously handled files, but he claimed that staff had taken corrective action and adjusted tax liabilities. He insisted, however, that the information he compiled as well as the files themselves could not be released to the public. Not only did they contain confidential tax return data, releasing them would "reveal Internal Revenue Service investigative techniques." That, of course, was precisely what investigators were after.[43]

CHAPTER FIFTEEN

OPERATION LEPRECHAUN: SEX AND POLITICS IN SOUTH FLORIDA

Even as the Internal Revenue Service responded to criticism of its Special Service Staff operations, another of its intelligence-gathering activities became public, prompting renewed complaints against IRS excesses and demands for change. This was Operation Leprechaun, an investigation involving sex and politics in South Florida. Even though Leprechaun was less blatantly political than many other IRS activities during the 1960s and 1970s, because of its timing and extensive coverage in the media it had a more dramatic impact on IRS procedures. It originated with the Intelligence Gathering and Retrieval System (IGRS), the product of the agency's broad fascination with intelligence capabilities which dated at least to the organized crime drive of the Kennedy years. Success had bred imitation, and IRS officials became caught up in their new law enforcement role. Indeed, the IRS was often the linchpin for many nontax criminal investigations. Although the Long hearings of the mid-1960s had alerted Internal Revenue leaders to real and potential problems with its intelligence operations, IRS officials apparently believed they had everything under control. Leprechaun demonstrated how easily they could come unraveled.

Operation Leprechaun was an outgrowth of a new IRS operation to gather "general intelligence" that lay outside of regular tax investigations. Formally established in May 1973, just months before the official demise of the SSS, the IGRS was designed to collect and store large amounts of intelligence in a computerized system that could spit out masses of data on command. By 1975 it had assembled information on 465,422 individuals and organizations from a wide range of sources. To the press and the public it seemed indistinguishable from Richard Nixon's Enemies List. A later investigation revealed that the IGRS "failed to supply any meaningful criteria for target selection or for the relevancy of the information to be gathered."[1]

This lack of criteria proved to be the undoing of the IGRS, as did its intent to collect intelligence information from unverified sources and in the absence of any specific allegations of wrongdoing. The material was supposed to have some relationship to "potential tax consequences," but no one evaluated it before entering it into the IGRS computers. Everything and everybody was indexed, merely because their names appeared in articles or reports. Most of the information came from news stories, but the IGRS also cultivated informants. Although the IRS called it an intelligence-gathering system, in effect it was a nationwide dragnet, indiscriminately collecting massive amounts of data that often had nothing to do with tax enforcement. Information on political activities, social life, even sexual activities and relationships found its way into IRS computers. The result was a massive data bank on the lives and habits of almost half a million Americans.[2]

Operation Leprechaun brought this intelligence gathering to light and caused a massive outcry against government snooping into private lives. It stimulated several investigations into IRS activities and ultimately led the IRS to curtail its intelligence-gathering operations. Leprechaun sprang directly from a 1971 investigation by the Miami, Florida, police department and the Dade County Department of Public Safety into political corruption in the Miami area. Originally part of the OCD and known as the "Market Connection," this effort was transferred to the IGRS in 1972 when the IRS chose its Jacksonville District as a pilot district for the IGRS. The IRS selected special agent John T. Harrison to be the principal agent on the case, and ultimately fed information from Leprechaun into the IRS computer system. He was part of a larger Justice Department strike force working on the project and was supposed to develop tax cases on public figures suspected of corrupt practices or of accepting bribes. Harrison chose the name "Operation Leprechaun" because he used green ink for his informant files and because he discovered that leprechauns were small mysterious individuals "who could reveal many secrets."[3]

According to Dougald McMillan, chief of the Miami strike force, there were plenty of secrets to discover. He believed that at least half of the city's judges and commissioners were corrupt. The strike force hoped to uncover information about that corruption and relied on the IRS to generate much of it. Guidelines for collecting the data were not precise, referring only to "meaningful information." The fact that the IGRS was outside the IRS tax collection system added to the confusion about what was to be collected and indexed. Aware of this confusion, the National Office issued guidelines in May 1973 that the information should involve "financial transactions with potential tax consequences" or relate to "illegal activities" with a potential to discover unreported or underreported income. Leprechaun operatives seem to have ignored those guidelines. Little screening of the raw data occurred, and this led to trouble. Even the IRS commissioner had his name indexed.[4]

Part of the problem stemmed from Justice Department demands to expand the strike force operation in the Jacksonville District, as well as agent Harrison's extensive use of informants. As early as 1972, even before formal establishment of the IGRS, Assistant Attorney General Henry Peterson and other Justice Department officials met with strike force representatives to urge them to expand their efforts and identify more targets. The project quickly expanded, and additional funding was provided to the special agent. Some of these funds, at least $15,000, went for informants. Agent Harrison had worked in the Miami area for several years and knew where to find confidential informants. He eventually recruited 261 individuals, a large percentage of them coming from the local Cuban community. Between 1972 and 1975 he obtained information from 34 paid and 28 unpaid informants. This led to files on hundreds of individuals and organizations. Harrison eventually produced 594 documents through his Leprechaun investigations. Fewer than half of them, however, contained information about taxable transactions, and even that information, according to a later investigation, "lacked sufficient specificity to indicate that the potential taxable transactions took place or that the information could be substantiated." Yet in November 1972 the director of the IRS Intelligence Division had told strike force representatives that "District offices have a responsibility to buy information and conduct surveillance. Greater emphasis should be placed on the development and use of informants." The assistant director of the Audit Division added that the "job you have is a significant developmental part of your career. Vigor and drive is important."[5]

To make matters worse, 23 percent of the documents collected included information on sexual habits or drinking activities, though some of those same documents also contained tax-related information of some kind. When news of the operation became public knowledge, its sex and drinking interests attracted considerable media attention and colored evaluations of the entire operation. The inclusion of that information reflected a lack of discipline and control over IRS intelligence-gathering activities. By allowing agent Harrison to work with the strike force in the absence of any IRS supervision, the IRS caused many of its own problems.[6]

This lack of control was apparent in the handling of informants. Agent Harrison even informed his superiors at one time that he had thirty-four informants but had not met many of them. Several were subinformants—informants developed by other informants—a situation both unorthodox and risky. One of his female informants turned out to be a double agent with a dubious past. An IRS-ordered review of these operations apparently did not curtail them. Several informants later testified that Harrison instructed them to develop information on sexual and drinking activities, though others denied they had received such instructions. Harrison later insisted that he gave no "blanket instructions" to his confidential informants to develop such information. But he admitted that "when the occasion warranted, I did request one or more informants to obtain the identity of a girl or boyfriend." He did this believing that an individual living in a fine apartment without sufficient income to support his or her lifestyle indicated a potential tax problem. He believed, moreover, that all personal information he received had "potential tax value." Whether or not Harrison was correct, his methods led to problems. In its own probe conducted in 1975, the IRS interviewed twenty of Harrison's informants. Five indicated that they had been requested to gather sexual information, two revealed that Harrison had asked them to search public records and develop background files, five reported being asked to gather political information, one indicated that her instructions included getting information on drinking habits, and four said they had conducted electronic surveillance.[7]

Many of these problems stemmed from confidential agent Carmen, an alias for Elsa Lourdes Patricia Arias G. de Castro Herrera Suarez-Reid Gutierrez, a thirty-three-year-old Cuban woman with three children who had been divorced four times. Previously a paid informant for the Secret Service as well as the Drug Enforcement Administration, Gutierrez claimed that Harrison showed her photographs of public officials during a secret meeting in a Holiday Inn on February 18, 1972, that he told her to "get something" on certain public officials, and that he talked about a particular individual being a homosexual. Later investigations also revealed that the IRS reimbursed Gutierrez for memberships in the local Mutiny and Playboy clubs. Despite the fact that Harrison later fired her after learning that she was about to divulge information from Operation Leprechaun to subjects of the probe, Gutierrez claimed that she had quit in disgust. In 1975, when she became a media celebrity in the Miami area, Gutierrez charged that Harrison had threatened her, her children, and her dog. Although Harrison denied all in congressional hearings, he admitted warning her that "the bad things she planned for others can also be planned for her." Regardless of who was telling the truth, the controversy gave the impression that the IRS was out of control and fueled demands for termination of the IGRS and an overhaul of IRS intelligence operations.[8]

Other problems stemmed from the nature of Operation Leprechaun itself and the "political" guidelines it provided. Speaking to strike force representatives, William Lynch, chief of the Organized Crime and Racketeering Section of the Justice Department, cautioned agents to be "very careful." They should not go out and hunt down governors, mayors, or congressmen. "Resist hunting big names," he warned. Leo Satterfield of Disclosure urged them to keep the list for disclosure clearance as small as possible. "We have to report to the Joint Committee [JCIRT] twice a year, and large numbers of names are questioned." The IRS did not want the operation to attract attention. It was to be a targeted operation, with the hope that targeted prosecutions would deter others. But agents had to be confused, especially when the IGRS brought in reams of data on thousands of individuals.[9]

Some of these problems surfaced in 1974 during an IRS study of the IGRS conducted by John Olszewski, director of the IRS Intelligence Division. Although the study found that the IGRS was meeting many of the objectives envisioned by the IRS and the strike force, it recommended sharper guidelines and pointed to the need for improved organization. Among its suggestions: background files and indexes should relate to specific subjects that were within the investigative jurisdiction of the district; subjects should have "potential tax administration purposes"; and better criteria needed to be developed for the inclusion of information in the computerized data banks. Management needed to review the indexes on a continual basis, routinely purge them every three years, and destroy all microfilm copies of records after five years. The greatest need was for systematic evaluation of the data to ensure that all materials were tax related. Two facts remained. First, none of these activities was driven by specific tax cases. The IRS maintained such an extensive data bank in hopes that the material would provide information for *potential* tax cases. An internal IRS audit of the Miami strike force in early 1974 reviewed the operation but concluded only that the strike force needed to collect delinquent taxes more promptly. Second, the guidelines for purging documents demonstrate that IRS staff either had no awareness of the legal responsibility to preserve the records of its activities or chose to destroy those records in defiance of that obligation.[10]

Targets for Leprechaun included Dade County State's Attorney Richard Gerstein as well as various political and media figures, including Miami Mayor Maurice Ferre, Metro Mayor Steve Clark, Joe Robbie (general managing partner of the Miami Dolphins professional football team), the hotelman Ben Novack, the entertainer Danny Thomas, and New York Jets quarterback Joe Namath. The Nixon White House apparently kept tabs on the operation through John Dean, who allegedly met several times with Thomas Lopez of the IGRS. The IRS later discovered from a subinformant that some of these intelligence activities were conducted at the request of White House officials, with the results "reported on at least one occasion to White House officials in a Key West motel."[11]

Two informants, Nelson Vega and Robert Novoa, later admitted that they had burglarized the office of Evelio Estrella, a Republican candidate for the House seat of Claude Pepper. Paid $100 a week as an informant, Vega was instructed to gather information on political candidates to "determine where they were getting their money for parties and other activities." During the Estrella burglary, the two men removed a filing cabinet in hopes that it would contain information of interest to the IRS. Harrison's files were later found to contain a manila envelope with original materials relating to Estrella's campaign, but Harrison never fully admitted that he recognized them. That same IRS investigation, however, concluded that special agent Harrison was not involved in the selection of targets, only in the nature of the information gathered. But electronic surveillance was conducted without the necessary Justice Department approval required by the IRS.[12]

After its 1974 study of the IGRS, the IRS appears to have lost interest in Operation Leprechaun and the work of the strike force until 1975, when allegations about these activities surfaced in Miami newspapers. This prompted several investigations by congressional committees and by the IRS itself. By this time, given the revelations about the illegal intelligence-gathering activities of several government agencies as well as the recent Watergate investigations, congressional and public interest in the matter was high and the exchanges heated. IRS protestations of ignorance or promises of tighter control failed to quiet critics.

Publication of details about Operation Leprechaun in the *Miami Herald* and the *Miami News* during the spring and summer of 1975 exposed the operation, aroused public concern, and embarrassed the IRS. In February 1975 the *Miami News* headlined: "IRS spied on Namath, Robbie, Gerstein as Nixon Enemies." The report argued that Operation Leprechaun was an extension of Nixon's Enemies List and cited a "key member" of the investigative unit as its source. Although other papers, like the *Philadelphia Bulletin*, had run stories about the operation, the Miami newspapers were close to the scene and produced a steady stream of sensationalized stories. The press reported that one source linked Leprechaun to the Watergate cover-up but justified it "by thinking that Nixon was the right thing for the country." Intelligence gathering was essential, the source argued, because many "subversive elements" were trying to "destroy the Democratic institutions in this country."[13]

Within a month the Miami press had found "Carmen" (Elsa Suarez-Reid Gutierrez), and new stories focused on charges that the IRS had used thirty-one undercover agents to investigate the sex lives of more than thirty prominent Miami residents, including three federal judges (Ellen Morphonios, Rhea Pincus Grossman, and Emmet Choate). Richard Gerstein, a state's attorney who had pursued the Miami side of Watergate, was also a primary target. Gutierrez told the press that both Harrison and Lopez had "insinuated" that she "should lure Gerstein into bed." By mid-March the press had discovered and publicized almost all the Leprechaun targets. The *Miami Herald* described Gutierrez as a woman with "a life as a sex bomb with a body tape recorder hidden where no gentleman would look [that] spanned three continents and four federal agencies." She had worked as a model as well as an informant and found undercover work exciting.[14]

Within days the press discovered another undercover agent, Elizabeth Bettner, who claimed to have knowledge of other IRS efforts to enlist prostitutes to have sex with targets of investigations and persuade them to talk on tape. Bettner admitted keeping a tape recorder behind her couch to record conversations with visitors, as well as spying on several state officials in Florida. Dougald McMillan, director of the Miami strike force, attacked the press for practicing "yellow journalism" and denied he had directed Operation Leprechaun. Nonetheless, to the dismay of IRS agents on the Miami strike force, he was recalled to Washington. McMillan was unpopular with Dade County officials, chiefly because many of them believed they were his targets. In early April the Miami press reported that IRS Commissioner Donald Alexander had admitted that the IRS (not the Justice Department) had "day-to-day control of the political sex-spying operation in Dade County." Alexander insisted, however, that the strike force identified targets for the operation. In July the press reported that the IRS had run another operation in Dade County while Leprechaun was under way. That was Operation Sunshine, which began in 1971 and ended in January 1973, and used IRS agents to spy on other IRS agents to see if they were accepting favors. In that operation, Harry "The Hat" Woodington collected information on the sex and drinking habits of hundreds of individuals. Officials also revealed that some of these operations and targets overlapped with Operation Rosebud, an investigation into narcotics trafficking.[15]

The Subcommittee on Oversight of the House Ways and Means Committee, chaired by Ohio Democrat Charles Vanik, launched one investigation of Operation Leprechaun. Complaining that Leprechaun raised "serious issues about the administration of the tax laws and the privacy of American citizens," Vanik energetically pushed the inquiry. He asked IRS Commissioner Donald Alexander to explain what the IRS was doing about the Miami allegations, who controlled the expenditure of funds for informants, if Miami-type operations were going on elsewhere, how such an operation could get started, how special agents were trained, and what the IRS was doing to review its operations to see if Leprechaun "had any relation" to activities such as the Special Service Staff and the enemies list.[16]

Alexander testified that the IRS was trying to find out what happened and who authorized Leprechaun. He also attempted to deflect blame from rogue IRS employees by asserting that the social and political turmoil of the sixties had led various government agencies to promote the "use of the Internal Revenue Service as a generalized tool for criminal law enforcement." He intended to pull the IRS back to its original tax-enforcement efforts and abandon nontax-related activities, and he admitted that Operation Leprechaun "was a mistake," as was the Special Service Staff. Later, in a speech before the tax section of the American Bar Association, Alexander reiterated his intention to remove the "inappropriate ornaments from the IRS Christmas tree." Referring to IRS investigations of various protest groups and dissidents during the 1960s, Alexander declared that the IRS should never again permit itself to be used as a "selective tool" for criminal enforcement. It jeopardized traditional IRS tax enforcement and revenue collection and eroded the public's faith in "an impartial, non-political tax system."[17]

Vanik's subcommittee was not satisfied with Alexander's eagerness to terminate these operations in the hope it would foreclose further congressional scrutiny. Subcommittee investigators therefore contacted Warren Williams, acting chief of the IRS Intelligence Division in the Jacksonville District office. They wanted more information about Operation Leprechaun, and Williams noted that their interest extended also to the status of special agent Harrison, to Project Haven (involving drug and banking activities in the Bahamas), and to Nixon confidante Bebe Rebozo. Other subcommittee investigators questioned lower-level IRS officials for the same information, and in early August 1975 this interest sparked a flurry of IRS memos about the investigation. Miami newspapers reported that Commissioner Alexander was under investigation by the FBI as well as by federal grand juries and congressional committees.[18]

Vanik opened hearings on IRS intelligence operations in order to "explore what the IRS is doing in gathering and using intelligence data and how these procedures relate to the legitimate needs of the IRS in administering the tax laws, as well as how they affect the basic rights of American citizens." He was particularly concerned about the IGRS data bank. With that in mind, he sent Donald Alexander an eight-page list of questions following his testimony on March 26, 1975. All related to Leprechaun. Vanik also wanted to know if the IRS had silently begun its own investigation more than two months before news about the operation surfaced in the press, and if so why the agency had kept it so quiet. At almost the same time, New York Democratic Congressman Charles Rangel launched investigations into the SSS files, an audit of twenty-eight civil rights workers in Mississippi, and the audits of private schools following the *Green v. Connally* decision. The IRS was under attack from several quarters. To make matters worse, the IRS itself seemed divided. Former Commissioner Randolph Thrower, taking a position clearly at odds with that of Alexander, noted that it would be "against the public interest and would be shocking to the public to find that where revenue agents, or special agents, had important information or evidence and could testify directly about criminal activity, that they would be available only for an income tax case, and would not be available for briberty, corruption, violation of other federal laws, and so forth."[19]

During his December 1975 hearings, Congressman Vanik criticized the IRS for its activities in Leprechaun—but he also strongly opposed Alexander's intent to shut down nontax IRS activities. Such a National

Office policy, he complained, would let white-collar criminals and organized crime figures run unchecked. Not only did the IRS have a legitimate role as a law enforcement agency, Vanik argued, Alexander's position had polarized IRS employees and IRS management over its efforts against criminal tax evaders. Even Attorney General Edward Levi criticized Alexander for creating "an absurd situation."[20]

In testimony before Vanik's subcommittee, various IRS officials who had investigated Operation Leprechaun defended the operation. Jeffrey Shapiro of the IRS Personnel Division testified that when he and Martha Broxton had reviewed documents in the Jacksonville District collected by the Inspection Division, they had found several improprieties but nothing criminal. They dismissed many allegations of misconduct as without merit, and cited "mitigating elements" that explained most of the other charges. Agent Harrison, they said, did not cause or create the problems. He was just "one of the cogs in the wheel" in a district that had long used improper procedures. Harrison had pursued nontax-related activities, but Shapiro claimed that he did so under IRS guidelines that were less restrictive than those currently in force. Shapiro's instructions, however, were only to review materials collected by the Inspection Division and not to conduct an investigation or interview individuals. In fact he ended up not only reviewing these materials but defending the entire operation. Even the "sex and booze aspects" were overstated and legitimate, he said. There could "conceivably be some kind of tax-relatedness issue," though he suggested none to subcommittee members.[21]

E. J. Vitkus, the assistant regional commissioner (Intelligence) for the IRS Southeast Region, was even more defensive about Leprechaun. Claiming that he had reviewed all the files, Vitkus testified that the operation had assessed about $7 million in tax liabilities at a cost of $25,000 to $50,000 per year. He also insisted that he and his staff had examined "every piece of paper they could lay their hands on" about the operation and could not cite "a single instance of abuse that grew out of Leprechaun." Operations like Leprechaun, he argued, were essential, and he attacked Alexander's characterization of the operation as a mistake as "premature and unfortunate." Vitkus's remarks revealed the deep split within the IRS over intelligence gathering and the strike force concept. They also contradicted part of an IRS Inspection report which revealed that "many of the documents indexed in the system did not meet the criteria of financial transactions or illegal activities with tax potential."[22]

Special agent John Harrison and his attorney, Charles Fishman, attacked the IRS for using Harrison as a scapegoat in order to avoid public criticism. The IRS knew that Harrison had done nothing wrong, Fishman charged, but "repeatedly and continually" issued statements about his improper conduct and the anomaly of Operation Leprechaun. For his part, Harrison testified that he originally set up a network of informers in May 1972, under instructions from the strike force. "My primary goal," he insisted, "was to gather tax-related information on organized crime, racketeering and corruption." Some of the information he received, he admitted, was not tax related and did in fact concern "sex and booze." But this was, he insisted, a minuscule part of the operation. Fishman attacked the IRS for trying to cover up its embarrassment over public revelations about Operation Leprechaun, and then publicly blaming Harrison. "I think if the committee were to examine the structure of the IRS," he testified, "the personnel structure of the southeast region, prior to March 1 of this year and examine the people who are there now, I think you will find that virtually every person in a position of authority is retired or has been transferred." Their retirements, he argued, were " 'forced' voluntary retirements."[23]

In response, Vitkus admitted that agent Harrison was blameless. He insisted that the IRS had tried to correct Leprechaun's problems and had done so before the appearance of news stories. Vitkus blamed "deficiencies at the Detroit Data Center" for delays and insisted that "the district was doing everything possible within the limits of its resources." He also cited the IRS Internal Audit findings of January 1974, which exonerated the IGRS from "improper practices or deficiencies." He was satisfied, he said, "that the system would have been properly screened and purged had not other circumstances intervened." And he insisted that he had seen nothing that led him to believe that "any personnel in Miami solicited information about the sex habits, drinking habits, and other personal matters relating to any taxpayer." In short, Vitkus now issued a ringing defense of all IRS actions in the face of congressional scrutiny.[24]

Representative Vanik was outraged at the vacillating and contradictory conduct of the IRS and its apparent effort to cover up embarrassing aspects of Leprechaun. He noted that Commissioner Alexander "properly directed" the IRS Inspection Service to investigate Operation Leprechaun when charges against Harrison first broke. But then Alexander and other National Office officials embarked on a "rush to judgment" against Harrison and IRS intelligence-gathering efforts and prejudiced subsequent investigations. The June Inspection report, consequently, was biased and "only served to pillory him [Harrison] further." Now the testimony of Shapiro and Vitkus appeared to "substantially vindicate" Harrison, and suggested that the National Office had suppressed evidence that could have cleared him. During this same time the National Office was in full retreat, reinforcing allegations against other IRS intelligence operations. Alexander, in turn, created new regulations about the use of paid informants and in effect shut down the other operations. The reservoir of informants was drying up, to the "detriment of tax law enforcement." In all these activities Vanik found one common thread: "You zero in on one or more individual special agents and prosecute them in public without benefit of complete investigation or administration or criminal due process; then you announce and execute new rules based on what the public has been led to believe." Yet those same IRS officials proclaimed their interest in protecting individuals' rights and purported to welcome congressional oversight. According to Vanik, the entire IRS policy was a disaster, and he exonerated agent Harrison of all charges.[25]

What of the reaction of the IRS itself? During 1975, Commissioner Donald Alexander spent much of his time testifying before congressional committees interested in IRS intelligence-gathering activities and Operation Leprechaun in particular. In a statement that revealed the enormous power held by individual Internal Revenue agents, Alexander testified that the IRS "didn't know that there was a Project Leprechaun." It knew only what officials had read in the newspapers, but it had treated the allegations seriously and had sent a "large squad" of inspectors to Miami. "But they didn't unearth this specific thing—this Project Leprechaun—until later." In fact, the initial IRS investigation in February 1975 seemed to operate in the dark not only about Leprechaun but about the IGRS itself. Much of its early attention was concentrated on possible White House involvement, prompted by the fact that the special Miami IGRS unit had been established during the Nixon administration and by the legacy of Watergate and the Enemies Lists. The IRS also sought first to investigate and rebut newspaper reports, then to conduct a broad investigation of the entire intelligence-gathering effort. The questions raised by investigators revealed that the IRS apparently had little or no knowledge about the structure, operation, or supervision of the IGRS. The IRS and its commissioner were clearly caught flatfooted and embarrassed.[26]

Alexander's testimony before Vanik's subcommittee that fall was equally defensive. He insisted that all IRS investigations of the Miami Intelligence office were being conducted by individuals who had never worked there; they would be closely supervised. Alexander also noted that the IRS had issued several reports on the operation and had referred all allegations of criminal wrongdoing to the Justice Department. For whatever reason, Internal Revenue staff chose not to take action against those who were accused of wrongdoing. The IRS had completed an Internal Audit investigation, but its Internal Security investigation remained incomplete. Approximately eight hundred auditors and inspectors had conducted these investigations. The National Office Review Program was evaluating the expenditure of confidential funds and had suspended payments to confidential informants until their investigation was complete. With what must have been great relief, Alexander reported that none of Leprechaun's targets were on the White House Enemies Lists or in the files of the SSS.[27]

Investigations of Operation Leprechaun by the Church Committee in 1975 and 1976 were more critical. Under close questioning, Commissioner Alexander admitted that the question of supervisory jurisdiction over strike forces was difficult to answer. The IRS wanted it, but Alexander's answers clearly revealed that the agency did not have it. Alexander defended the strike force concept but complained that IRS resources were being stretched and that the agency lacked control over its agents assigned to the strike forces. "What works in theory," he noted, "does not necessarily work in practice." Nonetheless Alexander defended the IRS. He told the committee that internal investigations of Leprechaun abuses had led management to begin imposing "restrictions upon intelligence gathering . . . to assure that non-tax-related information would not be gathered." Management could do a better job of controlling informants and agents. These controls, he admitted, might "actually impede the special agent in the performance of the normal IRS intelligence mission." Many of them would be unnecessary if the IRS could restrict its operations to tax enforcement.[28]

Despite tough questioning, Alexander faced a fairly sympathetic committee. It had sent only two of its staff members to Miami to investigate allegations against Leprechaun, and relied heavily on the IRS Inspection report. The committee largely rejected the accusations of Elsa Gutierrez, which were the most damaging charges against the IRS, but did discover some "improprieties" and blamed the IRS for failing to prevent or curtail them. The committee's investigators cited three reasons for the IRS failures: inadequate guidelines "for the recruitment and use of informants"; reliance "upon retrospective detection of abuse"; and agent John Harrison's "anomalous position outside the normal administrative structure" of the IRS. This last reason essentially supported Commissioner Alexander's assertion that the Justice Department, which had established the strike force, was really responsible for Operation Leprechaun.[29]

But a second round of hearings by Representative Vanik's subcommittee swung the final verdict against Alexander and in favor of the strike force concept. Justice Department officials defended their actions as well as those of the IRS, attacking critics of Operation Leprechaun as coming "about as close to the lynching of a law enforcement agency as anything I have ever seen." Dougald McMillan of the Justice Department's Criminal Division complained that "practically every two-bit hoodlum and shyster in the Miami area now screams 'Leprechaun' as some sort of vague defense at every opportunity." Investigators were discouraged. McMillan insisted that only through tax investigations could the Justice Department ever apprehend organized crime figures. Congressman Vanik agreed, praising McMillan as a "determined, aggressive prosecutor of organized crime figures" who was "tarred" by the distorted brush of Leprechaun. Vanik also attacked IRS management, charging that it had been a "major participant" in Leprechaun distortions. He blamed the agency for "excessive restrictions on tax information-gathering, the prolonged suspension of Operation Tradewinds," and other failures to prosecute illegal banking operations and drug trafficking aggressively.[30]

In February 1975 the IRS Inspection Division had launched its own investigation of Operation Leprechaun, and by June it had completed its report. The report criticized the IRS for its lack of management and internal control of Leprechaun. Agent Harrison had been given too much freedom, and the IRS had failed to supervise his activities and the use of agency funds. It also reported that IRS officials knew about some of the problems as early as 1972, even before they had formally established the project. District and regional management had failed to exercise their responsibilities. At the same time, however, the IRS tried to distance itself from much of what had happened, even to the point of citing that "Operation Leprechaun" was not an official IRS title given to the intelligence-gathering efforts, merely a term created by one special agent. It admitted, however, that Leprechaun was not a maverick operation. It was a part of the IGRS, though the report claimed it was a small part.[31]

> Internal audit tests, however, revealed many problems, including: a need to improve supervisory control over inputs to the IGRS indexing system; a need for improvement in the ability to retrieve and evaluate by entity the potential of information accumulated; a need for improve-

ment in compliance with existing instructions and a need for more specific instructions on the type of information that should be indexed as
well as the objectives for accumulating the information.[32]

This was sweeping criticism, but there was more. IRS investigators
found that the Jacksonville District had failed to change its procedures
in response to new regulations issued by the IRS National Office. This
apparently stemmed from a misinterpretation of those instructions
rather than from willful noncompliance. But, though similar problems
existed in the other test districts, in none of those other districts was information on sex and drinking collected and put into the system. Worse,
the IGRS indices did not "provide sufficient information to determine
whether a case has intelligence potential or whether the information is
of no value and should be destroyed."[33]

With respect to ties between Operation Leprechaun and the White
House, eighty-two employees of the IRS Jacksonville District prepared
signed affidavits that they had never forwarded information to the
White House. They denied knowing any IRS employee who had done
so. Special agent Thomas Lopez stated that he had met with various
White House personnel, including John Dean, but that those meetings
had concerned the narcotics trafficking program. Reviews of Lopez's diaries revealed no notations about other contacts with Dean or other
White House personnel. The internal investigation was perhaps ham-
pered by the fact that in 1974 the IRS had destroyed forty cubic feet of
records, including general background files older than five years, collateral investigation files more than one year old, and special investigative
equipment control records dating back to 1968. The destruction had
occurred before allegations about Operation Leprechaun had surfaced.[34]

The IRS report, released not only to the Treasury Department and
the Joint Committee on Internal Revenue Taxation but to relevant congressional committees and to the press, contained no conclusions or direct recommendations. It pointed to problems, but the IRS considered
it preliminary and promised further reports when they would not jeopardize ongoing investigations. The IRS also tiptoed around the issue of
special agent John Harrison. A memo from the Jacksonville District director to the National Office concluded that there was no "risk free,
clear-cut action that can be taken." Concerned about the impact of Harrison's actions on the IRS, but also aware that this was a highly sensitive
matter, officials decided simply to meet and review their options. The
IRS also decided to review all IRS operations in the state of Florida. In

the end, the IRS took no action against Harrison or other personnel involved in Operation Leprechaun. The IRS investigation, in short, seemed chiefly interested in finding a way out of the problem and in mitigating its damage.[35]

Other investigations reached mixed conclusions about Operation Leprechaun. A federal grand jury in Miami reported that the investigations of IRS intelligence agents did not violate taxpayers' civil rights, and later cleared Commissioner Alexander of any wrongdoing as well. It also branded many of Elsa Gutierrez's allegations as false and attacked the press for its reporting of Operation Leprechaun. The *New York Times* reported that the grand jury believed Miami newspapers had "knowingly" published false information and that at least one of its reporters had faked documents. The Miami press responded by labeling these reports as "untruths" and attacked the *Times'* allegations as "ludicrous." Howard Kleinberg, editor of the *Miami News*, said his newspaper would not be intimidated. By now the reputation of Elsa Gutierrez had fallen apart. She had remarried again, this time to a convicted marijuana dealer and attempted murderer who was currently serving eight years at a maximum-security prison in Florida. This was her fifth marriage, two of them to her first husband. In 1982, Daniel Heller, a lawyer for the *News*, was convicted of tax evasion in an investigation directed by Thomas Lopez. Five years later an appeals court reversed his conviction, and a judge later dismissed the entire case. The controversy died hard.[36]

The most important impact of Operation Leprechaun was IRS Commissioner Donald Alexander's decision to terminate all nontax-related investigations. Since taking office Alexander had faced revelations about the Special Service Staff and now the IGRS. He believed that both had operated outside normal IRS management channels, had led to serious abuses of IRS power, and had been irrelevant to the agency's mission. Although strike force operations had led to the conviction of several organized crime figures, the commissioner believed that in the process the IRS had lost control over investigative techniques and even its own agents assigned to the strike force. Individuals and organizations had been targeted for reasons having nothing to do with tax compliance problems. The IRS role, Alexander believed, was to find compliance problems that could be used as leverage for the prosecution of individuals targeted for nontax-related reasons.[37]

Alexander's decision to terminate IRS participation in several strike force operations currently under way in Miami and the Bahamas infuriated IRS intelligence officials and produced a revolt within IRS. Some of the officials tried to "get Alexander." Allegations appeared charging him with corruption, of being a "godfather to organized crime" and a friend of tax cheats for his termination of Operation Tradewinds, the investigation of banking and narcotics operations. Since he was a Nixon appointee, some suspected that he was covering up illegal activities by Nixon or Bebe Rebozo in the Bahamas banking industry. Alexander was sufficiently concerned about the charges that in the fall of 1976 he filed a Freedom of Information Act request to see his own IRS files as well as any files kept by the Customs Service.

Despite all the revelations of the 1970s, multiple congressional investigations, and internal upheaval, in 1982 the IRS would embrace a new "toughness" and *expand* its intelligence and undercover activities. This time, however, operations were decentralized—an administrative structure that had brought criticism of agency operations a generation earlier. The IRS returned to decentralized operations, even though the lack of effective oversight had resulted in significant abuses, in order to reduce the chance that its covert actions would attract the attention of the press, the public, or elected officials.[38]

CHAPTER SIXTEEN

CLEANING UP

After the revelations of the mid-1970s about intelligence gathering and the targeting of specific individuals and organizations, the IRS attempted to convince the American people that it was curtailing these operations and ending abuses. Congress was on the warpath, provoked by Nixon administration efforts to abuse the IRS, by the Enemies Lists, and by reports about IRS-driven covert operations like the Special Service Staff and Operation Leprechaun. While Congress demanded that the IRS be responsive, agency officials wrestled with the questions of how to maintain control of disclosure of its operations, and how to minimize negative publicity. The sheer volume of SSS files, and the lack of a comprehensive records management system, inevitably created delays. Although IRS Commissioner Donald Alexander had abolished the SSS, controversy about its operations was more intense than ever. Concerns about privacy, freedom of information, and constitutional rights led to crackdowns on intelligence gathering and provoked legislation to secure the confidentiality of income tax records.

The lack of centralized record-keeping at the IRS and the resulting compartmentalization of information led to the impression that no one was in charge of the agency's controversial operations. When congressional committees asked about SSS activities, all too often IRS officials had to confess that they knew little about them. They also feared that passage of the Freedom of Information Act meant that many IRS records formerly protected from disclosure might now become public. The IRS's concern, however, stemmed more from fear of revelations about its policies and investigations than from concern over specific wrongdoing. How the IRS operated, as much as what it accomplished in those operations, was the prize to be protected. In February 1975, for instance, the House Ways and Means Committee demanded that regulations governing IGRS data be made public. The IRS had suspended the IGRS in January, but no one seemed sure of its future status. Nonetheless the agency preferred to take care of its own affairs and not debate them in the glare of public scrutiny. To the public and to Congress, this sort of protective reaction hinted at a desire for secrecy, and secrecy bred suspicion.[1]

Commissioner Alexander responded to congressional concerns by endorsing the investigation of the SSS by the Joint Committee on Internal Revenue Taxation, arguing that tax "enforcement is too important to leave to the enforcers," and proposing "oversight, a vigilant press, constructive hearings . . . improved law," and "additional procedural safeguards" to prevent future use of the IRS for political purposes. These safeguards would also include a public log of all communications about taxpayers between the IRS and the White House or any government official. This public relations blitz was not entirely successful. Senator Vance Hartke, Democrat from Indiana, charged that the White House *did* send the IRS copies of the Enemies Lists, and that Alexander knew about the existence of the SSS as early as May 1973, not August as he had earlier testified. The commissioner defended the agency, claiming that just because the SSS maintained a file on an organization did not mean that it was subject to audit. This, of course, missed the underlying charge of critics: that the lists were too often compiled for nontax-related purposes. Investigations into the SSS also led the IRS to search for files it had created in the Ideological Organizations Project of the early 1960s, but they were not readily found in the National Office. The IRS apparently hoped to use those files to demonstrate that the SSS was based in part on precedent. Commissioner Alexander wearily suggested that "at the end of all these inquiries" he would like to take the SSS files to the "Ellipse and have the biggest bonfire since 1814."[2]

The Justice Department, meanwhile, opposed much of the proposed privacy legislation, arguing that it had found tax information crucial to its prosecutions of organized crime and corruption. The interaction between state and government agencies that stemmed from the sharing of tax return information was important; criminal investigations turned up tax violation, and IRS investigations of tax violations turned up criminal activities. While the IRS wanted to restrict dissemination of its tax files, the Justice Department wanted to continue business as usual. The press was stunned, and reporters raised the question of White House access to tax returns at President Ford's first news conference. The Justice Department position also angered congressional critics.

Connecticut Senator Lowell Weicker complained that for two years

Congress had been inactive despite massive intelligence operations that violated constitutional rights and extensive documentation of IRS wrongdoing; corrective action was long overdue. In 1974, Texas Senator Lloyd Bentsen proposed legislation to increase the confidentiality of tax returns that attracted widespread support. Extensive congressional hearings forced Richard Nixon to repeal two executive orders under which the IRS had been given permission to share farmers' income tax records with the Department of Agriculture. In 1974 Congress also passed a Privacy Act to prohibit any secret "Federal agency system of records about individuals." It required the president to report annually to Congress on these matters. But the act did not reform the decentralized IRS bureaucracy, which had failed to prevent the SSS abuses. Each IRS department remained responsible for "its own implementation and compliance with little or no supervision by anyone at the Department level." Nor did the act provide safeguards to prevent an organization formed to audit troublesome tax cases from developing the mentality of a full-scale intelligence operation, such as the SSS or the IGRS. A Privacy Protection Study Commission on Federal Tax Return Confidentiality reported that tax information seemed to be regarded as a "generalized government asset." It recommended that all "individually identifiable data" maintained by the IRS be restricted from disclosure by the IRS as well as by any agency with whom it might share tax data. Despite this defense of confidentiality, the commission did not investigate whether IRS disclosure of income tax information to the president or Congress was proper. The presumption remained that it was.[3]

The IRS had reservations about the 1974 Privacy Act, and an internal analysis of the act and its projected impact expressed those concerns. The act required the IRS to publish annually in the *Federal Register* "a notice of the existence and character of each system of records which it maintains," as well as how someone might access those records. Its disclosure restrictions, moreover, would likely force the IRS to curtail many current projects. With few exceptions, the IRS also had to allow individuals access to their own files. This meant that "many systems of records currently maintained by the Service would be accessible." Finally, all nontax information would have to be expunged from individuals' records, including reports from the FBI and police departments. The IRS argued that this would jeopardize interagency cooperation, including operations with the CIA and the FBI, such as COINTELPRO. Yet, as Arthur Harrigan, counsel to the Church Committee, concluded, operations like the SSS subjected "its targets to a systematic, disproportionate burden of tax enforcement" based on criteria that were not tax related. Even if the IRS argued that the criteria for enforcement were blind to a target's politics, the agency's enforcement efforts were not. "That SSS knew what it was doing and intended to accomplish non-tax goals through the application of the tax laws," Harrigan reported, was "apparent from the writings" of Paul Wright, its chairman.[4]

In the face of this barrage of criticism, the IRS overreacted. By 1975 internal IRS memoranda complained that the agency had surrendered to perceptions that it had a "storm trooper mentality." The IRS claimed to have stopped all intelligence-gathering operations, though this was not entirely true. Criminal income tax prosecutions had fallen off dramatically, however, and IRS insiders attacked Commissioner Alexander for going too far in order to appease critics. Although they agreed that the IRS should try to shed its "adverse image," critics within Internal Revenue believed that the agency needed to crack down on criminal activities and prosecute violators as it had done in its Organized Crime Program. Alexander was no Randoph Thrower, critics complained, and they suspected politics lay behind the change. They also expressed dismay at Alexander's termination of IRS investigations into offshore banking in the Bahamas, suspecting that the commissioner was covering up something for the man who appointed him—Richard Nixon. They urged a reversal of course, an increase in IRS law enforcement activities. Alexander argued in response that the IRS had assumed too many non-tax responsibilities. "There has been," he complained, "a tendency to hang ornaments on us as though we were a Christmas tree." Although Alexander agreed that the central mission of the IRS was the "administration and enforcement of the tax laws," he did not reveal why some investigations were continued and others were terminated.[5]

Still, when congressional committees investigated the IRS, its power overwhelmed them. The Internal Revenue Service even refused to turn over records to the General Accounting Office, and instead launched an audit of the investigator's taxes! Congress, however, moved quickly to authorize the GAO to audit the IRS. Commissioner Alexander concluded in August 1975 that the IRS could no longer openly oppose a GAO audit, hoping instead to limit its scope and seek protection "against a multiplicity of Congressional oversight activities." Even the Joint Committee, he reported, was "reconciled to something like this." In a last-ditch effort to protect its files, the IRS worked indirectly through the Senate Finance Committee, hoping to obtain legislation that at a minimum would require the GAO to go through one of the tax-writing committees to secure tax returns, without which it could not "undertake any significant audit effort." At the very least, the IRS hoped to prevent unauthorized disclosures of tax information and prevent the GAO from "second-guessing IRS." After it examined IRS records, the GAO characterized the IRS as a "monstrous, ungovernable and completely autonomous organization with awesome powers."[6]

In part to respond to public concerns, and in part to provide evidence of action that might silence its critics, the IRS claimed it was taking a number of steps to safeguard tax information, all the while ensuring that it retained control over its own documents and information about its actions. It reviewed procedures where it either shared information with or provided access for other government agencies. It required federal agencies authorized to inspect returns to examine them only in IRS offices, rather than providing the agencies with copies, and it took a series of steps to improve confidentiality of records shared with state tax officials. The agency also required all field agents to call to the attention of the National Office any effort by the White House to secure IRS information.[7]

In the wake of the SSS and Leprechaun revelations, the two biggest challenges to the IRS probably came from investigations launched by the Joint Committee on Internal Revenue Taxation, its congressional oversight committee, and by Congresswoman Bella Abzug. The IRS could not really escape scrutiny by the Joint Committee, so it cooperated, even in providing access to SSS files, in hopes of concluding the "investigation as soon as possible." The National Office gathered the SSS files from IRS field offices and made them available to Joint Committee staff in the IRS building in Washington. The Joint Committee looked at 770 names from the Enemies List and found that only about 3 percent also had SSS files. It released its report on June 5, 1975, amid charges from critics that its investigations had been lax. Eileen Shanahan of the *New York Times* complained that the Joint Committee had failed to interview too many key individuals who had applied political pressure. In response, staff director Laurence Woodworth not only disputed the charge but indicated that the Joint Committee's investigation remained active. In fact, though the Joint Committee's report seems almost preliminary, it did conclude that SSS files revealed a "lack of standard criteria governing their development or utilization, incorporation of information which was not evaluated or screened, and the concentrated accumulation of information on political activities."[8]

A problem for the Joint Committee, however, was that it could not estimate the extent of SSS punitive actions because FBI material was "commingled with the IRS files," and the FBI ignored IRS and Joint Committee requests to open its files. Secrecy begot secrecy. The Joint

Committee also failed to connect Roger Barth with a flow of information from the IRS to the White House, chiefly because Barth made all his requests by telephone and left no written records. Examination of cases referred to the field yielded more specific results, though the Joint Committee couched its findings in quiet understatement. It found evidence that the SSS had focused on a few groups, especially black militant and left-wing organizations, "to a greater degree than would seem to us to be justified on the basis of tax material." It also reported finding no evidence that the White House or Congress asked for the SSS to be established, though "IRS people at least feel that the pressure put on them to get after activist-type organizations" came from both sources. Either way, Laurence Woodworth reported, we "think that there are first amendment problems all the way up and down here."[9]

On the positive side, Woodworth reported that, based on a 10 percent random sample, the SSS had handled the war tax resistance cases appropriately. Denials of tax-exempt status would have occurred even without the SSS, though they had probably tried to influence judgments. This reflected a larger problem, in that the "cases that went into these [SSS] files were very loose, and the Service generally did not specify the standards to be used." Although these conclusions were based on only a sampling of SSS files, they were revealing nonetheless. The Joint Committee also concluded that FBI reports were irrelevant to tax enforcement, though they were often important in the delicate relationship between the SSS and the Exempt Organizations Branch. Woodworth found that SSS information was kept confidential, even within the IRS, unless disclosure was authorized in writing. Exempt Organizations could therefore use SSS information, but only as a source of leads and not as the specific basis for a ruling. The SSS, moreover, could stall any favorable approval of a tax exemption merely by objecting. The case then went to the Conference and Review staff, and then to the chief counsel who had to decide that a "favorable determination was appropriate." If he did, the case went for further review to the assistant commissioner (Technical). At that time the SSS could present its objections directly. This appeared, in essence, to grant the SSS a powerful role in determining tax exemptions should they choose to exercise it. In a decentralized bureaucracy, it was a stunning centralization of power.[10]

The Joint Committee concluded that the existence of a group like the SSS in the Internal Revenue Service "would appear questionable," noting that it "seemed inappropriate" for the IRS to focus on individuals or groups engaged in civil disobedience without information that they had violated tax laws. An internal audit report of the SSS for the period August 5, 1969, to June 1, 1972, took a different stance, questioning SSS policy not to refer cases to the field unless it had "financial information indicating potential tax liability." The director of the Collection Division took exception to this criticism, arguing that it was "not the mission of the staff to forward information which would trigger fishing expeditions."

The internal audit clashed with Donald Bacon's report that from its inception the SSS was interested primarily in dissidents, particularly black militant organizations and left-wing groups. More problematic was the Joint Committee's admission that though it had the "full and complete cooperation" of the IRS commissioner and his staff, it did "not have access to tax information" and was therefore "unable to fully deal with the impact of the SSS within the Internal Revenue Service." This was a revealing admission and a glaring omission.[11]

Congresswoman Bella Abzug's investigation was less extensive but much more adversarial. In late 1975 counsel for the Church Committee had first asked the IRS to explore the costs involved in releasing the names of all individuals and organizations in SSS files. Before doing this, the IRS would have to locate addresses for all of them and secure their permission to release the files. The IRS gave this possibility a good deal of attention, and numerous memoranda circulated throughout the National Office. Essentially the agency concluded that the idea was "unreasonable" because SSS files were so poorly organized and haphazardly compiled. Nonetheless the IRS dutifully reported that such an effort would cost about $653,000 but that the success rate in contacting these people would be quite low—and this only two years after abolition of the SSS! Bella Abzug then stepped into the spotlight. She chaired a Government Information and Individual Rights Subcommittee of the House Committee on Government Operations, and requested that the IRS supply the subcommittee with a list of the 11,458 names in the SSS files.[12]

Abzug was concerned chiefly about what use had been made of SSS files after the operation had been abolished, rather than what had occurred between 1969 and 1973. She quickly discovered that the IRS continued to use SSS files, though to "a limited degree." Worse, the agency admitted that it was "virtually impossible to determine" which SSS files had "intelligence information in them." Abzug also found that, while the IRS promised to retain these files until after all congressional investigations were complete, it intended to destroy them as soon as possible after that. Afraid that this would bury the past, Abzug opposed this plan and demanded to review SSS files. The IRS preferred to "let the files remain dormant and not attempt to make any notification." But it feared a strong reaction from the subcommittee and proposed trying to locate the 775 individuals and organizations whose files had been sent to the field. The agency recognized that noncooperation might provoke stronger reactions from Congress and stimulate suspicions of illegal activities and a cover-up. Yet the disclosure of any files would itself cause problems, especially since file material was so poorly referenced that sources of documents were "extremely difficult" to reconstruct. Something had to be done, because Abzug swept aside IRS complaints about mailing costs by asking how much money it had spent on the illegal operations of the SSS. Why couldn't the IRS undertake a notification program similar to what the Justice Department had done with victims of its COINTELPRO efforts?[13]

On July 23, 1976, the IRS mailed letters to 731 individuals and organizations asking permission to release their names. Two months later the post office had been able to find only 387 of them, and the IRS planned a second mailing. Most who received the letter asked for a copy of their file. The mailing also generated 366 "potential non-compliance leads" for the IRS, but Internal Revenue agents decided to refer only two of them (both potential fraud cases) to its service centers for processing. Concluding that it had met its responsibilities, for the next several years the IRS as well as other federal agencies repeatedly sought to destroy these and related files once the notification process was complete. IRS Commissioner Donald Alexander expressed concern that so long as the IRS retained SSS files, suspicions would lurk that it was using them. Abzug fought this tooth and nail, warning Alexander that just "to take the files and destroy them and have a bonfire has a lawless quality that I do not like." She put him on notice that the files were to remain intact. As a result, the SSS files were locked away in a vault where they remained undisturbed for fifteen years, until the IRS historian Shelley Davis stumbled upon them and recognized their importance. Those files became a crucial source for this book. More important, they are a haunting reminder of the power of the IRS to abuse the public trust.[14]

The Special Service Staff was the most egregious and least understood example of the Internal Revenue Service gone awry. During and immediately after the Watergate years the IRS faced scrutiny from congressional investigators and extensive media coverage that cast a harsh light on its operations and indeed on its institutional culture. The revelations of a systematic pattern of illegal activity directed against individuals and groups that criticized government policies shocked many

Americans, as did the attempts by the Nixon administration to make the IRS part of its campaign against its political opponents, which became the basis for one of the articles of impeachment that the House of Representatives adopted against the president. Evidence that the IRS was compiling nontax information about American citizens and sharing its files with the FBI and CIA was equally disturbing, as were revelations of surveillance activities that drew the IRS far from its statutory responsibilities of tax collection and enforcement. To a post–World War II generation that tended to see the U.S. government as a beneficent force, these were stunning developments. Lawrence O'Brien spoke for many when he characterized the political uses of the IRS as the most shocking aspect of Watergate—a pattern of abuse that threatened the very foundations of the republic.

But despite Capitol Hill hearings and the media spotlight, little permanent change ensued. Although the Tax Reform Act of 1976 limited the disclosure of tax return information to anyone outside the IRS, in subsequent years the agency remained a closed society. The IRS and its agents continued to possess near absolute power in investigating compliance with the tax code, and, as several hearings in the late 1980s and 1990s documented, too often wielded that power arrogantly. The agency continued to use the IRS code's disclosure restrictions not to protect the privacy of taxpayers and the integrity of the tax system, which was Congress's intent in writing the legislation, but as a shroud to deny public access to its records and prevent disclosure of its operations. Predictably, over the years the institutional culture of the agency tolerated a systematic pattern of abuse of taxpayers. Once again congressional hearings revealed the agency to be out of control, and taxpayer bills of rights were enacted in 1988 and again in 1996, when an Office of Taxpayer Advocate was also established. Two years later Congress adopted additional legislation designed to rein in the IRS and give taxpayers stronger rights in dealing with the agency. None of these efforts, however, has resulted in a careful, nonpartisan investigation of IRS records and operations. A generation after Watergate and revelations of the Special Service Staff, the potential for the politicization of the agency remains.

Notes

MANUSCRIPT COLLECTIONS, referred to in the notes, have been abbreviated as follows:

ADA Americans for Democratic Action

BHP Bertrand Harding Papers, Lyndon B. Johnson Library, Austin, Texas

BJHP Billy James Hargis Papers, University of Arkansas

DPP Drew Pearson Papers, Lyndon B. Johnson Library, Austin, Texas

EVLP Edward V. Long Papers, Western Historical Manuscripts Collection, University of Missouri, Columbia

HFP Henry Fowler Papers, Lyndon B. Johnson Library, Austin, Texas

HMP Henry McPherson Papers, Lyndon B. Johnson Library, Austin, Texas

HRP Henry S. Reuss Papers, Golda Meir Library, University of Wisconsin, Milwaukee

JFKP John F. Kennedy Papers, John F. Kennedy Library, Boston, Massachusetts

JJWP John J. Williams Papers, Morris Library, University of Delaware, Newark

JLRP Joseph L. Rauh, Jr., Papers, Library of Congress, Washington, D.C.

LBJP Lyndon B. Johnson Papers, Lyndon B. Johnson Library, Austin, Texas

LWP Lee White Papers, John F. Kennedy Library, Boston, Massachusetts

NA National Archives and Records Administration, Washington, D.C.

OFSAS Office Files of Secretaries, Under Secretaries, and Assistant Secretaries, 1932–1965, Department of the Treasury, Washington, D.C.

RCP Ramsey Clark Papers, Lyndon B. Johnson Library, Austin, Texas

RFKP Robert F. Kennedy Papers, John F. Kennedy Library, Boston, Massachusetts

SCP Sheldon Cohen Papers, Lyndon B. Johnson Library, Austin, Texas

TCHP Thomas C. Hennings Papers, Western Historical Manuscripts Collection, University of Missouri, Columbia

TCP Thomas Curtis Papers, Western Historical Manuscripts Collection, University of Missouri, Columbia

WHCF   White House Central Files
WHSF   White House Staff Files
WPP   Wright Patman Papers, Lyndon B. Johnson Library, Austin, Texas
WRP   Walter Reuther Papers, Archives of Labor and Urban Affairs, Wayne State University, Detroit, Michigan
WSP   William Simon Papers, Lafayette College Archives, Easton, Pennsylvania
WSPF–   Watergate Special Prosecution Force, Plumbers Task Force, Misuse of
IRS   the IRS, National Archives and Records Administration, College Park, Maryland

Introduction: Researching the IRS

1. Jerry Berman and Morton Halperin, eds., *The Abuses of the Intelligence Agencies* (Washington, D.C., 1975), pp. 86, 87. For some political uses of the IRS under Eisenhower, see Neal Smith, *Mr. Smith Went to Washington: From Eisenhower to Clinton* (Ames, Iowa, 1996), pp. 79–80.

2. See Athan Theoharis, "In-House Cover-up: Researching FBI Files," in Athan Theoharis, ed., *Beyond the Hiss Case: The FBI, Congress, and the Cold War* (Philadelphia, 1982), pp. 20–77.

3. Quoted in *Role of the Internal Revenue Service in Law Enforcement Activities*, Hearings Before the Subcommittee on Administration of the Internal Revenue Code of the Committee on Finance, U.S. Senate, 94th Cong., 2d sess. (Washington, D.C., 1976), p. 52.

4. Department of the Treasury, *Records Management in the Internal Revenue Service* (Washington, D.C., 1995), p. 3.

5. Ibid., p. 16. For "Operation Snowball," see Thomas Marusin, IRS Director of Freedom of Information, to the author, July 1, 1999.

6. *Records Management in the Internal Revenue Service*, p. 21. See also George Guttman, "IRS Records Management Program Panned by National Archives," *Tax Notes* (Jan. 1, 1996), 13.

7. John B. Cummings, Assistant Chief Counsel, Disclosure Litigation, to the author, June 20, 1996; Caplin's testimony is in *IRS Disclosure: Hearings Before the Subcommittee on Adminsitrative Practice and Procedure of the Committee on the Judiciary*, U.S. Senate, 93d Cong., 2d session (Washington, D.C., 1974), pp. 3–4.

8. Shelley Davis, *Unbridled Power: Inside the Secret Culture of the IRS* (New York, 1997), provides an account of my encounter with Parker and Raisch (pp. 252–254) as well as an overview of related research problems. Davis, the former IRS historian noted earlier, described her reaction to my account of the interview with Parker and Raisch: "At least I knew what I was up against: standard retaliation, trumped-up charges. By assigning Raisch and Parker to the investigation of me, the IRS laid the groundwork for a major grievance against it, because retaliation was so blatant a motive" (p. 254).

9. H. A. Williamson, Jr., to the author, December 8, 1995. He also asserted that the IRS was "not required to describe the nature of each document denied when processing a FOIA request."

10. Marcus Farbenblum, *The IRS and the Freedom of Information and Privacy Acts of 1974: The Disclosure Policies of the Internal Revenue Service and How to Obtain Documents from Them* (Jefferson, N.C., 1991), pp. 1, 28. This is an outstanding study that should be required reading for anyone seeking information on or from the IRS.

11. William A. Dobrovir, Attorney for the Petitioners [Tax Analysts, American Historical Association, Organization of American Historians], to IRS Commissioner Margaret Milner Richardson, July 18, 1996. Re: Petition for IRS Compliance with the FRA [Federal Records Act] and NARA Regulations. Copy in the author's possession.

12. Athan Theoharis, *A Culture of Secrecy: The Government Versus the People's Right to Know* (Lawrence, Kans., 1998), pp, 13, 22.

13. *Report on Administrative Procedures of the Internal Revenue Service, October 1975, to the Administrative Conference of the United States,* 94th Cong., 2d sess. (Washington, D.C., 1976), pp. 827, 832. Also see Berman and Halperin, *The Abuses of the Intelligence Agencies,* pp. 86, 88.

14. Jeff Schnepper, *Inside IRS: How Internal Revenue Works (You Over)* (New York, 1978), p. 187.

15. Davenport's comments are in *Role of the Internal Revenue Service in Law Enforcement Activities,* p. 245. For summaries of agents' activities see Frank Donner, *The Age of Surveillance: The Aims and Methods of America's Political Intelligence System* (New York, 1980), pp. 321–322.

Chapter One. The Early 1960s: A New Role for the IRS?

1. Bellino remains a somewhat shadowy figure. Pieces of his background can be found in the finding aid to the Carmine Bellino Papers, JFK Library; Clark Mollenhoff, *Tentacles of Power: The Story of Jimmy Hoffa* (New York, 1965), p. 91; Helen O'Donnell, *A Common Good: The Friendship of Robert Kennedy and Kenneth P. O'Donnell* (New York, 1998), pp. 118, 133, 141; Victor Navasky, *Kennedy Justice* (New York, 1971), pp. 404–405; and James Hilty, *Robert Kennedy: Brother Protector* (Philadelphia, 1997), p. 103.

2. For a summary of Bellino's inspections of IRS records, see D. O. Virdin to Burke Willsey, August 7, 1973, IRS (Sensitive): Miscellaneous folder: WSP. This was compiled by the IRS and covers 1961 through 1970.

3. Mortimer Caplin, Oral History Interview, November 1991 (prepared by Shelley Davis, IRS historian), pp. 20–21; *Federal Tax Return Privacy,* Hearings Before the Subcommittee on Administration of the Internal Revenue Code of the Committee on Finance, U.S. Senate, 94th Cong., 1st sess. (Washington, D.C., 1975), pp. 240; Mollenhoff, *Tentacles of Power,* p. 338; *Report on Administrative Procedures of the Internal Revenue Service, October 1975, to the Administrative Conference of the United States,* 94th Cong., 2d sess. (Washington, D.C., 1976), pp. 968–969; *IRS Disclosure,* p. 95; *Political Intelligence in the Internal Revenue Service: The Special Service Staff. A Documentary Analysis Prepared by the Staff of the Subcommittee on Constitutional Rights of the Committee on the Judiciary,* U.S. Senate, 93rd Cong., 2d sess. (Washington, D.C., 1974), p. 198. That Bellino had an office at IRS is noted in David Burnham, *A Law Unto Itself: The IRS and the Abuse of Power* (New York, 1989), p. 244.

4. Classified files of Secretary Dillon, 1961–1965, Box 6C-ES; folder: Secretary's Staff Meeting, February through May 1961, RG 56, NA; *Federal Tax Return Privacy* (1975), p. 127; Henry Hecht to Files, November 29, 1973, WSPF-IRS, Box 1, folder: Witness Statements: Mortimer Caplin; K. Martin Worthy to Randolph Thrower, April 22, 1970, WSPF-IRS, Box 11, folder: IRS–Opinions Relating to Disclosures of the Tax Returns to WH Staff, RG 460, NA; Memorandum of Robert Knight, in *IRS Disclosure,* pp. 194–195.

5. *The Internal Revenue Service: An Intelligence Resource and Collector.* Supplementary Detailed Staff Reports on Intelligence Activities and the Rights of Americans, Book III. Final Report of the Select Committee to Study Governmental Operations with Respect to Intelligence Activities, U.S. Senate, 94th Cong., 2d sess. (Washington, D.C., 1976), p. 871.

6. "Confidentiality of Tax Returns," *Report on Administrative Procedures of the Internal Revenue Service* (1976), pp. 901–902; Navasky, *Kennedy Justice,* pp. 50, 56; *Role of the Internal Revenue Service in Law Enforcement Activities,* p. 160.

7. Arnold Sagalyn to Secretary Dillon, November 30, 1961, Classified Files of Secretary Dillon, 1961–1965, Box 4C-ES, folder: Memos to the Secretary, 1961, part 2, RG 56, NA.

8. Memorandum: Re: Origins and Operation of the Organized Crime Drive, July 10, 1965, Box 83, folder: Criminal Division, RCP; *The Internal Revenue Service: An Intelligence Resource and Collector,* p. 869. Rogovin's comments are in *Role of the IRS in Law Enforcement Activities,* p. 52. See also Hilty, *Robert Kennedy,* p. 202.

9. For details on Alexander's 1988 interview, see Burnham, *A Law Unto Itself,* pp. 98–99.

10. Bertrand Harding to Mortimer Caplin, June 30, 1961, Box 1, folder: Reading File, 6/1/61–12/31/61, BHP; Hilty, *Robert Kennedy,* 282. Kennedy kept his intervention for the tax exemption so quiet that many activists did not know of it; see Harold and Virginia Fleming, *The Potomac Chronicle: Public Policy and Civil Rights from Kennedy to Reagan* (Athens, Ga., 1996), p. 35.

11. E. F. Preston, Assistant Commissioner (Administration) to Commissioner of Internal

Revenue Service, April 21, 1961, OFSAS, Records of Henry Fowler, Box 10-F, folder: IRS–Personnel (General), RG 56, NA.

12. Helen Lempart (O'Donnell's secretary) to Henry Fowler, August 29, 1962, in ibid., Box 9-F, folder: IRS–Commissioner's Advisory Group.

13. These cases during the Kennedy administration, including the Feldman case, are discussed in Bertrand Harding memos for the files of March 26 and 27, 1963, and November 23 and 25, 1964; Box 2, folder: reading file, Deputy Commissioner, Jan.–June 1963 and reading file, 7/1/64–12/31/64, BHP. In another instance, Robert Kennedy had intervened (after first recusing himself) in the case of James M. Landis, an old family friend, to negotiate a "more humane sentencing arrangement." See Hilty, *Robert Kennedy*, p. 477.

14. For the steel crisis, see Hilty, *Robert Kennedy*, p. 282; Roger Blough, "President Kennedy and Steel Prices," *The Benjamin F. Fairless Memorial Lectures* (New York, 1974), p. 89; and Roy Hoopes, *The Steel Crisis* (New York, 1963), pp. 67, 212–214. The charity ball question is in JFK to Dillon, January 5, 1962, OFSAS, Box 2C-ES, folder: Classified White House 1962, Classified Files of Secretary Dillon, 1961–1965, RG 56, NA. Caplin's replies are attached to this memo.

15. For a sample of this debate, see the *New York Times*, March 9, 1961, p. 12; March 19, 1961, p. 51; March 21, 1961, p. 8; and March 26, 1961, p. 60. Goldwater's speech is quoted in Donald Janson and Bernard Eismann, *The Far Right* (New York, 1963), p. 231. Some of this analysis appeared in my *The Other Side of the Sixties: Young Americans for Freedom and the Rise of Conservative Politics* (New Brunswick, N.J., 1997); see especially chapter 7.

16. *New York Times*, April 1, 1961, p. 1, and April 7, 1961, p. 15; "Wide-Swinging Bitter-Enders of the Right," *Newsweek* 57 (April 10, 1961), 38; "Subversion of the Right" and "Why They Crucify," *The Christian Century* 78 (April 12, 1961), 379–380, 443–444; Raymond Moley, "It Is Not Conservatism," *Newsweek* 57 (April 17, 1961), 114. The literature during 1961 is enormous. Other citations are in Andrew, *The Other Side of the Sixties*, pp. 262–264. The Kennedys' views are noted in the *New York Times*, Nov. 19, 1961, p. 1, and "Thunder Against the Right," *Time* 78 (November 24, 1961), 11–12.

17. An entire issue of *The Nation* is devoted to "The Ultras"; see vol. 194 (June 30, 1962). The quotation comes from p. 585. For the FBI's efforts against the right wing, see Athan Theoharis, *Spying on Americans: Political Surveillance from Hoover to the Huston Plan* (Philadelphia, 1978), p. 168, and *The Development of FBI Domestic Intelligence Investigations*. Supplemental Detailed Staff Reports of Intelligence Activities and the Rights of Americans, Book III. Final Report of the Select Committee to Study Government Operations with Respect to Intelligence Activities, U.S. Senate, 94th Cong., 2d sess. (Washington, D.C., 1976), p. 457.

18. "Address in Seattle at the University of Washington's 100th Anniversary Program, November 16, 1961," *Public Papers of the President: John F. Kennedy, 1961* (Washington, D.C., 1962), pp. 726, 727.

19. "Address in Los Angeles at a Dinner of the Democratic Party of California, November 18, 1961," ibid., p. 735.

20. For liberal concerns, see "Notes of an Oct. 18, 1961 Breakfast Meeting" of the Americans for Democratic Action board, reel 120, ADA Papers [microfilm]. Union concerns and their ties to the Kennedy administration are in Peter Levy, *The New Left and Labor in the 1960s* (Urbana, Ill., 1994), especially p. 24; and Victor Reuther, *The Brothers Reuther and the Story of the UAW* (Boston, 1976), p. 440. Part of the ensuing memorandum leaked to the press, but the full document was not publicly released until its publication in Reuther's book in 1976, long after both John and Robert Kennedy had died.

21. The intent of the memorandum is noted in the cover letter, Victor Reuther to Robert Kennedy, December 19, 1961, Box 41, folder: Walter P. Reuther, 1949, 1954–65, 1970, JLRP. A copy of the memorandum is in Box 377, folder 3, WRP. The quotations are from pp. 1 (emphasis in original), 2, 6. Hereafter this will simply be referred to as the Reuther Memorandum. By 1963, when the administration had acted on some of the memorandum's recommendations, requests for copies flowed into the Justice Department. Robert Kennedy's office provided copies until they ran out, but also concocted a cover story not only denying any connection to the memo but insisting that it had simply filed the memorandum without reading its contents. See Andrew F. Oehmann, Executive Assistant to RFK, to RFK, November 7, 1963, and Oehmann to Representative George E. Brown, Jr., December 10, 1963, Attorney General, Gen. Corresp., Box 48, folder: Reuther Memorandum 12/19/61, RFKP. Ironically, Nelson Lichtenstein's

splendid recent study of Walter Reuther, *The Most Dangerous Man in Detroit: Walter Reuther and the Fate of American Labor* (New York, 1995), has no mention of this topic. This and the next several pages are drawn from my *The Other Side of the Sixties*, pp. 154–157.

22. Reuther Memorandum, p. 6.

23. Ibid., pp. 15–17.

24. Ibid., pp. 18–21. For the Volker Fund, see Merrimom Cuninggim, *Private Money and Public Service: The Role of Foundations in American Society* (New York, 1972), p. 108.

25. Reuther Memorandum, pp. 21–24. The quotation is on p. 24.

26. An example of White's efforts are in "Confidential Report #1," November 28, 1961, Box 12, folder: The Radical Right, LWP. In his lengthy (386 pp.) oral history for the Kennedy Library, however, White failed to mention the right wing or his efforts to monitor it. Other efforts are noted in Theoharis, *Spying on Americans*, pp. 168–169, and *Army Surveillance of Civilians: A Documentary Analysis* (Washington, D.C., 1972), pp. 39, 76. This was prepared by the staff of the Subcommittee on Constitutional Rights, Committee on the Judiciary, U.S. Senate, 92d Cong., 2d sess. Robert Kennedy's remarks are in Edwin O. Guthman and Jeffrey Shulman, eds., *Robert Kennedy: In His Own Words* (Toronto, 1988), pp. 296–297.

27. "Internal Revenue Service Study of Ideological Organizations, December 31, 1965," FOIA. I have used this designation (FOIA) to refer to this and subsequent IRS documents received through various Freedom of Information Act requests. When they clearly came from a larger file within IRS, I have also used the file designation. The documents assembled using FOIA are housed in the John Andrew Collection, Archives and Special Collections, Shadek-Fackenthal Library, Franklin & Marshall College, Lancaster, Pennsylvania. David Burnham discusses some of this in *A Law Unto Itself*, pp. 270–276. In his *The American Police State: The Government Against the People* (New York, 1978), David Wise also makes brief mention of the project. For the question of ideology and taxation, see William J. Lehrfeld, "The Taxation of Ideology," *Catholic University of America Law Review* 19 (Fall 1969), 50–73. A good summary of the Church Committee, but one that says little about the IRS, is in LeRoy Ashby and Rod Gramer, *Fighting the Odds: The Life of Senator Frank Church* (Pullman, Wash., 1994), pp. 471 and *passim*. Even with the Church Committee, however, both the committee and the public focused their attention on Richard Nixon's abuses of the IRS rather than those of John Kennedy.

28. The IRS position on these issues is articulated in J. F. Worley, Chief, Exempt Organizations Branch, to John W. S. Littleton, Director, Tax Rulings Division, October 24, 1962, General Records of the Department of the Treasury, Office Files of Under Secretary Henry Fowler, 1961–1964, Box 17-F, folder: Tax Exemption—Correspondence with Congressman Patman, Records of Henry Fowler, RG 56, NA. White House agreement is noted in Commissioner Mortimer Caplin to Fowler, December 9, 1963, in the same file. This file also includes the background paper issued by the Public Information Office of the IRS, August 1962 (its public cover). For evidence that the IRS compartmentalized its projects to keep Patman in the dark, see Caplin to Patman, August 23, 1962, in the same file.

29. *Nominations.* Hearings before the Committee on Finance, U.S. Senate, 87th Cong., 1st sess. (Washington, D.C., 1961), pp. 5–15; Caplin Oral History, pp. 12–15, 67; *New York Times*, November 14, 1997.

Chapter Two. The Ideological Organizations Project

1. Information in this and the preceding paragraph is drawn from *Investigation of the Special Service Staff of the Internal Revenue Service*. Prepared for the Joint Committee on Internal Revenue Taxation (Washington, D.C., 1975), pp. 102–103; U.S. Senate, Select Committee to Study Government Operations with Respect to Intelligence Activities, *Final Report: Supplementary Detailed Staff Reports on Intelligence Activities and the Rights of Americans, Book III,* 94th Cong., 2d sess. (Washington, D.C., 1976), p. 891. Caplin's recollections are in his Oral History Interview, p. 15.

2. Although Arthur Schlesinger, Jr., in *Robert Kennedy and His Times* (Boston, 1978), carefully documents Robert Kennedy's use of the IRS in combating organized crime, and while he notes the existence of the Reuther Memorandum, he argues that the administration moved cautiously on it and omits all reference to the Ideological Organizations Project or any interest

in using the IRS against the right wing. See pp. 267, 283–284 for the IRS and organized crime, and p. 451 for the Reuther Memorandum. For evidence of Schlesinger's apparent ignorance of the project, see Acting IRS Commissioner Bertrand Harding to Schlesinger, June 27, 1963, FOIA.

3. *Final Report*, p. 892. Information on the CIA and FBI activities respecting the FPCC is in John Newman, *Oswald and the CIA* (New York, 1995), pp. 95, 238, 239, 243–244. Domestic CIA operations were, of course, a violation of the agency's charter. For Rogovin's CIA connection, see Taylor Branch, "Playing Both Sides Against the Middle," *Esquire* 86 (September 1976), 18.

4. Dean Barron to Ass't Commissioner (Compliance), March 9, 1962, FOIA. See also Bertrand Harding to Wright Patman, October 30, 1964, FOIA; Rogovin to Feldman, March 23, 1964, FOIA.

5. Barron letter of March 9, 1962; Rogovin to Feldman, March 23, 1964.

6. See Box 4, folder: Conference File: Washington, D.C., Regional Commissioners & Dist. Dir. Conf., November 6–8, 1961, BHP; IRS press release, September 7, 1962, Box 467, folder: Foundation Study, 1962, RG 128, NA.

7. Caplin to Fowler, May 14, 1962, Box 11-F, folder: IRS–Tax Exempt Organizations, Records of Henry Fowler, RG 56, NA. See also *The Internal Revenue Service: An Intelligence Resource and Collector*, p. 843.

8. Dean Barron, Audit Division, to Assistant Commissioner (Compliance), March 9, 1962, "Internal Revenue Study of Ideological Organizations, December 31, 1965, Part II," Series IIIA, Drawer 14, folder 14: 42, WSP.

9. Welch to A. G. Heinsohn, Jr., Cherokee Textile Mills, Sevierville, Tennessee, April 6, 1962, "Internal Revenue Study of Ideological Organizations, December 31, 1965," Series IIIA, Drawer 14, folder 14: 41, WSP.

10. Caplin to Kennedy, May 15, 1962, ibid., Series IIIA, Drawer 14, folder 14: 42, WSP.

11. Ibid.

12. For Fulbright, see Colin F. Stam, Chief of Staff, Joint Committee on Internal Revenue Taxation, to Fulbright, March 6, 1962, Box 468, folder: J. William Fulbright, RG 128, NA. The NAACP and church incidents are noted in Glenn Everett to Drew Pearson, January 31, 1961, Box F156 (2 of 3), folder: Internal Revenue, 1957–1961, DPP. The Bellino interest is noted in a June 5, 1962, note, Box 30, folder: Notes: Telephone, Telephone Notes, 1962, BHP. For the FBI, see Berman and Halperin, *Abuses of Intelligence Agencies*, p. 30.

13. Hauser to Caplin, November 19, 1962, WSPF–IRS, Box 11, folder: IRS–Opinions Relating to Disclosures of the Tax Returns to W. H. Staff, RG 460, NA. The Bellino issue surfaced again in the Nixon years. See K. Martin Worthy to IRS Commissioner Randolph Thrower, April 22, 1970, in the same file. Also see *IRS Disclosure* (1974), pp. 85–100.

14. Bacon to Caplin, February 6, 1963, "Internal Revenue Study of Ideological Organizations, December 31, 1965," Series IIIA, Drawer 14, folder 14: 41, WSP.

15. Caplin to Fowler, May 23, 1963, Classified Files of Secretary Dillon, 1961–1965, Box 16C-ES, folder: Classified Memos to Undersecretary, 1963, RG 56, NA.

16. Ibid.

17. Ibid. See also *Investigation of the Special Service Staff of the Internal Revenue Service*, p. 105. In his interview with the Joint Committee on Internal Revenue Taxation about this matter, Caplin did not recall this memo.

18. "Confidential Memorandum on Extremist Groups," July 11, 1963, "Internal Revenue Study of Ideological Organizations, December 31, 1965," Series IIIA, Drawer 14, folder: 14:42, WSP. See also Caplin to Fowler, May 23, 1963, Box 11-F, folder: IRS–Tax Exempt Organizations, Records of Henry Fowler, RG 56, NA; *Final Report*, p. 894n. Lowman's letter, dated January 30, 1965, is in the Tax Exemptions folder, BJHP.

19. *Investigation of the Special Service Staff*, pp. 14, 106–107. The expansion is noted in *Final Report*, p. 894. The White House meetings are recorded in handwritten notes on the Caplin to Feldman memo of July 11, 1963, Series IIIA, Drawer 14, folder 14: 42, WSP.

20. *Investigation of the Special Service Staff*, pp. 107–109. For one newspaper headline, see Erwin Knoll, "Taxpayers Subsidize Political Propaganda," *Newark Star-Ledger* (July 15, 1963), in Box 6, folder: Conference File: Washington, D.C., Regional Commissioners Conference, September 11–13, 1963, BHP.

21. Rogovin memorandum, August 21, 1963, "Internal Revenue Study of Ideological Or-

ganizations, December 31, 1965, Part II," FOIA. A copy of Feldman's study is in Memorandum for the President, 15 August 1963, Box 106, folder: Right Wing Movement, Part 1, Presidential Papers, President's Office Files, JFKP. The list of groups as of August 21, revised from two weeks earlier, included the Jane Addams Peace Association, the American Council of Christian Churches, the American Council of Christian Laymen, the American Economic Foundation, the American Enterprise Association, the American Good Government Society, America's Future, the Christian Anti-Communist Crusade, the Christian Echoes National Ministry, the Christian Freedom Foundation, the Circuit Riders, the Common Council for American Unity [then known as the American Council for Nationalities Service], the Council on Foreign Relations, the Foundation for Economic Education, the Four Freedoms Study Group, the League for Industrial Democracy, the Life Line Foundation, the National Education Program, the New School for Social Research, the Oxford Group–Moral Rearmament, Protestants and Other Americans United for Separation of Church and State, the Spindale Mills Foundation, and the Zionist Organization of America. The Freeman Charitable Foundation and the Educational Reviewer had been dropped. See "Ideological Organizations Proposed for First Phase of Audit Program," August 21, 1963, Box 6, folder: Conference File: Washington, D.C., Regional Commissioners Conference, September 11–13, 1963, BHP.

22. Rogovin Memorandum, August 21, 1963, "Internal Revenue Study of Ideological Organizations, December 31, 1965, Part II," FOIA.

23. Bacon Memo to Regional Commissioner, New York Regional Office, August 20, 1963, Box 6, folder: Conference File: Washington, D.C., Regional Commissioners Conference, September 11–13, 1963, BHP. (This is a sample letter.)

24. Ibid.

25. Rogovin to Regional Commissioners, August 27, 1963, FOIA.

26. Ibid. Rogovin did cite one example in which an oil refining company claimed more than $20,000 in contributions as deductions, including charging $2,000 in subscriptions for a John Birch Society publication to crude oil production.

27. The full list of 109 organizations, along with the list of 20 groups with applications pending, is in Rogovin to Caplin, September 9, 1963, "Internal Revenue Study of Ideological Organizations, December 31, 1965 (Part 2)," Series IIIA, Drawer 14, folder 14: 42, WSP. See also Rogovin to Director, Collection Division, September 10, 1963, Series IIIA, Drawer 14, folder 14: 40, WSP.

28. Bertrand Harding notes for October 22, 1963, Box 30, folder: Notes: Telephone, Telephone Notes, 1963 (1), BHP; William Hoover, Jr., to Williams, December 15, 1963, Box 79, folder 655, JJWP. See also *Investigation of the Special Services Staff of the Internal Revenue Service*, p. 109.

29. Conference Report, December 4, 1963, FOIA. That same day Caplin communicated the results of that staff conference to Secretary of the Treasury Douglas Dillon. For that, as well as Fowler's comments, see Staff Meeting Notes, December 4, 1963, Box 16C-ES, folder: file copy of Secretary's Staff Notes, 1963, Classified Files of Secretary Dillon, 1961–1965, RG 56, NA.

30. Conference Notes, January 4, 1964, FOIA.

31. The Rogovin link is in remarks by Vernon Acree of the IRS. See Series IIIA, Drawer 17, folder 17:58 [Watergate], WSP. For Feldman's comments, see *Investigation of the Special Service Staff*, p. 110. See also Rogovin to Feldman, March 23, 1964, FOIA.

32. Bacon to Secretary of the Treasury, August 17, 1964, "Internal Revenue Study of Ideological Organizations, December 31, 1965 (Part 2)," Series IIIA, Drawer 14, folder 14: 42, WSP.

33. Ibid.

34. "Internal Revenue Study of Ideological Organizations, December 31, 1965," Series IIIA, Drawer 14, folder 14: 41, WSP.

35. Ibid., folder 14: 42.

36. Bertrand Harding to Patman, October 30, 1964, FOIA. See also Harding to Treasury Secretary Dillon, December 10, 1964, Series IIIA, Drawer 14, folder 14: 42, WSP.

37. Rogovin to Harding, October 12, 1964, and Memorandum for File, A. W. Brisbin, October 13, 1964, "Internal Revenue Study of Ideological Organizations, December 31, 1965," Series IIIA, Drawer 14, folder 14: 42, WSP.

38. Conference Report, November 5, 1964, ibid. See also Harding to Treasury Secretary

Douglas Dillon, December 24, 1964, ibid., and Harding to Assistant Treasury Secretary Stanley Surrey, November 18, 1964, FOIA.

39. Ted Knap and Erwin Savelson, "Tax Men Probe Right-Wing Funds," *New York World-Telegram and Sun* (December 3, 1964), FOIA.

40. For an update of the IOP's progress, see Chief Counsel, IRS, to Secretary of the Treasury, February 8, 1965, "Internal Revenue Study of Ideological Organizations, December 31, 1965," Series IIIA, Drawer 14, folder 14: 42, WSP. A copy of Anderson's column from the *Washington Post* for March 3, 1965, was circulated within the IRS. See Carswell to Brisbin, March 3, 1965, "Internal Revenue Study of Ideological Organizations, December 31, 1965," Series IIIA, Drawer 14, folder 14: 42, WSP.

41. Carswell to Brisbin, ibid.; Sheldon Cohen, IRS Commissioner, to Secretary of the Treasury, March 8, 1965, ibid.

42. Rogovin to Surrey, April 20, 1965, "Internal Revenue Study of Ideological Organizations (Part 2)," FOIA.

Chapter Three. Prime Target: Billy James Hargis and the Christian Crusade

1. There is an enormous literature on the right wing in these years, much of it tendentious. For a summary of these issues in the Kennedy administration, see Andrew, *The Other Side of the Sixties*, pp. 126–154. Evidence that Hargis had attracted the Kennedy administration's attention is in Lee White's Confidential Report #5, February 6, 1962, Box 12, folder: The Radical Right, LWP.

2. For a lengthy summary of Hargis and his activities, see Group Research Special Report #11 (October 10, 1962), and Peter Schrag, "America's Other Radicals," *Harper's* 241 (August 1970), 35–37.

3. Group Research Special Report #11 (October 10, 1962), p. 4. See also Thomas H. Uzzell, "Billy James Hargis: A Pitch for God and Country," *The Nation* 194 (February 17, 1962), 140–142.

4. Group Research Special Report #11 (October 10, 1962), pp. 5–8. The analysis of Hargis's followers is in Harold Martin, "Doomsday Merchant on the Far, Far Right," *Saturday Evening Post* (April 28, 1962), 24.

5. *Christian Crusade vs. Internal Revenue Service: "A Landmark Decision"* (Tulsa, 1971), pp. 11–13. The next several paragraphs are drawn from this document.

6. Ibid., pp. 13–19.

7. "Internal Revenue Study of Ideological Organizations, December 31, 1965," Series IIIA, Drawer 14, folder 14: 41, WSP. See also Bertrand Harding, Acting IRS Commissioner, to Stanley Surrey, November 18, 1964, in Part II of the same documents; Series IIIA, Drawer 14, folder 14: 42, WSP.

8. "News from the Right," *Texas Observer* 56 (November 27, 1964), 13; clipping in Box 1557B, WPP. See also "IRS Forgets Fair Play in Crackdown Plans Against Right Wing," *Fort Lauderdale News*, November 24, 1964, p. 6; William F. Buckley, Jr., "Tax Exemption Quandary," *San Francisco Examiner*, December 29, 1964; "Taxation and the Right," *The New Guard* 5 (January 1965): 6. For IRS developments, see Bertrand Harding, Acting IRS Commissioner, to the Secretary of the Treasury, December 24, 1964, "Internal Revenue Study of Ideological Organizations, December 31, 1965," Part II, Series IIIA, Drawer 14, folder 14: 42, WSP. See also the IRS "Fact Sheet on Christian Echoes Ministry, Inc.," December 1, 1964, Box 335, folder: Sec. 501–Exemption from Tax on Corporations, 1964, RG 128, NA.

9. Carl Berryman, Jr., to Curtis, December 20, 1964, roll 406, folder 14119, Bertrand Harding to Curtis, December 11, 1964, folder 14118, TCP.

10. A copy is in the Tax Exemptions folder, BJHP. See also the editorial in the *Chattanooga News-Free Press* (November 13, 1966), p. 13, for additional Hargis comments about an impending dictatorship under Johnson and Humphrey. A copy is in Box 612C, folder: Tax Status, WPP.

11. See a November 16, 1964, Christian Crusade release, copy in roll 406, folder 14119, TCP. Also see Clyde Bickerstaff, IRS District Director, Oklahoma City, to Lybrand, Ross Bros. & Montgomery, April 29, 1965, Tax Exemptions folder, BJHP. Although this letter went out

over Bickerstaff's signature, it was written in Washington by IRS Chief Counsel Mitchell Rogovin; see General Counsel Memorandum 32993, March 22, 1965, FOIA.

12. Ibid.

13. Ibid.

14. Ibid.

15. Jones to Thurmond, May 19, 1965, and Callaway to Harold Hartstack, Chief, IRS Technical Coordination Branch, July 22, 1965, roll 162, folder 6432, TCP.

16. Lawrence B. Jerome, Chief, IRS Exempt Organizations Branch, to Charles Farnsley, August 16, 1965, and James F. Callahan, Chief, Conference Staff, IRS, to Lybrand, Ross Bros. & Montgomery, September 1, 1965. Both are in the Taxes–Exemptions folder, BJHP.

17. "Special Report: Christian Crusade's Fight to Retain Tax Exempt Status," *Christian Crusade* (August–September 1965), p. 13; copy in roll 162, folder 6432, TCP.

18. Cohen to Curtis, November 17, 1965; Curtis to Cohen, February 15, 1966; Byrnes to Cohen, February 16, 1966; all in roll 162, folder 6433, TCP. See also Callaway to Curtis, August 7, 1965, in roll 162, folder 6432, and Hargis to Curtis, March 28, 1966, roll 16, 2, folder 6434, TCP.

19. Cohen to Curtis, June 27, 1966, roll 162, folder 6436, TCP.

20. Ibid.

21. Albert Watson to Sheldon Cohen, October 18, 1966; Harold Hartstack, Chief, IRS Technical Coordination Branch, to Congressman M. Gene Snyder, July 12, 1967; Peter Dillon, Chief, IRS Technical Coordination Branch, to Snyder, September 7, 1967; John R. Barber, Chief, Rulings Section, Exempt Organizations Branch, to World Youth Crusade for Freedom, Inc., August 31, 1967. All are in the Tax Exemptions folder, BJHP. Hargis's efforts for Wallace are noted in Carter, *The Politics of Rage*, pp. 13–14.

22. A copy of this enclosure in a Christian Crusade publication is in roll 163, folder 6438, TCP. Emphasis is in the original.

23. H. B. Kelly, General Manager, Christian Crusade, to Dr. Leo M. Coleman, January 9, 1968; newspaper clipping in the file, *Tulsa Tribune*, January 20, 1968; "The Very Latest in the IRS Battle," Christian Crusade Memo, January 26, 1968; all in Tax Exemptions folder, BJHP.

24. Christian Crusade newsletter for March 1968; copy in Box 222, folder: Administrative Practice & Procedures, '67 (A–L), EVLP.

25. *Christian Crusade vs. Internal Revenue Service: "A Landmark Decision"* (Tulsa, 1971), pp. 27, 29.

26. LeRoy Blackstock to Hargis, January 9, 1973, Taxes–Exemptions folder, BJHP. Subsequent court actions are noted in Richard Barnes to Baron I. Shacklette, May 7, 1973, Box 1063C, folder: correspondence, WPP.

Chapter Four. The Ideological Organizations Project: Lessons Learned

1. "Internal Revenue Study of Ideological Organizations, December 31, 1965," FOIA. The following discussion of these organizations' cases is drawn from that same document. Much was redacted in the materials forwarded to me in response to my FOIA request, but a complete copy of the study is in Series IIIA, Drawer 14, folder 14: 41, WSP.

2. G.C.M. 32936, November 19, 1964, FOIA. Copies of these are also in Series IIIA, Drawer 14, folder 14: 42, WSP.

3. G.C.M. 32945, November 27, 1964, FOIA.

4. G.C.M. 32953, December 9, 1964, FOIA.

5. G.C.M. 32982, February 25, 1965, FOIA.

6. G.C.M. 32987, March 10, 1965, FOIA.

7. G.C.M. 33113, October 27, 1965, FOIA.

8. G.C.M. 33112, October 27, 1965, FOIA.

9. G.C.M. 33155, December 16, 1965, FOIA.

10. "Internal Revenue Study of Ideological Organizations, December 31, 1965," FOIA. A copy of this is also in Series IIIA, Drawer 14, folder 14: 41, WSP. I had to appeal the IRS's original redaction of "mass media."

11. Ibid.

12. Ibid. The next several pages draw upon this same study. I will footnote only when the sources change.

13. Ibid. The quotation is from Judge Clark in the 1941 case of *Girard Trust Co. v. Commissioner*, 122 F. 2d 108.

14. The next several pages draw upon the "Internal Revenue Study of Ideological Organizations, December 31, 1965." I will footnote only when the sources change.

15. Rogovin to Harold R. Swartz, Acting Commissioner (Technical), February 25, 1966; Swartz and Rogovin to IRS Commissioner, March 2, 1966; Director, Exempt Organizations and Pension Trust Division, to Chief, Exempt Organizations Branch, March 8, 1966. All are in "Internal Revenue Study of Ideological Organizations, December 31, 1965, Part 2," Series IIIA, Drawer 14, folder 14: 42, WSP.

16. For the status reports, see *Investigation of the Special Service Staff*, p. 110. Williams's request is noted in Cohen to Williams, August 14, 1968, JJWP.

17. *Investigation of the Special Service Staff*, pp. 112–113.

Chapter Five. Foundations, Politics, and Wright Patman

1. Patman's quote is in "The Question of Revising the Tax Status of Foundations: Pro and Con," *Congressional Digest* 48 (May 1969), 148.

2. Young's arguments are summarized in "Wright Patman, Foundations, and the Politics of Wealth and Poverty," paper presented at the ARNOVA Conference, November 9, 1996. Her *Wright Patman: Populism, Liberalism, and the American Dream* (Dallas, Tex., 2000) is the best biography of Patman; pp. 221–221 deal with Patman's connections with the IRS.

3. For the Ford Foundation, see Rebecca Lowen, *Creating the Cold War University: The Transformation of Stanford* (Berkeley, 1997), p. 194. A good discussion of the IRS's power is in Burnham, *A Law Unto Itself*, p. 17.

4. For the committee report, see *Tax-Exempt Foundations. Report of the Special Committee to Investigate Tax-Exempt Foundations and Comparable Organizations*, House of Representatives, 83rd Cong., 2d sess. (Washington, D.C., 1954), pp. 1, 3–4, 11–12 (for quotation).

5. Ibid., pp. 14, 16–19, 54, 56, 85, 116, 169. By "leftist" the committee meant someone "*who does not like what we have and wants to change it*"; see p. 202 (emphasis is in the original).

6. Ibid., pp. 421–423, 427–428.

7. For an overview of these changes, see Elias Clark, "The Limitation on Political Activities: A Discordant Note in the Law of Charities," *Virginia Law Review* 46 (1960), 439–446. The IRS did revoke the exemption of the Highlander Folk School in the late 1950s; see Karen Sue Conzett, "Female College Students' Perceptions of Their Role in the Civil Rights and Antiwar Movements of the 1960s," Ph.D. dissertation, University of Iowa, 1994, p. 45.

8. Waldemar Nielsen, *The Big Foundations* (New York, 1972), pp. 7–8; Young, "Wright Patman," pp. 2–3. A list of Patman's speeches is in Box 1413C, folder: Speeches on Foundations, WPP.

9. Informal Notes on the Secretary's Staff Meetings, July 21, 1961, Box 6C-ES, folder: Secretary's Staff Meeting, June through August, 1961, Classified Files of Secretary Dillon, 1961–1965, RG 56, NA; Young, "Wright Patman," pp. 4–5.

10. Wade Hobbs, Memo for the File, November 17, 1961, Box 8C-ES, folder: Classified Miscellaneous, 1961–1962, Classified Files of Secretary Dillon, 1961–1965, RG 56, NA. For the Joint Committee, see Julian Zelizer, *Taxing America: Wilbur D. Mills, Congress, and the State, 1945–1975* (New York, 1998), pp. 36–37.

11. Francis Lindley, President of the John Randolph Haynes and Dora Haynes Foundation, to Patman, September 8, 1961, Box 316A, folder: Haynes 1960–1961; Patman to D. L. Castle, November 18, 1961, and Castle to Patman, November 29, 1961, Box 312B, folder: Hudson, 1962–1964; all in the WPP. For the IRS, see Bertrand Harding's telephone notes for December 19, 1961, Box 29, folder: Telephone Notes, 1961; and A.W.B. to Mr. Hobbs, December 27, 1961, Box 1, folder: Reading File, Deputy Comm. June 1, 1961–December 31, 1961, BHP.

12. William H. Smith and Carolyn P. Chiechi, *Private Foundations Before and After the Tax Reform Act of 1969* (Washington, D.C., 1974), pp. 25–27.

13. *Congressional Record* 108, Part 11 (July 23, 1962), pp. 14427ff. The long quotation is on

p. 14428. Patman admitted at this time that this report had not been officially considered by the committee and was his alone; see p. 14474.

14. Ibid., p. 14428. The Wright Patman Papers contain numerous examples of these responses. See the exchange between Blake-More Godwin and Patman, July 26, 1962; July 30, 1962; August 2, 1962, Box 327A, folder: Libbey, 1960–1962; John Lyunn to Patman, October 10, 1962, Box 327C, folder: Lilly, 1960–1964; Paul Hemsoth to Patman, October 22, 1962, Box 327B, folder: Libby-Owens-Ford, 1960–1964; George W. Ryan to Patman, October 11, 1962, Box 313C, folder: Hormel, 1962–1964; and D. L. Castle to Patman, October 3, 1962, Box 312B, folder: Hudson, 1962–1964.

15. *Congressional Record* 108, Part 11 (July 23, 1962), pp. 14429–14434. The IRS response is reported in the *Wall Street Journal* (August 1, 1962), p. 1.

16. Informal Notes of the Secretary's Staff Meeting, July 30, 1962, Box 6C-ES, folder: File copy of Staff Meeting Notes, 1962, Classified Files of Secretary Dillon, 1961–1965, RG 56, NA.

17. Ibid.

18. *Congressional Record* 108, Part 13 (August 20, 1962), pp. 16996–16999.

19. Caplin's memo to Patman, August 23, 1962, is attached to Bertrand Harding to Under Secretary Fowler, August 23, 1962, Box 17-F, folder: Tax Exemption—Correspondence with Congressman Patman, Records of Henry Fowler, RG 56, NA.

20. IRS press release, September 7, 1962, Box 467, folder: Foundation Study, 1962, RG 128, NA; Harding to Caplin, October 26, 1962, Box 2, folder: Reading file, Deputy Comm., July 1962–December 1962, BHP; Caplin to Henry Fowler, October 30, 1962, Box 17F, folder: Tax Exemption–Correspondence with Congressman Patman, Records of Henry Fowler, RG 56, NA; Informal Notes of the Secretary's Staff Meeting, November 21, 23, 1962, and December 19, 1962, Box 6C-ES, folder: file copy of staff meeting notes, 1962, Classified Files of Secretary Dillon, 1961–1965, RG 56, NA.

21. *Tax-Exempt Foundations and Charitable Trusts: Their Impact on Our Economy* (Washington, D.C., 1962), pp. v, 1–3, 73.

22. Ibid., pp. v–vi, 14. The IRS had audited the Louis W. and Maud Hill Foundation but approved its returns and assessed no taxes; see A. A. Heckman, Executive Director, to Patman, October 12, 1962, Box 324C, folder: Hill, 1962, WPP.

23. Staff meeting notes for January 18, 1963, Box 16C-ES, folder: file copy of Secretary's staff notes, 1963, Classified Files of Secretary Dillon, 1961–1965, RG 56, NA; Fred J. Cook, "Foundations as a Tax Dodge," *The Nation* 196 (April 20, 1963), 321–322.

24. Cook, "Foundations as a Tax Dodge," pp. 322–323; Arnold Forster and Benjamin Epstein, *Danger on the Right* (New York, 1964), pp. 195–196.

25. Cook, "Foundations as a Tax Dodge," p. 324.

26. David Baird to Patman, September 7, 1962, Box 343B, folder: Baird: Summary by Olsher, Box 345A, folder 3: Winfield Baird Foundation–IRS; both in WPP.

27. John Littleton, Director, Tax Rulings Division, to the Lansing Foundation, January 18, 1963, Box 342C, folder: untitled; David Baird to H. A. Olsher, May 20, 1963, and Patman to Baird, June 28, 1963, Box 340C, folder: untitled [Baird Corporation]; WPP. Patman's complaints are in *Tax-Exempt Foundations and Charitable Trusts: Their Impact on Our Economy* (Washington, D.C., 1963), p. v.

28. Notes for Staff Meeting, October 23, 1963, Box 16C-ES, folder: file copy of Secretary's staff notes, 1963, Classified Files of Secretary Dillon, 1961–1965, RG 56, NA. For the tax-exemption issue, see Raphael Meisels, Manhattan District Director, to the Winfield Baird Foundation, May 13, 1959, and Caplin to the Winfield Baird Foundation, October 27, 1963, Box 342C, folder: untitled, WPP.

29. Harding to Fowler, October 28, 1963, Box 11-F, folder: IRS–Tax Exempt Foundations, Records of Henry Fowler, RG 56, NA.

30. William Ward, lawyer of Raskin and Downing, to Patman, December 6, 1963, and Patman to Baird, December 24, 1963, Box 342B, folder: untitled, WPP; *Tax-Exempt Foundations and Charitable Trusts: Their Impact on Our Economy* (1963), p. iii.

31. *Tax-Exempt Foundations and Charitable Trusts: Their Impact on Our Economy* (1963), p. iii. See also the report from an investigator-auditor of the Select Committee on Small Business, John J. Cronin, Jr., to H. A. Olsher c/o Wright Patman, May 4, 1964, Box 342 B, folder: untitled, WPP.

32. *Tax-Exempt Foundations and Charitable Trusts: Their Impact on Our Economy* (1963), pp.

iii. ix–xi, 11, 13; Caplin to Fowler, December 9, 1963, Box 11-F, folder: IRS–Tax Exempt Foundations, Records of Henry Fowler, RG 56, NA.

33. For the files, see H. A. Olsher Memorandum, February 10, 1964; Hyman Raskin to Patman, April 14, 1964; and Patman to Raskin, April 17, 1964; Box 342B, folder: untitled, WPP. The press release is in Box 342A, folder: untitled, WPP. For the hearings, see *Tax-Exempt Foundations and Charitable Trusts: Their Impact on Our Economy* (Washington, D.C., 1964).

34. A copy of Caplin's remarks is in Box 7, folder: Conf. File: Washington, D.C., Regional Commissioners–District Directors Conference, February 11–13, 1964, BHP. See also William Surface, *Inside Internal Revenue* (New York, 1967), p. 197.

35. Caplin's statement of July 22, 1964, is in Container #19, folder: Conference File, Exempt Organizations Hearings, 1964, BHP; see pp. 5, 9, 11, 17–18.

36. The briefing materials are in ibid.

37. Ibid. For a succinct description of the scope of IRS examinations, see Bertrand Harding's statement of September 1, 1964, in *Tax-Exempt Foundations and Charitable Trusts: Their Impact on Our Economy* (1964), p. 231.

38. *Tax-Exempt Foundations and Charitable Trusts: Their Impact on Our Economy* (1964), pp. 220–221, 273–275; *Tax-Exempt Foundations: Their Impact on Small Business*. Hearings before Subcommittee No. 1 on Foundations, Select Committee on Small Business, House of Representatives, 88th Cong., 2d sess. (Washington, D.C., 1964), p. 253.

39. *Tax-Exempt Foundations and Charitable Trusts: Their Impact on Our Economy* (1964), pp. 220–221, 273–275.

40. Surrey to Dillon, October 23, 1964, and Surrey to Dillon, October 31, 1964, Box 23C-ES, folder: Memos to the Secretary, September–October 1964, Classified Files of Secretary Dillon, 1961–1965, RG 56, NA.

41. "The Revenue Code and a Charity's Politics," *Yale Law Journal* 73 (1964), 663, 665.

Chapter Six. Robber Barons and Spies

1. For summaries of Hunt's activities, see Dan Carter, *The Politics of Rage: George Wallace, The Origins of the New Conservatism, and the Transformation of American Politics* (New York, 1995), p. 336; Harry Hurt III, *Texas Rich: The Hunt Dynasty, from the Early Oil Days Through the Silver Crash* (New York, 1981), pp. 179–180; and Chandler Davidson, *Race and Class in Texas Politics* (Princeton, 1990), pp. 66–67, 209–210. A fairly comprehensive study of Hunt's wealth is in Group Research, Inc., Special Report #6 (March 25, 1963).

2. Hurt, *Texas Rich*, pp. 180–184.

3. Ibid., p. 186.

4. Group Research, Special Report #6, p. 3; Davidson, *Race and Class*, p. 210. Hunt always capitalized LIFE LINE as the title of his new organization.

5. Gordon Moore, IRS agent, to Robert H. Dodman, President, Facts Forum, Inc., October 5, 1953, Box 1557A, loose materials, WPP.

6. Feldman, Memorandum for the President, August 15, 1963, Presidential Papers, President's Office Files, Box 106, folder: Right Wing Movement, Part 1, JFKP.

7. For the IRS chronology, see "Internal Revenue Study of Ideological Organizations, December 31, 1965," Series IIIA, Drawer 14, folder 14: 41, WSP.

8. A copy of the Life Line Foundation brief, as well as the 1962 IRS letter of revocation, is in Box 1557A, loose materials, WPP. Patman had asked the IRS for a copy; see Harding to Patman, March 17, 1964, in the same box. See also IRS Fact Sheet on Life Line Foundation, Inc., roll 162, folder 6435, TCP.

9. Patman to Hays, May 18, 1963, and Paul Green to Hays, April 30, 1963, Box 1557A, folder: Life Line Foundation Correspondence, WPP. Hays had earlier worked to revoke the tax exemption of Life Line's predecessor, Facts Forum, in the 1950s. See press release of September 4, 1954, Box 1550A, folder: Facts Forum, WPP. Seidman's advice is in Seidman to Olsher, November 13, 1963, Box 1550A, folder: Hunt, WPP. See also Hurt, *Texas Rich*, p. 253, and Young, "Wright Patman," p. 7.

10. Marquis Childs, "How Far Right Gets U.S. Subsidy," *Washington Post*, October 11, 1963, p. A22, copy in Box 1557A, folder: Life Line Correspondence, WPP; John Lindon to

Senator John Williams, November 7, 1963, Box 79, folder 646, JJWP; J. S. Seidman to Harry A. Olsher, November 13, 1963, Box 1550A, folder: Hunt, WPP; Hurt, *Texas Rich*, p. 186.

11. Robert G. Sherrill, "H. L. Hunt: Portrait of a Super-Patriot," *The Nation* 198 (February 24, 1964), 183, 188–189; Sherrill to Olsher, January 27, 1964, Box 1550A, folder: Sherrill, WPP. For a brief overview of the assassination charges, which are complex and shadowy themselves, see Aleksandr Fursenko and Timothy Naftali, *"One Hell of a Gamble": Khrushchev, Castro, and Kennedy, 1958–1964* (New York, 1997), pp. 348–349.

12. *Tax-Exempt Foundations and Charitable Trusts: Their Impact on Our Economy* (1964), pp. 224–232, 256–261.

13. Ibid., pp. 271–272, 248.

14. Ibid., pp. 236–237.

15. Fannie Warren to Patman, September 2, 1964, C. May Overton to Patman, September 2, 1964, and F. H. Love to Patman, April 1, 1965, all in Box 884A, folder: Foundations, WPP. See also Clay Cochran of the AFL-CIO to Patman, September 10, 1964, Box 1557A, loose material, WPP, and Young, "Wright Patman," pp. 7–8.

16. Surface, *Inside Internal Revenue*, pp. 202–203; Sheldon Cohen to Swartz and Rogovin, March 3, 1965, Box 10, folder: Correspondence, Official, 1965; Rosapepe to Patman, March 30, 1965, Box 1557A, loose material, WPP.

17. "The Tax Crackdown," *National Review* 17 (April 20, 1965), 315–316. See also the *Indianapolis Star* for August 9, 1965, clipping in Taxes–Exemptions folder, BJHP.

18. *Tax-Exempt Foundations and Charitable Trusts: Their Impact on Our Economy* (1962), pp. 3–4.

19. The best summary of these events is in Branch, "Playing Both Sides Against the Middle," p. 18.

20. Ibid.; Frances Saunders, *The Cultural Cold War: The CIA and the World of Arts and Letters* (New York, 1999), pp. 134–135, 143. See also Ben Whitaker, *The Foundations: An Anatomy of Philanthropy and Society* (London, 1974), pp. 144–155.

21. "Latin Study Group Here Controlled by the CIA," *Washington Post* clipping for February 18, 1961, copy in Box G264 (2 of 3), folder: CIA, DPP.

22. Samuel Berger to Patman, November 19, 1963, Box 339A, folder: Kaplan, 1962; and clipping from the *Texarkana Daily News*, August 31, 1963, Box 884A, folder: Foundations; both in WPP. See also Saunders, *The Cultural Cold War*, p. 134.

23. Conference File, Exempt Organization Hearings (Wright Patman), 1964, Container #19, BHP. Much of this discussion about the Kaplan Fund was off the record.

24. *Tax-Exempt Foundations: Their Impact on Small Business*, p. 182.

25. Ibid.

26. Ibid., pp. 182–183.

27. Ibid., pp. 184–187, 199.

28. Ibid., pp. 187–189.

29. Ibid., pp. 189–191.

30. Ibid., p. 191; "CIA Figures in Tax Probe," clipping from the *Texarkana Gazette* for September 1, 1964, Box 884A, folder: Foundations, WPP.

31. Excerpts from the *New York Times*, September 4, 1964, and the *Pittsburgh Post Gazette & Sun Telegraph*, September 7, 1964, are in *Tax-Exempt Foundations: Their Impact on Small Business* (1964), pp. 404–405.

32. Harding to Feldman, November 19, 1964, Box 2, folder: Reading File, Deputy Comm., July 1, 1964–December 31, 1964, and M. Rogovin memo for the file, October 9, 1964, Box 22, folder: Office Files, Memo for files; both in BHP. Harding's telephone notes for 1964 indicate a great deal of activity with respect to Patman and his hearings. See especially notes for October 1 and 2, 1964, both of which involved John Warner; Box 31, folder: Notes: Telephone, 1964 (1), BHP.

33. Helen Laville, "The Committee of Correspondence: CIA Funding of Women's Groups, 1962–1967," *Intelligence and National Security* 12 (January 1997), 104–105, 111–112, 113–114; Jacqueline Van Voris, *The Committee of Correspondence: Women with a World Vision* (Northampton, Mass., 1989), pp. 1, 44, 46, 49.

34. Christopher Simpson, *Science of Coercion: Communication Research and Psychological Warfare, 1945–1960* (New York, 1994), pp. 4, 81–82; Christopher Simpson, "U.S. Mass Communication Research, Counterinsurgency, and Scientific 'Reality,'" in William S. Solomon

and Robert W. McChesney, ed., *Ruthless Criticism: New Perspectives in U.S. Communication History* (Minneapolis, 1993), pp. 334–335, 347n. See also John Marks, *The Search for the "Manchurian Candidate": The CIA and Mind Control* (New York, 1979), pp. 149–159, and Christopher Simpson, ed., *Universities and Empire: Money and Politics in the Social Sciences During the Cold War* (New York, 1998), pp. xix, xxxiv. Cumings's remarks are in his essay "Boundary Displacement," in Simpson, *Universities and Empire*, pp. 171–172. See also David Wise and Thomas Ross, *The Espionage Establishment* (New York, 1967), p. 153.

35. Sol Stern, "CIA/NSA: A Short Account of International Student Politics and the Cold War with Particular Reference to the NSA, CIA, Etc.," *Ramparts* 5 (March 1967), 31. See also Angus MacKenzie, *Secrets: The CIA's War at Home* (Berkeley, 1997), pp. 19–20, 22. For information on the CIA reaction, see Donner, *The Age of Surveillance*, p. 328.

36. Williams to Dean Rusk, March 22, 1967; William Macomber, Jr., Assistant Secretary of State for Congressional Relations, to Williams, April 4, 1967; Carl Marcy, Chief of Staff, Senate Committee on Foreign Relations, to Williams, April 28, 1967; all in Box 24, folder 229, JJWP. Williams's correspondence with Sheldon Cohen was on September 28, 1966, with a reply from Cohen on March 8, 1967. For the determination that such funding should cease, see *National Intelligence Reorganization and Reform Act of 1978*. Hearings before the Select Committee on Intelligence of the U.S. Senate, 95th Cong., 2d sess. (Washington, D.C., 1978), p. 595.

37. Robert Sherrill, "Foundation Pipe Lines: The Beneficent CIA," *The Nation* 202 (May 9, 1966), 542–544, 556.

38. Berman and Halperin, *The Abuses of Intelligence Agencies*, p. 134; Wise and Ross, *The Espionage Establishment*, pp. 143–144, 155–156; "Foundation Cited as Conduit of CIA to Finance NSA," *Washington Post*, (February 16, 1967, clipping in Box G264 (2 of 3), folder: CIA, DPP. The list of CIA conduits is in a typescript report on Foundations and the CIA, Box 598B, folder: Foundations, WPP. See also George Morris, *CIA and American Labor: The Subversion of the AFL-CIO's Foreign Policy* (New York, 1967), pp. 151–152; *New York Times*, February 1, 1967, p. 26; February 19, 1967, pp. 1, 26, 32. Only a year earlier the *Times* had published a four-part series on the CIA but failed to mention any domestic activities or foundation conduits. See the issues for April 25–29, 1966.

39. *Washington Post*, February 20, 1967, p. E1; clipping in Box 742B, folder: Ford Foundation (1 of 2), WPP.

40. Richard Harwood, "O What a Tangled Web the CIA Wove," *Washington Post*, February 26, 1967, p. E1; clipping in Box 742B, folder: Ford Foundation (1 of 2), WPP.

41. Morris, *CIA and American Labor*, pp. 91–92; Stephen Rabe, *The Most Dangerous Area in the World: John F. Kennedy Confronts Communist Revolution in Latin America* (Chapel Hill, 1999), pp. 69, 88–89; Hobart A. Spalding, Jr., "US Labour Intervention in Latin America: The Case of the American Institute for Free Labor Development," in Roger Southall, ed., *Trade Unions and the New Industrialization of the Third World* (Pittsburgh 1988), pp. 270–271. For more on the CIA-AIFLD connection, see Philip Agee, *Inside the Company: CIA Diary* (New York, 1975), pp. 244–246, 252, 262, 305, 307, 311–312, 314, 321, 365, 376–377, 393, 485–486, 501–502, 549, 582, 610, 613, 620.

42. Scott to LBJ, March 22, 1967, Box 44, folder: Ramparts-NSA-CIA, NSF Security file, LBJ Library. Johnson's policy statement of March 29, 1967, is noted in the typescript report on Foundations and the CIA, Box 598B, folder: Foundations, WPP.

43. Patman, "The Free-Wheeling Foundations," *Progressive* 31 (June 1967), 27; typescript report on Foundations and the CIA, Box 598B, folder: Foundations, WPP.

44. Richard Albrecht to Simon, June 13, 1975, Series II, Drawer 9: Internal Memoranda: A-I, folder 9: 5, WSP.

45. Treasury Dept. Order No. 240, September 27, 1975, in ibid., folder 9: 8, WSP. For the Pike Committee, see *Proceedings of the Select Committee on Intelligence, U.S. House of Representatives*, 94th Cong., 1st sess. (Washington, D.C., 1976), Part 4, especially pp. 1356–1362.

Chapter Seven. Foundations: The Continuing Struggle

1. The Patman quotation is cited in "The Question of Revising the Tax Status of Foundations: Pro and Con," p. 148. For a good overview of the Ford Foundation's actions in this instance, see Nielsen, *The Big Foundations*, pp. 11, 421–425. Data on social-movement giving can

be found in J. Craig Jenkins and Abigail L. Halci, "Grassrooting the System?: The Development and Impact of Social Movement Philanthropy, 1953–1990," in Ellen Lagemann, ed., *Philanthropic Foundations: New Scholarship, New Possibilities* (Bloomington, Ind., 1999), pp. 229–256.

2. Ibid., p. 11; Taylor Branch, *Pillar of Fire: America in the King Years, 1963–65* (New York, 1998), p. 56. The IRS position is in A. L. O'Connell, Chief of the IRS Administrative Services Branch, to Allison T. French of the Florida Coalition of Patriotic Societies, June 24, 1966, folder: Taxes–Exemptions, BJHP.

3. John C. Chommie, *The Internal Revenue Service* (New York, 1970), p. 209; Irving M. Grant, "The Sierra Club: The Procedural Aspects of the Revocation of Its Tax Exemption," *UCLA Law Review* 15 (November 1967), 200–201, 215. For the Johnson White House interest in the activities of tax-exempt organizations, see Sheldon Cohen to Bill Moyers, March 4, 1966, Box 11, folder: Correspondence–Official, 1966, SCP; and Wright Patman to Hale Boggs, April 26, 1966, Box 1555A, folder: Misc. Correspondence, WPP. The Sierra Club attracted attention at this juncture in part because as it became more activist, its membership rolls swelled from 29,000 (1965) to more than 100,000 (1970). See also Michael Cohen, *The History of the Sierra Club, 1892–1970* (San Francisco, 1988), pp. 360–362, and Maurice Isserman and Michael Kazin, *America Divided: The Civil War of the 1960s* (New York, 2000), p. 120.

4. Mortimer Caplin, "Limitations on Exempt Organizations: Political and Commercial Activities," in Henry Sellin, ed., *New York University: Proceedings of the Eighth Biennial Conference on Charitable Foundations* (Albany, N.Y., 1967), pp. 269–272.

5. Ibid., pp. 273, 275–278.

6. Ibid., pp. 268–269.

7. Smith and Chiechi, *Private Foundations*, pp. 29–30.

8. Ibid., pp. 31–36; Thomas R. Allen, "The Treasury Report on Foundations: Methods of Enforcing Compliance," *Vanderbilt Law Review* 19 (June 1966), 610.

9. William C. Golden, "Legislative Proposals Concerning Private Foundations," *Indiana Law Journal* 41 (Summer 1966), 557; Cohen to Henry Fowler, April 22, 1965, Box 158, folder: Government Treasury, Dept. of Internal Revenue Service, 1965–66 (2 of 2), HFP; Commissioner of Internal Revenue, *Annual Report for 1965* (Washington, D.C., 1965), p. xiii; Cohen Memo, "Exempt Organizations [1966]," Box 228, folder: Comm. Back-up Book (2 of 3), SCP. For a strong endorsement of the Treasury Report over the solutions of Patman, see William T. Barnes, "The Treasury Department Report on Private Foundations," *Journal of Accountancy* 123 (February 1967), 34–40.

10. "Discussion Paper: Exempt Organization Audit Program," Box 4, folder: Commissioner's Advisory Group, 1967–68; Thomas Terry to Members of the Commissioner's Advisory Group, August 23, 1966, and Minutes of the Meeting of the Commissioner's Advisory Group, September 12–13, 1966, Box 5, folder: Comm. Advisory Group, 1966–67, SCP. See also Arnold Cutler, "Recent Developments in Foundation Tax Exemptions: Their Future Significance," in Sellin, *New York University*, p. 137.

11. Commissioner of Internal Revenue, *Annual Report for 1968*, p. 9; Briefing Book on IRS for Transition, November 1968, Box 181, SCP; Meeting of Commissioner's Advisory Group, June 13–14, 1968, Box 4, SCP.

12. "The Question of Revising the Tax Status of Foundations," pp. 138–139; Zelizer, *Taxing America*, p. 155; Chommie, *The Internal Revenue Service*, p. 208; *IRS Annual Report, 1969*, pp. 14, 20–21.

13. The quotations came from Howard Greenberg to Patman, May 19, 1969, Box 1032C, folder: Internal Revenue Service and Patman to Congressman Joe Evins, June 25, 1969, Box 1034A, folder: Foundations Study. See also Thrower to Patman, May 6, 1969, and June 10, 1969, Box 1032C, folder: Internal Revenue Service; Minutes of Meeting of Subcommittee No. 1, Foundations, July 30, 1969, Box 1033B, folder: Subcommittee of Foundations, Meetings. All are in WPP.

14. The "Frankenstein" quote is from Patman's statement of September 10, 1969, in Box 1413C, loose materials, WPP. For remarks from one critic, see Harley Watkins to Patman, September 19, 1969, Box 1039C, folder: Foundations–Ohio–Correspondence, WPP. Exchanges between Patman and the IRS are in Patman to Thrower, September 30, 1969; Acting IRS Commissioner William Smith to Patman, October 10, 1969; Thrower to Patman, October 31, 1969; Thrower to Patman, November 17, 1969; and Howard Greenberg to Patman, December 2, 1969; all in Box 1032C, folder: Internal Revenue Service, WPP.

15. Chommie, *The Internal Revenue Service*, p. 208; *Congressional Quarterly Almanac* 23

(Washington, D.C., 1967), pp. 1142, 1148. One ABC trustee took the Fifth Amendment eighty-three times; see Whitaker, *The Foundations*, p. 111.

16. L. A. Krupnick to H. S. Redeker, January 20, 1967, Box 1557A, folder: untitled, WPP. See also Redeker to John Shannon, February 17, 1967, ibid.

17. Cohen to Patman, October 23, 1967, Box 1558A, folder: IRS; Cohen to Patman, November 28, 1967, Box 1558B, folder: ABC; Cohen to Patman, October 26, 1967, Box 1558B, folder: IRS; Patman to A. J. Murray, Postal Inspector, November 14, 1967, Box 1035A, folder: Americans Building Constitutionally; Patman to Donald Irwin, September 11, 1967, Box 1557A, folder: untitled; Press release, October 11, 1967, Box 1560A, loose material; all in WPP. See also F. Emerson Andrews, *Patman and Foundations: Review and Assessment* (New York, 1968), p. 39.

18. Lawrence Tapper, Deputy Attorney General, to Patman, June 25, 1969; Patman to IRS Commissioner Randolph Thrower, January 28, 1970; Thrower to Patman, April 6, 1970; all in Box 1035A, folder: Americans Building Constitutionally, WPP.

19. George Webster, "The Mythology of Revocation: Deviation from Charter; Effect of Revocation on Operations and Contributions; Reinstatement; Positive Effects of Revocation," in Sellin, ed., *New York University*, pp. 250, 262. For Cohen, see Cohen to [Assistant Commissioner] Swartz, October 19, 1967, Box 11, folder: Correspondence, Official, 1967, SCP.

20. Ralph deToledano, "Once Again IRS Is Playing Politics with Tax Exemptions," *Human Events*, October 21, 1967, clipping in Senate Internal Security Subcommittee, Box 295, Subject Files, Tax Exemptions, RG 46, NA. Allan Brownfeld, "The Financiers of Revolution" (April 1969), copy in Box 591A, folder: foundations, WPP. See also William S. White, "Are Foundations Untouchable?" *Tulsa Daily World* clipping, May 12, 1969; *New York Times* clipping, May 16, 1967, and Mark Van Doren to "Friend," May 4, 1968, all in Tax Exemptions Folder, BJHP.

21. Jennifer Frost, "Participatory Politics: Community Organizing, Gender, and the New Left in the 1960s," (Ph.D. dissertation, University of Wisconsin, 1996), p. 115, note 87. For a list of specific Revenue Rulings pertaining to exempt status for particular foundations that demonstrated how whimsical IRS decisions appear, see "Notes: Regulating the Political Activity of Foundations," *Harvard Law Review* 83 (1970), 1847, note 20. The Rucker letter is in Box 1014, folder: American Enterprise, WPP.

22. Irwin Ross, "Let's Not Fence in the Foundations," *Fortune*, June 1969, pp. 148, 164, 172. The quotation is on p. 164. Also see Peter Frumkin, "Private Foundations as Public Institutions: Regulation, Professionalization, and the Redefinition of Organized Philanthropy," in Lagemann, *Philanthropic Foundations*, pp. 70–71.

23. "Background of the Commission on Foundations and Private Philanthropy," and Peter Peterson to Patman, August 11, 1969, Box 1032A, folder: Commission on Foundations and Private Philanthropy, WPP.

24. "Major Areas of Inquiry," May 5, 1968, draft, Box 157, folder: Commission on Foundations and Private Philanthropies, SCP. Commission members included Peter G. Peterson, Sheldon Cohen, Mrs. Patricia Harris, J. Paul Austin, Daniel Bell, Daniel P. Bryant, James Chambers, Thomas B. Curtis, Paul Freund, Martin Friedman, A. Leon Higginbotham, Lane Kirkland, Philip Lee, Edward Levi, Franklin Long, and A. S. Mike Monroney.

25. Robert Caulkins, "The Role of the Philanthropic Foundation," May 19, 1969, copy in ibid.

26. Jeffrey Hart, "The New Class War," *National Review*, September 9, 1969, pp. 897, 898, 900, 901. Pete Peterson sent a copy of the article to the Commission, and a copy is in Box 159, folder: Comm. on Foundations and Philanthropy, Correspondence, SCP.

27. "Summary of Recommendations to the Senate Finance Committee, October 22, 1969," in Box 159, folder: Comm. on Foundations and Philanthropy, Correspondence, SCP.

28. A succinct characterization of these debates is in Nielsen, *The Big Foundations*, pp. 14–17.

29. Ibid., pp. 373–374. See also Smith and Chiechi, *Private Foundations*, pp. 44–45.

30. Nielsen, *The Big Foundations*, p. 375; "Notes Regulating the Political Activity of Foundations," pp. 1849–1850. An outline of the bill's features with respect to political activity is in George Leibowitz, "Restraints on Political Action by Tax-Exempt Organizations Under the Tax Reform Act of 1969," Report from the Library of Congress Legislative Reference Service, September 18, 1970, copy in Box 1065C, folder: IRS Regulations and Rulings, WPP.

31. Nielsen, *The Big Foundations*, p. 19. See also "Notes Regulating the Political Activity of Foundations," pp. 1850–1861, for the political implications of these changes.

32. Nielsen, *The Big Foundations*, p. 13; Smith and Chiechi, *Private Foundations*, pp. 43–44; *Wall Street Journal*, February 28, 1969, p. 1. See also Anthony Lewis, "The Tax Bill and the Foundations," *New York Times*, October 31, 1969, clipping in Box 1640B, folder: Foundations, WPP; and Alexander Charns, *Cloak and Gavel: FBI Wiretaps, Bugs, Informers, and the Supreme Court* (Urbana, Ill., 1992), pp. 101, 103–104, 179 n83.

33. For a copy of the report and Patman's comments, see Box 159, folder: Commission on Foundations and Philanthropy, Parts I and II (1970), SCP, as well as Box 1032A, folder: Commission on Foundations and Private Philanthropy, WPP. Particularly revealing is the Peterson-Patman exchange: Peterson to Patman, February 5, 1971; Patman to Peterson, April 5, 1971; Peterson to Patman, June 30, 1971; and Patman to Peterson, July 6, 1971.

34. Patman memo of August 18, 1972, Box 1065B, folder: Memos–Foundations, WPP. A copy of the Thrower statement is in folder: Foundations: Ways and Means Testimony, in the same box. Later Treasury proposals are in Frederic Hickman to William Simon, October 11, 1973, Series II: Internal Memoranda, Drawer 9: Internal Memoranda, A-I, folder 9: 46, WSP.

35. Copies of the chief counsel reports are in Box 4, SCP. Analysis of the issue is in Michael Yaffa, "The Revocation of Tax Exemptions and Tax Deductions for Donations to 501(c)(3) Organizations on Statutory and Constitutional Grounds," *UCLA Law Review* 30 (1983), 160 n24. Thrower's remarks are in Thrower to the author, October 7, 1998. See also the *Wall Street Journal*, August 13, 1970, p. 11, for an announcement of the new IRS policies.

36. Quoted in Melvin Small, *The Presidency of Richard Nixon* (Lawrence, Kans., 1999), p. 163.

37. Yaffa, "The Revocation of Tax Exemptions," pp. 160–161, 169–170; Mark Silverblatt, "Denial of Tax Exempt Status to Southern Segregated Academies," *Harvard Civil Rights–Civil Liberties Law Review* 6 (December 1970), 179–180.

38. Lamar Alexander to Bryce Harlow, April 6, 1970, Nixon Project, WHCF, Subject File, FG 12, Dept. of Treasury, folder: EX FG 12-8 Internal Revenue Service (1/25/69–12/22/70), NA.

39. Peter Flanigan, Memo for Files, April 18, 1970; Harry Dent to Flanigan, May 12, 1970; Memorandum for the President, June 4, 1970; Leonard Garment memorandum to the President, June 6, 1970; Peter Flanigan memo to the President, June 29, 1970; all in ibid.

40. IRS Press Release, July 10, 1970, Nixon Project, WHCF, Subject File, FG 12, Dept of Treasury, folder: EX FG 12-8 Internal Revenue Service (1/25/69–12/22/70), NA; Yaffa, "The Revocation of Tax Exemptions," pp. 161–162; Thrower to the author, October 7, 1998. See also *Legislation to Deny Tax Exemption to Racially Discriminatory Private Schools*, Hearings Before the Committee on Finance, U.S. Senate, 97th Cong., 2d sess. (Washington, D.C., 1982), pp. 10,21.

41. Ehrlichman Memo for the President, July 18, 1970, Nixon Project, WHCF, Subject File, FG 12, Dept. of Treasury, folder: EX FG 12-8 Internal Revenue Service (1/25/69–12/22/70), NA; Thrower to the author, October 7, 1998. For another insider's view, see Leonard Garment, *Crazy Rhythm: My Journey from Brooklyn, Jazz, and Wall Street to Nixon's White House, Watergate, and Beyond* (New York, 1997), pp. 217–218. For a comprehensive chronology, see *Legislation to Deny Tax Exemption to Racially Discriminatory Private Schools*, pp. 275–278.

42. After 1971 the IRS issued a series of Revenue Rulings in an attempt to clarify and define what it meant to obey or violate the law with respect to private schools and "minorities." To follow this convoluted tale, which was never far from the surface of politics, see Yaffa, "The Revocation of Tax Exemptions," pp. 164–167, 170–173; Godfrey Hodgson, *The World Turned Right Side Up: A History of the Conservative Ascendancy in America* (Boston, 1996), pp. 174, 176–177, 187–188; *Tax-Exempt Status of Private Schools*, Hearings Before the Subcommittee on Taxation and Debt Management Generally of the Committee on Finance, U.S. Senate, 96th Cong., 1st sess. (Washington, D.C., 1979), pp. 1, 18–19, 23, 25, 41–55; and *Legislation to Deny Tax Exemption to Racially Discriminatory Private Schools*, pp. 3, 12–13. Subsequent problems, including the Bob Jones University case, are in Nolan to Connally, May 17, 1971, Series II, Drawer 9: Internal Memoranda: A-I, folder 9: 6; Alexander to Simon, January 18, 1975, Richard Albrecht to Simon, February 3, 1975, and Fred Hickman to Simon, May 15, 1975, Series II, Drawer 11, folder 15: Charles Walker (1 of 2); File memorandum, November 10, 1975,

and Albrecht to Simon, November 24, 1975, Series II, Drawer 9: Internal Memoranda: A-I, folder 9: 6; all in WSP. John Judis has argued that this policy launched the modern Christian right; see *The Paradox of American Democracy: Elites, Special Interests, and the Betrayal of Public Trust* (New York, 2000), p. 9.

43. Irving Louis Horowitz and Ruth Leonora Horowitz, "Tax-Exempt Foundations: Their Effects on National Policy," *Science* 168 (April 10, 1970), 228.

44. A copy of Thrower's speech of August 24, 1970, is in Box 1032C, folder: Internal Revenue, WPP.

45. For the criticism, see Nielsen, *The Big Foundations*, pp. 375n–376n. See also "Comments on Thrower Speech," Box 1032C, folder: Internal Revenue Service, WPP; Thrower to Patman, October 12, 1970, and Subcommittee Staff Director Michael Lemov to Patman, November 12, 1970, Box 1065B, folder: Memos-Foundations, WPP.

46. For examples of these reactions, see Walter Shipp, Acting Chief of the Exempt Organizations Branch, to Marshall Doty, Jr., August 5, 1969, Box 1032C, folder: Internal Revenue Service; S. B. Wolfe, Director of the IRS Audit Division, to Patman, August 12, 1969, Box 1035A, folder: Pearl S. Buck Foundation; *The Dan Smoot Report* 15 (November 24, 1969), copy in Box 1038A, folder: "S"; and Sam Cavnar to Patman, April 1, 1970, Box 1037A, folder: "A"; all in WPP. See also John Rarick to James Eastland, July 8, 1971, and Eastland to Rarick, July 16, 1971, Box 295, Senate Internal Security Subcommittee, Subject Files: Tax Exemptions, RG 46, NA.

47. Stuart H. Johnson, Jr., to Senator Gaylord Nelson, November 4, 1970, Box 1036A, folder: Lobbying by Tax-Exempt Organizations, Correspondence, and Joseph F. Shanahan to Randolph Thrower, December 20, 1970, Box 1032B, folder: Educational Institutions; both in WPP.

48. Thrower to Patman, October 28, 1970, and Harold Swartz, Acting IRS Commissioner, to Patman, July 23, 1971, Box 1035C, folder: Jerry Rubin Foundation, WPP. The Thrower letter also includes a copy of the fact sheet. See also Grace Lichtenstein, "Rubin's Tax-Exempt Foundation Target of IRS Legal Move," *New York Times*, January 10, 1971, clipping in Tax Exemptions folder, BJHP; Patman to Thrower, June 15, 1971, Box 1037A, folder: April tickle, WPP.

49. Thrower's thoughts are in Thrower to the author, October 7, 1998. For testimony and other related materials, see Michael Lemov to Patman, October 14, 1970; Statement by Mortimer Caplin, November 16, 1970; Lemov to Patman, November 17, 1970; all in Box 1033A, folder: Tax-Exempt Public Interest Law Firms, WPP. See also the *New York Times* editorial of November 20, 1970, clipping in Box 1036A, folder: Lobbying by Tax-Exempt Organizations–Articles, WPP. Also see the *IRS Annual Report* for 1970, p. 54.

50. Thrower's resignation was clearly a response to the political pressures on the Internal Revenue Service and involved more than the issue of tax exemptions for segregated schools. For comments on Thrower's resignation, see the *New York Times* for January 29, 1971, clipping in Box 1036A, folder: Lobbying by Tax-Exempt Organizations–Articles, WPP.

Chapter Eight. Politics, Two-way Mirrors, and Wiretaps in the Johnson Years

1. Robert Dallek, *Flawed Giant: Lyndon Johnson and His Times, 1961–1973* (New York, 1998), pp. 407–408; *Report on Administrative Procedures of the Internal Revenue Service* (1976), p. 988.

2. For LBJ and the Ideological Organizations Project, see Cohen to the author, June 14, 1994. On Phinney, see the *Wall Street Journal*, August 11, 1964, p. 19, and Phinney's oral history at the LBJ Library. On Cohen, see Surface, *Inside Internal Revenue*, p. 4; *Nominations*, Hearings Before the Committee on Finance, U.S. Senate, 89th Cong., 1st sess. (Washington, D.C., 1965), pp. 39, 41–43. The testimony of Cohen and Kolar is in *Federal Tax Return Privacy* (1975), p. 241; *Oversight Hearings into the Operations of the IRS* (Part 1, Hearings Before a Subcommittee on Government Operations, House of Representatives, 94th Cong., 1st sess. (Washington, D.C., 1975), pp. 792–793; *Confidentiality of Tax Return Information*. Hearing Before the Committee on Ways and Means, House of Representatives, 94th Cong., 2d sess.

(Washington, D.C., 1976), p. 131. For LBJ's retention of staff, see Emmette Redford and Richard McCulley, *White House Operations: The Johnson Presidency* (Austin, Tex., 1986), p. 16.

3. For data on White House requests for tax returns, see *U.S. Intelligence Agencies and Activities: Intelligence Costs and Fiscal Procedures.* Hearings Before the Select Committee on Intelligence (Part 1), House of Representatives, 94th Cong., 1st sess. (Washington, D. C., 1975), p. 604. For Baker's role, see his *Wheeling and Dealing: Confessions of a Capitol Hill Operator* (New York, 1978), pp. 43–44. The Watson episode is chronicled in Charns, *Cloak and Gavel*, p. 60. For information on the California and Texas inquiries, see Interview with Sheldon Cohen, October 17, 1973, Box 1, folder: Witness Statements–Sheldon Cohen; Henry Hecht to Jay Horowitz, September 27, 1973, Box 1, folder: Witness Statements–Randolph Thrower; Hecht to Files, December 4, 1973, Box 25, folder: William Smith; Hecht to Horowitz, October 9, 1973, Box 1, folder: Donald Bacon. All are in WSPF–IRS.

4. Cohen to LBJ, March 25, 1966, and Cohen to Marvin Watson, March 25, 1966, Box 11, folder: Correspondence, Official, 1966, SCP. See also the *Congressional Quarterly Almanac* 23 (Washington, D.C., 1967), pp. 1141–1142.

5. "HUAC and Tax Returns," *Washington Daily News,* June 27, 1967, clipping in Box 295, Subject Files: Tax Exemptions, Senate Internal Security Subcommittee, RG 46, NA.

6. These Sensitive Case Program directives are quoted in *IRS Disclosure*, pp. 53–54. The first (MS 12G-16) was dated September 8, 1964; the second (MS 8 [24] G-12) was issued November 2, 1964. The workings of the system are noted in Memorandum for the Files, July 28, 1964, Box 2, BHP.

7. *IRS Disclosure*, p. 54. For one example of these procedures in operation, see Joseph Barr (Under Secretary of the Treasury) to White House aide Marvin Watson, April 22, 1967. Marked "Eyes Only," this memo noted that the IRS was conducting an audit of the oil companies, clearly a topic of interest to the president. Box 166, folder: Government Treasury, Dept. of: Memoranda from Sec'y Barr, 1967, HFP.

8. For a rare report on "Operation Snowball," see David Sanford, "How Not to Give to the Politicians," *New Republic* 158 (February 17, 1968), 17–18. Pursuant to a FOIA request filed by the author, the Criminal Investigation Division of the IRS notified the Freedom of Information director that they found nothing, noting that before 1983 all such case files were destroyed every ten years. See Thomas Marusin to the author, July 1, 1999.

9. *The Internal Revenue Service: An Intelligence Resource and Collector*, p. 847. For a surviving example of this arrangement, see notes for March 3 and March 7, 1966, Senate Internal Security Subcommittee, Subject Files; National Security Agency, Box 179, RG 46, NA.

10. *Intelligence Activities and the Rights of Americans, Book II. Final Report of the Select Committee to Study Governmental Operations with Respect to Intelligence Activities* (Washington, D.C., 1976), pp. 79–81, 90, 93–94; *Report to the President by the Commission on CIA Activities Within the United States* (Washington, D.C., 1975), pp. 117–120.

11. Material on the Dolan case is in Jeff Shesol, *Mutual Contempt: Lyndon Johnson, Robert Kennedy, and the Feud That Defined a Decade* (New York, 1997), p. 232. Shesol notes that LBJ initialed these files, indicating that he had read them. See also Cohen to Hoover, March 9, 1965, Box 10, folder: Correspondence, Official, 1965, SCP; Angus MacKenzie, "Sabotaging the Dissident Press," *Columbia Journalism Review*, March–April 1981, p. 57; *The Internal Revenue Service: An Intelligence Resource and Collector*, pp. 848–849; and *Role of the Internal Revenue Service in Law Enforcement Activities*, p. 30.

12. The material on King and the SCLC was pieced together from several sources. See Branch, *Pillar of Fire*, pp. 197, 207–208, 580; *The Internal Revenue Service: An Intelligence Resource and Collector*, pp. 855–856; and David Garrow, *The FBI and Martin Luther King, Jr.: From "Solo" to Memphis* (New York, 1981), pp. 105, 114.

13. For the RFK incident, see Michael Beschloss, *Taking Charge: The Johnson White House Tapes, 1963–1964* (New York, 1997), p. 519. Cohen's comments are in Cohen to Clark, September 10, 1965, Box 10, folder: Correspondence, Official, 1965, and Cohen to Watson, April 13, 1966, Box 11, folder: Correspondence, Official, 1966, SCP.

14. The best summary of these efforts is in John Drabble, "COINTELPRO–WHITE HATE, the FBI, and the Cold War Political Consensus" (Ph.D. dissertation, University of California, Berkeley, 1997), pp. 223–224, 244, 260–261, 265–266. See also James Davis, *Spying on America: The FBI's Domestic Counterintelligence Program* (Westport, Conn., 1992), p. 89, and *The Internal Revenue Service: An Intelligence Resource and Collector*, p. 847.

15. *Oversight Hearings into the Operations of the IRS.* Hearings Before a Subcommittee of the Committee on Government Operations, House of Representatives, 94th Cong., 1st sess. (Washington, D. C., 1976), pp. 131–132, 152–153.

16. Briefing book, Box 19, folder: Conference File; Outside, DC Exempt Organizations Hearings, BHP; Cohen to Arthur Brisbin, et al., April 7, 1966, Box 11, folder: Correspondence, Official, 1966, SCP; Memo from Arthur Brisbin to Fowler, April 19, 1966, Box 158, folder: Government, Dept. of Treasury, IRS, 1965–66 (1 of 2), HFP.

17. Memo from C. D. Brennan to William Sullivan, February 3, 1969, quoted in *The Internal Revenue Service: An Intelligence Resource and Collector*, p. 851. For Gavin's problems, see Dallek, *Flawed Giant*, pp. 357–358, and William Gibbons, *The U.S. Government and the Vietnam War: Executive and Legislative Roles and Relationships*, Vol. 4 (Princeton, 1995), pp. 241,847. The army program is noted in a typescript dated April 18, 1971, Box 311, folder: Surveillance, Military; Matt Nimetz to Joseph Califano, March 6, 1968, Box 139, folder: White House 1/68 through 12/68 (2 of 2), RCP. See also *Federal Tax Return Privacy*, pp. 12–13, and Frank Donner, *Protectors of Privilege: Red Squads and Police Repression in Urban America* (Berkeley, 1990), p. 85.

18. *The Internal Revenue Service: An Intelligence Resource and Collector*, pp. 856–857.

19. Typescript report on Foundations and the CIA [1967?], Box 598B, folder: Foundations, WPP. The Russell confirmation is in a UPI wire report for February 21, 1967, copy in Box 44, folder: Ramparts-NSA-CIA, National Security File, Subject File, LBJ Library.

20. Confidential Memo for George Christian, the White House, from Jack Rosenthal, Special Assistant to the Under Secretary of State, February 15, 1967, Box 44, folder: Ramparts-NSA-CIA, National Security File, Subject File, LBJ Library. See also Richard Morgan, *Domestic Intelligence: Monitoring Dissent in America* (Austin, Tex., 1980), p. 178n; MacKenzie, "Sabotaging the Dissident Press," p. 57; Burnham, *A Law Unto Itself*, pp. 273–275. For Terry, see A Retired Revenuer to Drew Pearson, March 9, 1965, Box G286 (1 of 2), folder: Internal Revenue #2, DPP.

21. What LBJ knew is culled from Rostow to LBJ, February 18, 1967, Box 44, folder: Ramparts-NSA-CIA, National Security File, Subject File, LBJ Library; Cater to LBJ, February 21, 1967, Box 10, folder: CIA-Funding of Private Organization, NSF Agency File, LBJ Library. The Brzezinski call is noted in Harry McPherson to LBJ, February 18, 1967, Box 10, folder: CIA-Funding of Private Organization, NSF Agency File, LBJ Library. Also see *The Internal Revenue Service: An Intelligence Resource and Collector*, pp. 857–859, 862–863; Marks, *The Search for the "Manchurian Candidate,"* p. 203n.

22. Mitchell Rogovin Oral History, pp. 32–33, LBJ Library; Beschloss, *Taking Charge*, p. 160n; *Financial or Business Interests of Officers or Employees of the Senate.* Hearings Before the Committee on Rules and Administration, U.S. Senate, 88th Cong., 1st and 2d sess. (Washington, D.C., 1964), Part 1, pp. 25–26; Part 6, p. 556.

23. Beschloss, *Taking Charge*, p. 322; Charns, *Cloak and Gavel*, p. 96; Athan Theoharis, *From the Secret Files of J. Edgar Hoover* (Chicago, 1991), pp. 229–230.

24. *Financial or Business Interests*, Part 14, pp. 1305, 1311, 1357; Part 18, p. 1636; Part 26, p. 2197. Williams's testimony is in Part 21.

25. Ibid., Part 25, pp. 2157–2187; Robert M. Cipes, "The Wiretap War: Kennedy, Johnson and the FBI," *New Republic* 155 (December 24, 1966), 16–22. For FBI involvement in the Black case, see Theoharis, *From the Secret Files of J. Edgar Hoover*, pp. 153–176; Charns, *Cloak and Gavel*, pp. 36–43. Clark Mollenhoff later charged that LBJ used the IRS to try to shift the tax burden from Baker to Don Reynolds, a conduit for Baker's funds and a chief witness against him; see Mollenhoff, "Eyes Only" memo for IRS General Counsel, March 31, 1970, Box 24, folder: Clark Mollenhoff, WSPF-IRS.

26. Cipes, "The Wiretap War," p. 16.

27. Robert Bevan, Long's legislative assistant, to Morton Langstaff, December 28, 1961, Box 49, folder: wiretapping, 1961, EVLP. A draft of the article, "The Wiretap Story," is in Box 137 of the EVLP. The Supreme Court decision was *Olmstead v. United States*, 277 U.S. 438.

28. *Freedom of Information.* Hearings Before the Subcommittee on Administrative Practice and Procedure of the Committee on the Judiciary, U.S. Senate, 88th Cong., 1st sess. (Washington, D.C., 1964), pp. 172, 174, 176, 179, 189. The September 28, 1964, press release is in Box 26, folder: Government Snooping, EVLP.

29. Hank Messick, *Secret File* (New York, 1969), pp. 351–352; Burnham, *A Law Unto Itself*, p. 99; Arthur Schlesinger, Jr., *Robert F. Kennedy and His Times* (Boston, 1978), p. 760; Shesol, *Mutual Contempt*, pp. 349–350.

30. Harding to IRS General Counsel Belin, December 17, 1964, Box 2, folder: Reading File, 7/1/64–12/31/64, and Harding to Acree and Bacon, February 26, 1965, Box 3, folder: Reading File, Deputy Commissioner, January–June 30, 1965; both in the BHP.

31. *Washington Post*, April 5, 1965, clipping in Box 123, folder: Invasion of Privacy, EVLP.

32. A copy of the document is in Box 4, folder: Commissioner's Advisory Group, 1967–68, SCP.

33. Benjamin Rosenthal to Treasury Secretary William Simon, May 7, 1965, Series II, Drawer 9, folder 9: 4, WSP; Long to Jack Stapleton, Jr., June 14, 1966, Box 222, folder: 120K Admin. Practice & Procedure, '66 (S–Z), EVLP; Martin Kaplan and Naomi Weiss, *What the IRS Doesn't Want You to Know* (New York, 1995), p. 41.

34. Barr to Henry Fowler, June 12, 1965, and Barr to Fowler, June 14, 1965, Box 166, folder: Gov't Treasury, Memoranda from Sec. Barr, 1965–66 (2 of 2), HFP; Helen Dunlop to Long, June 15, 1966, Box 57, folder: Memos to Staff, 1965 (April–June), EVLP; Fowler and Nicholas Katzenbach memo to LBJ [1965], Box 22, folder: Executive Privilege, HMP. Katzenbach's testimony about the success of IRS sources in the OCD is in *Invasions of Privacy (Government Agencies)*, p. 1160.

35. Fowler and Katzenbach to LBJ [1965], Box 22, folder: Executive Privilege, HMP; Shesol, *Mutual Contempt*, p. 353.

36. Memorandum for Files, No. 9, June 23, 1965, Box 22, folder: Office Files: Memoranda for Files (BMH & IRS), BHP; Cohen to Fensterwald [1965], Lee White to LBJ, June 30, 1965, and Rogovin to White, July 6, 1965, Box 22, folder: Executive Privilege, HMP; Report of June 14–15 meeting, Box 4, folder: Commissioner's Advisory Group, 1965, SCP; Memo for the File, No. 8, June 21, 1965, Box 3, folder: Reading File, Deputy Comm., January–June 30, 1965, BHP.

37. Memorandum, July 10, 1965, Box 83, folder: Criminal Division, RCP; JUNE Memo, James Gale to Cartha DeLoach, May 27, 1966, in Theoharis, *From the Secret Files of J. Edgar Hoover*, p. 151.

38. *Invasions of Privacy (Government Agencies)*. Hearings Before the Subcommittee on Administrative Practice and Procedure of the Committee on the Judiciary, U.S. Senate, 89th Cong., 2d sess. (Washington, D.C., 1966), pp. 1118–1128.

39. Ibid., pp. 1130–1131, 1140–1141, 1155–1156, 1247; Edward V. Long, *The Intruders: The Invasion of Privacy by Government and Industry* (New York, 1967), pp. 118–119. The Intelligence Division bugged conference rooms in Albany, Albuquerque, Austin, Boston, Chicago, Detroit, Houston, Las Vegas, Milwaukee, Pittsburgh, Portland (Oregon), and San Francisco. The Alcohol and Tobacco Tax Division bugged rooms in Baltimore, Chicago, Dallas, Detroit, Montgomery (Alabama), Oklahoma City, and Seattle. Conference rooms bugged by the Internal Security Division were in Boston, Dallas, Detroit, Los Angeles, Newark, New York, Philadelphia, San Francisco, Seattle, and Washington, D.C. See Cohen to Long, July 26, 1965, Box 252, folder: Admin. Practice & Procedures, REF, 1965, EVLP. The FBI was also concerned about the extent of Long's investigation and tried to head off inquiries into mail covers by using a national security argument. See A. H. Belmont to Clyde Tolson, February 27, 1965, reprinted in *Hearings Before the Select Committee to Study Governmental Operations with Respect to Intelligence Activities of the United States Senate*, 94th Cong., 1st sess. (Washington, D.C., 1976), vol. 6, pp. 830–832.

40. *Invasions of Privacy*, pp. 1283, 1651; Messick, *Secret File*, p. 354.

41. From Cohen's statement before the Long Committee, July 13, 1965, copy in Box 4, folder: Commissioner's Advisory Group, 1967–68, SCP. Emphasis in the original.

42. Ibid.; *Wall Street Journal*, September 1, 1965, p. 1; Cohen to *Washington Post*, October 14, 1965, Box 29, folder 421, JJWP.

43. Cohen to Williams, October 22, 1965, Box 24, folder 421, JJWP; *Invasions of Privacy*, pp. 1657, 1770, 1827–1828. Rosapepe did scrutinize newspapers for their reporting of the hearings. See Rosapepe to Drew Pearson, November 24, 1965, Box G286 (1 of 2), DPP.

44. Long to Cohen, December 9, 1965, Box 174, folder: Invasions of Privacy, 1966 (2 of 2), SCP; "Administrative History of the Dept. of Justice During the Administration of LBJ," Box 139, folder: Wiretapping, RCP.

45. Cohen to Long, January 20, 1966, Box 174: Invasions of Privacy, 1966 (2 of 2), SCP. This included a copy of the report.

46. Ibid.

47. Ibid.

48. Ibid. Emphasis is in the original.

49. Ibid.

50. Ibid.

51. Spatz to Cohen, February 7, 1966, Box 174, folder: Invasions of Privacy, 1966 (2 of 2), SCP. Cohen forwarded this memo the following day to Attorney General Nicholas Katzenbach.

52. "How to Kill Big Brother," typescript in Box 172, folder: 120K–Administrative Practice & Procedures, EVLP. A copy of Long's Boston speech of June 10, 1966, is attached to a press release in Box 174, folder: Invasions of Privacy, 1966 (1 of 2), SCP.

53. The list of IRS Boston activities is from Long's June speech, Box 174, folder: Invasions of Privacy, 1966 (1 of 2), SCP. See also Cohen to Long, May 3, 1966, and Cohen to Bill Moyers and Marvin Watson, June 21, 1966, in the same file. Long's survey and statistical compilation is in *Government Dossier: (Survey of Information Contained in Government Files)*, Submitted by the Subcommittee on Administrative Practice and Procedure to the Committee on the Judiciary of the United States Senate, November 1967 (Washington, D.C., 1967), p. 7.

54. A copy of the article, "Big Brother in America," *Playboy*, January 1967, is in Box 158, folder: Gov't, Dept. of Treasury, IRS, 1967–68 (2 of 2), HFP.

55. Cohen, Memo for the Files, December 21, 1966, and Cohen to Fowler, December 21, 1966, Box 11, folder: Correspondence, Official, 1966; Conference Memorandum, December 28, 1966, and Telegram to Regional Commissioners, December 29, 1966, Box 174, folder: Invasions of Privacy, 1966 (1 of 2), SCP. A clipping of the *U.S. News & World Report* article for December 26, 1966, is in Box 123, folder: Invasion of Privacy, EVLP.

56. Mitchell Rogovin Oral History, pp. 38–39, 41–43, 46–48, LBJ Library.

57. The CIA reaction is in Marks, *The Search for the "Manchurian Candidate,"* p. 199n. For the government's investigation of Long, see Stennis to Henry Fowler, December 13, 1967, Box 158, folder: Government–Dept. of Treasury: Internal Revenue Service, 1967–68 (1 of 2), HFP; and D. O. Virdin to Burke Willsey, August 7, 1973, folder: IRS (Sensitive): Miscellaneous, WSP. See also the Commissioner's Weekly Report for July 6–12, 1967, Box 11, folder: Correspondence, Official, 1967, SCP.

58. Long's complaint is in Memorandum for the File, January 10, 1967, Box 11, folder: Corresp., Official, 1967, SCP. For Long's TV appearance, see Dan Miles to Long, February 17, 1967, Box 274, folder: Per. Corresp., 1967–68, "M," EVLP. Long's charge against the IRS is in the *Denver Post*, February 28, 1967, clipping in Box 123, folder: Invasion of Privacy, EVLP. For Cohen's defense of the IRS, see Cohen to Barr, March 13, 1967, Box 11, folder: Correspondence, Official, 1967, SCP; and Special Message from Cohen to all criminal investigative personnel, Box 158, folder: Government, Dept. of Treasury: Internal Revenue Service, 1967–68 (2 of 2), HFP.

59. *Right of Privacy Act of 1967*. Hearings Before the Subcommittee on Administrative Practice and Procedure of the Committee on the Judiciary, U.S. Senate, 90th Cong., 1st sess. (Washington, D.C., 1967), pp. 113, 114–115, 127. Cohen's response to Long is in Memorandum for the File, May 18, 1967, Box 11, folder: Corresp., Official, 1967, SCP.

60. For wiretapping, see Ramsey Clark to heads of executive departments and agencies, June 16, 1967, Box 139, folder: Wiretapping Memos, RCP; and Cohen Memo for the File, July 6, 1967, Box 11, folder: Correspondence, Official, 1967, SCP. IRS response to the FOIA is in *IRS Disclosure*, Appendix A, p. 169. Cohen's release of information is in Cohen to Long, July 11, 1967, Box 158, folder: Government, Dept. of Treasury, IRS 1967–68 (2 of 2), HFP.

Chapter Nine. Jimmy Hoffa, Senator Long, and the IRS

1. Handwritten notes, Box 22, folder: Raymond Kieley, WSFP–IRS; Cohen to Bacon, November 16, 1967, and Memo for the File, May 18, 1967, Box 11, folder: Official Correspondence, 1967, SCP. See also Charns, *Cloak and Gavel*, p. 92.

2. A good summary of this complexity is in Cipes, "The Wiretap War," pp. 16–22. In September 1963, Robert Kennedy summarized some of his OCD efforts before the Permanent Subcommittee on Investigations of the Senate Government Operations Committee; see Box 107, folder 27.7, EVLP. Hoover's remarks are in DeLoach to Tolson, January 17, 1966, RFK

FBI File, quoted in Hilty, *Robert Kennedy*, p. 519 n11. Additional background information is in Messick, *Secret File*, pp. 350–351.

3. Cipes, "The Wiretap War," pp. 17–18; Nicholas Von Hoffman, *Citizen Cohn* (New York, 1988), p. 302; Dick Anderman to Fensterwald, August 27, 1965, Box 123, folder: Invasion of Privacy, EVLP. Long's salute of Cohn is noted in A. Marie Hannon to Long, March 4, 1965, Box 252, folder: Admin. Practice & Procedures, 1965 (G-I), EVLP. Other letters in this box from Cohn to Long indicate that the two were on a first-name basis.

4. The summary of Hoffa's early connections is drawn from Mollenhoff, *Tentacles of Power*, see especially pp. 48, 55, and 57. See also Robert F. Kennedy, *The Enemy Within* (New York, 1960).

5. Dan Moldea, *The Hoffa Wars: Teamsters, Rebels, Politicians, and the Mob* (New York, 1978), pp. 4, 108; Mollenhoff, *Tentacles of Power*, pp. 4–5, 337; Walter Sheridan, *The Fall and Rise of Jimmy Hoffa* (New York, 1972), pp. 147, 151, 157, 165. Under Kennedy, Sheridan headed a special Hoffa investigative unit. This same Nixon-Hoffa scenario repeated itself in 1971, when Nixon released Hoffa from prison and immediately received the Teamsters Union endorsement for the 1972 election. By that time, moreover, Harold Gibbons was considered an enemy of the Nixon administration. See Rhodri Jeffreys-Jones, *Peace Now! American Society and the Ending of the Vietnam War* (New Haven, 1999), pp. 214, 289 n117.

6. Henry Hecht to Jay Horowitz [no date], Box 24, folder: Clark Mollenhoff, WSPF–IRS; Moldea, *The Hoffa Wars*, pp. 104, 260. For the Chotiner-Hoffa meetings, see entries for August 24 and 30 and September 18, 1971, in Box 16, folder: Murray Chotiner Diaries 1970-1972 (2 of 3), WSPF–IRS.

7. Moldea, *The Hoffa Wars*, pp. 7, 313, 316, 319–320, 351–352; Interview with Jane Thomas, John Dean's secretary, June 16, 1973, Box 26, folder: Jane Thomas, WSPF–IRS. The Kovens material is in Moldea, *The Hoffa Wars*, p. 293, and Dean to Colson, December 30, 1971, Box 17, folder: Colson Memos, WSPF–IRS. By the end of Nixon's term, Haig was also concerned about the possibility that Nixon was getting kickbacks from Mafia figures instrumental in the Southeast Asian drug traffic.

8. Sheridan, *The Fall and Rise of Jimmy Hoffa*, pp. 20–21, 255, 378; Dan Miles to Long [July 1963], Box 152, folder: Memos from Senator, July 1963, EVLP. For the Teamsters' resolution, see Gibbons to Long, March 11, 1965, Box 252, folder: Admin. Practice & Procedures, 1965 (G-I), EVLP.

9. Sheridan, *The Fall and Rise of Jimmy Hoffa*, pp. 380–381; *International Teamster* 61 (August 1964), 19–20.

10. Letters in Box 252 of the Edward Long Papers reveal the Long-Zagri relationship, as does Sheridan, *The Fall and Rise of Jimmy Hoffa*, p. 386. For the Hoffa trial, see Fred J. Cook, "The Hoffa Trial," *The Nation* 198 (April 27, 1964), 415–439.

11. "Bobbie Exposed: Secret Memos Show Kennedy Plotted to Blacken Hoffa's Name Before Prospective Jurors," *International Teamster* 61 (August 1964), 16–18; Baron to Long, March 8, 1965, Box 252, folder: Admin. Practices & Procedures, 1965 (A–F), EVLP; Sheridan, *The Fall and Rise of Jimmy Hoffa*, p. 397.

12. Bertrand Harding to Mitchell Rogovin, January 19, 1965, Box 3, folder: Reading File, Deputy Comm., January–June 30, 1965, BHP; Sheridan, *The Fall and Rise of Jimmy Hoffa*, p. 134.

13. The best summary of these efforts, from which this is taken, is in Sheridan, *The Fall and Rise of Jimmy Hoffa*, pp. 392, 399, 405–406. See also Mollenhoff, *Tentacles of Power*, p. 38, and Charns, *Cloak and Gavel*, p. 155 n39. Charns quotes Gale to DeLoach, May 23, 1966, for the Fred Black revelations. Black's call is noted in Kates to Miles, May 25, 1966, Box 61, folder: Memos to Senator 1966, EVLP.

14. For Shenker's quote, see the note to Long from his secretary [1966], Box 61, folder: Memos to Senator, 1966, EVLP. See also Sheridan, *The Fall and Rise of Jimmy Hoffa*, pp. 311, 415, 469, 481, 528. Long's disclaimer is in Long to Milton Shaber, April 17, 1967, Box 222, folder: Admin. Practice & Procedures, '67 (M–Z), EVLP.

15. William Lambert, "Strange Help-Hoffa Campaign of the U.S. Senator from Missouri," *Life* 62 (May 26, 1967), 26, 28.

16. Ibid., pp. 28–30, 76A–76B.

17. Dan Miles to Long, June 23, 1967, Box 274, folder: Personal Corresp., 1967–68, "M," EVLP. For Williams's views, see Memo for the Files, July 19, 1967, as well as Barron to

Williams, July 19, 1967, Box 41, folder 92, JJWP. Barron had recently written an extensive and critical article about the IRS for *Reader's Digest*. IRS Commissioner Sheldon Cohen had attacked the article as a collection of half-truths. See IRS press release, August 10, 1967, copy in Box 79, folder 645, JJWP.

18. *Congressional Record*, 90th Cong., 1st sess., vol. 113, part 15 (July 24, 1967), 19836–19839.

19. Ibid., p. 19845.

20. For the *Post-Dispatch*, see Bernard Fensterwald to Senator Thomas Hennings, Jr. [1967], folder 8200, TCHP; typescript of an article for the paper by Theodore Link [1967], Link to Williams, November 16, 1967, and Edward O'Brien to Williams, November 3, 1967, Box 41, folder 92, JJWP. The quotation is from Robert B. Curtis to Long, November 8, 1967, Box 275, folder: Congratulatory to Senator, EVLP.

21. George Hansen, *To Harass Our People: The IRS and Government Abuse of Power* (Washington, D.C., 1984), pp. 69–70; Burnham, *A Law Unto Itself*, p. 296. The IRS audits of Long and Fensterwald are noted in Robert Allen and Paul Scott, "IRS Retaliates Against Long," *Northern Virginia Sun*, May 15, 1968, clipping in Tax Exemptions–Publications folder, BJHP.

22. Allen and Scott, "IRS Retaliates Against Long."

23. Cohen's testimony and IRS expansion of the OCD are both in *Role of the Internal Revenue Service in Law Enforcement Activities* (1976), pp. 58–59, 111. For the new St. Louis investigations, see Denny Walsh, "A Two-Faced Crime Fight in St. Louis," *Life* 68 (May 29, 1970), 24–31. Cohen's remark is quoted in Messick, *Secret File*, pp. 364–365.

24. *Oversight Hearings into the Operations of the IRS (Part 1)* (1975), p. 448. For IRS reaction to the Freedom of Information Act, see Minutes of the Meeting of the Advisory Group, March 6–7, 1967, Box 5, folder: Comm. Advisory Group, 1966–67, SCP.

Chapter Ten. The Nixon Years: Tawdry Tales and Tattered Principles

1. *Newsweek*, October 15, 1973, clipping in Box 937A, folder: Howard Hughes Medical Institute, WPP.

2. John C. Whitaker memorandum to Bryce Harlow, February 21, 1969, Nixon Project, WHCF, Subject File, folder: EX FG 12-8 Internal Revenue Service (1/25/69–12/22/70), FG 12, Department of the Treasury, NA; *Wall Street Journal*, March 26, 1969, p. 1; Henry Hecht and Jay Horowitz, interview with Thrower, September 19, 1973, WSPF–IRS, Box 1, folder: witness statements–Randolph Thrower. These and other actions by the Nixon White House have spawned efforts to use psychobiography to understand what prompted them. I have avoided this approach. For one such example, however, see Vamik Volkan, Norman Itzkowitz, and Andrew Dod, *Richard Nixon: A Psychobiography* (New York, 1997). For more on Thrower, see Bob Kuttner, "The Taxing Trials of IRS," *New York Times Magazine*, January 6, 1974, clipping in Box 27, folder: Barth–NY Times & Star, WSPF–IRS.

3. Thrower to Mollenhoff, September 18, 1969, Box 11, folder: IRS–Opinions Relating to Disclosures of the Tax Returns to WH Staff, WSPF–IRS. For Barth's story, see interview with Roger Barth, November 9, 1972, Box 1, folder: Witness Statements–Roger Barth, WSPF–IRS.

4. Mollenhoff to Nixon, April 15, 1970, Box 24, folder: Clark Mollenhoff. See also Jay Horowitz to Bill Merrill, January 7, 1974, Box 20, folder: John Ehrlichman; Mollenhoff to Thrower, March 31, 1970, Box 17, folder: Murray Chotiner; Statement by Mollenhoff, Box 24, folder: Clark Mollenhoff; Interview with Randolph Thrower, September 19, 1973, Box 1, folder: Witness Statements–Randolph Thrower; all in WSPF–IRS.

5. Clark Mollenhoff, *Game Plan for Disaster: An Ombudsman's Report on the Nixon Years* (New York, 1976), pp. 106–108. One of the problems was that before the Tax Reform Act of 1976 the IRS had no "meaningful standards" by which to judge such requests from other government agencies. See *Disclosure of IRS Information to Assist with the Enforcement of Criminal Law*. Hearings Before the Subcommittee on Oversight of the Internal Revenue Service of the Committee on Finance, 97th Cong., 1st sess. (Washington, D.C., 1982), pp. 202–203.

Reports about Mollenhoff's access remain contradictory. According to K. Martin Worthy, former IRS chief counsel, Mollenhoff orally requested access in a late 1969 meeting with IRS Commissioner Randolph Thrower. Thrower demanded, however, that the request be in writing and that Mollenhoff sign it. It would cover only the examination of returns, not the copying of them. Former IRS Deputy Commissioner William Smith, on the other hand, insisted that the request was in the form of a memo to Thrower and did not indicate any particular reason for the request. Thrower then insisted that the request had to come from the president, but Mollenhoff's requests were never very specific. See Interview with K. Martin Worthy, October 17, 1973, Box 29, folder: Martin Worthy, and Interview with William Smith, October 16, 1973, Box 25, folder: William Smith; both in WSPF–IRS.

6. Ehrlichman to Kennedy, November 25, 1969; Paul Eggers to Kennedy, December 17, 1969; Kennedy to Ehrlichman, December 17, 1969, Nixon Project, WHFS, John D. Ehrlichman, Box 20, folder: IRS, NA.

7. Mollenhoff Witness File, folder: Wallace Tax Returns and Mollenhoff to Haldeman, March 21, 1970, Box 24, folder: Clark Mollenhoff, WSPF–IRS. The Chotiner leak to Anderson is noted in Anderson's *Washington Post*, June 26, 1974, column; clipping in the same file. See also Mollenhoff, *Game Plan for Disaster*, p. 109; Burnham, *A Law Unto Itself*, p. 250; and J. Anthony Lukas, *Nightmare: The Underside of the Nixon Years* (New York, 1976), pp. 147–148.

8. For a brief survey of the case, see Carter, *The Politics of Rage*, pp. 400–412. As Carter notes, Wallace abandoned all third-party efforts and announced his candidacy for the Democratic presidential nomination within twenty-four hours of the decision to halt the investigation. Nixon refused to admit any connection to this or almost any other IRS activity on his behalf. For the White House role, see Eileen Shanahan, "Nixon Asked Data on Wallace Tax, Panel Was Told," *New York Times*, July 17, 1974, clipping in Box 17, folder: Murray Chotiner, WSPF–IRS. A subsequent IRS investigation indicated that the leaks did not come from the IRS or from the Treasury Department. See *Statement of Information*. Hearings Before the Committee on the Judiciary, House of Representatives, 93rd Cong., 2d sess. (Washington, D.C., 1974), Book VIII, p. 3. IRS Commissioner Thrower believed that either Haldeman, Ehrlichman, or Nixon leaked the story, obviously for political purposes. Thrower's perception is in Interview with Thrower, September 19, 1973, Box 1, folder: Witness Statements–Randolph Thrower, WSPF–IRS. See also *Minority Memorandum on Facts and Law*. Hearings Before the Committee on the Judiciary, House of Representatives, 93rd Cong., 2d sess. (Washington, D.C., 1974), p. 121; Mollenhoff Witness File, folder: Wallace Tax Returns, WSPF–IRS; Thrower to Nixon, April 22, 1970, Nixon Project, WHSF, John D. Ehrlichman, Box 32, folder #7 (Clark Mollenhoff), NA. For Chotiner's role, see Interview with Clark Mollenhoff, November 7, 1973, Box 24, folder: Clark Mollenhoff, WSPF–IRS. Mollenhoff's own defense is in his *Game Plan for Disaster*, pp. 110–117. See also the affidavits of Thrower and Mollenhoff in *Federal Tax Return Privacy* (1975), pp. 141, 146–147. Nixon's efforts to deter Wallace failed; he was elected governor of Alabama in 1970 and remained a viable presidential candidate for 1972.

9. Worthy to Thrower, April 22, 1970, Box 11, folder: IRS–Opinions Relating to Disclosures of the Tax Returns to WH Staff, WSPF–IRS.

10. Ibid. Also see *Political Intelligence in the Internal Revenue Service: The Special Service Staff*, pp. 198–199.

11. Worthy Witness File, folder: Wallace Tax Returns, WSPF–IRS. For a later effort to address the confidentiality of tax returns, which came to approximately the same conclusion, see *Report on Administrative Procedures of the Internal Revenue Service*, pp. 972–977.

12. *Watergate and Related Activities, Phase I: Watergate Investigation*, Book 7. Hearings Before the Select Committee on Presidential Campaign Activities of the United States Senate, 93rd Cong., 1st sess. (Washington, D.C., 1973), p. 2798; "Draft Statement by Rogers Morton, 11 April 1970," and Democratic National Committee press release, April 12, 1970, Nixon Project, WHSF, John D. Ehrlichman, Box 32, folder #7 (Clark Mollenhoff), NA.

13. Williams's remarks are in the *Congressional Record* vol. 116, part 9 (April 16, 1970), 12226. Thrower's recollections of Barth are in Thrower to the author, October 7, 1998.

14. Mollenhoff to Nixon, Box 4, folder: PLME 3: Documentary Evidence/Summaries, WSPF–IRS.

15. Interview with Thrower, September 19, 1973, Box 1, folder: Witness Statements–Randolph Thrower; D. C. Dawkins, Memo of conversation, February 4, 1971, and Hecht note to file, October 3, 1973, Box 10, folder: Sensitive Case Reports, WSPF–IRS. See also Edward Schmults, Memo for file, July 31, 1973, Series IIIA, Drawer 17, folder 17: 58, WSP.

16. Confidential memo Dean to Haldeman, September 8, 1970, Nixon Project, WHSF, John Dean, Box 88, folder: Misc. Intelligence (1 of 2), NA. Also see Dean to Haldeman, August 22, 1970, in the same file.

17. Caulfield to Dean, September 11, 1970, Nixon Project, WHSF, John Dean, Box 88, folder: Misc. Intelligence (1 of 2), NA.

18. Flanigan to Haldeman, September 25, 1970, Nixon Project, WHCF, Subject File, FG 12, Dept. of Treasury, folder: EX FG 12-8 Internal Revenue Service (1/25/69–12/22/70), NA; Dean to Tom Huston, October 6, 1970, Nixon Project, WHSF, John Dean, Box 40, folder: Internal Revenue Service (2 of 2), NA.

19. Malek's report is attached to Huston to Dean, December 1, 1970, Nixon Project, WHSF, John Dean, Box 40, folder: Internal Revenue Service (2 of 2), NA; Confidential Memo, Haldeman to Dean, December 2, 1970, and Malek to Haldeman, December 4, 1970, ibid.

20. Dean to Haldeman, December 9, 1970, ibid.

21. Malek to Haldeman, December 15, 1970, ibid.

22. Ibid.

23. Thrower's recollections are in a letter to the author, October 7, 1998. See also Interview with Thrower, September 19, 1973, Box 1, folder: Witness Statements–Randolph Thrower, WSPF–IRS; Caulfield to Dean, September 25, 1970, Nixon Project, WHSF, John Dean, Box 39, folder: Internal Revenue Service (1 of 2), NA; *Statement of Information*, Book VIII, p. 53; and *Oversight Hearings into the Operations of the IRS*, Part 1 (1975), p. 286. For a brief look at ATF in these years see Donner, *Age of Surveillance*, p. 345.

24. Caulfield to Ehrlichman, October 27, 1970, Nixon Project, WHSF, John D. Ehrlichman, Box 16, folder: Jack Caulfield, NA.

25. Ibid. For a comment about Caulfield's qualifications, see Interview of Donald Bacon, August 30, 1973, Box 1, folder: Donald Bacon, WSPF–IRS. Ehrlichman had Harry Fleming request Caulfield's appointment as well on August 5, 1970; see Nick Akerman to the files, May 6, 1975, Box 4, folder: PLME 3: Documentary Evidence/Summaries, WSPF–IRS.

26. Walker to Secretary of the Treasury, November 4, 1970, in Nixon Project, WHSF, John D. Ehrlichman, Box 16, folder: Jack Caulfield, NA. Caulfield had initialed this memo, which was labeled "PERSONAL AND CONFIDENTIAL."

27. Caulfield to Ehrlichman, November 5, 1970, in ibid.

28. Caulfield to Ehrlichman, November 18, 1970, Nixon Project, WHCF, John Dean, Box 39, folder: Internal Revenue Service (1 of 2), NA. See also Ehrlichman to Walker, November 6, 1970, Nixon Project, WHCF, Subject File, FG 12, Dept. of the Treasury, folder: EX FG 12-8 Internal Revenue Service (1/25/69–12/22/70), NA; Tod Hullin, Memo for the Record, November 10, 1970, Nixon Project, WHSF, John D. Ehrlichman, Box 16, folder: Jack Caulfield, NA.

29. Caulfield to Ehrlichman, November 30, 1970; Bacon and Green to Thrower; both in Nixon Project, WHSF, John D. Ehrlichman, Box 16, folder: Jack Caulfield, NA.

30. Caulfield to Ehrlichman, December 2, 1970, ibid. For Caulfield's withdrawal, see Malek to Walker, December 4, 1970, in ibid., John Dean, Box 39, folder: Internal Revenue Service (1 of 2), NA.

31. Thrower to the author, October 7, 1998; *Statement of Information*, Book VIII (1974), pp. 55–58; *Oversight Hearings into the Operations of the IRS* (1975), p. 286. The White House–Thrower relationship is detailed in H. R. Haldeman notes for January–March 1970, Box 12, folder: IRS; Nixon to Connally, undated memo, Box 22, folder: Tod Hullin; Thrower interview, July 25, 1973, Box 4, folder: Computer Printout; Caulfield interview, July 13, 1973, Box 11, folder: Computer Printout–IRS; Interview with Fred Malek, January 2, 1974, Box 22, folder: Fred Malek; WSPF notes on Caulfield, Box 14, folder: Caulfield; all in WSPF–IRS.

32. *Baltimore Sun*, June 13, 1974, clipping in CCTF, Numerical File #6, folder: Wallace Tax Returns, WSPF–IRS; undated memo, Barth to Ehrlichman, Nixon Project, WHSF, John D. Ehrlichman, Box 20, folder: IRS, NA; transcript of telephone conversation, January 7, 1971, Connally and Ehrlichman, Nixon Project, WHSF, John D. Ehrlichman, Box 16, folder: John Connally, NA.

33. Albert Hunt, "Sociology and the IRS," *Wall Street Journal*, March 31, 1971, clipping in Nixon Project, WHSF, John D. Ehrlichman, Box 20, folder: IRS, NA.

34. Walters Witness File, folder: Johnnie M. Walters; Walters's notes for June 4, 1971, meeting with Ehrlichman, Box 27, folder: Walters's originals, WSPF–IRS.

35. Interview with Walters, August 29, 1973, Box 26, folder: J. M. Walters (1 of 2) and Kuttner, "The Taxing Trials of IRS," in Box 27, folder: Barth–NY Times & Star, WSPF–IRS. For more on Webster see the clipping from the *Washington Evening Star*, October 10, 1973, in Box 17, folder: Charles Colson, WSPF–IRS.

36. Caulfield to Dean, July 29, 1971, WHSF, John Dean, Box 40, folder: Internal Revenue

Service (2 of 2); Haldeman to Higby, September 14, 1971, WHCF, SMOF [Staff Member and Office Files], Larry Higby Alpha Subject Files, H. R. Haldeman, Box 261, folder: Dean IRS File; WHSF, Subject Files, John D. Ehrlichman, Box 21, folder: Gordon Liddy; all in Nixon Project, NA.

37. Haldeman notes, April–June 1971, and Liddy to Krogh, November 1, 1971, Box 12, folder: IRS; Strachan to Haldeman, December 1, 1971, Box 4, folder: PLME 3, Documentary Evidence/Summaries; WSPF–IRS. See also *Presidential Campaign Activities of 1972, Book 4. Senate Resolution 60.* Hearings Before the Select Committee on Presidential Campaign Activities of the U.S. Senate, 93rd Cong., 1st sess. (Washington, D.C., 1973), pp. 1682–1685.

38. H. R. Haldeman, *The Haldeman Diaries: Inside the Nixon White House* (New York, 1994), p. 564; press release, August 4, 1971, Box 495, folder: William Loeb, RG 128, NA; Liddy to Krogh, September 14, 1971, Nixon Project, WHSF, John D. Ehrlichman, Box 21, folder: Gordon Liddy, NA.

39. Nixon to Haldeman, March 12, 1973, Nixon Project, WHSF, President's Personal File, Box 4, folder: Memos–March 1973, NA.

40. *Confidentiality of Tax Return Information*, pp. 4, 6, 90, 91, 93, 94. The quotation is on p. 93.

41. Memo, Robert G. Dixon, Jr., Assistant Attorney General, Office of Legal Counsel, IRS, to Richard M. Fairbanks, III, Assistant Director, Domestic Council, March 19, 1973, Series IIIA, Drawer 14, folder 14: 40, Internal Revenue Service: 1973–1974, WSP.

42. Mollenhoff, *Game Plan for Disaster*, pp. 32, 38, 183.

Chapter Eleven. The Enemies List

1. *Investigation into Certain Charges of the Use of the Internal Revenue Service for Political Purposes.* Prepared for the Joint Committee on Internal Revenue Taxation by Its Staff (Washington, D.C., 1973), p. xiii; Berman and Halperin, *The Abuses of the Intelligence Agencies*, p. 88. Magruder's comment is from an October 17, 1969, memo to Haldeman; see *Warrantless Wiretapping and Electronic Surveillance—1974.* Joint Hearings Before the Subcommittee on Administrative Practice and Procedure and the Subcommittee on Constitutional Rights of the Committee on the Judiciary and the Subcommittee on Surveillance of the Committee on Foreign Relations, U.S. Senate, 93rd Cong., 2d sess. (Washington, D.C., 1974), p. 106.

2. *Statement of Information, Book VIII*, pp. 95, 99–100; *Presidential Campaign Activities of 1972, Book 3*, pp. 915–916.

3. *Presidential Campaign Activities of 1972, Book 4*, pp. 1461–1462, 1528. For a good introduction to this issue, see William Dobrovir, et al., *"Bribery, and Other High Crimes and Misdemeanors . . .": The Offenses of Richard M. Nixon: A Lawyer's Guide for the People of the United States of America* (Washington, D.C., 1973). Most studies of the Nixon administration at least mention the Enemies List; see particularly John R. Greene, *The Limits of Power: The Nixon and Ford Administrations* (Bloomington, Ind., 1992), pp. 128–129; Lukas, *Nightmare*, pp. 22–26, and David Wise, *The American Police State: The Government Against the People* (New York, 1976), pp. 328–329.

4. Nixon's early interest is in Hecht to Horowitz, August 23, 1973, Box 4, folder: PLME 3: Documentary Evidence/Summaries, WSPF–IRS. For the program's origins, see Henry Hecht to Henry S. Ruth, Jr., July 22, 1975, Box 1, folder: Legal and Factual Analysis, WSPF–IRS; *Warrantless Wiretapping*, p. 199; H. R. Haldeman, *The Haldeman Diaries: Inside the Nixon White House* (New York, 1994), p. 73. Some of this White House interest, as a later chapter will detail, led to IRS creation of the Special Service Staff, an entirely separate endeavor.

5. *Investigation into Certain Charges of the Use of the Internal Revenue Service for Political Purposes*, p. 3. Barth's views are in Interview with Roger Barth, November 9, 1972, Box 1, folder: Witness Statements–Roger Barth, WSPF–IRS. Thrower's concern is noted in Horowitz to the Files, September 29, 1973, Box 29, folder: Burke Willsey, WSPF–IRS. For a more complete story of Mollenhoff's activities, see *Report on Administrative Procedures of the Internal Revenue Service*, pp. 969–970, 1117–1121.

6. *Investigation into Certain Charges of the Use of the Internal Revenue Service for Political Purposes*, pp. 1–2; Schnepper, *Inside IRS*, pp. 146–148.

7. A list of names and the dates of requests is in Frank Martin, WSPF, to file, November 5,

1973, Box 4, folder: PLME 2: Investigative Correspondence; a list of income tax files requested in 1969 and 1970 is in Box 11, folder: Disclosure Staff; both in WSPF–IRS. See also *Investigation into Certain Charges of the Use of the Internal Revenue Service for Political Purposes,* p. 4.

8. Hecht to Files, 1973, Box 17, folder: Charles Colson; Investigation summary, Box 4, folder: Computer Printout; both in WSPF–IRS. For Nixon's comments, see Lukas, *Nightmare,* pp. 12–13.

9. Buchanan to Nixon, March 3, 1970, Box 23, folder: Buchanan Papers, WSPF–IRS.

10. Ibid.

11. *Watergate and Related Activities, Phase II: Campaign Activities, Book 10.* Hearings on Presidential Campaign Activities of the United States Senate, 93rd Cong., 1st sess. (Washington, D.C., 1973); quotations are on pp. 3914–3915, 3943, 3953–3954. For the SCLC, see Buchanan to Haldeman, December 9, 1970, Nixon Project, WHSF, John Dean, Box 40, folder: Internal Revenue Service (2 of 2), NA.

12. Haldeman, *The Haldeman Diaries,* p. 136; Haldeman notes, March 10, 1970, Box 4, folder: PLME 3: Documentary Evidence/Summaries, and Box 16, folder: Murray Chotiner Diaries (1 of 3), entry for May 1, 1970, WSPF–IRS. Memo from Colson for AEI file, July 11, 1970, Nixon Project, WHSF, John Dean, Box 9, folder: Correspondence File, Correspondence July 11–August 31, 1970, NA.

13. Walters to Dean, August 19, 1970; Richard Stakem, IRS Deputy Assistant Commissioner (Technical), to Walters, August 21, 1970; Dean to Walters, August 28, 1970; Walters to Dean, September 9, 1970; all in Nixon Project, WHSF, John Dean, Box 9, folder: Correspondence File, General Correspondence September 1–September 30, 1970, NA.

14. Higby to Chotiner/Dent, September 8, 1970, Box 12, folder: IRS, WSPF–IRS; Dean to Caulfield, September 21, 1970, Nixon Project, WHSF, John Dean, Box 9, folder: Correspondence File, General Correspondence, September 1–September 30, 1970, NA; Morton Mintz, "IRS Denies Pressure on Exemptions," *Washington Post,* October 25, 1970, clipping in Box 1033A, folder: Tax-Exempt Public Interest Law Firms, WPP; Robert M. Smith, "Nixon Picks Chief of Pollution Unit," *New York Times,* November 7, 1970, p. 1. The administration kept after Hartke; see Barth to Dean, October 8, 1971, Nixon Project, WHSF, John Dean, Box 39, folder: Internal Revenue Service (1 of 2), NA.

15. Memo, "Operation Alert: The American Security Council's Effort to Defeat United States Senate Candidates in the 1970 Elections," November 18, 1970, Box 1034B, folder: American Security Council, WPP.

16. The views of Watergate investigators are on a series of typed pages in Box 6, folder: file; the FBI perspective is in a secret memo from Jones to Bishop, November 25, 1970, Box 22, folder: Robert Mardian; both in WSPF–IRS. For background, see Lukas, *Nightmare,* pp. 35–36.

17. Interview with Larry Higby, October 5, 1973, Box 22, folder: Higby; Interview with Charles Colson, August 7, 1973, Box 17, folder: Charles Colson. A list of the memoranda is in Box 4, folder: PLME 3: Documentary Evidence/Summaries. All are in WSPF–IRS.

18. Dean to Buchanan, January 12, 1971, Nixon Project, WHCF, John Dean, Box 40, folder: Internal Revenue Service (2 of 2), NA. Attached to this is the memo from Huston to Dean.

19. Haldeman to Colson, March 16, 1971, and Colson to Haldeman, June 2, 1971, Box 12, folder: IRS; Anderson to Douglass Lee, ACLU Project on Privacy and Data Collection, August 3, 1973, Box 1, folder: ACLU Enemies, WSPF–IRS.

20. WSPF notes, Box 11, folder: Computer Printout–IRS and Sen. Fred Harris to Walters, February 15, 1971, and Dean to Colson, April 7, 1971, Box 4, folder: PLME 3: Documentary Evidence/Summaries, WSPF–IRS; Dean to Colson, May 13, 1971, Nixon Project, WHSF, John Dean, Box 40, folder: Internal Revenue Service (2 of 2), NA. Reports of Nixon's May meeting are in George Lardner, Jr., "Going After All the President's Enemies," *Houston Chronicle,* January 3, 1997. Additional material on the Fund for Investigative Journalism is in Caulfield to Dean, February 17, 1972, Box 14, folder: Caulfield documents; and Box 13, folder: Barth-Senate Testimony, WSPF–IRS.

21. Nick Akerman to the Files, April 11, 1975, Box 4, folder: PLME 3: Documentary Evidence/Summaries; Gordon to Acker, et al., June 25, 1971, Box 4, folder: Computer Printout, WSPF–IRS; Fred Fielding to Dean, June 8, 1971, Nixon Project, WHSF, John Dean, Box 39, folder: Internal Revenue Service (1 of 2), and Dean to Colson, June 14, 1971, Nixon Project, WHSF, John Dean, Box 2, folder: Correspondence File, June 1971, NA; *Statement of Information,*

Book VIII, p. 65; June 23, 1971, entry, Haldeman, *The Haldeman Diaries*, p. 305; Buchanan to Ehrlichman, July 8, 1971, Box 14, folder: Patrick Buchanan, WSPF–IRS.

22. *Statement of Information, Book VIII*, pp. 79, 80, 84, 86–87. See also material in Box 14, folder: Caulfield documents, WSPF–IRS.

23. Dean to Krogh, July 27, 1971, Box 23, folder: Weicker Agency Abuse Exhibits, WSPF–IRS.

24. Affidavit from Roger Barth, November 12, 1973, Box 5, folder: Institute for Policy Studies, WSPF–IRS.

25. Frank Martin, WSPF, to Files, October 30, 1973, ibid.

26. Rogovin to Ervin, September 28, 1973, ibid.

27. Buchanan to Haldeman, Ehrlichman, Colson, May 4, 1972, and Buchanan to Haldeman, January 20, 1972, Box 5, folder: Center for Corporate Responsibility, ibid. The issue arose after Russell Train testified before the House Ways and Means Committee in favor of such legislation. See David Keene to Buchanan, May 12, 1972, WHSF, SM&OF, Patrick J. Buchanan, Box 5, folder: Colson 1972 (2 of 5), Nixon Papers, NA. Keene considered this stance "politically myopic and possibly suicidal."

28. *Proposals for Administrative Changes in Internal Revenue Service Procedures*. Hearings Before the Subcommittee on Oversight of the Committee on Ways and Means, House of Representatives, 94th Cong., 1st sess. (Washington, D.C., 1975), p. 145. Details of the case are in Douglass Lea to Respondents to the Enemies List Study, November 30, 1973, Box 1, folder: ACLU Enemies; William Connett deposition, July 27, 1973, Box 3, folder: Depositions Taken in the Case of Center on Corporate Responsibility; Roy Kinsey deposition, July 30, 1973, Box 4, folder: Roy Kinsey; all in WSPF–IRS. See also E. Edward Stephens, "IRS and Political Pressure," *Washington Star-News*, May 12, 1974; Eileen Shanahan, "Tax Ruling Scores White House Role," *New York Times*, December 12, 1974, p. 1. An overall review of the case is in Frank Martin to Philip Heymann, July 19, 1973, and Henry Hecht to Phil Heymann and Bill Merrill, August 1, 1973, Box 5, folder: Center on Corporate Responsibility, WSPF–IRS.

29. Allen Matusow, *Nixon's Economy: Booms, Busts, Dollars, and Votes* (Lawrence, Kans., 1998), pp. 97–98; Christopher Matthews, "Nixon on Tape: Go After 'Rich Jews,'" *San Francisco Examiner*, December 8, 1996, found online at http://www.sfgate.com/cgi-bin/article/cgi?file=/examiner/archive/ in 1999. For Goldberg, see *Federal Tax Return Privacy*, pp. 135–137.

30. For protestations of innocence, see Colson to Fred Thompson and Sam Dash, June 28, 1973, Box 4, folder: PLME 2: Investigative Correspondence and Interview with Larry Higby, July 30, 1973, Box 5, folder: PLME 4: Witness Statements, WSPF–IRS. Development of the scheme is noted in Hecht to Horowitz, October 12, 1973, Box 1, folder: Legal and Factual Analysis; Interview with Murray Chotiner, December 20, 1973, Box 17, folder: Murray Chotiner; and Strachan to Haldeman, August 17, 1971, Box 12, folder: IRS; all in WSPF–IRS. For the National Movement for the Student Vote, see handwritten note of March 28, 1972, Box 18, folder: John Dean, WSPF–IRS.

31. An account of this meeting is in Caulfield's notes, Box 1, folder: Jencks Material for Larry, and in Akerman Memo for the Files, Box 15, folder: Caulfield (1 of 2); WSPF–IRS.

32. Nixon's comments are on the September 8, 1971, tape; see Stanley Kutler, ed., *Abuse of Power: The New Nixon Tapes* (New York, 1997), p. 29. Colson's efforts are noted in Box 4, folder: Computer Printout, WSPF–IRS; *Statement of Information*, pp. 103, 105, 111. Pressures on Dean are in Box 4, folder: PLME 3: Documentary Evidence/Summaries, WSPF–IRS; Wilson to the File, October 5, 1971, Nixon Project, WHSF, John Dean, Box 40, folder: Internal Revenue Service (2 of 2), NA.

33. Caulfield to Dean, October 15, 1971, and October 20, 1971, *Warrantless Wiretapping*, pp. 115, 118. Fielding to Dean (handwritten note on the 10/15/71 Caulfield to Dean memo, Box 19, folder: Dean . . . rec'd October 25, 1973, WSPF–IRS; Dean to Strachan, October 20, 1971, Nixon Project, WHSF, SM&OF, H. R. Haldeman, Box 204, folder: John Dean III–October 1971, NA.

34. The characterization of Strachan is in Interview with Joan Blend, June 29, 1973, Box 26, folder: Gordon Strachan; Strachan's complaint about intelligence is in Strachan to Higby, October 20, 1971, Box 12, folder: W.H.–Newsday, WSPF–IRS. On the talking paper, see Akerman to the Files, April 28, 1975, Box 4, folder: PLME 3: Documentary Evidence/Summaries, WSPF–IRS. Other political efforts included challenging the tax exemptions of labor unions because of their partisan political activities; see John Kilcullen to Dean, December 8, 1971,

Nixon Project, WHSF, John Dean, Box 39, folder: Internal Revenue Service (1 of 2), NA. Doar's comments are in the *New York Times*, July 23, 1974, p. 24.

35. Gordon to Acker, et al., November 11, 1971, Box 4, folder: Computer Printout; L. F. Satterfield, Memo for File, December 13, 1971, Box 13, folder: Correspondence Provided–Roger Barth; Rustin to Douglas Lea, August 14, 1973, Box 1, folder: ACLU Enemies; all in WSPF–IRS.

36. Fensterwald to Archibald Cox, July 25, 1973, Box 4, folder: PLME 2: Investigative Correspondence, WSPF–IRS; Memo for Files, August 2, 1973, and Walter Mondale to Meade Whitaker, August 17, 1973, Series IIIA, Drawer 17, folder 17: 58, WSP. For the activities of Caulfield and Barth, see Interview with Anthony Ulasewicz, October 1, 1973, Box 14, folder: Caulfield Documents; Jay Horowitz to the files, December 3, 1973; handwritten notes, Box 18, folder: Anne Dawson; all in WSPF–IRS. Also see *Intelligence Activities*, p. 22, and Douglas Caddy, "Did Judge Sirica Cause the Watergate Cover-up?," personal memoir in typescript, p. 49, Douglass Caddy Papers. Ambrose had at one time been in charge of the Federal Narcotics Bureau, where he apparently developed ties to gun-running across the Mexican border into Texas in a deal linked to the Mafia and the CIA. See Pete Brewton, *The Mafia, CIA and George Bush* (New York, 1992), p. 156.

37. For a description of the system, see Memo to the Files, May 24, 1974, Box 23, folder: (b)(7)(c), #3, WSPF–IRS. Additional information is in Fensterwald to Philip Lacovara, April 1, 1974, Box 20, folder: Bernard Fensterwald; FBI memo, September 4, 1973, and FBI Memo, October 11, 1973, Box 4, folder: PLME 2: Investigative Correspondence, WSPF–IRS. Fensterwald may have had an axe to grind here; Acree had called him a "madman" that year; see Interview with Caulfield, June 22, 1974, Box 15, folder: Caulfield, WSPF–IRS. For Acree's efforts, see the transcript from the ABC-TV program on the IRS, March 21, 1975, *Federal Tax Return Privacy* (1975), p. 259.

38. Handwritten notes re: Colson/IRS, Box 17, folder: Charles Colson; Confidential Memo to Marge Acker, et al. from Joanne Gordon, June 2, 1972, Box 4, folder: PLME 2: Investigative Correspondence; Memo from Gordon to Acker, et al., May 16, 1972, Box 4, folder: Computer Printout; Colson to Dean, May 30, 1972; Frank Martin to the Files, September 11, 1973, Box 29, folder: David Wilson; WSPF–IRS; John Dean testimony, *Presidential Campaign Activities of 1972, Book 4*, p. 1479; Lukas, *Nightmare*, p. 18; *Wall Street Journal*, June 13, 1975, p. 1. The request to the FBI is in Henry Ruth, WSPF, to Clarence Kelley, FBI Director, September 17, 1973, Box 4, folder: PLME 2: Investigative Correspondence, WSPF–IRS. Additional efforts to infiltrate and discredit the VVAW are noted in Andrew Hunt, *The Turning: A History of Vietnam Veterans Against the War* (New York, 1999), p. 151.

39. "Proposed White House Staff Activities in the Internal Security Area," Box 12, folder: IRS, WSPF–IRS.

40. Haldeman, *The Haldeman Diaries*, pp. 489–490, 492; Kutler, *Abuse of Power*, pp. 112–113; Nixon to Haldeman, August 9, 1972, Box 4, folder: PLME 3: Documentary Evidence/Summaries, WSPF–IRS.

41. Colson to Dean, June 12, 1972, Box 18, folder: John Dean, WSPF–IRS. Gibbons's support of McGovern also meant that he was an opponent of Nixon supporter and Teamsters icon Jimmy Hoffa. As noted in a previous chapter, Hoffa's presence seems ubiquitous throughout this period.

42. Interview with William Timmons, November 20, 1973, Box 26, folder: William Timmons; Jay Horowitz to Bill Merrill, January 7, 1974, Box 20, folder: John Ehrlichman. The Walters quote is in Interview with Walters, Box 26, folder: J. M. Walters (1 of 2). All are in WSPF–IRS.

43. Horowitz to Merrill, January 7, 1974, Box 20, folder: John Ehrlichman and Horowitz to Phil Lacovara, November 6, 1973, Box 5, folder: PLME 5: Legal & Factual Analysis, WSPF–IRS. Dean's request and Walters's actions are noted in Johnnie M. Walters, note, September 11, 1972, Box 5, folder: Enemies List–500, WSPF–IRS and *Investigation into Certain Charges of the Use of the Internal Revenue Service for Political Purposes*, pp. 3–4. The Connecticut incident is in Frank Martin to Roger Witten and Thomas McBride, June 29, 1973, Box 1, folder: Plumbers Task Force Investigation of IRS–Correspondence, WSPF–IRS. At this same time the White House worried about proposed hearings by Wright Patman's House Banking and Currency Committee on fund-raising by the Committee to Re-Elect the President. Through John Dean, they moved to block the hearings. See *Presidential Campaign Activities of 1972, Book 3*, pp. 959–960. A revealing discussion among the Watergate special prosecutors

about potential criminal charges in the case of the Enemies Lists is in Robert Palmer to Philip Locavara and Jay Horowitz, November 29, 1973, Box 5, folder: PLME 5: Legal & Factual Analysis, WSPF–IRS.

44. *Minority Memorandum on Facts and Law*, pp. 121–123; Horowitz to the Files, re: interview with John Dean, December 3, 1973, Box 18, folder: John Dean, WSPF–IRS. Haldeman's comment is from a September 8, 1972, oval office tape, quoted in Kutler, *Abuse of Power*, pp. 133–134.

45. Transcript of September 15, 1972, meeting, Box 10, folder: September 15, 1972, tape (1 of 2), WSPF–IRS. In its reporting of the taped conversation, the White House deleted the IRS material. See the *Wall Street Journal*, May 30, 1974, p. 22. Copies of the Enemies Lists are in *Investigation into Certain Charges of the Use of the Internal Revenue Service for Political Purposes*, Appendices A and B.

46. For Walters's actions, see Hecht to Horowitz, September 18, 1973, Box 26, folder: J. M. Walters (1 of 2), WSPF–IRS. The Nixon-Haldeman exchange, November 13, 1972, at Camp David, is in Kutler, *Abuse of Power*, pp. 176–177.

47. See Burnham, *A Law Unto Itself*, pp. 216–221 for the ITT affair. The University Centers for Rational Alternatives case is noted in Flanigan to the Staff Secretary, December 24, 1969, and January 15, 1970, WHCF, Subject File, FG 12, Dept. of Treasury, folder: EX FG 12-8 Internal Revenue Service (1/25/69–12/22/70), Nixon Project. The other cases are in Box 4, folder: Computer Printout and Akerman to the Files, May 6, 1975, Box 4: folder: PLME 3: Documentary Evidence/Summaries, WSPF–IRS.

48. Hecht to Horowitz, re: interview with Thrower, September 19, 1973, Box 1, folder: Witness Statements–Randolph Thrower; Hullin to Haldeman and Zeigler, September 2, 1970, Box 4, folder: PLME 3: Documentary Evidence/Summaries; Horowitz to Merrill, January 7, 1974, Box 20, folder: John Ehrlichman; all in WSPF–IRS. Material on Smith is in Gerth, "Nixon and the Mafia," p. 67; Kirkpatrick Sale, *Power Shift: The Rise of the Southern Rim and Its Challenge to the Eastern Establishment* (New York, 1975), pp. 58–59, 201–202; Denny Walsh and Tom Flaherty, "Tampering with Justice in San Diego," *Life*, March 24, 1972, clipping in Box 26, folder: David Stutz, WSPF–IRS; and Walters's notes, Box 26, folder: Walters, WSPF–IRS. For Alessio, see Ovid Demaris, *Poso Del Mundo: Inside the Mexican-American Border, from Tijuana to Matamoros* (Boston, 1970), pp. 170–181, 190–201, 204–205, 214–216; Sale, *Power Shift*, p. 57.

49. The Graham case can be pieced together from several sources. See Hecht to Files, October 18, 1973, Box 22, folder: Higby; Horowitz to Files, November 12, 1973, Box 1, folder: Witness Statements–Roger Barth; and Akerman to Files, May 6, 1975, Box 4, folder: PLME 3: Documentary Evidence/Summaries; all in WSPF–IRS. See also Haldeman memo for John Dean, August 30, 1971, WHSF, SMOF, H. R. Haldeman, Box 261, folder: Dean IRS File (L. Higby Alpha Subject Files), and Caulfield to Dean, September 30, 1971, WHCF, John Dean, Box 39, folder: Internal Revenue Service (1 of 2), Nixon Project, NA; Kutler, *Abuse of Power*, pp. 30–31; *Statement of Information, Book 8*, p. 145.

50. For the Wayne incident, see Caulfield to Dean, October 6, 1971 in *Federal Tax Return Privacy*, pp. 129–130, 132, 133–134; handwritten notes, Box 20, folder: Geibel, WSPF–IRS.

Chapter Twelve. Dangerous Relationships: The Rebozo-Hughes-O'Brien Connection

1. The best outline of these connections is in Gerth, "Nixon and the Mafia," pp. 32, 35. See also Sale, *Power Shift*, p. 22, and Leslie Waller, *The Swiss Bank Connection* (New York, 1972), pp. 145–148.

2. Gerth, "Nixon and the Mafia," pp. 32, 34; Warren Hinckle and William W. Turner, *Deadly Secrets: The CIA-Mafia War Against Castro and the Assassination of J.F.K.* (New York, 1992), p. 337. This was originally published in 1981. See also Moldea, *The Hoffa Wars*, p. 105. Nixon withdrew all his correspondence with Rebozo from his pre-presidential papers, so the exact nature of their early relationship remains unclear.

3. Sale, *Power Shift*, pp. 224–227; Gerth, "Nixon and the Mafia," pp. 35, 64; Hinckle and Turner, *Deadly Secrets*, pp. 164–165, 226. For more on Artime, see Juan Carlos Rodriguez, *The Bay of Pigs and the CIA* (Melbourne, Australia, 1999), pp. 24–25; Morris Morley, *Imperial State and Revolution: The United States and Cuba, 1952–1986* (Cambridge, England, 1987), p. 155;

and Fabian Escalante, *The Secret War: CIA Covert Operations Against Cuba, 1959–62* (Melbourne, Australia, 1995), pp. 32–33, 36, 43.

4. Gerth, "Nixon and the Mafia," pp. 36, 64; Hinckle and Turner, *Deadly Secrets*, pp. 352, 363; List of Areas to Be Resolved, October 26, 1971, Box 7, folder: *Newsday* Investigation Documentary Evidence, WSPF–IRS.

5. Sale, *Power Shift*, pp. 203, 227; Gerth, "Nixon and the Mafia," pp. 32, 42, 64; Waller, *The Swiss Bank Connection*, p. 36. Material on the Parvin Foundation is in Demaris, *Dirty Business*, pp. 308–313. The foundation had several notable figures on its board of directors, including Justice William O. Douglas, Robert Hutchins, and Harry Ashmore. The IRS later investigated both Parvin and the foundation, and Parvin was on the Justice Department's organized crime list.

6. Gerth, "Nixon and the Mafia," pp. 65–68; Sale, *Power Shift*, pp. 201–205n, 226. See also Rebozo to Ehrlichman, November 2, 1971, Box 7, folder: Newsday Investigation–Documentary Evidence, WSPF–IRS. Information on Intertel is in Akerman to Files (re: Interview with Tad Szulc), July 28, 1973, Box 26, folder: Tad Szulc, WSPF–IRS and in Hinckle and Turner, *Deadly Secrets*, pp. 338–339. For more information on the links between these individuals, see Waller, *The Swiss Bank Connection*, pp. 122–135.

7. WSPF Chronological Report: References to Joseph Woods, Box 29, folder: Joseph Woods; Akerman to Files (undated), Box 15, folder: Caulfield (1 of 2); Haldeman to Strachan, October 11, 1971, and Akerman to Files, April 11, 1975, Box 4, folder: PLME 3: Documentary Evidence/Summaries; Akerman to Files, May 12, 1975, Box 18, folder: John Dean; "Inventory of and Notes on: Political Matters Memos," December 2, 1971, Box 1, folder: Legal and Factual Analysis; all in WSPF–IRS. Caulfield's prospectus is in Box 18, folder: Anne Dawson, WSPF–IRS.

8. Box 4, folder: Computer Printout, WSPF–IRS.

9. Henry Hecht to Files, December 10, 1973, re: Interview with Robert Greene, Box 7, folder: Newsday Investigation–Witness Statements WSPF interviews, WSPF–IRS.

10. Hecht to Files, December 10, 1973 (Interview with Robert Greene), and Horowitz to Files, November 27, 1973 (Interview with Fred Fielding), ibid.; Ehrlichman to Dean, July 21, 1971, and Action Paper, July 26, 1971, Box 4, folder: PLME 3: Documentary Evidence/Summaries; Akerman to Files, May 12, 1975, Box 7, folder: Newsday Investigation–Legal and Factual Analysis, WSPF–IRS.

11. Thrower interview, July 25, 1973, Box 4, folder: Computer Printout; Akerman to Files, May 12, 1975, Box 7, folder: Newsday Investigation–Legal & Factual Analysis; WSPF–IRS. *Brief on Behalf of the President of the United States.* Hearings Before the Committee on the Judiciary, House of Representatives, 93rd Cong., 2d sess. (Washington, D.C., 1974), p. 13. Caulfield also burned most of his notes and documents that he did not take home; see Marc Lackritz to Terry Lenzner (re: Conversation with Anne Dawson), February 19, 1974, Box 18, folder: Anne Dawson, WSPF–IRS.

12. Horowitz to Files, December 4, 1973, Box 7, folder: *Newsday* Investigation Documentary Evidence; Mitchell to Dean, September 7, 1971, Box 4, PLME 3: Documentary Evidence/Summaries; Caulfield to Dean, September 10, 1971, Box 19, folder: Dean . . . rec'd October 25, 1973, first half; Interview with Leon Green, Box 7, folder: Newsday Investigation–Misc. notes by a staff attorney, WSPF–IRS. For the Nixon-Haldeman discussion, which occurred on September 14, 1971, in the Oval Office, see Kutler, *Abuse of Power*, p. 32. Walters's denial is in Box NNR-A, Rm. 6310 (Walters Witness File), folder: Johnnie M. Walters, WSPF–IRS.

13. Copies of the articles are in Box 7, folder: "Newsday." For Fielding, see Horowitz to Files (re: Interview with Fielding), November 27, 1973, Box 20, folder: Fred Fielding. Mitchell's comments are in Martin and Hecht to Files (re: Interview with Mitchell), January 14, 1974, Box 23, folder: John N. Mitchell. For the audits, see Jay Horowitz to Bill Merrill, January 7, 1974, Box 20, folder: John Ehrlichman and Horowitz to Robert Morvillo (John Caulfield's attorney), May 20, 1974, Box 4, folder: PLME 2: Investigative Correspondence; Lea to Respondents to the Enemies List Study, November 30, 1973, Box 1, folder: ACLU Enemies. All are in WSPF–IRS. See also *Statement of Information, Book VIII*, p. 165.

14. Higby to Dean, October 8, 1971; Haldeman to Higby, October 19, 1971; Higby to Haldeman, October 21, 1971; all in Box 4, folder: PLME 3: Documentary Evidence/Summaries, WSPF–IRS. See also *Warrantless Wiretapping*, p. 98. Material on the hiring of private investigators is in John J. Doermer to James Juliana, October 29, 1971, and Juliana to Paul Wagner (of Wagner & Baroody), December 6, 1971, Box 7, folder: "Newsday," WSPF–IRS.

15. For information on Operation Tradewinds, Project Haven, and Project 3, see *Oversight Hearings into the Operations of the IRS* (1975), pp. 190–192, 241, 905, 925. See also Alan Block, *Masters of Paradise: Organized Crime and the Internal Revenue Service in the Bahamas* (New Brunswick, N.J., 1991), p. 12.

16. Box 6, folder: Notes of Interviews with IRS personnel (1 of 2), WSPF–IRS; Affidavit of Richard Danner, July 5, 1973, loose folder: IRS (Sensitive): Bebe Rebozo Investigations: 1973–1974, WSP; Block, *Masters of Paradise*, pp. 120–128. For skimming methods, see Box 22, folder: Keeney's Las Vegas Work Plans/ Briefings, WSPF–IRS. For more detail on the contributions to Nixon through Rebozo, see Ovid Demaris, *Dirty Business: The Corporate–Political Money–Power Game* (New York, 1974), pp. 268–272.

17. Alexander to Simon, May 23, 1973, loose folder: IRS (Sensitive): Bebe Rebozo Investigations: 1973–1974, WSP.

18. Walters to Shultz, February 23, 1973, and Notes for Briefing Secretary, March 3, 1972, Box 27, folder: Walters's Originals; Woodward and Bernstein, "Ehrlichman Tells Senate Panel of Pressure on IRS," *Washington Post*, July 11, 1974, clipping in Box 26, folder: Johnnie M. Walters (2 of 2); Jay Horowitz to files, re: Interview with Roger Barth, Box 1, folder: Witness Statements–Roger Barth; WSPF–IRS. See also Lukas, *Nightmare*, p. 365, and Block, *Masters of Paradise*, p. 224.

19. Jay Horowitz, Memo to Files, Box 9, folder: O'Brien Tax Inquiry (1 of 2) and Mary DeOreo to Terry Lenzner, May 13, 1974, Box 25, folder: G. P. Shultz, WSPF–IRS. Acree later denied the charges, but the Watergate Special Prosecution Force remained unconvinced. See *Newsweek* 84 (July 29, 1974), 29–30.

20. Memo from MEH to Simon, May 1, 1974, and Kelley to Alexander, August 1, 1973, both in folder: IRS (Sensitive): Bebe Rebozo Investigation: 1973–1974, WSP; Alexander to Simon, May 23, 1973, Box 9, folder: Summer '72 Interest in O'Brien (2 of 2), and Memo of September 21, 1973, Box 14, folder: Caulfield Interviews & Testimony. All are in WSPF–IRS.

21. Walters to Shultz, February 23, 1973, Box 25, folder: Shultz; Lackritz to Lenzner (re: Conversation with Anne Dawson, Caulfield's secretary), February 19, 1974, Box 15, folder: Caulfield; Akerman to the Files, May 6, 1975, Box 4, folder: PLME 3: Documentary Evidence/Summaries; all in WSPF–IRS. For the 1956 loan, see Sale, *Power Shift*, pp. 216–217.

22. For material on the Sensitive Case Report, see Box 9, folder: Summer '72: Interest in O'Brien (1 of 2), WSPF–IRS. A memorandum of the interview by informant LA-72-231 is in the same file. Donald Nixon actively used his name to create opportunities for himself; see Demaris, *Dirty Business*, pp. 272–274.

23. Hinckle and Turner, *Deadly Secrets*, pp. 21, 23, 335; Michael Ewing, *Coincidence or Conspiracy?* (New York, 1977), pp. 334–335. For Colson's concerns, see notes on an interview with Robert Bennett, Box 4, folder: Computer Printout, WSPF–IRS. Walters's assessment is in Walters to Shultz, February 23, 1973, folder: IRS (Sensitive): Bebe Rebozo Investigations: 1973–74, WSP.

24. Levoy G. Venable, Hughes Project, Status Report, May 22, 1972, and Assistant Commissioner (Compliance) to Walters, September 1, 1972, both in Box 9, folder: Summer '72: Interest in O'Brien (1 of 2), WSPF–IRS. See also notes on Laxalt interview, December 19, 1973, Box 4, folder: Computer Printout and Jack Anderson, "Senate Probes Hughes Contributions," *Washington Post*, September 20, 1973, p. B11, clipping in Box 5, folder: Enemies List–500, WSPF–IRS. Haig's remark is in Kutler, *Abuse of Power*, p. 592. This is from a tape-recorded conversation in the oval office on June 7, 1973.

25. Bennett to Dean, July 30, 1971, Dean to Walker, August 4, 1971, Box 1063A, loose materials, WPP.

26. Walker to Dean, August 17, 1971, ibid. The details of these transactions are complex and beyond our concern here, but see Demaris, *Dirty Business*, pp. 260–266.

27. Ehrlichman to Dean, January 25, 1972, Box 4, folder: PLME 3: Documentary Evidence/Summaries, WSPF–IRS. Barth's notes are in Box 12, folder: IRS, WSPF–IRS. The Rosenberg release (March 14, 1972) is in Box 937A, folder: Howard Hughes Medical Institute, WPP. See also Fred Hickman to William Simon, July 1973, Series II, Drawer 9: Internal Memoranda: A-I, folder 9: 46, WSP; Morton Mintz, "Bid for Hughes Institute Tax Break Is Kept Secret," *Miami Herald*, October 28, 1973, clipping in Box 1056C, folder: foundations, WPP; Patman to Shultz, October 15, 1973, Box 937A, folder: Hughes Medical Institute, WPP.

28. James Hogue, Special Assistant to the Secretary of the Treasury for Legislative Affairs, to Patman, October 19, 1973, Box 607C, folder: Hughes Foundation; Shultz to Patman, Octo-

ber 29, 1973, Box 1063A, folder: loose material; Morton Mintz, "White House Had Role in Hughes Case," *Washington Post*, November 7, 1973, clipping in Box 1056C, folder: Rebozo–73; all in WPP. The exchange between Patman and Hickman is in Box 61, folder 44, HRP. See also Akerman to the Files, April 11, 1975, Box 4, folder: PLME 3: Documentary Evidence/Summaries, WSPF–IRS.

29. Nixon's concern is noted in the March 4, 1970, entry in Haldeman, *The Haldeman Diaries*, p. 134. Williams's remarks are in the *Congressional Record*, vol. 116, pt. 9 (April 16, 1970), 12218–12228.

30. Nixon to Haldeman, January 14, 1971, in Akerman to the Files, April 28, 1975, Box 4, folder: PLME 3: Documentary Evidence/Summaries. A background and biographical sheet on O'Brien is in Box 10, folder: Karelitz and O'Brien Cases (2 of 2); Horowitz to the Files (no date), Box 9, folder: O'Brien Tax Inquiry (1 of 2). All are in WSPF–IRS.

31. Jay Horowitz to Files (re: Interview with Roger Barth), November 12, 1973, Box 1, folder: Witness Statements–Roger Barth; "Lawrence F. O'Brien: Returns Reviewed 1969–1971," Box 10, folder: Karelitz and O'Brien Cases (2 of 2); both in WSPF–IRS. The chronology of O'Brien's audits is in Box 4, folder: Computer Printout, WSPF–IRS. See also Horowitz to the Files (no date), in Box 9, folder: O'Brien Tax Inquiry (1 of 2) and Horowitz to Merrill, January 7, 1974, Box 20, folder: John Ehrlichman, WSPF–IRS.

32. The August 3 Nixon-Ehrlichman discussion is in Kutler, *Abuse of Power*, pp. 118–119. For Walters's remarks, see "Lawrence F. O'Brien: Returns Reviewed 1969–1971," Box 10, folder: Karelitz and O'Brien Cases (2 of 2), WSPF–IRS. The link between the O'Brien matter and the hope to appoint Barth IRS deputy general counsel is noted in Tod Hullin to Ron Brooks, July 20, 1972, in Akerman to the Files, May 6, 1975, Box 4, folder: PLME 3: Documentary Evidence/Summaries, WSPF–IRS.

33. Shultz's views of the affair are in Henry Hecht to Files (re: Interview with Shultz), April 8, 1974, Box 25, folder: Shultz, WSPF–IRS. Walters's affidavit is in Box 26, folder: J. M. Walters (1 of 2), WSPF–IRS. For the agents' actions, see Horowitz to the Files (no date), Box 9, folder: O'Brien Tax Inquiry (1 of 2), WSPF–IRS. Walters's remarks are quoted in notes of an interview on February 28, 1974, Box 9, folder: O'Brien Tax Inquiry (2 of 2), WSPF–IRS.

34. Nixon tape for August 3, 1972 in Kutler, *Abuse of Power*, pp. 114–116; Larry O'Brien Oral History, p. 41, LBJL; Haldeman to Nixon, August 9, 1972, in Akerman to the Files, May 6, 1975, Box 4, folder: PLME 3: Documentary Evidence/Summaries, WSPF–IRS. For O'Brien's later reaction, see his testimony of May 7, 1975, in *Postal Inspection Service's Monitoring and Control of Mail Surveillance and Mail Cover Programs*. Hearings Before the Subcommittee on Postal Facilities, Mail, and Labor Management of the Committee on Post Offices and Civil Service, House of Representatives, 94th Cong., 1st sess. (Washington, D.C., 1975), p. 67. Baker's comments are in his *Wheeling and Dealing*, pp. 252–256.

35. McGowan, Memo of meeting with Commissioner Walters, August 29, 1972, Box 9, folder: Summer '72: Interest in O'Brien (1 of 2), and Horowitz to the Files (no date), Box 9, folder: O'Brien Tax Inquiry (1 of 2), WSPF–IRS.

36. Dean's remarks are in Box 4, folder: Computer Printout. See also Hecht and Horowitz to Phil Lacovara and Peter Kreindler, November 28, 1973, Box 10, folder: September 15, 1972, tape (1 of 2), and Horowitz to Merrill, January 7, 1974, Box 20, folder: John Ehrlichman. All are in WSPF–IRS. The story of the tape is in *Statement of Information, Book VIII*, pp. 331, 333, 335. Nixon's comments to Buzhardt are on a June 5, 1973, tape; see Kutler, *Abuse of Power*, p. 580. Comments from the minority counsel are in *Minority Memorandum on Facts and Law*, pp. 124–125.

37. The March 30, 1973, oval office tape, in Kutler, *Abuse of Power*, pp. 290–291, deals with Weicker. Nixon's fantasizing is in Nixon to Haig, July 7, 1973, Nixon Project, WHSF, President's Personal Files, Box 4, folder: Memos–July 1973, NA.

38. Bacon is quoted in Bob Kuttner, "The Taxing Trials of IRS," *New York Times Magazine*, January 6, 1974, clipping in Box 27, folder: Barth–NY Times & Star, WSPF–IRS.

39. Hanlon to Alexander, July 13, 1973, Folder 1: Senate Select Committee on Presidential Campaign Activities–IRS Involvement, WSP; Hanlon to Alexander, July 23, 1973, Series IIIA, Drawer 17, Folder 17: 58: Watergate: 1973 (July 1974), WSP.

40. Alexander to Cox, October 2, 1973, Box 4, folder: PLME 2: Investigative Correspondence, WSPF–IRS.

41. Cox to Alexander, October 10, 1973; Cox to Alexander, October 15, 1973; Jaworski to Alexander, November 20, 1973; all in Box 4, folder: PLME 2: Investigative Correspondence,

WSPF–IRS. See also Robert Bork to Alexander, November 21, 1973, Box 11, folder: Disclosure Staff, WSPF–IRS.

42. Whitaker to Petersen, November 29, 1973, Box 4, folder: PLME 2: Investigative Correspondence, WSPF–IRS.

43. Lea to Patman, July 30, 1973, Box 535A, folder: Enemies Lists, WPP; Akerman to the Files, December 3, 1973, Box 1, folder: ACLU Enemies, WSPF–IRS; *Federal Tax Return Privacy.* Hearings Before the Subcommittee on Administration of the Internal Revenue Code of the Committee on Finance, United States Senate, 94th Cong., 1st sess. (Washington, D.C., 1976), pp. 17, 19–20.

44. *Investigation into Certain Charges of the Use of the Internal Revenue Service for Political Purposes,* pp, 11–12; Francis Geibel, Assistant Commissioner (Compliance) to Commissioner Alexander, July 23, 1973, Series IIIA, Drawer 17, folder 17: 58, WSP. See also Schnepper, *Inside IRS,* pp. 159–162, and Wise, *The American Police State,* pp. 332–333. Jarriel's remarks are in the transcript from a March 21, 1975, ABC-TV program on the IRS, quoted in *Federal Tax Return Privacy* (1975), p. 261.

45. Watergate Special Prosecution Force, *Report* (Washington, D.C., 1975), pp. 66–67. The Schmults-Abzug exchange is in *Access to Records.* Hearings Before a Subcommittee of the Committee on Government Operations, House of Representatives, 93rd Cong., 2d sess. (Washington, D.C., 1974), pp. 223–227. House Judiciary Committee comments are in *Federal Tax Return Privacy,* p. 154. Information on the Senate Select Committee on Intelligence Activities came from comments by Barbara Banoff, former staff counsel to the committee. See Larry Zelenak, "Headline-Grabbing Pols Hurt Agency Probe: Banoff," *Harvard Law Record* 63 (December 1976), 3.

46. Hecht to Files, December 7, 1973, Box 1, folder: Plumbers Task Force Investigation of IRS–Planning and Coordination; Hecht to Ruth, February 19, 1974, Box 29, folder: Burke Willsey; WSPF–IRS. See also *New York Times,* July 17, 1974, p. 17, for information on the Judiciary Committee.

47. Richard Albrecht, IRS General Counsel, to William Simon, September 5, 1974, Series IIIB, Drawer 19, folder 19: 37, Disclosure of Tax Information: 1974, WSP; Testimony of Donald Alexander, *Surveillance.* Hearings Before the Subcommittee on Courts, Civil Liberties, and the Administration of Justice of the Committee on the Judiciary, House of Representatives, 94th Cong., 1st sess. (Washington, D.C., 1975), pp. 632–648; Howard Baker, September 25, 1975, Hearings Before the Select Committee to Study Governmental Operations with Respect to Intelligence Activities (Vol. 2: the Huston Plan), U.S. Senate, 94th Cong., 1st sess. (Washington, D.C., 1976), pp. 110–111.

Chapter Thirteen. The Special Service Staff: An IRS Enemies List

1. Robert Wall, "Why I Got Out of It," in Pat Watters and Stephen Gillers, eds., *Investigating the FBI* (Garden City, N.Y., 1973), p. 380.

2. Davis, *Unbridled Power,* pp. 78, 94–95. SSS files, for instance, include a 1990 obituary of the historian William Appleman Williams, as well as obituaries for historians Charles M. Wiltse and Evelyn Leffler. Apparently someone at the IRS tracked SSS targets until their death. See SSS files, FOIA, 9166A–9166B. (I will use this citation practice throughout. It refers to the fourteen-thousand-plus pages of SSS files I obtained through a Freedom of Information Act request. The IRS numbered the pages at the time of my FOIA. All materials are in the John Andrew Collection, Archives and Manuscripts, Shadek-Fackenthal Library, Franklin & Marshall College.) One note on terminology is important. The SSS, which I will use throughout, was first called the Activist Organizations Committee, then the Special Service Group, and finally the Special Service Staff. The name changes, however, carried with them no changes in function or operation.

3. A copy of the memo is in *Intelligence Activities, Vol. 3.* Senate Resolution 21. Hearings Before the Select Committee to Study Governmental Operations with Respect to Intelligence Activities, U.S. Senate, 94th Cong., 1st sess. (Washington, D.C., 1976), pp. 46–47. See also *People & Taxes* (October 1975) and the *New York Times,* October 3, 1975, clippings in SSS files, FOIA, pp. 10829 and 2360.

4. Virdin to Harold Snyder, May 2, 1968, SSS files, FOIA, p. 11330. For an example of IRS

harassment, see the *Washington Post*, May 17, 1968, clipping in Senate Internal Security Sub-committee, Subject Files, Box 274, folder: Students for a Democratic Society, January to June 1968, RG 46, NA. Several August 1968 FBI memos detail the use of IRS information in the COINTELPRO effort; see *Intelligence Activities and the Rights of Americans, Book 2* (1976), p. 10.

5. D. O. Virdin, Memo for the File, August 28, 1968, and September 11, 1968; Virdin to Deputy Commissioner William E. Williams, November 22, 1974; McClellan to Henry Fowler, September 19, 1968; all in SSS files, FOIA, pp. 1056, 1057, 1058, 1059–1061. The last memo included a list of the groups requested. They were: SNCC, The Student Voice, the Sojourner Motor Fleet (Atlanta), the Southern Education and Research Institute (Atlanta), CORE, SDS, the Black Panther party, the Revolutionary Action Movement (Philadelphia), the Deacons for Defense and Justice (Jonesboro, Louisiana), the Nation of Islam, the Afro-American Research Institute (New York), the Southern Conference Education Fund, the Progressive Labor party, Rosen Publishing Company (New York), Tri-Line Offset Company (New York), the Medical Committee for Human Rights, the Fund for Education and Legal Defense (New York), the Minutemen, the American Nazi party, the United Klans of America, the White Knights of the KKK (Laurel, Mississippi), and the National States Rights party (Savannah, Georgia). See Box 10, folder: Special Service Group (IRS), (3 of 3), WSPF–IRS.

6. DeLong to Seufert, January 9, 1969, SSS files, FOIA, p. 12662. For the Fact Sheet, see pp. 1039–1044 in the same files.

7. Virdin, Memo for File, March 18, 1969, Box 10, folder: Special Service Group (IRS), (3 of 3); and Bacon to Regional Commissioners, March 25, 1969, Box 10, folder: Special Service Group (IRS) (2 of 3), WSPF–IRS; Virdin, Memo for File, April 2, 1969, and R. G. Clucas to Virdin, April 8, 1969, SSS files, FOIA, pp. 1311, 1313. An annotated list of codes and comments is in SSS files, FOIA, p. 8255.

8. *The Internal Revenue Service: An Intelligence Resource and Collector*, pp. 900, 907–908; *Oversight Hearings into the Operation of the IRS (Part 1)*, pp. 789–790.

9. Special Investigator to Chief, Enforcement Branch, May 7, 1969, in *Political Intelligence in the Internal Revenue Service: The Special Service Staff*, p. 119; Special Report: Militant-Subversive Organizations for Senate Committee on Government Operations, May 12, 1969, SSS files, FOIA, pp. 9350, 9353.

10. Special Report, May 12, 1969, p. 9353.

11. Ibid., pp. 9354, 9363.

12. Interview with Thrower, September 19, 1973, Box 1, folder: Witness Statements: Randolph Thrower, WSPF–IRS; D. O. Virdin, Memo for File, May 26, 1969, and May 28, 1969, Box 10, folder: Special Service Group (IRS) (3 of 3), WSPF–IRS; Bacon to Spatz, May 28, 1969, SSS files, FOIA, p. 531.

13. Deputy Assistant Commissioner (Compliance) to Donald Bacon, May 29, 1969, *Political Intelligence in the Internal Revenue Service*, p. 312; D. O. Virdin, Memo for File, June 4, 1969, Box 10, folder: Special Service Group (IRS) (3 of 3), WSPF–IRS. A June 12 meeting on this issue focused on the IRS Black Panther party file, which included information from the Central, Mid-Atlantic, and Western regions. The group wanted to review the file before turning anything over to the McClellan Committee. See D. O. Virdin, Memo for File, June 12, 1969, SSS files, FOIA, p. 1349.

14. Statement of Dr. Laurence Woodworth, Chief of Staff, Joint Committee on Internal Revenue Taxation, *Internal Revenue Service Intelligence Operations*. Hearings Before the Subcommittee on Oversight of the Committee on Ways and Means, House of Representatives, 94th Cong., 1st sess. (Washington, D.C., 1975), p. 73; *Investigation of the Special Service Staff of the Internal Revenue Service*, pp. 5, 16–18, 23–24; Huston to Nixon, June 18, 1969, Nixon Project, WHSF, WHCF, Confidential files, Box 18, folder: [CF] FG 12-8 Internal Revenue Service (1969–1970), NA. Shelley Davis, in *Unbridled Power*, pp. 82–83, dates the beginning of the SSS from the hearings on the Black Panthers.

15. *The News American*, June 22, 1969, clipping in SSS files, FOIA, p. 2381; D. O. Virdin, Memo for File, June 23, 1969, and June 25, 1969, Box 10, folder: Special Service Group (IRS) (3 of 3), WSPF–IRS; Fact Sheet: Establishment of SSS (August 7, 1973); Bacon memo, June 25, 1969; both in SSS files, FOIA, pp. 1039–1044, 706. A complete copy of the Bacon memo is also in Box 10, folder: Special Service Group (IRS) (3 of 3), WSPF–IRS. Bacon later added other organizations to the list: see D. O. Virdin, Memo for File, June 26, 1969, in the same file. A sample of replies is in the same file. At least one respondent also included material on CORE, the Revolutionary Action Movement (Philadelphia), the Nation of Islam, the Minutemen, and the

American Nazi party; see Snyder to Bacon, June 30, 1969. For Powell's testimony, see *Investigation into Certain Charges of the Use of the Internal Revenue Service for Political Purposes*, p. 14.

16. *Political Intelligence in the Internal Revenue Service: The Special Service Staff*, p. 9. Charles Jones, ed., *The Black Panther Party Reconsidered* (Baltimore, 1998), pp. 368–369, also traces the origins of the SSS to the White House.

17. Hughes's activities are noted in SSS files, FOIA, p. 1011; *Investigation of the Special Staff of the Internal Revenue Service*, pp. 20–21; *The Internal Revenue Service: An Intelligence Resource and Collector*, p. 878; and Davis, *Unbridled Power*, pp. 85, 86. For the memo, see Bacon to Barth, July 1, 1969, Box 10, folder: Special Service Group (IRS) (3 of 3), WSPF–IRS.

18. Bacon to Barth, July 1, 1969.

19. Ibid.

20. D. O. Virdin, Memo for the File, July 2, 1969, SSS files, FOIA, pp. 610–611; *The Internal Revenue Service: An Intelligence Resource and Collector*, p. 882.

21. S. B. Wolfe to Meehan, July 2, 1969, SSS files, FOIA, p. 1376; *The Internal Revenue Service: An Intelligence Resource and Collector*, p. 883; Wise, *The American Police State*, pp. 326–327; *Political Intelligence in the Internal Revenue Service: The Special Service Staff*, p. 13.

22. *The Internal Revenue Service: An Intelligence Resource and Collector*, pp. 879–880; *Investigation of the Special Service Staff of the Internal Revenue Service*, pp. 38, 121.

23. D. O. Virdin, Memo for the File, July 8, 1969, SSS files, FOIA, p. 619; *Investigation of the Special Service Staff of the Internal Revenue Service*, pp. 38–39; undated memo, "Special Service Staff Case Procedure," SSS files, FOIA, p. 2382; Bacon to Hoover, undated [1969], SSS files, FOIA, p. 928.

24. Snyder to Meehan, July 9, 1969; Bacon to Regional Commissioners, July 14, 1969; D. O. Virdin, Memo for File, July 29, 1969; Virdin to William E. Williams, November 22, 1974. All are in SSS files, FOIA; see, respectively, pp. 625, 10799–10802, 572, 1008–1009.

25. IRS actions can be determined by matching the following sources with one another: Bacon to Regional Commissioners, July 14, 1969, Box 10, folder: Special Service Group (IRS) (2 of 3), WSPF–IRS (which contains the full list of fifty-five organizations) and the same memo in SSS files, FOIA, pp. 9341–9343. See also handwritten notes, July 14, 1969, SSS files, FOIA, pp. 8328–8330.

26. SSS files, FOIA, pp. 605, 1001–1002. Putnam later denied much of this; see *Investigation of the Special Service Staff of the Internal Revenue Service*, pp. 22–23, and *Internal Revenue Service Intelligence Operations*, p. 97.

27. Bacon to Ass't Comm. (Data Processing), Ass't Comm. (Technical), Chief Counsel, All Compliance Division Directors, July 18, 1969, SSS files, FOIA, p. 601; *Warrantless Wiretapping and Electronic Surveillance*, pp. 90–91; *Political Intelligence in the Internal Revenue Service: The Special Service Staff*, pp. 11–12.

28. Memo of July 22, 1969, in *The Internal Revenue Service: An Intelligence Resource and Collector*, p. 882; Talking Paper, July 24, 1969, SSS files, FOIA, pp. 593–596. Virdin's definition of "highest levels" is in Affidavit of Donald O. Virdin, SSS files, FOIA, p. 1003. Roger Barth secured a copy of this memo and forwarded it to Tom Huston at the White House; see Virdin to Burke Willsey, April 10, 1974, SSS files, FOIA, p. 10576.

29. The minutes are in Virdin, Memorandum for File, July 24, 1969, SSS files, FOIA, pp. 587–590. The report, "Special Service Staff: Its Origin, Mission and Potential," is in SSS files, FOIA, 1265–1266.

30. Virdin, Memorandum for File, July 24, 1969, SSS files, FOIA, pp. 587–590.

31. Virdin to Wright, July 29, 1969; Virdin, Memo for File, July 29, 1969; Affidavit of Donald O. Virdin, November 29, 1974; Virdin, Memo for File [meeting minutes], July 29, 1969; Virdin to Snyder, July 31, 1969; all in SSS files, FOIA, pp. 573–574, 575, 1003–1004, 563–564, 560, respectively. While Virdin praised Wright to Snyder, he later indicated that much of that praise was gratuitous and not very sincere. See Meehan, Memo for File, November 23, 1974, SSS files, FOIA, p. 1007. In *Unbridled Power*, IRS historian Shelley Davis characterizes Wright as a fanatical zealot; see p. 87.

32. Kent Brown, Acting Assistant Regional Commissioner, ATF, Western Region, to Regional Commissioner Western Region, August 1, 1969; Collection Division to Paul Wright, August 4, 1969; Internal Revenue Agent [name redacted] to Chief, Los Angeles Intelligence Division, August 4, 1969; W. J. Bookholt, Regional Commissioner Southeast Region, to Assistant Commissioner (Compliance), August 8, 1969; all in SSS files, FOIA, pp. 3022, 3043, 547, 551–552, 4951–4952, 3051–3054, respectively.

33. D. J. Brennan, Jr., to William Sullivan, FBI, August 15, 1969, in *Intelligence Activities, Vol. 3*, p. 43; *Intelligence Activities and the Rights of Americans, Book 2*, pp. 255–256; Memo for File, August 8, 1969, SSS files, FOIA, p. 11327. The Office of International Operations also became interested in the SSS, designating an OIO contact person; see D. O. Virdin, Memo for File, August 6, 1969, SSS files, FOIA, p. 544.

34. A copy of Thrower's speech is in SSS files, FOIA, pp. 3185–3191.

35. Weekly Progress Report, August 14, 1969; Wright to Green, August 20, 1969; both in SSS files, FOIA, pp. 549–550, 838–840.

36. Wright to Green, August 20, 1969, SSS files, FOIA, p. 840; *Investigation of the Special Service Staff of the Internal Revenue Service*, pp. 37–38; Virdin, two Memos for File, both August 25, 1969; Thrower to Williams, August 26, 1969; Collection Division to District Director, Atlanta, August 27, 1969; all in SSS files, FOIA, pp. 538, 540, 4937–4938, 535, respectively. Wright's comment is in *The Internal Revenue Service: An Intelligence Resource and Collector*, pp. 881–882.

37. Minutes of the Justice Department Civil Disturbance Group, October 1, 1969, SSS files, FOIA, p. 526; *Political Intelligence in the Internal Revenue Service: The Special Service Staff*, pp. 38–39. The SSS files contain copies of both guides, partially annotated by SSS staff members. See SSS files, FOIA, pp. 1701–1790.

38. The document, "United States Army Military Assistance School, Military Assistance Advisor Department," is in SSS files, FOIA, pp. 12989–13006. See also Green to Paul Wright, undated memo [1969], SSS files, FOIA, pp. 12981–12987; *Political Intelligence in the Internal Revenue Service: The Special Service Staff*, p. 131.

39. Bacon to Regional Commissioners, October 8, 1969, SSS files, FOIA, pp. 521–525. The organizations targeted this time were: Afro-American Industries, the Black Economic Development Conference, the Black Peoples Unity Movement, the Black Student Union, the Black United Front, the Brown Berets, the California Migrant Industry, the Camden Christian Crusade, the Foundation for Community Development, FORCE, the Founding Church of Scientology, the Garfield Organization, Har-You, Hope Development, the Los Angeles Black Congress, the Moving the Movement Fund, the New Left Movement, the Police Malpractice Complaint Center, the United Black Brotherhood, the United States Committee to Aid the National Liberation Front of South Vietnam, U.S. Inc. "United Slaves, Inc.," and the Welfare Rights Organization. See Box 10, folder: Special Service Group (IRS) (2 of 3), WSPF–IRS. See also Charles Hulberg to Green, Bacon, Thrower, and Wright, October 8, 1969; William Smith to Patman, October 10, 1969; and Patman to Smith, October 13, 1969, SSS files, FOIA, pp. 933–936. A handwritten record documenting the results of investigations into all the ninety-nine organizations is in SSS files, FOIA, pp. 13358, 13364–13366.

40. Wright to Assistant Commissioner (Compliance), October 23, 1969, SSS files, FOIA, pp. 845–847; *Investigation of the Special Service Staff of the Internal Revenue Service*, pp. 60–63.

41. Meeting with Civil Disturbance Group, October 7, 1969; Memo from Assistant Commissioner (Compliance) and Assistant Commissioner (Data Processing) to Deputy Commissioner, undated [1969]; both in SSS files, FOIA, pp. 527, 2044–2047.

42. Assistant Commissioner (Compliance) and Assistant Commissioner (Data Processing) to Deputy Commissioner, undated [1969], SSS files, FOIA, pp. 2047–2093; "Feasibility Study and Chronology," SSS files, FOIA, p. 2208. See also the Operating Procedures Guide Transmittal by L. B. Jerome, Chief of the Exempt Organizations Branch, November 13, 1969, SSS files, FOIA, pp. 852–855.

43. Notes on various demonstrations are in SSS files, FOIA, pp. 5166–5167. See also, in the same files, Memo of November 18, 1969, W. A. Bates, District Director, Reno, to Regional Commissioner, Western Region, p. 7027; District Director, Portsmouth, to Assistant Commissioner (Compliance), November 20, 1969, p. 519; Paul Wright to the Assistant Commissioner (Compliance), November 25, 1969, pp. 2242–2245; District Director, Brooklyn, to Assistant Commissioner (Compliance), November 25, 1969, p. 518; Bacon to Cole, November 25, 1969, p. 3218; Donald Virdin buckslip, December 1, 1969, p. 516. Cole's reply to Bacon, December 17, 1969, in in Box 11, folder: Special Service Staff, WSPF–IRS.

44. J. Norris to P. Wright, January 14, 1970; Mrs. F. R. Mosley to files, February 3, 1970; Thrower to James Rowley, Director, U.S. Secret Service, January 26, 1970; D. G. Elsberry to Mr. Jack, January 28, 1970; all in SSS files, FOIA, pp. 1805–1817, 11283, 944, 12658–12661, respectively. See also Wright to Barth, February 4, 1970, in *Political Intelligence in the Internal Revenue Service: The Special Service Staff*, p. 139.

45. Chief, Exempt Organizations Branch, to Chief, Exempt Organizations Examination Branch, October 5, 1970, SSS files, FOIA, pp. 9249–9252. See also the following memos in these files: Saul Reuben Memo of October 6, 1970, p. 9246; Walter Shipp to Nunez, October 8, 1970, p. 9257; Bacon to Thrower, October 13, 1970, pp. 9234–9236; Bacon to Representative Ichord, September 24, 1970, p. 9238; Thrower to Representative Ichord, October 14, 1970, p. 9237.

46. Richard Schwartz, Regional IRS Counsel, to K. Martin Worthy, IRS Chief Counsel, February 24, 1970, and Dean J. Barron to Chief Counsel, April 19, 1972, SSS files, FOIA, pp. 5316, 5312. See also Virdin to Bacon, September 22, 1970, p. 496, in the same file. The list of Panther bank deposits is in SSS files, FOIA, p. 11178.

47. See the following documents in SSS files, FOIA: D. O. Virdin, Memo for File, February 25, 1970, p. 952; D. O. Virdin, Memos for File, February 27, 1970, and March 2, 1970, p. 11274; Virdin to Wright, March 2, 1970, pp. 945–951; Memo for File, September 16, 1974, pp. 10903–10904. See also Virdin, Memo for File, April 8, 1970, Box 10, folder: Special Service Group (IRS) (3 of 3), WSPF–IRS.

48. Bacon to IRS Commissioner, May 26, 1970, SSS files, FOIA, p. 4205; *Political Intelligence in the Internal Revenue Service: The Special Service Staff*, pp. 24–25, 218.

49. D. O. Virdin, Memo of Understanding, June 16, 1970, SSS files, FOIA, p. 865. These files also contain excerpts of a Senate document, *Report of the Subcommittee to Investigate the Administration of the Internal Security Laws and Other Internal Security Laws* (1973), that outlines the United States Servicemen's Fund investigation; see p. 2009. For material on Fall River, see *Extent of Subversion in the "New Left" (Fall River, Mass.)*. Hearings Before the Subcommittee to Investigate the Administration of the Internal Security Act and Other Internal Security Laws of the Committee on the Judiciary, U.S. Senate, 91st Cong., 2d sess. (Washington, D.C., 1970), pp. 761–762; Paul Cowan, Nick Egleson, Nat Hentoff, *State Secrets: Police Surveillance in America* (New York, 1974), pp 6, 53. Material on war tax resisters is in *Investigation of the Special Service Staff of the Internal Revenue Service*, pp. 13, 50–51, 89. For charges of theft of documents, see *Daily World* (July 14, 1970), clipping in SSS files, FOIA, pp. 7719–7722. Evidence of IRS targeting the underground press is in Angus MacKenzie, *Secrets: The CIA's War at Home* (Berkeley, 1997), pp. 3–4.

50. Nixon's request for a review is in *National Security, Civil Liberties, and the Collection of Intelligence: A Report on the Huston Plan*, Final Report of the Select Committee to Study Governmental Operations with Respect to Intelligence Activities, Book III (Washington, D.C., 1976), pp. 923–996. Hoover's characterization of Huston is in Small, *The Presidency of Richard Nixon*, p. 56; see also William Safire, *Before the Fall: An Insider's View of the Pre-Watergate White House* (New York, 1975), pp. 227, 296–297 and Stanley Kutler, *The Wars of Watergate: The Last Crisis of Richard Nixon* (New York, 1990), p. 96, for more on Huston. See also Huston to Barth, August 14, 1970, in *Political Intelligence in the Internal Revenue Service: The Special Service Staff*, p. 143. There are many copies of the status report available; see Thrower to Huston, September 19, 1970, Box 11, folder: Special Service Staff, WSPF–IRS; SSS files, FOIA, p. 1501; *Presidential Campaign Activities of 1972*, Book 3, pp. 1340–1345.

51. Status Report on the Special Service Group, SSS files, FOIA, p. 1206.

52. Huston to Haldeman, September 21, 1970, Box 19, folder: Dean . . . rec'd October 25, 1973, WSPF–IRS; Hearings Before the Select Committee to Study Governmental Operations with Respect to Intelligence Activities, Volume 2: The Huston Plan, U.S. Senate, 94th Cong., 1st sess. (Washington, D.C., 1976), pp. 11–12, 29, 31.

Chapter Fourteen. The SSS: In the Trenches and Under Fire

1. *Report on Administrative Procedures of the Internal Revenue Service*, pp. 963–967. For the FBI, see the testimony of Charles Brennan, former director of the FBI Domestic Intelligence Division, Hearings Before the Select Committee to Study Governmental Operations with Respect to Intelligence Activities, Volume 2: The Huston Plan, p. 120. See also *The Internal Revenue Service: An Intelligence Resource and Collector*, pp. 854–855; Donner, *The Age of Surveillance*, p. 327.

2. For the Rustin material, see SSS files, FOIA, pp. 3005–3015; material on Wilkins and Jordan is on pp. 3029–3037 and 3024, respectively. Peace activists information is on pp.

3016–3019. Targeting of black groups is in *Internal Revenue Service Intelligence Operations*, p. 66. For leaks, see Ron Koziol, "IRS Probes Funding of Radicals, Leftist," *Chicago Tribune*, November 29, 1970, clipping at p. 8472; and Wright to Assistant Commissioner (Compliance), December 2, 1970, pp. 8469–8470. Material on the AFSC is in SSS files, Center for National Security Studies, N-7. Information on the Moratorium Committee is in SSS files, FOIA. See D. O. Virdin, Memo for File, May 21, 1971, p. 674, and a newspaper clipping, *Washington Post*, May 29, 1971, p. 673. Information on FBI cooperation is in *Political Intelligence in the Internal Revenue Service: The Special Service Staff*, p. 36. Tabulations of correspondence from various agencies is in SSS files, FOIA, pp. 12114–12115.

3. D. O. Virdin, Memo for File, March 26, 1971, Box 11, folder: Special Service Staff, WSPF–IRS.

4. Minutes of Joint Meeting, March 26, 1971, SSS files, FOIA, pp. 4186–4187; Mardian to Rolapp, April 1, 1971, *Federal Tax Return Privacy* (1976), p. 52. IRS procedures were included in an undated memorandum, Commissioner CP:C:D to Assistant Commissioner (Compliance), SSS files, FOIA, p. 697.

5. Davis, *Unbridled Power*, p. 91; *Political Intelligence in the Internal Revenue Service: The Special Service Staff*, pp. 22–24, 251; D. O. Virdin, Memo for File, April 15, 1971, SSS files, FOIA, pp. 700–701. In the same files, see Sam Ervin to Henry Peterson, November 29, 1973, pp. 8888–8898. Hoover's request is noted in D. O. Virdin, Memo for File, February 22, 1972, SSS files, FOIA, pp. 11295–11296.

6. Peterson to Ervin, February 1, 1974, in *Political Intelligence in the Internal Revenue Service: The Special Service Staff*, pp. 252–253; *Investigation of the Special Service Staff of the Internal Revenue Service*, pp. 58–59, 60, 67. See the SSS files, FOIA, for a September 29, 1975, memo on the Subject Data Listing, pp. 2941–2942. The same files contain lists of taxpayers sent to ISD from the SSS, in a November 25, 1974, memo. pp. 1368, 1523–1527.

7. Bacon to Assistant Commissioner (Data Processing), June 29, 1971, p. 871, and Bacon to Assistant Chief of Staff for Intelligence, Dept. of the Army, July 22, 1971, in the same files. Also see Bacon to Barth, August 2, 1971 in *Political Intelligence in the Internal Revenue Service: The Special Service Staff*, p. 148.

8. *Political Intelligence in the Internal Revenue Service: The Special Service Staff*, pp. 261–262.

9. Ibid., pp. 263–265. Another example of such targeting just by the SSS is in SSS files, FOIA, pp. 1988–1989, involving an individual who had "allegedly aided and abetted individuals to evade service under the Selective Service Acts." The SSS targeted the individual because he "has pacifist views."

10. *Political Intelligence in the Internal Revenue Service: The Special Service Staff*, pp. 28, 271; SSS files, FOIA, pp. 810, 2031–2042, 4610–4613, 9101–9103. One example of a search request is Wright to Ralph Morgan, Division of Earning System, Social Security Administration, August 21, 1972, SSS files, FOIA, pp. 21581–21591.

11. *Investigation of the Special Service Staff of the Internal Revenue Service:*, p. 89n; Wright to Director, Collection Division, January 12, 1972, SSS files, FOIA, pp. 12392–12398.

12. The reports are in SSS files, FOIA, pp. 811–814, 3095–3101.

13. For Thrower's comments, see *Role of the Internal Revenue Service in Law Enforcement Activities*, p. 147. SSS activities against the underground press are noted in Wright to Director, Collection Division, January 12, 1972, SSS files, FOIA, pp. 12392–12398; see also handwritten notes, pp. 3108–3115; undated SSS document [1975?], pp. 2520–2521; and *Investigation of the Special Service Staff of the Internal Revenue Service*, pp. 39, 90. Ironically, former IRS official Mitchell Rogovin represented many of these groups against the IRS; see Wright to Leon Green, 1971, SSS files, FOIA, p. 3026.

14. Loeb to Wright, January 14, 1972; Assistant Commissioner (ACTS) to IRS Commissioner, April 12, 1972; Wright to Acting Assistant Commissioner (Compliance), January 5, 1972, SSS files, FOIA, pp. 2030, 4209, 872–876, respectively. A congressional committee claimed that the IRS oversight committee (Joint Committee on Internal Revenue Taxation) did not learn of SSS functions until 1973, and then only after stories about the group appeared in the press; see *The Internal Revenue Service: An Intelligence Resource and Collector*, p. 880. If true, one wonders how they missed the story in the *New York Times* on January 13, 1972, where the IRS acknowledged the existence of the SSS.

15. Wright to Director, Collections Division, May 25, 1972, SSS files, FOIA, p. 3214. A copy of the memo, Assistant Chief, Office Branch to All Office Branch Supervisors, Reviewers, Interviewers and TSR's, March 7, 1972, is in SSS files, FOIA, 3216.

16. "For Agenda, Charlottesville AC/RC Conference, 11/1–11/2/72," SSS files, FOIA, p. 4212. Concern about foreign intervention is in an undated, multipage outline and notes prepared before the conference, SSS files, FOIA, p. 2893.

17. Undated, multipage outline and notes prepared before the conference, SSS files, FOIA, pp. 2895–2901.

18. Ibid., pp. 2901–2906. IRS staff redacted all examples provided to the commissioners.

19. "Special Service Staff: Its Origin, Mission and Potential," in *Intelligence Activities, Vol. 3: Internal Revenue Service*, pp. 39–41.

20. "Special Service Staff: Exhibits for Discussion Paper" (Commissioner Walters's copy), SSS files, FOIA, pp. 7405–7502. In fact, a listing of the organizations sent to the field in December 1972 was an exact copy of the organizations originally targeted by the SSS; see Chief, Intelligence Division, to District Director, St. Louis District, December 6, 1972, in *Intelligence Activities, Vol. 3: Internal Revenue Service*, pp. 48–52.

21. Ray F. Harless to Assistant Commissioner (Inspection), April 16, 1973, SSS files, FOIA, p. 912. In the same files, see IRS Manual Supplement, August 14, 1973, pp. 4615–4616, and a brief outline of resistance problems, pp. 4391–4393.

22. All this information comes from SSS files, FOIA. See "Special Service Staff: Its Origin, Mission and Potential," pp. 1276–1277; Walters to J. Elton Greenlee, Acting Assistant Secretary for Administration, January 2, 1972, pp. 8478–8479; Walters to Greenlee, January 24, 1972, pp. 3071–3073; Walters to Greenlee, February 16, 1972, pp. 1984–1986.

23. Pickering to Chief, Compliance and Special Programs, June 30, 1972, SSS files, FOIA, pp. 2210–2212.

24. Ibid., pp. 2212–2216; Dean Barron, Assistant Commissioner (ACTS), to Deputy Commissioner, August 24, 1972, and Robert Goldsmith and Ronald Pickering to Barron, July 28, 1972, SSS files, FOIA, pp. 4583–4584, 2232–2234.

25. Ervin to Alexander, December 5, 1973, SSS files, FOIA, p. 10682; Francis Geibel, Assistant Commissioner (Inspection), to Raymond Harless, Deputy IRS Commissioner, August 16, 1972, Box 11, folder: Special Service Staff, WSPF–IRS; *Political Intelligence in the Internal Revenue Service: The Special Service Staff*, pp. 20–21; Barron to the Deputy Commissioner, August 24, 1972 SSS files, FOIA, pp. 2229–2230.

26. Pickering, Memo to Files, October 27, 1972; David Tippets, Memo to the File, November 22, 1972; ADP Handbook Supplement, December 11, 1972; all in SSS files, FOIA, pp. 2225–2227, 2240, 13295–13296, respectively.

27. Assistant Commissioner (ACTS) to Deputy Commissioner, February 9, 1973; Wright to Director, Collection Division, February 13, 27, and 28, 1973; Dean Barron, Assistant Commissioner (ACTS), to Harless, June 6, 1973, and Harless's response of the same date; all in SSS files, FOIA, pp. 4228–4230, 4231–4234, 4239–4241, 4237–4238, 915, 6348, respectively.

28. Notes of a meeting on Service Center security, November 6, 1972; Internal Management Document from the District Director, Salt Lake City, November 20, 1972; Flynn to All Directors, December 18, 1972, SSS files, FOIA, pp. 820–821, 823–824, 743–745, respectively.

29. *Internal Revenue Service Intelligence Operations*, pp. 75–76; Ervion to Pierce, May 21, 1973, and Moody to Alexander, May 23, 1973, SSS files, FOIA, pp. 752 and 751, respectively; *Political Intelligence in the Internal Revenue Service: The Special Service Staff*, p. 5.

30. *Political Intelligence in the Internal Revenue Service: The Special Service Staff*, pp. 5–8. Alexander to Ervin, June 28, 1973, pp. 757–761; Ervin to Alexander, July 5, 1975, p. 10990; both in SSS files, FOIA. For details on the access procedures, see Bob Kuehling, Memo for File, April 9, 1974, SSS files, FOIA, p. 2811.

31. R. G. Clucas, Memo for File, June 4, 1973, p. 985; D. C. Dawkins to Harless, June 6, 1973, unnumbered page; both in SSS files, FOIA.

32. Willsey to Alexander, June 22, 1973, SSS files, FOIA, pp. 4376–4377; *Investigation of the Special Service Staff of the Internal Revenue Service*, p. 41. Figures on SSS activity are in *Political Intelligence in the Internal Revenue Service: The Special Service Staff*, pp. 174–175.

33. Alexander to Ervin, July 10, 1973, Box 11, folder: Special Service Staff, WSPF–IRS; Ervin to Alexander, July 12, 1973, SSS files, FOIA. pp. 3085–3091; Wright to Alexander, August 7, 1973, SSS files, FOIA, pp. 4251–4252. Shelley Davis failed to find evidence of any study, and Alexander himself could not remember one. The likelihood is that the study in question was the Willsey investigation; see Davis, *Unbridled Power*, pp. 95–96.

34. *The Internal Revenue Service: An Intelligence Resource and Collector*, pp. 884–885; *Intelligence Activities and the Rights of Americans, Book 2*, p. 95; *The Evolution and Organization of Intel-*

ligence Activities in the United States (Laguna Hills, Calif., 1980), p. 288; Memorandum of Understanding, August 15, 1973, SSS files, FOIA, pp. 1449–1451. In the same files, see "SSS: Outline of Task Force Recommendations," August 17, 1973, pp. 1180–1183. Lists of SSS files on individuals that were included or excluded, with names redacted, are on pp. 1839–1925.

35. Task Force meeting notes for August 31 and September 7, 1973; SSS (Phase-Out/Phase-In) Task Force Recommendations, 1973. For the weeding of files, see Wright to Director, Collection Division, September 24, 1973. All are in SSS files, FOIA, pp. 1176, 1178, 1184–1188, 1192–1193, respectively.

36. Interview with Burke Willsey and John Hanlon, September 6, 1973, Box 1, folder: Witness Statements–Burke Willsey; Alexander to Ervin, September 24, 1973, Box 11, folder: Special Service Staff; both in WSPF–IRS. The internal IRS memorandum, Assistant Commissioner (ACTS) to Commissioner, 1973, is in SSS files, FOIA, pp. 771–787. The list of additional interrogatories is in SSS files, FOIA, pp. 8906–8916.

37. Alexander to James Chenoweth, Acting Assistant Commissioner (Inspection), October 15, 1975; Leon Levine to IRS Public Affairs Office, November 28, 1973; Wright to Director, Collections Division, December 20, 1973; all in SSS files, FOIA, pp. 430, 419–420, 1201, respectively. Wright's resignation and vault changes are noted in *Political Intelligence in the Internal Revenue Service: The Special Service Staff*, p. 343. See also Davis, *Unbridled Power*, p. 97. Having reviewed about fifteen thousand pages of SSS files obtained through the Freedom of Information Act, I would describe the files as chaotic and disorganized rather than incomplete.

38. Ervin to Alexander, January 28, 1974, and Continuation of Response, March 1974; SSS files, FOIA, pp. 8900–8902, 9058–9075. See also Jack Anderson, "Jane Fonda Wins Bout with IRS," *Washington Post*, March 13, 1974, p. D19, clipping in Box 5, folder: IRS Enemies–Press Clippings, WSPF–IRS.

39. Satterfield to Flanagan, April 6, 1974, SSS files, FOIA, pp. 10641, 9124–9125. Other examples of file topics are in *Political Intelligence in the Internal Revenue Service: The Special Service Staff*, pp. 31–32, 43–47.

40. Willsey to Ms. Dorothy Glancy, Subcommittee Counsel, May 16, 1974; Glancy to Willsey, May 21, 1974; Ervin to Alexander, May 22, 1974; all in SSS files, FOIA, pp. 11031, 11033–11035, 7666 respectively. See also Alexander to Ervin, May 24, 1974, Box 11, folder: IRS–Opinions Relating to Disclosures of the Tax returns to WH Staff, WSPF–IRS; Glancy to Ervin, May 29, 1974, in *Political Intelligence in the Internal Revenue Service: The Special Service Staff*, pp. 212–214; Willsey to Glancy, May 30, 1974; Alexander to Attorney General William Saxbe, May 30, 1974; both in SSS files, FOIA, pp. 11042–11043, 11045.

41. Alexander to all IRS officials, August 9, 1974; S. F. Satterfield, Memo for File, August 26, 1974; Robert Kuehling to Mr. Marvillo of the GAO, September 3, 1974; *New York Times* clipping for November 18, 1974, all in SSS files, FOIA, pp. 9826, 10620, 2782–2786, 10878, respectively.

42. IRS news release, November 18, 1974; L. F. Satterfield, Memo for File, November 27, 1974; Thomas Glynn, Assistant to the Commissioner, to Charles Gibb, Chief of the Disclosure Staff, November 29, 1974; Thomas Davis, Acting Director, Collection Division, to Glynn, December 3, 1974; buckslip from Frank Malanga to Miss Alpern, December 1974; all in SSS files, FOIA, pp. 1386–1387, 10782, 10774, 4206, 9519–9537, respectively. Even the assistant to the commissioner, Thomas Glynn, apparently did not know much about SSS operations in 1974; see Glynn to Gibb, December 27, 1974, SSS files, FOIA, p. 2450. An appeal for help to all regional commissioners from John Hanlon, Assistant Commissioner (Compliance), January 10, 1975 is in these same files, pp. 10757–10758.

43. Civil Action No. 74-216, "Complaint for Declaratory and Injunctive Relief and for Money Damages"; Harold Flanagan, Director, Disclosure Division, to Assistant Commissioner (ACTS), January 10, 1975; Affidavit of William C. Rankin, Jr., April 22, 1974; all in SSS files, FOIA, pp. 12125–12138, 7069, 387–390, respectively. Shelley Davis is the source for the claim that no copy of the Rankin study exists. Another example of such a suit is one filed by Walter Teague III and the Indochina Solidarity Committee against Donald Alexander and a lengthy list of IRS officials, For details, see Davis, *Unbridled Power*, p. 97, as well as *Federal Tax Return Privacy*, pp. 34–40; John J. McCarthy, Chief, General Litigation Section, Tax Division, Dept. of Justice to WSPF, April 2, 1975, and Jay Horowitz to Peter Kreindler, April 8, 1975, in Box 6, folder: Tom Charles Huston, WSPF–IRS.

Chapter Fifteen. Operation Leprechaun: Sex and Politics in South Florida

1. *The Internal Revenue Service: An Intelligence Resource and Collector*, pp. 843, 897. Destruction of IRS files relating to Operation Leprechaun has created difficulties evaluating the operation. According to one investigation, in 1974 the IRS destroyed forty cubic feet of records. It also established guidelines in October 1974 calling for systematic file destruction of background files older than five years, records of collateral investigations more than a year old, and "special investigative equipment control records" before October 1, 1968. See *Operation Leprechaun*, p. 414.

2. *The Internal Revenue Service: An Intelligence Resource and Collector*, pp. 904–905; Schnepper, *Inside IRS*, pp. 119–120.

3. *The Internal Revenue Service: An Intelligence Resource and Collector*, pp. 911–912. The pilot test ran from May 1, 1972, until May 4, 1973, when IRM 9390 formally established the IGRS. See *Operation Leprechaun*. Hearings Before the Subcommittee on Oversight of the Committee on Ways and Means, House of Representatives, 94th Cong., 1st and 2d sess. (Washington, D.C., 1976), p. 407. Miami is in the Jacksonville IRS District.

4. *Operation Leprechaun*, pp. 408–410; *The Internal Revenue Service: An Intelligence Resource and Collector*, p. 913. For McMillan's argument, see the June 28, 1972, memo in N-5: Operation Leprechaun, CNSS.

5. *Operation Leprechaun*, pp. 152–157. The quotation is on p. 157. The comments to the strike force are in the Minutes of the Strike Force Representatives Seminar, November 14, 1972, Investigation of "Operation Leprechaun," N-5: Operation Leprechaun, CNSS.

6. *Operation Leprechaun*, p. 157.

7. Ibid., pp 160, 162–163; *The Internal Revenue Service: An Intelligence Resource and Collector*, p. 915.

8. *Operation Leprechaun*, pp. 162–163. For information on Gutierrez, see Schnepper, *Inside IRS*, pp. 113, 126.

9. Minutes of the Strike Force Representatives Seminar, November 14, 1972, N-5: Operation Leprechaun, CNSS.

10. "IRS Study Results," *Operation Leprechaun*, pp. 499–500. For the audit, see *Oversight Hearings into the Operations of the IRS* (Part 1), p. 520.

11. *Oversight Hearings into the Operations of the IRS* (Part 1), pp. 503–504. For IRS discoveries, see notes on a telephone call from Donald Alexander in Henry Ruth to Jay Horowitz, April 11, 1975, Box 4, folder: PLME 2: Investigative Correspondence, WSPF–IRS.

12. *The Internal Revenue Service: An Intelligence Resource and Collector*, pp. 915, 919; Schnepper, *Inside IRS*, p. 125.

13. *Miami News*, February 1, 1975, pp. 1A, 4A. I want to thank Bruce Bates for providing me with photocopies of the key Miami newspaper stories.

14. *Miami Herald*, March 15, 1975, pp. 1A, 18A; March 16, 1975, p. 26A; March 17, 1975, pp. 1B–2B.

15. *Miami News*, March 19, 1975, pp. 1A, 7A; March 28, 1975, p. 4. *Miami Herald*, April 8, 1975, pp. 1, 8; July 8, 1975, unnumbered page. *Miami News*, July 9, 1975, p. 9.

16. *Internal Revenue Service Intelligence Operations*, pp. 1–3.

17. Ibid., p. 6. Alexander's remarks before the bar association are in *Operation Leprechaun*, pp. 208–218; the quotations come from pp. 209 and 211.

18. *Internal Revenue Service Intelligence Operations*, pp. 6, 46–47. For Vanik's interest in Rebozo and other matters, see Warren Williams memo, August 19, 1975, and the memo of August 8, 1975, by Robert Smoot of the IRS, SSS Files, FOIA, pp. 10277, 10239–10249.

19. *Internal Revenue Service Intelligence Operations*, p. 1; Vanik to Alexander, April 3, 1975, SSS files, FOIA, pp. 10096–10103. See also Vanik to Alexander, July 1, 1976, SSS files, FOIA, page unnumbered. Thrower's remarks are in SSS files, FOIA, p. 2671.

20. *Operation Leprechaun*, pp. 1–2.

21. Ibid., pp. 8–11, 15.

22. Ibid., pp. 51, 55, 410.

23. Ibid., pp. 70–72, 75, 89.

24. Ibid., pp. 105–106, 109–111. Vanik later charged that Alexander pressured him to retire, which he did on March 12, 1976; see the testimony of James Woischwill, Group Manager of the Miami IRS office, in ibid., p. 569.

25. Ibid., pp. 96–97.

26. *Oversight Hearings into the Operations of the IRS* (Part 1), pp. 244–245, 503–511.

27. *Operation Leprechaun*, pp. 186, 188–189.

28. *Internal Revenue Service Intelligence Operations*, pp. 14–15, 19, 84.

29. Ibid., pp. 911, 913, 920. For information on Alexander's portrayal of Leprechaun as a creature of the Justice Department, see *Operation Leprechaun*, pp. 631–632.

30. *Operation Leprechaun*, pp. 637, 642–643, 665.

31. "Investigation of Operation Leprechaun," June 23, 1975, pp. 1, 13–16, 21, N-5: Operation Leprechaun, CNSS.

32. Ibid., p. 3.

33. Ibid., pp. 4, 6.

34. Ibid., pp. 7–8.

35. Richard Albrecht to Secretary Simon, June 25, 1975, Series II, Drawer 9: folder 9: 5: Richard R. Albrecht (General Counsel): 1975 (June–August), WSP; District Director, Jacksonville, to William E. Williams, Deputy IRS Commissioner, August 15, 1975, in *Operation Leprechaun*, pp. 35–37; IRS press release, September 29, 1975, Series IIIB, Drawer 23, folder 23: 18: Internal Revenue Service: 1974–1975, WSP.

36. *New York Times*, January 6, 1977, pp. 1, 13; *Miami Herald*, January 7, 1977, p. 1; *Miami News*, January 6, 1977, pp. 1, 10, and August 25, 1980, p. 3A. The Heller case is discussed in Burnham, *A Law Unto Itself*, pp. 143–144.

37. *The Internal Revenue Service: An Intelligence Resource and Collector*, pp. 837–838.

38. For the internal IRS revolt, see the *Wall Street Journal*, September 29, 1975, IRS FOIA. Charges against Alexander are noted in the *Miami Herald*, February 9, 1976, p. 21A. The *Herald* also reported Alexander's FOIA request; see November 2, 1976, p. 7A. See also Donner, *The Age of Surveillance*, pp. 344–345, and Gary Marx, *Undercover: Police Surveillance in America* (Berkeley, 1988), pp. 5, 235 n4. That the problems in the area remained real was revealed in a 1979 Treasury Department study, which estimated that $4.5 billion in excess cash found its way into two Federal Reserve banks in Florida, largely in denominations of $20 and $100. See *Disclosure of IRS Information to Assist with the Enforcement of Criminal Law*, p. 36.

Chapter Sixteen. Cleaning Up

1. Robert Kuehling to Thomas Glynn, January 30, 1975, SSS files, FOIA, p. 2509. In the same files, see "Freedom of Information–Background," pp. 10400–10409, and an untitled document from the Oversight Committee of the House Ways and Means Committee, p. 2444. The IRS also suspended at least two other programs: Project Mercury, which involved secret reports to the IRS on every Western Union money order valued at more than $1,000, and a program with the CIA whereby that agency supplied the IRS with the names of all American citizens who traveled to North Vietnam so that the IRS could audit their taxes. See clipping from the *Chicago Tribune* for October 3, 1975, SSS files, FOIA, p. 2361. Other evidence of IRS interest in Vietnam War protesters is in Buckslip of May 30, 1975, to Bob Kuehling, SSS files, FOIA, pp. 12373–12375.

2. Alexander to Hartke, March 3, 1975, SSS files, FOIA, pp. 6500–6536. For efforts to find the earlier records, see Thomas Glynn, Assistant to the Commissioner, to Albert St. Jean, Staff Assistant to the Director, Audit Division, March 20, 1975, and Glynn to Howard Schoenfeld, Technical Adviser, Employee Plans/ Exempt Organizations, March 25, 1975, pp. 1613–1616, 1618, in the same files. See also *Intelligence Activities, Vol. 3: Internal Revenue Service*, pp. 8, 24; *Internal Revenue Service Intelligence Operations*, p. 48.

3. Testimony of Harold Tyler, Jr., Deputy Attorney General, Before the Senate Committee on Finance, Subcommittee on Administration of the Internal Revenue Code, April 21, 1975, copy in SSS files, FOIA, pp. 10547A. In the same files, see F. J. Spiegelberg, Jr., Memo for File, April 28, 1975, p. 10446, and Bentsen press release, April 28, 1975, p. 10456. See also *The Privacy Act of 1974: An Assessment* (Washington, D.C., 1977), Appendix 4, pp. 10, 29–30. The issue of farmers' tax returns is in "Proposed Revision of Section 6103," SSS files, FOIA pp. 9862–9865, and Statement of Representative Jerry Litton, *Proposals for Administrative Changes in Internal Revenue Service Procedures*, p. 4. For the Privacy Commission report, see *The Citizen as Taxpayer. Appendix 2 to the Report of the Privacy Protection Study Commission* (Washington,

D.C., 1977), pp. 2, 4, 31; Privacy Protection Study Commission, *Personal Privacy in an Information Society* (Washington, D.C., 1977), p. 541. A compilation of their recommendations is in *Surveillance Technology*, pp. 478–485. This battle for confidentiality was a protracted one. For its persistence from the 1960s, see Jon Weiner, "'National Security' and Freedom of Information: The John Lennon FBI Files," in Athan Theoharis, ed., *A Culture of Secrecy* (Lawrence, Kans., 1998), pp. 83–96. For Ford, see *Report on Administrative Procedures of the Internal Revenue Service*, pp. 970–971; Schnepper, *Inside IRS*, pp. 182–184. Ford actually favored broadening presidential authority over tax returns.

4. "Analysis of the Privacy Act of 1974," undated document, SSS files, FOIA, pp. 9867–9899. Harrigan's comments are in his draft report to the Church Committee, 1975, SSS files, FOIA, pp. 7741–7750; the quotations are on pp. 7749 and 7750.

5. David Macdonald, Assistant Secretary (Enforcement Operations and Tariff Affairs) to Deputy Secretary Gardner [1975], *Oversight Hearings into the Operations of the IRS* (1975), pp. 593–601, 3–4.

6. The IRS-GAO struggle is documented in a series of memoranda in Series II, WSP. See Alexander to Deputy Treasury Secretary Stephen Gardner, August 5, 1975, and Richard Albrecht and Warren F. Brecht to Treasury Secretary Simon, August 28, 1975, Drawer 9, folder 9: 5; Alexander to Gardner, November 18, 1975, and Albrecht to Simon, November 25, 1975, Drawer 9, folder 9: 6; Albrecht to Simon, May 21, 1976, Drawer 8, folder 9: 8; Laurence Woodworth to Elmer Staats, Comptroller General of the U.S., October 16, 1976, Drawer 23, folder 23: 19.

7. Maxwell Green, Roy Carden, and Lee Butcher, "The IRS: Everybody's Big Brother," *Texas Business*, p. 22, clipping in SSS files, FOIA, p. 6753; "Actions to Tighten Confidentiality of Tax Data" [1975], SSS files, FOIA, pp. 9851–9852.

8. W. E. Williams, Deputy IRS Commissioner, to All Regional Commissioners, January 6, 1975; Acting Commissioner (Compliance) to Thomas Glynn, Assistant to the Commissioner, February 20, 1975; handwritten notes to Carl Bates of the Joint Committee, April 1, 1975, all in SSS files, FOIA, pp. 6, 2845, 2842, respectively. See also Eileen Shanahan's story in the June 5, 1974, *New York Times*, p. 30; *Surveillance Technology. Policy and Implications: An Analysis and Compendium of Materials.* A Staff Report of the Subcommittee on Constitutional Rights of the Committee on the Judiciary, U.S. Senate, 94th Cong., 2d sess. (Washington, D.C., 1976), p. 132.

9. *Federal Tax Return Privacy* (1976), p. 21; *Internal Revenue Service Intelligence Operations*, pp. 85, 87, 90.

10. *Internal Revenue Service Intelligence Operations*, pp. 93–94, 83–84; *Investigation of the Special Service Staff of the Internal Revenue Service*, p. 95. A breakdown of the cases referred to the SSS by the Exempt Organizations Branch is in this Joint Committee report, p. 99; they indicate that the SSS did not always exert its influence successfully.

11. *Investigation of the Special Service Staff of the Internal Revenue Service*, pp. 112, 79, 46–47, 1–2. A percentage breakdown of SSS sources of information is on p. 48. The IRS's claim to the confidentiality of tax information, which it used in denying the Joint Committee on Internal Revenue Taxation's request for access to documents, is one that it continues to use today. In 1995 the IRS refused to allow even the National Archives and Records Administration to review its files when the Archives attempted to fulfill its responsibility to evaluate the status of records management at the Internal Revenue Service.

12. Arthur Harrigan to Tom Glynn, October 31, 1975; Robert Hudgins, Chief, Operations Analysis, Management and Resources Branch of IRS ACTS, to Director, Planning Staff, October 31, 1975; Kuehling to Glynn, December 12, 1975; Abzug to Alexander, May 17, 1976; all in SSS files, FOIA, pp. 2484, 2488–2490, 2476–2479, 2470, respectively.

13. Anita Alpern, Assistant Commissioner (Planning and Research), to Meade Emory, Assistant to the Commissioner, June 3, 1976; James Owens, Deputy Assistant Commissioner (ACTS), Memo to File, June 9, 1976; Grant Newman, Assistant Commissioner (ACTS), to Commissioner, June 18, 1976; all in SSS files, FOIA, pp. 2496–2504, 2507, 2458–2464, respectively. Drafts of letters for various IRS options and responses are in these files. See also *Notification to Victims of Improper Intelligence Agency Activities.* Hearings Before a Subcommittee of the Committee on Government Operations, House of Representatives, 94th Cong., 2d sess. (Washington, D.C., 1976), pp. 104–105, 110–113.

14. Delivery data is in S. B. Wolfe, Assistant Commissioner (Compliance), to Alexander, September 24, 1976, and Director, Collection Division, to Acting Assistant Commissioner

(ACTS), January 13, 1977, SSS files, FOIA, pp. 3234 and 3316. The file destruction controversy can be followed in Alexander to Representative Richardson Preyer, February 23, 1977, SSS files, FOIA pp. 6698–6699; *Notification to Victims of Improper Intelligence Agency Activities*, pp. 99–101, 277–279, 282–283, 313–314.

Index